Musica mechanica organoedi.

Musical mechanics for the organist.

by
Jacob Adlung

edited for publication by
Johann Lorenz Albrecht

with commentary by
Johann Friedrich Agricola

English translation by
Quentin Faulkner

PART I

Zea E-Books
Lincoln, Nebraska
2011

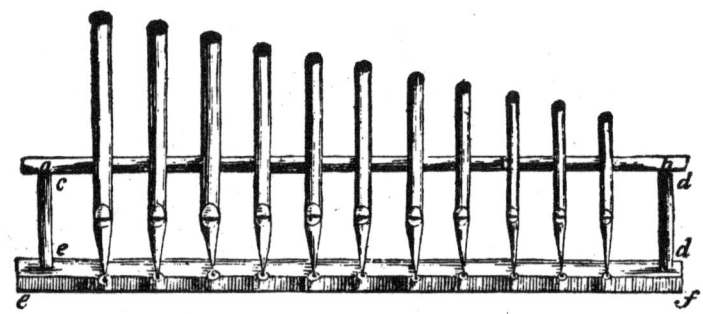

ISBN 978-1-60962-013-4 [Part 1 of 3]

English translation, notes, etc. copyright © 2011 Quentin Faulkner.

Design, layout, and composition, based on the 1768 edition, by Paul Royster.
Set in IM Fell DW Pica typeface, developed and furnished by Igino Marini.

The Fell Types
www.iginomarini.com

Zea E-Books are published by the University of Nebraska–Lincoln Libraries.
http://digitalcommons.unl.edu/zea/

Contents

PART 1

Part 1 includes all of "Volume One" of the original 1768 Berlin edition, except the Stoplists from Chapter 10.

Preface to the Translation [Q. Faulkner]	ix–xvi
Acknowledgements [Q. Faulkner]	xvii–xviii
Notice [Q. Faulkner]	xix
Preliminary Matters concerning the Art of the Keyboard in General	3–6
Chapter 1. Concerning the Nature, Uses, Methods and Aids of Mechanics	7–15
Chapter 2. Concerning the Outer Case of the Organ	16–27
Chapter 3. Concerning the Windchest	28–35
Chapter 4. Concerning the Other Internal Components of the Organ, with the Exception of the Pipes	36–39
Chapter 5. Concerning the Bellows and Wind Ducts	39–50
Chapter 6. Concerning the Pipework in General	50–69
Chapter 7. Concerning the Stops in General, and Each One of Them in Particular	70–159
Chapter 8. Concerning the Use of the Stops	160–173
Chapter 9. Contracting for and Building an Organ	173–181
Chapter 10. Concerning the Stoplist	182–196

Pages 1–196 are German-English facing 2-page spreads.
The stoplists collection from Chapter 10 appears in [Part 3] of this edition.

Preface to the Translation

Jacob Adlung, the author of *Musica mechanica organœdi*, was born in Bindersleben near Erfurt in Thuringia (central Germany) on January 14, 1699; he died in Erfurt on July 5, 1762. Happily, quite a lot is known about his life and career, since his comprehensive autobiography was published in the Foreword to Vol. II of *Musica mechanica organœdi*. As a result of his native intelligence and disciplined lifestyle, Adlung rose from humble beginnings to become a musician and scholar of considerable erudition. After preparatory studies in Erfurt, he matriculated at the University of Jena, where he pursued the study of philosophy, mathematics, languages and theology. Having already undertaken musical studies in Erfurt, he came under the influence of Johann Nicolaus Bach (J.S. Bach's cousin), organist of the Jena Stadtkirche. Immediately upon his return to Erfurt in 1727, he won the post of organist at the Predigerkirche, upon the death of the incumbent, Johann Heinrich Buttstedt. That post he kept until his death, supplementing his income by teaching keyboard and languages, by making and selling keyboard stringed instruments, and by offering courses in philology, mathematics and philosophy.

What sort of man was Adlung? The picture that emerges from his autobiography and his writings reveals a character at once ambitious, energetic, inquisitive, and multitalented: in mathematics, theology, teaching, and mechanics, as well as in music. Yet it also reveals a man who was rather officious and a bit of a pedant (consider his belabored explanation of deriving a square whose area is the same as a circle, §.97-99, an explanation undertaken, as §.99 shows, only to reveal his mathematical prowess); a man methodical to an extreme (who in §.177 lists any number of places where a 16′ Principal may be found) and possessing a stunted sense of humor (read his comments on the cat-organ in §.554). Adlung's pedantic streak, however, together with his fascination (one might say, his obsession) with mechanics, is much to our benefit. It is they that we have to thank for the exhaustive and invaluable information about 18th-century organs that he gives us in his publications.

In addition to some organ compositions that survive in manuscript, Adlung published a number of treatises; these are listed in the Foreword to Vol. II (pp. XV-XVI). There are a number of smaller items, as well as two major ones, *Anleitung zu der musikalischen Gelahrtheit* (*Introduction to Musical Learning*, Erfurt, 1758; hereafter referred to as *Anleitung*) and *Musical mechanica organœdi* (*Musical Mechanics for the Organist*, Berlin, 1768; hereafter referred to as *Mmo*). Of the two, *Anleitung* has by far the broader scope; it includes information on music history and bibliography, music and mathematics (including problems of temperament), organ history, registration and

construction (largely plundered from the yet unpublished manuscript of *Mmo*[1]), other instruments (both keyboard and non-keyboard), the art of singing, figured bass, Italian tablature (modern score), improvisation and composition.

Mmo's field is far more limited than that of *Anleitung*; for that reason, *Mmo* treats in considerably greater detail the matters it addresses. It focuses primarily on the organ, from the perspective of the information an organist might need to know about the instrument. More specifically, it encompasses the following:

- an evaluation, from an 18th-century perspective, of earlier works on its subject: Praetorius, Werkmeister, Mattheson, Niedt, Kircher and others
- an appreciation of the organ: its value and regard
- the history of the organ
- a thorough description of all the parts of an organ, and all facets of the organ-builder's art, including definitions of several hundred organ stops.
- suggestions about organ registration: the use and combination of stops, and how to go about choosing what stops an organ shall have
- advice to those who intend to purchase an organ: cost, advantages and faults, testing, maintenance and repair
- temperament and tuning
- construction and assessment of other keyboard instruments, notably the harpsichord and clavichord with pedal
- stoplists of almost 90 organs of various types and sizes (most of them in Germany).

One of *Mmo*'s most valuable features is its attempt to be a compendium of information from earlier sources. Adlung not only recorded his own ideas and observations, but incorporated those of every previous major German publication that treats the organ, beginning with Praetorius's *Syntagma musicum* (1619). This attempt at comprehensiveness is interesting for two reasons: first, because it gathers information from so many diverse sources, and second, because in commenting on his predecessors Adlung offers yet another perspective (closer to the sources than any commentary from our time) on the matters they treat. *Mmo* is therefore, more than any other contemporary publication, a mirror of the state of knowledge and preferences concerning the 18th-century German organ. This statement is all the more significant in that during this period the organ in Germany (more specifically in Thuringia) was undergoing rapid and profound changes, resulting in characteristics that set it in marked contrast to earlier organ types: a reduction in the number of reed stops, especially in the manuals; the abandonment of the Rückpositiv; the proliferation of colorful flue stops at 8′ pitch; the early appearance (before 1700) of narrow-scale string stops; little concern for the case as a sound-reflecting enclosure; the predilection for prominent third-sounding ranks, both independent and as components of mixtures; less emphasis on higher-pitched

---

1. See the Foreword to Vol. II, p. XVII.

stops in the pedal; and the appearance of a Glockenspiel. In retrospect, it is evident that 18th-century Thuringian organ design was the most progressive of its time, often foreshadowing typical romantic organ traits by 100 years or more.[2]

Those profound changes, resulting in a whole new epoch of organbuilding (the nineteenth century), are the most persuasive explanation for *Mmo*'s limited influence on succeeding generations. Radical new developments in pipe scales, in bellows (magazine bellows), in reeds (free reeds), in mechanics (octave couplers, detached consoles), as well as the introduction of various means of swelling and diminishing the tone [3]— all these were just around the corner in 1768. Johann Ulrich Sponsel's *Orgelhistorie* (Nürnberg, 1771) is indebted to *Mmo*, but then Adlung's work was fresh from the press. The only other treatise that bears the trace of Adlung's work is J.J. Seidel's *Die Orgel und ihr Bau* (Breslau, 1843). The order in which Seidel treats the various aspects of organbuilding is clearly derived from *Mmo* (Seidel's purpose in writing his book was similar to Adlung's: to acquaint organists and church officials with sound organbuilding practices without, however, offering sufficiently detailed information to build organs). Its actual contents, however, unmistakably identify it as a work of the early nineteenth century. A quirk of history did, though, extend *Mmo*'s influence to an obscure by-way of American organbuilding history. Johann Traugott Wandke (1808-70), who emigrated from Silesia to Round Top, Texas, in 1855, built seven small pipe organs in central Texas. A notebook in Wandke's hand contains, among other miscellanea, excerpts from *Mmo*, specifically portions of chapters 9 and 13.[4]

Unlike *Anleitung*, *Mmo* is a posthumous publication. The complicated tale of its genesis and circuitous route to press is told in the Foreword to Vol. II. The title page of Adlung's manuscript stated that he began to write it in Jena in 1726,[5] and (in the words of the book's first editor, J.L Albrecht) "the work grew to be a manuscript of 820 very clearly written...pages."[6] Several clues in the work itself suggest that Adlung continued to pursue the project for at least a quarter of a century. In Adlung's enumeration of the organs in Hamburg that are to be found in Mattheson's Appendix to Niedt (Chap. 10, §.301), the organ at St. Michaelis is listed as "d)," followed by a statement in parentheses, "This organ has been destroyed by fire." If this remark is part of Adlung's work (as it appears to be) and not that of a subsequent editor, then it suggests that Adlung was still collecting and recording stoplists as late as the early 1750's (the Schnitger organ at the Michaeliskirche in Hamburg, the instrument whose stoplist appears in Mat-

---

2. For a more detailed analysis of these characteristics, see: Quentin Faulkner, "Jacob Adlung's *Musica mechanica organœdi* and the "Bach Organ," in: *Early keyboard Studies Newsletter* (pub. by the Westfield Center for Early Keyboard Studies), Vol. V, No. 2, May 1990. See also: Winfried Schrammek, "J.S. Bach und die Aufklärung," in: *Bach-Studien 7* (Leipzig: VEB Breitkopf & Härtel 9c.1982]), pp. 192-211.
3. See: Peter Williams, *The European Organ 1450-1850* (London: Batsford [1966], p. 166.
4. See: Gerald David Frank, *The Life and Work of Johann Traugott Wandke* (Harrisville, New Hampshire: The Boston Club Chapter of the Organ Historical Society, 1990), pp. 35f. & 59f.
5. See the Foreword to Vol. II, p. XVI.
6. *Ibid.*

theson's Appendix to Niedt, was destroyed by fire in 1750). Adlung also mentions the destruction of this organ in Chap. 7, §.146 (under "Flute à bec/Flute douce"). In 1753 Johann Mattheson gave the money for a new organ to replace it. The stoplist of that new organ is found later in the list of organs at Hamburg; it was added to *Mmo*, however, not by Adlung, but by J.F. Agricola, the book's second editor. In §.285, under St. Stephani in Bremen, there is a *Nota Bene* stating that the organ there was destroyed by fire on Dec. 6, 1754. Although it is impossible to be certain, this *N.B.* looks very much as if it were added by Agricola. These various bits of circumstantial evidence suggest an approximate terminus for Adlung's work with the stoplists, and indeed on *Mmo* as a whole. Such a terminus also tallies with the publication of Adlung's *Anleitung* in 1758; the author may well have abandoned work on *Mmo* in the early 1750's in order to concentrate on producing *Anleitung*.[7] Adlung's closing remark concerning the stoplist of the organ at St. Maximi in Merseburg, §.309, confirms that he was still collecting stoplists as late as 1752.

Although Adlung continued to work on the project throughout most of his life, it was still in manuscript form at the time of his death. His heirs turned the manuscript over to Johann Lorenz Albrecht.[8] Albrecht (1732-73) was an author, composer, Cantor and Music Director at the Marienkirche in Mühlhausen; like Adlung, he held an M.A. in philosophy. We do not know why Albrecht undertook the task of editing the manuscript and preparing it for print; he must have enjoyed a close friendship with Adlung, and perhaps also with Adlung's family. The task must indeed have been burdensome, and lengthy as well, since Albrecht found the manuscript overrun with marginal notes [9] and had to copy out the entire work (of course by hand) to fashion a suitable printer's copy.[10] In this process, Albrecht added a considerable number of editorial notes (labelling them with Arabic numerals: 1, 2, 3, etc.); both the character of these notes, however, as well as Albrecht's express testimony,[11] make it clear that he did not alter in any way the original text. This copy he submitted to the Berlin printer Friedrich Wilhelm Birnstiel to consider for publication.

Birnstiel was not entirely satisfied with the manuscript as he received it (for what reasons, we do not know[12]); therefore he turned it over to Johann Friedrich Agricola for further editing.[13] Agricola (1720-1774) was a student of J.S. Bach from 1738-41, during his student years at the University of Leipzig. Thereafter he moved to Berlin, working with J.J. Quantz and C.P.E. Bach. Frederick the Great eventually named him

---

7. Chapters 6-10 of *Anleitung* are largely duplicated in the later *Mmo*; Adlung apparently plundered his *Mmo* manuscript to include this material in *Anleitung*.
8. See the Publisher's Preface to the First Volume, as well as the Foreword to Vol. II, p. XVII-XVIII.
9. See the Foreword to Vol. II, p. XVI.
10. *ibid.*, p. XVII.
11. *ibid.*, pp. XVIII-XIX.
12. The reason may lie in Albrecht's relative youthfulness (he was only 36 years old when the volumes were published in 1768), in Agricola's greater professional and social stature, or in Birnstiel's long association with Agricola.
13. See the Foreword to Vol. II, p. XIX.

Royal Prussian Court Composer. Birnstiel had a longstanding connection with the students and admirers of J.S. Bach in Berlin. It was he who first published Bach's chorale settings, under the title *Vierstimmige Choralgesänge*, in two volumes: a volume of 100 published in 1765 (ed. F.W. Marpurg and C.P.E. Bach), and a second volume of 100 in 1769 (ed. J.F. Agricola). Agricola must have been working on the second volume at the time J.L. Albrecht submitted Adlung's work for publication; it was quite natural for Birnstiel to seek Agricola's editorial assistance with *Mmo*.

Agricola adopted the same editorial policy in the second editing process that Albrecht had followed in the first. He did not alter the original text, but added a number of additional notes and supplementary material, labelling his contributions with (**) or (less often) with letters of the Greek alphabet. His notes reveal just how faithful a disciple of J.S. Bach Agricola was. It is only in Agricola's notes that Bach is mentioned, and in every instance Bach is cited as an authority to modify or refute an opinion Adlung has expressed. As a result, Agricola's notes are of major significance in understanding Bach's views on organ design and construction. In a broader sense, however, the inestimable value of the entire *Mmo* as a mirror of Bach's opinions is assured, since by undertaking the task of editing the work Agricola gave it his tacit stamp of approval. We may thus assume that, aside from Agricola's relatively few contradictions, *Mmo* is in some measure a credible witness to J.S. Bach's ideas about the organ.

The multiple levels embodied in *Mmo* are a feature that many subsequent readers have missed; some modern scholars, for example, have quoted Agricola's remarks concerning J.S. Bach and attributed them to Adlung. To prevent this sort of confusion in the translation, each original editorial note (in addition to being labelled with the same sign as in the original text) ends with the name of its author in brackets. The added notes, creating three clearly defined layers of material, contribute greatly to the value of the work, since they represent ideas and opinions both 40 years later than Adlung's and (in Agricola's case) markedly more sophisticated and cosmopolitan (cf., e.g., Adlung's remarks on the cornet in §.132 with Agricola's lengthy note following). The modern translator's commentary, a fourth layer of material, appears as side-notes at the right of each page of the translation.

Although the Publisher's Preface to the First Volume suggests that the two volumes of *Mmo* were intended to be bound separately, in the surviving exemplars the two volumes are bound as one. The first volume ends with an extensive list (almost 100 pages) of 17th- and 18th-century German organ stoplists. It appears that Adlung's original intention was to assign a new paragraph number to each stoplist. Subsequent additions to the stoplists eventually rendered those numbers meaningless and superfluous.

One of the greatest challenges the translation has presented is the achievement of a written style that communicates some of the flavor of the original text. Although Luther's translation of the German Bible (1521f.) laid the foundation for modern German literary style, German was just beginning to come into its own as a literary lan-

guage during the 18th century. To cite an illustration: Praetorius's learned, scholarly treatment of the history of music is published in Vol. I of the *Syntagma musicum*—in Latin. It is only the practical advice on making music, in Vols. II & III, that is written in German (with a liberal lacing of Latin and Greek terms to express that which the prevailing German vocabulary lacked). Adlung's German is marked both by regional peculiarities and by the use of colloquialisms that would never pass muster in a modern scholarly publication—for a particularly striking instance of this, see "Bourdon," §.124. Albrecht tacitly acknowledges the distance between Adlung's German and that of the next generation when he writes, "Perhaps many readers might have wished to see in this Musical Mechanics this or that place more precisely worded or more elegantly written, and I cannot deny that I myself often expressed that wish during the process of copying the work."[14] Adlung's sentences are at times cryptic, and at times he quotes sources without understanding them.[15] His train of thought is at times interrupted by parenthetical observations that he fails to enclose in parentheses. The translation makes an attempt to interpret the more confusing of these instances, either by means of the modern footnote apparatus, or by supplementing the text with additional words or phrases in brackets. The process of translation has made it clear, however, that in some instances we are unlikely ever to know precisely what Adlung meant.

Since Adlung intended *Mmo* to be a compendium of information on the organ, he quotes extensively from earlier publications. Yet, despite Adlung's expressed fear of being accused of plagiarism,[16] his quotes are often not enclosed in quotation marks, and they frequently take the form of close paraphrases. Since Adlung is normally conscientious about citing his sources, the translator has not felt obliged to indicate the extent of the quote or how literal it is.

In its manifest attempt to adhere to empirical scientific methodology, Adlung's work betrays the influence of the dawning Enlightenment. Due to the publication's early date, however, it is not surprising that many of Adlung's scientific and etymological explanations are naive, fanciful and at times entirely mistaken. Some of the most obvious errors and misunderstandings have been identified in footnotes, but no systematic attempt has been made to correct the text.

※ ※ ※

A number of peculiarities about Adlung's text need further explanation. Consider first this sentence from the Foreword to Vol. II, p. XVI: "...*Anleitung zu der musikalischen Gelahrtheit*....2 Alphab. 9 Bogen in 8vo..." The literal translation is "*Anleitung*...2 Alphabets [and] 9 sheets in octavo." The meaning of this cryptic description requires further elucidation.[17] A common way of referring to the size and extent of a

---

14. Foreword to Vol. II, p. XVIII.
15. See Chap. 7, note [159].
16. See §.429.
17. The translator is indebted to Mr. James Wallmann for his kindness in supplying the explanation that follows.

book in Adlung's day was by how it was printed. One large sheet (*Bogen*) of paper was folded once across the long side to produce two folio leaves or four pages; folded a second time across the first fold to make four quarto (4°) leaves or eight pages; or folded a third time across the second fold for eight octave (8°) leaves or 16 pages. In a duodecimo (12°) book, a sheet was folded to make twelve leaves or twenty-four pages. Each gathering or signature (that is, one printed sheet) was signed by successive letters of the alphabet, twenty-three letters in all (A to Z, omitting J, U and W). Within a gathering, the recto of each leaf—at least in theory—was distinguished by a numerical suffix indicating that leaf's position in the gathering or signature: A1, A2, A3, etc. (In practice, the first leaf of a gathering was signed by the letter alone, without "1," and the leaves at the end of a signature were rarely signed at all.) Once twenty-three signatures had been reached and the first alphabet exhausted, letters were doubled (Aa) or tripled (Aaa) as necessary. This would have been readily understood by the readers of Adlung's day, a time when books were commonly purchased unbound, in signatures or gatherings, the purchaser seeing to it that the book was finished by the bookbinder. Thus the reference to "two alphabets plus nine signatures in octave" means that *Anleitung* required a total of 53 signatures: twice through the alphabet (for a total of 46 sets), plus 7 additional signatures, Aaa1-8 to Ggg 1-8. The other two signatures (to bring the total to 9, as recorded by Albrecht) are occupied by the title page, dedication, foreword and introduction at the beginning of the volume, a total of 15 leaves or two signatures (minus one leaf). For all practical purposes this numbering system is often irrelevant, since the pages of the text are also numbered with consecutive Arabic numerals.

Throughout *Mmo* Adlung makes constant reference to old units of measure and money: *Schuh* (foot), *Zoll* (inch), *Elle* (ell), *Rthlr.* (*Reichsthaler*), *Ohm*, etc. In the case of the first three, for each of which there is an exactly equivalent word in English, the translation adopts the English word. In the case of many others, the translation retains the original German. In any case, the reader must not think that the unit of measure, whether in English or German, is identical to its modern counterpart (if indeed it has one). Before the advent of standard systems of measurement (gradually adopted across Europe during the 19th century), units of measure with the same name could vary quite widely from one country or region to another. Therefore any attempt to give modern equivalents would rest on guesses (likely inaccurate ones) on the part of the translator. A compact source that offers documentable modern equivalents for old units of measure is: Fritz Verdenhalven, *Alte Maße, Münzen und Gewichte aus dem deutschen Sprachgebiet*. Neustadt an der Aisch: Verlag Degener & Co., 1968.

Finally, there is the matter of the generic and technical senses of the term *Flöte*. In §.145, under "Flöt or Flöte," Adlung writes: "... in the past, before reeds became fashionable, all wind instruments (Pfeifwerk) were called "flutes". Later on, when reed instruments were introduced, the word "flute" was used for all wind instruments that were not reeds. Thus Praetorius divides all stops into flutes and reeds; consequently principals, mixtures, gedakts, etc., are actually flutes in the general sense." Though he

does not make it clear in §.145, Adlung also adheres essentially to this method of classification; by this time, however, the term "flute stop" seems to be applied more specifically to all flues except principals (i.e., both flute and string stops).[18] For an example, in §.172, under "Offenflöt," Adlung writes: "Offenflöt means *aperta* [open] or *tibia aperta* [open flute] in Latin... There is also an Offenflöte in the Marienkirche at Danzig, where it is called Viol at the same time and is a 3′; thus it would be an open Quintflöte; see Praetorius, *l.c.*, p. 162." Defining "Offenflöt" as meaning merely "open," as well as equating a Viol with a Quintflöte, are both indications that Adlung (and Praetorius) use the word "Flöt" in both a generic sense (i.e., "flue stop") and a technical sense (i.e., "flute"). Thus the translation distinguishes between the generic and technical senses of the term *Flöt* or *Flöte*, wherever this distinction is clear from the text, by translating "Flöt" as either "flute" or "flue", and "Flötwerk" as either "flute stop" or "flue stop."

---

18. J.F. Agricola, *Mmo*'s final editor, is quite specific in this regard. In a lengthy article concerning organ stops and registration, Agricola divides flue stops [Pfeifenwerk] into principals and flutes (p. 491), and then indiscriminately lists both flute and string stops in the category of "flutes" (pp. 493ff.). See: Friedrich Wilhelm Marpurg, *Historisch-Kritische Beyträge zur Aufnahme der Musik*, Vol. III, Part 6 (Berlin: Gottlieb August Lange, 1758), pp. 486-518.

Acknowledgements

A great number of people have graciously and generously offered me their expert help in understanding and interpreting the many challenges and puzzles this translation has presented. I am grateful to all of them for their time, their advice, and their patience. If I have inadvertently omitted mentioning names of persons that should by right be in this list, I ask for their kind pardon, and assure them that the fault lies not in any ingratitude on my part, but rather in the scope of the project.

> Prof. Neil Adkin, Classics Department, University of Nebraska-Lincoln
> American Historical Society of Germans from Russia, Lincoln, Nebraska
> The staff of the Bayerische Staatsbibliothek, Munich, Germany
> Mr. Gene Bedient, organbuilder
> Prof. Konrad Brandt, Evangelische Hochschule für Kirchenmusik, Halle/Saale, Germany
> Prof. Anita Breckbill, Music Librarian, University of Nebraska-Lincoln
> Mr. Bradley Brookshire, harpsichordist
> Ms. Lynn Edwards Butler, Director Emerita, Westfield Center for Early Keyboard Studies, for years of patient help and wise counsel.
> Mr. Robert Cornell, organbuilder
> Deutsche akademische Austauschdienst
> Prof. Michael Eberth, Hochschule für Musik, Munich, Germany
> Frau Rosemarie Eberth
> Prof. Dr. Jürgen Eppelsheim, Ludwig-Maximilians-Universität, Munich, Germany, for many hours' wrestling with the most challenging passages of *Mmo*.
> Dr. Mary Murrell Faulkner
> Prof. Raymond Haggh, School of Music, University of Nebraska-Lincoln
> Prof. Dieter Karch, Dept. of Modern Languages, University of Nebraska-Lincoln
> Frau Kettmann, Bibliothekarin, Evangelische Hochschule für Kirchenmusik, Halle/Saale, Germany
> Prof. John Koster, Conservator, National Music Museum, Vermillion, South Dakota
> Prof. Joseph Kraus, School of Music, Florida State University, Tallahassee, Florida
> Dr. Laurence Libin, Research Curator, Department of Musical Instruments, Metropolitan Museum of Art, New York City
> The Administration of the Ludwig-Maximilians-Universität, Munich, Germany, especially Frau Musselmann
> Prof. Susan Messerli, Music Librarian, University of Nebraska-Lincoln

Ms. Jill Montgomery

National Endowment for the Humanities, for a Travel to Collections grant, summer 1990.

Prof. George Ritchie, School of Music, University of Nebraska-Lincoln

Prof. Paul Royster, Coordinator of Scholarly Communications, University of Nebraska-Lincoln Libraries, for his enthusiasm and creativity in preparing this digital publication.

Prof. Dr. Hans-Joachim Schulze, Director, Bach-Archiv Leipzig

Prof. Priscilla Silz, Westminster Choir College, Princeton, New Jersey

Prof. William Small, Department of Modern Languages, University of Maine, Bangor, Maine

Ms. Louise Small

Prof. Pamela Starr, School of Music, University of Nebraska-Lincoln

Mr. George Taylor, Organbuilder

Herr Günter Trobisch, instrument-maker

College of Fine and Performing Arts, University of Nebraska-Lincoln, for a faculty development leave

Prof. Harald Vogel, North German Organ Academy; Hochschule für Künste Bremen

Mr. James L. Wallmann

Herr Christian Wegscheider, organbuilder

Prof. Dr. Christoph Wolff, Department of Music, Harvard University; Director, Bach-Archiv Leipzig

Marlene M. Wong, Head of Werner Josten Library, Smith College, Northampton, Massachusetts

Prof. Jean-Claude Zehnder, Schola Cantorum Basiliensis, Basel, Switzerland

Notice

Mmo's complicated genesis, and in particular its posthumous publication, are the most likely reasons for a large number of words and passages whose meaning is ambiguous and/or unclear. Even with the generous, patient counsel I have received from those with special expertise, I have all too often been unable to arrive at an incontestable translation of Adlung's text.

These instances are indicated in dark red type in the electronic edition of the translation (http://digitalcommons.unl.edu/zeabook/6/), and show as gray in the printed version (3 volumes; available from http://www.lulu.com/spotlight/unllib).

Among the advantages of electronic publishing is the opportunity it affords to alter and correct such words and passages. The translator and publisher would be grateful for suggested corrections and clarifications, but they reserve the right to accept or reject them as they see fit.

Quentin Faulkner

MUSICA MECHANICA ORGANOEDI.

Das ist:

Gründlicher Unterricht

von

der Struktur, Gebrauch und Erhaltung, ꝛc.

der Orgeln, Clavicymbel, Clavichordien

und

anderer Instrumente,

in so fern
einem Organisten von solchen Sachen etwas zu wissen nöhtig ist.

Vorgestellet von

M. Jakob Adlung,

weil. der Churfürstl. Maynzis. Akademie nützlicher Wissenschaften in Erfurt ordentl. Mitgliede,
des evangel. Rathsgymnasii ordentl. Lehrer, wie auch Organisten an der evangel.
Raths- und Predigerkirche daselbst.

Aus
der hinterlassenen Handschrift des seel. Hrn. Verfassers in Ordnung gebracht
mit einigen Anmerkungen und einer Vorrede versehen,
und zum Drucke befördert

von

M. Johann Lorenz Albrecht,

kaiserl. gekrönten Dichter, Collegen der vierten Classe am Gymnasio, wie auch Cantor und Musikdirektor
bey der oberstädtischen Hauptkirche, Beatä Mariä Virginis, zu Mühlhausen in Thüringen,
und der hochlöbl. deutschen Gesellschaft zu Altdorf Ehrenmitgliede.

Nebst zwey Tabellen und vielen Figuren.

Berlin,

gedruckt und verlegt von Friedrich Wilhelm Birnstiel, königl. privil. Buchdrucker,

1768.

MUSICAL MECHANICS FOR THE ORGANIST.

That is:

Fundamental Instruction
concerning

the Structure, use, and Maintenance, etc.

of Organs, Harpsichords, Clavichords
and

other Instruments
to the degree
that it is necessary for an organist to know something about such things.
set forth by

Jakob Adlung, M.A.
formerly a regular member of the Mainz Electoral Academy of Practical Sciences at Erfurt,
regular instructor in the Protestant Municipal Gymnasium, as well as organist of the
Protestant Municipal Predigerkirche.

Put into order
from the manuscript left by the late author, provided with a
number of notes and a preface, and
conveyed into print
by

Johann Lorenz Albrecht, M.A.
Imperial Poet-Laureate, Colleague of the Fourth Class at the Gymnasium, as well as Cantor and Director
of Music of the Principal Church of the Blessed Virgin Mary in the upper town at Mühlhausen in
Thuringia, and Honorary Member of the eminent German Society at Altdorf.

Together with two charts and many figures.

Berlin,
printed and published by Friedrich Wilhelm Birnstiel,
Printer by appointment to his Royal Majesty,
1768.

Vorbericht des Verlegers,
zum
Ersten Bande.

Das Buch, deffen erster Band hierbey geliefert wird, ist nicht allein zum Nutzen angehender, auch wol mancher schon lange im Amte gewesener Organisten, und aller anderer Liebhaber des größten, vollständigsten und künstlichsten unter allen musikalischen Instrumenten, der Orgel; sondern auch zum Besten der Ausüber und Freunde der Clavicimbel, Clavichorde, und anderer Instrumente, welche vermittelst der Tasten klingend gemacht werden, geschrieben worden. Sein Verfasser ist, wie der Titel schon sagt, der seel. Hr. Jacob Adlung, Professor und Organist an der Predigerkirche zu Erfurt: ein Mann der mit einer guten Gelehrsamkeit auch große Einsichten in die theoretische und praktische Musik verbunden hatte.

Der Verleger war anfänglich willens das ganze Werk auf einmal zu liefern; und des Hrn. M. Johann Lorenz Albrecht in Mühlhausen, der das Manuscript dieses Buchs von den Adlungischen Erben erhalten, es mit verschiedenen Anmerkungen vermehret, und dem Verleger zum Drucke überlassen hatte, ausführliche Vorrede dazu, sollte es begleiten.

Allein, da dieses Buch die Stärke eines bequemen Quartbandes zu sehr überschreiten würde: so hat sich der Verleger entschlossen, es in zween Bände zu theilen; und giebt also hiermit den ersten aus.

Publisher's Preface
to
the First Volume

The book whose first volume you see before you is not only written for use by prospective as well as more advanced organists, many of whom have long held positions, and for all other admirers of the organ, that greatest, most perfect and artistic of all musical instruments; but it is also written for the best among the performers and friends of the harpsichord, clavichord and other instruments that are made to sound by means of keys. The author of the book is, as the title indicates, the late Mr. Jacob Adlung, Professor and Organist at the Predigerkirche in Erfurt, a man in whom were united sound learning and great insight into theoretical and practical music.

The publisher was at first of a mind to deliver the entire work at once, accompanied by a lengthy preface written by Mr. Johann Lorenz Albrecht, M.A., of Mühlhausen, who received the manuscript of this book from Adlung's heirs, augmented it with various notes, and entrusted it to the publisher to print.

However, since a single quarto volume would be too weak for the entire book, the publisher has decided to divide it into two volumes, of which the first is before you.

Vorbericht.

Die geneigten Leser desselben werden die Unbequemlichkeit, daß nicht alles, was die Orgel betrift, in diesen ersten Band hat gebracht werden können, weil sonst der zweyte gar zu schwach geworden seyn würde, von sich selbst einsehen, und entschuldigen.

Auf künftige Ostermesse g. G. soll der zweyte Band, nebst des Hrn. Albrecht Vorrede, und das Register zum ganzen Werke, unfehlbar nachfolgen.

Anitzo wird nur noch angemerkt, daß, auf des Verlegers Verlangen, von dem Königl. Preußis. Hofcomponisten, Hrn. Johann Friedrich Agricola, nicht nur noch einige nöthige Anmerkungen und Erläuterungen hie und da beygefüget, sondern auch zum Kapitel von den Orgeldispositionen, welches das Zehnte ist, noch verschiedene andere nicht im Druck bekannte Dispositionen berühmter Orgeln zugesetzt, und die, so man noch in andern Büchern gedruckt findet, welche aber Hr. Adlung nicht angeführet hatte, zum Theil auch nicht hatte anführen können, angezeigt worden sind.

Die Zusätze des Hrn. Agricola unterscheiden sich von den andern entweder durch vorgesetzte (**), oder durch kleine griechische Buchstaben. Es ist dadurch eine Sammlung von Orgeldispositionen entstanden, welche die vollständigste ist, die man bis itzo hat: und man glaubt Kennern und Liebhabern der Orgeln dadurch nicht mißfällig geworden zu seyn.

Berlin, am 1sten Oktobr. 1767.

der Verleger.

MVSICA

Preface.

Thus not everything that pertains to the organ could be included in this first volume; otherwise the second volume would have been too insubstantial. The sympathetic reader will, we trust, understand this inconvenience and excuse it.

The second volume will follow without fail, God willing, by next Easter, together with Mr. Albrecht's preface and an index to the entire work.[†]

In addition it should be noted that, at the publisher's request, the Royal Prussian Court Composer, Mr. Johann Friedrich Agricola, has not only contributed a number of necessary notes and comments here and there, but has also added various other organ specifications (some of which have not yet appeared in print, others that appear in other books, but were not or could not be included by Mr. Adlung) to the chapter on organ specifications, that is, Chapter 10.

The contributions of Mr. Agricola may be distinguished from the rest of the book by the (**) preceding them, or by small Greek letters. Thus has been created the most complete collection of organ specifications that has appeared to date; thereby we hope that connoisseurs and admirers of the organ will not be displeased.

Berlin, October 1, 1767.

the Publisher.

[†] The two volumes seem to have been bound as one when the treatise was finally published.

MVSICA
MECHANICA
ORGANOEDI.

MUSICAL
MECHANICS
FOR THE ORGANIST

PRAELIMINARIA.
Von
der Clavierkunst überhaupt.

Von der Musik überhaupt will ich anjezo nichts reden, weil davon alle musikalische Lehrbücher angefüllet sind. Sie wird in die theoretische und praktische Musik eingetheilet. Jene zeigt, wie eine Melodie und Harmonie regelmäßig zu setzen, und nimmt ihre Gründe aus der **Physik, Moral** und **Mathematik,** wenigstens was die **Harmonicam** betrift: Diese aber applicirt sothane Anweisung, und bestehet im würklichen Componiren, oder der componirten Sachen Execution nach solchen Principiis. Unter so vielen Instrumenten, worauf solche Execution verrichtet wird, sind diejenigen oben an zu setzen, welche mit Clavieren versehen sind, als auf welchen die vollkommenste Harmonie hervorzubringen. Diese sind z. Er. **Orgeln, Clavikordien, Clavessins, Clavicitheria, Spi-**
nette,

PRELIMINARY MATTERS
concerning
the Art of the Keyboard in General.

I do not intend to speak about music in general, since all musical textbooks are full of this sort of thing. Music is divided into theoretical and practical matters. The former indicates the rules and procedures governing melody and harmony, and is based upon physics, ethics and mathematics (at least as far as harmony is concerned). The latter however, puts this instruction to practical application, and consists of actual composition, or the execution of such matters as pertain to composition according to given principles. Among the many instruments upon which the results of such activity may be realized, pride of place must be accorded to those that are provided with keyboards, since they are capable of producing the most perfect harmony. These instruments are, for example, organs, clavichords, harpsichords, clavicitheria, spinets, lute harpsichords,

nette, Lautenwerke, Violdigambenwerke u. d. gl. Und eben deswegen wird mehr zu einem Trakteur solcher Instrumente erfordert, als zu andern, so, daß man wegen der Weitläuftigkeit der Lehren schon vorlängst vier Theile daraus gemacht hat, da man die Lernenden hat unterwiesen 1) in Generalbasse, 2) in Choralen, 3) in der italienischen Tabulatur, 4) in der Fantasie. Denn wenn ich sagen soll, wie es mir deucht; so hat ein Organist, wenn er recht seyn soll, eben das zu wissen nöthig, was die Componisten sonst sich allein zuschreiben.¹) Und was ist denn die Fantasie? Ist es nicht eine stete Compositio extemporanea, die eben so regelmäßig und reine seyn muß, als andere Arten? Die Chorale können gleichfalls eine Compositio extemporanea genennet werden, wenn einer dieselben nicht aus dem Choralbuche, oder aus der Memorie, sondern aus eigener Invention traktirt. Es wäre nur zu wünschen, daß die Lehrmeister ihren Schülern dasjenige recht ordentlich, deutlich und gründlich beybrächten, was zu diesen vier Theilen gehöret; aber wieweit dies geschehe, wissen wir alle. Gesetzt aber, es wäre damit zur Richtigkeit; so dünket mir doch, es sey, über die allgemeine Anleitung zur Musik, die allhier sonderlich accurat zu geben, noch ein nöthiges Stück, nemlich die Mechanica, vergessen. Ob diese für Organisten gehöre, wird im folgenden 1 Kap. untersucht werden. Jezo sage ich nur dies, daß die Orgelmacher freylich diese Dinge accurater inne haben müssen, als ein Organist, deswegen es auch die Orgelmacherkunst heißt: allein,

ein

---

¹) Der berühmte Herr Organist Schröter in Nordhausen läßt sich hierüber also vernehmen und schreibt: „Ein vollkommener Organist muß nicht weniger als ein tüchtiger „Kapellmeister verstehen. Und von beyden gilt das bekannte Sprichwort: Nicht alle „sind gute Köche, die lange Messer tragen." S. Mizlers musikal. Bibliothek. 3 B. 2 Theil. S. 252.

keyed gambas, and the like. For this reason, more is demanded from one who plays such instruments than from others. Due to the complexity of the subject, it was long ago divided into four areas: students must be instructed 1) in figured bass, 2) in hymn-playing (in Choralen*), 3) in Italian tabulature,† and 4) in improvisation. To be honest, as I see it, an organist (if he is competent) must be just as knowledgeable as a composer.[1] For what indeed is improvisation? Is it not continuous extemporaneous composition, that must be just as orderly and refined as other types [of composition]? Playing hymns can also be called extemporaneous composition, if one plays them not out of a hymnbook, nor from memory, but using his own improvisatory skills. One could only wish that teachers would impart to their students everything that pertains to these four areas in an organized, clear and thorough fashion; we all know, however, how infrequently this happens. Even supposing this instruction were properly given, though, I do believe that there is yet one other area that needs to be imparted very accurately in any general introduction to music, and that is usually forgotten, namely, the area of mechanics. Chapter 1 following addresses whether this pertains to organists. For now I will say only that an organbuilder must of course understand these things more thoroughly than an organist (hence we refer to the "art of organbuilding"); nevertheless, an organist must

* meaning accompanying any monophonic congregational singing.

† Adlung's *Anleitung zu der musikalischen Gelahrtheit*, pp. 699f., tells us that by this term Adlung means learning to read notes on staves (i.e., modern musical notation), as opposed to the letters of north German tabulature, particularly in keyboard works (in contrast to figured bass or chorale playing).

---

1) The well-known Nordhausen organist Schröter‡ is of the same opinion; he writes: "An accomplished organist must understand no less than a proficient Kapellmeister. The same saying holds true for both: "Not everyone who carries a long knife is a good cook." See Mizler's Musikalische Bibliothek, Vol. 3, Part 2, p. 252. [Albrecht]

‡ Christoph Gottlieb Schröter (1699-1782).

ein Organist muß es auch wissen. Daß man es die **Orgelmacherkunst** nennt, ob man schon auch andere Instrumente nebst der Orgel hier antrift, geschiehet eben deswegen, weswegen ein Organist ein **Organist**, und nicht ein **Spinettist** ꝛc. genennet wird, weil die Orgel das vornehmste Instrument ist, daß also der Name a potiori hergenommen wird. Was sonst die Orgelmacherkunst in sich begreife, kann man z. Ex. lesen in **Johann Caspar Trosts Weissenfelsischen Orgel. Kap. 1.** Sie erfordert einen guten Grund in der **Mathematik**, weil sie stets mit Aus- und Abmessungen zu thun hat. Es gehören viel Handwerke dazu. Es muß einer ein guter **Tischler, Klempener, Schmidt,** u. s. w. seyn. Nicht weniger muß auch ein guter Orgelmacher die **Metalle** und **Holzarten** aus der **Physik** verstehen; er muß **drechseln** können: sonderlich aber wird erfordert, daß er die **Architektur** gründlich inne habe.²) Es haben auch die Orgelmacher desfalls besondere Priuilegia, und heißet diese Sache kein Handwerk, sondern eine **Kunst**. Von den Iuribus und Priuilegiis der Orgelmacher soll man nachschlagen den Traktat de Iuribus et Priuilegiis Musicorum Hrn. **Johann Caspar Trosts**, wie er ihn allegirt Kap. 1. S. 3. der Weissenfelsischen Orgel.

Ich habe hier gesucht den Lernenden zu dienen, denen solche Lehrherren nicht beschert sind, von welchen sie dergleichen erfahren könnten: wird es aber von den Liebhabern der edlen Musik wohl aufgenommen; so bin ich mit Gott

---

²) Von den Eigenschaften eines rechtschaffenen Orgelbauers hat Herr Joh. Adam Jacob Ludwig, Postsekretär in Hof, einen feinen Traktat geschrieben, welchen hierbey zum Nachlesen bestens empfehle. Er ist zu Hof 1759. auf 2 Bogen in 4to gedruckt worden.

also be familiar with them. We call it the "art of organbuilding," even though we thereby are referring to other instruments in addition to the organ. Why? For the same reason that an organist is called an organist, and not a spinettist; because the organ is the most distinguished instrument, and thus its name is given pride of place. Johann Caspar Trost's book, *Beschreibung der Orgel zu Weissenfels*, Chap. 1,* describes what is included in the art of the organbuilder. It demands a good background in mathematics, because it is constantly concerned with measurements and dimensions. There is a great deal of handwork connected with it; one must be a good wookworker, metalworker, blacksmith, etc. No less must a good organbuilder understand the physical properties of various types of metal and wood. He must be skilled at the lathe. But it is especially necessary that he have a thorough understanding of architecture.2) For this reason organbuilders have garnered special recognition (Privilegia), and their work is called not a craft, but an art. Concerning the privileges and responsibilities of the organbuilder one should consult the treatise *de Iuribus et Privilegiis Musicorum* by Johann Caspar Trost, which he refers to in Chapter I, p. 3, of [the treatise on] the Weissenfels organ.

* "Was zu der Orgelmacher=Kunst gehöre" ("That which pertains to the Art of Organbuilding"), pp. 1-3.

In this book I have sought to be of service to students who are not blessed with proper teachers from whom they can learn these things. But since admirers of fine music may well also study my work, with God's help I have determined to sketch out the re-

2) Mr. Johann Adam Jacob Ludwig, Postal Official in Hof, has written an excellent treatise on the attributes of a genuine organbuilder; one would be well-advised to read it. It was published in Hof in 1759 as a quarto in two signatures.† [Albrecht]

† i.e., 16 pages; for an explanation of this method of book manufacture, see the Translator's Preface.

entschlossen, die übrigen Theile der Clavierkunst auch zu entwerfen, daß endlich alles, was zu einem tüchtigen Organisten gehöret, deutlicher und weitläuftiger abgehandelt werde,[3] als woran leider ein großer Mangel, theils aus Unwissenheit, theils aus Neid und Bosheit, theils aus Faulheit der Organisten, welchen es aber gewiß keine große Ehre ist, von andern sich in ihr Scibile eingreifen zu lassen, da ihrer doch so eine große Menge in der Welt gewesen, und noch sind. Doch es sey wie ihm wolle: Wir wollen eins nach dem andern vornehmen.

[3] Was der sel. Herr Professor Adlung zu leisten versprochen, dasselbe ist bereits im Jahr 1758 in Erfüllung gebracht worden, nemlich in der zu Erfurt edirten nützlichen Anleitung zu der musikalischen Gelahrtheit; als in deren praktischem Theile alles hinlänglich abgehandelt ist, was zur Bildung eines tüchtigen Organisten erfordert wird.

maining aspects of the art of the keyboard, so that everything that pertains to a competent organist may finally be treated more clearly and in more adequate detail,[3] [a topic] in which regrettably there is a great deficiency, in part due to ignorance, in part due to jealousy and malice, in part due to the laziness of organists who consider it by no means a great honor to let others intrude upon their expertise. Of such there have been and continue to be a great number in the world. But be that as it may, we will consider each thing in its turn.

[3] The late Prof. Adlung's promise is already fulfilled in his useful *Anleitung zu der musikalischen Gelahrtheit*, published in Erfurt in the year 1758; in its section on practice he treats quite adequately what is required for the training of a competent organist. [Albrecht]

Das I. Kapitel.

Von der Natur, Nutzen, Methode und Hülfsmitteln in der Mechanik.

Inhalt.

§. 1. Von des Worts (*mechanica*) Etymologia und Homonymia. §. 2. Synonymia. §. 3. Ob diese Lehre nöthig sey? §. 4. Die Nothwendigkeit wird bewiesen aus dem Regiesterziehen. §. 5. Weil sonst die Orgel leicht ruiniret wird. §. 6. Den Orgelmachern suche ich keinen Tort zu thun. §. 7. Von der Methode und Eintheilung dieser Lehren. §. 8. Von den Hülfsmitteln, sonderlich vom Reisen. §. 9. Von Prätorii Syntagmate. §. 10. Werkmeisters Paradoxal-Discurse; Organum grüningense; Orgelprobe. §. 11. Boxbergs Görlitzer Orgel; Matthesons Orcheftre; Niedts P. II. §. 12. Kircheri Musurgia; Ianowka; Bendeleri Organopoeia; Trosts Weissenfelsische Orgel.

§. 1.

Das Wort Mechanica ist dem Ursprunge nach griechisch: denn μηχανή heißt unter andern so viel, als machina, instrumentum, &c. So kann z. E. ein Uhrwerk eine machina, μηχανή, heissen u. s. w. Daher wird μηχανικός, mechanicus, geleitet, welches im foeminino μηχανική hat, und worunter τέχνη, ars, eine Kunst, verstanden wird; ist also τέχνη μηχανική die Kunst allerhand machinas, instrumenta u. s. w. zu verfertigen. Μηχανικός, mechanicus, heißt der Künstler, welcher die Wissenschaft und Geschicklichkeit besitzt, allerhand machinas zu verfertigen. Es wird aber das Wort Mechanica mehrern Künsten beygelegt: denn
wer

Chapter I.

Concerning the Nature, Uses, Methods and Aids of Mechanics.

Contents:

§.1. Etymology and homonyms for the word "mechanica." §.2. Synonyms. §.3. Is it necessary to learn about mechanics? §.4. Choosing the [appropriate] stops proves its necessity. §.5. Otherwise the organ might easily be damaged. §.6. I do not seek to do any harm to organbuilders. §.7. Concerning the methods and classification of this knowledge. §.8. Concerning the aids [in gaining this knowledge], especially travel. §.9. Concerning Praetorius's *Syntagma*. §.10. Werkmeister's *Paradoxal-Discurse*; *Organum gruningense*; *Orgelprobe*. §.11. Boxberg's *Görlitzer Orgel*; Mattheson's [*Neu-eröffnete*] *Orchestre*; Niedt's [*Musicalische Handleitung*], Part II. §.12. Kircher's *Musurgia*; Janowka; Bendeler's *Organopoeia*; Trost's *Weissenfelßische Orgel*.

§. 1.

The word "mechanica" is Greek by origin; for μηχανή means, among other things, the same as "machine" or "implement". For example, a clock-work can be called a machine, μηχανή. Thence is derived μηχανικοσ, *mechanicus*, the feminine form of which is μαηχανικὴ,* by which is implied τέχνη, *ars*, "art"; thus τέχνη μηχανικὴ is the art of constructing all sorts of machines or implements. Μηχανικὸσ, *mechanicus*, refers to the artist who possesses the knowledge and skill to construct all sorts of machines. The word *mechanica* is often

* sic; should be μηχανικὴ.

wer weis nicht, was die Mechanica bey den Mathematicis sey? Wem ist unbekannt, daß man einen erfahrnen Goldarbeiter, einen guten Tischler, und überhaupt einen berufenen Künstler, der NB. in die Augen fallende Machinas verfertiget, einen Mechanicum nennt? [4]) Aber ich nehme das Wort etwas enger, und verstehe dadurch eine Wissenschaft, diejenigen Werkzeuge, deren sich ein Organiste zu bedienen pfleget, und welche allerdings auch Machinae genennet werden können, zu machen, zu erhalten, und zu verbessern.

§. 2.

Einen andern Namen wußte ich diesem Theile der Clavierwissenschaft nicht zu geben, der ausgedruckt hätte, was ich darunter begreife. Organopoeiam, oder Orgelmacherey konnte ich ihn nicht nennen, obwol besagtes Wort nicht gar unbekannt ist; und so hat z. B. Bendeler einen Traktat von solcher Materie benennet. Hier wollen wir nicht sowol Orgeln machen, oder machen lernen, als nur einigermaaßen davon urtheilen, wenn sie gemacht werden, oder zu machen sind; auch gedenken wir nicht allein von den Orgeln zu reden, sondern auch von andern Instrumenten, die ein Organist zu kennen besondere Ursache findet. Um der letztangeführten Ursache willen konnte ich auch das Wort Organographia nicht brauchen, welches eine Beschreibung der Orgeln andeutet, weil wir unsere Gedanken auf etwas mehrers gerichtet haben. Uebrigens hat Michael Prätorius in Syntagmate Tom. II. die letzte Benennung gebraucht, da er doch nicht nur von Orgeln, sondern auch von andern musikalischen Instrumenten geschrieben. Wollte man auf die eigentliche Bedeutung des Worts ὄργανον sehen; so könnte diese Benennung sowol als die vorige beybehalten werden; sintemal dadurch ein jedes Instrument bedeutet wird, es sey eine Orgel, oder etwas anders. Es müßte aber dabey noch angemerket werden, daß insbesondere anjetzo von solchen Instrumenten geredet werde, die der Organiste, als ein Organiste, zu brauchen pflegt; und dies ist es auch, was bey unserer Benennung *Mechanica* zu erinnern, damit einer nicht die Struktur, z. Ex. einer Harfe, Laute, Violin u. s. w. allhier zu finden vermeyne, obschon diese und andere mehr zu der Mechanica Musica mit gezogen werden müßten, wenn man das Wort in weitläuftigerm Verstande annehmen wollte. Die hernach zu erzählenden Kapitel dieses Werks werden noch deutlicher zu erkennen geben, was ich dadurch verstehe.

§. 3.

Es fragt sich hierbey, ob solche Erkenntniß der Mechanicae einem Organisten nicht nur nützlich, sondern auch nöthig sey? Ich antworte, ohne mir desfalls Bedenkzeit auszubitten: Ja. Wie rare Vögel aber dergleichen Organisten sind, beweißt die Erfahrung. Denn wie ich zuvor allbereits erinnert; (s. die Präliminaria,) so pflegt ein Lehrmeister, wenigstens hier zu Lande, seinen Untergebenen weiter nichts vorzutragen

---

[4]) *Andreae Reyheri* Theatrum Latino-Germanico-Graecum, S. 1393. welcher das Wort *Mechanicus* durch opificem eorum operum, quae manu fiunt, erkläret.

applied to a number of arts; who could be ignorant of its use in mathematics, or who could be unaware that a skilled goldsmith is called a mechanic, or a fine cabinetmaker, or indeed any qualified artist who constructs any of the machines that one can see? 4) I define the word, however, somewhat more narrowly, and understand it to mean knowing how to make, preserve and repair those implements that are of service to an organist and that can indeed be called "machines."

§. 2.

I can think of no other name to give this branch of keyboard science that could express what I mean. I could not call it *organopoeia*, or organbuilding, although this term is certainly not unfamiliar; in fact, Bendeler has used this term as the title of a treatise on such matters.* Here we are not so much concerned with building organs, or learning to build them, as we are to report in some measure how they are made, or should be made. In addition, we intend not only to speak about the organ, but also about other instruments that an organist in particular needs to know about. For this very same reason I also could not use the word *organographia*, since it connotes a description of the organ, while we have set our sights rather more broadly than that. I am aware that Michael Praetorius in his *Syntagma*, Vol. II,† has used this term to denote not only matters pertaining to the organ, but to other musical instruments as well. If one considers the actual meaning of the word ὄργανον [organon], then one might regard it as synonymous with *mechanica*, since it [basically] denotes any instrument, be it an organ or anything else. I want to make it clear, however, that here I will speak primarily about those instruments that an organist as such is likely to use. One need only remember that the use of the term *mechanica* here excludes any discussion of, for example, the structure of a harp, a lute, a violin, etc., even though these and many others besides must be considered under "musical mechanics," if one wishes to consider the term in its broadest sense. The following chapters of this book will continue to clarify what I mean.

* Johann Philipp Bendeler, *Organopoeia, oder Unterweisung, wie eine Orgel nach ihren Hauptstücken ... zu erbauen*. Frankfurt und Leipzig: Calvisius [c.1690].

† Praetorius, Michael, *Syntagma musicum*, Vol. II, *De Organographia*. Wolfenbüttel: Holwein, 1618/1619.

§. 3.

Here one might ask, "Is it necessary or even useful for an organist to be knowledgeable about mechanics?" Without a moment's hesitation I answer, "Yes." Practical experience will verify, however, what rare birds such [well-informed] organists are. As I have already observed (see the Preliminary Matters [above]), it is not usual, at least in these parts, for a teacher to introduce his charges to anything beyond figured bass,

4.) see Andreas Reyher's *Theatrum Latino-Germanico-Graecum*, p. 1393, where the word *mechanicus* is defined as "a worker with his hands." [Albrecht]

gen als den Generalbaß, Choral, etwas von der italienischen Tabulatur (da sie nicht einmal eine Beschreibung von einer Picce geben) und etwas von der Fantasie. Und damit nicht jemand meyne, als sey die Schuld auf die Lernenden zu geben, welche aus unzeitiger Menage die Information allzubald quittirten; so berufe ich mich auf die Contrakte, da die Organistenkunst vor eine gewisse Geldsumme überhaupt verdungen wird; ich verwette, es werden wenige oder gar keine seyn, darinnen dieser Disciplin mit einem Worte gedacht wird. Die Ursache ist, weil vielen eine solche Erkenntniß fehlet, oder weil, wenn die Information überhaupt verdungen wird, man fein bald davon kommen will; oder man denkt, es müßte alsdann ein mehres von dem Discipul gezahlet werden, durch welche Theurung man seinen Applausum verlieren dürfte. Bey vielen ist die Ursache, weil sie den Nutzen und Nothwendigkeit der Doktrin nicht genugsam einsehen.

§. 4.

Daß aber dergleichen Lehren unumgänglich nöthig sind, kann aus folgendem zur Gnüge erhellen. Ein jeder Künstler und Handwerksmann muß ja seine Instrumente kennen, und würde z. Ex. ein Tischler übel zurechte kommen, wenn er seine mannigfaltigen Höbel nicht nennen, oder einen von dem andern unterscheiden könnte; oder wenn er so viel Wissenschaft nicht besäße, daß er das Hobeleisen nach Nothdurft ein- oder auswärts ziehen könnte. Ein Organist muß den Ohren mit steten Veränderungen zur Kützelung dienen, da er bald dies bald ein ander Register hören läßt; wie soll er denn seiner Pflicht ein Genüge leisten, wenn er die Register nicht kennt, und nicht weis, wie ein jedes klingt, oder was man damit thun solle? Ja, sagt man, die Register muß einer freylich kennen lernen, und das kann durch den Gebrauch und Zuschauen geschehen, wenn die Lehrmeister solche ziehen. Antwort: Gut; das gehört auch zur Mechanica. Also ist die Nothwendigkeit dieses Stücks in so weit bewiesen. Daß aber aus dem Zusehen ein Lehrschüler gescheid werden solle, kann ich mir nicht einbilden. Denn man zieht nicht oft die Register einzeln, damit man vernehme, wie ein jedes eigentlich klinge; und allezeit kann ja der Lehrling nicht dabey seyn. Auch sind in einer Orgel oft die wenigsten Register, wie kann er denn durch das Gehör derselben Natur kennen lernen? Daher es denn kommt, daß einer auf einer fremden Orgel nicht mehr zu ziehen weis, als was er auf seiner zu ziehen gewohnt gewesen. Also muß man nothwendig in Beyseyn verständiger Leute sich prostituiren.

§. 5.

Ich erfordere aber über die Erkänntniß der Register auch die Wissenschaft anderer Dinge, und solches darum, damit ein Liebhaber des Claviers sein Instrument durch Unvorsichtigkeit nicht verderbe, sondern es zu erhalten wisse, auch wo ja etwas von Kleinigkeiten zu verbessern wäre, es selbst zu corrigiren geschickt sey, damit nicht der Kirche oder sich zum Schaden um aller Kleinigkeiten willen der Orgelmacher oder Mechanicus müsse bemühet werden, zumal verschiedene solcher Leute gar gewissenlos verfahren, und

hymn playing, something about Italian tablature* (though they may never give a description of an actual piece) and something about improvisation. Lest anyone think, however, that students are at fault for forgetting what they have learned, thinking it to be so much old-fashioned baggage, one need only take note of the contracts that require an organist to exercise his art for a given sum of money. I will wager that few or none of them mention a single word about this subject.† There are a number of reasons for this: many [organists] are simply lacking in this knowledge; or if the contract stipulates expertise in this area, an organist will soon try to get out of it; or an applicant may think that such expertise would call for a higher salary and thus cause him to lose favor. Yet it is often the case that organists simply do not adequately appreciate the usefulness and necessity of such knowledge.

* See the footnote in the Foreword that explains this term.

† i.e., few contracts require an understanding of the mechanics of the organ and other keyboard instruments.

§. 4.

Here is why such knowledge is absolutely necessary: every artist, every craftsman, must surely be acquainted with his tools. For example, one would surely think ill of a cabinetmaker who could not name or distinguish between his various planes, or who did not possess the expertise necessary to draw his plane in first one direction and then another as required. In order to tickle his listener's ears, an organist must serve up constant variety by letting the listener hear first this and then that stop. How is he going to be able to fulfill satisfactorily this obligation if he does not know the stops, if he does not know the sound each of them produces nor what he should do with them? Someone may say, "Of course the stops must be learned, but that can be accomplished through practice and observation as the teacher uses them." My answer: "Fine! That belongs to the area of mechanics as well; the necessity of this matter is thus proven." I simply cannot imagine, however, that a student could learn discrimination merely through observation; for one does not often use the stops singly, so that one can perceive how each of them actually sounds, and furthermore, a student cannot be constantly at his teacher's side. In addition, there are often very few stops in an organ; how then is the student to learn the qualities [of all sorts of stops] by listening? The result is that on an unfamiliar organ such a student knows only to pull those stops that he has been used to pulling where he practices. He therefore unavoidably embarrasses himself in the presence of knowledgeable people.

§. 5.

Above and beyond a knowledge of stops, however, I also require an acquaintance with other matters, in order that a keyboard practitioner may not damage his instrument through carelessness, but rather understand how to preserve it, and even be skillful enough to execute minor repairs on it, so that he does not put the church or himself to the bother and expense of calling the organbuilder, the *mechanicus*, for trifling repairs. Ignorant people often do this without thinking, thus making a mountain out

aus einer Mücke einen Elephanten machen, sich folglich alles theuer genug bezahlen lassen, sonderlich wenn man dieselbe von andern Orten muß holen lassen. Ferner wird von einem Organisten gar oft verlangt eine Disposition zu machen; einen Contrakt zu verfertigen; einen Orgelbau zu dirigiren; eine Orgel zu probiren; ein Claviford u. d. gl. zu beziehen u. s. w. O, wie bestehet da mancher so gar kahl, und begeht solche Schnitzer, welche die Gemeinden oft in langer Zeit nicht verwinden können! Zumal wenn es zur Orgelprobe kömmt; da siehet man seinen Gräuel, und rechtschaffene Orgelmacher müssen mit großen Verdruß ihre Arbeit von einem Ignoranten tadeln lassen, welche doch was zu reden haben wollen, um ihre paar Thaler nicht umsonst einzustecken.[5]) Mehr thue ich nicht hinzu, um die Nothwendigkeit zu beweisen. Es beliebe der Musikliebende diese Abhandlung selbst durchzublättern; so wird sich die Lust gar bald finden; und da ich nicht läugne, daß etliche Kapitel für andern zu wissen nöthig sind; so kann ich es auch keinem Organisten verdenken, wenn er dieselben am fleißigsten lieset: nur wolle man das andere nicht gar bey Seite setzen. Also ist die Erkenntniß der Register nöthiger, als des übrigen Orgelbaues; der Orgelbau ist doch noch nöthiger, als die Historie der Orgeln, ɼc.

§. 6.

Ob ich bey allen Orgelmachern viel Dank verdienen werde, lasse ich dahin gestellet seyn, wenigstens lassen sich manche gar sehr bitten, wenn sie etwas von ihren Dingen offenbaren sollen, weil sie nicht leiden können, daß man ihnen in die Karte guckt. Allein, ich lasse mich nichts abschrecken, sondern werde allen meinen Lehrschülern diese Lehren inculciren, wenn sie die Zeit und die Kosten daran wenden wollen; denn wenn ein Orgelmacher redlich ist, und folglich die Kirchen in keinem Stücke zu berücken sucht; so kann ihm mein Bemühen nicht entgegen seyn; indem es ihn nichts schadet, wenn ein Organist dergleichen Erkenntniß hat. Ich werde auch soviel nicht beybringen, daß jedermann eine Orgel wird bauen können, und daß die Nahrung der Orgelmacher dadurch geschwächt werde. Hat aber ein Orgelmacher aus Bosheit oder Unwissenheit im Orgelbauen etwas versehen; so schreibe er sich es selbst zu, wenn ein nach diesen Lehren gewitzter Organist dergleichen Betrügereyen entdecket. Und um derer Willen habe ich diese Arbeit meistens übernommen; frage auch wenig darnach, ob solche über meine Arbeit süß oder sauer sehen.

§. 7.

---

[5]) Sonderlich prostituiren sich die Leute in Vorschreibung der Register nicht wenig, wenn sie von dem und jenem etwas gehöret haben, und nicht recht wissen, wie es damit aussiehet; denn da kann mancher zur Oktave eine Koppeldone, oder Thubal, oder Jubal setzen, wenn er nicht weis, daß alles eins sey, und denkt dabey Wunder wie schön und klug er seine Sachen gemacht habe. Der Herr von Mattheson sagt deswegen ganz recht, daß es dem Organisten keinen Schaden thue, des Orgelmachers Wesen zu approfondiren (d. i. zu untersuchen.) S. Orchestre P. III. cap. III. S. 259.

of a molehill and incurring considerable expense to boot, especially when [the organbuilder] must be summoned from a distance. In addition, an organist is quite often requested to draw up a stoplist, prepare a contract, act as an organ consultant, examine an organ, string a clavichord or some such. O what a sorry excuse many of them* are, committing such blunders that it takes a congregation years to recover from them. When the final examination of the new organ is carried out, then the consultant's outrageous ignorance comes to light. The honest organbuilder must to his dismay suffer his work to be criticized by an ignoramus, who wants to have something to say so that he can pocket his few dollars.5) Enough about the necessity of such knowledge; I'll say no more. Music lovers need only peruse this treatise themselves to awaken their interest. Since I cannot deny that some chapters treat matters that are necessary for others to know, I cannot blame any organist for reading these the most carefully; the rest however ought not to be completely ignored. Being informed about the stops is more important [to an organist] than anything else in organbuilding; but knowing about organbuilding is more important than knowing about the history of the organ, etc.

> * i.e., organists who act as consultants.

§. 6.

It is a legitimate question whether organbuilders will thank me for my pains. Many of them are very concerned about having their affairs made public, because they are afraid of having trade secrets betrayed. Yet I will not let myself be detered, but will rather inculcate all my students with this knowledge, if they want to take the time and trouble to learn it. If an organbuilder is honest, and as a consequence does not try to cheat churches in any way, then my efforts to educate organists will do him no harm. I will not teach so much that anyone would be able to build an organ, and thereby diminish the livelihood of an organbuilder. On the other hand, if any builder has out of malice or ignorance made a mistake in his work, then he must blame himself if an organist made knowledgeable by what I have taught discovers the fraud. Anyway, I have undertaken this work primarily for the sake of such [organists], and do not really care if it pleases organbuilders or not.

---

5) The bunglers especially embarass themselves when in drawing up a stoplist they have only an imperfect understanding of the qualities of various stops. To an "Octave" they add a "Koppeldone," a "Thubal," or a "Jubal,"† not realizing that these are all the same stop, and then marvel at their clever choices. Mr. Mattheson is quite right in saying that it would do an organist no harm to investigate the art of organbuilding; see his [*Neu-eröffnete*] *Orchestre*, Part III, Chap. III, p. 259. [Albrecht]

> † see the descriptions of these stops in Chapter VII below.

§. 7.

Von der Eintheilung und Methode dieser Abhandlung ist zu merken, daß ich die Paragraphen des Nachschlagens wegen nach der Reihe fortzählen will, damit ich zu seiner Zeit nur den §phum anführen könne, und mich an die Kapitel nicht zu kehren habe. Um aber dem Gedächtnisse zu rathen, kann doch das ganze Werk in etliche Kapitel getheilet werden, welches folgende seyn sollen:

Das 2. Kapitel.
Von dem äußerlichen Gehäuse der Orgeln.

Das 3. Kapitel.
Von der Windlade.

Das 4. Kapitel.
Von dem andern Eingeweide der Orgel, das Pfeifwerk ausgenommen.

Das 5. Kapitel.
Von den Bälgen und Windführungen.

Das 6. Kapitel.
Von dem Pfeifwerk überhaupt.

Das 7. Kapitel.
Von den Registern überhaupt und von einem jeden insonderheit.

Das 8. Kapitel.
Vom Gebrauch der Register.

Das 9. Kapitel.
Von Verding- und Bauung einer Orgel.

Das 10. Kapitel.
Von der Disposition.

Das 11. Kapitel.
Von den Unkosten bey einer Orgel.

Das 12. Kapitel.
Vom äußerlichen Zierath einer Orgel.

Das 13. Kapitel.
Von andern Vollkommenheiten und Fehlern einer Orgel.

Das 14. Kapitel.
Von der Temperatur.

Das 15. Kapitel.
Von der Stimmung der Orgeln.

Das 16. Kapitel.
Von der Ueberlieferung und Probe der Orgeln.

Das 17. Kapitel.
Von der Windprobe und andern mechanischen Instrumenten eines Organisten.

Das 18. Kapitel.
Von der Erhaltung und Temperatur der Orgel.

Das 19. Kapitel.
Von der Historie der Orgeln.

Das 20. Kapitel.
Von den andern Instrumenten, die ein Organist zu kennen nöthig hat, überhaupt: item von Positiven.

Das 21. Kapitel.
Von allerhand Regalen.

Das 22. Kapitel.
Von dem Clavicymbel, Clavicytherio, Spinett, Instrument und Cembal d'Amour.

Das 23. Kapitel.
Von Violdigambenwerken, Claviergamba, Geigenwerk und Leyer.

Das 24. Kapitel.
Vom Organo portatili, Wasserorgel und Hänflings Claviatur; auch Xylorgano.

Das 25. Kapitel.
Von Lautenwerken und Glockenspielen.

Das 26. Kapitel.
Von dem Clavikordio und Pedal.

Das 27. Kapitel.
Von andern Instrumenten, und der Stimmung beseyteter Instrumente.

Das 28. Kapitel.
Von etlichen curiösen Materien.

§. 7.

Concerning the classification and procedure followed in this treatise, note that for purposes of reference I intend to number paragraphs consecutively, so that in referring to a passage I will be able to cite only the number of the paragraph in question, without mentioning the chapter. As an aid to the memory, however, the entire work has been divided into various chapters, as follows:

CHAPTER 2.
Concerning the outer case of the organ

CHAPTER 3.
Concerning the windchest

CHAPTER 4.
Concerning the other internal parts of the organ, except the pipework

CHAPTER 5.
Concerning the bellows and wind ducts

CHAPTER 6.
Concerning the pipework in general

CHAPTER 7.
Concerning the stops in general and each of them in particular

CHAPTER 8.
Concerning the use of the stops

CHAPTER 9.
Concerning contracting for and building an organ

CHAPTER 10.
Concerning the stoplist

CHAPTER 11.
Concerning the cost of an organ

CHAPTER 12.
Concerning the exterior decoration of an organ

CHAPTER 13.
Concerning the merits and faults of an organ

CHAPTER 14.
Concerning temperament

CHAPTER 15.
Concerning the tuning of organs

CHAPTER 16.
Concerning the delivery and examination of organs

CHAPTER 17.
Concerning the windgauge and other mechanical tools of [use to] an organist

CHAPTER 18.
Concerning the maintenance and repair* of organs

CHAPTER 19.
Concerning the history of organs

CHAPTER 20.
Concerning other instruments an organist needs to be familiar with; also about positivs.

CHAPTER 21.
Concerning regals of all types

CHAPTER 22.
Concerning the harpsichord, clavicytherium, spinet, instrument, [arpichord]† and cembal d'amour

CHAPTER 23.
Concerning the Violdigambenwerk, Claviergamba, Geigenwerk and hurdy-gurdy

CHAPTER 24.
Concerning the organon portatile, the water-organ and Hänfling's claviatur, as well as the xylorganum

CHAPTER 25.
Concerning lute harpsichords and carillons

CHAPTER 26.
Concerning the clavichord and the pedal-clavier

CHAPTER 27.
Concerning other instruments, and the tuning of stringed [keyboard] instruments

CHAPTER 28.
A discourse on certain curious matters.

---

* The word found here is *Temperatur*, but the heading of Chap. 18 reads "Reparatur." This error is noted in the *errata* at the end of the book.

† This instrument is listed in the title of Chapter 22 below; it seems to have been inadvertently omitted here.

Kap. I. Von der Natur, Nutzen, Methode

§. 8.

Ich habe, wie dieser Entwurf zu erkennen giebt, mir viel vorgesetzt; doch hoffe ich von allen das Nöthigste beyzubringen: Weil es aber ohnmöglich ist, alles aus den Fingern zu saugen, so will ich kürzlich von denjenigen Hülfsmitteln Erwähnung thun, welche bey dieser Traktation können mit Nutzen gebraucht werden. Hieher ziehe ich das Reisen eines Organisten, welches sonderlich dieser Lehren wegen nöthig ist. Denn im Generalbasse, Fantasie, Choralen, italienischen Tabulatur, ꝛc. kann man richtige Principia setzen, und daraus das übrige erkennen: aber in dieser Lehre, sonderlich wenn es die Untersuchung der Orgelregister betrift, sind viel Sachen durch den Augenschein und durch das Gehör zu erkennen, welche man nie beysammen in einer Stadt findet; folglich muß man sie anderswo aufsuchen. Dies ist die Ursach, warum ich bey den Registern, die man nicht überall antrift, die Oerter beygesetzt, wo sie zu sehen. Doch läugne ich nicht, daß durch die Fantasie vielerley Register und Strukturen der Orgeln und Pfeifen können erdacht werden, wie es denn zuweilen geschiehet: aber das kann durch die Kräfte meines Verstandes nicht erkannt und erkläret werden, was durch allerhand Namen in der und jener Orgel eigentlich angedeutet wird; dieses muß man sich mündlich zeigen lassen, oder man muß auf Reisen solche Sachen aufsuchen. Und damit man wisse, wo etwas zu hören; so sollen im 10ten Kapitel etliche Dispositionen beygefüget werden, sammt den Namen der Städte, wo dergleichen Orgeln zu finden. Hat jemand Gelegenheit bey einem Orgelmacher oder Mechanico etwas zu sehen, oder eine Orgel durchzusuchen wenn sie gebauet oder reparirt wird, der lasse solche Gelegenheit nicht vorbey.

§. 9.

Doch alles dieses reicht nicht hin; sondern die Schriften berühmter und in diesen Dingen erfahrner Männer können auch vieles Licht geben, welche ich nach der Reihe erzählen will, soviel mir derselben für diesesmal beyfallen.

Michael Prätorius, weiland Fürstl. Braunschweig-Lüneburgischer Kapellmeister zu Wolfenbüttel, hat ein Werk in 4to geschrieben, Syntagma musicum genannt, Ao. 1614. Er hat das Werk in vier Tomos getheilet, wiewol nur drey zum Vorschein gekommen, darinn wird Tomo II. von der Organographia, oder von der Beschreibung der musikalischen Instrumente gehandelt. Er gibt sowol von der Beschaffenheit der alten als auch der neuen Orgeln Nachricht, und die Struktur der Pfeifen kann man daselbst im Risse sehen. Dies ist das Hauptbuch bey der Mechanica musica. Der Kürze wegen werde ich es allegiren: Præt. Synt. T. II. Eben dieser Prätorius hat auf der letzten Seite des 2ten Tomi einen Traktat von Verdingung, Bauen und Lieferung einer Orgel versprochen, welcher aber zurückgeblieben.[6]) Von diesem

Prä=

---

[6]) Es ist mir aus der Verlassenschaft des Hrn. Verfassers das Manuscript vom Prätorio, mit in die Hände gekommen, welches derselbe S. 341. der Anleitung zu der musikal. Gelahrt

§. 8.

I have my work cut out for me, as is evident from the foregoing sketch. I hope to impart the essentials of it all. Yet, because it is impossible to explain everything in writing, I want to mention briefly those extra means that may help to make this treatise even more useful. First, an organist ought to travel; travel is especially necessary to understand fully the knowledge imparted here. For figured bass, improvisation, hymn-playing, Italian tabulature and such, are governed by exact rules from which one may proceed to a complete understanding; but in matters pertaining to musical mechanics, especially as regards the study of organ stops, many things can only be understood by seeing and hearing. These things are seldom found together in the same city, and so one must travel to hear them. This is why I have listed the places where the more unusual registers can be examined. I do not deny that (as sometimes is the case) it is possible in the course of extemporizing to gain a conception of all sorts of stops and designs of organs and pipes; but my ability to understand these will not help to reveal or clarify what is really meant by the various stop names in this or that organ. These things can only be explained by word of mouth,* or experienced by actual visits to organs. So that one may know where to hear various [stops], Chapter 10 contains a number of stoplists, together with the names of the cities where the organs in question are to be found. If anyone has the opportunity to observe an organbuilder (a *mechanicus*), or to examine an organ as it is being built or repaired, he should by all means take advantage of it.

* i.e., on the spot, by a teacher to a student.

§. 9.

But even all this is not enough. The writings of famous men, men experienced in these matters, will also shed much light on the subject. I will now proceed to describe in turn whatever I know at the present about each of these.

Michael Praetorius, the late Kapellmeister to the Duke of Braunschweig-Lüneburg at Wolfenbüttel, wrote a book in quarto in the year 1614, entitled *Syntagma musicum*. He divided it into 4 volumes, although only three were published; of these, volume 2 deals with *organographia*, that is, with the description of musical instruments. In it one may find information about the characteristics of old as well as new organs, and may see for oneself sketches of pipe structures. This is the primary book for musical mechanics. For brevity's sake I will refer to it as "Præt. *Synt*. Vol. II."† Praetorius himself promised on the final page of vol. 2 a treatise on contracting for, building and delivering an organ, but this was not forthcoming.6) My treatise on Italian Tabula-

† In fact, Adlung almost always refers to this source as "Praetorius".

---

6) There has come into my hands from the author's estate a manuscript of Praetorius, the one mentioned on p. 341 of the *Anleitung zu der musikalischen Gelahrtheit*, that concerns the Delivery and

Prätorio kann nachgelesen werden, was in meiner italienischen Tabulatur [7] beygebracht worden ist. Der erste Tomus des vorhin erwähnten Syntagmatis musici ist ganz lateinisch; der andere aber, den wir allhier brauchen, ist deutsch, und kann also von allen gelesen werden.

§. 10.

Aus diesem Prätorio hat etwas angeführet Andreas Werkmeister, weiland Königl. Preuss. Inspektor über alle Orgeln im Fürstenthum Halberstadt, und Organist zu St. Martini in Halberstadt, der Ao. 1706. gestorben, in den Paradoxaldiscursen von der Hoheit der Musik, ꝛc. welche zu Quedlinburg in 4to, Ao. 1707. nach seinem Tode herausgekommen, da er im 16. Kapitel, S. 83. und folg. von der Einfalt der alten Orgeln handelt. Noch besser aber ist seine Beschreibung der Grüningischen Orgelwerks zu brauchen, welche Ao. 1705. in 4to heraus ist, unter dem Titul: „Organum grüningense rediuinum, oder kurze Beschreibung des in der „Grüningischen Schloßkirchen berühmten Orgelwerks, wie dasselbe Anfangs „erbauet und beschaffen gewesen: und wie es itzo ist renoviret und merklich „verbessert worden;" da hat er die Fehler und Vollkommenheiten der Orgeln gar aufrichtig und deutlich angezeiget. Es ist deutsch und nicht dicke, [8] daher es, wie seine übrigen Schriften für wenig Geld zu kaufen, mit geringer Mühe durchzulesen, und zuweilen gar zu gut zu nutzen ist. Ebenderselbe hat auch eine Orgelprobe geschrieben, so das principalste Werk in dieser Mechanica mit ist. Dieser Traktat ist Ao. 1681. in 12. herausgegeben; [9] aber sehr mangelhaft: daher der Autor Ao. 1698. sie vermehrt

heit anführet, und von der Lieferung und Beschlagung oder Probirung einer Orgel handelt. Es sind zwar nicht mehr, als 3 geschriebene Bogen, welche aber viel Gutes in sich fassen. Die Schreibart ist der Prätorianischen gleich, so, daß es fast für dasjenige Werkchen zu halten, welches hier oben angeführet worden. Vielleicht entschließe ich mich künftig, dies nützliche Ueberbleibsel des Alterthums der Vergessenheit zu entreissen, und durch den Druck gemein zu machen.

[7] Die hier vom Hrn. Verfasser angeführte italienische Tabulatur ist nicht mehr vorhanden; sondern im Jahr 1736. mit verbrannt, wie aus dessen Lebenslauf zu ersehen, den ich in die kritischen Briefen über die Tonkunst, nach seinem eigenen Entwurf, einrücken lassen. (S. den 4ten Theil des 2ten Bandes des kritis. Br. S. 454. und folg.) Man kann aber dagegen mit Nutzen dasjenige nachlesen, was im 16. Kap. der Anleitung zu der musikalischen Gelahrtheit hiervon geschrieben worden; ob man gleich dasjenige daselbst vermißt, was der Hr. Prof. von Prätorio geschrieben zu haben hier erwähnet.

[8] Die Beschreibung des Orgelwerks faßt, nebst Titulblat und Dedication nicht mehr als 3½ Bogen in sich. Ausser diesen ist noch ein besonderer Bogen dabey, auf welchem das Schloß und große Faß zu Grüningen beschrieben werden.

[9] Daß etliche damals Werkmeistern beschuldiget, als habe er sich eines andern Mannes Arbeit zugeeignet, und solche unter seinem eigenen Namen herausgegeben, hat der Hr. Verfasser in der Anleitung zu der musik. Gelahrth. S. 342. Anmerk. p. imgl. in dieser Abhandlung §. 429. angeführt.

ture imparts some information about Praetorius that you may wish to consult. The first volume of the abovementioned *Syntagma musicum* is entirely in Latin, but the second one, the one we are using here, is in German, and thus anyone can read it.

§. 10

Andreas Werckmeister, former Royal Prussian Inspector of all organs in the Principality of Halberstadt and Organist at St. Martini in Halberstadt, who died in 1706, has cited some [information] from Praetorius in his *Paradoxal-Discursen von der Hoheit der Musik*,* published posthumously at Quedlinburg in quarto in 1707, in the 16th chapter, pp. 83f., where he speaks of the lack of sophistication of old organs. Of even greater use, though, is his description of the organ at Gröningen,† published in quarto in 1705 under the title *Organum gruningense redivinum*,‡ *oder Kurze Beschreibung des in der grüningischen Schloßkirchen berühmten Orgelwerks, wie dasselbe Anfangs erbauet und beschaffen gewesen: und wie es itzo ist renoviret und merklich verbessert worden*,§ in which he has indicated very honestly and clearly the faults and merits of organs. It is in German, and not large, and thus (like his other writings) it may be purchased quite cheaply, read with little trouble, and often be of considerable use. The same author has also written an *Orgelprobe*,‖ which is another of the main works on the subject of mechanics (*Mechanica*). This treatise was published in 1681 in duodecimo, but very defective. Therefore the author published an expanded version in 1698 in

Examination or Testing of an Organ.¶ It is only three manuscript signatures in length, yet contains much of value. Since the writing style is similar to that of Praetorius, I consider it to be the very same treatise that is mentioned above. Perhaps in the future I will resolve to snatch this useful little remnant of a past age out of oblivion and make it available to all in print. [Albrecht]

7) The treatise on Italian Tabulature mentioned here by the author no longer exists. It was burned in 1736, as may be noted in his autobiography, sketched by Adlung himself, which I have had entered in [Friedrich Wilhelm Marpurg's] *Kritische Briefe über die Tonkunst* (see the fourth part of the second volume of the *Kritische Briefe*, p. 454f.**). [As a substitute for it] it would be useful to consult what is written about Italian tabulature in the 16th chapter of the *Anleitung zu der musikalischen Gelahrtheit*, although one will not find there what the author here mentions having written about Praetorius. [Albrecht]

8) The description of the organ, together with the title page and dedication, encompasses no more than 3½ signatures.†† In addition there is one extra signature on which there is a description of the palace and the great cask at Gröningen. [Albrecht]

9) The author [Adlung] relates that at that time some people accused Werckmeister of appropriating another man's work and publishing it under his own name; see *Anleitung zu der musikalischen Gelahrtheit*, p. 342, note p, as well as §.429 below. [Albrecht]

---

* "Paradoxical Discourses on the Nobility of Music."

† A palace east of the city of Halberstadt in Thuringia; not to be confused with the city, Groningen, in the Netherlands.

‡ sic; should be *redivivum*.

§ "The Gröningen Organ Reborn; or a Short Description of the Famous Organ in the Gröningen Palace Church, how it was first Built and Constituted, and how it has now been Renovated and notably Improved;" English translation and commentary by Marcos Fernando Krieger (Doctoral Document, University of Nebraska-Lincoln, 1998; VDM Verlag, 2009).

‖ "Examination of an Organ," or "Organ Testing."

¶ The treatise has been published in a modern edition as : Michael Praetorius and Esaias Compenius, *Orgeln Verdingnis*. (Kieler Beiträge zur Musikwissenschaft, hrsg. Friedrich Blume, Heft 4. Wolfenbüttel & Berlin: Georg Kallmeyer, 1936). A second modern edition with an English translation and a helpful preface has also been published: Vincent Panetta, "An Early Handbook for Organ Inspection: the 'Kurtzer Bericht' of Michael Praetorius and Esaias Compenius" (in: *The Organ Yearbook*, Vol. XXI (1990), pp. 5-33). Mr. Panetta has also published a detailed account of this treatise's influence on subsequent manuals regarding the testing of organs: "Praetorius, Compenius, Werckmeister: A Tale of Two Treatises" (in: *Church, Stage, and Studio: music and its contexts in seventeenth-century Germany*, ed. Paul Walker. Ann Arbor, MI: UMI Research Press, c. 1990, pp. 67-85). See also §.239.

** The lengthier autobiography that Albrecht includes in the Foreword to the *MMO*, Vol. II (below) likewise records the destruction of this treatise.

†† i.e., 28 pages; see Translator's Preface above.

in 4to drucken lies. Sie ist durchgängig deutsch, und hat den Titel: „Andreä Werk=
„meisters, Benic. Cherusci p. t. Musici und Organisten zu St. Martini in Halber=
„stadt, erweiterte und verbesserte Orgelprobe, oder eigentliche Beschreibung, wie
„und welcher Gestalt man die Orgelwerke von den Orgelmachern annehmen, probiren,
„untersuchen und denen Kirchen liefern könne; auch was bey Verdüngniß eines neuen
„und alten Werks, so da zu renoviren vorfallen möchte, nothwendig in Acht zu nehmen
„sey, nicht nur einigen Organisten, so zur Probirung eines Orgelwerks erfordert wer=
„den, zur Nachricht: sondern auch denen Vorstehern, so etwan Orgeln machen oder
„renoviren lassen wollen, sehr nützlich. Quedlinburg, 1698. 11. Bogen in 4to, oh=
ne das Titulblat, Dedication, Vorreden und Ehrengedichte, welche zusammen auch
noch 2 Bogen und 3 Quartblätter betragen.[10] Er hat das Werk in 32. Kapitel ein=
getheilet, die zu gehöriger Zeit zum Nachlesen allegirt werden sollen. Seine Sachen
sind gut; doch könnte manches zuweilen ordentlicher seyn. Seine übrigen Schriften
sind im forschenden Orchestre des Herrn von Mattheson S. 143. erzählt; zu unserm
itzigen Vorhaben aber dienen sie nicht.

§. 11.

Ein wichtiges Hülfsmittel ist auch die Beschreibung der Görlitzer Orgel,
welche Christian Ludwig Boxberg, der Organist daselbst, Ao. 1704. in 4to drucken
lassen, da die Einweihungspredigt M. Gottfried Kretschmars voran gedruckt, auch
die äußerliche Gestalt des Werks in Kupfer vorgestellet ist. Gewiß, man findet dar=
innen schöne Anmerkungen, welche wir zu seiner Zeit nicht vergessen wollen.

Etwas weniges hat der Herr von Mattheson in seinem Orchestre P. III. c. III.
§. 3. beygebracht.[11] Mit bessern Nutzen kann allhier gebraucht werden der zweyte
Theil von Nieds Handleitung zur Variation des Generalbasses, sonderlich die zwote
Auflage welche gedachter Herr von Mattheson, Ao. 1721. zu Hamburg auf 26½ Bo=
gen in länglicht 4to, besorget, und mit vielen Zusätzen und Ausbesserungen, wie auch
einem Anhange von mehr als 60 Orgeldispositionen bereichert: denn dabey findet man
hin und wieder gute Anmerkungen, welche zur Kenntniß der Orgelstimmen vieles bey=
tragen können.

§. 12.

Athanasius Kircherus, der bekannte Jesuit, hat in seiner Musurgia, die
Ao. 1650. in Folio zu Rom in 5½ Alphab. heraus ist, auch etwas davon. Und da
das

---

[10] Ao. 1716. kam diese Orgelprobe nochmals heraus, und Mizler bediente sich dieser Ausga=
be, als er das Buch recensirte. S. musik. Bibliothek, des 1sten Bandes 4ten Theil. S. 28.
Endlich wurde dies Werkchen Ao. 1754. in Leipzig abermals auf 7 Bogen in 8vo herausgegeben;
welche Ausgabe allen andern vorzuziehen. Vermehrungen sind nicht dazu gekommen, und die
Dedication, wie auch eine Vorrede und Ehrengedichte, sind weggelassen.

[11] Mehr hieher gehöriges findet man im 24. Kap. des 3ten Theils des vollkommenen Kapell=
meisters.

quarto. It is entirely in German and bears the title: *Andreä Werkmeisters, Benic. Cherusci p[ro].t[empore]. Musici und Organisten zu St. Martini in Halberstadt, erweiterte und verbesserte Orgelprobe,** "being a proper Description of how and in what Form One should Accept an Organ from an Organbuilder, Try it Out, Examine it and Turn it Over to a Church; also What must necessarily be Considered in Contracting for a New Organ or for an Old One (in Case it Needs Renovation), not only to Advise those Organists who are Requested to Examine an Organ, but also very Useful to those Authorities who Wish to have an Organ Built or Renovated."† Quedlinburg, 1698. 11 sheets in quarto, not counting the title page, dedication, preface and complimentary poems, which together occupy another two sheets plus three quarto leaves.10) He has divided the work into 32 chapters, [and the reader may profitably] consult them when they are mentioned at the appropriate time [in this treatise]. His points are well made; on the other hand, much of it could be better organized. His remaining writings are described in Mr. Matheson's *Das Forschende Orchestre*, p. 143; they do not contribute anything, however, to matters under consideration here.

§. 11.

Another important aid is the *Beschreibung der Görlitzer Orgel*,‡ published by the organist there, Christian Ludwig Boxberg, in quarto in 1704, prefaced by a dedicatory sermon [delivered] by Gottfried Kretschmar, M.A., as well as a copper plate of the organ façade. It certainly contains some fine remarks, which we will not forget to mention at the appropriate time.

Mr. Matheson has spoken only briefly [on the subject of organ mechanics] in his [*Neu-eröffnete*] *Orchestre*, Part III, chap. III, §.3.11) Of greater use in this regard is the second part of Niedt's [*Musicalischer*] *Handleitung* [*von der*] *Variation des General-Basses*,§ especially the second edition, the publication of which was supervised by the abovementioned Mr. Matheson in Hamburg in 1721, on 26½ signatures in oblong quarto.¶ This edition contains many additions and improvements, as well as an appendix enriched by more than 60 organ stoplists. Good remarks are found here and there [throughout the appendix], remarks that can contribute much to an understanding of organ stops.

§. 12.

Athanasius Kircher, the well-known Jesuit, has also spoken somewhat of these matters in his *Musurgia*, published in folio at Rome in the year 1650, in 6½ alpha-

---

* "The Expanded and Improved "Organ Testing" of Andreas Werkmeister, Musician from the Cheruskan [Village of] Benneckenstein, presently Organist at St. Martini in Halberstadt."

† All of this is a quote from the title page of the *Orgelprobe*.

‡ "Description of the Organ at Görlitz." The full title reads *Ausführliche Beschreibung der Grossen Neuen Orgel In der Kirchen zu St. Petri und Pauli allhie zu Görlitz*... (A Detailed Description of the Large New Organ in the Church of St. Peter and Paul in Görlitz), Görlitz: Johann Gottlob Laurentius, 1704. A facsimile may be found in: *Die Sonnenorgel der evangelischen Pfarrkirche St. Peter und Paul zu Görlitz: Festschrift zur Orgelweihe am 12. Oktober 1997* (Görlitz, 1997). English translation and commentary by Mary Murrell Faulkner (Doctoral Document, University of Nebraska-Lincoln, 2000; VDM Verlag, 2009).

§ "Musical Handbook on Variety in Performing Figured Bass."

¶ i.e., 204 pages; see Translator's Preface above.

---

10) This *Orgelprobe* was again reprinted in 1716, and Mizler made use of this edition when he reviewed the book; see *Musikalische Bibliothek*, Vol. I, Part 4, p. 28.‖ This little volume was republished a final time in Leipzig in 1754, but this time on 7 sheets in octavo; this edition is preferable to all the others. No additions have been made to it, and the dedication, preface and complimentary poems have been omitted. [Albrecht]

11) More on this subject is to be found in chapter 24 of the third part of his *Volkommene Kapellmeister*. [Albrecht]

‖ actually pp. 27f.

das Werk in 10 Bücher getheilet ist; so gehet uns sonderlich das 6te an, und zwar dessen Pars III. cap. III. pag. 506. da er von der Struktur und Eigenschaften der Orgeln handelt. Er hat auch von Clavicymbel und andern Instrumenten geredet, welche Stellen an gehörigen Orte angeführet werden sollen. Er schreibt lateinisch.

Ferner hat Janowka in seinem Clave S. 90. und folg. etwas von den Orgeln, und zeigt unter andern auch die Klugheit im Registerziehen. Von andern Instrumenten hat er ebener Maaßen gehandelt, welche man bey ihm nach der alphabetischen Ordnung leicht finden kann. Er schreibt schlecht Latein.

Johann Philipp Bendelers Organographia, von der Orgelmacherkunst, ist zu Frankfurt und Leipzig (ohne Jahrzahl) in 4to herausgegeben worden.

Johann Caspar Trost, hat eine Beschreibung der Weißenfelßischen Orgel in 12. edirt, davon der vollständige Titul also lautet: „Ausführliche Beschreibung des „neuen Orgelwerks auf der Augustusburg zu Weißenfelß, worinnen zugleich enthalten, „was zu der Orgelmacherkunst gehöre, wie nach allen Stücken eine Orgel disponirt, „vermittelst des Monochordi rein gestimmt und temperirt, die Stimmen auf allerhand „Art verwechselt, und ein neu Orgelwerk probirt werden solle, ꝛc. von Johann Caspar „Trost, jun. Nürnberg 1677. in 12." Ist also schon eine alte Orgel. Er war ein Sohn des alten Johann Caspar Trosts, Curiae Electoralis Halberstad. Advocati ordinarii et Organoedi ad D. Martini; die Orgel aber hat Christian Förner von Wettin gebauet, und die Disposition derselben kömmt unten im 10. Kap. vor. Sein Vater, Johann Caspar Trost, hat ein Examen organi pnevmatici contra sycophantas mit Kupfern zu ediren versprochen; it. Beschreibung vieler Orgeln, welche Schriften aber wol im Manuscript mögen geblieben seyn. Endlich sind auch allhier zu gebrauchen die Schriftsteller von der Temperatur: wir wollen einige alsdann erst namhaft machen, wenn wir im 14. Kapitel von der Temperatur zu reden haben.[12]) Was sonst beyzufügen wäre, das soll in dieser Abhandlung an gehörigem Orte selbst angemerket werden.

Das

---

[12]) Zu denen bis daher angeführten Schriften sind noch folgende zu setzen. Als:

α) Werner Fabricii, ehemaligen Organisten zu St. Nikolai in Leipzig, Unterricht, wie man ein neu Orgelwerk, obs gut und beständig sey, nach allen Stücken, in- und auswendig examiniren, und so viel möglich probiren soll. Frankfurt und Leipzig, 1756. 5¼ Bogen in 8vo.

β) Johann Adam Jacob Ludwigs, Postschreibers zu Hof, Gedanken über die großen Orgeln, die aber deswegen keine Wunderwerke sind. Leipzig, 1761. 2 Bogen in 4to.

γ) Ebendesselben Trakt. von unverschämten Entehrern der Orgeln. Erlangen, 1764. 2½ Bogen in 4to.

bets.* This work is divided into 10 books, of which the sixth is of special interest to us, more particularly [Vol. I], Part III, chapter III, p. 506, in which he treats the structure and characteristics of organs. He also speaks about harpsichords and other instruments, and his remarks will be noted at the appropriate places in this book. The work is in Latin.

Furthermore, [Thomas Balthasar] Janowka includes something about the organ in his *Clavis [ad Thesaurum Magnae Artis Musicae]*,† pp. 90f; among other things he teaches how to be skillful at registration. He has also treated other instruments to some degree; these can be found easily since they are in alphabetical order. The book is in poor‡ (schlecht) Latin.

Johann Philipp Bendeler's *Organographia*§ was published at Frankfurt and Leipzig (without date) in quarto.

Johann Caspar Trost [Jun.] has published a description of the Weissenfels organ in duodecimo, the complete title of which reads as follows: "*Ausführliche Beschreibung des neuen Orgelwerks auf der Augustusburg zu Weissenfelß*,¶ "in which is also Contained: What Pertains to the Art of Organbuilding; how an Organ is Arranged in All its Parts; how it is purely Tempered and Tuned by means of the Monochord; how the Stops are varied in all Sorts of Ways; how a New Organ should be Tested, etc. By Johann Caspar Trost, Jr., Nuremberg, 1677, in duodecimo." This is already an old organ. Trost was the son of the elder Johann Caspar Trost, Official Counsel to the Halberstadt Electoral Curia and Organist at St. Martini. Christian Förner of Wettin built the organ,‖ however, the stoplist of which is found below in chapter 10. The elder Trost promised to publish a book *Examen organi pneumatici contra sy[n]cophantas* with copper plates, as well as a "Description of many organs," but these writings must have remained in the manuscript stage. Finally, the writers on temperament also are useful to this subject; we will name several of these later on, when we discuss the subject of temperament in chapter 14.[12] Any additional sources will be mentioned at the appropriate place in this treatise.

---

12) To the abovementioned writings must be added the following:
  α) Werner Fabricius, former organist at St. Nikolai in Leipzig: *Unterricht, wie man ein neu Orgelwerk, obs gut und beständig sey, nach allen Stücken, in- und auswendig examiniren, und so viel möglich probiren soll*.** Frankfurt and Leipzig, 1756. 5½ signatures in octavo.
  β) Johann Adam Jacob Ludwig, Postal Official at Hof: *Gedanken über die grossen Orgeln, die aber deswegen keine Wunderwerke sind*.†† Leipzig, 1762. 2 signatures in quarto.
  γ) By the same author, a treatise: *Den unverschämten Entehrern der Orgeln*.‡‡ Erlangen, 1764. 2½ signatures in quarto. [Albrecht]

---

* For an explanation of this term and the method of book manufacture from which it derives, see the Translator's Preface above.

† "Key to the Treasury of the Great Art of Music."

‡ In older German documents, the word "schlecht" may also mean "simple" (cf. modern German "schlicht").

§ "Concerning the Art of Organbuilding."

¶ "A Detailed Description of the New Organ at the Augustusburg at Weissenfels."

‖ at the Augustusburg in Weissenfels.

** "Instruction in how to examine a new organ internally and externally, whether it is good and durable in all its parts, and to test it insofar as is possible." Fabricius died in 1679; this publication appeared posthumously, 77 years after his death.

†† "Thoughts upon Large Organs that nevertheless Leave Much to be Desired."

‡‡ "To Those who Shamelessly Defame Organs."

Das II. Kapitel.
Von dem äusserlichen Gehäuse der Orgel.
Inhalt.

§. 13. Difinition der Orgel. §. 14. Ob die Orgel nützlich? §. 15. Ob der Pracht der Orgeln zu verwerfen? §. 16. Etymologia des Worts Orgel. §. 17. Die Eintheilungen der Orgeln. §. 18. Der Fuß der Orgeln. §. 19. Stockwerke, Felder, u. s. w. §. 20. Eintheilung der Orgeln. §. 21. Von dem Clavier. §. 22. Von den Koppeln. §. 23. Anzahl der Palmularum. §. 24. ihre Eintheilung und Namen. §. 25. Der Unterschied der Oktaven §. 26. andere Theile der Tastatur. §. 27. Von dem Pedal. §. 28. Von dessen Federn, Anzahl und Namen der Palmuln. §. 29 Die Lage und Pedalbank. §. 30. Die registratura manubria. §. 31. Die Thüren und Tafeln.

§. 13.

Eine Orgel ist ein solches musikalisches Instrument, da durch Niederdrückung der Palmulen das Pfeifwerk geöfnet wird, damit es von dem Winde angeblasen werde, und einen gewissen Sonum von sich hören lasse, zur Ergötzung des Gehörs und Beförderung der Ehre Gottes. Durch diese Beschreibung hoffe ich die Orgeln von allen andern musikalischen Instrumenten zu unterscheiden; sintemal keine, als des Organisten Instrumente, durch die Claviere und Palmuln regieret werden, und unter diesen nennt man eine Orgel, wenn das Pfeifwerk durch das Blasen des Windes aus den Bälgen einen Klang von sich gibt. Das aber dergleichen Werke die Ohren kitzeln, lehrt eines jeden Erfahrung, und brauchen wir die Zeit nöthiger, als daß wir dabey uns aufhalten sollten.

§. 14.

Ob aber die Ehre Gottes dadurch befördert werde, hat einigen bedenklich geschienen. Die Reformirten gehen von uns darinnen ab; indem sie aus der Musik und Orgel entweder nichts, oder doch wenig machen: sie sind aber nicht alle eines Sinnes. Die anhaltischen Reformirten rechnen die Orgel unter die Stücke, so des römischen Abgottes, Baals, Feldzeichen seyn; (conf. Dedekenni Consil. P. I. p. m. 1146.) aber in Berlin haben sie in ihren meisten Kirchen Orgeln, it. in Hanau und andern Oertern mehr. Unter den Lutheranern selbst sind einige so weit gegangen, daß sie die Orgeln sehr herunter gesetzt. Und dazu sind sie meistens durch den großen Misbrauch verleitet worden, der sich in unserer Kirche dabey eingeschlichen; da vielmal an die Andacht und Ehre Gottes nicht gedacht, sondern blos die fleischliche Kützelung der Ohren und die Ehre des Organisten gesucht wird. Allein dieser Misbrauch darf den rechten Gebrauch der Orgeln nicht aufheben, weil ein solcher modus procedendi niemals gebilliget wird: denn sonst müßte man auch die unschuldigsten Sachen verwerfen. Es ist auch besagter Misbrauch nicht allge-

Chapter II.
Concerning the Outer Case of the Organ.

Contents:

§.13. Definition of an organ. §.14. Whether [the organ] is useful? §.15. Whether the splendor of organs is objectionable? §.16. The etymology of the word "organ". §.17. The classification of organs. §.18. The base of an organ. §.19. Case levels, pipefields, etc. §.20. The divisions of an organ. §.21 The keyboards. §.22. The couplers. §.23. The number of keys. §.24. Their classification and names. §.25. The designation of octaves. §.26. Other parts of the keyboard. §.27. The pedal. §.28. The pedal springs, and the number and name of the keys. §.29. Positioning the pedals; the [organ] bench. §.30. The stopknobs. §.31. Doors and panels.

§. 13.

An organ is a musical instrument in which keys, being depressed, bring pipes into operation through wind pressure, and thus produce a certain sound for the delight (Ergötzung*) of the sense of hearing and the advancement of God's glory. By this description I hope to distinguish the organ from all other musical instruments, since the only instruments an organist plays are those operated by keyboards and keys, and among these the one called "organ" is the one in which pipes are made to sound by the pressure of wind from bellows. A certain amount of experience will reveal that such an instrument can delight the ear; but our time is better spent [on other matters] than developing that topic.

* This word also has the connotation "re-creation," "making anew," "restoration."

§. 14.

It has appeared questionable to some, however, whether this [instrument] does indeed advance God's glory. Herein those of the Reformed persuasion differ from us,† in that they consider music and the organ of either little or no value. Not all of them, though, are of the same opinion. The Reformed Church of Anhalt considers the organ among those objects that are banners of Roman idolatry or of Baal (cf. Dedeken's *Consil.*,‡ P. I., p.m. 1146), but the Reformed in Berlin, as well as in Hanau and elsewhere, have organs in most of their churches. Even among the Lutherans there are those who have gone so far as to greatly disparage the organ. Most of these have been misled by the great abuses that have crept into our churches; often devotion and God's glory are not the aim, but merely the carnal delight of the ears and the glory of the organist. Yet this abuse ought not to invalidate the correct use of the organ, because such a *modus operandi* has never been approved of; for otherwise one would have to object to

† i.e., those who belong to the Lutheran Church.

‡ Dedeken, Georg, *Thesauri consiliorum et decisionum*...Jena: Hertel, 1671.

allgemein, und finden sich hin und wieder noch ehrliche Organisten, die sich ganz eines andern zu bescheiden wissen. Und gesetzt, es wäre aller Organisten Herz mit dem Hochmuthsteufel so besessen, daß sie blos ihre Eigenliebe durch ihr Spielen zu befördern suchten; was kann dies der Musik schaden? Wenn keine allzulustige, oder profane Melodien gehöret werden, welches solchen lustigen Brüdern noch wol zu verbieten; so schadet der in dem Herzen verborgene Hochmuth eines Organisten denen Zuhörenden so wenig, als der Ehrgeiz eines Predigers. Zu wünschen wäre es, daß auch in diesem Stücke des Gottesdienstes mehr Andacht gespüret würde; aber deswegen schaft man die Orgeln eben so wenig mit Recht ab, als das Predigen. Doch was halte ich mich hierbey auf, da von andern diese Wahrheit schon gar deutlich bewiesen ist. Man schlage die Autores nach, die von dem Nutzen und Nothwendigkeit der Musik überhaupt gehandelt; sonderlich aber, was den Gebrauch der Orgeln betrift, verdient gelesen zu werden M. Gottfr. Kretschmar in der Einweihungspredigt der görlitzischen Orgel, vornehmlich S. 20. u. folg. imgl. S. 12. It. Prätorius Syntag. T. II. P. I. membr. IV. c. 15. it. T. II. P. III. c. I. daß ich andere der Kürze halben nicht nenne. [13]

§. 15.

Das würden endlich die meisten sich bereden lassen, es wären die Orgeln nicht gar zu verwerfen, zumal da die Gottesmänner, David, Salomo ꝛc. auch viel Instrumenta musica erfunden und in dem Tempel gebraucht: Was nun wider die Orgeln möchte eingewendet werden, das wird sich alles auch auf solche Instrumente appliciren

---

[13] Folgende drey Predigten verdienen hierbey zum Nachlesen bestens empfohlen zu werden.

α) **Gottlob Kluge**, Orgelpredigt, welche den 15. December, als am 3ten Adventsonntage des 1754sten Jahres, bey Einweihung der im Evangelischen Bethhause zu Neumarkt erwünscht erbauten neuen Orgel über den 150sten Psalm gehalten worden. Breßlau, 1756. 5 Bogen in 4to. Diese Predigt ist eine kräftige Vertheidigung des singenden- und klingenden Gottesdienstes. Ausser diesem fasset sie allerhand merkwürdige Nachrichten, und nutzbare Anmerkung über einige Orgelstimmen, wie auch die Disposition in sich.

β) **Jonathan Hellers**, Prediat von der weisen und treuen Hand Gottes bey der Sorgfalt der Menschen für einen Gott wohlgefälligen Gottesdienst, bey öffentlicher zahlreichen Versammlung in der Oberpfarrkirche zu St Marien (in Danzig) am 4ten Advents-Sonntage 1760. da die neu erbauete große Orgel Gott geheiliget ward, gehalten. Danzig, 1761. 3 Bogen in 4to, ohne die Zuschrift, welche auch einen Bogen anfüllt. Diese Predigt giebt der vorigen nichts nach: aber von dem Orgelwerke selbst trift man nichts dabey an, auch nicht einmal die Disposition.

γ) **Bernhardt Sebastian Große**, Pr. Die heiligen Verrichtungen in dem Hause des Herrn, wurden den 10ten Sonntage nach Trinitatis 1763. in der Ilmenauischen Stadtkirche bey der Einweihung der neuen Orgel vorgestellet, und mit einer kurzgefaßten Orgelgeschichte zum Druck übergeben. Eisenach, 1765. Die Predigt faßt 2 Bogen, und die kurzgefaßte Orgelgeschichte nebst der Disposition ½ Bogen in 8vo in sich: beydes aber wird sich nicht ohne rührendes Vergnügen lesen lassen.

Ch. II. Concerning the Outer Case of the Organ.

the most innocent things. This sort of abuse is also not everywhere prevalent; here and there upright organists are still to be found who know how to conduct themselves quite differently. And even if the hearts of all organists were so possessed by devilish arrogance that they only sought to bolster their own egos through their playing, how could that harm the music? If no jolly or profane tunes are heard (and these should surely be forbidden our more merry colleagues), then the arrogance hidden in an organist's heart can do no more harm than the ambition of a preacher. It would be desirable if greater devotion could also be sensed in this aspect of the worship service; but it would be just as wrong to do away with organs for this reason as to do away with preaching. Yet why should I go on about this, when others have already clearly established the truth of it. It would be best to consult the authors who have treated the value and necessity of music in general; in regard to the use of the organ, however, the following are especially worthwhile: Gottfried Kretschmar, M.A., in the dedicatory sermon for the Görlitz organ, particularly pp. 20f. as well as p. 12; Praetorius, *Syntagma*, Vol. II,* part I, Membr. IV, chapter 15, [p. 346;] as well as vol. II, part II, chapter I, [pp. 82f.] I will forbear mentioning other sources for the sake of brevity.[13)]

* sic; should read "Vol. I".

§. 15.

Most people will finally come to the conclusion that organs really ought not to be condemned, in particular since godly men such as David and Solomon have both devised many musical instruments and also used them in the temple.† For the same objections that are lodged against the organ must also be applied to other instruments as

† cf. I Chronicles 15:16f.; 16:4f.; 23:5; 25:1f.: II Chronicles 5:12f.

---

13) The following three sermons are recommended as being especially worthwhile to consult in this regard:

α) Gottlob Kluge, an Organ Sermon on the 150th Psalm, delivered on the 15th of December 1754, the third Sunday of Advent, on the occasion of the dedication of the long awaited new organ in the Protestant House of Worship in Neumarkt. Breslau, 1756. Five signatures in quarto. This sermon is a powerful defence of voices and instruments in worship. In addition it also contains all sorts of noteworthy information and useful remarks about several organ stops, as well as the stoplist.

β) Jonathan Hellers, A Sermon on the wise and faithful handiwork of God evident in the conscientious exercise of worship that is acceptable to God, delivered publicly before a great throng in the Main Parish Church of St. Mary, Danzig, on the fourth Sunday of Advent, 1760, upon the occasion of the dedication of the newly-built great organ. Danzig, 1761. 3 signatures in quarto, not including the dedication, which occupies yet another signature. This sermon is in no way inferior to the one above [by Kluge], but it includes nothing about the organ itself, not even the stoplist.

γ) Bernhardt Sebastian Große, Holy Acts in the House of the Lord, a sermon delivered on the 10th Sunday after Trinity 1763 at the dedication of the new organ in the Stadtkirche at Ilmenau, and then printed together with a brief history of the new organ. Eisenach, 1765. The sermon occupies 2 signatures, and the brief history of the organ together with the stoplist another half signature, all in octavo. Both cannot fail to move and delight the reader. [Albrecht]

ciren laſſen, welche doch niemand leicht verwerfen, noch beſagte Männer darum ſtrafbar nennen wird. Aber wenn gefragt wird: ob es recht ſey, daß man ſo große Werke, mit ſo großen Unkoſten, und unmäßiger Pracht erbaue? ſo findet ſich dabey ein ſtärkerer Widerſpruch; indem viele gedenken, was die Jünger zu Bethanien dem Weibe vorrückten: es könne dieſes denen Armen gegeben werden, und gehöre nicht zum Weſen einer Orgel. Dieſe Vorwürfe haben einen guten Schein; und das erſte anlangend, ſo bin ich nicht in Abrede, daß es unverantwortlich ſey, die Sorge für die armen Glieder unſers Heilandes bey Seite zu ſetzen, und alles an ſolche Dinge zu hängen. Wenn aber die Armen gebührend verſorget worden, und durch Gottes Segen ſo viel übrig bleibet, warum ſollte man es nicht an den Gottesdienſt wenden dürfen? Daß es nicht zum Weſen einer Orgel gehöre, wenn ſie koſtbar und wohlgeputzt ausſiehet, muß ich zwar geſtehen; allein deshalben iſt es nicht unrecht. Gehört es doch auch nicht zum Weſen eines Kleides, daß das Tuch 2 oder mehr Thaler koſte; daß es mit goldenen Balletten und Knöpfen prange ꝛc. und doch kann ſolches mit der Andacht gar wohl beſtehen, ſi cetera ſint paria. Oder beym Gottesdienſte zu bleiben; ſo gehöret es auch nicht zum Weſen des Altars oder Kanzel, daß ſie mit Statuen, koſtbaren Gemählden und zierlichen Decken prangen; und doch wird dieß als etwas indifferentes angeſehen. Daß aber dabey die rechte und innerliche Sabbathsfeyer wohl beſtehen könne, giebt Gott durch die Einrichtung des Gottesdienſtes im alten Teſtamente genugſam zu erkennen, welcher auf deſſen Befehl gewiß ſo koſtbar und prangend angerichtet worden, daß wir heut zu Tage einen ſo herrlichen nimmer antreffen werden. Und ob dieſes gleich im neuen Teſtamente kein Gebot iſt; ſo iſt doch auch kein Verbot da, wenigſtens ſieht man aus dem alten Bunde, daß es Gott gar wohl leiden könne, welches ich anjetzo eben beweiſen wollte. S. Kretſchmars Einweihungspredigt: und wie bey einem ſchönen Kleide der Königin Eſther dennoch ein demüthiges und frommes Herz ſeyn konnte; ſo kann auch bey einem ſchönen Gottes hauſe und propern Gottesdienſte die Andacht wohl beſtehen.

§. 16.

Das deutſche Wort Orgel kömmt her von dem lateiniſchen ORGANUM: dieſes aber iſt, dem Urſprunge nach griechiſch ὄργανον. Ὄργανον aber bedeutet ein jedes Inſtrument, womit etwas gemacht wird, und kömmt her von ἔργον, opus, ein Werk, quaſi ἔργανον. Ἔργον aber kann von dem hebräiſchen אָרַג, texuit, oparatus eſt, er hat gewirket, hergeleitet werden, welches alſo das erſte Stammwort des Vocabuli Orgel ſeyn mag. (Conf. Becmanni Origin. lat. linguae. p. m. 787.) [14] Es wird aber die

---

[14] Werth iſt dasjenige zu leſen, was Caſpar Calvör de Muſica, ac ſpeciatim eccleſiaſtica, Cap. 5. §. 11. p. 61. der Edition in 12. Ao. 1702 ſchreibt. Der fragt: ob nicht vielleicht ſowol dieſes Wort, als auch die Sache ſelbſt, griechiſcher Herkunft ſey? Und anſtatt, daß andere Organum erklären κατ᾽ ἐξοχὴν pro opere elegantiſſimo et exellentiſſimo, ſagt er: Die Griechen hätten dem Bacchus zu Ehren die orgia (ὄργια) gefeyert, welches mit Springen verrichtet

well. No one will lightly object to the latter, nor blame the men cited above* on their account. The question also arises whether it is fitting to construct such large instruments at such great expense and with such excessive splendor? In that same vein is yet a stronger protest, in that many consider how the disciples rebuked the woman at Bethany: "This could have been given to the poor,"† and thus ought not rightfully be applied to [the purchase of] an organ. These objections appear to be well-founded, and I would indeed agree that it would be irresponsible to neglect caring for our Savior's faithful poor, and to put all [the money] into organs. When the poor are appropriately cared for, however, and through the blessing of God a certain amount remains, why should this not be applied to the service of God in worship? I will indeed admit that it is not essential that an organ have a shiny, expensive appearance; but it is not wrong if it does. Is it not appropriate that an article of clothing, if its cloth should cost 2 or more Talers, be decked with shiny golden sequins and buttons? And yet, all things being equal, such attire is held to be consistent with an attitude of devotion. Or, still speaking about worship, is it not considered appropriate that an altar or pulpit be resplendent with statues, valuable paintings and elegant cloths; yet no one seems to consider this improper. God has given ample evidence through the institution of worship in the Old Testament (which at his command was assuredly arranged in an expensive and splendid way such as we never encounter nowadays ‡) that a proper and heartfelt observance of the sabbath is not inconsistent with [outward splendor]. And even if there is no command to this effect in the New Testament, there is certainly no prohibition; at least one may see from the Old Testament that it does not displease God, as I have just tried to demonstrate above. Note Kretschmar's dedicatory sermon:§ "Just as a humble and pious heart could exist within the beautiful dress of Queen Esther,¶ so may true devotion exist within a beautiful house of God and a proper service of worship."

* i.e., King David and King Solomon.

† John 12:5.

‡ cf. I Chronicles 22:6f.; 23:2f.;

§ see above, §.11.
¶ See the Book of Esther, Chap. 5f.

§. 16.

The German word "Orgel" [i.e., organ] is derived from the Latin *organum*; this in turn originates in the Greek οργανον. Οργανον, however, means any instrument or tool by means of which something is made, and is derived from εργον, *opus*, or "work" (as though the word were εργανον). Εργον can in turn be derived from the Hebrew אָרַג, *texuit, oparatus* [sic] *est*, "he has worked," which may therefore be the root of the word "organ." (cf. Becmann's *Origin. lat. Linguae.*‖ p.m. 787).[14] The term *organum* or οργανον is used to refer to the organ itself, however, both because of its excellence and because it is the ideal for most musical instruments, in that it contains the trombone, trumpet, bassoon, viol da gamba, etc. The word *Werk* is also used in its absolute sense in referring to an organ or *Orgelwerk*, e.g., "They are building a fine *Werk*," by

‖ Becmann, Christian, *De originibus latinae linguae...* Wittenberg, 1609.

---

14) It is worthwhile to read what Caspar Calvör writes in his *de Musica, ac speciatim ecclesiastica*, Chap. 5, §.11, p. 61, published in 1702 in duodecimo. He asks if perhaps both this work and also the [instrument] itself might be of Greek origin. And in contrast to the way others explain the word itself to mean "a most elegant and excellent creation" (κατ εξοχην, *pro opere elegantissimo et exellentissimo*), he says: the Greeks celebrated the *orgia* (οργια) in honor of Bacchus; these were carried

die Orgel κατ᾽ ἐξοχὴν organum ὄργανον benennet, wegen der Vortreflichkeit, und weil sie ein Begrif ist der meisten musikalischen Instrumente: denn darinne finden wir die Posaune, Trompet, Fagott, Violdigamba, ꝛc. Ueber die Benennung Orgel und Orgelwerk, sagt man auch Werk absolute, e. g. sie bauen ein schön Werk, d. i. eine schöne Orgel. Sonst weis ich kein Synonymum. Organum pnevmaticum (ein Windinstrument) ist gleich viel. De Chales Mund. mathem. To. III. sagt gar oft Organum pithaulicum.

Hebräische Namen der Orgel sollen seyn: עוּגָב und עֻגָב, derer gedacht wird, 1 B. Mose Kap. 4. v. 21 Hiob Kap. 30. v. 31. Psalm 150. v. 4. ꝛc. Von עָגַב amare, quia sono ardentes ciet adfectus et amores עֲגָבִים dictos, so das Targum giebt per *canticum canticorum*, Ezech. Kap. 33. v. 31. wie Prätorius schreibt Tom I. P. I. Membr. IV. c. VIII, da es andere auch חָלִיל nennen wollen, a הוּל vel חָלַל privare, evacuare, weil die Pfeifen hohl sind; Esaia Kap. 5. v. 12. Kap. 30. v. 29. ubi quidam *organum* exponunt: allein alles dieses ist nicht hinlänglich bewiesen, und wer weis, was sie für Instrumente dadurch verstanden haben. Vergl. M. Kretschmars Einweihungspredigt der Görlitzer Orgel.

§. 17.

Es werden die Orgeln in Ansehung der verschiedenen Größe in große, kleine und mittelmäßige getheilet. Die kleinen führen einen besondern Namen, nemlich, Positiv; wovon unten im 20. Kapitel gehandelt wird. Wir bleiben itzt bey den ordentlichen Orgeln. Die Theile einer solchen Orgel sind verschieden. Es lassen sich äusserliche und innerliche dabey bemerken. Die innern werden im folgenden Kapitel beygebracht. Itzo erzählen wir die äusserliche Gestalt einer Orgel, und finden folgende Stücke zu betrachten:

§. 18.

Zu unterst liegt der Fuß, welches der Grund der Orgel ist, und eben das prästiren muß, was die Schwellen an einem Hause zu leisten haben. Man verfertiget denselben von starken Säulen oder Balken, und dieses auf allen vier Seiten, welche denn nach Zimmermannsart auf den Ecken befestiget werden: Um aber desto sicherer zu verfahren; so heftet man die einander entgegen liegenden Schwellen mit mehrern Zwerchsäulen zusam-

---

wurde, und wozu man den ὀργιαστήν, celebratorem solcher orgiorum nöthig hatte. Der ist nun wol ohne Zweifel ein Spielmann, und des ganzen Chors Anführer gewesen. —— Daher kommen die andern griechischen Worte: ὀργιάζω, ὀργάζομαι, orgia celebro, &c. It. ὀργασμοί, ceremoniae, &c. Wie nun der ὀργιαστής mit der Pfeife und tanzend dem übrigen Chor vorgieng; so muthmaße ich (sagt Calvör) daß unsere Künstler, weil sie mit den Pfeifen ihrer Maschine bey der Feyer eines Festes dem Volke vorspielen, sonderlich wenn gesungen wird, den alten Namen der ὀργιαστής bekommen, woraus nach der Zeit Organist geworden, und das Instrument, worauf sie spielen, hat den Namen Organon bekommen.

Ch. II. Concerning the Outer Case of the Organ.

which is meant "a fine organ." Beyond this I know of no synonym. *Organum pneumaticum* (a "wind instrument") amounts to the same thing. De Chales in his *Mundus mathematicus*, Vol. III, often refers to the *Organum pithaulicum*.*

 The Hebrew names for the organ are said to be עֲגָב and עִיגָב, as mentioned in the book of Genesis, Chap. 4, v. 21, Job, Chap. 30, v. 31, Psalm 150, v. 4, etc., from עָגַב, "to love", because by the sound the burning affections and passions, called עֲגָבִים, are set in motion, whence the Targum refers to the song of organs† in Ezekiel, Chap. 33, v. 31; [all of this is from] Praetorius, [*Syntagma musicum*,], Vol. I, Part I, Membrum IV, chap. VIII[, p. 108]. Others try to derive it from חָרִיר, from הוּרר or חָרַר, "to deprive of", "empty out", because the pipes are hollow; or from Isaiah, Chap. 5, v. 12 [and] Chap. 30, v. 29, by which some have explained [the term] *organum*.‡ None of this is sufficiently well proven, however, and [anyway] who knows what sort of instruments they understood [these words] to signify. Cf. Kretschmar's dedicatory sermon for the organ at Görlitz.

§. 17.

With regard to their various sizes, organs are categorized into large, small and middle-sized. The small ones have a specific name, "Positiv, " and are dealt with in Chapter 20 below. Only regular "organs" are discussed here. The parts of an organ are many and various, both exterior and interior. The next chapter treats the interior; now we turn our attention to the exterior form of an organ, and note the following parts:

§. 18.

At the bottom lies the base/lower case, the foundation of an organ, which must fulfill the same function as the joists of a house. It is fashioned out of strong pillars or beams on all four sides, anchored at the corners according to the techniques of carpentry. In order to make it all the sturdier, however, the opposing joists are braced by several diagonal beams, a technique well-known to craftsmen and thus not necessary to

---

* de Chales, Vol. III, pp. 17-21.

† Adlung writes *canticum canticorum*, "Song of Songs"; Praetorius, Adlung's source, writes *Canticum Organorum*, "the song of organs".

‡ Adlung's paragraph up to this point is a free quote, heavily abbreviated and partially translated into German, from Praetorius, *Syntagma musicum*, Vol. I, p. 108. The material it treats is obscure and inconsequential, as Adlung states in the next sentence.

---

out with leaping dances, for which the "οργιασησ", the *celebrator* [celebrant] of such orgies, was necessary. This person was doubtless a minstrel, and the director of the whole choir. — — Thence come the other Greek words, οργιαζω, οργαζομαι, *orgia celebro* [I celebrate the orgies], as well as οργασμοι, *ceremoniae* [ceremonies], and the like. Now, since the οργιασησ with his piping and dancing must have preceeded the whole choir, so I conjecture (says Calvör) that our artists, because they perform before the populace on the pipes of their instrument (Maschine) at the celebration of a feast (especially when singing is involved), got the old name οργιασησ, which in time was transformed into "organist"; the instrument upon which they play likewise got the name *Organon*. [Albrecht]

sammen, wie die Werkleute wohl wissen, und hier nicht nöthig anzuführen ist. Nachdem die Form der Orgel seyn soll, nachdem wird die vorderste Schwelle verfertiget, entweder in gerader Linie, oder auf beyden Seiten aus- oder einwärts gebogen, in der Form eines halben Zirkels.

§. 19.

Auf diesen Fuß werden perpendikulare Säulen aufgerichtet, je nachdem die vorgeschriebene Form der Orgel es erfordert. Das ganze Gebäude wird auch wol in **Stockwerke** getheilet, da das untere Stockwerk von dem Fuße bis an die erste Windlade reicht, darauf wird auf gleiche Art das andere gebauet, (wenn nemlich mehr als ein Clavier zu verfertigen ist) das reicht von der ersten bis zur andern Lade, u. s. f. Oben drauf kömmt die **Krone** zu liegen, welches ein Gesimse ist; wie denn alle Stockwerke durch starke Simswerke pflegen unterschieden zu werden. Es wird aber die Ordnung der Stöcke gar sehr verändert, indem bey einer Orgel, die z. E. zwey Claviere haben soll, zuweilen beyde Laden übereinander zu stehen kommen, zuweilen kömmt eine in die Mitte etwas erhaben, die andere aber wird auf beyde Seiten vertheilet, u. s. f. Ferner werden die auswärtsstehenden Pfeifen entweder in einem Felde, oder ohne Unterschied gesetzt: oder man theilet sie in gewisse Felder und Thürme, da zwischen eine gewisse Anzahl Pfeifen ein hölzerner Unterschied angebracht wird. Wenn die Pfeifen in gerader Linie stehen, nennt man es ein **Feld**: wenn sie aber einen halben Zirkel, oder einen Triangul ꝛc. vorstellen; so heißt man es einen **Thurm**. Von dem Pfeifwerke selbst ist Kap. 6. zu reden.

§. 20.

Weil demnach, wenn mehr Claviere sind, als eins, gleichsam etliche Orgeln sich beysammen finden; so unterscheidet man sie nach der Größe, und nach der Lage. Was zu dem obern Claviere gehöret, heißt das **Oberwerk**; was vor uns steht, wird das **Brustwerk** oder die **Brust** genennet; was hinter dem Rücken zuweilen gebauet ist, heißt das **Rückpositiv**. Diese Rückpositive waren sonst weit mehr im Gebrauche, als itzo, da man alles in ein Gebäude bringet, welches auch viel besser ist. Unterdessen ist der Name bey uns eingeschlichen, daß man die kleinen Werke, oder das geringste Clavier in der Orgel, sammt dem, was dazu gehöret, oft das Rückpositiv nennet. Sind mehr als zwey Claviere vorhanden; so wird das eine auch das **mittlere Werk** genennet.

Das eine Clavier hält ordentlich die vornehmsten und schärfsten Register in sich, daher dasselbe zuweilen das **Hauptmanual**, das **Hauptwerk**, it. das **Werk** κατ' ἐξοχήν genennet wird, es mag nun oben oder unten liegen. Z. Ex. in der Orgel zu St. Stephani in Bremen finden sich 3 Claviere, da eins das **Werk**, das andere das **Oberwerk**, das dritte die **Brust** heißt. Das Oberwerk ist nicht allemal vor das vornehmste zu achten, sondern es liegt nur oben. Die wichtigsten Register, damit man recht

voll-

describe here. The front beam is built in the shape that the organ is to assume, either in a straight line or bent inwards or outwards on both sides in the form of a crescent.

§. 19.

Upon this footing perpendicular pillars are erected, each following the prescribed form required by the organ. The entire structure is normally divided into levels, of which the lowest extends from the footing to the first windchest; the second is built on top of it in the same way. If the organ is to have more than one keyboard, then the second extends as far as the second windchest, and so forth. On the very top sits the "crown," which is a cornice; in fact, it is customary to demarcate all the levels with heavy moldings. The arrangement of the levels is however quite variable; in a two-manual organ, for example, sometimes the chests stand one above the other, at other times the one in the middle is rather more prominent/slightly raised and the other is divided on both sides, etc. Likewise the façade pipes are either displayed in a single undivided field/flat, or they are divided into distinct flats and towers, each group of pipes separated by a wooden divider. If the pipes stand in a straight line, then they are referred to as a "flat;" if, however, they appear as a half-circle or a triangle, then they are known as a "tower." Chapter 6 will discuss the actual pipes themselves.

§. 20.

Wherever there is more than one keyboard, it follows that several organs* are found together; these are then distinguished by their size and their position. Whatever belongs to the upper keyboard is called the Oberwerk;† whatever stands directly in front of the organist is called the Brustwerk or Brust;‡ that division occasionally built behind the organist's back is called the Rückpositiv.§ Rückpositivs were much more in use in earlier times than at present; the entire organ is nowadays in one case, which is much better. The name meanwhile continues to creep into use, in that smaller divisions or the least substantial manual of an organ with everything belonging to it is often called the Rückpositiv. If there are more than two manuals, one of them may be called the Mittlere Werk¶ ["middle-work"].

One keyboard normally contains the most prominent and aggressive stops, and is therefore called the Hauptmanual, Hauptwerk, or simply the Werk,‖ no matter where it is located. In the organ at St. Stephen's in Bremen, for example, there are three keyboards, the Werk, the Oberwerk, and the Brust. "Oberwerk" does not always connote the most prominent manual, but only that it is located on top. The most important stops, the ones used for improvising in full textures (recht vollstimmig), as well as for

---

* i.e., divisions.

† "upper-division".

‡ "breast-division" or "breast".

§ "back-positive".

¶ "middle-division".

‖ "primary manual", "primary division", or simply "the instrument".

vollstimmig fantasirt, liegen im Werke; und was dergleichen mehr ist. Ich führe es nur an, damit man im Registerziehen sich besser finde. Sonst wird eine Orgel entweder eine ganze, oder halbe, oder Viertelorgel genennet, welches von den verschiedenen Principalen herrühret, und also bey der Lehre von den Principalen soll berühret werden.

§. 21.

Die Claviere betreffend, so sind sie ordentlich von aussen zu sehen, entweder oben, daß sie mit den Handen gespielet werden, oder unten, woselbst den Füßen ihre Verrichtung angewiesen wird. Jenes heißt insbesondere das Manual; dieses aber das Pedal. Zuweilen liegt auch wol eins von den Manualclavieren inwendig, wie z. Er. in Eisenach.

Das Wort Claviere kömmt her von dem lateinischen Worte Clavis, ein Schlüssel, weil durch die Claviere die Windladen geöfnet werden, daß der Wind die Pfeifen anblasen kann. Ein Stück von diesen Schlüsseln wird clavis (a *claudo* vid. *Becm.* orig. lat. ling. p. 365.) genennet, auch palmula, (vid. *Becm.* ib. p. 800. it. *Ianowka* in Claue p. 96.) von palma, eine kleine Hand; it. ein Ruder, welchem letztern diese Claues nicht unähnlich sind. Man nennet sie auch Tangenten u. s. w. Eine solche Palmula ist ein länglichtes Hölzchen, in der Breite eines Daumens; in der Dicke hat der Mechanicus kein Gesetz vor sich. Das Holz ist Linden, welches sich am besten arbeiten läßt, sich nicht verwirft, und dabey leichte ist. Doch wird von etwas besserm Holze, oder von Elfenbein ein subtiles Blat darauf fournirt, sowol der Sauberkeit, als der Dauerhaftigkeit halben. In der Mitte und an dem hintern Ende sind diese Palmulen in eisernen oder meßingern Stiften beweglich, rc. Viel sage ich nicht davon: ein jeder kann es täglich sehen. Der ganze Innbegrif, oder eine ganze Reihe der Palmularum heißt ein Clavier: Wo demnach mehr Reihen sind, da sind auch mehr Claviere. Mann nennet auch eine solche Reihe die Claviatur; it. Clauiarium, Taftaturam, abacum organicum, abacum polyplectrum &c. (Conf. *Ianowka* loc. cit. *Kircheri* Musurg. L. VI. P. III. c. III. §. 1.) Abacus, schlecht hin, sagt *de Chales* an einigen Orten seines §. 16. bekänntgewordenen Buches. Clauiatura und Clauiarium kommen auch von Clauis her: Taftatura aber ist im lateinischen Lexiko nicht zu finden, sondern es kömmt von dem italienischen Tasto ein Grif, Anrührung, it. die Claviere an einem Instrument. Abacus heißt sonst ein Credenztisch, Tresor, Rechentisch, Bretspiel, u. s. w. Abacus organicus ist ein abacus auf der Orgel. Abacus polyplectrus ist πολύς, multus, viel, und plectrum, πλῆκτρον, welches das Instrument ist, dessen sich die Zitherschläger in Berührung der Sayten bedienen; und werden solche Benennungen auf die Orgelclaviere appliciret.

§. 22.

Die Palmulae sind von einer Breite, und die verschiedenen Claviere müssen recht auf einander passen; denn es werden dieselben oft zusammen gekoppelt, daß wenn das

Ch. II. Concerning the Outer Case of the Organ.

other types [of improvisation], are found in the Werk. I only mention this as an aid to a better understanding of registration. Furthermore, an organ is also referred to as a whole-, a half- or a quarter-organ; this stems from the length of its principal pipes, and is thus treated under the discussion of Principals.*

*§.177.

§. 21.

The keyboards are ordinarily visible outside the case,† either above, where they are played with the hands, or beneath, where they are operated by the feet. The former is specifically referred to as the manual, the latter as the pedal. At times one of the manual keyboards lies within the organ, as for example at Eisenach.‡

† Later in the treatise Adlung treats automatic instruments that have an internal keyboard; see §.549.

The word *Claviere* ["keyboards"] is derived from the Latin word *Clavis*, a key, because it is by means of keyboards that the windchests are opened so that wind may blow into the pipes. A single one of these keys is called *clavis* (from *claudo*; see Becmann, *Orig. Lat. Ling.*,§ p. 365), also *palmula* (see Becmann, ibid., p. 800; also Janowka in his *Clavis*, p. 96) from *palma*, a little hand, also an oar (since the shape of a key is not unlike that of an oar¶); it may also be called a Tangent,‖ etc. This *Palmula* is an oblong strip of wood, about the width of a thumb, but of no standard thickness (organ-builders follow no rules in this). It is made of linden wood, which is easy to work, does not warp, and is light as well. However, it is faced with a better-quality wood or a thin ivory wafer for neatness and durability. Each key moves upon an iron or brass pin, either in the middle or at the back end. Since this can easily be observed at any time, there is no need to say any more about it. All of these together, an entire row of keys, is called a keyboard. Where there are more rows, then, there are more keyboards. Such a row [of keys] is also known as a *Claviatur*, *Claviarium*, *Tastatura*, *Abacus organicus* or *Abacus polyplectrus* (cf. Janowka, *loc. cit.*, Kircher's *Musurgia*, Book VI, Part III, chap. III, §. 1 [, p. 506]. At several places in his book (described in §.16), de Chales simply says *abacus*. *Claviatura* and *Claviarium* are also derived from *clavis*. *Tastatura*, however, is not to be found in a Latin dictionary; it comes from the Italian *tasto*, a grasp or touch, or the key of an instrument. *Abacus* otherwise means a credenza, vault, desk or board-game; *Abacus organicus* is therefore an *abacus* on the organ. *Abacus polyplectrus* is a compound of πολυς, *multus*, "much/many", and *plectrum*, πληκτρον, the implement that a zither player uses to pluck the strings; this term is then applied to organ keyboards.

‡ Johann Limberg's *Das in Jahr 1708 lebende und schwebende Eisenach* (Eisenach, 1712, p. 150) helps to clarify this curious assertion: "Two years ago [the organ in the Georgenkirche] was made much more splendid. It has five manuals, together with the pedal. Four of the manuals lie together in front, above the pedal. The fifth has its action (Angehänge) behind the instrument (Wercke), so that two of the manuals can be played upon simultaneously;" see §.288.

§ see §.16, note 12.

¶ This assertion is more understandable if one takes into account the shape that keys assumed in early organs, depicted in §.486.

‖ In Chapter 26, the chapter dealing with the construction of the clavichord and pedal clavichord, there is some inconsistency in the meaning of the term "Tangent"; see the note to §.572.

§. 22.

The keys are of the same width and the various keyboards must fit together precisely one atop the other, since keyboards are often coupled; in that case when one is

eine gedruckt wird, auch das andere, zuweilen auch wol das dritte mit niederfällt. Die gemeinste Art sie zu koppeln ist, da unten an die Palmulas kleine Hölzerchen mit Leime bevestiget werden, etwa einen Finger dick, auch so breit, und 1 Zoll lang; alsdann werden dergleichen auch an denen Palmulis des untern Claviers bevestiget, doch so, daß sie oben zu stehen kommen. Sie werden so abgerichtet, daß diese zweyerley Koppelhölzchen neben einander vorbeystreichen, und wenn das obere Clavier gerühret wird, es das untere nicht mit berühre: wenn aber das obere Clavier hinterwärts geschoben wird; so treten die obern Klötzchen just über die Hölzchen des andern Claviers, daher durch des obern Niederdrückung auch das andere niederfallen muß. Und so wird es auch gehalten, wenn mehr, als 2 Claviere zu koppeln sind. Daraus folgt, daß, wenn man das untere Clavier berühret, das obere dadurch nicht angeschlagen werde, weil das Drücken unterwärts geschiehet. Ferner siehet ein jeder, daß man die Hände nicht darf auf dem Oberwerke haben, wenn man dasselbe schieben will, weil die Hölzchen gegen einander stoßen, und endlich abbrechen würden: auf dem untern Claviere aber können die Hände ohne Schaden bleiben, weil in dem Schieben die Hölzchen über einander wegpaßiren. Das Koppeln der Claviere geschiehet auch wol so, daß das obere geschoben wird, und doch von dem untern niedergezogen wird durchs Spielen; denn die obern Abstrakten haben besondere Mütterchen oder Schlingen, darein die untern sich hängen. So ists in Naumburg zu St. Wenceslai und St. Otmari. Da muß man die Hände auf keinem Claviere haben. Andere machen ihre Koppel durch blinde Claviere, dabey die Tastatur unbeweglich liegt; weil aber dieses vielerley Ungelegenheit verursacht; so hält man heut zu Tage wenig oder nichts davon. Dies blinde Clavier, wie man es nennt, wird durch einen Zug zwischen die Claviere gestellt, dabey die Mannigfaltigkeit der Züge wohl zu merken, um des rechten Weges nicht zu verfehlen. Bisweilen thut es eins von den Register-Manubriis, zuweilen gehen auf beyden Seiten des Claviers Hölzer heraus, welche beweglich sind, und nach dem Organisten zu, oder vorwärts auf beyden Seiten zugleich müssen bewegt werden, wenn das Koppeln vor sich gehen soll. Zuweilen sind zwey Zapfen an dem Vorsetzbrette des einen Claviers vorn heraus, welche auch auswärts gezogen werden, wenn man koppeln will. Die erste von diesen drey Arten habe ich z. Ex. gesehen in der Michaeliskirche in Erfurt; die andern in der Universitätskirche zu Jena, wie auch in Zwezen; die dritte in der Kirche St. Andreä zu Erfurt. Es gibt aber noch andere Arten zu koppeln. Man koppelt auch wol drey Claviere zusammen, und spielt auf denen Mittelsten, wie z. Ex. in Gera, it. zu Waltershausen. [15])

§. 23.

Die Anzahl der palmularum ist auf einer Orgel nicht wie auf der andern. Die uralten Orgeln hatten nur 15 palmulas, hernach hat man derer stets mehrere gemacht,

bis

---

[15]) Dieser Umstand findet sich auch an der Orgel in unser hiesigen Obermarktskirche B. M. V. wo alle drey Claviere zusammengekoppelt, und durch die Bespielung des Mittelsten können zum Klange gebracht werden.

being depressed, it must operate a second and at times even a third. The most common means of coupling is this: small blocks, about the width and breadth of a finger and an inch long, are glued to the underside of the keys. Identical blocks are then also glued atop the keys of the keyboard beneath. They are so constructed that both sets of coupling blocks usually pass by each other; thus when the upper keyboard is played it does not come into contact with the lower one. If, however, the upper keyboard is shoved backwards, these blocks move into position exactly above those of the other keyboard; thus when the upper key is depressed, then the lower one must fall as well. The same sort of arrangement is used to couple more than two keyboards together. Naturally, if one plays the lower keyboard the one above it is not affected, since the lower key is depressed. In addition, it is obvious that one must be careful not to depress the upper keyboard while shoving it, or else the blocks will collide and finally break off. No damage will occur, however, if the hands are depressing [keys on] the lower keyboard, since the blocks will simply slide into position one atop the other. The manual coupling system may also be constructed so that, when the upper keyboard is shoved [into position], [its keys] are pulled down when one plays on the lower manual; in this case the upper manual's trackers have special little nuts or eyes that the lower [manual's trackers] hook into. St. Wenceslaus and St. Ottmari in Naumburg have this sort of arrangement. No key must be depressed on any manual [while this coupler is being engaged]. Others build their coupling mechanisms using blind keyboards;* with this [system] the keys do not move. Nowadays this arrangement is in disfavor, since it causes all sorts of inconveniences. The blind keyboard, as it is called, is drawn between the keys by means of a drawknob; since there are [already] so many drawknobs [on an organ], one needs to be careful not to miss the right one. Sometimes it is included as one of the manual drawknobs, while at other times there are moveable wooden [knobs] that the organist must simultaneously push or pull on either side of the keyboard† to couple or uncouple the manuals. At times there are also two pegs that protrude from one keyboard's thumper board, and these must be shoved outwards to engage the coupler. I have seen the first of these three types, for example, in the Michaeliskirche at Erfurt; the second in the University Church at Jena as well as in Zwesen; and the third at the St. Andreas' Church in Erfurt. There are other ways to construct couplers as well. It is also quite possible to couple three manuals together; in this instance one plays on the middle manual, as for example at Gera and also at Waltershausen.[15]

§. 23.

The number of keys varies from organ to organ. Primitive organs had only 15 keys, and gradually this number has been increased to 49, although some have only 48, since

* These seem to be something different from the blind keyboard mentioned by Werner Fabricius (*Unterricht, wie man ein neu Orgelwerk, obs gut und beständig sey, nach allen Stücken, in- und auswendig examiniren, un so viel möglich probiren soll*. Frankfurt and Leipzig, 1756, p. 18), a device Fabricius says is designed to keep the Brustwerk from projecting so far forward as to hinder performance on the keyboard.

† i.e., on the key cheeks.

[15]) This is also the case with the organ in the Obermarktskirche of the BVM here,‡ in which all three manuals can be coupled together and played from the middle one. [Albrecht]

‡ in Mühlhausen, where the author of this note, Johann Lorenz Albrecht, was Cantor and Director of Music.

Kap. II. Von dem äusserlichen Gehäuse der Orgel. 23

bis man auf 49. gekommen: wiewol etliche noch 48. palmulas haben, da ihnen das große Cis fehlet; etlichen mangelt auch das große Dis; etlichen mangelt auch Fis und Gis, an deren statt D und E unter den chromatischen palmulis sind; an einigen fehlen auch wol etliche von den obersten clauibus, da die untere Oktav, auch zuweilen die obere, kürzer wird, weswegen man alsdann zu sagen pflegt: es hat kurze Oktav. Aber das ist nur noch bey alten Orgeln zu finden, in welchen bald dieß bald jenes fehlt. Die neuern gehen ordentlich bis auf 48 und 49 etliche noch höher, da sie cis, d, auch wol dis und e aus der dreygestrichnen Oktave mitnehmen. z. E. in Eisenach.

§. 24.

Es sind zweyerley palmulae, niedrige und erhabene, diese liegen zwischen jenen inne, und ragen fingersdicke vor jenen in die Höhe. Die nennet man am bequemsten Claues chromaticas, die niedrigen aber Claues diatonicas. Andere nennen jene Semitonia, oder, welche besser Griechisch verstehen, Hemitonia; aber es sind dieses keine richtige Benennungen. Die Namen der Palmulen sind mit den Namen der Noten einerley, indem sie durch das a b c d e f &c. von einander unterschieden werden. Und vom C machen wir ordentlich den Anfang und benennen die 49 palmulas mit den dazwischen liegenden clauibus chromaticis also:

C.	Cis.	D.	Dis.	E.	F.	Fis.	G.	Gis.	A.	B.	H.
1	2	3	4	5	6	7	8	9	10	11	12
c.	cis.	d.	dis.	e.	f.	fis.	g.	gis.	a.	b.	h.
13	14	15	16	17	18	19	20	21	22	23	24
c̄.	c̄is.	d̄.	d̄is.	ē.	f̄.	f̄is.	ḡ.	ḡis.	ā.	b̄.	h̄.
25	26	27	28	29	30	31	32	33	34	35	36
c̿.	c̿is.	d̿.	d̿is.	ē̄.	f̿.	f̿is.	ḡ̄.	ḡ̄is.	ā̄.	b̿.	h̿.
37	38	39	40	41	42	43	44	45	46	47	48
c̿̄.											
49											

Es ist einerley ob ich cis oder g mahle; und so mit andern.

§. 25.

Mehr hiervon wird anderswo geredt. Also siehet man, daß, wenn man durch ist, wieder von vorn angefangen werde: um aber aller Verwirrung vorzukommen, hat man einem jeden Absatze einen besondern Namen beygelegt, und die palmulas von C an bis an das andere c exclusiue, mit den Namen große bemerkt. Demnach spricht man das große C, große D, u. s. w. Von dem andern c bis zum dritten nennet man es blos, z. Er. das bloße c, das bloße d, ꝛc. weil man keine Striche darüber machet. Von dem dritten bis zum vierten nennet man es eingestrichen. Z. Er. das eingestrichene c, d, e, u. s. f. Und da die tiefsten palmulae durch große Versalbuchstaben vorgestellet

Ch. II. Concerning the Outer Case of the Organ. 23

they lack the low C#. Some organs also lack the low D#, or even F# and G# as well. In this last instance the notes D and E* occupy these chromatic keys. There are also organs that lack some of the notes at the top of the keyboard; thus the lowest as well as the highest octave is shorter. Hence it is said, "It has a short octave." Today, though, one encounters this only in old organs, in which this or that is lacking. Newer organs normally have 48 or 49 keys, and some have even more, when c#''' and d''', or even d#''' and e''' are included, e.g. at Eisenach.†

§. 24.

There are two kinds of keys, lower and raised, the latter lying between the former and projecting upward the thickness of a finger above them. The most convenient term for the latter is "chromatic keys," and for the former "diatonic keys." The [chromatic keys] are also referred to as *semitonia*, or better in Greek, *hemitonia*; but there is no specific name for the [lower keys]. The names of the keys are identical with the names of the notes, being distinguished one from the other by the letters a b c d e f etc. And now, beginning with great C, here are the 49 keys in order, including the intervening chromatic keys:

C	C#	D	D#	E	F	F#	G	G#	A	B-flat	B
1	2	3	4	5	6	7	8	9	10	11	12
c	c#	d	d#	e	f	f#	g	g#	a	b-flat	b
13	14	15	16	17	18	19	20	21	22	23	24
c'	c#'	d'	d#'	e'	f'	f#'	g'	g#'	a'	b-flat'	b'
25	26	27	28	29	30	31	32	33	34	35	36
c''	c#''	d''	d#''	e''	f''	f#''	g''	g#''	a''	b-flat''	b''
37	38	39	40	41	42	43	44	45	46	47	48
c'''											
49											

How one depicts c# or any other note is immaterial.‡

§. 25.

We will say more about this subject elsewhere. You will note that the series of notes keeps repeating itself. In order to avoid any confusion, however, each series has been given a special name. The keys from C up to but not including c are given the name "great," so that one speaks of "great C, great D," etc. [The keys] from c to c' are referred to as "plain,"§ e.g., "plain c, plain d," etc., because there is no line above them.¶ From c' to c'' is called "one-stroke," e.g., "one-stroke c, d, e," etc.‖ Note that the lowest keys are distinguished by the use of capital letters, while the succeeding series

* The publication has "D and C," but this is surely an error (probably a misreading of Adlung's manuscript). What Adlung is describing here is the short octave, a common arrangement for the lowest octave of keyboard instruments up through the 17th century that was rapidly becoming obsolete during his day.

† at the Georgenkirche; see §. 288.

‡ This remark only makes sense in the German original —"Es ist einerley ob ich *cis* oder ƒ mahle; und so mit andern."—since Adlung recognizes two equivalent ways to write c-sharp: *cis* or ƒ.

§ The word Adlung uses is "bloss;" the English equivalent in this instance is "tenor:" "tenor c, tenor d," etc.

¶ Adlung indicates the strokes that accompany the pitch letters as lines above the letters; the more usual practice today is to place small strokes after the pitch letter.

‖ 35 Modern English labels these notes "c one, d one, d three," etc.

let werden, die in andern Absatze durch Currentbuchstaben; so macht man über solche Currentbuchstaben im dritten Absatze einen kleinen Strich; daher es eingestrichen heißt. Hierauf folgen zwey Striche, das sind alsdann die 2 gestrichenen Claues vom vierten c bis zum fünften. Das 5te c allein, hat drey Striche, und heißt das dreygestrichne c. Wollte man die Tastatur oben weiter ausdehnen, so würden die folgenden auch 3 Striche führen. Die Orgelmacher, wenn sie ein 8füßiges Werk vor sich haben, nennen das große C das 8füßige, darauf folgt daß 4füßige c, dann das 2füßige, dann das 1füßige, und endlich das ½füßige. Soviel aber das Große größer ist, als das kleinere so viel geht nach Proportion den andern auch ab. Diese Absätze nennet man auch Oktaven, daher man sagt: die bloße, die eingestrichne, die zweygestrichne, ꝛc **Oktave.**

§. 26.

Zu beyden Seiten des beweglichen Claviers finden sich zuweilen Knöpfe, Schrauben, oder sonst etwas, wodurch man das Koppeln besorgt. Unter die palmulas wird ein Tuch bevestiget durch Leim, damit die palmulae kein Rasseln verursachen, wenn sie müßten auf das bloße Holz fallen. Zwischen den Clavieren wird ein Bretchen angeheftet oder angeschraubet, welches man das Vorsetzbrett nennet. An die palmulas werden Stifte geschlagen, woran die Abstrakten durch Schrauben bevestiget werden; aber das ist was innerliches. Bey dem untern Claviere findet sich bisweilen eine Reihe Stangen unter der Tastatur von beliebiger Länge, diese machen das sogenannte Druckwerk aus, wovon wo anders geredet werden soll, weil es was innerliches ist. Es wird aber zuweilen von aussen über dieselben ein Brett geheftet, oder angeschraubet, damit man in der Noth dazu kommen könne.

§. 27.

Das Pedal hat den Namen von Pes, ein Fuß, weil es sich unter den Füßen des Organisten befindet, auch mit den Füßen getreten wird. Hierbey finden sich die palmulae, welches die nach der Reihe liegenden langen Hölzer sind, und ebenfalls, wie bey den Manualen, claues genennet werden. Sie sind ordentlich oblongae, 2 Finger breit, und hoch, von beliebiger Länge, weil daran dem Hauptwerke nichts entgehet, ob sie 4, oder 5, oder 6 viertel Ellen lang sind. Diese palmulae sind wie bey den Manualen, zum Theil erhaben, zum Theil aber gerade. Jene nennet man chromatische, diese aber diatonische claues. Das äusserste Ende derselben unter der Bank ist auf einem Ramen in Stifte geleget, darinn sie bewegt werden können, über solche Reihe Stifte legt man eine Leiste, um die Unreinigkeiten abzuhalten. Hier sind die palmulae alle gleich hoch, eine halbe viertel Elle ohngefehr von der Erde erhoben. Diese Höhe ist willkührlich. Aber das andere Ende wird in viereckigten oder länglichten Kerben, oder Scheiden beweglich gemacht, welche in ein Brett geschnitten werden, doch die Kerben der diatonischen clauium zuweilen etwas tiefer, etwann also: ▢▢▢▢ ꝛc.

Als-

of notes all use lower-case letters; thus to label the notes of the third octave one makes over them a small stroke, and so they are called "one-stroke." The notes of the following series, from the fourth c up to the fifth c, are called "two-stroke." The fifth c alone has three strokes, and is thus called the "three-stroke c". If the keyboard extends higher, the notes following also bear three strokes. Organbuilders call great C in an 8-foot division "8-foot C," the next c "4-foot c," then "2-foot c," "1-foot c," and finally " ½-foot c;" the smaller pipe is always half the size of the larger. These series [of notes] are called "octaves," and so we speak of "the tenor octave," the "one-stroke octave," the "two-stroke octave," etc.

§. 26.

On both sides of the keyboard that shifts there are sometimes knobs, screws or some such [device] to operate the coupling system. A strip of fabric is glued beneath the keys, so that the keys do not strike bare wood when they fall and thus create a clatter. A strip of wood is fastened or screwed between the keyboards, called the thumper board. Pins are driven into the keys, to which the trackers are attached by means of screws; but this belongs to the inner [workings*]. Beneath the keys of the lowest manual there is found at times a row of stickers, of an unspecified length; these constitute the so-called sticker action which, since it belongs to the inner [workings], will be discussed elsewhere.† At times, though, a front panel is fastened or screwed on to cover them, so that one can get at them when necessary.

* Thus it is discussed in succeeding chapters instead of here.

† see §.52.

§. 27.

The pedal derives its name from [Latin] *pes*, "foot", since it lies under and is operated by the organist's feet. Just as the manuals, the notes of the pedal are called *claves* or keys; they are a row of long pieces of wood lying parallel to each other. They are usually oblong in shape, two finger-widths broad and deep, but of unspecified length, since it makes no difference whether they are 1, 1¼ or 1½ ells‡ long. Just as in the manuals, some of these keys are lower and some are raised; the latter are called "chromatic," the former "diatonic" keys. The outer ends of them, under the bench, are set upon pins in a frame, upon which they can be moved. A board is placed over this row of pins to keep them from getting dirty. At this point§ the keys are all of equal height, elevated about an eighth of an ell from the floor; this height is arbitrary. The other ends, however, travel within square or oblong slots or sheaths that are cut into a board. The slots of the diatonic keys, however, are sometimes placed a bit lower, rather like this:

‡ Adlung continues to refer to this old unit of measure throughout the book. The word may be translated as "yard," but such a translation would be misleading. Just like many other old standards of measure, this one varied considerably according to time and place, but in central Germany it would have been between .564 - .579 meters (cf. Fritz Verdenhalven, *Alte Maße, Münzen und Gewichte aus dem deutschen Sprachgebiet*. Neustadt an der Aisch: Degener, 1968, pp. 21-22).

§ i.e., under the back of the bench.

Kap. II. Von dem äusserlichen Gehäuse der Orgel. 25

Alsdann setzt man etwas auf die chromatischen, damit sie erhaben werden, und da die diatonischen etwan so aussehen möchten:

So sehen die chromatischen also aus:

Wiewol, wenn man den Zapfen *a* an dem obern Aufsatze machen wollte; z. Er.

so könnten die Kerben von einerley Höhe seyn; welches auch bisweilen geschiehet.

§. 28.

Unter den Palmulis liegen meßingene, oder eiserne Federn von Drat, und zwar unter deren innerem Ende; da man zuweilen 1, und zuweilen 2 und mehr Federn unter jeder palmula findet, wodurch sie, wenn sie niedergetreten worden, wieder aufwärts getrieben werden. Es haben diese Federn folgenden Form:

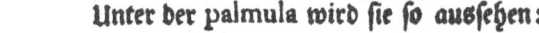 da die Spitze *a* in die palmulam, *b* aber in ein unten angemachtes Zwergbrettgen bevestiget ist. In *c* ist das Drat 2 oder mehrmal in zirkelrunder Form gewunden. Diese Federn merke man einmal für allemal: denn so oft wir der Federn hinführo gedenken werden, sind es dergleichen. Unter der palmula wird sie so aussehen:

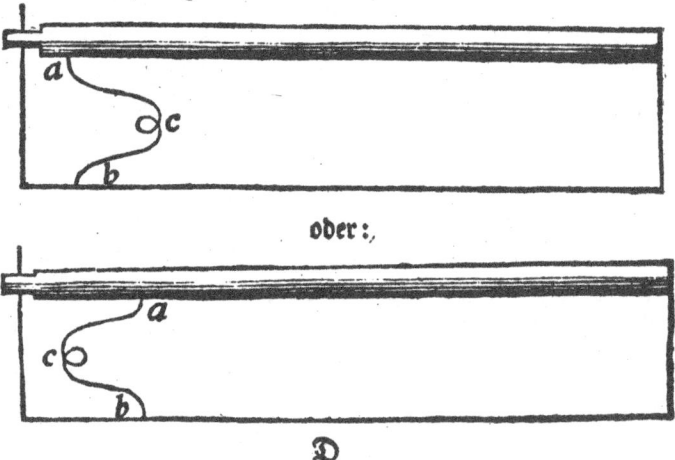

D Dieses

Ch. II. Concerning the Outer Case of the Organ.

The chromatic keys must then be built up, so they are raised. Then the diatonic keys might look something like this:

while the chromatic keys look like this:

Although if the tabs at *a* were to extend from the raised portion, as in the following diagram:

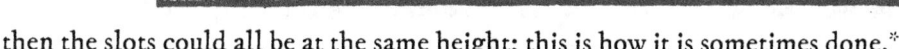

then the slots could all be at the same height; this is how it is sometimes done.*

§. 28.

Under the inner end of the [pedal] keys lie springs of brass or iron wire. At times one, at times two or more of these springs are found under each key; when the key is depressed, they push it up again. The springs take the following shape: The pointed end *a* is inserted into the key, while the pointed end *b* is fastened to a cross-board anchored beneath. At *c* the wire is bent two or more times into a circular form. Whenever springs are mentioned in this treatise, it is this form that is meant; therefore please take careful note of it now. They look like this under the [pedal] keys:

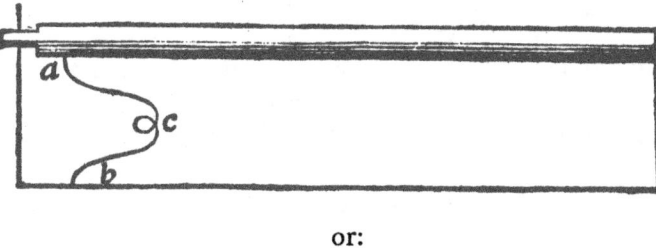

or:

* Adlung seems to have this exactly backward. If the tabs extended from the risers, then the slots for the chromatic keys would have to be higher than those for the diatonic keys. If, on the other hand, the tabs on all the keys extended directly behind the slats, the slots could indeed all be at the same height.

26 Kap. II. Von dem äusserlichen Gehäuse der Orgel.

Dieses Brett in *b* gehet unter allen palmulis durch, und ruhet auf beyden Seiten auf Leisten, wodurch der hintere Rahmen und das Kerbenbrett zusammen verbunden werden, und worinne hernach die palmulae enthalten sind, daß es ein parallelogrammum formirt. Die Zahl der palmularum ist nicht einerley.

Die **Erfindung** des **Pedals** wird **Bernhardo**, einem Deutschen zugeschrieben, der aus Deutschland dergleichen nach Venedig überbracht, und zwar wie **Prätorius** in Synt. Tom. II. P. III. c. V. p. 96. meldet Ao. 1470. **Prinz**, in Hist. mus. setzt c. 10. §. 29. das Jahr 1472. Und da hatte man nur 8 claves, nemlich von H bis h. Nach der Zeit hat man die chromatischen claves dazu gethan, und auch die Zahl sonst vermehret, daß die gemeinste Zahl itzo 24. ist; denn man hebt vom C an bis zum $\bar{c}$, läßt aber gemeiniglich das große Cis aussen. Wenn dasselbe dabey ist, sind deren 25. Bisweilen thut man cis und d auch dazu, da denn 27 claves werden. Etliche gehen noch höher. Z. Er. die Weissenfelßische, welche bis ins f hinauf gehet. In etwas alten Orgeln mangelt auch das Dis. Aber die gemeineste Claviatur ist diese:

C.	Cis.	D.	Dis.	E.	F.	Fis.	G.	Gis.	A.	B.	H.
1	2	3	4	5	6	7	8	9	10	11	12
c.	cis.	d.	dis.	e.	f.	fis.	g.	gis.	a.	b.	h.
13	14	15	16	17	18	19	20	21	22	23	24
c̄.	c̄is.	d̄.									
25	26	27									

Vom ersten C bis zum andern heißt es die **große Oktav**; vom andern c bis zum dritten die **bloße Oktav**, und vom dritten bis zu Ende die **eingestrichene Oktav**, wie bey den Manualen. Die Kerben worinne die palmulae laufen, werden Scheiden genennet, und diese sind meistentheils mit Tuch ausgefuttert, daß es nicht rassele. Man macht solche palmulas aus Lindenholz, wie die Manuale, aus eben derselben Ursach.

§. 29.

Die beste **Lage** ist, daß das mittlere c perpendikulariter unter dem mittlern $\bar{c}$ des Manuals liege. Denn weil man sich doch mitten vor das Clavier setzt, warum sollte ich nicht die 2 Oktaven des Pedals auf beyden Seiten gleich eintheilen? Ein Bein ist ja so lang, als das andere.

Ueber oder vor die Palmuln kömmt die **Pedalbank** zu stehen, welche von willkürlicher Länge, Breite und Form ist. Ordentlich werden sie bey uns oben kürzer gemacht als unten, etwan also:

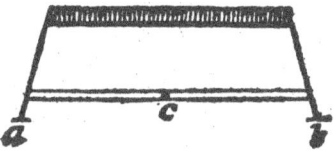

Die

This [cross-]board at *b* extends under the keys from one side to the other, and rests at both sides upon rails that connect the rear frame and the slotted board. This structure forms a rectangle (*parallelogrammum*) that holds the pedal keys in position. The number of pedal keys is not the same [in every organ].

The invention of the pedal is ascribed to Bernhard, a German, who brought it from Germany to Venice in the year 1470, as Praetorius reports in *Syntagma musicum*, Vol. II, Part III, chap. V, p. 96. Printz, in his *Historische Beschreibung der Edelen Sing= und Kling=Kunst*, chap. 10, §.29, [pp.113-4,] gives the year as 1472. At that time there were only 8 keys, B to b.* Over the course of time the chromatic keys were added, and the [total] number [of keys continued to] increase, so that nowadays the most common number is 24: C to c′, usually without C#.† If the C# is included, then there are 25. Sometimes c#′ and d′ are added, in which case there are 27 keys. Some organs go even higher, for example, the one at Weissenfels‡ that extends upward to f′. Some old organs also lack low D#. The most common [pedal] keyboard, however, is as follows:§

C	C#	D	D#	E	F	F#	G	G#	A	B-flat	B
1	2	3	4	5	6	7	8	9	10	11	12
c	c#	d	d#	e	f	f#	g	g#	a	b-flat	b
13	14	15	16	17	18	19	20	21	22	23	24
c′	c#′	d′									
25	26	27									

* Thus there were no chromatic pitches.

† Low C# was commonly omitted up until the 18th century, since low C# pipes were expensive to build and were seldom required to play the music of the time.

‡ in the Augustusburg; see §.354 and the stoplist of this organ in Chapter 10, §.315.

§ The total number of pedal notes Adlung gives here is 27, a number that contradicts the one he has just given several sentences earlier as the most common number, i.e., 24.

From the first C to the second is called the "great octave," from the second to the third the "tenor octave," and from the third to the uppermost key the "one-stroke octave," just as with the manuals. The slots in which the keys travel are called "sheaths" (Scheiden); these are usually lined with cloth to prevent clattering. The pedal keys are made of linden wood, just like the manual keys, and for the same reason[s].¶

¶ see §.21

§. 29.

The best position [for the pedalboard] is such that the c in the middle of it‖ lies directly under the middle c′ of the manuals. For since the organist sits at the midpoint of the manual keyboard, why shouldn't the two octaves of the pedal be divided equally on both sides of him? After all, one leg is just as long as the other.

‖ i.e., tenor c.

The organ bench (Pedalbank) is placed over or in front of the keys: its length, breadth and shape are arbitrary. In this region they are ordinarily built shorter on top than at the bottom, rather like this:

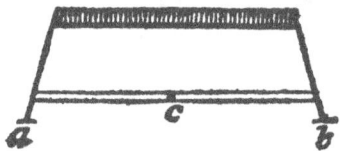

Die Höhe ist so zu messen, daß die ordinäre Länge der Füße das Pedal bequem erreichen kann. An die Füße der Bank *a b* wird eine starke Leiste *c* angemacht, etwas von den palmulis erhaben, doch nicht viel, darauf die Beine ruhen.

§. 30.

Endlich sind unter den äusserlichen Theilen noch die Manubria der Registerzüge, die auf beyden Seiten des Claviers auf mancherley Art erscheinen. Die gemeinste Struktur ist: daß man Knöpfe von Holz verfertiget, etwas stark, daß die Registraturstangen einen Zoll dicke darein gesteckt und mit Stiften bevestigt werden können. Doch findet man auch solche auf andere Art formiret. Wenn man die Register dadurch aufziehen will, ziehet man sie heraus, und durch das einwärts Drücken werden die Register wieder verschlossen. Selten findet man das Gegentheil; wie ich mich denn nur einer einzigen Orgel zu erinnern weis, da die Register durch das Eindrücken der Manubriorum aufgezogen werden. Manubrium heißt sonst ein Griff, Handhabe, 2c. von Manus die Hand. Die gewöhnliche Gestalt ist diese: Man macht aber die Manubria auch von Meßing, Eisen, 2c. Es finden sich auch andere Figuren, als da sehen manche so aus: ohngefehr Daumens breit, und etwan einen $\frac{1}{2}''$ dick; wenn sie aber nicht von Holz sind, sondern von Meßing oder Eisen; so können sie gar dünne seyn. Diese werden zuweilen auswärts gezogen; zuweilen aber schiebet man sie in einem langen Ritze in die Höhe, zuweilen unterwärts, zuweilen auf die Seite; zuweilen sind etliche Arten der Manubriorum an einer Orgel. Doch sind alle diese Arten nicht sonderlich mehr im Gebrauch.

§. 31.

Alle diese bisher erzählten Theile finden sich auch bey den Rückpositiven, welche hinter dem Organisten zu finden, nur daß das Clavier an dem Hauptwerke zugleich anzutreffen; die Register aber sind hinter dem Rücken des Organisten auf beyden Seiten.[16]) Endlich findet man äusserlich noch die Bretter und Tafeln, womit diejenigen Oerter der Orgel zugemacht sind, wo kein Pfeifenwerk befindlich ist; und damit man, so oft als es nöthig, in die Orgel kommen könne: so werden Thüren angebracht, vorne, auf den Seiten und hinten. Oben über der Orgel findet man auch bisweilen ein Dach von Brettern, oder ein ausgespanntes Tuch, um dadurch zu verwehren, daß nicht so viel Koth in das Pfeifwerk falle.

---

[16]) Dies befindet sich nicht an allen Orgeln ohne Ausnahme. Z. Ex. in der Orgel der Oberstädtischen Hauptkirche B. M. V. allhier zu Mühlhausen ist es nicht so; sondern die Manubria zu den Registern des Rückpositivs sind alle vorne in die Reihe der übrigen mit angebracht.

Ch. II. Concerning the Outer Case of the Organ.

The height should be the average distance at which the feet can most comfortably reach the pedals. A strong board is fastened to both of the bench's side-supports, *a* and *b*, a bit above the keys, but not too high, so that the [organist's] legs may rest on it.

§. 30.

The last of the exterior parts [to be discussed] are the drawknobs that operate the stops; these appear on both sides of the keyboards in various configurations. The most common way to build them is to make knobs of wood, quite sturdy, inserting the [stop-]rods about an inch into them and fastening them with pins. They are found, however, in other shapes as well. By pulling them out, the stops are made to sound; by pushing them in the stops are shut off. One seldom finds the reverse; in fact, I can remember only one organ in which the ranks of pipes were made to sound by pushing in the stops. "Manubrium" comes from [Latin] *manus*, hand, and means a grip or handle. The most common shape is this: Drawknobs may also be made of brass, iron, etc. There are also other shapes; many of them look like this: , about the width of a thumb and about half an inch thick. If they are not made of wood, however, but rather out of brass or iron, then they can be very thin. These [metal drawknobs] are at times pulled outwards; or sometimes they are shoved upwards, downwards, or sideways within long slots. Sometimes there are several varieties of drawknobs on the same organ. But all these variants are not much in use anymore.

§. 31.

All of the parts thus far described are also found in the Rückpositiv, [a division] that is located behind the organist. Its keyboard is situated in the main case with [the other keyboards], but the stops are on both sides behind the organist's back.[16] Finally there are, of course, the exterior boards and panels that cover those parts of the organ not occupied by [display] pipes. In order that one may gain access to the organ when necessary, doors are constructed in front, on the sides and in back. On top of the organ case there is built at times a cover of boards, or a cloth is stretched over it, to prevent filth from falling into the pipes.[*]

---

16) This arrangement is not found on all organs without exception. For example, it is not the case with the organ of the Principal City Church of the B.V.M. here in Mühlhausen;[†] here the drawknobs for the Rückpositiv stops are arranged with the other stops in front [of the organist].[‡] [Albrecht]

---

[*] This statement reflects the 18th century's increasing abandonment of the case as a sound reflector, one of the primary characteristics of organs prior to this time; the organ case entirely enclosed except at the front was by Adlung's day a rapidly vanishing phenomenon.

[†] Johann Lorenz Albrecht was Cantor and Music Director at the Marienkirche in Mühlhausen.

[‡] i.e., on the main case at either side of the keyboards.

Das III. Kapitel.
Von der Windlade.

Inhalt.

§. 32. Von dem Namen. §. 33. Von der Größe. §. 34. Von deren Unterschiede, Schenkeln und Kanälen. §. 35. Von den Spünden und Parallelen. §. 36. Die Dämme und Stifte. §. 37. Das Polystomaticum. §. 38. Wie der Wind beysammen zu erhalten. §. 39. Von dem Windkasten. §. 40. Von den Paraglossis und deren Federn auch Stiften. §. 41. Die Säcke. §. 42. Die Spünde und deren Vorschläge. §. 43. Von getheilten Laden. §. 44. Von den Pfeifenstöcken und Stockschrauben. §. 45. Von den Springladen. §. 46. Von den Stöcken, Ventilen, Drückeln, Parallelen, ꝛc. derselben.

§. 32.

Der Haupttheil einer Orgel ist die Windlade; wodurch dasjenige Behältniß des Windes verstanden wird, aus welchem derselbe unmittelbar in die Pfeifen gelassen wird. Sie heißt auch canon musicalis, secretum organicum, ein Orgelgeheimniß, weil sie vor den Zuhörern das Geheime in der Harmonie verbirgt, wie Janowka in claue p. 6. es erkläret. Secretum organi ist gleichviel. Es heißt auch dieselbe Secretum uentorum, weil sich daselbst der Wind verbirgt. S. Kirchers Musurgia. L. VI. P. III. c. III. §. 1. sonderlich pag. 512. Es ist aber von sothaner Windlade der Windkasten zu unterscheiden; denn dieser ist das Vorgemach, worein der Wind aus den Kanälen spatziret, bis er durch gewisse Oefnungen in jene gelassen wird.

§. 33.

Von der Windlade kann gelesen werden, was Werkmeister davon in der Orgelprobe geschrieben. Z. Ex. Kap. V. VIII. XVII. XVIII. Prätorius Tom. II. p. 107. und folg. it. p. 159. und folg. Was hieher gehöret ist folgendes: Die ordinaire Struktur ist diese: Man nimmt eichene Bohlen, die etliche Jahre gelegen und recht dürre sind, und füget sie zusammen nach der Tischlerkunst in Form eines Kastens, daran die Höhe kaum 4 oder 5 Finger, in die Quere, austrägt, die Länge aber ist willkürlich, und richtet man sich darnach ob man große oder kleine Pfeifen darauf setzen will, welche wenig oder viel Raum einnehmen. Also kann sie 2. 4. 5. 6. ꝛc. Ellen lang seyn. Die Breite richtet sich nach der Menge der Register. Und da in einer Orgel oft etliche Laden sind; so sind sie ihrer Länge und Breite nach meistentheils unterschieden. Sie formiren ordentlich ein Viereck, oder ein Quadratum oblongum. Die Theile derselben sind: Der Boden, die Seiten-Rahmen und das obere Theil.

Chapter III.
Concerning the Windchest.

Contents:

§.32. Its name. §.33. Its sizes. §.34. Its dividers,* bars and channels. §.35. The sponsels and sliders. §.36. The spacers and pins. §.37. The table (Polystomaticum). §. 38. Making the windchest airtight. §.39. The pallet box. §. 40. The pallets, their springs and their guide-pins. §. 41. The pouches. §.42. The bungboards and their stays. §.43. Divided chests. §.44. The toeboards and their screws. §.45. Spring chests. §.46. Their toeboards,† stop pallets, stop-pallet pins, stop rods, etc.

* Cf. §.358

† Adlung in fact discusses the spring chest's toeboards at the end of §.45.

§. 32.

The primary component of an organ is the windchest, the container that holds the wind, from which the wind proceeds directly into the pipes. It is also called the *canon musicalis* [or] *secretum organicum*, the "organ's secret," because it conceals the secret of the harmony from the listeners, as Janowka explains in his *Clavis*, p. [9]6,‡ *Secretum organi* means the same thing. It is also called the *Secretum ventorum*, because it hides the wind within itself; see Kircher's *Musurgia*, Book VI., Part III, chap. III, §.1, [p. 506,] and especially p. 512. It is necessary, however, to distinguish such a windchest from the pallet box; the latter is the antechamber into which the wind passes from the wind ducts, and which feeds the former through certain openings.§

‡ Janowka, pp. 96-7, says, "Canon Musicalis à Vitruvio sic dictus, aliàs secretum Organicum, est principale membrum totius Organi, aut positiv etc., quod ab Auditoribus secretum Harmoniae abscondat (The *Canon Musicalis*, so called by Vitruvius, otherwise known as the *secretum Organicum*, is the principal component of the entire organ or positiv, etc., because it conceals the secret of the harmony from the listeners).

§ i.e., those covered by the pallets.

§. 33.

One may read what Werkmeister writes about the windchest in his *Orgelprobe*, e.g., Chapters 5, 8, 17 and 18, and in Praetorius, [*Syntagma musicum*,] Vol. II, pp.107f., as well as pp. 159f. Here is what one ought to know about it. The most common construction is as follows: oak planks that have been stored for several years and are well-cured are joined together into the shape of a box, using the skills of cabinetry. This box is barely 4 or 5 finger-widths high, in cross-section, but of indeterminate length, depending on whether large or small pipes are to be set on it, and how much room they require. It may be 2, 4, 5, 6 or more ells in length. The width is determined by the number of stops. There are often several chests within the same organ, and they usually vary in their length and breadth. The windchest normally takes the shape of a square or a rectangle, and consists of the following parts: the bottom, the side walls (Seiten-Rahmen) and the upper part.

Kap. III. Von der Windlade. 29

§. 34.

Es sind die Windladen hauptsächlich zweyerley: Schleifladen und Springladen. Ehe die ersten waren, hat man die letzten mit großer Mühe erfunden, und in den Niederlanden, auch anderwärts gebraucht; wie denn auch in den neuen Orgeln solche Springladen zuweilen angetroffen werden. Doch sind die Schleifladen weit gebräuchlicher, leichter und begreiflicher, daher ich von denselben erst rede. Der Boden derselben wird von guten Bohlen gemacht, und wohl verwahret. Auf allen Seiten werden eichene Rahmen aufgesetzt, alsdann wird der Boden in soviel Theile getheilt, als das Clavier palmulas hat. Diese Theile werden durch aller Orten wohlpassende Unterscheide von Holz von einander unterschieden, welche hölzerne Rahmen denen Seiten-Rahmen gleich hoch und meistentheils parallel sind, und die Schenkel genennet werden. Die Höhlen oder Kämmerchen die daraus auf der Lade entstehen, nennt man Cancellen, derer so viel sind, als palmulae auf dem Clavier, und also heut zu Tage gemeiniglich 49, wenn es die Manuallade ist; aber die Pedalladen haben dererselben 25, 26 oder 27. Jede Cancelle ist so lang als die Lade breit ist; die Breite aber ist verschiedentlich, nachdem große oder kleine claues darauf zu stehen kommen, und nachdem die Lade selbst länger oder kürzer ist.

§. 35.

An dem einen Ende, zuweilen an beyden Enden, hat jede Cancelle unten auf dem Boden eine längliche Oefnung, so $\frac{1}{4}$ oder $\frac{1}{2}$ ꝛc. Elle lang ist. Die Breite aber ist zuweilen kaum der Breite eines Daumens gleich, zuweilen aber wie 2 Finger ꝛc. dadurch kann der Wind aus dem Windkasten in die ganze Cancelle fahren. Die Cancellen werden oben zugespündet, indem nach der Tischlerkunst die Schenkel auf beyden Seiten eingefalzt werden, in welche Einschnitte lange eichene Latten zu legen und wohl zu verwahren sind, damit kein Wind heraus kommen könne. Das nennet man Spünde; und sagt man also: die Cancellen werden oben zugespündet. Denn ein Spund ist in unsere mechanica ein vorgesetztes Brett oder Stück Holz, dergleichen wir noch mehr bekommen werden. In diese Spünde werden Löcher gebohret, und zwar in eines so viel, als man Register auf solche Lade bringen will. Wenn also der Wind in die Cancelle kömmt; so bläset er in alle darauf gebohrte Löcher, und folglich in die darauf gesetzten Pfeifen: also würden aller Register Pfeifen, welche auf einem claue und Cancelle stünden, zusammen gehöret werden, wenn nicht die Registraturen darauf zu liegen kämen, wodurch einige von diesen Löchern nach Belieben bedeckt, andere aber eröfnet werden. Diese Registraturen sind ebenfalls von Eichenholz, und in einer länglicht viereckigten Form; welche $\frac{1}{2}$ Daumen dicke ohngefehr, und etwan 2, 3, bis 4 Fingerbreit gemacht werden. Die Länge ist der Länge der Lade gleich. Diese Leisten legt man zwerch über alle Cancellen, daß dadurch von jeder Cancelle ein Loch bedeckt werde; und soviel Löcher jede Cancelle hat, oder so viel Stimmen auf der Lade stehen sollen, so viel werden auch solcher Leisten übergelegt.

D 3   §. 36.

Chapter III. Concerning the Windchest.

§. 34.

There are two primary types of windchests: slider chests and spring chests. The latter were invented before the former with much effort, and were used in the Low Countries and elsewhere. But spring chests are still encountered now and then in new organs. Since the slider chest is however far more usual, easy* and comprehensible, I will discuss it first. Its bottom board is constructed of sturdy planks, tightly joined together. Oak side walls are erected on all sides [of it], and then the bottom board is divided into as many sections as the keyboard has keys. These sections are separated from each other at all points by carefully fitted wooden dividers, that are just the same height as the side walls and run for the most part parallel to them; these are called bars (Schenkel).† The resulting cavities or small chambers on the chest are called channels. There are as many of these as there are keys on the keyboard, that is to say, nowadays usually 49 for a manual chest‡ and 25, 26 or 27 for a pedal chest.§ Each channel is as long as the chest is wide. Its width, however, is variable, according to whether large or small pipes (claves) are to stand on it, and also according to the greater or lesser length of the windchest itself.

* either to build or to understand (or both); Adlung writes "leichter," thus even leaving open the possibility that he might mean "lighter, less in weight."

† See §.358.

‡ See §. 23 & §.24 above.
§ See §.28 above.

§. 35.

At one end (or at times at both ends) of the bottom board of each channel there is an oblong opening, about a quarter or a half an ell long. Its width is sometimes hardly equal to that of a thumb; at other times, however, it may be up to 2 fingers or more in width. Through this opening the wind can flow out of the pallet box into the entire channel. The channels are sealed on top by grooving the bars on both sides using the techniques of cabinetry, and then inserting long oak slats into these grooves and fastening them tight, so that no wind can escape. These [slats] are called sponsels (Spünde), and so it is said that the channels are sponselled on top. For a sponsel in organbuilding is a covering board or piece of wood, of which we will encounter yet other [types].¶ As many holes are bored into the sponsels as there are to be stops on that chest. Then when the wind passes into the channel, it blows through all of these holes that have been bored, and consequently into all the pipes set upon them. Thus the pipes of every stop that stood on the same key and channel would sound simultaneously, were it not for the sliders (Registraturen) that lie atop [the sponsels], by means of which certain holes may be opened and others stopped at will. These sliders are likewise of oak, and of oblong, rectangular shape, about half the thickness of a thumb and 2, 3 or even 4 fingerwidths wide. Their length is identical to the length of the chest. These wooden strips are set crosswise over all the channels, so that each strip covers one hole of each channel. However many holes each channel has (that is, however many stops stand on the chest) determines the number of such overlying strips that are necessary.

¶ See §.42; the German word "Spund" has two equivalent English meanings: sponsel and bung-board.

§. 36.

Diese Register heißen Registratura, Canones, Systemata. S. Kirchers Musurg. l. c. sie werden auch genennet Regulae, weil sie einem Lineale nicht ungleich sind; it. Parallelen, weil sie einander parallel liegen. De Chales nennet sie ordines. (Tom. III. de Musica.) In diese Parallelen bohret man soviel Löcher, als Cancellen sind, und zwar also, daß alle Löcher unter den Parallelen in den Cancellenspünden zugleich auf alle Löcher des übergelegten Parallels passen. Wenn demnach die Löcher auf einander treffen; so geht der Wind aus der Cancelle in die Pfeife über den Parallelen: wenn aber die Parallele hinter oder vorwärts gezogen wird; so treffen die Löcher nicht auf einander, sondern die Unterschiede zwischen den Löchern der Parallelen kommen auf die Löcher der Cancellen, und bedecken sie; da muß der Wind zurücke bleiben. Damit aber die Parallelen sich nicht auf die Seite schieben; so werden zu beyden Seiten von eben dergleichen Holze Klötzer oder Dämme bevestiget, zwischen welchen die Parallelen hinter und vorwärts geschoben werden können. Diese Dämme sind mit den Parallelen einerley Dicke, oder etwas sehr weniges dicker; die Länge ist willkürlich; die Breite ist so groß, als der Raum zwischen 2 Parallelen. Und um den Raum zu schonen, pflegt man 2 Parallelen hart aneinander zu legen, alsdann die Dämme oben und unten; hernach wieder ein Paar Parallelen, ꝛc. damit aber dieselben Parallelen nicht über die Löcher hingezogen werden; so werden an dem äussersten Theile oder Spitze starke meßingene oder eiserne Stifte in die Lade geschlagen, oder ein Damm vorgesetzt, und in den Seiten werden dergleichen deswegen eingeschlagen, damit man sie nicht allzuweit herausziehe, sondern präcise so viel, als erfordert wird, daß Loch auf Loch zu stehen komme, oder nicht.

§. 37.

Anstatt der Spünde in den Cancellen findet man auch zuweilen ein Brett über die ganze Lade gelegt, wodurch alle Cancellen bedeckt werden, und worein auch die Löcher gebohret werden, welche sonst in den Spünden sind: Und hierauf kommen die Parallelen zu liegen. Bisweilen sind die Spünde da, und solches Brett auch oben drüber, da die Löcher auf einander passen, und da oben hernach die Parallelen liegen. Dieses Brett nennt man das Fundamentalbrett; it. das cribrum oder Sieb, und ist dasselbe ¼" oder ⅜" dick. S. Janowka. S. 31. Kircher in Musurgia nennet es polystomaticum, von πολύ multum und στόμα, os, weil es viele Oefnungen hat. Doch wird solches Brett wenig mehr gebraucht, weil es große Ungelegenheiten verursacht.

§. 38.

Zuweilen werden in den Cancellen anstatt der untern größern Oefnung soviel Löcher gebohret, als Register auf jeder Cancelle stehen, und in diese setzt man eben so viel Röhren, oder Windkanäle, welche bis in die Spünde reichen, und oben durch die Parallelen,

Chapter III. Concerning the Windchest.

§. 36.

These sliders (Register) are called *Registratura*, *Canones*, or *Systemata*. In Kircher's *Musurgia*, l.c., they are called *Regulae*, since they are not unlike a ruler, and also *Parallela*, since they lie parallel to each other. DeChales calls them *ordines* (in Vol. III [of his *Cursus*] *de Musica* [pp. 20-21]). Into these sliders are bored as many holes as there are channels, in such a way that all the holes in the underlying channel-sponsels line up precisely with all the holes of the slider lying over them. Then when the holes are aligned, wind passes from the channel through the slider and into the pipes. If, however, the sliders are drawn one way or the other, then the holes are not aligned; rather, the solid spaces between the slider holes come to rest over the holes of the channels, and cover them. Thus the wind is held back [from the pipes]. In order that the sliders do not shift to one side or the other, they are anchored on both sides by blocks or spacers, likewise of oak, between which they may be drawn back and forth. These spacers are of the same thickness as the sliders, or a tiny bit thicker; their length is arbitrary, and their width is as great as the space between two sliders. In order to save space, 2 sliders are usually set right against each other, with spacers on either side; then another set of 2 sliders, etc. To prevent the sliders from being drawn beyond the holes, strong brass or iron pins are driven into the far end of the chest, or a spacer is extended and the same sort of pins are driven into its sides. Thus the sliders are prevented from being drawn out too far, but rather only precisely as far as is required to allow the holes to be aligned or not.

§. 37.

Instead of [individual] sponsels for each channel, [some builders] set a sheet of wood over the entire chest, by which all the channels are covered. Into this sheet are bored all the same holes that would otherwise be found in the sponsels. The sliders are then set in place upon this sheet. Sometimes such a sheet is made and laid atop the sponsels, with the holes of each of them corresponding precisely; the sliders then lie on top. This sheet is called the table (Fundamentalbrett), or the *cribrum*, sieve, and is itself ½ or ⅔ of an inch thick (see Janowka, p. 31). In his *Musurgia* [p. 506], Kircher calls it a *polystomaticum*, from πολύ, "many" and σόμα* os [mouth], since it has so many openings. Such a wooden sheet is seldom used anymore, however, since it causes many problems.

* sic; should be στόμα.

§. 38.

In place of the large opening on the underside of the channel, there are at times bored as many holes as stops on the channel. In each of these holes is set a tube or wind conduit. These conduits extend up into the sponsels, and are covered on top by the

len, unten aber durch die Ventile im Windkasten bedeckt werden, dergleichen Struktur in der Görlitzer Orgel sich befindet und sehr gut ist; davon hernach. Ebendaselbst wird auch einer treppenförmigen Windlade gedacht: weil ich sie aber nicht gesehen, und auch von Borbergen nicht deutlich beschrieben finde; so habe ich keinen deutlichen Begrif davon. Endlich ist auch die ganze Windlade wohl mit Leim auszugiessen, damit der Wind nicht durch die Poros des Holzes durchschleiche. Kann man die Materie mit etwas vermischen, wodurch zugleich die Würmer abgehalten werden; so ist es noch besser. Der Herr Casparini hat bey der görlitzischen Orgel eine Massam dazu gebraucht, die Invetriatur genannt; wovon Borberg in deren Beschreibung etwas meldet, mehr aber nicht zu sagen weis, als daß es eine Massa, Kitt oder Firniß sey, so meistens aus dem bolo armenico, camphora und vielen andern dergleichen Sachen bestehe, welche mit starkem Brandtewein aufgelöst und zum Gebrauch zugerichtet werde. Etliche haben es nachmachen wollen; es hat aber die Probe nicht gehalten; denn des Hrn. Casparini Invetriatur wird auch nicht weggestoßen, wenn man gleich das damit bestrichene Brett auf den Kanten abhobelt. — Man überklebt auch den obern Theil der Lade mit Leder, um allen Ungleichheiten vorzukommen; doch ist dieses nicht allzunöthig, wenn die Lade accurat abgerichtet ist. So viel von der Lade.

§. 39.

Es folget der **Windkasten**, der von *Kirchern* l. c. Receptaculum uentorum, ein Aufenthalt der Winde genannet wird. Es ist dieses dasjenige Behältniß, worein der Wind aus den Kanälen gebracht wird. Er liegt unter der Lade, von welcher er in der Breite etwan ¼ oder ⅓ Elle, oder auch wol mehr, einnimmt: die Länge aber ist der Länge der Laden gleich; die Dicke ist verschiedentlich, je nachdem viel Wind darinne aufzufangen ist, und folglich nachdem man viel Register hat. Man macht doch diesen Kasten inwendig so weit, daß man mit der Hand hinein kommen kann. Er wird von starken Brettern gemacht, und ist eben so wohl zu verwahren, und mit Leim auszugiessen, als die Windlade. Man belegt ihn mit Papiere, darauf die Ventile schlagen. Es hat dieser Kasten eine oder mehrere große Oefnungen in viereckigter Form, und so groß, als die Windkanäle dick sind: denn dadurch wird der Wind hineingebracht; aus dem Kasten aber gehet der Wind weiter durch die Oefnungen der Lade in die Cancellen oder Röhren.

§. 40.

Damit aber nicht alle Cancellen und das ganze Register, oder alle claues zugleich gehöret werden; so bedecket man diese Oefnungen mit den **Ventilen**. Es finden sich aber viel Ventile in der Orgel, auch derselben vielerley Arten. Man nennet alles dasjenige ein Ventil, wodurch der Wind an einem Ort eingelassen, oder abgehalten wird; denn es kömmt her von Ventus, der Wind. Die Ventile des Windkastens heißen insbeson-

sliders and underneath by pallets in the pallet box. This system is found in the organ at Görlitz, and is quite fine; more about it later.* This same organ is also reported to have a windchest with a terraced construction. Since I have not seen it, however, and since Boxberg does not describe it clearly, I do not have a clear conception of it.† Finally, the entire windchest is to be liberally smeared with glue, so that the wind does not escape through the pores of the wood. It is even better if this glue can be mixed with some other [substance] to prevent [damage from] borers. In the Görlitz organ Mr. Casparini‡ has used a substance for this purpose called *Invetriatur*. Boxberg mentions this in his description of the organ, but says nothing other than that it is a substance, putty or varnish consisting mostly of Armenian bole,§ camphor and many other similar ingredients, prepared for use by being dissolved in strong spirits.¶ Several others have tried to copy it, but their attempts have not stood the test, since Mr. Casparini's *Invetriatur* is not shaved off when the edges of a board that has been impregnated with it are planed. — Leather is then glued onto the upper surface of the chest, to insure a perfectly even surface. This [procedure], however, is not really necessary if the chest has been constructed precisely [to begin with]. Enough about the windchest.

* See §.41 below.

† See Boxberg, pp.[8-9]; for a further discussion of this arrangement, see: Ernst Flade, *Gottfried Silbermann*. Leipzig: Breitkopf & Härtel, 1953, p. 29, n. 80.

‡ Eugen Casparini (1623-1706), the organbuilder.

§ A soft, fine red clayey earth found in Armenia, also used as a coloring material in the making of size for soldering; Adlung refers to it elsewhere as "rothen Bolus;" see §.323.

¶ See Boxberg, pp.[11-12]; this entire passage is loosely quoted from Boxberg.

§. 39.

Next comes the pallet box, called by Kircher, *l.c.*, the "abode of the wind" (Receptaculum ventorum). This is the container into which the wind flows from the wind ducts. It lies underneath the windchest, taking up a space about ¼ or ½ an ell or more wide within it. Its length is the same as the length of the chest. Its depth (Dicke) varies, according to how much wind it must hold, that is, how many stops there are. The interior of this pallet box is constructed deep enough to allow a hand to reach into it. It is made of strong boards, just as tightly fastened together and smeared with glue as the windchest. It is lined with paper, upon which the pallets strike [when they close]. This pallet box has one or more large rectangular openings, the size of the wind ducts, through which the wind enters; the wind then passes through the openings in the windchest and into the channels or tubes.

§. 40.

These openings are covered by [what are generally speaking called] ventils, so that all the channels and stops, or all the keys, do not sound at once. There are many types of ventils in an organ; anything is called a "ventil" that admits or blocks the entrance of wind. [The word] is derived from [Latin] *Ventus*, "wind." The ventils of the pallet box are specifically called "pallets" (*paraglossae*); see Janowka, [*Clavis*,] p. 96. They are long strips lying parallel to each other, that cover the openings into the

besondere Paraglossae, S. Janowka. S. 96. und sind lange Leisten, welche einander parallel liegen, womit die Oefnungen der Lade zugedeckt werden; folglich sind sie etwas breiter, als die Oefnungen. Hinten werden sie mit Leder und Leim bevestiget, und damit sie nicht allzuschwer werden; so macht man sie kaum Daumens dick, und unten etwas conisch, daß der Wind sie nicht allzuhart andrücke, und überzieht sie oben mit Leder oder Tuch, daß sie accurater zudecken. Man macht sie von reinem Tannenholz, dessen Adern abwärts stehen, weil das Holz solchergestalt zum Verwerfen nicht so geneigt ist, als wenn die Adern seitwärts stehen. Unter dieselben setzt man solche Federn, dergleichen Kap. 2. §. 28. beschrieben worden, wodurch sie angedruckt werden, doch so, daß man sie auch aufziehen kann. Mehr als eine Feder zu jedem Ventil nimmt man nicht leicht. Damit diese Ventile oder Paraglossae sich nicht verwerfen, oder seitwärts lenken; so schlägt man zu beyden Seiten fast Fingerslange meßingene Stifte ein, zwischen welchen sie können beweget werden; oder von vornen nur einen, der in der Schlinge sich beweget.

§. 41.

An diese Paraglossas werden Drate bevestiget, welche durch des Windkastens Boden durchgehen, und vermittelst der Abstrakten an die Palmulas des Claviers gehen, durch deren Niederdrückung diese Ventile aufgezogen werden, daß der Wind hinein kommen kann. Damit aber neben dem Drate durch die Löcherchen kein Wind durch den Boden des Windkastens schleiche; so macht man um diese Drate Säckchen von Leder, und bevestiget es an dem Drate und auf dem Boden. Meistens werden dadurch die Ventile in die Länge aufgezogen, also:

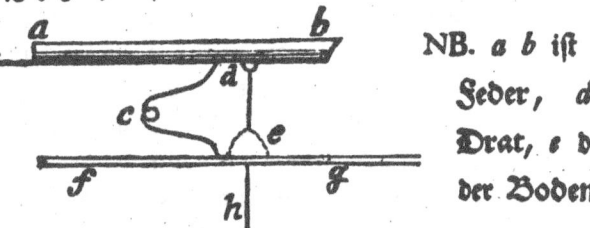

NB. *a b* ist das Ventil, *c* die Feder, *d h* das aufziehende Drat, *e* das Säckchen, *f g* der Boden des Kastens.

Wenn aber, wie §. 38. erwähnet worden, jeder clavis in jedem Register seinen eigenen Kanal hat; so werden solche Röhren am besten durch paraglossas bedeckt und der Wind in alle zugleich gelassen, wenn die Ventile in der Breite aufgezogen werden, da sie denn blos von den Stiften und Federn können gehalten werden, etwan also:

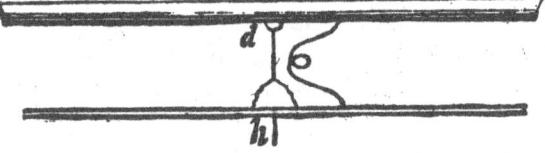

Doch es läßt sich durch den Riß nicht wohl vorstellen. Besiehe Bozbergs Beschreibung der Görlitzer Orgel.

§. 42.

windchest. Thus they are slightly wider than the openings. At their back ends they are fastened [to the underside of the windchest] with leather and glue, and are barely the thickness of a thumb, to keep them from being too heavy. Their sides are beveled, to keep the wind from pressing so hard against them. So that they close [the openings] more tightly, they are covered with leather or cloth. They are fashioned out of knot-free pine wood, with the grain running vertically/crosswise, since in this form the wood is not as prone to warp as when the grain runs horizontally/lengthwise. Under these are placed springs such as have been described in Chapter 2, §.28; the springs press them upward, but not so firmly that they are difficult to pull down. One ought to think twice before placing more than one spring under each pallet. In order to keep the pallets or "paraglossae" from warping or slipping sideways, brass pins, each almost a finger-length long, are driven in on either side of them; between which the pallets then can travel. At times only one pin is driven in front of each pallet, and this [single pin] moves in an eyelet.*

* protruding from the front of the pallet.

§. 41.

Wires are affixed to these pallets, that pass through the bottom board of the pallet box and are connected to the keys of the keyboard by means of trackers. When the keys are depressed, the pallets are drawn open, thus allowing the wind to enter [the channels]. So that no wind can escape through the small holes drilled into the bottom board of the pallet box to allow passage of the wires, leather pouches are set around the wires; these are attached to the wire and to the bottom board. Normally the pallets are pulled down long-ways, thus:

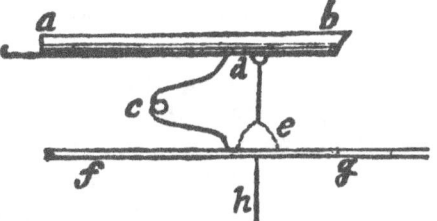

N.B. *a b* is the pallet, *c* the spring, *d h* the wire that pulls [the pallet] open, *e* the pouch, and *f g* the bottomboard of the pallet box

If, however, each key has its own conduit for each stop, as mentioned in §.38,† then it is best to cover these tubes with pallets that admit the wind into all of them simultaneously. In that case the pallets are drawn down sideways, since they can be held in place by just the pins and springs,‡ something like this:

† in connection with the organ at Görlitz.

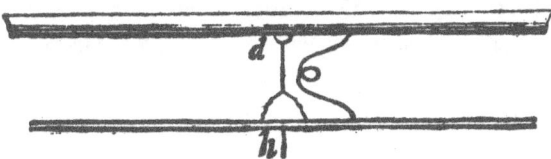

This cannot, however, be made clear by this sketch; consult Boxberg's *Beschreibung der Görlitzer Orgel*.§

‡ i.e., they are not fastened to the bottom of the windchest by a piece of leather, as described above in §.27. See: Flade, *Silbermann*, p. 29, n. 80. Adlung's presentation might give the impression that this sort of arrangement was common; in fact, it was quite unusual, and Agricola in a note to §.365 reports some experts as having asserted that this feature was to blame for the Görlitz organ's heavy action.

§ See Boxberg, p.[9] (who explains the matter no more clearly than Adlung does).

Kap. III. Von der Windlade.

§. 42.

Der äusserste Theil des Windkastens wird nicht wie die andern Seiten mit Rahmen vest verwahret, sondern er wird mit Spünden verschlossen; welches länglichte viereckigte Bretter oder Leisten sind, mit Leder überzogen, daß sie besser passen; mit Rinken oder Riemen versehen, daran man sie herausziehen kann, damit man im Nothfall zu den Ventilen kommen könne. Damit aber die Gewalt des Windes diese Spünde nicht heraustreibe; so werden sie mit Vorschlägen verwahret; welches kleine eiserne Haspeln sind.

§. 43.

Diese Schleifladen nennet man auch gespündete Laden, wenn sie kein Fundamentalbrett oder cribrum haben. Sonst machte man sie zuweilen von ganzen eichenen Bohlen, und durchbohrete sie in die Breite anstatt der Cancellen, und von oben herunter anstatt der Löcher in den Spünden: allein die macht man nicht mehr.

Es ist eben nicht nöthig, daß jedes Clavier nur eine Lade habe; vielmehr treffen wir oft Orgeln an, da die Laden getheilt sind, und auf beyden Seiten der Orgel stehen: aber ein Registerzug öfnet sie beyde zugleich. Zuweilen ist die Lade getheilet, die Theile aber stehen neben einander, und jeder Theil hat seinen eigenen Zug, also, daß, wenn auch würklich nur 4 Register in der Orgel sind, man doch 8 manubria zu ziehen hat. 2c.

§. 44.

Auf den Parallelen können die Pfeifen unmittelbar nicht stehen, sonst könnte man sie nicht hin und her ziehen; sondern es werden auf diese Parallelen die Pfeifenstöcke gesetzt, welches Bohlenstöcke sind $1\frac{1}{2}$" dicke. (NB. die Striche " bey einer Zahl bedeuten Zolle, ein Strich aber ' einen Fuß.) Unter diesen schleifen sich die Parallelen aus und ein; daher man es Schleifladen nennet. Die Pfeifenstöcke macht man so lang, daß die Pfeifen etlicher clauium darauf stehen können, und zwar, daß man den Stock mit seinen Pfeifen commode abheben und forttragen könne. Sind die Pfeifen allzuklein; so bringet man die Stöcke, ihrer Breite nach, über mehr als ein Register: doch nicht allezeit. Sind die Pfeifen allzugroß, daß man an einer zu heben hat; so muß man sie abnehmen, wenn der Stock herab zu schrauben ist. Demnach macht man einen solchen Pfeifenstock von beliediger Länge. Ein Register hat zuweilen auf einem claue mehr als eine Pfeife; folglich muß über einem Loche der Parallel der Stock von unten her zwar nur ein Loch haben, dadurch der Wind in die Pfeife geht: aber oben hat er so viel Löcher, als Pfeifen darauf zu stehen kommen. Der Stock aber wird an dem Theile, da die Pfeifen stehen, durchbohret, daß der Wind durch das allgemeine untere Loch zu allen Pfeifen kommen könne. Auf den Seiten spündet man alles wieder zu,

wenn

Chapter III. Concerning the Windchest.

§. 42.

The side of the pallet box that faces forward is not shut up tightly in frames, as are the other sides; rather it is closed up with bungboards.* These are oblong rectangular boards or strips, covered with leather for a tighter fit. They are provided with rings or straps so that they may be pulled out, thus allowing access to the pallets if needed. To keep the wind pressure from forcing these seals out, however, they are fastened with bung stays, which are small iron hasps.

*cf. §.35.

§. 43.

Slider chests are also referred to as "sponselled" chests if they have no table.† Sometimes they used to be made of solid oak planks, chiseled out across the breadth [of the plank] in place of channels, and with holes bored through on top in place of the holes in the sponsels. This procedure, however, is no longer in use.

† See §.37.

It is by no means necessary that each keyboard have only one chest. It is much more usual to encounter organs with divided chests, one on each side of the organ, but with drawknobs that operate them both simultaneously. At times the chest is divided, but the sections stand right next to each other, and each section has its own drawknob; in this case, if an organ actually has only 4 stops, then there are 8 drawknobs to draw.‡

‡22 cf. §.259.

§. 44.

The pipes cannot stand directly on the sliders, or otherwise the sliders could not be moved back and forth; rather the sliders are covered by the toeboards, planks about 1F12 " thick (N.B. The strokes " after a number mean "inches," and one stroke ' means "a foot"). The sliders slide back and forth under the [toeboards], and thus it is called a "slider chest." The toeboards are made long enough to accommodate the pipes of a number of keys, in such a way that the board together with its pipes can easily be lifted out and removed. If the pipes are very small, then the toeboards are made wide enough to hold more than one stop (though not always). If the pipes are very large, so that they have to be lifted singly, then they must be removed before the toeboard is unscrewed and lifted off. With all this in mind, the toeboards are made the appropriate length. At times a stop has more than one pipe to a key; consequently the toeboard must have only one hole underneath (corresponding to the single hole in the slider, through which the wind passes into the pipe), but as many holes on top as there are pipes. In this case the [upper] part of the toeboard, where the pipes stand, is drilled in such a way that the wind may proceed from the common hole beneath into

wenn man die Kammern des Stockes fertig hat. Ein Pfeifenstock möchte etwan so aussehen:

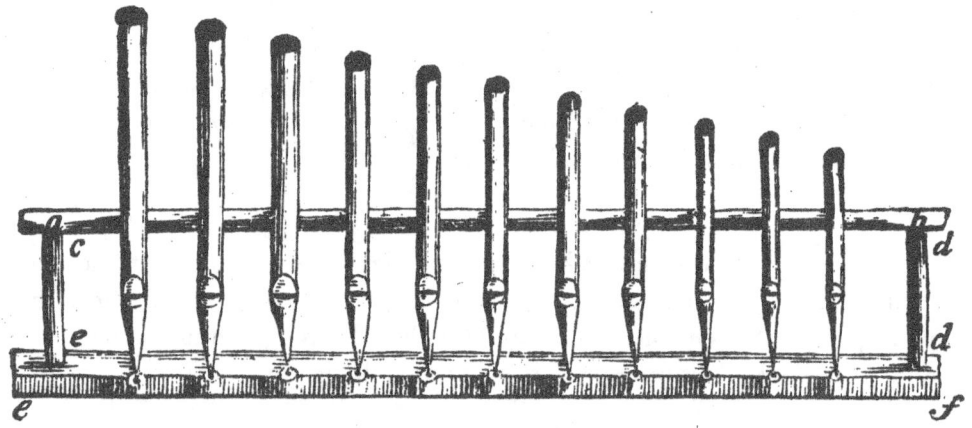

Diese Stöcke, werden auf die Parallelen gesetzt, und ruhen am meisten auf den Dämmen, damit die Register besser gezogen werden können. Daß sie aber nicht umfallen; so werden sie in die Windlade geschraubt mit hölzernen Schrauben. Die untersten Löcher müssen just auf die Löcher der Registratur passen, wenn diese aufgezogen ist. Ueber den Löchern der Spünde aber stehen sie allezeit perpendiculariter. Wenn die Pfeifen allzuenge stehen; so werden die Löcher nicht in einer geraden Linie gebohret: denn auf solche Weise hätten die Pfeifen keinen Raum; sondern auf folgende Art:

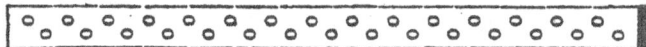

Und eben so müssen alsdann auch die Löcher der Parallelen und der Spünde seyn.

§. 45.

Es folgen die Springladen, woraus viele etwas recht Großes machen, und es für ein Geheimniß achten. Ja mancher Organist nähme nicht viel Geld, wenn er es jemanden zeigen sollte; und Werkmeister in der Orgelprobe Kap. 17. sagt, daß nicht alle Orgelmacher sie kennen. In Erfurt ist keine, als auf dem Dom. Prätorius melder Tom. II. S. 170. daß zu St. Johannis in Lüneburg, und S. 179. daß im Stift St. Blasii zu Braunschweig dergleichen Laden gestanden. Zu Weissenfelß in der Augustusburg sind 3 Laden von dieser Gattung: Und Biermann in Organographia Hildesiensi pag. 2. 4. 6. 23. 24. giebt uns die Nachricht, daß allda auch Springladen zu sehen. Sie sind schön, wenn dieselben von einem tüchtigen Meister verfertiget werden, weil man vor dem verdrüßlichen Durchstechen gesichert ist: aber wenn sich ein schlechter Arbeiter untersteht, dergleichen zu machen; so erwecken sie viel Verdruß, welches

Werk=

34 Chapter III. Concerning the Windchest.

all the pipes. When these chambers in the toeboards are completed, then all the sides are again sealed up.* A toeboard should look something like this:

* to make them airtight.

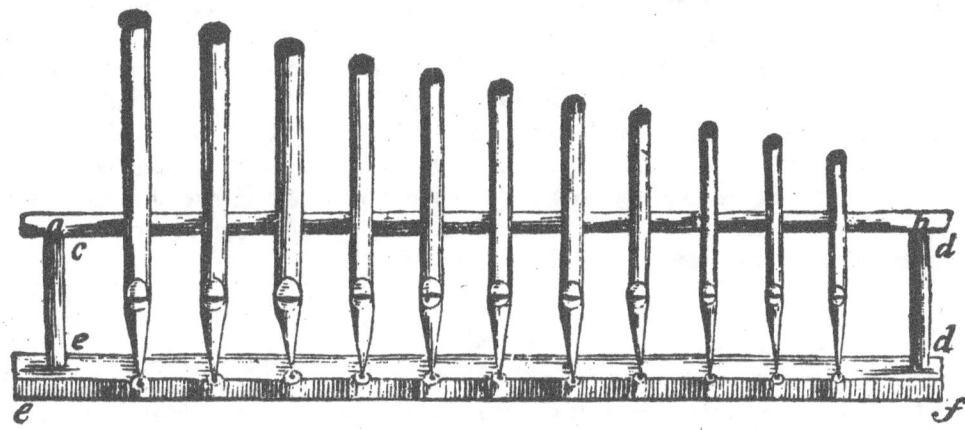

These toeboards are set atop the sliders, but rest for the most part upon the spacers, so that the stops may be drawn more easily. They are affixed to the windchest with wooden screws to keep them from falling over. The holes on the underside must correspond exactly to those in the sliders when they are drawn out. They of course always stand directly over the holes in the sponsels. If the pipes stood too close to each other, they could become too crowded; thus the holes are not bored in a straight line, but in the following fashion:

The holes in the sliders and sponsels must then also conform to this configuration.

§. 45.

Now we come to the spring chest,† which many people make a great deal of and treat like a secret. Indeed, many an organist would demand a pretty penny for showing it to someone, and Werkmeister in his *Orgelprobe*, Chap. 17, says that not all organ builders are familiar with it. There is only one example in Erfurt, at the Cathedral. Praetorius [in his *Syntagma musicum*], Vol. II, pp. 170 and 179, reports that such chests are found in Lüneburg in the Johanniskirche and at the Collegiate Church of St. Blasius at Braunschweig. In the Augustusburg at Weissenfels there are 3 chests of this type. And Biermann in his *Organographia Hildesiensis*,‡ pp. 2, 4, 6, 23 and 24, reports that spring chests may also be observed [at Hildesheim, Woltingenroda and Heiningen]. They are fine when they are constructed by a competent master, since it is then certain that they will be free of irritating runs. When a poor craftsman undertakes to make them, though, they can be extremely annoying, as Werkmeister remarks in his

† See also §.356.

‡ Johann Hermann Biermann, *Organographia Hildesiensis Specialis* (Hildesheim: Schlegel, 1738).

Werkmeister in der Orgelprobe Kap. 17. und 18. angemerkt, und die daher entstehende Unlust nicht groß genug zu beschreiben weis. Der Unterschied dieser Laden von der Schleiflade bestehet darinn: Nichts wird geändert als der obere Theil der Lade, die andern Theile sind eben so, wie sie vorhin erzählet worden. Anstatt daß die Cancellen mit Spünden verspündet werden, kommen die Pfeifenstöcke unmittelbar auf die Cancellen zu stehen. Und da also die Cancellen und Stöcke durch die Breite der Lade gehen; so hat jeder clavis seinen Stock, auf welchem von jedem Register die zu dem claue gehörigen Pfeifen stehen. Da in der Schleiflade die Register distincte auf die Stöcke gesetzt werden, und zwar in die Länge der Laden; so kommen sie in die Breite zu stehen, daß z. Ex. auf einem Stocke das C vom Principale, vom Gedakt, Quint, ꝛc. stehet, auf dem andern Stocke das Cis vom Principale, vom Gedakt, Quint, ꝛc.

§. 46.

An diesen Stöcken sind viel gar kleine Ventile, für jede Pfeife ein Ventil, sonst würde der Wind in alle Register eines clavis zugleich blasen: die Ventile aber decken die Löcher zu. Wenn aber in einem Register mehr Pfeifen zu einem claue gehören, als eine; so haben sie zusammen nur ein Ventil: z. Ex. da in der Mixtur 4 Pfeifen zu *d* gehören: so ist auch zu diesen 4 Pfeifen, die auf einem Stocke stehen, unten am Stocke nur eine Oefnung, und diese wird durch ein Ventil bedeckt. Wenn nun ein Register klingen soll; so muß in jedem Stocke das Ventil zu der Pfeife des Registers eröfnet werden, und das geschiehet durch die Register oder Parallelen, welche aber, wie ein jeder aus der vorigen Erzählung schließen kann, zwischen den Füßen der Pfeifen gehen müssen. Zu jeden Ventil in den Stöcken ist ein Drückel, oder durch den Stock auf das Ventil gehender Stift, durch welchen vermittelst der Parallelen die Ventile, folglich auch die Register oder Stimmen auf- und zugezogen werden: denn unter jedem Ventile stehet eine Feder, welche dasselbe wieder andrückt, daher die Ventile wieder für das Loch des Stockes springen; und deswegen nennet man es Springladen. Eine Nachricht von solchen Laden hat Werkmeister l. c. Kap. 17. und 18. Was für Incommoditäten daher entstehen, soll unten vorkommen; jezo lernen wir nur alle Theile der Orgel kennen. Bisweilen stehen die Pfeifen so, daß man die Stöcke herausnehmen kann, ohne das Pfeifwerk. S. Werkmeister l. c. p. 40. Soviel von der Windlade.

Chapter III. Concerning the Windchest.

Orgelprobe, Chaps. 17 and 18, and it is hardly possible to describe the disgust they engender. The difference between this chest and the slider chest is as follows: only the upper part of the chest is altered; the other parts remain just as they have been described above. Instead of the channels being covered with sponsels, the toeboards sit directly on top of the channels. Since both channels and toeboards thus extend across the breadth of the chest, each key then has its own toeboard, upon which the pipes of every stop belonging to that specific key stand. In contrast to the slider chest, where each register is set upon its own toeboard, i.e., across the length of the chest, here [in a spring chest] the toeboards lie across the breadth [of the chest]. This means, for example, that on one toeboard sit the C of the Principal, the Gedakt, the Quint, etc., while on the next toeboard sit the C# of the Principal, Gedakt, Quint, etc.

§. 46.

On the toeboards there are many tiny [stop-]pallets, one for each individual pipe; otherwise the wind would blow into all the pipes of a given key at once. The pallets however cover the holes. If a stop has more than one pipe per key, all the pipes together still have only one pallet. For example, in a Mixtur there may be 4 pipes for the note "d"; but on the underside of the toeboard on which they sit there is only one opening, and it is covered by only one pallet. If one of these stops is to sound, then for each toeboard the pallet under the pipes of that stop must be opened. This is accomplished by means of stop rods, but now (as anyone can deduce from what has been said above) these must move between the feet of the pipes. For each [stop-]pallet there is a stop-pallet pin in the toeboard, a pin that passes through the board and contacts the [stop] pallet. By means of the stop rods these are made to operate the pallets, and consequently the stops may be sounded or silenced. Under each pallet there stands a spring that provides a counter-pressure, so that the pallets once again snap shut over the holes in the toeboard; this is why it is called a "spring chest." Werkmeister reports on these chests, *l.c.*, Chaps. 17 and 18. The inconveniences that arise from them will be discussed below,* but for now we will continue to become familiar with all the components of the organ. At times the pipes are positioned so that the toeboards may be taken out without removing the pipes; see Werkmeister, *l.c.*, p. 40. So much for the windchest.

* See §.356.

Das IV. Kapitel.
Von dem andern Eingeweide der Orgel,
das Pfeifwerk ausgenommen.

Inhalt.

§. 47. Das Pfeifenbrett. §. 48. Die Abstrakten. §. 49. Die Wellenbretter. §. 50. An deren Stellen man auch Rahmen gebraucht. §. 51. Wie die Abstrakten an die Claviere gemacht werden. §. 52. Von den Druckwerken. §. 53. Die gebrochnen Claviere. §. 54. Die Gänge, Treppen, ꝛc. sonderlich die Windführungen. §. 55. Noch andere Windleitungen. §. 56. Die Schiebstangen und andere Theile der Registratur.

§. 47.

Durch das innere Eingeweide verstehe ich das Pfeifenbrett, die Abstrakten, die Wellen und Wellenbretter, die Registerstangen, ꝛc. wovon beyläufig zu lesen ist, was Werkmeister in der Orgelprobe hat. Kap. 7. S. 15.

Das Pfeifenbrett ist zweyerley Art. Ueberhaupt dienet es dazu, daß die größten Pfeifen destoweniger umfallen und die Kleinern nicht zerschlagen, auch für sich keinen Schaden nehmen. Es kann aber dieser zu besorgende Schade auf mancherley Weise verhütet werden; denn man pflegt entweder zwischen einer Reihe Pfeifen einen Rahmen oder Leiste aufzurichten, daran die Pfeifen angehängt werden, indem an die Leiste, welches auch ein Brett seyn kann, Häkchen, an die Pfeifen aber ein Angehänge, oder umgekehrt, gemacht wird. Man nennet die Häkchen auch Oeschen. S. Werkmeisters grüningische Orgelbeschreibung. §. 14. und 29. Oder man nimmt ein Stück Brett, und schneidet so viel zirkelrunde Löcher hinein, als Pfeifen auf einem Stocke stehen, und unten bevestiget man es auf dem Stocke mit 2 Füßen, und steckt die Pfeifen dadurch: alsdenn kann man es mit dem Stocke zugleich abheben. Wenn die Pfeifen sehr lang sind, muß man wol 2 Pfeifenbretter zu einem Stocke haben. Werkmeister gedenket, daß das Pfeifenbrett vielerley Namen habe, s. Orgelprobe Kap. 8. S. 20. aber er fügt sie nicht bey. Im vorhergehenden 3. Kapitel dieser Abhandlung §. 44. habe ich die Figur des Pfeifenbrettes vorzustellen gesuchet, da denn *a b* das Peifenbrett vorstellet; *c* und *d* sind die Füße, die im Stocke *e f* befestiget sind.

§. 48.

Von den Säckchen in dem Windkasten, und den dadurch gehenden Draten, wodurch die Paraglossae oder Ventile aufgezogen werden, ist §. 41. geredet worden. Damit aber durch die Palmulas Tastaturae dieses verrichtet werden könne; so kommen die Abstrakten (auf französisch: Abregés) darzwischen, welche von abstrahere, abziehen, also

genennet

Chapter IV.

Concerning the Other Internal Components of the Organ,
with the Exception of the Pipes.

Contents:

§. 47. The pipe rack. §.48. The trackers. §.49. The rollerboards. §.50. Frames may be used in their place. §.51. How the trackers are attached to the keyboards. §.52. Concerning backfall actions. §.53. Interrupted backfall actions. §.54. The walkways, stairs, etc., and in particular the wind ducts. §.55. Other wind conduits. §.56. The trace-rods and other components of the stop action.

§. 47.

By the "internal components" I mean the pipe rack[s], the trackers, the rollers and rollerboards, the trace-rods, etc, about which, by the way, you may read more in Werkmeister's *Orgelprobe*, Chap. 7, p. 15.

There are several kinds of pipe racks. Their primary purpose is to prevent the largest pipes from falling over, thus smashing the smaller pipes and also damaging themselves. There are a number of ways, however, to keep this damage from happening. One way is to erect a frame or wooden rail between a row of pipes,* on which the pipes are hung. To accomplish this, the strip (which may also be a board) is provided with small hooks and the pipes with eyes, or vice versa. The little hooks are also called eyelets ; see Werkmeister's *Organum Gruningense redivivum*, §.14 and 29. Another way is to take a piece of wood and cut as many round holes in it as there are pipes on a toe board. This is then fastened beneath onto the toe board with two feet, and the pipes pass through it; then it can be lifted off together with the toe board. If the pipes are very long, then there must be two pipe racks for each toe board.† Werkmeister mentions that the pipe rack has a number of names (see his *Orgelprobe*, Chap. 8, p. 20), but does not say what they are. Above, in Chapter 3, §. 44 of this treatise, I have attempted to present a drawing of a pipe rack; in it, the pipe rack is designated *a b*, while *c* and *d* are the feet that are fastened to the toe board *e f*.

§. 48.

The pouches in the pallet box, together with the wires that pass through them and draw open the Paraglossae or pallets, are discussed in §. 41. These wires are connected to the keys of the keyboard by means of trackers (Abstrakten) (Abregés in French). The name comes from [the Latin] abstrahere, "to pull away." These are the

---

* Adlung's use of the word "between" becomes clearer after considering what he has said about the arrangement of pipes on the toeboard, at the end of §. 44 above. The pipe rack would then pass between the two rows of pipes that comprise a rank.

† presumably one of each of the types mentioned immediately above in this paragraph.

genennet werden. Dies sind die langen subtilen hölzernen Stangen, die oben an das Drat unter dem Windkasten bevestiget sind, und herunter hangen. Sie werden einen Finger breit, und kaum den vierten Theil so dick gearbeitet, daß sie recht leichte seyn mögen: jedoch ist dahin zu sehen, daß sie durch allzudünnes Abhobeln nicht etwan abreissen, oder unvermuthet Schaden nehmen. Man nennt den ganzen Begriff der Abstrakten die **Traktur**, von trahere, ziehen. Die Abstrakten selbst heißen auch pilotides; und Janowka p. 97. beschreibt sie so: *Pilotides* sunt filâ intra organum, quae inter palmulas et paraglossas mediana: d. i. die *Pilotides* sind Faden innerhalb der Orgel, welche zwischen den Palmulis und Ventilen sind. Es werden dieselben, wenn sie sehr kurz sind, auch zuweilen von Drat gemacht; die langen aber von Holz: Und weil sie zuweilen 1, 2, 4, 5 und mehr Ellen lang sind, nachdem die Laden hoch vom Claviere liegen; so könnten sie durch Schlottern oder Schwanken viel Ungelegenheit verursachen, sich verwirren, und zum Heulen Anlaß geben. Diesem allen wird durch die Kämme entgegen gegangen; denn man bevestiget hinter den Pilotidibus Bretter von beliebiger Breite, schneidet Kerben darein, in deren jeder eine von diesen Pilotidibus sich ohne Drücken auf und nieder bewegt; so können sie sich nicht verwirren. Besiehe die folgende Figur. §. 49. Und daß die langen Abstrakten nicht zu schwer werden, und wider des Organisten Willen die Ventilen aufziehen; so bevestiget man zuweilen, nicht aber allezeit, an dieselben subtile Federn, dergleichen im Windkasten sind, die helfen sie wieder in die Höhe ziehen, damit die Ventilfeder das Ventil leichter andrücke. Damit man auch inwendig durch das Hin- und Wiedergehen ihnen keinen Schaden thun; so findet man bisweilen kleine Bretter angemacht, welche dieses verhindern.

§. 49.

Wenn die Laden nicht breiter wären als die Tastatur, oder Claviere, und allezeit perpendikulariter, auch unzertheilt über denselben geleget werden könnten, auch die Pfeifen von der Größten bis zur Kleinsten in der Ordnung auf der Lade folgten, wie die claves auf einander folgten; so könnten diese Pilotides von dem Windkasten herab hangen, und unten ohne fernere Weitläuftigkeit an die Palmulas bevestiget werden. Dieses aber geschiehet niemals; es würde auch sonderlich bey etwas großen Werken unmöglich seyn: oder wenn es ja zuweilen möglich wäre; so würde es doch viel Unheil nach sich ziehen. Daher kömmt es, daß man die Cancellen und Pfeifen nach Gefallen ordnet, und die Abstrakten herunter hangen läßt, unten aber durch besondere Wellen sie an den clavem befestiget, er mag stehen wo er will. Die Wellen sind runde Walzen, von beliebiger Dicke, etwan Daumens dick, wenn sie von Holz sind. Diese werden auf beyden Enden mit Stiften versehen, welche in kleinen Löcherchen zu beyden Seiten laufen; denn man nimmt ein Brett, und bevestiget dieses an gehörigen Orte in der Orgel, und darein bevestiget man kleine Arme von Holz oder Eisen, oder Meßing, in dieser Form wie Tab. I. fig. 1. zu sehen; und in diesen daran befindlichen zirkelrunden Löchern laufen die

Ch. IV. Other Internal Components, Except the Pipes. 37

long thin wooden shafts that are fastened at the top to the wire under the pallet box, and hang down. They are about a finger's width broad, and are cut only about a quarter of that width thick, so that they may be as light as possible. It is necessary to be careful when planing them, however, lest they get too thin and break or are inadvertently damaged. The whole complex of trackers is called "the action" (die Traktur), from [Latin] trahere, "to pull." The trackers themselves are also called *pilotides*; on p. 97 [of his *Clavis*] Janowka describes them thus: "*Pilotides sunt fila intra organum, qua inter palmulas et paraglossas mediana,*" that is: "The *pilotides* are cords within the organ, that lie between the keys and the pallets." When they are very short they are sometimes made of wire, but the long ones are of wood. Because they are at times 1, 2, 4, 5 or more ells long (according to how high the chests lie above the keys), they can cause a lot of trouble by swaying and wobbling, or becoming entangled, and giving rise to ciphers. These are all remedied by the guide rails (Kämme*), boards of arbitrary width that are fastened behind the trackers. Notches are cut into these boards, and in each notch one of the trackers is free to move up and down without friction. In this way [the trackers] cannot become entangled; consult the figure below in §. 49.† To keep the long trackers from becoming too heavy and pulling the pallets open against the organist's wishes, delicate springs like those in the pallet box are sometimes (though not always) fastened to them. These springs help pull them up again, so that the pallet spring presses more lightly on the pallet. In order to keep them from being damaged by anyone climbing around inside [the organ], small boards are sometimes installed to protect them.

* literally "combs;" in his *Anleitung*, p. 356, Adlung calls these "Füßgen" (literally, "little feet")

† Adlung does not mention guide rails in §. 49, nor does he depict them in the accompanying Table I. Apparently he is merely suggesting that the reader look at the entire mechanism (shown in Fig. 3) to note how easily the trackers might become entangled.

§. 49.

If chests were never any wider than keyboards, and could always be placed directly above the keyboards without being divided, and if pipes were always arranged on chests from largest to smallest in the same order as the keyboard, then the trackers could hang down from the pallet box and be fastened directly to the the keys without any further complications. This, however, is never the case; it would be impossible, especially in larger organs, or if it might at times actually be possible, it would nevertheless be the cause of much trouble. Therefore the channels and pipes are arranged at will, and the trackers hang down under them, but they are connected to the keys, wherever they are, by means of special rollers beneath [the pallet box]. These rollers are round cylinders of varying thickness (about the thickness of a thumb, if they are made of wood). They are provided with pins at either end that rotate in small eyelets at both ends. [These eyelets are held by] a board mounted at an appropriate place in the organ, to which are fastened small arms of wood, iron or brass, of the shape indicated in Tab. I, fig. 1. The round eyes are fixed to these arms, and in them rotate the pins in

Stifte der Wellen also: fig. 2. Da ist *a b* das Wellenbrett, darein die Brachia oder Arme *e* und *f* bevestiget, *c d* ist die Welle, *g* und *h* aber derselben Stifte, die in den brachiis laufen. Diese Wellen haben jede 2 Arme. Z. Ex. in *i* und *k*, an deren einem die Abstrakte von oben herab gemacht ist, an dem andern aber von unten herauf. Der erste wird unter die Cancelle gemacht, der andere aber über den clauem, der zu derselben Cancelle gehöret: also mag die Cancelle liegen wo sie will; so kann doch durch die Niederdrückung der Palmulae die Welle herum gedrehet, und durch die Abstrakten am andern Arme das dazu gehörige Cancellchen geöfnet werden. Ich will vom Windkasten an bis auf das Clavier es also vorstellen. Man besehe Tab. I. fig. 3. Ueber diese Vorstellung wird ein Orgelmacher freylich lachen; denn sie ist nicht nach der Kunst gemacht. Ich will aber den Lernenden zeigen, wie man durch Wellen die Cancellen mit ihren clauibus verbinden kann, sie mögen übrigens liegen wo sie wollen. *r* bedeutet die Pfeifen, und die andern Buchstaben darunter ihre Namen nach dem Sono. *a b* ist der Windkasten; *q* die herabhangenden Abstrakten; *x* die in die Breite gelegten Wellen; *y* die andern Abstrakten von den Wellen bis an das Clavier; *m* und *n* schliessen das Clavier ein, unter welchem die Namen der Palmulen stehen. Zuweilen ist auch dies noch nicht genug; sondern es werden mehr Absätze und Wellenbretter gemacht, bis man endlich zu den Clavieren kömmt.

§. 50.

Anstatt des Wellenbretts bedienet man sich bisweilen mit grosser Commodität eines eichenen Rahmens, an welchen man die Wellen bevestiget. Auch werden die Wellen nicht von Holz gemacht, sondern von langen runden dünnen eisernen Stangen, daß sie nicht so viel Raum einnehmen; alsdann werden auch wol die Brachia, oder Wirbel, worinne sie beweget werden, von Meßing oder Eisen gemacht. Besiehe die Beschreibung der görlitzer Orgel. Es liegen aber die Wellenbretter und die Wellen zuweilen in die Länge, je nachdem die freye Invention des Orgelmachers die Sache gut befindet. Solcher Wellen und deren Bretter oder Rahmen sind oft viel darinnen, theils für das Manual, theils für das Pedal; zumal wenn die Laden getheilet sind, welches bey dem Pedale fast allezeit geschiehet.

§. 51.

Endlich werden die untern Abstrakten an die Palmulas des Manuals oder Pedals also bevestiget. Man schlägt ein Drat in die palmulam, gleich hinter dem Vorsetzbrette, macht dasselbe krumm wie einen Haken oder Schlinge, und an das Ende der pilotidis macht man dergleichen auch, und hänget es also zusammen. Das Drat kann mit der Zange auf- oder nieder gebogen werden, bis die palmula hoch genug stehet. So findet man es bey etlichen Alten. Jetzo aber macht man alles durch Schrauben; denn es wird eine subtile Schraube von Meßingdrat in die palmulam geschlagen, nemlich der **Vater**, cochlea mas, wie man sie nennet: oben an die Abstrakte kömmt eine horizontale

the rollers. In fig. 2, *a b* is the roller board, to which the arms *e* and *f* are fastened; *c d* is the roller, *g* and *h* the pins that rotate in the arms. Each of these rollers has two arms, e.g., at *i* and *k*. The tracker that hangs down from above is connected to the first of these, while the second holds a tracker that hangs down from it. The first of these arms is attached under the [appropriate] channel, and the second is attached over the key that belongs to that channel. Thus, no matter where the channel is located, its key can open it, since depressing the key turns the roller, [transferring the pull] to the tracker [attached] to the other arm, and thus opening the appropriate channel. In Tab. I, fig. 3, I have depicted this [action] from the pallet box all the way to the keyboard. Organbuilders will of course laugh at this diagram, for it is not skillfully and precisely drawn. I only intend to show learners, though, how channels are connected with the appropriate keys, no matter where they might lie, by means of the rollers. [In this figure,] *r* signifies the pipes, while the other letters underneath signify the pitch names; *a b* is the pallet box, *q* is the trackers hanging down; *x* are the rollers, [running parallel] to the broad side [of the case]*, *y* the other trackers from the roller to the keyboard; *m* and *n* form the bounds of the keyboard, under which stand the names of the keys. At times even this is not sufficient and even more offsets and roller boards are made to connect [the pallet box and] the keyboard.

* This seems to be the correct sense of this obscure phrase; cf. its use in §.575, where it clearly means "across the breadth of the [clavichord's] soundboard."

§. 50.

Instead of a roller board, an oak frame may at times prove very serviceable and advantageous, a frame to which the rollers are fastened. The rollers are also not [always] made of wood, rather [they can be] long, thin, round iron rods that do not take up as much space [as wooden rollers]. In this case the arms or pins in which they rotate are made of brass or iron (see [Boxberg's] *Beschreibung der Görlitzer Orgel*, [p. 9]). Sometimes the roller boards and rollers lie [parallel to] the narrow side [of the case] (in die Länge†), according to whatever the organbuilder's inventiveness finds most advantageous. There are often a number of rollers and roller boards or frames in an organ, some for the manuals, some for the pedal, especially if the chests are divided, as is almost always the case with the pedal.

† Adlung's meaning is unclear. The expression as translated here (corresponding to the phrase "in die Breite..." in the preceding paragraph) would seem to apply to an organ whose keyboard is on the side of the case. Such organs do indeed exist, but Adlung never mentions them. It is also possible that "in die Breite..." refers to rollerboards perpendicular to the ground, while "in die Länge" denotes rollerboards parallel to the ground (i.e., under the chest).

§. 51.

Finally the trackers in the lower part [of the case] are fastened to the manual or pedal keys. A wire is driven into the key directly behind the thumper board, and then bent into a hook or loop; the same thing is done at the end of the tracker, and then one is hung on the other. The wire can be bent up or down with pliers until the key stands at the right height. At least this is the way it is done in certain old [organs]. Nowadays it is all done by means of screws. A thin brass screw is driven into the key, the so-called "male screw" or *cochlea mas[culina]*.‡ Above it on the tracker there is a loop, [set]

‡ *Cochlea* means "snail" in Latin, in reference to the spiral threads on the screw.

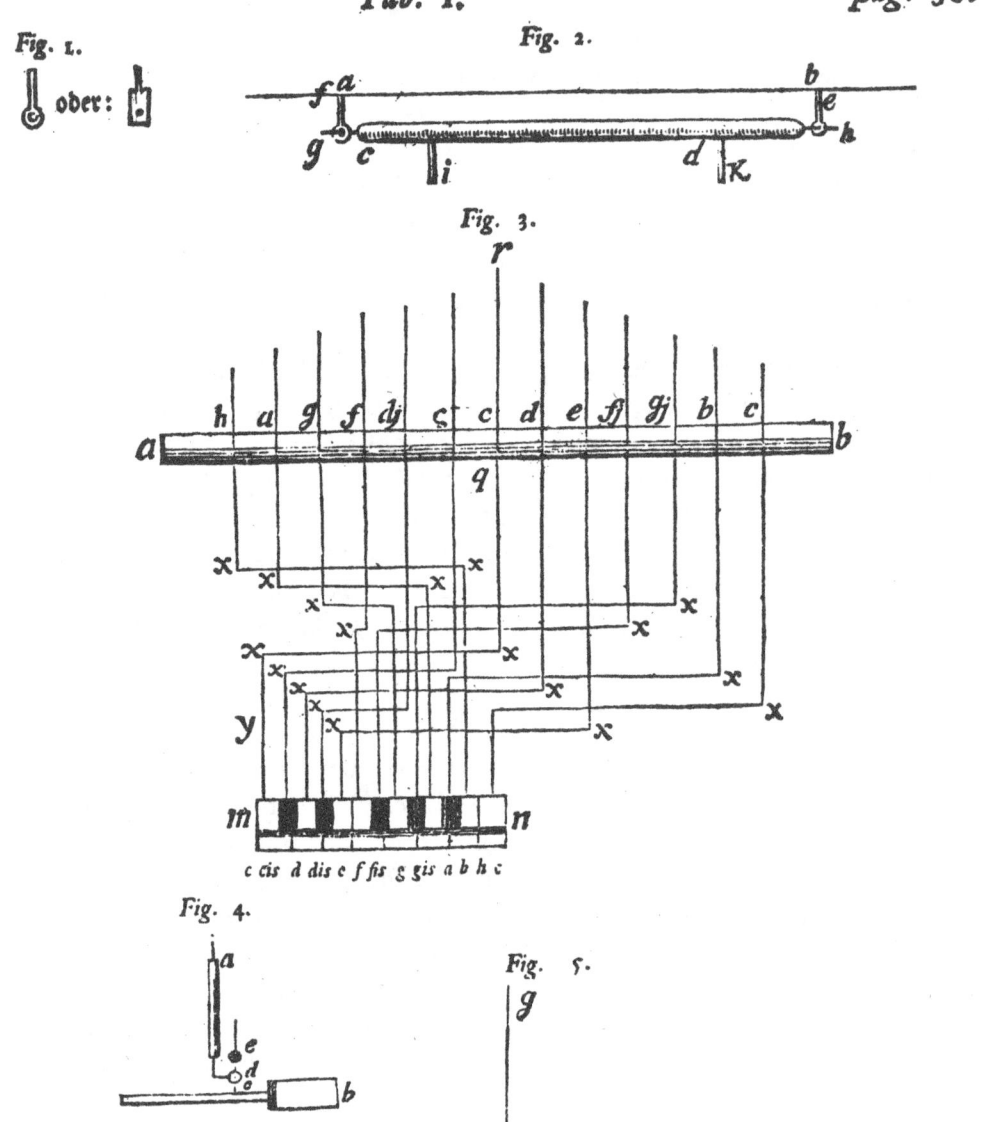

Tab. I. pag. 38.

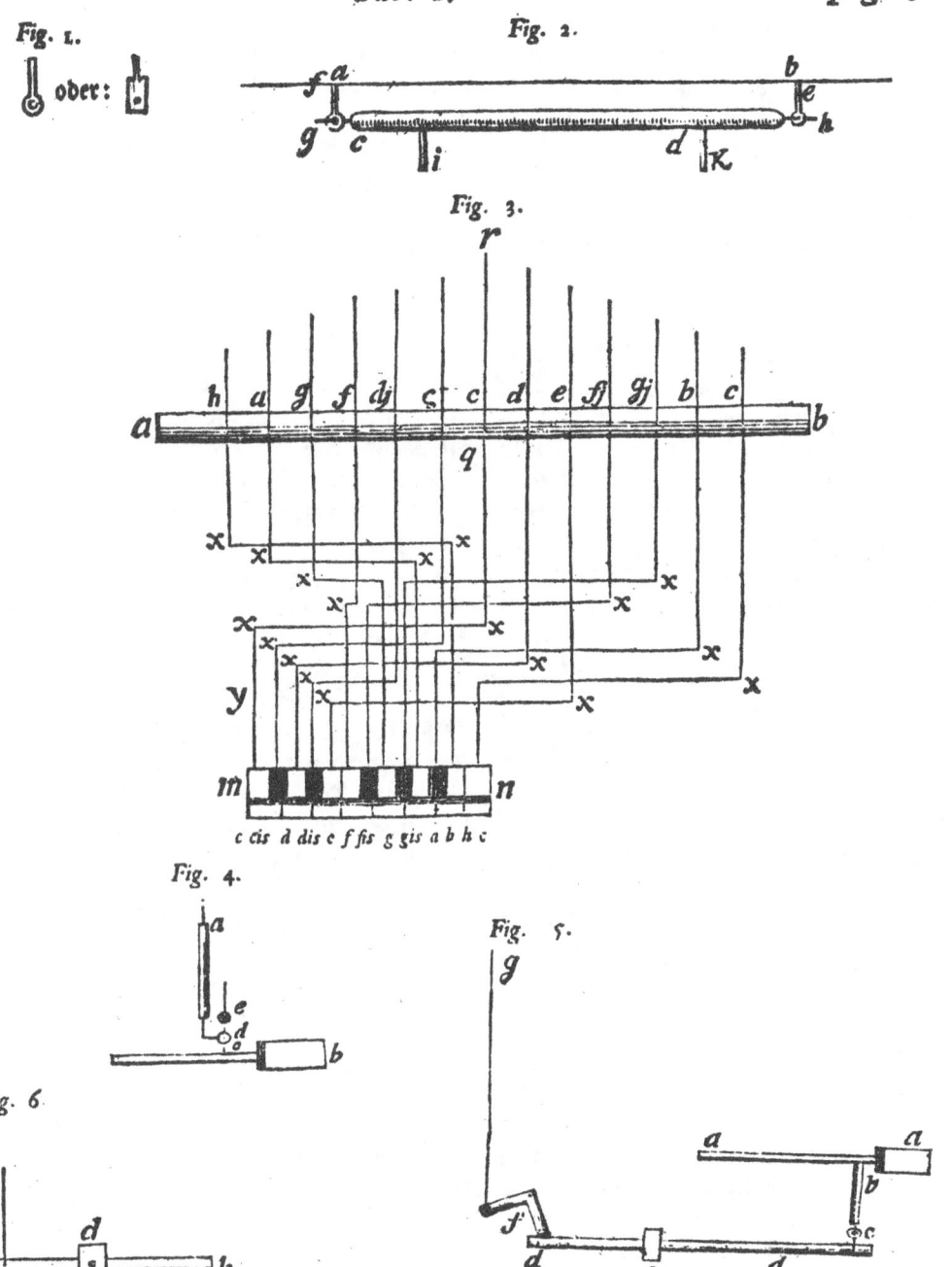

tale Schlinge, dadurch die Schraube blos gesteckt wird; und an die Schraube schraubt man die cochleam foeminam oder die Schraubenmutter, welche von dickem Pfund=leder ist, und so breit, daß sie zwischen den Abstrakten Raum genug hat. Es siehet so aus, wie bey fig. 4. *a* ist die pilotis; *b* die palmula; *c* die cochlea mas; *d* die Dratschlinge an der pilotide, wodurch die Schraube nicht geschraubt, sondern blos durchgesteckt wird; *e* ist die Mutter von Leder, die über der Schlinge angeschraubt wird. Anstatt der Dratschlinge an den pilotidibus macht man zuweilen eine lederne Schlinge, und schraubt über dieselbe ebenfalls das Mütterchen an; das verursacht kein solches Rasseln.

§. 52.

Wenn mehr als ein Clavier ist; so bekömmt das untere Clavier lange Schrauben, daß sie durch die palmulas, des obern durchreichen, und also hinter den Schrauben des andern auch gemacht werden auf vorige Art. So ist es z. Er. in der Jenaischen Colle=gen=Orgel. Und also bekömmt man lauter Zugwerke, das ist, die die Abstrakten un=mittelbar abwärts ziehen. Aber es finden sich zuweilen auch Druckwerke, welche fol=gende Theile haben. Hinter dem Claviere hangen die Abstrakten herab, welche an Win=kel bevestiget werden. An diesen Winkeln ist eine Stange unter dem Claviere bis vor geführt, in welcher ein rundes Löchelchen zu sehen. Hernach nimmt man subtile hölzer=ne Stangen, welche selten über ¼ Elle lang sind, diese berühren mit dem obern Theile die Palmulam, an das untere Theil wird eine cochlea mas gemacht; die man in das vorgedachte Löchelchen setzt, und unten abermal auf die vorige Art die Mutter daran schraubt über dem Löchelchen, so hoch, daß die palmula die rechte Höhe bekomme. Wenn nun die palmula gedruckt wird; so druckt sie die Stange, diese die untere große Stange, daher der hintere Winkel sich regt, und dadurch wird die Traktur bis zu de=nen Ventilen beweget. Man sehe eine Vorstellung bey Tab. I. fig. 5. Z. Er. *a* soll das Clavier, oder nur eine palmula andeuten; *b* das Stängelchen; *c* die Mutter sammt der cochlea mari; *d* die unter dem Clavier weggehende Stange; *e* das hypomochlium, oder der Ort, darinn sich die vestliegende Stange bewegt; *f* der Winkel; *g* die pilotis. Diese Druckwerke sind ordinär, wo Rückpositive stehen, nemlich hinter dem Rücken des Organisten; doch auch zuweilen wo 2 Claviere sind, obschon der Bau beysammen ist. Ich habe auch kleine neue Orgeln gesehen mit einem Claviere, da auch Druckwerke waren, weil man aufwärts keinen Raum gehabt, sondern alles Eingeweide unter dem Claviere anbringen müssen.

§. 53.

Die Claviere selbst liegen auch zum Theil inwendig, indem ihre Stangen meistens sehr lang sind, und hinten in dem Rahmen werden sie in Stiften beweget, und zu bey=den Seiten wohl verwahrt und auf Säulen gelegt. Und damit man zu allem kommen, und das Clavier heraus heben könne, so wird über den Clavieren der äusserliche Theil also gemacht, daß man ihn heraus heben könne.

Die

horizontally, through which the screw is inserted. A nut or *cochlea fœmi[ni]na* is then screwed onto the screw; [it is] made of thick, heavy leather and is narrow enough to fit between the trackers. It is illustrated in fig. 4: *a* is the tracker; *b* the key; *c* the male screw; *d* the wire loop on the tracker, through which the screw is merely inserted, not screwed; *e* is the leather nut that is screwed on above the loop. Instead of a wire loop on the trackers, some builders make a leather loop and then screw the nut on over it; this prevents any rattling.

§. 52.

If there is more than one keyboard, then the lower keyboard is fitted with long screws that pass through the keys of the upper manual, behind the screws of the latter; these [long screws] are then connected as has been described above. This is how, for example, the organ in the Collegenkirche at Jena is built. The result is a pure suspended action (Zugwerke), in which the trackers pull directly downwards. But there are also backfall actions (Druckwerke*), that work as follows: the trackers hang downward† behind the keyboard, and are fastened [at the bottom] to squares. Onto [the other side of] these squares are attached [lever-]rods that reach forward under the keyboard. A small round hole may be seen in [the forward end of] these rods. [The action is] then [completed by] thin wooden rods,‡ seldom more than a ¼ of an ell long;§ their tops contact [the underside of] the keys, and to their bottoms are affixed male screws. A nut is put on the screw, and the screw is set into the abovementioned hole. Then the nut is adjusted so that the key stands at the proper level. Now when the key is depressed, it presses down upon the rod; this in turn depresses [the forward end of] the long [lever-]rod down below. This causes the square at the rear [end of the lever-rod] to move, and the tracker then transmits this action to the pallet. This is illustrated in Tab. I, fig. 5: *a* is the keyboard (or rather, a single key), *b* is the thin [wooden] rod, *c* is the nut [set upon] the screw, *d* is the rod that passes under the keyboard, *e* is the fulcrum, the point at which the rod is affixed and pivots, *f* is the square, and *g* is the tracker. Such backfall actions are common where there are Rückpositivs that stand behind the organist's back. But they are also to be found at times in two-manual organs, even though the instrument is contained within a single case. I have also seen small new one-manual organs in which there were backfall actions, because the builders had no room above, and so had to construct all of the interior components¶ under the keyboard.

§. 53.

The keys themselves lie in part within the organ, since their levers (Stangen) are normally quite long. At the back end they move upon pins in a frame which is well secured at both sides and set upon posts. In order to permit easy access to everything and to allow the keyboard to be lifted out, the outer panel above the keyboard∥ is constructed so that it may be lifted out.

---

* It is common today to use the term "suspended action" to describe any action in which the keys are pivoted at the tail, even those with stickers (such as the *Druckwerk* described here), so that the weight of the key helps the player to open the pallet and likewise prevents the pallet from closing too quickly. Apparently this distinction was not important to Adlung.

† from the pallet box or rollerboard.

‡ i.e., the stickers.

§ Here Adlung is describing a backfall action for a division in the main case; later in the paragraph he mentions this type of action in connection with the Rückpositiv (where backfall actions are often found in modern mechanical organs).

¶ i.e., the action as well as the chest and the pipes.

∥ Where the music rack is located.

Kap. IV. Von dem andern Eingeweide der Orgel,

Die claues oder palmulae sind inwendig zuweilen gebrochen, nämlich so, wie bey Tab. I. fig. 6. da denn, wenn die palmula *a* niedergedruckt wird, so begiebt sich deren Hinterstes in *b* in die Höhe, und nimmt das darauf liegende besondere Stück auch mit in die Höhe; also gehet des andern Theils hinterstes Ende in *c* niederwärts, weil es in *d* in einem unbeweglichen Punkte bevestiget ist, doch so, daß es um dasselbe sich bewegen kann. Weil also *c* niedergeht, so muß die Abstrakte *e*, die daran hängt, auch mit nieder, und folglich die Welle, die obern pilotides und endlich das Ventil des Windkastens. Und dergleichen Inventionen haben die Orgelmacher noch viel, wobey ich mich aber nicht aufhalte; ein Organist bekümmert sich mehr um andere Dinge.

§. 54.

Zu dem Eingeweide gehören auch die Säulen und Bevestigungen, worauf die Laden und übrigen Theile zu liegen kommen, it. die Streben, die das Orgelgebäude von innen halten helfen. Ferner die Gänge, die man, wo der Raum es verstattet, um die Laden macht, von Bohlen oder Brettern, daß man zu allen Theilen der Orgel kommen kann; it. die Treppen oder Leitern, die uns in die Höhe führen, aus einem Stock in das andere. Auch siehet man inwendig noch die Kanäle, die aus den Bälgen nach dem Windkasten gehen. Aus den Bälgen geht meistens ein großer Kanal, aber hernach zertheilt er sich in so viel kleinere Armen, als sich Windladen in der Orgel befinden, daß der Wind zugleich in alle Laden der Orgel kommen kann. Sind die Laden groß; so sind auch diese Kanäle groß, und zuweilen ist es nur einer, zuweilen sind deren 2, 3 und mehr, dadurch der Zufall des Windes geschwinder und stärker wird. Es müssen also auch in den Windkasten soviel Oefnungen gemacht, und die Kanäle darein gesteckt, doch mit Leder wohl verwahret werden, das kein Wind neben den Kanälen aus dem Kasten kommen könne. Ein solcher Kanal heißt auch portavento; ist ein italienischer Name, von portare, tragen, und vento der Wind, weil der Wind vermittelst eines solchen Kanals an gehörigen Ort getragen oder befördert wird. It. canalis uentorum; it. anemotheca, von ἄνεμος, uentus der Wind, und τίθημι pono, ich setze. Besiehe Kirchers Musurg. l. c.

§. 55.

Man hat auch andere Windführungen darinnen, z. Ex. aus dem Kanal nach dem Tremulanten, nach dem Stern oder Zimbelglocken, welches letztere eine lange Röhre ist aus dem Kanal bis zu dem Sternrade; wovon unten mehr folgt. Auch sind Windführungen von der Lade weg; denn man setzt nicht alles Pfeifwerk auf die Lade, sondern vorn in das Gesicht, in die Thürme u. s. f. bald höher und bald tiefer als die Lade; alsdann führt man den Wind aus der zu jeder Pfeife gehörigen Cancelle durch hölzerne oder ander Röhren von Metall zu der Pfeife, daß sie zugleich mit angeblasen wird, wenn die Cancelle voll Wind ist.

§. 56.

The keys or *palmulae* are sometimes interrupted within the case, as is illustrated in Tab. I, fig. 6. When the key *a* is depressed, its back end *b* rises, bearing with it the rear backfall. The back end of the backfall, at *c*, moves downward, since it is fastened to a stationary point *d* (but it can of course move upon that point). Because *c* falls, the tracker *e* that is connected to it must also move downward, and consequently the roller, the trackers beyond it, and finally the pallet in the palletbox. Organbuilders have come up with many other inventions such as this, but I will not dwell on them, since other matters are of greater importance to an organist.

§. 54.

To the interior components belong likewise the posts and supports upon which the chests and other parts rest, as well as the props that steady the organ case from the inside. There are also the walkways, beams or boards that are constructed about the chest as room permits, to grant access to all parts of the organ. Likewise there are stairs or ladders that lead upward from one level to the next. Inside the organ one may also see the wind ducts that run out of the bellows to the pallet box. Usually just one large trunk runs from the bellows, that then branches into as many smaller ducts as there are windchests in the organ. Thus the wind is distributed evenly to all the chests of the organ. The size of the ducts is proportionate to that of the chests. Sometimes there is only one duct [to a given chest], sometimes 2, 3 or more, so that the supply of wind may be more rapid and steady. The pallet box must be provided with the requisite number of openings to receive the ducts, and [the points at which they meet must be] tightly sealed with leather so that no wind may escape from the pallet box at these joints. Such a duct is also called a *portavento*, an Italian name coming from *portare*, "to carry", and *vento*, "the wind", since the wind is carried or channeled where it is needed by means of such a duct. It is also known as *canalis ventorum* or *anemotheca*, from ἄνεμος, *ventus*, "the wind", and τίθημι, *pono*, "I place." See Kircher's *Musurgia*, loc. cit. [p. 506].

§. 55.

There are also other wind conduits inside the case, for example, the one leading from the duct to the tremulant; also the one leading to the Zimbelstern, which is a long tube from the duct to the revolving star (more on this below*). There are also wind conduits running out of the chest, since not all pipes sit [directly] on the chest, but in the façade, in the towers or the like, at times above, at times below the chest. In this case the channel belonging to a pipe is fitted with a wooden or metal tube that bears the wind to the pipe; thus when the channel is filled with wind, the pipe sounds immediately.

* See §.133, under "Cymbel."

das Pfeifwerk ausgenommen.

§. 56.

Noch ist übrig, von den Registern zu reden. Da finden sich folgende Theile: An den manubriis sind die Schiebstangen; (ich rede itzt von der ordentlichen Art, da man die manubria horizontal heraus zieht) diese sind durch Arme und Stifte an die Wellen gemacht, die mit dem andern Arme oder Wirbel bisweilen unmittelbar die Register oder Parallelen aus der Lade ziehen; am gewöhnlichsten aber geschiehet es durch andere Stangen und Wellen, nach der Invention eines jeden Orgelmachers, als welcher am besten wissen muß, wo sich ein jedes von diesen innern Theilen hinbringen läßt. Nachdem aber die manubria traktirt werden, (wovon §. 30.) nachdem werden auch die innern Theile verschiedentlich seyn. Die Wellen aber haben oben und unten sehr starke Stifte, welche in einem Brette beweglich sind.

Das V. Kapitel.
Von den Bälgen und Windführungen.

Inhalt.

§ 57. Theile der Bälge. §. 58. Ihre Platten. §. 59. Deren Verbindung. §. 60. Die Faltenbälge. §. 61. Das Balgventil. §. 62. Das Kanalventil. §. 63. Bevestigung der Platten. §. 64. Der Calculaturclavis. §. 65. Das Balghaus. §. 66. Die Scheiden, Treppen und Querstangen. §. 67. Die Vorschläge und das Balgregister. §. 68. Das Gewicht der Bälge. §. 69. Pedal- und Manualbälge. §. 70. Zahl der Bälge und deren Beschaffenheit bey den Alten. §. 71 Calcant. §. 72. Das Gegengewicht. §. 73. Die Kanäle. §. 74. Die Ventile darinnen.

§. 57.

Was Bälge sind, ist vorhin einem jeden bekannt, indem dergleichen bey allen Schmieden können gesehen werden. Ja fast in allen Küchen führet man Blasbälge, um das Feuer damit anzublasen, an welchen die Haupttheile sich eben sowol, als bey unsern Bälgen, finden müssen. Diese Orgelbälge sind zweyerley: Faltenbälge und Spanbälge. Von den Spanbälgen will ich erst reden; weil dies die gewöhnlichsten sind. Die Form anlangend, so sind sie länglicht-viereckigt. Die Theile sind: die obere und untere Platte, die Seiten, Balgventil, Oefnung gegen den Windkanal, Kanalventil, Leisten, Calculaturclavis.

§. 58.

Die Platten werden von zusammengefügten dicken Bohlbrettern gemacht, sowol die obere als untere; die gar kleinen können auch von Brettern seyn. Nachdem die Bälge groß werden sollen, nachdem macht man die Platten groß. Die Länge übertrift

die

with the Exception of the Pipes.

§. 56.

The only thing now remaining is to discuss the stop [action]. It consists of the following parts: [attached] to the stop knobs are the trace-rods (now I am speaking only of the ordinary kind, where the knobs are drawn outward horizontally*). These trace-rods are attached to trundles by means of arms and [center-]pins. The [trundle's] other arm or rotating peg pulls the slider in the chest outward, sometimes directly, but most commonly by means of further rods and trundles, according to the inventiveness of each organbuilder, who must understand how to dispose each of these internal parts to best advantage. The internal parts differ, though, in accordance with how the stop knobs are operated (see §.30). The trundles are fitted at the top and bottom with very strong pins, that rotate in boards.

* i.e., those of a slider chest, in contrast to the stop levers of a spring chest or to the other varieties Adlung discusses above.

Chapter V.
Concerning the Bellows and Wind Ducts.

Contents:

§.57. Parts of the bellows. §.58. Their boards. §.59. Their bindings. §.60. Multi-fold bellows. §.61. The bellows valve. §.62. The wind duct valve. §.63. Braces for the boards. §.64. The bellows pole. §.65. The bellows frame. §.66. The slots, steps and cross-rails. §.67. The latches and the bellows stop. §.68. The bellows-weight. §.69. Pedal and manual bellows. §.70. The number of bellows and their structure in old organs. §.71. The bellows-pumper. §.72. The counterweight. §.73. The wind ducts. §.74. The duct ventils.

§. 57.

Everyone already knows what bellows are, since they may be seen at any blacksmithy. Indeed, bellows are kept in almost every kitchen to fan the fire, and their principal parts there are just the same as the ones found in organs. Organ bellows are of two types: multi-fold bellows and wedge* bellows. I shall begin by discussing the wedge bellows, since they are the most common. They are rectangular in shape, and have the following parts: the top and bottom boards, the sides, the bellows valve, the opening into the wind duct, the wind duct valve, the strips† and the bellows pole.

* i.e., single-fold.

† That brace the boards.

§. 58.

The boards, both top and bottom, are made of thick planks joined together; very small ones may be made of boards instead. They are the same dimensions as the bellows themselves. The length is for the most part half again the width, but there are bellows

42 Kap. V. Von den Bälgen und Windführungen.

die Breite meistentheils um die Hälfte, und hat man Bälge die 5′ breit und 10′ lang sind; (der Strich über der Zahl bedeutet Schuhe,) oder 6′ breit und 12′ lang. Doch hat man sie auch kürzer und schmäler; wie denn auch keine Nothwendigkeit ist, daß die Länge sich gegen die Breite allezeit wie 2 zu 1 verhalten müsse. Je größer man sie haben kann, je besser ist es, sonderlich was die Länge betrift.

§. 59.

Das vordere Theil der zwo Platten wird durch starkes Leder und Roßadern, wie auch durch eiserne Gelenke, mit einander verbunden. Roßadern sind theils Riemen von Pferdhäuten, theils würkliche getrocknete Pferdadern, Sehnen oder Flechsen aus den Füßen, welche zum Halten besser sind als das gemeine Leder, welches bald reißet und den Wind durchläßt. Die Seiten werden auch zusammen gefüget; doch wird an die obere Platte mit Leder und Roßadern ein Brett befestiget, welches vornen ganz schmal, hinterwärts aber stets breiter ist, also:

Dergleichen wird auch an der andern Seite angemacht, daß sie abwärts hängen. Und damit es beweglich sey; so wird es an die Platte nur mit Leder und Roßadern verbunden. Dergleichen wird auch an der untern Platte auf sothane Art bevestiget, doch aufwärts; und endlich werden diese 2 Seitbretter selbst in der Mitte auf eben diese Art mit einander verbunden, das wird hernach, wenn der Balg sich zusammen thut, eine Falte. Die Platten werden auch hinten, durch 2 Bretter, so oben und unten auf die vorige Art bevestiget, mit einander verbunden, und diese Falten werden ordentlich einwärts angebracht, selten auswärts. S. §. 375. Und so ist die Form oder das Corpus fertig.

§. 60.

Was in diesem, im vorhergehenden, und folgenden Paragraphen vorkömmt, läßt sich auch bey den Faltenbälgen appliciren; nur daß die Seiten anders sind, als welche anstatt einer Falte etliche bekommen, da auf die vorige Art ein kleineres Brett, als man zuvor bedurfte, an die obere und untere Platte befestiget wird. An diese zwey Bretter werden eben also noch oben und unten 2 andere gemacht, an diese wieder andere, nachdem der Balg viel oder wenig Falten haben soll. Endlich werden die mittelsten Falten mit einander verbunden. Hinten ist es auf gleiche Art. Der aufgezogene Faltenbalg siehet also aus:

Der niedergegangne so:

Ch. V. Concerning the Bellows and Wind Ducts.

that are 5′ wide and 10′ long or 6′ wide and 12′ long* (the stroke above the number means "feet"). They may be either shorter or narrower, however, since it is not necessary that the length always be twice the width. The larger they can be the better, particularly as regards length.

* i.e., there are some bellows that are twice as long as they are wide.

§. 59.

The forward edges of the two boards are bound together by strong leather and horse veins as well as by iron hinges. Horse veins are in part straps of horsehide, in part actual dried horse veins, tendons or sinews taken from the feet. These are more durable than common leather, that soon splits and lets the wind escape. The sides are also joined together, but in this way: a board is fastened onto the top board with leather and horse veins. This board is very narrow in front, growing increasingly broader towards the rear, thus:

The other side [of the top board] is given the same treatment, and both boards hang downward. They are fastened to the [top] board only with leather and horse veins in order to remain movable. The same sort of boards are also fastened to the bottom board, in the same way, but [extending] upwards. Finally the two side-boards [on each side] are connected to each other in the middle, in the same way. Thus when the bellows collapses, it becomes a fold. The back edges of the boards are likewise fastened together with two boards, one above and one beneath, in the same way as above. The boards are usually constructed to fold inward, rarely outward. See §.375.† This completes the shape of the body.

† for further information about the bellows.

§. 60.

What is said in paragraphs 59, 60 and 61 also applies to the multi-fold bellows, the only difference being that the sides [of the multi-fold bellows], instead of having one fold, have smaller boards‡ fastened to the top and bottom boards. To each of the two boards on each side are affixed yet two more boards, then others to these and so forth, depending on whether the bellows is to have fewer or more folds. The middle folds are finally bound together, and then the entire process is repeated at the back. The inflated multi-fold bellows looks like this:

‡ i.e., narrower than those of the wedge bellows.

When it is collapsed it looks like this:

Der aufgezogene Spanbalg aber so: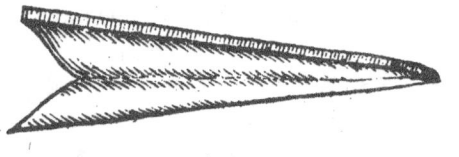

Und der niederliegende auf diese Weise: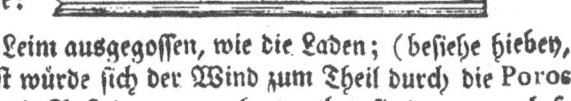

Alle Bälge werden durchaus wohl mit Leim ausgegossen, wie die Laden; (besiehe hiebey, was §. 39. gesagt worden.) denn sonst würde sich der Wind zum Theil durch die Poros verliehren. Etliche Bälge sind nicht mit Roßadern verwahret; aber sie dauren auch so nicht, wie die andern.

§. 61.

In den Balg wird durch Aufziehen der Wind gezogen, und zwar durch eine Oefnung, welche an der untern Platte gemacht wird, groß oder klein, nachdem der Balg ist. Diese Oefnung ist ordentlich ein länglicht Quadrat, also: ▭ An der einen langen Seite wird eine starke Pappe bevestiget, doch also, daß sie auf- und niedergebogen werden könne; oder was man sonst dazu nehmen will. Sie muß aber inwendig angemacht werden, damit beym Aufziehen des Balges der äussere Wind diese Klappe einwarts aufthun und sich in den Balg ziehen kann. Wenn aber der Balg wieder nieder gehet; so drückt der inwendige Wind die Klappe an, daß also derselbe nicht wieder hier herauskommen kann. Dies ist das Balg- oder Fangventil, (siehe was §. 40. von den Ventilen überhaupt gesagt worden,) weil es den Wind in den Balg läßt. Wenn die Bälge groß sind; so muß auch diese Oefnung groß seyn, damit auf einmal der Balg vom Winde erfüllet werden könne; folglich müßte die Klappe sehr breit seyn, aber weil sie sich alsdann leicht verwerfen könnte; so pflegt man das Ventil doppelt zu machen, auf beyden Seiten eine Klappe, welche in der Mitte bevestiget werden kann. Also:

Auf solche Art wird der Wind gefangen.

§. 62.

Und wie dieses Ventil fast oben, wo der Balg sich aufthut, angebracht wird; so pflegt man unten eine andere viereckigte Oefnung zu machen, dadurch der Wind aus dem Balge in den Kanal geführet wird. Weil es aber eben so wohl geschehen könnte, daß der aufziehende Balg den Wind durch diese Oefnung aus den Kanälen an sich ziehe, als leichte es geschiehet durch die Balgventile; so werden bey dieser Oefnung abermal Ventile

Ch. V. Concerning the Bellows and Wind Ducts.

An inflated wedge bellows, though, looks like this:

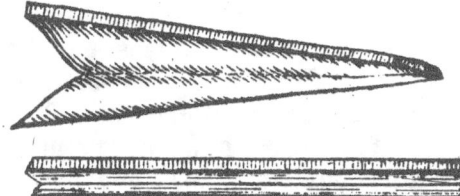

And when it is collapsed it looks like this:

All the bellows are thoroughly smeared all over with glue, just like the chests (see in this regard what has been said in §. 39), for otherwise some of the wind would escape through the pores. Some bellows are not fastened together with horse veins, but these are not as durable as others.

§. 61.

When the bellows are inflated, wind is drawn into them through an opening in the lower plate, proportionately larger or smaller according to the size of the bellows. This opening is usually a rectangle: ▭ A sturdy paste-board flap (Pappe*) is fastened on the long side [of the rectangle], in such a way that it can flop up and down. Another material may be used instead. It must be attached on the inside, however, so that when the bellows is inflated the wind being drawn in forces it inward as it rushes into the bellows. Then when the bellows begins to compress, the pent-up wind presses the flap shut, so that none can escape. This [flap] is the bellows- or feeder valve (consult what has already been said about valves in general in §. 40), since it lets the wind into the bellows. If the bellows is large, then the opening must also be large, so that the bellows may immediately be filled with wind. Consequently the flap must be very wide. But because it is then prone to warp, it is customary to make a double valve, with flaps on both sides that are attached in the middle, thus:

In this way the wind is held captive.

§. 62.

Since this feeder valve is located at the back end, where the bellows expands, it is customary to put another rectangular opening at the other end, through which the wind is channeled out of the bellows into the wind duct. Since the expanding bellows would inevitably draw the wind back out of the duct through this opening (just as easily as it can through the feeder valve), here again valves are attached at the opening.

* This word literally means "pasteboard" or "cardboard." Adlung may have intended to write "Klappe" (flap), since he subsequently uses that word several times in this paragraph without explaining it.

44　Kap. V. Von den Bälgen und Windführungen.

Ventile angebracht, welche Klappen in dem Kanale bevestigt sind, auch in dem Kanale sich aufthun; und also kann der Wind des Balges sie in den Kanal aufblasen, so geht der Wind hinein: Aber wenn der Balg den Wind des Kanals an sich ziehen wollte; so würde der Wind des Kanals wegen seiner Elasticität das Ventil nach dem Balge zu treiben, und das Loch bedecken. Dies ist das Kanalventil. Daher es geschiehet, wenn etwas zwischen diese Klappe kömmt, daß sie nicht anpassen kann; so zieht der Balg den Wind aus dem Kanale an sich, und raubet den andern Bälgen den Wind durch den Kanal.

§. 63.

So weit ist der Balg fertig. Aber damit die Platten nicht springen, krumm werden, oder sich verwerfen, so werden oben und unten starke Leisten übergelegt: oder, welches noch besser, man schraubet rechte Säulen auf, wodurch allem Unheil vorgebogen wird; wie denn auch alle verdächtige Oerter mit Leder überzogen werden.

§. 64.

Die Aufhebung des Balges geschiehet auf vielerley Art. Bey kleinen Positiven, oder Regalen hebt man ihn zuweilen mit den Händen auf. Ordinär aber wird ein Calculaturclavis angebracht; der den Namen von calcare, treten, herleitet. Dies ist eine Stange von verschiedener Länge und Dicke, welche zuweilen über- oder unter dem Balge weggehet bis ausserhalb des Balghauses. Deren hinterster Theil wird an die obere Platte des Balges bevestiget durch eine Kette oder Strick, wenn der Calcalaturclavis über dem Balge weggehet; wiewol zuweilen eine hölzerne Stange dazu gebraucht wird. Mitten durch diesen clauem, oder wohin man es sonst machen will, geht ein Loch, und durch dieses ein Nagel von Holz, oder besser von Eisen, da wird der clauis auf einer Säule bevestiget, als auf einem unbeweglichen hypomochlio. Wenn nun der clauis vornen gedruckt oder getreten wird; so bleibt dieser mittlere Theil stehen: aber da der clauis um diesen Nagel sich bewegt; so geht der hintere Theil des clauis in die Höhe, und nimmt die obere Platte mit: und auf solche Weise wird der Balg aufgezogen. Z. Er.

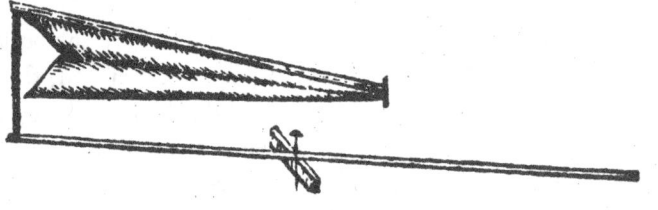

Wenn aber der Calculaturclavis unter dem Balge weggehet, so muß die obere Platte allezeit durch eine Stange gehoben werden. Also:

§. 65.

44   Ch. V. Concerning the Bellows and Wind Ducts.

These are flaps fastened into the duct, opening into it. Thus the wind in the bellows can blow them open to enter the duct, but when the bellows begins to draw the wind back from the duct, then due to its elasticity that wind forces the valve back against the bellows and thus closes the hole. This is the wind duct valve. If something gets into this flap that keeps it from fitting tightly, then it can happen that the bellows draws the wind back out of the duct, and robs the wind from the other bellows through the duct.

§. 63.

At this point the bellows is complete. However, so that the boards do not split, get out of alignment or warp, strong strips are fastened over them at the top and bottom; or even better, solid timbers are screwed onto them to prevent any kind of trouble. Then any suspicious spots* are covered over with leather.

* i.e., spots that might be prone to leak.

§. 64.

The inflation of the bellows is acomplished in a number of ways. With little positives or regals they are at times lifted manually. Ordinarily, though, a bellows pole is attached, whose name derives from [Latin] *calcare*, "to tread." This is a pole of varying length and thickness that passes at times over, at times under the bellows, and then out of the bellows frame. If the bellows pole passes over the bellows, its far end is fastened to the top board of the bellows by a chain or rope, although at times a wooden rod is used for this purpose. In the middle of the bellows pole, or wherever else is convenient, there is a hole, and through this [hole] passes a wooden (or better, an iron) nail. By this nail the pole is attached to a post, an immobile fulcrum. If the treading pole is then pushed or trodden down at the near end, its midpoint remains fixed (rotating upon the nail), and thus the far end of the pole rises, lifting with it the top board. In this way the bellows is inflated; for example:

If however the bellows pole passes under the bellows, then the top board must always be lifted by means of a rod, thus:

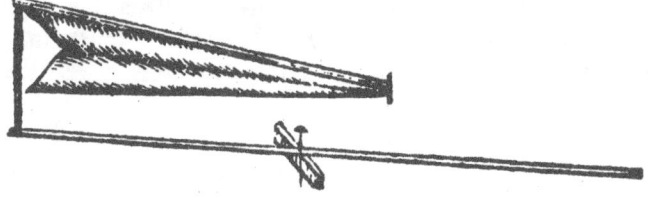

§. 65.

Für die Bälge wird eine Stelle abgesondert und auf allen Seiten mit Brettern verwahret, daß nichts dazu kommen könne. Wenn derselben wenig sind, so können sie zuweilen neben einander liegen: wo aber der Raum dieses nicht gestattet; so muß ein besonderes Gerüste aufgeführet werden, darauf sie über einander zu liegen kommen; 2 und mehr fach, doch daß zwischen allen so viel Raum bleibe, daß sie sich bequem aufthun können; doch nicht perpendikulär der clauium wegen. Dieses ist das Balghaus. Die Calculaturclaves werden alle in einer Linie neben einander, gerade unter jeden Balg gelegt, weil die Stangen auf und nieder geführet, und dadurch der Balg aller Orten gehoben werden kann. Eine Oefnung oder Thür läßt man zu den Bälgen, damit man im Nothfall dahin kommen könne.

§. 66.

Auf einer Seite, da die Spitze des Calculaturclavis hervorraget, beschlägt man das Gebäude auch mit Brettern: es sind aber dabey noch folgende Theile zu merken. Die Scheiden oder Ritze, welche perpendikulariter von oben abwärts durch die vorgeschlagenen Bretter des Balghauses geschnitten sind, dadurch der clauis oder Stange ausser dem Balghause hervorgehet, und von aussen kann getreten werden. Die Weite der Scheide richtet sich nach der Dicke der Stange; die Länge aber nach dem Aufthun des Balges, so, daß wenn derselbe hoch genug aufgezogen, der clauis zugleich am untern Ende der Scheide sich finde, daß der Balg nicht abgehoben oder zerrissen werde: wenn aber der Balg sich zusammen legt, daß der clauis zu gleicher Zeit accurat das obere Ende berühre. Damit der, welcher die Balken tritt (der Calcant, von calcare, treten,) hinauf kommen könne; so wird zuweilen eine hohe Bank vor die claues gelegt, doch so, daß dieselben vor derselben sich abwärts treten lassen; oder man legt zwischen 2 und 2, oder zwischen alle Bälge kleine Treppen, darauf man hinauf laufen kann. Zuweilen sind die Treppen da, doch etwas erhaben, und die Bank ist auch dabey. Damit der Calcant mehr Force haben, und nicht herab purzeln möge, so werden oben dicke Stangen angemacht, um sich daran halten zu können. Sie sind so hoch über den Calculaturstangen, das der Calcant sie doch in Händen haben kann; wenn er gleich mit dem claue oder der Stange ganz herunter gelaufen.

§. 67.

Es finden sich dabey zuweilen Vorschläge, wodurch man hölzerne Haken verstehet, die vor den Balg geleget werden, damit er unten bleiben muß. An den meisten Bälgen aber findet sich dieses nicht, sondern wenn man sie nicht braucht, so laufen sie aus. Auch findet man zuweilen eine besondere Säule oder Brett, womit man die Bälge, oder deren Claves verschließt, daß sie keiner treten kann. Auch findet man Orgeln, da durch einen Registerzug alle Bälge, um sie treten zu können, zugleich geöfnet, und auch

Ch. V. Concerning the Bellows and Wind Ducts.

§. 65.

A space is partitioned off for the bellows and closed in on all sides with boards, so nothing can get into it. When the bellows are few in number, then they are sometimes placed next to each other. Where space does not permit this, however, then a special frame must be erected, upon which the bellows rest, stacked 2 or more atop each other. Yet there must remain enough room between each that they may comfortably be inflated; and the bellows may not lie directly over each other because of the bellows poles. This [structure] is the bellows frame. The bellows poles all lie in a line next to each other, each one under the bellows it operates; then the poles are moved up and down, thus making it possible to inflate the entire series of bellows. An opening or a door is provided into the bellows [chamber], so that they may be accessible in case of need.

§. 66.

The structure is also covered with boards on the side from which the ends of the bellows poles protrude; but on this side there are several other parts to take note of, as follows. First are the slots, clefts that are cut vertically from top to bottom through the boards covering the bellows frame. Through these the bellows poles protrude from the bellows chamber, so that they may be trod from the outside. The width of a slot is determined by the thickness of the pole, and its length by the rise of the bellows. That is, when the bellows is sufficiently inflated, the pole is then at the lower end of the slot, thus preventing the bellows from being lifted [off its mounting] or torn apart. When the bellows is collapsed, however, the pole should then just touch the upper end [of the slot]. So that the one who pumps the bellows (the Calcant, from *calcare*, "to tread") may get atop [the poles], a high bench is sometimes set in front of the poles, positioned so that the poles may be trodden downward right in front of it. Alternatively, small stairs are erected between every bellows or every two bellows, on which to clamber up. At times the steps are there (though somewhat raised) as well as the bench.* In order to allow the pumper to exert greater force and to keep him from tumbling down, thick rails are erected up top for him to hold onto. They are high enough above the bellows poles for the pumper to hold onto with both hands as he rides the pole downwards.†

§. 67.

At times latches are provided, wooden hooks that are placed in front of the bellows to latch them down. Most bellows do not have these, however, but simply collapse when they are not being used. Occasionally there is a special post or board that locks either the bellows or their poles, so that no one may tread them. There are also organs where a drawknob either releases or locks all the bellows at once, either to allow or to

---

* i.e., since the stairs are somewhat raised above the floor level, the pumper walks back and forth on a bench, from which he climbs onto the stairs.

† Standing upon the pole with his feet.

46   Kap. V. Von den Bälgen und Windführungen.

auch wieder verschlossen werden, daß der Calcant nicht mehr treten kann; dergleichen zu Bückeburgk ist, oder doch zu Prätorii Zeiten war, der in seinem Synt. T. II. P. V. S. 185. dessen gedenkt, da er von pag. 161. an und folg. viel Orgeldispositiones hat.

§. 68.

Wie aber nicht durch eine jede Bewegung der Luft ein Sonus oder Schall verursacht wird, sonst müßte man des Menschen Stimme beständig hören, auch der andern Thiere, weil sie den Athem stets aus- und einziehen, sondern es gehöret eine gewisse modification der Luft dazu, durch die Gurgel, Zunge u. s. w.; auch eine starke Bewegung der Luft, daß nemlich die Luft erst in der Enge sey, und hernach mit Force heraus gehen und sich expandiren könne: Also ist es auch bey den Orgeln. Denn wenn der Wind aus dem Balge ohne Zwang in die Cancellen schleichen sollte, so würde es wenig oder nichts effektuiren: vielmehr muß man den Wind mit einer Gewalt aus dem Balge in das Pfeifenwerk treiben. Daher legt man das Gewicht hinten auf die Bälge, um den Balg mit einer Force nieder zu drücken, welches Gewicht von gemeinen Steinen, Backsteinen, Bley ꝛc. seyn kann. Auf einen Balg legt man alsdann so viel Gewichte, als auf den andern, daß der Wind vollkommen gleich werde: es wird aber hierbey billig voraus gesetzt, daß die obern Platten also gearbeitet worden, daß sie auf allen Bälgen gleiche Schwere haben. Damit aber das aufgelegte Gewicht im Aufziehen des Balges nicht herab hutsche, so werden Leisten vorgeschlagen. Ob aber viel oder wenig Gewicht darauf liegen müsse, das ist durch die Windprobe zu erforschen; denn daran siehet man, ob der Wind die verlangten Grade halte, und ob er in allen Bälgen vollkommen gleich sey. Doch ist es nicht in allen Orgeln gleich; weil nach Beschaffenheit des Pfeifwerks, nach der Größe der Kirchen u. s. f. auch der Wind stärker oder schwächer, folglich das Gewicht schwerer oder leichter gemacht wird. Das übrige davon wird unten folgen: jezo lernen wir nur alle Theile der Orgel einigermaßen kennen.

§. 69.

Die Bälge werden zuweilen in Pedal- und Manualbälge getheilet, [17]) da etliche, wenigstens 2, ihren Wind blos in die Manualladen, andere aber, deren abermals wenigstens 2 seyn müssen, blos in die Pedalladen schicken. Zuweilen geht der Wind zusammen, er kann aber durch einen Zug getheilet werden, wie z. Ex. in Waltershausen. Zuweilen aber gehören alle Bälge für alle Laden. Wenn im ersten Falle das ganze Werk zu spielen ist, oder das Pedal und Manual zugleich; so müssen auch von beyden Gattungen Bälge getreten werden: hier aber thut ein Balg eben die Dienste. Wenigstens zween Bälge müssen seyn, oder auch soviel bey jeder Gattung: denn sonst würde man keinen Wind haben, so lange man sich mit dem Niedertreten des Balges beschäftiget. Es wäre denn, daß man Doppelbälge anbrächte, dergleichen die Schmiede in ihren Werkstätten haben: die aber in großen Orgelwerken nicht Mode, und auch nicht brauchbar sind.

§. 70.

[17]) So findet man es hier in Mühlhausen in der Hauptkirche B. M. V. mit 3 und 3.

prevent the pumper from operating them. This is such [a device] at Bückeburg, or at least there was in Praetorius's day, since he mentions it in his *Syntagma*, Vol. II, Part V, p. 185 (pp. 161ff. of this publication contain many organ stoplists).

§. 68.

Not every motion of the air produces a sound; otherwise voices of humans and other animals would be heard continuously, since they constantly inhale and exhale. Rather, sound is produced by modifying the air in certain ways, by means of the throat, the tongue and such, but also by forcing the air into motion, first by compressing it and then by forcibly expelling it and letting it expand. This is the case with organs. For if the wind were simply to creep out of the bellows without being forced into the wind channels, then it would accomplish little or nothing. Rather the wind must be forced out of the bellows into the pipes. Therefore a weight is placed on the back end of the bellows, to forcibly press it downwards. This weight may be ordinary stones, bricks, lead, etc. An equal amount of weight is placed upon each bellows, so that the wind is perfectly even (it goes without saying that the upper boards of all the bellows are likewise constructed to be of the same weight). Slats are nailed on to keep the imposed weight from sliding downward as the bellows are drawn upward. Exactly how much weight must be set upon them is determined by the wind gauge.* By this means it can be ascertained whether the wind keeps the required degree [of pressure], and whether it is perfectly equal in every bellows. The wind pressure, though, is not the same in every organ; it must be greater or less (and thus the weight must be heavier or lighter) depending on the nature of the pipes, the size of the church, etc. More about this later;† now we are simply becoming familiar with all the components of an organ in summary fashion.

* See §.460 below.

† Chap. 16, §.441-3. Adlung also discusses matters pertaining to bellows in Chap. 13, §.370ff.

§. 69.

The bellows are at times divided into pedal and manual bellows.[17] In this case, some bellows (at least 2) deliver wind only to the manual chests, while others (again at least 2) deliver it only to the pedal chests. Sometimes the wind runs to all chests but can be divided by a stop, as for example at Waltershausen. Sometimes, however, all the bellows serve all the chests. When the bellows are divided and the entire organ is to be played, both manuals and pedal simultaneously, then both types of bellows must be pumped, for then only one bellows [at a time] is serving [each chest]. There must be at least 2 bellows, or 2 of each type,‡ or otherwise there would be no wind while the bellows are being inflated. One might consider constructing double bellows§ of the type that blacksmiths have in their smithies, but these are neither fashionable nor serviceable in large organs.

‡ i.e., manual and pedal.

§ Perhaps Adlung means a type of feeder bellows: two wedge bellows, one of which moves, the other of which is stationary.

(17) Such is the case here in Mühlhausen in the Hauptkirche B.V.M., in which there are three of each type. [Albrecht]

Kap. V. Von den Bälgen und Windführungen. 47

§. 70.

Die Anzahl der Bälge wird nicht determinirt, sondern das dependirt theils von ihrer Größe, theils von der Größe der Orgeln, und theils von dem Willen des Orgelbauers. Die Alten hatten gar kleine Bälge, daher sie derer desto mehr haben mußten. Prätorius l. c. cap. IX. pag. 103. sagt, daß zu Halberstadt in der von ihm beschriebenen alten Orgel 20, zu Magdeburg aber 24 Bälge wären, gar klein, fast wie unsere heutigen Schmiedebälge, an Größe und Proportion 3′ bis 4′ lang. Sie wurden auch nicht durch Bley regieret, sondern durch ein solches Mittel, daß man allezeit zu 2 Bälgen eine Person zum Treten gebraucht, und wenn mit dem einen Fuße der eine Balg durch die Schwere des Calkanten niedergetreten, so ist der andere mit dem andern Fuße wieder in die Höhe gezogen worden, daß also zu 24 Bälgen 12 Personen seyn mußten. Oder, wie Werkmeister, der diese Rudera auch gesehen, es erzählet in den Paradoxaldiscursen Kap. 16. p. 83. u. folg. so hat der Calkant müssen auf die Bälge treten, bis sie nieder gewesen, darnach sind auf jedem Balge hölzerne Tritte, wie Schuhe, gemacht gewesen, womit die Bälgetreter sie wieder aufziehen müssen. — — Jetzo aber macht man alles auf eine bessere Art, so, daß ein Calkant genug ist, und wenn der Bälge noch soviel wären; doch hat man nicht eben so viel Bälge nöthig, weil man sie heutiges Tages viel größer macht. Also findet sich im Schloß zu Grüningen ein Werk von 59 Stimmen, und doch hat es nur 4 Bälge, wie Matheson im Anhange zum 2ten Theil der Niedtischen Handleitung zur Variation des Generalbasses die Disposition anführet: aber Werkmeister, der diese Orgel vor und in der Reparatur beschrieben, zählt der Bälge achte. Sie müssen nach der Zeit größer, und ihrer weniger gemacht worden seyn. Doch finden sich in Erfurt auch wenig Bälge bey ziemlich starken Orgeln. Also sind zum Predigern 3; zum Reglern 5; andere haben derer mehr. z. Ex. zu St. Dominico in Prag sind 12 Bälge; doch sind auch daselbst 71 Stimmen. Eben so viel Bälge sind zu 50 Stimmen im Dom zu Upsal. Zu 54 Stimmen finden sich 16 Bälge, zu St. Marien in Lübeck. S. Mathesons Anhang zum Niedt.

§. 71.

In kleinen Orgeln, wo nicht Raum ist, legt man die Bälge auch wol auf den sogenannten Himmel der Kirche, oder doch so in die Höhe, daß man sie nicht treten kann, sondern mit Stricken ziehen muß. Zuweilen legt man sie in das untere Theil der Orgel; zuweilen hinter dieselbe, und läßt sie aufheben; und daß man sie nicht allzuhoch aufhebe; so werden von einer Falte zur andern Bänder angebracht. Wenn man in kleinen Positivchen gar keinen Raum hat; so macht man auch einen doppelten Balg, da man beständig Wind hat, ob man schon stets den einen Balg drückt oder tritt. Es mag im übrigen ein Balg getreten, gehoben oder gezogen werden; so heißt doch die dazu bestellte Person ein Calcant, welches eigentlich einen Tretenden bedeutet. Etliche nennen ihn: Sine me potestis nihil facere, d. i. ohne mich könnet ihr nichts thun; welches aber Beer, als einen Misbrauch

Ch. V. Concerning the Bellows and Wind Ducts.

§. 70.

There is no set number of bellows; it depends in part on their size, in part on the size of the organ, and in part on the wishes of the organbuilder. Our ancestors had very small bellows, and so there had to be all that many more of them. In describing the old organ at Halberstadt, Praetorius (loc. cit., Chap. IX, p. 103) says that it had 20 bellows, while the one at Magdeburg had 24, but these were very small, 3′ to 4′ long in size and [of] proportionate [width], almost like our present-day blacksmith's bellows. They were not weighted with lead, but by assigning one person to tread every two bellows; while the weight of the treader collapsed one of them with one foot, the other foot would draw the other one upward. Thus there had to be 12 people for 24 bellows. Or as Werkmeister (who also saw these relics) explains it in his *Paradoxal=Discourse*, Chap. 16, p. 83f.,[*] the pumper had to tread the bellows until they were collapsed, and then draw them up again by means of wooden treadles, like shoes, that were constructed on each bellows. — — Nowadays, though, bellows are made in a better way, so that one pumper is sufficient [to operate] any number of them. On the other hand, not as many bellows are necessary, since they are constructed much larger today. Thus in the palace at Gröningen there is an organ with 59 stops that nevertheless has only 4 bellows, according to Mattheson's stoplist in his Appendix to the second part of Niedt's *Handleitung zur Variation des Generalbasses*.[†] Werkmeister, however, who has described this organ before and after its repair, gives the number as 8;[‡] subsequently they must have been made larger, thus requiring fewer of them. Likewise at Erfurt there are quite powerful organs with only a few bellows: at the Predigerkirche there are 3, at the Reglerkirche 5, while others have more of them. E.g., at St. Dominic's in Prague there are 12 bellows, but of course that organ has 71 stops. That same number of bellows serves 50 stops in the Cathedral at Uppsala. At St. Mary's in Lübeck there are 16 bellows for 54 stops; see Mattheson's Appendix to Niedt.[§]

[*] actually p. 84.

[†] See p. 173; but there it appears that Mattheson's note refers to the organ at Elmshorn, not that at Gröningen.

[‡] *Organum gruningense redivivum*, §.6.

[§] p. 190.

§. 71.

In small organs where there is not enough room, the bellows may also be placed in the church's attic, or at least high up enough that they cannot be trod, but must be pulled [upward] by ropes. Sometimes they are placed in the lower section of the organ [case], or behind it, and they are lifted. To insure that they are not drawn up too high, straps are attached between the folds. If in a small positiv there is really no room at all, then a double bellows is built, that provides a constant supply of wind even though only one bellows is being depressed or pumped.[¶] In sum, a bellows may be trod, lifted or drawn up.[||] The person entrusted with this task is called a "Calcant", meaning a bellows treader. Some people call him "Sine me potestis nihil facere," i.e., "Without me you can do nothing." Beer, however, in Chap. 54 of his *Musikalische Discurse*,[**]

[¶] This refers to a single feeder bellows that supplies a reservoir or well.

[||] These correspond to the placement of the bellows, as Adlung has just described it. If the bellows are on the floor, they may be lifted manually; if they are placed high up, they may be drawn up by means of a rope and pulley; if they are somewhat elevated above the floor level, to allow the action of a bellows pole, then they are trod.

[**] p. 185.

48 Kap. V. Von den Bälgen und Windführungen.

brauch der Worte Christi, im 54 Kap. der musikalischen Discurse mit Recht bestraft. In der Stiftsorgel St. Severi in Erfurt, it. zu St. Wenceslai in Naumburg, findet sich eine andere Art die Bälge zu treten; denn es liegen dieselben auch hoch; doch anstatt der Stricke hat man starke Latten in rimis, mit einem hervorragenden Zahne, darauf man tritt, also:

Oben ist diese Stange an den Calculaturclaven bevestiget, und lauft zwischen zwoen Leisten abwärts, wenn auf den Zahn *a* getreten wird. Durch Treppen steigt man in die Höhe; und was die Einbildungskraft der Orgelmacher noch mehr an die Hand giebt. So werden z. Er. in der Augustusburg zu Weissenfelß die drey Bälge, welche 9′ lang und 4½′ breit sind, auf eine besondere Art, mit neun eisernen Ketten, auf 3 großen hölzernen Walzen, da von der einen ab- und auf eine andere aufgewunden wird, und mit 3 Rädern gezogen; welches besser zu sehen als zu beschreiben ist. S. Trosts Beschreibung der weissenfelßischen Orgel. S. 16.

§. 72.

Endlich sind auch die Gegengewichte (antipondia) nicht zu vergessen. Hier wollen wir sie nur kennen lernen. Man bevestiget hinter dem Balge in gewissen Säulen, oder wie es sich schickt, Stücke Holz oder Stein, oder was sich am besten gebrauchen läßt: dieses muß aber um seine Are beweglich seyn. Dessen oberer Theil wird durch Stricke an die obere Platte des Balges verbunden, etwann also:

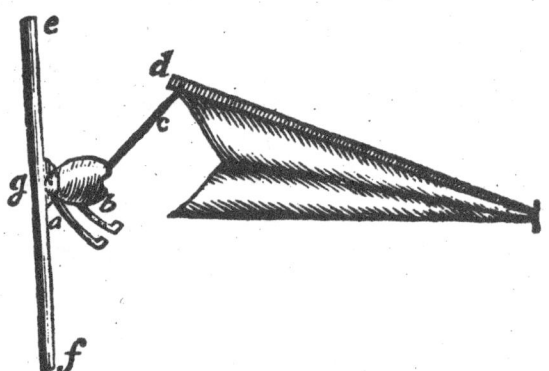

Wenn der Balg niederliegt; so liegt das Gegengewicht auch tiefer, weil dessen natürliche Schwere nach dem centro der Erden drückt. Wird der Balg bis in *d* aufgezogen, so wird durch den Strick *c* das Gewicht *b* mit aufgezogen, weil es an der Säule *e a f* bevestiget ist, und bey *g* sich bewegt. Also hilft es den Balg wieder abwärts ziehen. Das heißt das Gegengewicht. Was davon zu halten, kömmt unten vor. s. Werkmeisters Orgelprobe. Kap. 20. S. 46.

§. 73.

48 Ch. V. Concerning the Bellows and Wind Ducts.

rightly criticizes this as a misuse of Christ's words.[*] In the organ of the Collegiate Church of St. Severus in Erfurt, and also at St. Wenceslaus in Naumburg, there is yet another way to pump the bellows. There the bellows are located up high, but instead of ropes there are heavy slats [travelling] in slots, fitted with protruding pegs to be trod down, thus:

Up top these rods are fastened to the bellows-poles, and they travel down between two [guide-]strips when someone steps on the peg *a*. Steps are supplied to climb up [high enough to operate this apparatus]. There are other bellows mechanisms as well, depending on the organbuilder's imagination. For example, in the Augustusburg at Weissenfels the 3 bellows, each 9′ long and 4½′ wide, are operated in a special way, by 9 iron chains that are wound back and forth around 3 great wooden rollers, drawn by 3 wheels; this is better seen than described;[†] see Trost's *Beschreibung der weissenfelssischen Orgel*, p. 16.

[*] John 15:5.

[†] Most of this vague sentence is quoted directly from Trost's book; Adlung himself may not have been able to visualize the mechanism it describes.

§. 72.

Finally, the counter-weights or *antipondia* should not be forgotten, though here we will only become acquainted with them. These are pieces of wood, stone or some other easily available material, fastened to special posts or whatever surface is handy behind the bellows. Each one, however, must be movable upon an axis. The upper part [of the weight] is linked with a rope to the upper bellows-board, thus

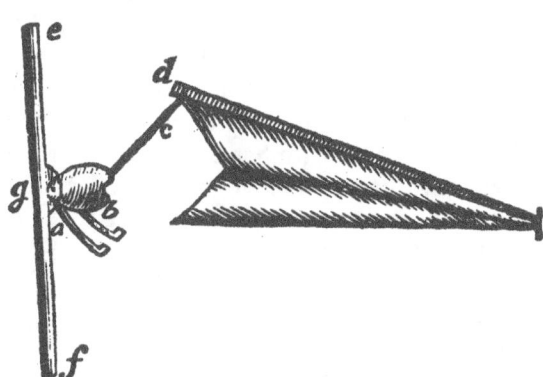

When the bellows collapses, then the counterweight falls, due to the force of gravity. As the bellows is drawn upward to point *d*, the rope *c* draws the weight upward with it, since the weight is affixed to the post *e a f* and moves at point *g*. Thus it helps to draw the bellows downward. This is what a counter-weight is. An evaluation of them will follow below;[‡] see Werkmeister's *Orgelprobe*, Chap. 20, p. 46.

[‡] See §.371ff.; see also Adlung's description of the organ in the Stadtkirche at Jena, §.302.

Kap. V. Von den Bälgen und Windführungen.

§. 73.

Es folgen die **Windkanäle**, die den Wind von den Bälgen nach der Orgel führen. Wenn die Bälge mit Winde versehen, so gehen unter der Oeffnung derselben, davon §. 62. gesagt ist, Kanäle weg, und fangen den Wind aus den Bälgen auf; und diese haben die §. 62. beschriebenen **Kanalventile** in sich. Hernach aber laufen diese Kanäle zusammen in einen großen Kanal, der zuweilen 2 Schuh, auch wol mehr, auch weniger, dick und hoch ist. Oder die Pedalbälge schicken ihren Wind in einen besondern Kanal, die Manualbälge auch. In oder nicht weit vor der Orgel theilen sich diese Kanäle in kleinere Arme, deren einer nach dieser, der andere nach jener Windlade zu gehet. Zuweilen gehen etliche Arme nach einer Lade; doch alle in den Windkasten. Die Kanäle sind viereckigt, von Brettern oder Bohlen gemacht, und wohl verbunden, auch mit Leder überlegt, wo die Fugen sind, und durchaus mit der Masse bestrichen, wovon §. 38. zu lesen, damit ja der Wind sich nicht verschleiche. An dem äussern Hauptkanal wird ein Loch gebohrt, etwa Fingers dick, darein man die **Windprobe** [18] steckt, um den Wind, so oft es nöthig, abmessen zu können: doch mag das Loch seyn, wo es will, so muß es, nach den principiis der Mechanik, stets einerley Effekt haben. Ausser dem Gebrauch verwahrt man das Loch mit einem Zäpfchen, bis man es braucht.

§. 74.

In den Kanälen liegen zuweilen mancherley **Ventile**. Denn etliche Orgeln haben ein **Hauptventil**, wodurch die ganze Orgel, das Pedal und Manual zugleich schweiget, wenn gleich die Bälge getreten, die Register offen, und die palmulae niedergedrückt sind. Dieses Ventil liegt in dem Hauptkanale, und schließt den Wind aus, daß er gar nicht zur Orgel kommen kann. Wo aber die Pedalbälge a part sind, da hat man auch ordentlich zwey Hauptventile, eins für alle Manuale, welches in den Hauptkanal der Manualbälge gelegt wird, und das andere für das Pedal. Zuweilen wird in die besonderen Kanale, die nach jeder Lade gehen, ein Ventil gelegt, daher ein Clavier klingt, das andere aber nicht. Zuweilen hat ein Clavier mehr Ventile als eins; zuweilen sind diese besondern Ventile da, und die vorigen allgemeinen auch, welches desto besser ist. Insgesammt nennet man dieses **Sperrventile**. Insbesondere bekommen sie auch Namen von den Theilen, welche sie versperren. Z. Ex. das **Brustventil**, **Pedalventil** u. s. w. In der Görlitzer Orgel sind 9 Ventile. Als 1) zum Hauptwerke, 2) zum Oberwerke, 3) zur Brust, 4) zum großen Seitenbasse, 5) zum kleinen Seitenbasse, 6) zum Hinteroberbasse, 7) zum Hinterunterbasse, 8) zu beyden Engeln über dem Brustpositive, 9) zu der Calcantenglocke. Dabey noch andere seyn könnten. Die Orgel zu Königsberg, im Löbenicht hat 4 Sperrventile, und 1 Hauptventil, damit alles auf einmal kann abge-

---

[18] Die Beschreibung der **Windprobe** hat der Hr. Verfasser bis ins 17. Kap. versparet, allwo sie §. 460. erfolget.

Ch. V. Concerning the Bellows and Wind Ducts.

§. 73.

Next are the wind-ducts that carry the wind from the bellows to the organ. When the bellows are provided with wind, then it is borne away through the opening described in §.62 into the ducts. In these are found the duct-valves described in §.62. Thereupon these ducts all run together into one large trunk, two feet deep and wide, more or less. Or the pedal bellows may send their wind into a separate duct, and the manual bellows send theirs into another. Either within the organ or slightly before they reach it, these trunks branch out into smaller ducts, one leading to one windchest, one to another. Sometimes several of these branch-ducts lead to one chest; but all of the ducts end at the pallet boxes. The ducts are quadrangular, being made of boards or planks tightly joined, overlaid with leather at the joints, and thoroughly smeared with glue (as described in §.38) to keep the wind from seeping out. On the exterior of the main trunk a hole is bored, about the width of a finger, into which the windgauge is inserted[18] whenever necessary, in order to measure the wind pressure. Wherever the hole is located, it must, according to the principles of mechanics, register the same result. When it is not being used, the hole is stopped with a plug until it is again needed.

§. 74.

In the ducts there are from time to time various ventils. Some organs have a main ventil by which the entire organ, manuals and pedal alike, is silenced, even though the bellows are being pumped, the stops are pulled, and the keys are being depressed. This ventil is located in the main trunk, and blocks the wind so that none of it can enter the organ. Wherever the pedal bellows are separate, there are usually two main ventils, one for all the manuals (set into the main trunk of the manual bellows) and the other for the pedal. Sometimes the ducts that lead into each separate chest each have a separate ventil, in which case one keyboard can sound while another cannot. At times a keyboard has more than one ventil, and at other times both the particular ventils as well as the universal ventils (described above) are provided, which is all the better. These ventils are known collectively as cut-out ventils. They also receive more specific names from the divisions that they block off, for example, the "Brustventil," the "Pedalventil," etc. In the Görlitz organ there are 9 ventils, as follows:* 1) for the Hauptwerk, 2) for the Oberwerk, 3) for the Brustpositiv, 4) for the great Seitenbass, 5) for the small Seitenbass, 6) for the Hinteroberbass, 7) for the Hinterunterbass,† 8) for both angels above the Brustpositiv,‡ and 9) for the Calcant-bell.§ There could be others, as well. The organ in the Löbenichtkirche at Königsberg has 4 cut-out ventils and one main ventil so that everything can be blocked off at once. Then there are those malicious or-

---

18) The author has saved the description of the windgauge for chap. 17, where it will be found in §.460. [Albrecht]

---

* The list of ventils is taken directly from Boxberg, p.[5].

† This and the previous 3 divisions all belong to the pedal; see the stoplist in Chap. 10, §.301.

‡ On pp. [5–6] Boxberg reports: "The two small angels that sit above the Brustpositiv, in front of the middle Hauptwerk [pipe] flat, are put to especially good use. Each one has a trumpet in its mouth, yet this single pipe produces eight absolutely clearly perceptible pitches of the 8' Hautbois that stands in the Brust[werk]..."

§ The device by which the organist signals the bellows pumper to begin or to cease winding the organ. It is of course not a ventil, nor does Boxberg list it as one; its inclusion here is the result either of misunderstanding or oversight.

abgeschlossen werden. Sonst haben manche tückische Orgelmacher noch heimliche Ventile in solchen Kanälen, die sie nach der Zeit schelmischer Weise halb zuziehen, ohne daß jemand davon etwas gewahr wird; dadurch entgeht dem Werke der zulängliche Wind, es wird unrein ꝛc. und scheint ganz verdorben. Dadurch wollen sie die Gemeinden glaubend machen, als sey die Lade nichts nutz, und müsse man eine neue machen, die sie hernach anstatt der noch guten alten hinsetzen, sich ihre Arbeit brav bezahlen lassen, und die vorige Lade wo anders anbringen. Diese Spitzbübereyen sind von ehrlichen Orgelmachern weit entfernet, und wenn der Direktor des Baues beständig bey der Verfertigung und Zusammensetzung der Theile gegenwärtig ist, so kann ein solcher Betrug wol verhütet werden. S. Werkmeisters Organum grüningense rediuiuum. §. 71. it. Orgelprobe Kap. 24. S. 59. Die vorigen guten Ventile werden durch Registraturen auf- und zugeschlossen, welche meistens unter den andern Registern ihren Platz nehmen, da an den Manubriis die Stangen, Wellen und andere Theile sind, bis an den Sitz des Ventils, welches alsdann dadurch geöfnet wird.

Das VI. Kapitel.
Von dem Pfeifwerke überhaupt.

Inhalt.

§. 75. Welche Instrumente die ersten gewesen. §. 76. Namen der Pfeifen. §. 77. Theile dieses Kapitels. §. 78. 79. 80. 81. Wörter-Erklärung. §. 82. Proportion der Pfeifen. §. 83. 84. Was F, Fach, Repetiren, Dito, Aufschnitt und Intonation sey. §. 85. Materie der Pfeifen. §. 86. Silber und Gold. §. 87. Eisen, Zinn, Bley. §. 88. Das Gießen der Pfeifen. §. 89. Proportion der Länge und Weite. §. 90. Figur, Loth, und Labium des corporis. §. 91. Der Fuß. §. 92. Der Aufschnitt. §. 93. Die Intonation. §. 94. Oeschen und Bärte. §. 95. Materie der hölzernen Pfeifen. §. 96. Figur. §. 97. Verwandlung des Zirkels ins Quadrat. §. 98. In der Figur vorgestellt. §. 99. Eben das bey den conischen Pfeifen. §. 100. 101. Andere hölzerne Pfeifen. §. 102. 103. Der Fuß und andere Dinge. §. 104. 105. Von dem Schnarrwerk. §. 106. 107. 108. Von den gedeckten Pfeifen. §. 109. Allerhand Oefnungen derselben. §. 110. Das Kröpfen der Pfeifen, und die schwellenden Register.

§. 75.

Weil alle Pfeifen einige Affectiones unter sich gemein haben, oder doch einige derselben; so ist nöthig davon zu reden, ehe wir die Register selbst nach der Reihe betrachten. Den Ursprung der Pfeifen leitet man nicht unbillig von den Vögeln her, als welche die Menschen haben singen hören, und daher auf die Erfindung der Pfeifen gefallen sind. Die heil. Schrift führt als den ältesten Künstler in dieser Sache den Jubal an; ob aber die Sayteninstrumente eher erfunden worden, als die Blasinstrumente, daran liegt uns nichts. Diese aber scheinen simpler, und daher leichter zu erfinden; wiewol
die

ganbuilders who put secret ventils into the ducts, that they roguishly close halfway at some later time, without anyone being aware of it. Thus sufficient wind is denied the organ, and it sounds out of tune and completely ruined.* In this way they try to make the congregation believe that the chests are worthless and must be replaced. Then they proceed to replace the still sound chests with old ones, get well paid for their work, and carry off the good chests somewhere else. Such chicanery is far beneath honest organbuilders, and when the director† of the project is present for the construction and erection of the parts, then such deception can be avoided; see Werkmeister's *Organum Gruningense redivivum*, §.71, as well as his *Orgelprobe*, Chapter 24, p. 59. The good ventils described above are opened and closed by stops that are usually located under the other stops, since the stopknobs are connected to rods, trundles and other parts until they reach the location of the ventil and thus open it.

* See also §.381 and §.240.

† See §.240.

Chapter VI.
Concerning the Pipework in General.
Contents:

§.75. Which instruments were first. §.76. Names of the pipes. §.77. Sections of this chapter. §.78. 79. 80. 81. Explanation of terms. §. 82. Proportions of the pipes. §. 83. 84. What *F*, *Fach*, *Repetiren*, *Dito*[sic], *Aufschnitt*, and *Intonation* are. §.85. Materials used for pipes. §.86. Silver and gold. §. 87. Iron, tin and lead. §.88. Casting the pipes. §.89. Proportion of the length and width. §. 90. Shaping, soldering and [fashioning the] upper lip of the [pipe] body. §.91. The foot. §.92. The cut-up. §.93. The voicing. §.94. Eyelets and beards. §.95. Materials [used] for wooden pipes. §.96. An illustration. §.97. Conversion of a circle into a square. §.98. Illustrated in a figure. §.99. The same [applied to] conical pipes. §.100. 101. Other wooden pipes. §.102. 103. The foot and other matters. §. 104. 105. Reed pipes. §. 106. 107. 108. Stopped pipes. §. 109. Various openings in them. §.110. Mitering the pipes, and stops that swell [in volume].

§. 75.

Since all pipes, or at least a number of them, have certain affinities in common, it is necessary to speak of these before considering each stop individually. It is not unreasonable to derive the origin of pipes from birds that humans heard singing; this suggested to them the invention of pipes. Holy Scripture cites Jubal* as the oldest artist in this matter. Whether stringed instruments were invented before winds does not concern us. The latter would appear to be less complex, and thus easier to invent,†

* Genesis 4:21: "His [Jabal's] brother's name was Jubal; he was the father of all those who play the lyre and pipe."

† This statement may reflect the less technically advanced state of wind instruments at the time Adlung was writing (the 1720's), in contrast to the more highly developed strings: Stradivarius had already created his violins, while valved brass instruments and the Boehm flute were yet to come.

die Menschen casu fortuito auf den Klang eines Fadens so wol zuerst fallen können, als auf das Pfeifwerk.

§. 76.

Den Namen der Pfeife anlangend; so sagt man im Niederdeutschen auch Pipe, und ist also Bärpfeife und Bärpipe einerley. So ists auch bey andern. Die Lateiner haben zwey Wörter, die am meisten bekannt sind: fistula und tibia. Das erste wollen einige von φυσάω, inflo, ich blase an, herleiten; das andere heißt ein Schienbein, und ist wol wegen der Aehnlichkeit der Form denen Pfeifen solcher Name beygeleget worden, als die solchen langen Röhren nicht ungleich sind. Etliche machen zwischen fistula und tibia einen Unterschied, daß das letzte solche Pfeifen andeute, die durch mancherley Löcher ihren Sonum verändern können, z. Ex. die Hautbois, Querflöten u. d. gl.; die fistulae aber thäten dieses nicht. Z. Ex. die Pfeifen in der Orgel. Es wird aber von andern dieser Unterschied nicht beobachtet. Das hebräische Wort ist נקב (nekeph) von perforare, durchlöchern, weil alle Pfeifen durchlöchert sind. Συριγξ, bedeutet bey den Griechen auch so viel, und mag wol von dem Zischen einer Pfeife herstammen. S. Prätorius Synt. Mus. T. I. P. II. Membr. II. c. III. pag. 326. da er de *fistula* handelt; c. IV. pag. 331. und folg. handelt er de *tibia*, als welche er von jener unterscheidet, und sagt, das dieser im Hebräischen חליל, hol, respondire. Apollo, oder Pallas, oder Marsyas, oder Hyagnis sollen sie erfunden haben. Kircher in Musurgia L. VI. P. III. c. 2. u. folg. nennt aber fistulas, wo die mancherley Löcher sind, daher er S. 497. von der fistula tristoma, die 3 Löcher hat, handelt, und S. 499. de fistala hexastoma, die 6 Löcher bekömmt, rc. Die Querpfeife nennet er tibiam militarem, die auch viel Löcher hat. Von fistula kömmt das bekannte Fistuliren her, da einer ein Falset singt, oder, wie es andere ausdrücken, da einer mit halber Stimme singt. S. Matthesons Crit. Mus. Tom. I. pag. 111. not. (g.) Ob die Blasinstrumente den Besayteten, oder diese, jenen vorzuziehen, davon lese man, was Kuhnau im musikal. Quacksalber S. 417. und 431. vorträgt.

§. 77.

Wir bekümmern uns um solche Dinge nicht viel, sondern merken nur an, daß die große Mannigfaltigkeit des Pfeifwerks nach und nach aufgekommen, und das noch heut zu Tage viele neue Arten desselben üblich werden. Da aber die Orgeln so alt nicht sind, als andere Instrumente; so ist leicht zu erachten, daß die Orgelmacher von andern Instrumenten Gelegenheit genommen, allerhand Arten der Pfeifen in den Orgeln anzubringen. Und dabey wollen wir itzo stehen bleiben, als die wir uns um nichts, als Orgelpfeifen zu bekümmern haben. Doch wollen wir in diesem Kapitel lauter generalia abhandeln, welche nach der verschiedenen Art der Pfeifen unter sich selbst unterschieden sind. Daher wir handeln:

Ch. VI. Concerning the Pipework in General.

although humans might just as easily have stumbled first upon the sound made by a string as by a pipe.

§. 76.

Regarding the name "pipe"* (Pfeife), Low German says *Pipe*, and thus Bärpfeife and Bärpipe are the same. It is the same with other [instruments or stops] as well.† Latin has two widely-known words, *fistula* and *tibia*. Some derive the first of these from φυτάω, *inflo*, "I blow into." The other means "shin-bone," and may well have gotten this name from the shape of its pipes, that are not unlike long tubes such [as shin-bones]. Some make a distinction between *fistula* and *tibia*, using the latter term to denote pipes that have a number of holes to alter their sound (e.g., the oboe, transverse flute, and the like), and the [former term,] *fistula*, for those without this capability (e.g., the pipes in an organ). Others do not recognize this distinction. The Hebrew word is נֶקֶב (nekeph), from *perforare*, "to perforate," since all pipes are perforated. Σύριγξ [*syrinx*] in Greek means the same thing, and may well stem from the hissing noise made by a pipe. In his *Syntagma Musicum*, Vol. I, Part II, Membrum II, Chap. III, p. 326, Praetorius treats the *fistula*; in Chap. IV, p. 331f., he treats the *tibia*, which he differentiates from the *fistula* by saying that it corresponds to the Hebrew חָדִיד, "hollow." He credits its invention to Apollo, or Pallas [Athene], or Marsyas or Hyagnis.‡ Kircher, in his *Musurgia*, Book VI, Part III, Chap. 2f. [pp. 497f.], calls *fistulas* those [pipes] that have a number of holes; thus on p. 497 he treats the *fistula tristoma*, that has 3 holes, on p. 499 the *fistula hexastoma* that has 6 holes, etc. The transverse flute, that also has many holes, he labels *tibia militarem*. From *fistula* comes the well-known expression *fistuliren*, meaning to sing in falsetto or, to say it another way, to sing in half voice;§ see Mattheson's *Critica Musica*, Vol. I, p. 111, note *g*. Concerning whether brass or stringed instruments are to be given pride of place, see what Kuhnau says in his *Musikalischer Quacksalber*, p. 417[f.] and 431[f.].

§. 77.

Such matters need not concern us much; only take note that a great variety of pipes¶ has gradually been developed, and many new types are in use nowadays. Since the organ is not as old as other instruments, it is easy to understand how organbuilders have seized the opportunity to introduce all sorts of pipes from other instruments into the organ. Here we will let the matter rest, since we are concerned only with organ pipes. The rest of this chapter we will devote solely to general matters, by which the various types of pipes are distinguished from each other. Thus we will treat:

---

* Adlung uses this term throughout the following two paragraphs in a generic sense: "pipe" as the prototype of wind instruments.

† e.g., Hohlpfeife and Holpipe.

‡ The last two named are the legendary inventors, masters and propagators of the art of the Greek *aulos*, or reed pipe. It is a subsequent mistranslation of this term into Latin as *tibia* that caused Praetorius to link their names with the flute.

§ *Fistelstimme* in German signifies the falsetto voice.

¶ i.e., wind instruments.

Kap. VI. Von dem Pfeifwerke überhaupt.

1.) Von den Eigenschaften, welche allen Pfeifen gemein sind.
2.) Von denen, welche bey den metallenen Pfeifen zu beobachten.
3.) Von dem, was insonderheit bey den hölzernen Pfeifen vorkömmt.
4.) Von den Schnarrwerken.
5.) Von den gedeckten Pfeifen.

Denn bey uns sind ordentlich die Pfeifen entweder aus Metall, oder aus Holz: Sie sind weiter entweder Flöt= oder Schnarrwerke: Sie sind endlich entweder offen oder gedeckt.

§. 78.

1.) Was das erste anlanget; so sind etliche termini zu erklären, welche in dieser Abhandlung zuweilen vorkommen. Ein Fuß ist von mancherley Art. Die Rheinländischen sind ordentlich $\frac{1}{2}$ Elle groß; und deren werden 16 auf eine Ruthe genommen, zuweilen 15. it. 14. Die Ellen aber selbst sind auch verschiedener Größe. Ein geometrischer Fuß ist größer: Denn die geometrae theilen die Ruthe in 10 Theile, welche sie Füße nennen; müßte also 1 geometrischer Fuß $1\frac{3}{5}$ Rheinländisch halten, das ist fast eine Elle, wenn nemlich die rheinländische Ruthe 16' lang angenommen wird. Hier merke man nur die Zeichen. (°) bedeutet die Ruthe, als 2°, 2 Ruthen. (') aber die Schuh, oder Fuß, als 2' Fuß. Jeder Fuß wird wieder in 10 Theile oder Zolle getheilet, das bedeuten die 2 Striche über einer oder mehrern Zahlen, als 3'', drey Zoll, it. 12'', 12 Zoll, 4° 5' 7'', sind 4 Ruthen, 5 Schuhe und 7 Zoll. Auf solche Weise werden wir es der Kürze wegen allegiren. Hier behalten wir meistens die Rheinländischen, da ein Daumen mit seiner Breite ohngefehr einen Zoll austrägt: aber wenn die Rechnungen vorkommen; so bedienet man sich der Geometrischen, als welche, wegen der Decimalrechnung, bequemer sind. Sonst bedeutet das Wort Fuß bey der Pfeife den untersten Theil, wo sie angeblasen wird.

§. 79.

Ein Zirkel ist ein runder Kreis, dessen Theile alle gleich weit von einem gemeinen Centro oder Mittelpunkt entfernet sind. Diese Linie um das Centrum heißt die Peripherie, oder der Umkreis. Die längste Distanz eines Punkts vom andern Punkte in der Peripherie, heißt der Diameter, oder Durchmesser, welche Linie allein durch das Centrum gezogen wird. Deren Hälfte, das ist die Linie vom Centro bis zur Peripherie heißt der Semidiameter. Ein Cylinder ist ein solcher Körper der zwar in die Dicke zirkelrund ist, aber nicht in die Höhe; dabey aber durchaus von gleicher Weite ist. Z. Er.

Ch. VI. Concerning the Pipework in General.

1). the characteristics that all pipes have in common.
2). the characteristics to be noted in metal pipes.
3.) those that appear particularly in wooden pipes.
4.) reed pipes.
5.) stopped pipes.

It is our normal practice, then, to make pipes either of metal or of wood; furthermore, they are either flue or reed pipes (Flöt-* oder Schnarrwerke); and finally, they are either open or stopped.

* Agricola uses this designation in a more restrictive sense; see Supplement to Chap. 10, p. 286, n. ‡ (Altenburg stoplist)

§. 78

1.) Regarding the first of these,† there are a number of terms that need to be explained, since they appear from time to time in this treatise. A foot (Fuß) can be a number of different lengths. That of the Rhineland is normally a half-ell long, and there are 16 of them within a rod (though at times only 15 or 14). Ells themselves, however, are also of various sizes. A geometric foot is larger, since the geometrists divide the rod into 10 sections that they call "feet." Thus one geometric foot must be considered equivalent to 1 3/5 Rhineland feet, in other words, nearly an ell, if the Rhineland rod is considered to be 16′ long.‡ Here one need note only the signs:§ (°) means a rod, and thus 2° is 2 rods. (′) signifies foot, and thus 2′ is 2 feet. Each foot is further divided into 10 sections or inches, which are indicated by two strokes above [and after] one or more numbers: 3″ is 3 inches, 12″ is 12 inches. 4°, 5′, 7″ is 4 rods, 5 feet and 7 inches. We will adopt this method for the sake of brevity. For the most part we will follow the Rhineland [system], in which the width of a thumb is about one inch. When the calculations appear,¶ however, we will make use of the decimal system, since it computes by decimals and is thus more convenient. Note that the word "foot" also means the lowest section of a pipe, where it is winded.

† i.e., the characteristics that all pipes have in common.

‡ For more precise information on old units of measure, see: Fritz Verdenhalven, *Alte Maße, Münzen und Gewichte aus dem deutschen Sprachgebiet*. Neustadt an der Aisch: Verlag Degener & Co., 1968. Adlung is assuming that the rod is a constant measurement, and thus the size of a foot must vary, according to how many feet are in a rod. Note that in Vol. II of the *Syntagma musicum*, on the verso of the title page of *Theatrum Instrumentorum*, Praetorius depicts a ruler half a *Schuh* in length, divided off into *Zolle*.

§ Adlung is writing only for the organist, not for the organbuilder; thus understanding differences in measurements is not essential.

¶ in §.97.

§. 79.

A circle is a round ring, any part of which is equidistant from a common center or midpoint. This line around the center is called the *Peripherie* or circumference. The greatest distance from one point to another upon the circumference is called the diameter, a line that must always pass through the center. Half of the circumference, i.e., a line from the center to the circumference, is called the radius. A cylinder is a form that is circular in its width, yet not in its height, which is constantly of the same width, e.g.:

Kap. VI Von dem Pfeifwerke überhaupt. 53

So sind die meisten Pfeifen. Ein Conus ist auch rund: aber dabey spitzig an einem Ende, am andern breit, etwan also: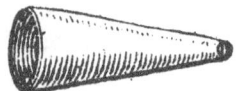

Wenn oben die Spitze des Coni abgeschnitten ist; so ist es ein Conus truncatus, also:

Wenn alle Winkel und alle Seiten auf diese Art ☐ gleich sind; so ist es ein Quadrat oder Viereck: sind aber die Winkel gleich und die Seiten ungleich; so ist es ein quadratum oblongum, ein länglicht Viereck, z. Er. ▭ oder ▯.

§. 80.

So misset man die Körper aus, und beschreibt ihre Größe und Form. Aber bey den Orgelpfeifen wird auch der Sonus gemessen. Denn man hat eine Pfeife etwan 8′ hoch und in gehöriger Weite angeblasen, und ihrem Sonum observirt: so oft man nun diesen Klang die Höhe oder Tiefe nach, bey einer andern auch antrift; so oft nennet man es auch 8′, wenn gleich nach der veränderten Weite das corpus kürzer oder länger ist, als 8′. Und so auch bey andern. Dieser terminus wird gar oft vorkommen in folgenden Kapiteln: dabey merke man überhaupt, daß man allezeit das Register nach dessen größesten Pfeife, oder nach dem großen C. benennet, wenn es so weit hinunter gehet. Z. Er. Principal 4′, oder 4 F, it. 4 Fuß. Da ist die größte Pfeife, oder das große C 4 Fuß lang. Gemshorn 8′, eben so. Doch verstehet man nicht allemal eine mathematische Höhe, sondern wenn die tiefste Pfeife den achtfüßigen Sonum von sich giebt; so ist es genug deswegen auch oft dazu gesetzt wird; 4′ Ton; 8′ Ton, ꝛc. ꝛc. Was aber in der Weite zuweilen fehlet, das wird in der Länge wieder ersetzt, und was in der Länge zu wenig ist, das wird in der Weite wieder beygebracht. Es ist also ein Unterschied unter den Redensarten 4 Fuß, und 4 Fuß Ton. Jene zeiget an, es sey das corpus von solcher Größe, wo nicht in der Länge, doch in der Weite: Diese aber deutet an, es habe die Pfeife zwar einen so tiefen sonum, als eine 4füßige zu haben pfleget, aber deren Körper sey viel kleiner. Und diese Art zu reden kömmt bey gedeckten Registern und Schnarrwerken oft vor. Also heißt das Gedakt 8 F. Ton, da dessen größte Pfeife ohngefehr nur 4′ ist: aber durch das Decken bekömmt die Pfeife eine Tiefe wie eine 8füßige. So hat auch der 16füßige Subbaß die größte Pfeife nur 8′ groß. Auch hat solchergestalt in Schnarrwerken das 8füßige Regal oft gar kleine Pfeifen, kaum etliche Zolle lang. Also kömmt es auf den sonum an.

Ch. VI. Concerning the Pipework in General.

Most pipes assume this shape. A cone is also round, but pointed at one end and wide at the other, rather like this: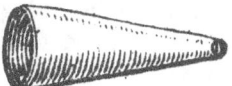

If the tip of the cone is cut off on top, then it is a truncated cone, thus:

If all angles and all sides are equal like this illus., then it is a square ▢ ; if however, the angles are equal and the sides unequal, then it is a rectangle, e.g. ▭ or ▯ .

§. 80.

That is how to measure the body [of a pipe] and to describe its size and shape. But with organ pipes the pitch is also measured. Someone first sounded a pipe about 8′ tall and of a normal width, and took note of its pitch. Now whenever anyone encounters a sound this low or high in another [pipe], he calls it 8′, even though the body of the pipe is [actually] shorter or longer than 8′ due to the variable width. The same holds true for other [pitches]. This term will appear again and again in the following chapters. With regard to it, take note that a stop is always designated by its largest pipe, the great C, if it goes down that low; for example, Principal 4′, or 4 F. or 4 Foot. In this case, the largest pipe, or the great C, is 4 feet long. The same is the case with Gemshorn 8′. This does not always mean an [exact] mathematical height, but rather that the lowest pipe produces an eight-foot pitch; thus [8′] suffices [as a designation]. For this reason, though, there is often added [the indication] 4′ pitch, 8′ pitch, etc. What may at times be lacking in the width is made up for in the height, and what is lacking in the height is made up for in the width. Thus there is a distinction between the expressions "4-foot" and "4-foot pitch." The former indicates that the body of the pipe is of that size (more or less, depending on the width). The latter, however, denotes that the pipes have as low a pitch as is usual in a 4-foot pipe, but that their bodies are much smaller. This way of speaking is often applied to stopped registers and to reeds. Thus a Gedakt is said to have 8 F. pitch, even though its largest pipe is only about 4′ [tall], and it only attains the depth of an 8-foot pipe by being stopped. In the same way, the largest pipe of the 16-foot Subbass is only 8′ long. Thus also among the reeds the 8-foot Regal often has very small pipes, barely a few inches long. So everything depends on the pitch.

§. 81.

Doch hört man diese zweyerley Redensarten oft vermischen, daß man von offenen Pfeifen sagt: Fußton. Z. Er. Gemshorn 4 Fußton; Quinte 3 Fußton, u. s. w. welches nur mit 4' und 3' ꝛc. könnte angedeutet werden. Hingegen, da in Gedakten und Schnarrwerken die Körper selten die Höhe haben, die mit dem sono überein kömmt, sondern ordinär viel kleiner sind, da pflegt man ordentlich zu sagen: 8 Fußton, 16 Fußton, und s. f. anzuzeigen, der Ton deute zwar ein so großes corpus an: aber würklich sey es nicht so groß. Doch läßt man das Wort Ton oft weg, und sagt, z. Er. Gedakt 8 Fuß, anstatt 8 Fußton, u. s. w. So stehet es gemeiniglich auch an den Manubriis der Register. Wer aber die Register weis, ob sie offen, oder gedeckt, oder Schnarrwerke sind, der wird auch sogleich zu beurtheilen wissen, ob die angegebene Größe von dem sono zu verstehen, oder auch zugleich von dem corpore der größten Pfeife des Registers.

§. 82.

Es wird aber der Fuß der Pfeife niemals mit gerechnet; sondern blos der obere Theil vom Aufschnitte an bis an die Höhe. Daher z. Er. die Pfeife 1' hoch seyn kann, der Fuß aber ist wol noch eins so groß: denn dessen Größe ist willkürlich. Ferner kann man aus der größten Pfeife auch die Größe der andern in eben dem Register, determiniren. Und zwar so oft man eine Oktave höher gestiegen, so sind die Füße der Pfeife nur die Hälfte zu nehmen. Z. Er. wenn das untere C, 16' ist; so ist das c nur 8', das $\bar{c}$ aber 4', das $\bar{\bar{c}}$ 2', das $\bar{\bar{\bar{c}}}$ 1', das $\bar{\bar{\bar{\bar{c}}}}$ $\frac{1}{2}'$ ꝛc. Wenn die Quinte 6' angegeben wird im C, so ist sie beym c 3', beym $\bar{c}$ $1\frac{1}{2}'$, beym $\bar{\bar{c}}$ $\frac{3}{4}'$, beym $\bar{\bar{\bar{c}}}$ $\frac{3}{8}'$ ꝛc. folglich allezeit die Hälfte kleiner. So verhält sichs auch in andern Tönen. Z. Er. wenn ich weis, daß im 8füßigen Principal die Quarte zum C, oder das F 6' hält; so wird das bloße f 3' halten, das $\bar{f}$ $1\frac{1}{2}'$, das $\bar{\bar{f}}$ $\frac{3}{4}'$: Denn daß die Quarte f, nicht aber die Quinte g diese Größe habe, ist aus dem Monochord klar.

§. 83.

Das F oder f, bedeutet also zuweilen so viel als Fuß: aber es wird auch gesetzt für fach; und dies letztere kömmt in solchen Registern vor, da auf einem jeden claue mehr als eine Pfeife sich befindet, ob es schon nur ein Register ist. Z. Er. Mixtur 6 fach, d. i. dies Register hat auf jedem claue sechs Pfeifen: Rauschpfeife 3 fach, d. i. es stehen drey Pfeifen auf jedem claue, folglich ist dies Register 3 fach, so, wie jenes 6 fach war. Wenn also das f bey Registern stehet, die mehrfach zu machen sind; so wird es meistens nicht Fuß, sondern fach bedeuten. Es werden zuweilen diese Register gar klein gemacht, so, daß das große C kaum $1\frac{1}{2}'$ oder noch kleiner ist. Daher die obern Oktaven so kleine Pfeifen bekommen müßten, daß man sie gar nicht zur Intonation

Ch. VI. Concerning the Pipework in General.

§. 81.

Yet one often hears these two expressions confused, so that open pipes are said to be at "__-foot pitch;" for example, Gemshorn four-foot pitch, Quinte 3-foot pitch, etc., that could be indicated simply by 4′ and 3′. On the other hand, since the bodies of stopped pipes and reeds are seldom of the full height indicated by the pitch, but are usually much smaller, it is usual to speak of "8-foot pitch" or "16-foot pitch," and thus to indicate that the pitch suggests a body of that size, but that it is actually not that tall. Yet the word "pitch" is often omitted, e.g., "Gedakt 8-foot" instead of "8-foot pitch." Ordinarily this is also the way it appears on the stop-knobs. Anyone who is familiar with the stops, whether they are open or stopped or reeds, will then of course be able to judge whether the size indicated means only the pitch, or the body of the stop's largest pipe as well.

§. 82.

The foot* of the pipe is never included in stating the pitch, but only the upper part from the cut-up to the top. Thus, for example, a pipe may be 1′ tall, while its foot is nearly another foot tall (since the foot's length is arbitrary). In addition the sizes of the other pipes in the stop can be determined from the largest pipe. That is, the footage of the pipe is to be halved with every octave higher the stop rises. For example, when the lowest C is 16′, then tenor c is only 8′, c′ is 4′, c″ is 2′, c‴ is 1′, c⁗ is ½′, etc. If the Quinte is indicated as 6′ at low C, then it is 3′ at tenor c, 1½′ at c′, ¾′ at c″, ⅜′ at c‴, etc., that is, consistently smaller by one half [the length]. [Pipes at] other pitches proceed by the same ratio as well. For example, if I know that the fourth above low C in an 8′ Principal, that is the F, is 6′ high, then the tenor f will be 3′, the f′ 1½′, and the f″ ¾′. The monochord makes it clear that it is [actually] the fourth [above c], f, and not the fifth, g, that is this size.†

* See §.91 below.

† This remark reflects the fact that many old organs bear mutation stop indications whose fractional lengths are rounded off to the nearest whole number, resulting in the Quinte being labelled "6′," "3′," "1½′." Subsequently most builders adopted the more precise practice of labelling quints with fractional numbers, e.g., 5⅓′, 2⅔′, 1⅓′.

§. 83.

The [letter] F or f is sometimes the abbreviation for "foot." But it may also stand for "ranks" (fach). The latter appears in stops that have more than one pipe [sounding] for each note (even though it is in fact only one stop). For example, "Mixtur 6 fach" means that this stop has six pipes for each note; "Rauschpfeife 3 fach" means that there are three pipes for each note. Consequently the latter stop is "3 ranks," just as the former is "6 ranks." Thus if [the letter] f is found on compound stops, it does not usually mean "foot," but rather "fach." At times these stops‡ are made [up of] very small [pipes], so that the great C is barely 1½′ or even smaller. Therefore the upper octaves would have to have such small pipes that they could not be made to speak.

‡ i.e., the mixtures.

Kap. VI. Von dem Pfeifwerke überhaupt. 55

tion bringen könnte. Z. Ex. in den Mixturen sind etliche Pfeifen im C kaum $\frac{1}{2}'$ lang, daher sie im c nur $\frac{1}{4}'$ halten, im $\bar{c}$ $\frac{1}{8}'$, im $\bar{\bar{c}}$ $\frac{1}{16}'$, im $\bar{\bar{\bar{c}}}$ $\frac{1}{32}'$. Nun theile man doch 1 Fuß in 32 Theile, und nehme einen solchen Theil zum corpore der Pfeifen, wie groß wird es werden? Daher kömmt es, daß man die Register repetiren läßt; das heißt, wenn die Pfeifen zu klein werden; so nimmt man die Mensur der vorigen Oktav noch einmal. Z. Ex. es wird ein Scharf durchgeführet bis auf das $\bar{\bar{c}}$; so nimmt man vom $\bar{\bar{c}}$ bis $\bar{\bar{\bar{c}}}$ eben die Größen, die von $\bar{c}$ bis $\bar{\bar{c}}$ gebraucht worden. Zuweilen heben die Register beym $\bar{c}$ schon an zu repetiren, und beym $\bar{\bar{c}}$ wieder. Zuweilen wird nur die untere Oktav gearbeitet, und in c bis $\bar{c}$, it. von $\bar{c}$ bis $\bar{\bar{c}}$, rc. bis hinaus wird allezeit die Mensur der untersten Oktav behalten. Daraus wird man verstehen was es sey, wenn Kap. 7. der repetirenden Zimbel gedacht wird, u. d. gl.

§. 84.

Es wird auch der terminus *dito* gefunden. Z. Ex. zu St. Ansgarii in Bremen stehet: Trommet 16′, dito 8′, das ist auch eine Trommet, doch in verschiedener Größe. Also bedeutet das Wort *dito* allezeit das vorhergehende Register. Der Aufschnitt der Pfeifen ist, da man zwischen den labiis eine Oefnung macht. Die Intonation ist, da man der Pfeife den gehörigen Klang giebt. Das Silpen ist, wenn die Pfeife sich überbläset. Das Kröpfen der Pfeifen wird §. 110. erkläret. Mehrere Kunstwörter werden im Folgenden hin und wieder vorkommen.

§. 85.

2.) Nun fragt sichs: Woraus macht man denn die Pfeifen? Außer der Orgel kann man fast alles darzu gebrauchen, alle Metalle, als Gold, Silber, Zinn, Bley, Kupfer, Eisen, Erz, Meßing, auch andere Dinge, als Glas, Erde,[19] Stein, Holz, Federn, Hörner, Schalen der Bäume, Papier,[20] rc. Das meiste läßt sich auch in den Orgeln appliciren, nur daß nicht alles Mode ist. Die Federn sind zu klein; die Erde, oder Töpferarbeit, wie auch das Glaß, sind zerbrechlich, und übel einzustimmen. Die Schalen der Bäume sind nicht beständig, auch

[19] Hierunter verstehet man den Thon, wie ihn die Töpfer verarbeiten. Die Frankfurter Zeitungen 1751. No. 144. thaten von einem solchen Werke Erwähnung, welches ein Töpfer zu Mayenburg in der Priegnitz, nahe bey Pritzwalk, Namens Weidner, auf eine sehr künstliche Art verfertiget, dessen Pfeifen alle von Thon gemacht worden, und auf welchem so schön, deutlich und rein könne gespielet werden, als auf der besten Orgel von Zinn. Es war ein Werk von 3 Registern.

[20] Ein Positiv von 6 Stimmen, dessen Pfeifen von purem Papiere sind, hat ehemals der berühmte Casparini der Aeltere, in die kaiserl. Kunstkammer zu Wien verfertiget; wie solches Boxberg in der Beschreibung der Görlitzer Orgel berichtet.

Ch. VI. Concerning the Pipework in General.

For example, some pipes in mixtures are barely ½' long at great C; therefore they are proportionately ¼' at tenor c, ⅛' at c', ¹⁄₁₆' at c'', and ¹⁄₃₂' at c'''. Now, if one were to divide one foot into 32 parts, and take one of those parts as the body of a pipe, just how large would it be? Thus it is that these stops are made to repeat. In other words, when the pipes get too small, then they again assume the scale of the previous octave. For example, a Scharf is carried up to c''; then from c''* to c''' it assumes just the same size that it had from c' to c''. Sometimes the ranks already begin to repeat at c', and then again at c''. Other times only the lowest octave is used, repeating itself from tenor c to c', then again from c' to c'', etc., so that the scale of the lowest octave is maintained throughout. From this one may understand what is meant by the "Repeating Zimbel" and other such stops mentioned in Chap. 7.†

* Here and at other similar places in this paragraph it is unclear whether the breaking back is between b and c or between c and c#.

† See §.184 and 134.

§. 84.

You will also encounter the term *dito*. For example, at St. Ansgarius's in Bremen‡ there stands: Trommet 16', *dito* 8', meaning likewise a Trommet, but of a different size. The word *dito* thus always means "the preceding stop." The "cut-up" is the opening made between the lips of a pipe. "Voicing" means giving the pipe its proper sound. Mis-speaking (Das Filpen) is when the pipe overblows (sich überblaset§). Mitering the pipes is explained in §.110. A number of [other] technical terms will appear now and then in the following [pages].

‡ The stoplist is given in Mattheson's Appendix to Niedt, Part II, p. 159; see Chap. 10 below under "Bremen."

§ But elsewhere Adlung seems to draw a distinction between *filpen* and *überblasen*; see Chapter 28, pp. 179-180.

§. 85.

2.) Now the question arises, "Of what materials are pipes made?" For pipes apart from the organ¶ almost anything may be used: all [kinds of] metals, such as gold, silver, tin, lead, copper, iron, bronze, brass, and other materials such as glass, earth,[19] stone, wood, quill, horn, treebark, paper[20], etc. Most of these could also be used for organ pipes, but it is not customary to use all of them. Quills are too small; earth (or pottery), as well as glass, is fragile and troublesome to tune. Treebark is not durable,

¶ i.e., wind instruments.

---

19) By this is meant clay, such as is worked by a potter. The *Frankfurter Zeitungen*, 1751, No. 144, made mention of an organ with pipes of this material, that was constructed in a very artistic way by a potter named Weidner, at Mayenburg in the Priegnitz, near Pritzwalk. Its pipes were all made of clay, and they sounded as beautiful, clear and pure as those of tin in the best organs. This organ had three stops. [Albrecht]

20) Some time ago the famous elder Casparini‖ built a positive of 6 stops in the the imperial *Kunstkammer* at Vienna, whose pipes were entirely of paper; Boxberg reports this in his *Beschreibung der Görlitzer Orgel* [p. 1]. [Albrecht]

‖ Eugen Casparini (1623-1706)

56 Kap. VI. Von dem Pfeifwerke überhaupt.

auch in solcher Menge und vollkommenen Figur, oder so groß, als man sie benöthiget ist, nicht leicht zu haben; welches letztere auch von den Hörnern der Thiere zu sagen ist. Von Steinen dergleichen viel zu machen, ist sehr mühsam. Es bleibt also ordentlich bey den Metallen und beym Holze. [21] Meßing ist sehr hart zu arbeiten, auch gar theuer; daher es wenig gebraucht wird. Es findet sich aber eine ziemliche Menge desselben in der grüningischen Schloßorgel, da die corpora aller Schnarrwerke von starkem Meßing sind, und auf 6 Centner wiegen; welches sehr kostbar ist. S. Werkmeisters Organ. grüning. redivivum. Doch dauren solche Pfeifen viel länger, als andere, ja sie verderben nimmer. Mehrere Exempel kommen im folg. Kap. vor.

§. 86.

Das Silber ist noch kostbarer, daher man wol zuweilen einzelne Pfeifen von Silber antrift; nicht leicht aber ganze Orgeln von Silber. [22] Das Gold ist noch kostbarer, und wird man es desto weniger zu Orgelpfeifen gebrauchen. [23] Wir bleiben gemeiniglich beym Zinn, Bley und Eisen. Vom Holze soll hernach geredet werden.

§. 87.

Das Eisen anlangend; so wird es zu einem breiten und etwas subtilen Bleche geschlagen, welches Blech hernach die ihm gehörige Form bekömmt. Das Zinn ist wegen der Härte etwas schwer zu hobeln; aber es giebt gut Pfeifwerk, sonderlich das englische Zinn; welches aber bey uns wenig gebraucht wird, weil es theuer ist. [24] Wir haben ordentlich das Bergzinn. Weil das Zinn theuer ist, auch sich so gut nicht arbei-

---

[21] Man findet zwar bisweilen auch Stimmen von anderer Materie. Denn es meldet Prätorius im 2ten Tomo S. 185. daß zu Bückeburgk Offenflöt 4′ von Elfenbein; und zu Hessen auf dem Schlosse Kleinprincipal 4′ von Elfenbein und Ebenholz anzutreffen sey. S. 92 gedenket Prätorius gar eines Orgelwerks, da die Laden, Pfeifen, Clavier und Blasbälge von Glaß oder Alabaster gewesen. In Mantua soll auch eine Orgel von Alabaster stehen. S. Reinholds einige zur Musik gehörige Gedanken bey Gelegenheit einer neuen Orgel. Dresden, 1736. 4to. S. 23. Anmerk. bbb. Daß von Thon und Papier dergleichen gemacht worden, ist aus der 19. und 20. Anmerk. zu ersehen, und von Silber und Gold werden die zwo folgenden Anmerk. etwas melden. Alles dieses aber ist unter die Seltenheiten zu rechnen.

[22] Im Dom zu Mayland in Italien soll doch eine silberne Orgel stehen, wie solche D. Joh. Melchior Götze in Werkmeisters Parentation anführet. It. zu Friedrichsburg. S. Reinholdt l. c.

[23] Doch gedenkt kaum angeführter D. Götze l. c. daß der Kaiser Michael Curopalates zu Constantinopel eine goldene Orgel habe aufrichten lassen. Man sehe auch M. Gottfr. Kretschmars Görlitzer Orgelpredigt. S. 14.

[24] In der Görlitzer Orgel soll das englische Zinn zu allen im Gesicht stehenden Registern gebraucht worden seyn, als zum Principal 16′, 8′, 4′, und im großen Principalbasse 32′, zum clave F 24′, Tromba 8′, Jungfernreal 4′. S. Boxbergs Beschreibung.

56 Ch. VI. Concerning the Pipework in General.

nor is it easily available in such quantity, size or perfect form as would be necessary; the same can be said of animal horn. Making many pipes of stone is very tedious. Thus the usual materials to be used are metals and wood.[21] Brass is very hard to work, and also very expensive; thus it is little used. There is, however, a goodly amount of it in the palace organ at Gröningen; the resonators of all the reed pipes are of heavy brass, totaling 6 hundredweight, which is very costly (see Werkmeister's *Organum gruningense redivivum* *). On the other hand, such pipes will last much longer than others; indeed, they will never corrode. Several more examples will appear in the following chapter.

* §.5.

§. 86.

Silver is even more costly, and so single pipes of silver are at times to be met with, but seldom an entire organ of silver[22] Gold is even more costly, and is all the less frequently used for organ pipes.[23] Tin, lead and iron are most commonly used. [The use of] wood will be discussed below.

§. 87.

As for iron, it is beaten into a wide and rather thin sheet (Blech†), and then given the proper shape. Because of its hardness tin is rather difficult to plane, but it produces good pipes, especially English tin--but the latter is seldom used here, since it is expensive.[24] Normally we use native tin. Because tin is both expensive and troublesome

† When Adlung uses this term, here and elsewhere in the book, he almost surely means *Weissblech*, sheet iron that is plated with tin in order to hinder rust, in contrast to *Schwarzblech*, sheet iron not plated with tin. Occasionally he is specific in this regard, writing Weissblech; more often, however, he writes the generic "Blech."

---

[21]) Sometimes ranks are made of other materials as well. In [his *Syntagma*], Vol. II, p. 185, Praetorius reports that the open flute 4′ at Bückeburg is of ivory, and the Kleinprinzipal 4′ in the palace at Hesse‡ is of ivory and ebony. On p. 92 [of Vol. II] Praetorius mentions an entire organ with chests, pipes, keyboard and bellows of glass or alabaster. There is also said to be an alabaster organ in Mantua; see Reinholdt's *Einige zur Musik gehörige Gedanken bey Gelegenheit einer neuen Orgel* (Dresden, 1736, quarto), p. 23, note ddd. Notes 19 and 20 [above] reveal that pipes may be made of clay or paper, and the two following notes will report something about silver and gold. All of these, however, are to be considered rarities. [Albrecht]

[22]) At Milan Cathedral in Italy there is said to be an organ of silver, as reported by Dr. Joh. Melchior Götze in Werkmeister's eulogy.§ The same holds true at Friedrichsburg;¶ see Reinholdt, *l.c.*|| [Albrecht]

[23]) Yet Dr. Götze, just cited above, mentions [on pp. 3-4] that the Emperor Michael Curopalates had an organ of gold built at Constantinople. See also p. 14 of the *Görlitzer Orgelpredigt* by Gottfried Kretschmar, M.A. [Albrecht]

[24]) English tin is said to have been used in the Görlitz organ for all stops that stand in the façade, i.e. for the Principals 16′, 8′ and 4′, the great Principalbass 32′ up to 24′ F, the Tromba 8′ and the Jungfernre[g]al 4′. See Boxberg's *Beschreibung der Orgel zu Görlitz* [pp. 2-4]. [Albrecht]

‡ See Praetorius, p. 189. This organ, built in 1610 by Esaias Compenius, is now in the castle church in Frederiksborg, Denmark.

§ Götze (or Goeze), Johann Melchior, *Der Weit=berühmte Musicus und Organista Wurde Bey Trauriger Leich=Bestellung... Andreae Werckmeisters...*, p.4.

¶ The stopknobs of the Compenius organ at Frederiksborg, Denmark, are made of pure silver.

|| See Albrecht's note 21) in §. 85 above,

Kap. VI. Von dem Pfeifwerke überhaupt. 57

arbeiten läßt; so wird meistentheils Bley dazu genommen. Dieses ist wohlfeil, und läßt sich auch am besten arbeiten, biegen, hobeln, ꝛc. Doch hat es den Fehler, daß es so schön nicht aussiehet, als das Zinn; daß es sehr schwer ist; sonderlich daß es so lange nicht dauret: denn der Salpeter setzet sich gar bald an, besonders an dem Fuße, und durchfrißt das Bley, daß es in etlichen Jahren ganz unbrauchbar wird. Daher man ordinär Zinn darunter menget, damit es besser dauren möge. Diejenigen Pfeifen, die ins Gesicht zu stehen kommen, erhalten ordentlich mehr Zinn, auch wol pur Zinn; dahingegen die Innwendigen aus schlechterer Materie verfertiget werden können. Diese massam aus zusammengeschmolzenen Zinn und Bley nennet man Metall. Es kömmt zwar sonst dies Wort dem Zinn, Bley, Gold, ꝛc. zu: aber wenn im Orgelbau von Metalle geredet wird; so verstehet man allezeit diese Vermischung. Ob viel oder wenig Zinn dazu gethan werden soll, dependirt von denen die den Orgelbau dirigiren. Man nennet aber dieses die Legirung, it. das Loth, da man z. Ex. sagt: das Pfeifwerk soll 12löthig, 10löthig u. s. w. seyn. D. i. unter 12 Loth Metall ist das 12te Bley, unter 10 Loth ist das 10te Bley, das übrige lauter Zinn. Andere sagen 12löthig sey, wenn 12 Loth Zinn und 1 Loth Bley wären, zusammen 13 Loth, u. s. w. Daher man sich bey Orgelcontrakten nicht vergehen darf. (*)

(*) Dies ist undeutlich, und scheinet gar unrichtig zu seyn. Der gemeinste Gebrauch ist, daß man durch die genannte Zahl, die Zahl der Lothe des Zinnes bemerkt, und 16 immer für die höchste Zahl der Lothe, welche zur Zusammensetzung gehören, oder gleichsam für das ganze annimmt. Also ist 16löthig Zinn, ganz rein Zinn. 14löthig ist wo 14 Loth Zinn und 2 Loth Bley sind; 10löthig, wenn 10 Loth Zinn und 6 Loth Bley sind. So findet man es in allen etwas umständlichen Dispositionen berühmter Orgelbaumeister z. Ex. eines Trost, Friderici, und anderer mehr, angegeben. Einige behaupten daß man ganz reines Zinn nicht zu Orgelpfeifen arbeiten könne. Andere z. Ex Hr Joh. Gottlieb Schramm in Berlin, beweisen, daß es, obwol mit mehrerer Mühe und Fleiß, gar wohl gearbeitet werden könne.

§. 88.

Es haben so wol die metallenen als auch die hölzernen Pfeifen zwey Haupttheile, nemlich: das corpus und den Fuß. Die Metallenen werden aus Platten gemacht. (Von den Eisernen oder Blechernen ist §. 87. gedacht worden.) Aber das Zinn und Bley wird durch den Guß zu breiten Platten gebracht. Dieses geschiehet auf der Gießlade. Man machet nemlich einen Kasten, so lang und breit, als es die Länge und Breite der Pfeifen erfordert, stellet ihn auf Füße, und thut Sand darein, welcher recht gerade liegen muß, ohne alle Ungleichheiten, und recht horizontal, sonst würde die flüßige Materie nach einem Ende mehr laufen, als nach dem andern, folglich würde das Blat an einem Ende dicker, als an dem andern. Darauf läßt man das im Feuer geschmolzene und wohl gesäuberte Metall laufen, soviel, daß der Kasten oder Lade an allen Orten etwas bekömmt, und zwar in gehöriger Dicke. Wenn die Masse geronnen ist; so thut man sie weg, und gießet mehr. Es insinuiren sich aber zuweilen die Sandkörner in das Metall, und verderben hernach die Hobel; ja etliche verbergen sich gar,

und

Ch. VI. Concerning the Pipework in General.

to work, lead is used most of the time for [making pipes]. It is cheap and the easiest to work, to bend, to plane, etc. It has, however, some shortcomings: it is not as attractive in appearance as tin, it is very heavy, and most important, it is not very durable. Saltpeter* very soon sets in, especially at the foot, and eats away the lead, so that after a number of years it becomes totally unusable. Usually, therefore, tin is mixed in with it, to give it greater durability. Those pipes that are to stand in the façade normally get more tin, or even pure tin, while on the other hand the interior pipes may be fashioned of an inferior material. This alloy of tin and lead fused together is called "pipe-metal" (*Metall*). Indeed, this word (*Metall*) is also used to denote tin, lead, gold, etc., but when we speak of *Metall* in organbuilding, it is always this alloy that is meant. Whether more or less tin should be used in it depends on those who are building the organ. This is called the alloy (Legirung) or weight† (Loth); thus, for example, the expression "the pipes shall be 12-weight, 10-weight, etc." In other words, 12-weight pipe-metal is 1/12th lead, 10-weight is 1/10th lead, while the rest is pure tin. Others say 12-weight is when the metal is 12 parts tin and 1 part lead, thus 13 parts total. Therefore one ought not to be misled by organ contracts.(*)

* See Vol. II, §.383, and Chap. 28, pp. 173f.

† See also §.245.

> (*) This is unclear, and appears to be totally incorrect. The most common usage is that the stated number indicates the number of parts of tin, with 16 being the greatest number of parts in the alloy, that is, [the greatest number of parts] for the whole. Thus 16-weight tin is completely pure tin, and 14-weight is 14 parts tin and 2 parts lead, and 10-weight is 10 parts tin and 6 parts lead. This is the case in all of the more detailed stoplists drawn up by famous master-organbuilders, such as Trost, Friderici and others as well. There are some who insist that completely pure tin cannot be made into organ pipes; others, for example Mr. Joh. Gottlieb Schramm in Berlin, demonstrate that it certainly can be made [into pipes], although with considerable trouble and diligence. [Agricola]

§. 88.

Both metal as well as wooden pipes have two main parts, namely the body and the foot. The ones of *Metall* are made from sheets (ones of iron or sheet iron have been mentioned in §.87). But tin and lead are made into wide sheets by casting.‡ This takes place on the casting table. A tray is fashioned, of the width and length required by the pipes; it is set upon legs, and filled with sand that must lie completely smooth, without any unevenness, and perfectly horizontal—otherwise more of the molten material would run to one end than to the other, and thus one end of the sheet would be thicker than the other. Then the pipe-metal, having been melted and thoroughly refined in the fire, is poured out in sufficient quantity that the box or tray is completely covered by an even layer of the proper thickness. When the alloy has set, then it is removed, and the casting process is repeated. At times, however, grains of sand become imbedded in the metal and subsequently damage the plane. Indeed, some actually get com-

‡ In contrast to iron that is beaten into sheets.

und verursachen hernach einen zitternden sonum, daß man solche Pfeifen oft gar nicht brauchen kann. Daher andere anstatt des Sandes reine Asche nehmen, wodurch solchem Unheil vorgebogen wird. Casparini hat bey der görlitzer Orgel die Gießlade noch anders gemacht, indem er das Metall auf bloße Leinwand gegossen, welche mit einer von ihm erfundenen Materie bestrichen worden, sonst sie bald würde Schaden genommen haben. Boxberg sagt, daß diese Art zu gießen zwar nicht so geschwinde zugehe, als auf dem Sande; doch habe er in einem Tage zu den großen Pedalpfeifen 38 Centner Zinn gießen sehen, ohne daß die Leinwand schadbar worden. Er lobt es, weil die vorgedachten incommoda dadurch vermieden werden, und über dies die Blätter auf beyden Seiten sehr glatt fallen, und haben auf der einen Seite nicht mehr Narben als auf der Leinwand sind; die leicht wegzubringen.

§. 89.

Hernach nimmt man mit dem Hobel alle Ungleichheiten weg,[26]) und schneidet die Blätter ab, so lang und breit, als es die Natur eines jeden Registers erfordert. Man darf nur die Länge und Weite der größten Pfeife haben; (wie §. 82. gedacht worden,) so findet man daraus die Proportion aller clauium in demselben Register. Doch merke man überhaupt, daß die corpora der kleinen Pfeifen in den obern Oktaven gemeiniglich etwas weiter gemacht werden, als es die Proportion erfordert; hingegen laßt man es in der Länge fehlen. Dadurch bekommt man eine leichtere Intonation; sie quiksen auch nicht so jämmerlich. Damit die Orgelmacher desto geschwinder arbeiten können; so reißen sie die Proportion aller Pfeifen in einem Register auf ein Brett, nach der Länge so wol, als nach der Breite, und darnach schneiden sie die Pfeifenblätter. Ein solches Brett nennen die Orgelmacher das Mensurbrett. Von der Proportion der Breite gegen die Länge der Pfeifen kann man nachlesen *Kircheri* Musurg. L. VI. P. III. c. 3. p. 510. welches wir aber den Orgelmachern überlassen. Ueberhaupt findet man, daß die enge Mensur einen anmuthigern Klang verursacht, als die weite: aber die engen Pfeifen sind schwerer zur Intonation zu bringen, und jeder Orgelmacher macht sie nicht gerne. S. *Prätorius* Synt. T. II. P. IV. c. II. p. 142. Wenn die Blätter der kurzen Gießlade

---

[25]) Der Hr. Verfas. hat in der Anleitung zur musikal. Gelahrtheit, S. 371 u. 529. angemerkt, daß man die gegossenen Platten, ehe man sie hobelt und zuschneidet, durch das Hämmern härter machen könne; jedoch erinnert er auch dabey, daß das Zinn in diesem Falle nicht gar zu spröde seyn dürfe.

[26]) In der Anleitung zur musikal. Gelahrtheit, S. 370. m. schreibt der Hr. Verfasser dieses Umstandes wegen nachfolgende gegründete Anmerkung, welche ich hierbey zu wiederholen für dienlich erachte. Sie heißt so: „Die Gießlade muß viel länger seyn, als die längste „Pfeife werden soll, und nach der Weite der dicksten Pfeife muß sich die Breite „der Lade richten, weil es nicht fein ist, wenn die Körper aus mehr Stücken „zusammen gestickt sind."

pletely buried and afterwards cause a fluttering sound [in the pipe], to the extent that pipes often become completely unusable. Thus others make use of pure ashes in place of sand, which prevents such trouble. For the Görlitz organ Casparini made the casting table in a different way; he cast the metal onto a plain canvas cloth smeared with a substance he invented (otherwise [the cloth] would quickly have gotten damaged). Boxberg says* that this method of casting does not proceed as quickly as upon sand, to be sure; yet he observed 3,800 lbs. of tin being cast in one day for the pedal pipes, without the canvas getting damaged. He praises it, since it avoids the abovementioned disadvantages, and moreover the sheets [of pipe-metal] turn out very smooth on both sides, having on the one side† no more pits than are on the canvas cloth, which are easily removed.

* as recorded in *Beschreibung der Görlitzer Orgel*, p.[7].

† i.e., the side underneath.

§. 89.

After this any unevenness is removed with a plane,[25] and the sheets are cut to the dimensions required for each specific stop. Only the length and width of the largest pipe are needed (as has been mentioned in §.82); from these are determined the proportions of all the pipes in that stop. Take note, however, that the bodies of the small pipes are usually made [of] somewhat wider [scale] in the upper octaves than the proportion requires, and thus are made shorter in length. It is easier to voice the pipes by doing this, and they do not squeal so miserably. So that organbuilders may work all the more quickly, they sketch the proportions, the length as well as the width, of all pipes in one stop upon a board, and then cut the sheets for the pipes according to this [sketch]. Organbuilders call such a board a "scaling-board." One may consult Kircher's *Musurgia*, Book VI, Part III, Chap. 3, p. 510 concerning the proportion of the pipes' widths to their lengths; but we will leave such things to the organbuilders. In general one discovers that a narrow scale produces a more pleasant sound than a broad one. The narrow pipes, however, are more difficult to coax into speech, and no organbuilder likes to make them; see Praetorius, *Syntagma*, Vol. II, Part IV, Chap. II, p. 142.‡ If a short casting table does not allow the sheets to get long enough, then several pieces of sheet are soldered together, although this is not particularly commendable.[26]

‡ Here Praetorius is speaking expressly of *reed* pipes, not flues. The page citation should read "p. 143," not "p. 142."

25) The author remarks in his *Anleitung zur musikalischen Gelahrtheit*, p. 371, [note *n*.] & p. 529, that the cast sheet may be made harder by hammering it before planing and cutting it, but he cautions that in doing this the tin not be allowed to get too brittle. [Albrecht]

26) With respect to this situation, in the *Anleitung zur musikalischen Gelahrtheit*, p. 370[, note] m, the author writes the following well-founded remark, which I consider useful to repeat at this point. It reads thus: "The casting table must be much longer than the longest pipe is to be, and the width must be determined by that of the widest pipe, since it is not neat if the [pipe] body is patched together out of several pieces." [Albrecht]

lade wegen nicht lang genug werden, löthet man etliche Stücke Platten zusammen; wiewol es nicht eben zu loben.²⁶)

§. 90.

Hernach giebt man der Platte die ihr zukommende Figur, und zwar werden etliche cylindrisch, etliche aber bekommen eine kegelförmige Figur, doch wie coni truncati, welches aus §. 79. deutlich seyn wird. Denn man nimmt hölzerne Walzen, in der Dicke, daß die Blätter sich darum legen lassen, in cylindrischer oder kegelförmiger Figur, und darum windet man die Blätter. (Man hat aber noch andere Figuren der metallenen Körper, die aber Kap. 7. beyzubringen sind.) Hernach löthet man die Enden der Blätter zusammen. Dieses wird auf folgende Weise verrichtet: Man nimmt einen eisernen Kolben, macht ihn in Kohlen glüend, und fasset etwas vom Loth, und überziehet die Fuge, wodurch sie verbunden werden. Und damit es besser halten möge, so nimmt man Silberloth. Doch damit durch dasselbe das Pfeifencorpus nicht zugleich zerschmolzen werde; so beschmieret man die beyden Enden des Blats mit rother Menge, welche nach der Löthung wieder kann und soll abgewaschen werden, auf daß es besser anzusehen sey. Zuweilen läßt man diese Farbe dran, sonderlich mitten in der Orgel, da es niemand siehet. Endlich wird das Labium oder Lefze formirt. Man nimmt nemlich einen hölzernen Cylinder; der aber an einem Ende breit geschnitten, also: und stellet ihn in die Pfeife, und druckt das Blat an, nach einer proportionirten Höhe, nachdem die Pfeife kurz oder lang ist. Dies ist die obere Lefze, oder Labium. Die untere kömmt an den Fuß.

§. 91.

Hernach bekümmert man sich um den Fuß, welcher conus fistulae deswegen genennet wird, weil er bey metallenen Flötenwerken allezeit wie ein conus truncatus aussiehet, also: Dessen Blatt wird eben so gegossen, wie der Körper, doch gemeiniglich stärker, daß er die Pfeifen tragen könne. Hernach giebt man dem Blatte die kegelförmige Gestalt, da man es um einen hölzernen conum windet, es verlöthet wie das corpus, auch ein labium hinein druckt, wie an jenem. Die Länge ist willkührlich und thut es nichts zum Klange, ob der Fuß 1 Elle, oder $\frac{1}{4}$ Elle lang ist; nachdem man Raum hat, oder Staat damit machen will, nachdem macht man ihn kurz oder lang. Der spitzigste Theil ist so dick, das er in das Loch des Pfeifenstocks gesetzt werden kann: der breiteste Theil aber hat die Breite des Körpers, und dahinein kömmt der Kern zu liegen, welches eine metallene Platte ist, deren Peripherie etwas kleiner ist, als die Circumferenz des Fußes, indem der Kern hineingeleget wird. An der Seite, wo er gegen dem labio des Fußes stehet, wird er gerade geschnitten, daß er dem labio recht parallel stehe; doch ist dessen Schärfe etwas schrade, daß das untere Theil weiter hervor ragt nach dem labio; als das obere, so, daß man zwischen den Kern und dem

§. 90.

Next the sheet is given its proper shape; some pipes receive a cylindrical shape, others a conical shape (or rather that of a truncated cone, as will be clear from §.79). The sheets are wrapped around wooden rollers of cylindrical or conical shape, that are thick enough so that the sheets can fit around them. (There are, though, other shapes for metal pipes, but these are described in Chapter 7.) Next the edges of the sheet are soldered together. This is accomplished in the following manner: a soldering iron is heated red-hot in coals, then tipped with solder and drawn over the joint, sealing it. Silver solder is used so that the is joint more durable. However, to keep the body of the pipe from melting when this is done, both edges of the sheet are smeared with red size (rother Menge*). The size can and should be washed off when the soldering is completed, for appearance's sake; at times the stain is left on the pipes, especially inside the organ where no one sees it. Finally, the lip is formed. A wooden cylinder is cut wide at one end, thus: and inserted into the pipe. The sheet is then pressed in to a height proportionate to the length of the pipe. This is the upper lip, or *Labium*. The lower [lip] is part of the foot.

* Menge = Mennige. The context suggests that what Adlung means is Armenian bole; see §.38.

§. 91.

The next thing to be concerned with is the foot, called "the cone of the pipe," because in metal flue pipes it always looks like a truncated cone, thus: A sheet is cast for it, just like the body's, but usually stronger, so that it can bear [the weight of] the pipe. Next the sheet is given a conical shape by wrapping it around a wooden cone; then it is soldered and impressed with a lip, in the same manner as the body. The length is arbitrary, since it makes no difference to the sound whether the foot is an ell high or only a 1⁄4 ell. It may be made as short or long as desired, either to fill up space or for purposes of display. The pointed end is blunt enough to be set into the hole in the toe board. The broad end, though, is the width† of the body, and inside it sits the languid, a [circular] metal plate whose diameter is somewhat smaller than the circumference of the foot into which it is set. On the side next to the lip of the foot the languid is cut straight, so that it lies exactly parallel to the lip. Its edge, however, is somewhat sharp, so that the bottom of it protrudes further toward the lip than the top, [leaving just enough room] in a small pipe to see between the lip and the languid (in larger pipes, however, the slit may be larger). The languid is made quite strong, so

† i.e., the diameter.

dem labio in dem kleinen Pfeifwerke durchsehen könne: in großen aber kann der Ritz größer werden. Der Kern wird etwas stark gemacht, daß ihn die Gewalt des Windes nicht in die Höhe biege; auch wird er rings herum wohl verlöthet. Endlich löthet man auf die vorige Art den Fuß und Körper zusammen, daß die beyden Lefzen auf einander stoßen: zwischen beyden aber liegt der Kern.

§. 92.

Nun folget der Aufschnitt der Pfeife. Denn es muß ein orificium oder Oefnung darein gemacht werden, und das geschiehet an dem obern labio, von welchem man ein Stück abschneidet, so breit als dasselbe ist, und die Höhe richtet sich theils nach der Breite, theils aber nach der Art des Registers. Doch ist die Höhe nie so groß, als die Breite. Je kleiner der Aufschnitt der Höhe nach ist, desto schärfer wird der Klang: aber diese Pfeifen silpen oder überblasen sich gern. In Grobgedackten, oder dergleichen stumpfen Registern wird der Aufschnitt hoch, daher da der Aufschnitt, der Breite nach, den 4ten Theil der Peripherie der Pfeife in sich hält; so ist die Höhe zuweilen der 3te Theil von der Breite des labii, zuweilen der 4te Theil, zuweilen $\frac{2}{5}$; je nachdem das Register es mit sich bringt. S. Kirchers Musurg. L. VI. P. III. C. III.

§. 93.

Nun folgt die Intonation, wodurch bedeutet wird, wenn man die Pfeifen recht zu ihrem Klange bringet. Wenn die Pfeifen enge sind, so ist sie schwerer als sonst. Bisweilen schlagen sie nicht an, da man ihnen hilft durch Biegung der labiorum und des Kerns; zuweilen schlagen sie zu scharf an, da schneidet man sie weiter auf; zuweilen schlagen sie allzustumpf an, da sind sie verschnitten, und ist ihnen nicht zu helfen, man müßte denn ein Stück an das obere labium löthen, und hernach den Aufschnitt ändern: man thut aber besser, wenn man anstatt dieser Flickerey eine neue Pfeife macht. Zuweilen zittern die Pfeifen, und was für Umstände bey der Intonation sich mehr finden.

Man kann etliche Pfeifen, sonderlich die engen so intoniren, daß zwey Töne zugleich gehöret werden, als zuweilen die Oktave, zuweilen die Quinte; das letzte geschiehet ordentlicherweise bey der Quintatön, davon sie auch diesen Namen bekommen. Das metallene Pfeifwerk kann leichter zu einer reinen und schönen Intonation gebracht werden, als das Hölzerne, welches selten so schön klingt, als das Metallene. Doch können etliche Orgelmacher die metallenen Pfeifen so intoniren, daß sie wie Holz klingen, und hingegen die Hölzernen so einrichten, daß sie am Klange einer metallenen Pfeife nicht das geringste nachgeben; welche Kunst an Casparini gelobet wird, welcher 40 Jahr daran studiret. Besiehe die Görlitzer Orgelbeschreibung, da der Inventriatur die meiste Ursach beygelegt wird. (*)

(*) Hr. Gottfried Heinrich Trost pflegte bey einigen Registern, absonderlich im Pedale, die von Holz waren, zu diesem Ende dünne zinnerne Blätter auf die hölzerne Kerne zu leimen.

that the force of the wind does not bend it upwards, and it is soldered firmly [to the foot] all around. Finally, the foot and the body are soldered together in the manner described above, so that both lips touch each other; between them both, though, lies the languid.

§. 92.

Now comes the cut-up of the pipe; for an *orificium* or opening has to be made in it, and this is done by cutting a piece out of the upper lip, as wide as the lip itself, and of a height determined in part by the width [of the mouth] and in part by the kind of stop. Yet the height is never so great as the width. The lower the cut-up is, the keener the sound, though such pipes tend to be unstable and overblow (filpen oder überblasen sich gern]. In a Grobgedackt or other such dull-sounding register the cut-up is high, and therefore, since the width of the cut-up* is a quarter of the pipe's circumference,† the height [of the cut-up] is sometimes a third the width of the lip, sometimes a quarter, sometimes two thirds, all according to the nature of the stop (see Kircher's *Musurgia*, Book VI, Part III, Chap. III).

* i.e., the width of the mouth

† It is not clear whether Adlung intends this remark to apply to all pipes or only to the stopped pipes he is discussing at the moment.

§. 93.

Next comes the voicing, by which is meant coaxing the pipes to sound properly. If the pipes are narrow, they are more difficult [to voice] than otherwise. Sometimes they do not speak, and must be helped by bending the lip and the languid. Sometimes they speak too stridently, and must be cut up further. Sometimes they sound very dull; then they are overcut, and this cannot be amended except by soldering a patch to the upper lip, thus allowing the cut-up to be altered. Instead of this patchwork, though, it would be better to make a new pipe. At times a pipe['s speech] may flutter; and there are other difficulties attendant upon voicing, as well.

Certain pipes, especially narrow ones, may be voiced to produce two tones at once, at times an octave,‡ at times a fifth. The latter is regularly the case with the Quintatön, whence its name. Metal pipes can be more easily coaxed into pure and beautiful speech than wooden pipes, which seldom sound as beautiful as metal ones. Some organbuilders, however, can voice metal pipes to sound like wooden ones, and conversely regulate the wooden ones so that they are in no way inferior to the sound of metal pipes. Casparini is especially praised for this art, which he studied for 40 years. Consult [Boxberg's] *Beschreibung der Görlitzer Orgel*,§ which credits this mostly to the Invetriatur.(*)¶

‡ in addition to the fundamental.

§ pp.[11] & [15].
¶ See §.38 above.

(*) Mr. Gottfried Heinrich Trost used to glue thin tin plates onto the wooden languids of some wooden stops, especially in the pedal, for the purpose [of making wooden pipes sound like metal ones]. [Agricola]

Kap. VI. Von dem Pfeifwerke überhaupt. 61

Am meisten siehet man darauf, daß die Pfeife augenblicklich anschlage. Wo die Pfeifen schwer zur Intonation zu bringen, da löthet man zu beyden Seiten der labiorum Bärte an, welches länglicht viereckigte metallene Platten sind, in großen Pfeifen zuweilen Daumens breit, und wol noch eins solang, in kleinen Pfeifen aber kleiner. Sie heißen auch alae, Flügel, auch auricolae, Ohrläpplein, und halten den Wind zu beyden Seiten an. Bey der Quintatön, Gedackten und engen Pfeifwerk findet man sie am meisten: zuweilen auch an der Violdigamba, doch wer sie ohne Bärter macht, der verdienet mehr Lob; indem dies ein Zeichen ist, daß entweder die Mensur der Pfeifen, oder der Aufschnitt nicht allzurichtig sey.

§. 94.

Man löthet auch Oeschen oder Haken an die Körper des Pfeifwerks, daran man dasselbe an eine Leiste oder Brett hangen kann, daß sie nicht umschmeißen. Kann aber das Peifwerk in einem Pfeifenbrette stehen; so braucht man dergleichen nicht.

§. 95.

3.) Von den hölzernen Pfeifen. Da fragt sichs erstlich: Was für Holz dazu zu nehmen? Antw. Die Natur eines jeden Holzes giebt uns die Antwort in den Mund. Das Erlenholz vermodert, wenn es nicht in sumpfigten Oertern stehet; Eben= und Brasilienholz ist hart zu arbeiten, dabey auch sehr kostbar; Eschen= und Ilmen= wie auch Pappelholz ist ebenfalls schwer zu arbeiten. Die Tanne bleibt fein gerade, und ist gut zu arbeiten: aber die Würmer gehen sie bald an. Cedern= und Cypressenholz läßt sich auch gut arbeiten, und ist auch von den Würmern frey; und was in der Physik mehr vom Holze gemeldet wird. Die drey leztern Arten schicken sich gut zum Pfeifwerke; doch muß man das Tannenholz durch die massam (§. 38.) vor den Wurmern verwahren. Das Cedern= und Cypressenholz ist beydes hier zu Lande viel zu rar, als daß man große Werke davon aufführen sollte, daher man es selten gebraucht. In der Görlizer Orgel ist die Quintatön 16' und die Onda maris meist von Cypressenholz, sonderlich in den obern clauibus. Es ist auch dieses Holz weder bey kalt= und feuchten Wetter, noch bey warm= und trockenen einiger Veränderung unterworfen. Das Tännenholz, und, welches gleiche Natur hat, das Fichtenholz wird also bey uns gebraucht. Das Eichenholz kann aber auch einige Dienste thun. Auch hat man Stimmen von Ebenholz, Birnbaum, Ahorn und Elsebeern, welche im Folgenden näher werden bekannt gemacht werden.

§. 96.

Das Holz nun schneidet man in Bretter, oder nimmt schon geschnittene Bretter, läßt sie recht dürre werden, welches zuweilen etliche Jahre erfordert, hobelt sie auf beyden Seiten gerade, und füget deren viere nach der Tischlerkunst accurat zusammen, daß es ein viereckigter Kanal werde, nach der Länge und Weite, welche das Register erfordert. Wie breit die Seiten seyn müssen, ist denen bekannt, welche die Weite in

H 3 den

Ch. VI. Concerning the Pipework in General. 61

The most important thing is to make the pipe speak instantaneously. When a pipe is difficult to coax into speech, then beards are soldered to both sides of the lips. These are rectangular metal plates, sometimes the width of a thumb in large pipes, and twice that long, but smaller in little pipes. They are also called *alae*, "wings," or *auricolae*, "earlobes," and they channel the wind at both sides [of the lip]. They are mostly found on Quintatöns, Gedackts and narrow-scaled pipes, and sometimes also on the Violdigamba--though anyone who makes them without beards deserves more credit, since they are a sign that either the scale or the cut-up of the pipes is not quite right.

§. 94.

Eyelets or hooks are soldered to the bodies of the pipes; then they can be hung upon a strip or board so they do not topple over. These are not needed, though, if the pipes can stand in a pipe-rack.*

* See also §.47 and §.44.

§. 95.

3.) Concerning wooden pipes: the first question is "What sort of wood should be used for them?" The characteristics of each of the woods gives us the answer straightway. Alderwood molds if it does not stay in marshy places. The hardness of ebony and brazilwood make them difficult to work with, and they are also very expensive. Ash and elm, as well as poplar wood, are likewise hard to work with. Fir remains nice and straight and is easy to work with, but worms get into it quickly. Cedar and cypress are also easy to work with, and are free of worms. There are other things as well that [the study of] physics can tell us about wood. The three types last-named are well suited for making pipes, but fir wood must be protected from worms by the compound [described in] §.38. Cedar and cypress wood are much too rare in this country to be employed extensively in building organs, and thus are seldom used. The Quintatön 16' and the Onda maris in the Görlitz organ are mostly of cypress, especially the upper notes.† This wood is not subject to any change, either in cold, damp weather or in warm and dry. Thus fir as well as spruce‡ (which has the same characteristics) are used here. Oak wood can also be of some service.§ Stops have also been constructed of ebony, pearwood, maple and wild service-tree (Elsebeern¶); more specific information about these will be given below.||

† cf. Boxberg, *Beschreibung der Görlitzer Orgel*, p.[15].

‡ For a discussion of the characteristic differences among fir, spruce and pine, as well as the linguistic equivalents of these types of wood in other European languages, see: Frank Hubbard, *Three Centuries of Harpsichord Making* (Cambridge, Mass.: Harvard University Press, 1967), pp. 202f.

§ See §.103 below.

¶ "Elsebaum" can also mean "alder-tree."

|| See the discussion of individual stops in Chapter 7.

§. 96.

The wood is now cut into boards (or boards that are already cut are used) and allowed to cure thoroughly, which sometimes takes several years. Both sides are planed straight, and then four of them are precisely joined together, using cabinetry skills, to create a rectangular channel of the length and width required by the stop. Those who

den runden metallenen Pfeifen verstehen, und die die quadraturam circuli in der Geometrie zu finden gelernet haben, soviel möglich. Man muß den Innhalt der Rundung einer solchen runden Pfeife erst wissen, welcher aber auf folgende Weise gefunden wird. Ich fasse nämlich den Diameter des Zirkels oder der Peripherie, und sage in der Regula trium, wie sich 100 zu 314 verhält, so verhält sich der Diameter zu der Peripherie. Oder so: wie sich 7 zu 22 verhält, so verhält sich der Diameter zu der Circumferenz.

§. 97.

Ich will das ganze Werk durch ein Exempel erklären. Ich will einen kurzen Maaßstab, einen Schuh vorstellend, nebst den Zollen und Linien hinreißen. s. Tab. II. fig. 1. Eine Tertia oder Linie ist der 10te Theil eines Zolles. Der Schuh aber ist in 10 Zolle getheilt. Will man nun mit dem Zirkel etwas messen, so fasse man es, und trage es hinüber, da ein Fuß hinten in die obere Linie gesetzt werden muß, der andere aber muß eine heruntergehende Linie treffen, daher wenn es oben nicht trift, daß ein Fuß die Linie äusserst berühret, der andere Fuß aber kommt zu stehen wo eben diese Zwerchlinie durch eine andere durchschnitten wird. Alsdann sehe ich, was über der abwärts gehenden Linie stehet, das giebt die Zolle: Was aber vor der Zwerchlinie steht, das giebt die Tertien oder den zehenden Theil vom Zolle etlichemal. Ob es schon nicht allzuschön noch accurat werden wird; so dient es uns doch, das Problema zu solviren. Es sey also der Zirkel Tab. II. fig. 2. Der Zirkel stellt die Peripherie oder Rundung und Umkreis der metallenen Pfeifen vor. Die gerade Linie bc ist der Diameter, und mag er von oben herab oder in die Breite gezogen werden, so bekömmt er allezeit gleiche Länge, wenn er nur allezeit gerade, und zwar durch das Centrum oder Mittelpunkt a gezogen wird. Nun fragt sich, wenn eben dieses Register von Holz gemacht werden sollte, um das Metall zu schonen, wie groß würden die Bretter genommen werden in der Breite? (denn die Länge wird eben so, wie in den metallenen, gefunden.) Und wie groß würde das Quadrat der Pfeife werden?

Der Diameter bc wird nach dem Maaßstabe lang gefunden 2′ 5″ 6‴, oder 2 Schuh, 5 Zoll, 6 Tertien. Daraus findet man die Petipherie durch die Regel de tri. Entweder so:

Wie 100 zu 314 so 2 5 6 zu der Peripherie

```
      3 1 4
     ──────
     1 0 3 4
       2 5 6
       7 6 8
     ──────
     ⌐8 0 3 8 4⌐
```

L 100

Die

62 Ch. VI. Concerning the Pipework in General.

understand [how to give] round metal pipes their [proper] diameter and have learned adequately how to transform the area of a circle into a rectangle will know how wide to make the sides. One must first know the area of the circle of such a round pipe, which may be found by the following method: namely, I take the diameter of a circle or its circumference (Peripherie), and state according to the rule of *pi*: the diameter is related to the circumference as 100 is to 314, or as 7 is to 22.

§. 97.

I will clarify the entire matter by means of an example. I will sketch out a little scale, representing a foot, showing the inches and *Linien* on it; see Table II, fig. I. A *Tertia* or *Linie* is a tenth of an inch,* and a foot is divided into 10 inches. If one now wishes to measure something with a compass, he should take it and position it so that one point rests on the right side of the upper line† and the other point touches one of the vertical lines in such a way that, if it does not exactly meet it at the top, it should come to rest wherever a horizontal line is intersected by another.‡ Then I note what [number] stands above the vertical line; this is the [number of] inches. [The number] that stands in front of the horizontal line, however, gives the [number of] *Tertien* or tenths of an inch.§ Although this will not be all that accurate, it will serve to solve the problem. Table II, fig. 2, shows the circle that represents the circumference of a metal pipe. The straight line *b c* is the diameter; whether it is drawn vertically or horizontally, it is always of the same length, as long as it is always straight and passes through the center or midpoint *a*. Now the question is: If this stop¶ were to be made of wood, in order to save [on] metal, how wide would the boards‖ have to be? (For the length will be just the same as that of the metal pipes.) And how large would the square pipes be?

According to the scale, the diameter *b c* will be found to be 2′ 5″ 6‴, or 2 feet, 5 and 6/10 inches. From this the circumference is computed by the rule of *pi* [in one of two ways], either thus:

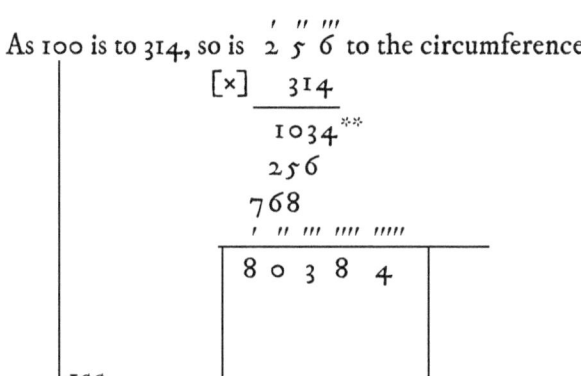

* Adlung is thus dividing a foot (Schuh) into 10 inches (Zolle) and each inch into 10 *Tertiae* or *Linien*; each of these, then, is 1/100 of a foot. See §.78 above.

† i.e., on the upper right hand corner of the scale, marked by 0.

‡ i.e., the next previous vertical line.

§ Or, to explain it more clearly: position the compass on the top of the scale and with one point on 0 and the other on 10; this is a foot. Measure how many feet there are in the diameter of the circle (fig. 2); in this case there are 2 plus a remainder (it is this remainder that Adlung is describing how to measure). Set the compass points on both ends of the the remainder; then transfer the compass to the scale and put one point on the upper right hand corner (at 0). The other point turns out to fall not exactly on one of the inch marks, but between 5 and 6. To find out how many additional 100ths of an inch the remainder is, drop the second compass point down on the scale until it meets the vertical line that descends from 5. It meets that line where the horizontal line no. 6 intersects it. Thus the diameter is 2 feet, 5 "inches," and 6 "tenths of an inch."

¶ whose pipe is represented by the circle.

‖ i.e., each one of the four sides.

** sic; the number should be 1024, but the total below it is correct.

Tab. II. pag. 62.

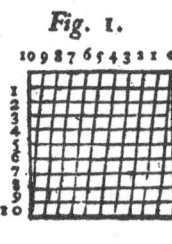
Fig. 1.

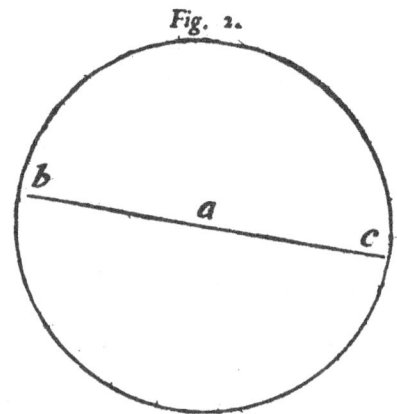
Fig. 2.

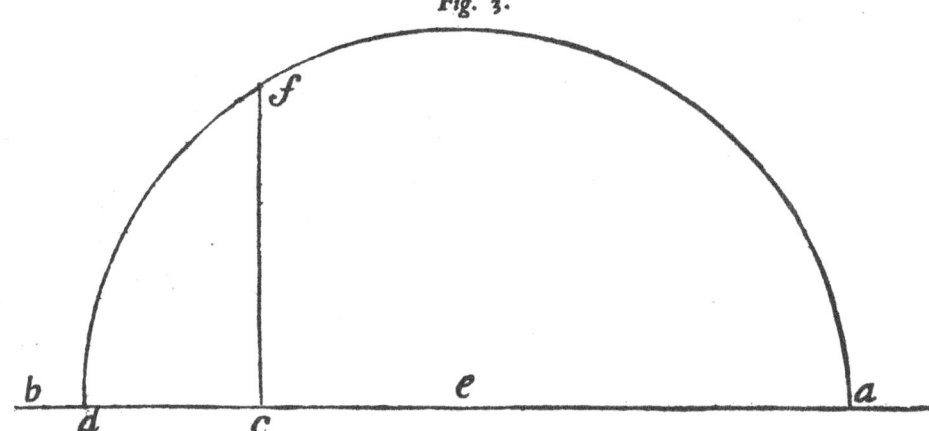
Fig. 3.

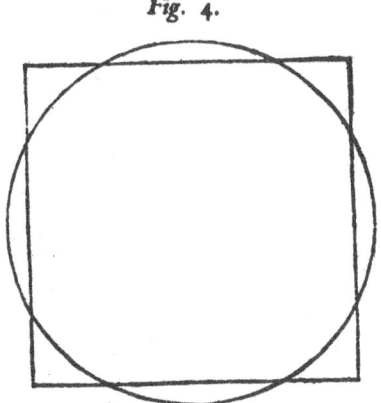
Fig. 4.

Tab. II. pag. 62.

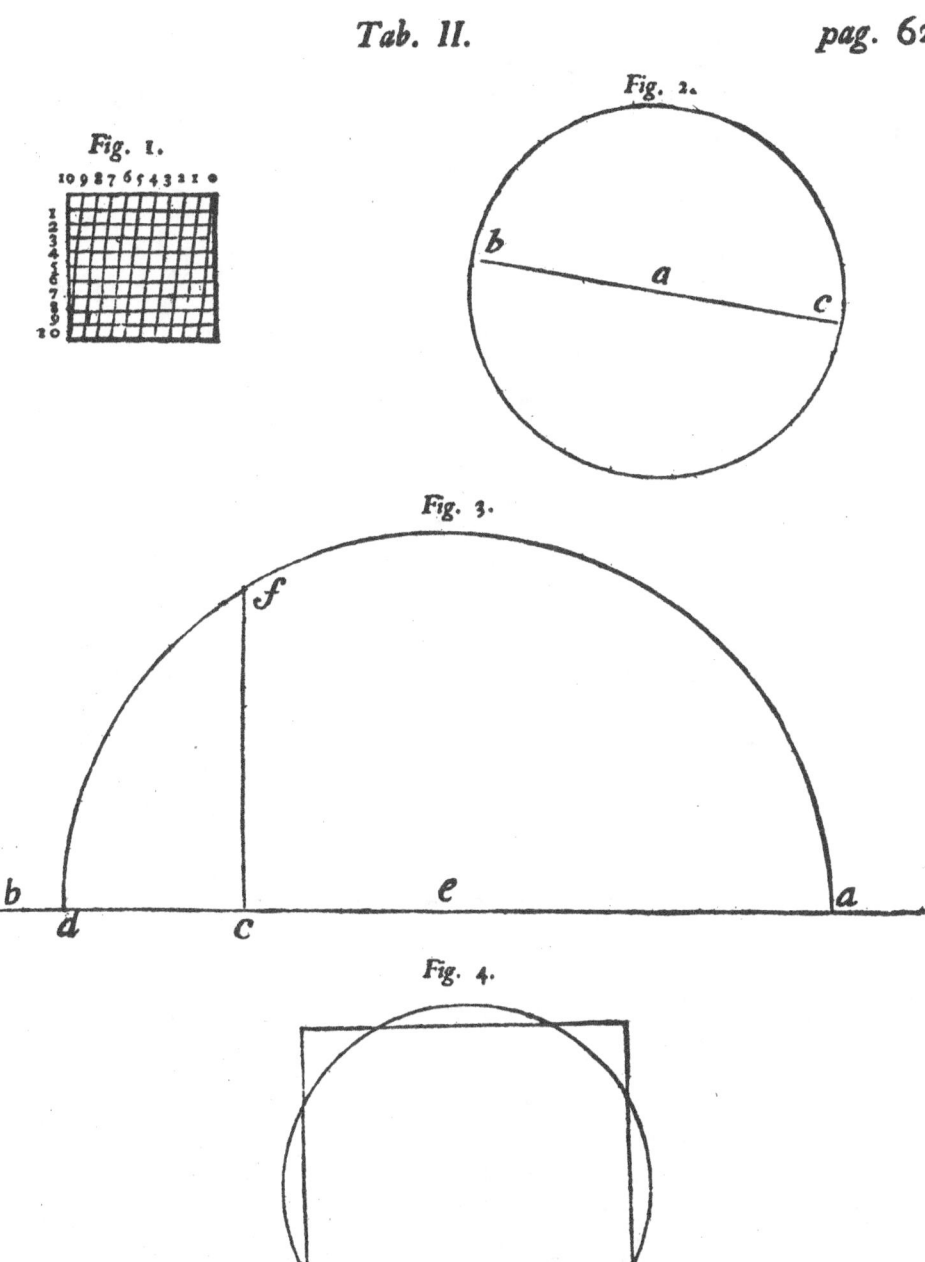

Kap. VI. Von dem Pfeifwerke überhaupt.   63

Die Peripherie hält aufs genaueste 8 Schuh, 3 Tertien, 8 Quarten und 4 Quinten. In allen Exempeln bleibt der erste und andere Satz 100 und 314. Der 3te Satz wird der Diameter, so groß er etwann gefunden wird. Dann werden die 2 letzten mit einander multiplicirt, und die Summe durch den ersten dividirt.

Oder anstatt der zwey ersten Sätze nehme man 7 und 22. z. E.
Wie 7 zu 22, so 2′ 5″ 6‴ zu der Peripherie.

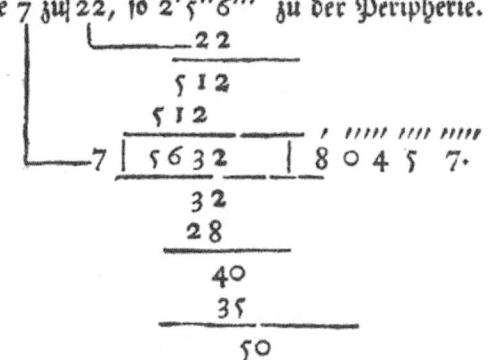

```
              22
             512
             512
        ┌─────────┐    ′ ″ ‴ ″″ ‴‴
       7│  5632   │   8 0 4 5 7.
              32
              28
              40
              35
              50
```

Die Peripherie wird etwas weniges größer, als bey der ersten Operation, so aber nicht merklich ist. Die erste ist accurater.

Nun suche ich durch das Halbiren die halbe Peripherie, und ziehe eine gerade Linie, so lang, als die halbe Peripherie gefunden worden, und den semidiametrum darunter,

```
          ′  ″  ‴  IV  V
          8  0  3  8  4

          ′  ″  ‴  ″″ ‴‴
          4  0  1  9  2   halbe Pe-
                          ripherie nach der ersten
                          Operation.
```

———————————————————————
halbe Peripherie.
                              ———————————
                              semidiameter.

Zwischen diesen beyden Linien muß eine media proportionalis gefunden werden, die kleiner ist als die große, und größer, als die kleine, und sich verhält zu der kleinen, wie die große sich zu der zu findenden mittlern verhält. Man ziehe eine gerade Linie *a b*, fasse die halbe Peripherie mit dem Zirkel, und trage sie von *a* nach *b*, daß sie sich in *c* endige. Hernach fasse man den semidiameter mit dem Zirkel, und setze ihn auch auf dieselbe Linie von *c* nach *b*, daß er sich in *d* endige. Das Stück der Linie *d a* theile man in 2 gleiche Theile, und ziehe aus der Mitte *e* einen halben Zirkel von *a* nach *d*. Alsdann richte man in *c*, wo sich die halbe Peripherie und der semidiameter berühren, eine gerade Linie oder ein Perpendikel auf, nach dem Bogen, daß sie den Bogen schneide in *f*. Diese Linie *c f* bis an den Bogen ist eben die media proportionalis, und die rechte

Breite

Ch. VI. Concerning the Pipework in General. 63

The circumference is precisely 8 feet, 3 ¹⁄₁₀₀ths, 8 ¹⁄₁₀₀₀ths, and 4 ¹⁄₁₀₀₀₀ths. In every instance the first and second principal numbers remain 100 and 314. The third principal number is the diameter, at the size it is computed to be. Then the last two [numbers*] are multiplied and their product is divided by the first [number].†

Or in place of the first two principal numbers, 7 and 22 may be used; for example:
As 7 is to 22, so is 2′ 5″ 6‴ to the circumference

<small>* i.e., the second and third numbers just mentioned.</small>
<small>† i.e., 100.</small>

```
           ×]  2 2[
               5 1 2
               5 1 2      ′  ″  ‴  ⁗  ⁗′
        7 | 5 6 3 2 | 8 0  4  5  7.
               3 2
               2 8
                 4 0
                 3 5
                   5 0
```

The circumference will [turn out to] be a little bit larger than with the first method, but not enough to make any difference. The first [method] is more accurate.

Now I divide by 2 to find half of the circumference, and draw a straight line exactly one half the length of the circumference; next [I place a line] half [the length of] the diameter under it.

```
            ′  ″  ‴  IV  V
          | 8  0  3  8   4
            ′  ″  ‴  ⁗  ⁗′
          | 4  0  1  9   2      is half the cir-
                                 cumference according to the first
                                 method.
```

_____
half the circumference.   _____
                            radius (*semidiameter*).

A mean proportion must be found between these two lines; it will be shorter than the longer [line] and longer than the shorter [line], and will be related to the smaller as the larger is related to the mean proportion to be computed. One draws a straight line *a b*,‡ measures the half-circumference with the compass, and transfers it to *a b* [beginning at *a*], so that it ends at *c*. Next one measures the radius with the compass, placing it on the same line [*a b*] from *c* toward *b*, so that it ends at *d*. One bisects the line segment *d a* [naming the mid-point *e*] and constructs an arc from *a* to *d*, using *e* as the center. Then at *c*, where the half-circumference and the radius meet, one constructs a straight line or a perpendicular upward toward the arc, so that it intersects the arc at *f*. This line *c f* [from the line *a b*] up to the arc is the mean proportion and the proper

<small>‡ Here Adlung is referring to Table II, fig. 3, on p. 62.</small>

64   Kap. VI. Von dem Pfeifwerke überhaupt.

Breite des Quadrats, oder die innre Breite eines jeden Bretts. Die Figur sehe man Tab. II. fig. 3.

§. 98.

Daß ich alle Processe in Perpendicular-Linien ziehen, Abtheilungen machen, und alle solche Kleinigkeiten hersetzen sollte, wird niemand verlangen. Ich präsupponire solche Dinge, und zeige das Hauptwerk. Diese Linie c f ist die Seite des Quadrats der Pfeife, wenn alle Seiten derselben gleich lang werden, wie ordinär geschiehet. Wollte ich ein Quadrat daraus machen, oder die ganze Seite der Pfeife vorstellen; so kann es leicht geschehen, wenn ich eine gerade Linie ziehe, von solcher Länge als c f ist, und zu beyden Seiten von gleicher Höhe perpendicula ziehe, auch oben die Linie überreisse. Will ich sehen, ob wol der Innhalt dieses Quadrats dem Innhalte der Rundung der Pfeife gleich sey; so kann aus dem centro des Quadrats der vorige Zirkel beschrieben werden, wie Tab. II. fig. 4.

Da fällt es auch einigermaßen in die Augen, daß die Weite des Quadrats dem Zirkel gleich sey; denn was dem Zirkel entgehet auf einer Seite, das wird durch das andere wieder ersetzt.

Wenn nun ein Orgelmacher die Intonation verstehet; so können die meisten Stimmen mit wenigen Kosten von Holz gemacht werden, s. §. 93. Wer aber die nicht zu geben weis, daß der Klang nicht metallen wird, der läßt es billig bleiben, es sey denn, daß die Art des Registers einen solchen hölzernen Klang erfordere.

§. 99.

Wenn aber die metallenen Pfeifen eine konische Figur haben; so gibt es eine doppelte Arbeit. Z. Ex. wenn die 8füßige Spitzflöte von Holz zu machen ist, die so aussiehet:

So muß man den Diameter des obern Zirkels a nehmen, daraus den Inhalt derselben Peripherie finden, und daraus ferner das obere Quadrat der hölzernen Pfeife, nach der vorigen Operation. Hernach muß man auch den untern größten Zirkel gleichfalls ins Quadrat bringen, und die Bretter alsdann darnach schneiden, so:

Auf solche Art sucht man die Proportion der größten Pfeifen. Sollte aber das corpus der Pfeife des Raums wegen länglicht viereckigt werden müssen; so kann man dieses Quadrat zum Oblongo machen, nach den principiis der planimetriae. Die Orgelmacher aber geben sich soviel Mühe nicht, sondern sie suchen das Quadrat des Zirkels durch Hülfe der Mechanik, doch auch ziemlich accurat, zu finden. Sie theilen nemlich den

deme-

Ch. VI. Concerning the Pipework in General.

width of [each side of] the square (the width of each board on the inside [of the pipe]). The figure is shown in Table II, fig. 3.

§. 98.

No one will expect me to set down all the details of such procedures, drawing perpendicular lines and making sections. I am presupposing such things, and only indicating basic concepts. The line cf is one side of the square pipe, presuming that all of its sides are equal, as is ordinarily the case. If I want to make a square out of it, that is, to represent all sides of the pipe, then all I need to do is simply draw one straight line the length of cf, draw two equally long perpendicular lines, one at either end of it, and then connect the two perpendiculars with a line at the top. If I want to be sure that the content of this square is equal to that of the circular pipe, then I describe the initial circle around the center of the square, as illustrated in Table II, fig. 4.

The eye will then be able to perceive that the width* of the square is roughly that of the circle, since what the circle loses in some places is made up in others.

* i.e., the area.

If an organbuilder understands voicing, then most of the ranks can be made less expensively out of wood (see §.93). Anyone who does not know how to imbue them with the sound of metal [pipes], though, should leave well enough alone, unless a particular register requires the sound that wood gives.

§. 99.

If the metal pipes have a conical shape, then the work is doubled.† For example, if an 8-foot Spitzflöte that looks like this:

† in order to construct square wooden pipes of an identical scale.

is to be rendered in wood, then the area within the circumference of the upper circle a must be found and then [translated] into the upper square of the wooden pipe, according to the method [described] above. Then in the same way the larger lower circle [b] must likewise be translated into a square. Then the boards must be cut according to these measurements, thus:  This is the way to compute the scale of the largest pipes. If however due to space [limitations] the body of the pipe must be made rectangular, the square can be transformed into a rectangle using the principals of surface measurement. Organbuilders, though, do not go to all this trouble; rather they compute a square from a circle with the aid of mechanics, and indeed quite accurately. That is, they divide the diameter of the circle into eight parts, discard

diametrum des Zirkels in acht Theile, werfen einen solchen Theil davon, und nehmen die übrigen sieben Theile für die Breite der Seiten im Quadrat an, daraus sie gar gut ein Quadrat, und hieraus, wo es nöthig, ein oblongum reißen können. Und so würde das vorige Quadrat fast eben so, nach der mechanischen Operation, geworden seyn.

§. 100.

Wie sie dann hingegen aus einer hölzern Quadratpfeife auf mechanische Art eben so leicht eine runde metallene zu machen wissen, wenn sie die Seite des Quadrats in sieben Theile theilen, und hernach zu der Länge noch ein solches Theilchen thun; denn dasselbe wird der Diameter des zu findenden Zirkels, aus dessen Mitte hernach der Zirkel leichtlich gezogen wird: und sind diese zwo Operationen gegen einander gleichsam eine Probe, ob man richtig procediret habe.

§. 101.

Man findet aber auch hölzerne Pfeifen, die von außen keine Breite und viereckigte Figur, sondern eine runde, präsentiren. Also stehet in Tondorf, einem erfurtischen Dorfe, der Subbaß von Holz im Gesichte, und zwar in Form einer runden metallenen Pfeife, und ist silberfarbig angestrichen, daß es von fern dem Metall gleich scheinet. Allein, es sind die Blätter inwendig doch viereckigt, nur daß die 2 im Gesicht stehenden Ecken abgestoßen sind. Doch habe ich auch hölzerne Pfeifen inwendig rund gesehen, da die Blätter in Form eines Kanals ausgebohret, und hernach zusammen geleimet waren, diese werden der innern Weite nach, wie die Metallenen gemacht. Die Körper der hölzernen Schnarrwerke werden eben so gemacht. Denn der rechte Unterschied der Flöt- und Schnarrwerke ist im Fuße.

§. 102.

Wenn der Körper richtig ist; so wird er wohl ausgegossen, daß ja kein Wind durchschleiche. s. §. 38. Dies wiederfährt auch den Füßen. Diese Füße werden verschiedentlich gemacht, weil es gleich viel gilt, wenn nur der gehörige Wind zur Pfeife kömmt. Denn man machet entweder dieselben konisch, wie bey den Metallenen, welches sonderlich geschiehet bey dem Pfeifwerke, dergleichen §. 101. ich in Tondorf gesehen habe. Diese Füße sind aber mit dem Körper, oder mit dessen Seitenbrettern von einem Stücke: denn anlöthen kann man sie nicht. Diese Bretter werden unter dem labio spitzig gemacht, daß nach Abstoßung der Ecken ein conus heraus kömmt. Oder man endet das corpus der Pfeifen unter dem labio inferiori, und verwahret dasselbe Ende mit einem viereckigten Brett, bohret ein Loch durch dessen Mitte, und steckt eine runde Röhre hinein, deren äußere Spitze auf den Pfeifenstock zu stehen kommt.

§. 103.

Der Kern ist gemeiniglich von Eichenholz, und hat eine viereckigte Figur, und dessen äußerste Seite beym labio stehet von demselben eben so weit ab, als in dem metallenen §. 91. erfordert wird. Die Labia werden über und unter dem Kerne in das

one of those parts, and use the remaining seven parts as the width of each side of the square; in this way they can very serviceably derive a square, and from it a rectangle, if need be. The square that results from mathematical computation turns out to be almost exactly the same as that derived from this mechanical procedure.

§. 100.

On the other hand, [organbuilders] just as readily know how to make a round metal pipe from a square wooden one by using this mechanical method, whereby they divide one side of the square into seven parts, and then add yet one more of these parts to the length. The result is the diameter of the circle in question, by means of which the circle may easily be drawn. These two procedures in tandem constitute as it were a test of whether the computations have been done correctly.

§. 101.

There are also wooden pipes that do not present a flat, quadrangular shape externally, but rather a round one. In Tondorf, a village belonging to Erfurt, a wooden Subbass stands in the facade, indeed shaped like round metal pipes and painted silver, so that from a distance it looks like metal. Internally, however, the sides are quadrangular, and the two corners exposed to view have simply been planed off. Yet I have also seen wooden pipes that are internally round, whose sides have been bored out in the shape of a channel and then glued together. These have the same internal dimensions as metal pipes. Bodies of wooden reed pipes are constructed in the same way; the only real difference between flue and reed pipes is in the foot.

§. 102.

When the body is correctly [aligned], then it is liberally smeared [with glue], so that no wind can escape (see §.38); the same is done to the foot. The feet [of wooden pipes] are constructed in various ways, since the only thing that matters is that sufficient wind reaches the pipes. One way is to make them conical, as in metal pipes. This is a peculiar characteristic of [wooden] pipes such as I have seen in Tondorf, [described in] §.101. In this case, though, the feet are of one piece with the body, or rather with its side-boards, since they cannot be soldered. These [side-]boards come to a point under the lip, so that the planed-off corners devolve into a cone. Another way [to make pipe feet] is to end the body of the pipe under the lower lip, close up the end with a quadrangular board, bore a hole through the middle of this board, and insert a round tube into it, the other end of which rests on the toe-board.

§. 103.

The languid is usually of oak, quadrangular in shape, and its front edge is the same distance from the lip as is required in metal pipes (see §.91). The lips are cut into the wood above and below the languid, and to make it especially sharp and durable the

66   Kap. VI. Von dem Pfeifwerke überhaupt.

Holz geschnitten, und daß das untere sonderlich scharf und dauerhaft sey, nimmt man unter dem Kern ein viereckigtes Eichenbrett. Von der Intonation ist nichts mehr anzuführen, als was §. 93. gesagt worden.

§. 104.

4.) Es folgen die Schnarrwerke oder Narrwerke, wie sie andere nennen, weil sie sich oft verstimmen, und daher dem Organisten viel Mühe und Verdruß machen. (**) Die **Körper** derselben sind meistens, wie bey dem andern Pfeifwerke, von **Zinn, Metall, Meßing, Holz** oder **Blech**; daher allhier nichts davon zu sagen. Was aber insbesondere von dem und jenem Register zu sagen seyn mögte, das gehöret zum folgenden Kapitel. Die Füße machen den vornehmsten Unterschied, und der von ihrer Struktur entstehende schnarrende Klang: da in dem Flötwerk dergleichen Zittern oder Schnarren so deutlich nicht vernommen wird. Es kommen hier bey den Füßen vor: der Stiefel, das Mundstück, das Blatt, der Drücker, die Schrauben, die Vorschläge, ꝛc. Der Stiefel ist ein viereckigtes oder rundes corpus von beliebiger Höhe, auf allen Seiten von Brett oder Meßing gemacht. Unten wird eine Oefnung und darein eine Röhre gemacht, dadurch man den Stiefel auf den Stock setzt. Oben ist er geöfnet, damit das Mundstück hineingesetzt werden kann, daß es durch den Stiefel den Wind empfängt. In den Stiefel kömmt der Kopf zu stehen, welches ein viereckigtes oder rundes Holz oder Metall ist, mitten durchbohret, da denn durch dieses Loch eine metallene Röhre, das Mundstück genannt, gesteckt und bevestiget wird. Diese hat die Form eines Gänseschnabels, und wird mit Zinn ausgegossen, auch zuweilen mit Leder überzogen, damit es nicht allzusehr knastere oder rassele; doch in manchen Registern, sonderlich in kleinen, ist dieses nicht. Dieses Mundstück wird bedeckt mit einem meßingenen Blatte, in der Breite und Länge des Mundstücks; und in großen Pfeifen zuweilen Daumens breit, aber kaum $\frac{1}{4}$ Gran oder Gerstenkorn dicke; die kleinern Pfeifen bekommen, nach Proportion, kleinere und dünnere. Es siehet dieses Blatt der Zunge nicht ungleich, und wenn der Wind hinein bläset, giebt es sich durch beständiges Zittern bald an das Mundstück, bald von demselben; eben als wenn der Mensch das R mit seiner Zunge stark ausspricht, da dieselbe auch beständig zittert. Deswegen heissen auch die Schnarrwerke Zooglossa, vom griechischen ζῶον ein Thier, und γλῶσσα, die Zunge. S. *Kircheri* Musurg. L. VI. P. III. C. III. Probl. VIII.

(**) In vielen alten Orgeln Deutschlands, z. Ex. in der St. **Catharinenkirchen** Orgel in **Hamburg**, und in andern mehr; und noch in vielen neuen herrlichen Orgeln **Frankreichs**, sind der Rohrwerke eine ziemlich große Anzahl. Der größte Orgelkenner, und Orgelspieler Deutschlands, und vielleicht Europens, der seel. Kapellmeister B a ch, war ein großer Freund davon: der mußte doch wol wissen, was und wie darauf gespielet werden könne. Ist die Commodität mancher Organisten und mancher Orgelbauer wol Ursach genug, so schöne Stimmen zu verachten, zu schimpfen, und auszumärzen?

§. 105.

Ch. VI. Concerning the Pipework in General.

lip below the languid is a quadrangular oak board. There is nothing more to be added about voicing beyond what has been said in §.93.

§. 104.

Next are the reed pipes (Schnarrwerke), or "fool's-pipes" (Narrwerke*), as some people call them, since they often get out of tune and thus cause a lot of fuss and bother for the organist.(**)† The bodies of reed pipes are, as in other pipes, usually of tin, pipe-metal, brass, wood or sheet iron; thus we need say no more about them here. Anything in particular that may need to be said about this or that stop will be taken care of in the following chapter. The principal difference is in the foot, and in the rattling sound that is produced by its structure; in flue pipes this vibration or rattle is not perceived so clearly. The components of the foot are: the boot, the shallot, the tongue, the tuning wire, the screws, the latches, etc. The boot is a quadrangular or round body of arbitrary height, all sides of which are constructed of boards or of brass. At the bottom there is an opening to which a tube is attached, by which the boot is set into the toe board. It is open at the top so that the shallot can be inserted into it and thus receive wind from the boot. Into the boot is inserted the block, a quadrangular or round piece of wood or metal with a hole bored through the middle; a metal tube called the shallot is then inserted and fastened into this hole. [The shallot] is shaped like a goose's beak, cast of tin and at times covered with leather to keep it from clattering and rattling so much (many ranks, though, especially small ones, do not have this). The shallot is covered by a brass tongue, identical in size to it. In large pipes [the tongue] is sometimes the width of a thumb, but barely a ¼ of a grain or barleycorn thick; the smaller pipes receive proportionately smaller and thinner ones. This tongue is not unlike an [animal] tongue in appearance, and when the wind blows into it, it sets up a constant vibration against the shallot, just as when a person pronounces a [rolled] "r" with a lively tongue (which is also a sort of constant vibration). For this reason, reed pipes are also called *Zooglossa*, from the Greek ζῶον, an animal, and γλοσσα, the tongue (see Kircher's *Musurgia*, Book VI, Part III, Chap. III, Prob. VIII [pp. 513-4]).

(**) In many old organs in Germany, for example in the organ at St. Catharine's Church in Hamburg‡ and in others as well, and also in many magnificent new organs in France,§ there is a relatively large number of reed stops. The greatest organist and organ expert in Germany, and perhaps in all of Europe, the late Kapellmeister [J.S.] Bach, was a great friend of reeds. He knew very well what could be played on them and how to do it. Is the convenience of some organists and builders sufficient cause to scorn, revile and eliminate such lovely stops? [Agricola]

---

* a play on words in German.

† In this regard Adlung reveals himself as progressive; his apparent lack of enthusiasm for reed stops (as revealed in this remark) presages the gradual reduction in the number of reed stops, already apparent in most "modern" stoplists Adlung reproduces; e.g., the Garnisonkirche, Berlin (§.285), built in 1725 by Joachim Wagner: 51 stops, of which 3 ½ in the manuals and 4 in the pedal are reeds. This paucity of reeds became increasingly characteristic of German organs in general until the advent of the 20th-century *Orgelbewegung* (Organ Reform Movement). It is to counter Adlung's remarks, then, that Agricola adds the note that follows.

‡ 58 stops, 17 reeds; see Mattheson's *Appendix* to Niedt, Part II, pp. 176-7, as well as under "Hamburg" in Chap. X below.

§ See p. 288, note *t* (Agricola's note on his translation of Dom Bedos's assessment of the new organ at St. Martin in Tours).

Kap. VI. Von dem Pfeifwerke überhaupt. 67

§. 105.

Damit aber diese Zunge nicht allzuweit von dem Mundstücke weiche, oder gar heraus falle; so wird für das letzte durch zwischengesteckte Hölzer ein Mittel geschaffet: jenem aber wird vorgebogen durch die Krücke oder Drücker, welcher auch filum und aulozonum heißt. s. Kircher l. c. Dieser Drücker wird durch den Stock gesteckt, daß er sich schwerlich auf und nieder bewegen läßt, und mitten bey der Zunge wird er krum gebogen, also: [figure] damit nicht das Drat, sondern die untere Krümme *a* das Blatt andrücke. Je weiter der Drücker durch den Hammer (womit auf den Haken *b* geschlagen wird, der ausser dem Stocke zu sehen ist,) unterwärts getrieben wird, desto mehr drückt er das Blatt unten an, und desto weniger und gedränger gehet der Wind durch, und desto höher gehet die Pfeife: Tiefer aber gehet sie, wenn der Drücker auswärts gezogen wird. Bey den Krücken braucht man auch zuweilen mit gutem Effekt die Schrauben, dadurch eine solche Krücke auf ein Haar und gar genau vermittelst eines Stimmschlüssels auf- und unterwärts geschraubet wird. Weiter ist auf dem Stocke eine blecherne oder metallene Röhre, darüber wird die Pfeife gesetzt: und damit die Gewalt des Windes die Pfeife nicht in die Höhe treibe; so macht man Schrauben in den Stock, in die Pfeife aber Häkchen oder Schlingen, durch welche die Schraube reicht, und über der Schlinge wird die Mutter angeschraubet, welche von Leder ist, wie oben geschahe bey den Abstrakten an dem Clavier, §. 51. Dergleichen kömmt auf einer, auch zuweilen auf 2 Seiten daran. Daß aber nicht der Stock mit der Pfeife heraus falle; so wird er an den Stiefel mit Vorschlägen bevestiget, wie oben bey den Spünden geschahe, §. 42. Der Stiefel aber wird fest eingeleimet und niemals heraus genommen: denn wenn etwas zu ändern ist; so kann man nur den Stock und Pfeife abheben.

Weiter ist unserm Zwecke nach von den Schnarrwerken nichts zu melden, als daß die Körper derselben zuweilen gar klein sind, und doch einen tiefen Ton von sich geben: das macht aber die Einrichtung der Blätter, und das Andrücken des Drückers. Daher einem solchen Schnarrwerke die Zahl der Füsse zwar beygeleget wird: aber der Körper hat sie nicht, sondern man muß es ordentlich von dem Sono verstehen. Doch sagt man absolute oft z. Ex. Posaune 16 Fuß, und ist doch wol nur 12 Fuß groß. Daher man sagen sollte: 16 Fußton; aber der Gebrauch lehret ein anders.

§. 106.

5.) Alles Pfeifwerk ist entweder offen oder gedeckt. Von jenem ist bisher geredet worden; von dem Gedeckten soll nun noch etwas weniges folgen. Gedeckte Pfeifen sind die, deren oberste Oefnung zugemacht ist, daß der Wind nicht oben heraus kommt, sondern wieder zurück und zum labio heraus gehen muß, daher er eine gedoppelte Reise thut, und also seinen sonum ohngefehr um die Hälfte tiefer hören läßt. Als

Ch. VI. Concerning the Pipework in General.

§. 105.

Wooden wedges are used to prevent the tongue from falling out altogether. It is prevented from traveling too far from the shallot by the tuning crook wire, also called *filum* and *aulozonum* (see Kircher, *l.c.*). This tuning wire passes through the block (Stock*), making it rather stiff to raise or lower. At the middle of the tongue it is bent thus: so that the crook *a* at the bottom, rather than the wire itself, presses against the tongue. A hammer is used to drive the tuning wire downwards at the hook *b* (which protrudes from [the top of] the block), and the further down it is driven, the further down it presses the tongue. As this happens, the wind is more and more impeded and compressed, and the [pitch of the] pipe rises higher and higher. The pitch falls, however, as the tuning wire is drawn upward. Sometimes a screw operated by a tuning key is used to good advantage to raise and lower the crook absolutely precisely. Also on the block is a tube made of sheet iron or pipe metal, over which the resonator is fitted. To keep the force of the wind from blowing the resonator off, it is provided with hooks or loops, through which screws pass into the block; then a leather nut is screwed [onto the screw] over the loop, in the same way that trackers are fastened to the keyboard (see §.51). Such screws are sometimes on one, sometimes on both sides [of the resonator]. To keep the block and resonator from coming out [of the boot] together, the block is fastened to the boot with latches, the same as with the bungboards described above (see §.42). The boot, however, is tightly glued together,‡ and never taken apart, for when anything needs to be adjusted the block and resonator are simply lifted off together.

* This may be a mistake; "Stock" means "Toeboard." But note: Boxberg writes "Stöckgen" to refer to the block of the Posaune at Görlitz!

‡ Here Adlung is thinking specifically of a wooden boot.

Our purposes do not require reporting anything else about reed pipes, except that their resonators are sometimes very small and still produce a low pitch. This is caused by the structure of the tongue and the pressure of the tuning wire. The number of feet is written after [the name of] such a reed rank, to be sure; yet the resonator is not that tall, rather the number must be construed as referring to the pitch. This is nevertheless often expressed in absolutes, for example, "Posaune 16′," even though it is only 12 feet high. It would be more proper to say "16-foot pitch;" but usage teaches us otherwise.

§. 106.

5.) All pipes are either open or stopped. The former have already been discussed; it remains to say a few words about stopped pipes. Stopped pipes are those whose upper opening has been sealed off, so that the wind cannot get out at the top, but rather must return and pass out of the lip. Thus it makes twice as long a journey, and as a consequence the pitch is heard approximately twice as low (um die Halfte tiefer) [as

wenn z. Er. das c̄ gedeckt wird; so giebt es den Klang c von sich, eine Oktave tiefer. Es werden daher solche Pfeifen nach dem Klange, nicht aber nach der Länge des Körpers gemessen, und sagt man z. Er. Quintatön 8', da der Körper doch nur 4' ist; solche Pfeifen gehen aber allezeit schwächer; denn da die Luftwirbel von der Decke wieder zurück gestoßen werden, und ehe sie wieder in der Pfeife herunter durch das labium zu unserm Ohre kommen; so sind sie sehr geschwächt. Es thut auch etwas dazu, daß die gedeckten Register einen weiten Aufschnitt bekommen, welches den Klang ohne dies stumpf macht, nach §. 92.; denn dadurch wird von dem zwischen dem Kern und untern labio durchdringenden Winde soviel weggeführet, daß er nicht in die Pfeife kömmt. Eben daher werden an die meisten gedeckten Register Bärte gemacht, wodurch der allzuhäufig abmarschirende Wind zurückgetrieben wird.

§. 107.

In den metallenen Pfeifen wird das Decken durch den Hut verrichtet. Denn man verfertiget einen Cylinder von beliebiger Höhe, nachdem die Pfeife groß oder klein ist, etwan 2'', oder 3'', 4'', 6'', ꝛc. hoch; der Diameter aber wird etwas größer, als der Diameter der Pfeife; denn er muß über die Pfeife just passen, daß er gedränge auf sie gesetzt werden könne. Den Cylinder löthet man zusammen, und bedeckt die eine Oefnung mit einer runden Platte, eben wie die Cylinder von Metall, welche eingelöthet wird. Dies deckt man auf die Pfeife. Wenn man den diametrum zu groß genommen; so muß man den Hut (denn so nennt man den Deckel) mit Leder füttern, daß er just anschließe. Ziehet man ihn aufwärts, so wird die Pfeife gleichsam verlängert, und daher tiefer: drückt man aber den Hut nieder, so wird die Pfeife kürzer, und folglich ihr sonus höher.

§. 108.

In hölzernen Pfeifen macht man einen viereckigten Stöpsel, der in die Pfeife etwas gedränge kann eingesteckt werden. Oder, wenn er zu klein gerathen, umwindet man ihn mit Leder, und steckt ihn in die Pfeife. Daß man aber die Pfeifen tiefer oder höher stimmen könne, oder den Stöpsel heraus ziehen und hinein drücken möge, wird eine Handhabe an den Stöpsel gemacht, also: *a* ist der Stöpsel in der Pfeife; *b* aber die Handhabe.

§. 109.

Die gedeckten Pfeifen bekommen zuweilen andere Löcher, entweder oben in der Decke, oder am Körper. Denn oben an der Decke macht man oft eine kleine Oefnung, und steckt noch ein kleines Pfeifchen, oder metallenes Röhrchen hinein, welches nach Proportion der Pfeifen bald lang bald kurz ist. Diese Register nennet man Rohrflöten. Das Pfeifchen in der grössern Pfeife nennet man paraulum, auch achimene. Dieses Pfeifwerk klingt ordinär stärker als das andere gedeckte. Die Größe und Proportion der kleinen Pfeifen wird den Orgelmachern überlassen, s. *Kircheri* Muturg. l. c. S. 512.

the length of the pipe would indicate]. For example, if c′ is stopped, it produces the pitch c, an octave lower. Therefore such pipes are measured* by their sound and not by the length of their bodies. Thus a Quintatön is stated as 8′, even though its body is only 4′ [tall]. Stopped pipes are always softer [than other pipes]; the column of air is thrust back down into the pipe by the cover before it reaches our ears by passing through the lip, and so the sound is much diminished. Another factor that contributes to this [softness] is that stopped ranks are given a high cut-up. [This practice] automatically makes the tone dull (see §.92.), since a great deal of the wind passing between the languid and lower lip escapes and never enters the pipe. For that very reason beards are attached to most stopped ranks, by which the wind that otherwise escapes too copiously is forced back [into the pipe].

* i.e., assigned a pitch in numbers of feet.

§. 107.

Stopping a metal pipe is accomplished by means of a cap. A cylinder is fashioned, of variable height according to the size of the pipe, say, 2", 3", 4", 6", etc., tall. Its diameter must be somewhat greater than the diameter of the pipe, since it must fit snugly over the pipe. The cylinder is soldered together, and one of its open ends is covered by soldering onto it a round plate of the same metal as the cylinder. It is then set upon the pipe, covering it. If its diameter is too great, then the cap (this is what the cover is called) must be lined with leather, so that it grips firmly. If it is drawn upwards, then the pipe is, as it were, lengthened, and its pitch lowered; if the cap is pushed down, the pipe becomes shorter and consequently its pitch rises.

§. 108.

For a wooden pipe a quadrangular stopper is fashioned, to be inserted rather snugly into the pipe. If it turns out to be too small, it is wrapped with leather before being inserted into the pipe. In order to allow the pipe to be tuned sharp or flat, that is, to enable the stopper to be drawn out or pushed in, the stopper is provided with a handle, thus: *a* is the stopper in the pipe, *b* the handle.

§. 109.

Sometimes the stopped pipes are provided with other holes,† either in the cap on top or in the body. The cap is often provided with a small opening into which a tiny pipe is fitted, a little metal tube, proportionately longer or shorter according to the length of the pipe. This stop is called a Rohrflöte. The tiny pipe in the larger pipe is called a chimney (*paraulum*) or *achimene*.‡ Such a stop normally sounds louder than other stopped [pipes]. The size and proportion of the small pipes§ are left to organ-

† in addition to the mouth.

‡ See: Kircher, Vol. I, p. 512. Kircher writes: "a pipe … that the French call *Achemenee*," an obvious reference to the French term "Flûte à cheminée."

§ i.e., the chimneys on the pipes.

Kap. VI. Von dem Pfeifwerke überhaupt.

S. 512. Probl. 5. Zuweilen ragt das kleine Pfeifchen durch den Hut der größern Pfeife hervor, zuweilen sieht man aussen nichts, als das runde Löchlein. Die Schnarrwerke, wenn sie gedeckt sind, bekommen zuweilen am Körper kleine Löcher, zumal die kleinen Regale mit den meßingenen; die Vox humana, nach gewisser façon gemacht; u. à. m. Dadurch wird der Klang auswärts geführt, da die Schnarrwerke sonst keine labia haben, da der Wind heraus könnte. *Kircherus* nennt die gedeckten Pfeifen fistulas clausas, d. i. verschlossene Pfeifen. Daß aber nicht nur in offenen, sondern auch in gedeckten Registern die ganz großen Pfeifen etwas schwach klingen, das macht, weil der Wind durch das viele Anschlagen in einer langen Reise durch so große Körper geschwächt wird: in Schnarrwerken aber ist das nicht.

§. 110.

Manche Pfeifen werden gekröpft. Das muß auch erklärt werden. Man versteht dadurch, wenn die Pfeifen nicht in einer Linie in die Höhe fortgeführet werden, wegen Mangel des Raums, sondern in die Breite, z. Er. also:

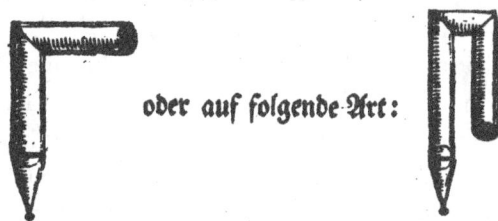

oder auf folgende Art:

Dies thut an sich dem Klange nicht allzuviel Schaden, es ist aber ein Uebelstand. Doch wo der Raum nicht ist, da muß man es wol leiden. Es geschiehet sowol bey metallenen, als auch bey andern Pfeifen. Endlich, damit das Kapitel aus werde, gedenket auch die Critica Musica *Matthesonii* Tom. II. p. 150. der schwellenden Register in der St. Magnuskirche in London, deren Ton immer stärker wird, je länger man aushält: ich weis aber nicht, wie das geschiehet.

builders (see Kircher's *Musurgia*, loc. cit., p. 512, Prob. 5). Sometimes the tiny pipes* stick up through the caps of the larger pipes; other times nothing can be seen on the exterior except the little round hole.† If reed pipes are stopped, their resonators are at times provided with little holes, especially the little Regals with brass [resonators], the Vox humana (constructed in certain ways), and others as well. In this way the sound is allowed to get out; otherwise reed pipes have no lips through which the wind can escape. Kircher‡ calls stopped pipes *fistulas clausas*, i.e., "sealed pipes." Very large pipes, not only in stopped ranks but also in open ones, sound somewhat weak. This is because the wind grows weak through encountering so much resistance in its long journey through such a large body. This, however, does not hold true for reed pipes.

§. 110.

Some pipes are mitered; this needs explaining. What it means is that pipes do not proceed upward in a [straight] line, but horizontally, due to a lack of room; for example:

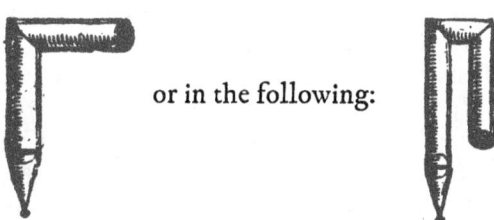 or in the following:

This in itself does not do all that much harm to the tone; it is, however, undesirable. One must put up with it, though, when space is lacking. It is done to metal pipes as well as to others.§ Finally, to end the chapter, Mattheson's *Critica Musica*, Vol. II, p. 150, mentions a swelling stop at St. Magnus's Church in London, in which the longer one holds [a note or chord], the louder the sound gets; I do not know, however, how this is accomplished.¶

* i.e., the Rohrflöte chimneys.

† i.e., the chimneys extend downward from the cap into the interior of the pipe.

‡ pp. 510-11.

§ i.e., wooden pipes.

¶ In the passage Adlung cites from *Critica Musica*, Mattheson is reporting on one of the earliest attempts at a swell division. The organ at St. Magnus's Church, London Bridge, built by Abraham Jordan & Son and announced in the *Spectator* for February 8, 1712, had a small swell organ, in effect an echo division with a sliding shutter operated by a pedal.

Das VII. Kapitel.
Von den Registern überhaupt, und von einem jeden insonderheit.

Inhalt.

§. 111. Dies Kapitel ist nach dem Alphabet gesetzt. §. 112. Die unterschiedlichen Gattungen der Register. §. 113. Alle Register wird man schwerlich hier finden. §. 114. Die Subsidia, deren man sich allhier bedienet hat. §. 115. bis 211. Stehen sie alphabetischer Ordnung, und kann man sie leicht finden. §. 212. Für einen Organisten ist das genug. §. 213. Die Namen aus allerhand Sprachen habe ich nicht alle untersucht.

§. 111.

Für einen Organisten ist dieses Kapitel das nöthigste. Es wird aber darinne bloß gemeldet, was jedes Register der Form und Klange nach für andern besonders habe; die gemeinen Eigenschaften aber werden aus dem 6ten Kapitel präsupponirt, sonst dürfte dieses Kapitel allzulang gerathen, welches ohne dies ziemlich weitläuftig ist. Da nun der Register eine große Menge ist; so deucht mir am besten zu seyn, wenn deren Namen nach dem Alphabet hierher gesetzt, und erkläret werden; denn auf solche Weise kann man von einem jeden die verlangte Nachricht augenblicklich finden. Ein Register hat zuweilen etliche Namen, daher die Hauptnachricht an einem Orte stehet, auf welchen ich hernach bey den andern verweise. Was den Registern für Namen beygeleget werden. S. - §. 36.

§. 112.

Der Unterschied der Register ist aus dem 6ten Kapitel klar, weil das eine diese Natur, Form und Klang hat, das andere aber eine andere. Daher nach eines jeden Invention die Anzahl der Register kann vermehret werden. Ein Register hat zuweilen mehrerley Formen; und haben die Orgelmacher gar verschiedene Principia. Die Namen derselben sind theils deutsch, theils lateinisch, theils holländisch, ꝛc. und man hat sie ihnen gegeben vom Klange, Figur, Größe, ꝛc. u. s. w. Es ist aber bis dato bey etlichen eine ziemliche Confusion. Z. Ex. das Bordunregister ist bey manchen ein Schnarrwerk, bey andern ein Flötregister, welches nicht seyn sollte.

§. 113.

Alle Register in der Welt wird man hier wol nicht finden: Denn aller Orgeln Dispositionen habe ich weder gelesen, noch selbst gesehen: und die hernach zu erzählenden Subsidia geben nicht von allen Instruktion. So werde ich auch nicht alle Arten der Strukturen beybringen können, weil jeder Orgelmacher fast etwas anders hat. Manches Re-

Chapter VII.
Concerning the Stops in General, and Each One of Them in Particular.

Contents:

§.111. This chapter is arranged alphabetically. §.112. The various categories of stops. §.113. All the stops are not to be found here. §.114. The sources that have been used here. §.115-211. [The stops] arranged in alphabetical order, so they may be located easily. §.212. This is sufficient for an organist. §.213. I have not investigated all the [stop] names in various languages.

§. 111.

This chapter is the one most necessary for an organist. What are reported here are the special properties of each stop that distinguish it from others as regards shape and sound. Common characteristics, however, are presupposed from Chapter 6, otherwise this chapter would go on too long; it is already quite extensive without them. Since there is such a multitude of stops, it seemed best to me to arrange and explain their names here alphabetically; in this way information required about any one of them can be found immediately. At times one stop has several names, in which case the main entry stands in one place, and is then cited under the [synonyms]. For names that are synonymous with "stop", see §.36.*

* Adlung considers "stop" and "slider" [the actual means by which the "stopping" is effected) to be equivalent, and writes the same term, *Register*, for both; thus he begins §.36 (where he is writing about sliders) with the statement, "These sliders/stops (Register) are called *Registratura*, *Canones*, or *Systemata*."

§. 112.

The difference between the stops is made clear in Chapter 6, since each one has a different nature, shape and sound. Thus the number of stops can be increased by each succeeding new invention. At times a stop has several forms; each organ builder follows his own very different principles. The names themselves are in part German, in part Latin, in part Dutch, etc., and have originated from the sound, shape, size, etc.[, of the pipes]. Up to the present a certain confusion has prevailed about some of them. For example, many call the Bordun stop a reed, while others call it a flue stop; this ought not to be.

§. 113.

All the stops in the world are certainly not to be found here, since I have neither read all organ stoplists nor seen [the organs] themselves; nor do the sources described below provide instruction about all of them. Thus I will not be able to describe all types of structures [of pipes], since almost every organbuilder has something dif-

Kap. VII. Von den Registern überhaupt und insonderheit. 71

Registers Name, nicht aber dessen Natur, ist nur bekannt, daher durch die folgenden Zeiten noch viel wird verbessert werden müssen; doch wird man Zeugs genug allhier finden. Den Gebrauch der Register spare ich bis ins 8te Kapitel; die Fehler und Vollkommenheiten jedes Register insbesondere trage ich allhier mit vor.

§. 114.

Die Hülfsmittel, deren ich mich theils bedienet, sind folgende: Prätorii Syntagma thut die besten Dienste, als worinnen nicht nur die Register genennet, sondern deren Struktur, sammt der Proportion jedes Registers gegen das andere, auch deutlich beschrieben ist; ja er hat die größeste Pfeife von einem jeden im Risse vorgestellet, welches ich hier nicht thue, sondern mich dorthin beziehe; zumal da ich keinen Orgelmacher lehren will. Die Traktation des Prätorii findet sich Tom. II. Part. IV. cap. II. von pag. 124. bis pag. 148. Etliche Register die er beschreibt, sind fast, oder gänzlich, abgekommen; in alten Orgeln aber trift man sie zuweilen noch an, daher sie nicht vorbey zu gehen. Etliche Register sind nach der Zeit Mode worden, daher er sie damals noch nicht beschreiben können: denn sein Syntagma ist im Jahre 1618. zu Wolfenbüttel bereits gedruckt worden. [27]) Viel Register sind auch beschrieben in dem Organo grüningensi des Herrn Werkmeisters, und in Borbergs Beschreibung der Görlitzer Orgel, wie auch in denen Schriften, die §. 10. u. s. erzählet worden. [28]) Andere Dispositionen geben einem zwar den Namen zu erkennen, doch wo die Beschreibung fehlet, hilft es weiter nichts, als daß man, wenn der Weg uns an solche Oerter trägt, Gelegenheit nimmt, solche Register zu hören und zu betrachten. Und gewiß ohne Reisen wird man nicht alles verstehen. Der Klang kömmt auf die Empfindung an, und wo diese mangelt, so wird man nicht überzeugt, daß man ein Register kenne.

Nun folgen sie nach dem Alphabet. [29])

§. 115.

Acuta. s. Mixtur.
* Adler (ein) S. 394.
* Aequal-Principal, ist das Principal 8 Fuß. ibid. [30])   * Ag=

[27]) Dieß ist nur von dem zweyten Tomo zu verstehen: denn der erste ist 1615. zu Wittenberg, und der dritte 1619. zu Wolfenbüttel, ans Licht getreten.

[28]) Solchen ist noch beyzufügen M. Jo. Baptist Samber, von welchem der Herr Verf. in der Anleitung zur musikal. Gelahrtheit S. 341. Nachricht giebt.

[29]) Diejenigen Namen, vor welchen ein * stehet, habe aus des Herrn Verf. Anleitung hier zur Ergänzung mit eingerückt, damit in diesem Kapitel nichts fehlen möchte; doch habe ich nicht alles von Wort zu Wort abschreiben und hierher setzen, sondern nur anzeigen wollen, wo man das in besagter Anleitung hieher gehörige dort finden, und selbst nachschlagen könne, weswegen ich auch die Seite jedesmal dabey angezeiget. Ueberhaupt wird es nicht ohne Nutzen seyn, wenn man das 7te Kap. aus der Anleitung bey diesem 7ten Kapitel stets vor Augen hat.

[30]) Im 153. §pho dieses Werks gedenket der Herr Auctor eines Registers, welches Aequal Gemshorn genennet wird, und auch mit zu obiger Rubrik gerechnet werden kann.

Ch. VII. Concerning Stops in General and in Particular

ferent. Many a stop is known to me only by its name and not by its character, and thus a great deal remains to be improved in the following pages; but there is still plenty of material to be found here. The use of the stops is reserved for Chapter 8, but the merits and faults of each stop in particular are set forth in this chapter.

§. 114.

The resources of which I have made use in part are as follows: Praetorius's *Syntagma [musicum]* is of the most value, since not only are the stops enumerated in it, but their structures are clearly described, together with the proportion of each stop in comparison with the others. He has even gone so far as to provide a sketch of the largest pipe of each [stop]. Here I do not do that, but instead make reference to him, since it is not my intention to train organbuilders. Praetorius's treatment is found in Vol. II, Part IV, chap. II, from pages 124 to 148. Certain stops that he describes are almost or completely obsolete, but they are still encountered now and again in old organs, and thus ought not to be passed over. Certain stops have become fashionable in more recent times, and thus he could not yet describe them, since his *Syntagma* was already published at Wolfenbüttel back in the year 1618.[27] Many stops are also described by Mr. Werkmeister in his *Organum gruningense* and in Boxberg's *Beschreibung der Görlitzer Orgel,* as well as in those publications mentioned in §.10f. [above][28] Other stoplists indeed give the names [of the stops], but when there are no descriptions there is nothing left to do but to take the opportunity to hear and examine such stops if one happens to travel to the places where they are. Certainly it is impossible to understand everything without travelling. Knowing a sound depends on experiencing it, and where [experience] is lacking one cannot be certain of a stop's characteristics.

[The stops] are now presented alphabetically.[29]

§. 115.

ACUTA. See Mixtur.
* ADLER (an [Eagle]). p. 394.
* AEQUAL-PRINCIPAL, is the same as the 8′ Principal. [30]

---

27) This applies only to Volume II, since the first [volume] appeared at Wittenberg in 1615 and the third at Wolfenbüttel in 1619. [Albrecht]

28) To these are to be added [those by] Mr. Jo. Baptist Samber, which the author describes in the *Anleitung zu der musikalischen Gelahrtheit,* p. 341. [Albrecht]

29) The names preceded by an * I have inserted here from the author's *Anleitung* as a supplement, so that nothing might be lacking in this chapter. I have not, though, copied and placed here everything word for word. I wanted only to indicate where in the aforementioned *Anleitung* the reader might inform himself about [the stop] in question, and thus in each case I have also cited the page. It would be most useful always to have the seventh chapter of the *Anleitung* at hand [when consulting] this chapter 7. [Albrecht]

30) In §.153 below the author mentions a stop by the name of Aequal Gemshorn that can also be included under this heading [Albrecht].

Kap. VII. Von den Registern überhaupt und insonderheit.

* Agges. ibid.
* Allerley Vogelgesang. ibid.
* Alteration. S. 395.

Angelica, von angelus ein **Engel**, angelica vox, die **Engelsstimme**, ist muthmaßlich ein lieblich intonirtes Schnarrwerk. 31) Ich habe sie niemals gesehen, auch in keiner Orgeldisposition angetroffen: sie soll sich aber in einigen Orgeln, die der Orgelmacher Stumm aus Sulzbach verfertiget, befinden. (s. **Anleitung** l. c. Anmerk. c.)

* Angusta. S. 395.
* Anthropoglossa. ibid.
* Anzug. ibid.
* Aperta. ibid.

§. 116.

Apfelregal, ist, wie alle Regale, ein Schnarrwerk. Es wird auch **Knopfregal** genennet, weil es wie ein Apfel auf dem Stiele, oder wie ein Knopf aussiehet. Das größte corpus ist etwann 4" hoch, und doch giebt es einen 8füßigen Ton. Es hat eine kleine Röhre, an der Größe wie sein Mundstück, und auf derselben Röhre einen runden hohlen Knopf voller kleinen Löcher, gleich einem Biesem-Knopf gebohret, da der sonus wieder herausgehen muß. Es ist nach Regalart lieblicher und stiller als ein ander Regal. s. Prätorii Syntagm. Tom. II. p. 148. **Köpflinregal** ist davon wohl zu unterscheiden. s. unten §. 163.

§. 117.

31) Man will sönst die Menschenstimme allezeit durch ein Schnarrwerk in den Orgeln vorstellen: da man aber auch den Engeln gemeiniglich eine Menschenstimme beyzulegen pfleget, und zwar eine Discant- oder Weiberstimme, so annehmlich, als man erdenken kann; so dürfte wol ein solches Schnarrwerk, (wenn es ja dergleichen seyn soll, wie der Herr Verfasser muthmaßet) über 4 Fuß groß dem Klange nach nicht gemacht werden: denn die Menschenstimme, wenn der Tenor oder Baß vorzustellen ist, hält ordentlich 8 Fuß Ton. Die besondere Annehmlichkeit kann sie aus einer besondern Struktur des Körpers, des labii, des Mundstücks, u. s. w. bekommen, etwann wie die Stimme eines Menschen. Ob es aber eben nöthig sey, die Engel als Weiber und Diskantisten vorzustellen, weis ich nicht. Denn es hat von uns keiner einen Engel reden oder singen hören, daß man daraus die Beschaffenheit einer solchen Stimme hätte beurtheilen können. Und eigentlich kann ihr Klang dem unsern nicht gleichen, weil sie als Geister ihre Gedanken einander auf eine viel subtilere Art, als durch die groben Luftwirbel, offenbaren können. Wenn aber in der Bibel die Engel mit den Menschen reden, so geschiehet es in angenommenen menschlichen Körpern. Man lieset aber an keinem Orte in der Bibel, daß sich die Engel in der unvollkommenen Statur eines Knaben, oder in der Gestalt einer Weibesperson, präsentiret; wohl aber lieset man, daß sie als vollkommene Mannspersonen sind gesehen worden. Wenn nun ihre angenommene Statur, Natur ꝛc. männlich ist, und folglich auch ihre organa, mit welchen das reden und singen verrichtet wird, männlich sind: warum sollte man ihnen nicht auch eine vollkommene, und einem Manne wohlanstehende Stimme beylegen, etwann den Tenor oder Baß? Dergleichen gar vernünftige Vorstellung von dieser Sache thut der Herr v. **Mattheson** in Critica mus. Tom. II. p. 319. Und solchergestalt hätte man keiner besondern angelicae nöthig; sondern die **Menschenstimme** wäre auch zugleich die **Engelsstimme**.

Ch. VII. Concerning Stops in General and in Particular

* AGGES. ibid.

* ALLERLEY VOGELGESANG [various sorts of bird calls]. ibid.

* ALTERATION. p. 395.

ANGELICA, from *angelus*, an angel, *angelica vox*, the voice of an angel, is apparently a sweetly voiced reed.[31] I have never seen it or encountered it in any organ stoplist. It is said to be found, however, in several organs built by the organbuilder Stumm* from Sulzbach (see *Anleitung*, loc. cit.,† note "c").

* ANGUSTA. p. 395.

* ANTHROPOGLOSSA. ibid.

* ANZUG. ibid.

* APERTA. ibid.

§. 116.

APFELREGAL is, like all regals, a reed stop. It is also called Knopfregal, because it looks like an apple on a stem, or like a knob. The largest resonator is about 4" tall, yet it produces an 8′ pitch. It has a small tube, the size of its shallot, upon which sits a round, hollow knob full of small holes, bored just like a braided button (Biesem = Knopf), since the sound must [be able to] escape. It is gentler and quieter as compared with other regals. See Praetorius's *Syntagma*, Vol. II, p. 148. It is indeed to be distinguished from the Köpflinregal; see §.163 below.‡

---

* probably Johann Michael Stumm (1683-1747), founder of the Stumm family organbuilding dynasty.

† i.e., p. 395.

‡ Actually §.162; presumably by oversight, there is no §.163.

§ Albrecht's meaning is not clear. Adlung uses the term lip (*labium*) only in reference to flue pipes (cf. §.84; 90-93; 102-3). Albrecht may be referring here to the reed tongue.

---

31) There have been continuous attempts to represent the human voice by means of an organ reed stop. It is also customary to attribute to angels a human voice, namely a treble or female voice, as charming as may be conceived. Such a reed, however, may not be built larger than 4′ as regards pitch (if it is indeed the same as the author supposes), since the Vox *humana* [stop], if it is to represent a tenor or bass, is normally found at 8′ pitch. It may attain a special charm, reminiscent of a human voice, through a special structure of its body, lips§ (*labii*), shallot, etc. I do not know whether it is really necessary to represent angels as women or trebles. For none of us has heard an angel speak or sing, by which we might judge the characteristics of such a voice. And actually their sound cannot be compared to ours, since they as spirits may reveal their thoughts to each other in a far subtler way than through coarse sound waves (Luftwirbel). If however in the Bible angels speak with humans, this comes about through their assuming human form. Nowhere does the Bible state, however, that angels present themselves in the immature stature of a boy or in female form; indeed, it states than they have been seen as mature males. Now if their assumed stature and nature is masculine, and thus also the organs by which they speak and sing, why ought they not also to be assigned a mature and appropriately masculine voice, either tenor or bass? Mr. Mattheson adduces the same highly reasonable exposition of this matter in his *Critica musica*, Vol. II, p. 319. And thus nothing especially angelic would be necessary; rather the human voice would be equivalent to the voice of an angel. [Albrecht]

Kap. VII. Von den Registern überhaupt und insonderheit. 73

§. 117.

Assat 2'. Diesen Namen führet ein Register zu Hildesheim, wie Prätorius l. c. S. 199. in der Disposition von Hildesheim beybringt. Was daraus zu machen weis ich nicht. Weil Prätorius es aber nicht beschreibt, so halte ich dafür, es sey verdruckt, oder an der Orgel verschrieben, und soll vielleicht Nassat heissen, wovon unten §. 169. zu reden. Zwar scheinet 2' sich nicht dazu zu reimen: doch hat man unten in dem kaum angeführten §. 169. dergleichen mehr. Assat 1½' hat er S. 194. auch.

§. 118.

Bärpipe, oder Bärpfeife; Pipe und Pfeife ist einerley. Man schreibet auch Bähr- Baar, it. Behrpfeife. Es ist ein Schnarrwerk, welches auf mancherley Art gemacht wird, daß man dem Brummen des Bären am nächsten kommen möge. Man findet sie gemeiniglich 16' auch 8' Ton; denn wollte man sie kleiner arbeiten, so würden sie ihren Namen verliehren. Sie klingen ganz in sich, und respondiren dem stillen Brummen des Bären mit einer brummenden Intonation. Sie haben zwar keine hohe Körper, aber dagegen sind sie ziemlich weit, und als zwey zusammen gestürzte Trichter, wenn sie NB. von Metall oder Blech gearbeitet sind: von Holz aber werden sie etwas anders gearbeitet. Sie können auf mancherley Art verfertiget werden: ihre Eigenschafft aber ist, daß sie unten enge, und alsobald gerade in die Weite ausgestreckt werden müssen. Prätorius l. c. hat auf der 38. Tabelle fünferley Figuren von diesem Register mitgetheilet, welche ich dem Leser zu Gefallen hierher setzen will. z. E.

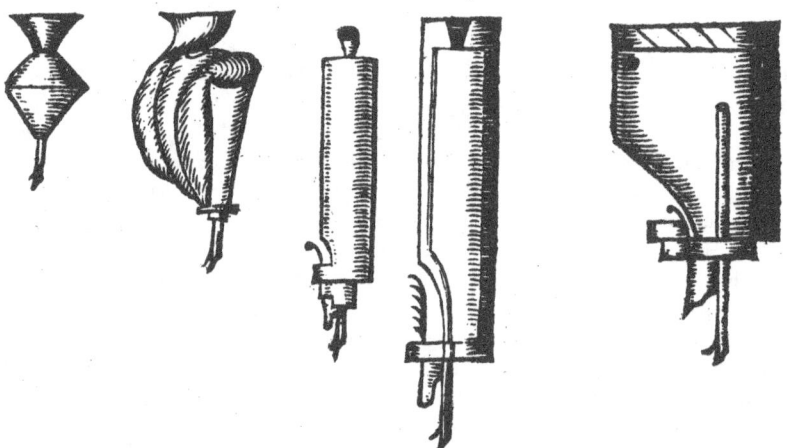

Welche Art dem Bären am nächsten kömmt, die muß ein Orgelmacher erwählen. Dies Orgelregister bekommt man nicht oft zu sehen. Es wird z. Ex. angetroffen in der grossen Orgel zu St. Nicolai in Hamburg; in der Orgel zu St. Jacobi daselbst; in der

K St.

Ch. VII. Concerning Stops in General and in Particular

§. 117.

ASSAT 2′. A stop at Hildesheim bears this name, as stated by Praetorius, *loc. cit.*, p. 199, in the Hildesheim stoplist. I do not know what to make of it. Since Praetorius does not describe it, I consider it to be a misprint, or incorrectly written on the organ, and that it should probably read "Nassat," which is discussed in §.169 below. "2′" indeed does not seem to make sense with it; but there is more about this in §.169 just cited. On p. 194 [Praetorius] also lists ASSAT 1 ½′.[*]

[*] Praetorius writes: "Assat uf die Quinten" ("Assat" at the fifth).

§. 118.

BÄRPIPE, or BÄRPFEIFE (PIPE and PFEIFE are the same). BÄHR-, BAAR- and BEHRPFEIFE are also found. This is a reed, built in many forms, that approximates the growling of a bear. It is normally found at 16′ or 8′ pitch, for if it were to be made smaller it would lose its name. It has quite a muffled sound, corresponding with its growling tone to the quiet growling of a bear. Its resonator is indeed not very tall, but on the other hand it is quite wide, and is built as two funnels thrust together, if it is made of pipe metal or sheet iron; if of wood, it is constructed somewhat differently. It may be constructed in many ways; its peculiar characteristic is, however, that it is narrow at the bottom and must gradually broaden out as it rises. Praetorius, *loc. cit.*, gives five different shapes for this stop in Table 38;[†] these I have reproduced below for the reader's convenience:

[†] of the "Theatrum Instrumentorum," at the end of Vol. II.

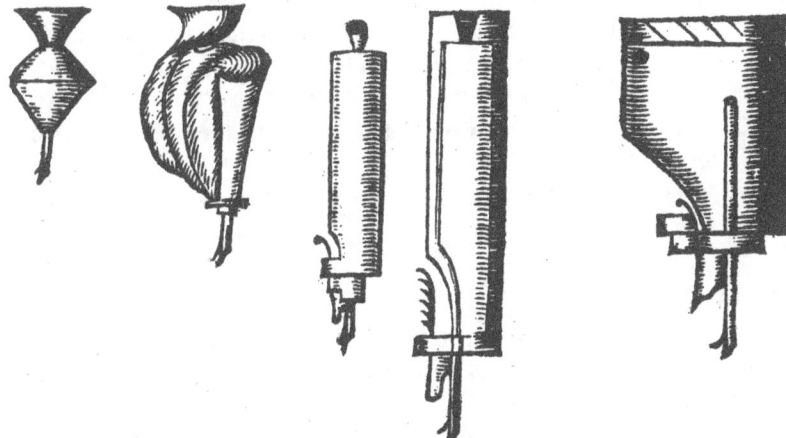

An organbuilder must choose which of these types approximates most closely [the sound of] a bear. This organ stop is not found frequently. It is encountered, for example, in the large organ at St. Nicolai in Hamburg, and in the organs of St. Jacobi,

74 Kap. VII. Von den Registern überhaupt und insonderheit.

St. Catharinen Orgel daselbst; in der Orgel zu St. Petri daselbst; in der Dom-Orgel eben daselbst. Zu St. Marien in Lübeck, wie auch zu St. Petri und zu U. L. Fr. daselbst. Zu St. Johannis und St. Lamberti in Lüneburg. An allen diesen Oertern ist sie 8 Fußton. Werkmeister sagt in Organo Grüningensi rediv. §. 46. daß zu Prätorii Zeiten die Bärpfeifen oder Krumhörner wären Vox humana genennet worden. (Mehr s. in der Anleitung S. 396. Anmerk. h).

§. 119.

Balgglocke, s. §. 125. bey Calcant.

Balgregister. Also benenne ich das Register welches nach den Bälgen gehet, und dieselben alle zugleich los läßt, auch wieder verschleußt, daß der Calcant nicht mehr treten kann. Daß dies möglich sey, zeiget der Effect, weil Prätorius S. 185. in seinen Dispositionen meldet, daß dergleichen sich in Bückeburgk befinde. Sonst habe ich keins gesehen, auch nichts davon gehöret.

§. 120.

Barem. Ist ein Gedakt: sonderlich aber bekommen die still intonirten 8' und 16' diesen Namen. Stillgedakt 8' hat gleiche Bedeutung. Das Musicirgedakt in der Stadtorgel in Jena heißt Barem. S. Prätorius Tom. II. p. 164. Desgleichen ist Barem 16 Fuß zu Eisenach in der Hoforgel, wo Stillgedakt 8' in eben dem Claviere stehet.

Baß. Absolute wird zwar nicht ein Register so heißen; aber bey andern wird es oft gefunden, als Subbaß, Posaunbaß, ꝛc. sonderlich im Pedale, da man alles Bässe nennen kann, wenn die Pfeifen schon noch so klein sind, als: Bauerflötenbaß, dessen größtes Körperchen kaum 1' oder 1½' groß ist; Mixturbaß, Dezehmbaß, ꝛc. Wenn Flötedouce 4' im Manual stehet, und auch von eben der Größe im Pedal; so heißt sie in diesem Flötedoucenbaß, ꝛc.

Basse de Cromorne, s. in Cromorne und in Fagotto.

§. 121.

Basson ist mit Fagott einerley, daher davon bey Fagott zu reden ist.

Bassanelli sind Schnarrwerke, welche Werkmeister in Organo grüning. §. 46. unter die fast unbekannt gewordenen Stimmen zählet. Prätorius beschreibt sie im zweyten Tomo S. 41.

* Bassaune und Bassune. Anleit. S. 397.

* *Basse contre*. S. Contrabaß.

Bäuerlein, Bäuerlin, Bauerflöt, ist alles einerley. Bauerflötbaß heißt das Register, wenn es im Pedale stehet. Etliche schreiben Päurlin, s. Prätor. l. c. S. 140.

St. Catharinen, St. Petri and the Cathedral, all in the same city; likewise in Lübeck at St. Marien, St. Petri, and [Kirche zu] Unsrer Lieben Frau;* in Lüneburg at St. Johannis and St. Lamberti. In all these places it is at 8′ pitch. Werkmeister in his *Organum gruningense redivivum*, §.46, states that in Praetorius's time Bärpfeifen or Krummhorns were called *Vox humana* (for further information, see the *Anleitung*, p. 396, note h).

* i.e., in Praetorius's stoplist. "St. Marien" (referring to the same church) reveals that the source is Mattheson's stoplist.

§. 119.

BALGGLOCKE, see §.125 under "Calcant."

BALGREGISTER. This is what I call the stop that leads to the bellows, unlocking them all at the same time, and also locking them again, so that the pumper can no longer pump them. That this is possible is shown by their effect, since Praetorius on p. 185 in his stoplists reports that this stop is found in Bückeburg. I have never seen or heard of it anywhere else.

§. 120.

BAREM is a Gedeckt; in particular, though, the quietly voiced 8′ and 16′ are given this name. Stillgedakt 8′ means the same thing. The Musicirgedakt† in the Stadtkirche at Jena is called Barem. See Praetorius, Vol. II, p. 164.‡ The Barem 16′ in the court organ at Eisenach, where there is a Stillgedakt [8′] in the same manual, is the same sort of thing.

† i.e., the quiet Gedackt on which figured bass is realized in ensemble playing; see §.150.

‡ Praetorius writes: "Barem is an 8′ Gedackt (Aequalgedackt), very quietly and gently voiced."

BASS. No stop is ever called by this name alone, but it is often used in connection with other [stop names], such as Subbass, Posaunbass, etc. This is especially true in the pedal, where everything may be labeled "Bass," no matter how small the pipes are, such as the Bauerflötenbass, whose largest little pipe is barely 1 or 1 ½′ high, or Mixturbass, Detzehmbass, etc. If there is a 4′ Flötedouce in the manual and also one of the same size in the pedal, then the latter is called Flötedoucebass.

BASSE DE CROMHORNE, see under Cromorne and under Fagotto.

§. 121.

BASSON is the same as Fagott, and is thus discussed under Fagott.

BASSANELLI are reeds that Werkmeister in his *Organum gruningense*, §.46, includes among those stops that have become almost extinct. Praetorius describes it in Vol. II, p. 41.§

§ Here Praetorius is describing the instrument, not the organ stop.

* BASSAUNE and BASSUNE. *Anleitung*, p. 397.
* BASSE CONTRE. See Contrabass.

BÄUERLEIN, BÄUERLIN, BAUERFLÖT are all the same. The stop is called Bauerflötbass if it appears in the pedal. Some [authors] write Päurlin; see Praetorius, *loc. cit.*,

Kap. VII. Von den Registern überhaupt und insonderheit.

S. 140. Es ist weiter nichts, als ein Gedakt, oder Rohrflöt; doch gar klein, etwan 1′ oder 1½′ oder 2′ groß: läßt sich aber wohl hören. Zu Bernau in der Mark ist Baurpfeif, oder Blockflöt; sonst aber sind diese Stimmen divers. S. den Prätorius S. 177. Ebenderselbe hat auch S. 200. in der Disposition der Orgel im Kloster zu Riddageshausen angeführt Nachthorn oder Baurbäßlein 2′ oder 1′. Die Bauerflöt heißt beym Werkmeister S. 55. der Orgelprobe auch fistula rurestris, it. Feldflöt, welche letztere nach §. 142. sonst was besonders ist. S. a. Samber S. 153. Sie wird meistens im Pedal angetroffen. S. Niedts zweyten Theil, nach der Matthesonischen Ausgabe, hin- und wieder, und Prätor. S. 140. und 141. In der Reglerkirche zu Erfurt ist sie 1′; zu Colberg in der heil. Geistkirche ebenfalls; zu Königsberg im Kneiphof oder Dom ist sie 1½′, daselbst heißt sie Bauerpfeife, und ist also eine Quinte. In der Pfarrkirche zu Danzig, it. zu St. Marien in Lübeck, auch in der Altstädter Orgel in Königsberg trift man sie 2′ an. Die besten Bauerflöten werden gemacht von den Rohrflöten; da man Rohrflöt 1′ dazu nimmt. S. Prätor. l. c. S. 141. 2fach soll sie zu Görlitz seyn: es soll aber wol 2 Fuß heißen, oder ist verdoppelt, um ihr eine rechte Stärke zu geben. Prätorius gedenkt S. 126. in der Tabelle auch eines Bauerrohrflötenbasses, oder Rohrschell 1′, da der Deckel ein paraulum oder Röhrchen hat.

§. 122.

Behrpipe,
Beerpfeife, rc. } S. §. 118. bey Bärpipe.

Blockflöt. Was Flöten überhaupt sind, wird in F. §. 144. und folg. erklärt. Wie sie ausser der Orgel aussiehet, kann man im Prätorio finden. Es wäre zwar gut, wenn man hier die Aehnlichkeit zeigen könnte: allein, weil es zu weitläuftig ist; so betrachten wir sie, wie alle Register, nur in der Orgel. Blockpfeife, Blockpipe. Plockpfeife, ist eben so viel; it. Plochflöt. Es ist dabey einige Uneinigkeit. Denn etliche nennen das Gemshorn also: aber das ist nicht recht. S. Prätorius l. c. S. 135. welcher sagt, daß die Spitzflöten 4′ des Klanges halber Plockflöten genennet werden könnten: denn so klingen sie wie die Plockpfeifen. Dabey lese man, was eben daselbst von den Spitzflöten oder Gemshörnern gesagt wird. „Diese, sagt er, „macht ein verständiger Meister nicht kleiner, als 2′. Etliche haben andere Plockflö-„ten, fast auf Querflöten Art, also, daß das corpus noch eins so lang wird, als sonst „die rechte Mensur es mit sich bringt, ohnzugedeckt; daher sich dieselbe in die Oktave „überblasen muß." Die Spitzflöten hat Prätorius im Risse auf der 37. Tabelle also vorgestellet:

Ich habe dies Register angetroffen in Lübeck zu St. Marien 8′; zu St. Petri und im Dom

Ch. VII. Concerning Stops in General and in Particular 75

p. 140. It is nothing other than a Gedeckt or Rohrflöt, but very small, about 1′, 1 ½′ or 2′ in size, but pleasant to listen to. At Bernau in the Mark [Brandenburg] there is a Baurpfeif or Blockflöt, but otherwise these stops are different. See Praetorius, p. 177; also on p. 200 in the stoplist of the organ in the Monastery at Riddagshausen he has indicated a Nachthorn or Baurbässlein 2′ or 1′. In Werkmeister's *Orgelprobe*, p. 55, the Bauerflöt is also called *fistula rurestris* or Feldflöt, the latter of which is otherwise something different according to §.142 [below]. See also Samber, [Vol. II,] p. 153. It is usually encountered in the pedal. See various citations in Part Two of Niedt's [*Handleitung zur Variation des Generalbasses*] in Mattheson's edition, and Praetorius, p. 140 and 141. In the Reglerkirche at Erfurt and at Colberg in the Heilig-Geisteskirche it is a 1′ [stop]; at Königsberg in the Kneiphof or Cathedral it is called Bauerpfeife and is 1 ½′, and thus a quint. In the Pfarrkirche at Danzig, at St. Mary's in Lübeck and also in the Altstädter[kirche] organ in Königsberg it is found at 2′. The Bauerflöte is best constructed as a Rohrflöte, and at 1′. See Praetorius, *loc. cit.*, p. 141. It is reported as a 2 rank stop at Görlitz;* but that should probably read "2 foot", or [perhaps] it is doubled to give it adequate strength. In the Table, p. 126, Praetorius also mentions a Bauerrohrflötenbass or Rohrschell 1′, in which the cap has a *paraulum* or little chimney.†

* See Boxberg, p.[4].

† This final clause is not found in Praetorius.

§. 122.

Beerpipe
Beerpfeife, etc. } see §.118 under Barpipe.
Blockflöt. §.144f.‡ explains in general what flutes are. Praetorius shows what they§ look like outside the [context of an] organ. It would be good to show the similarity¶ here, but because this would be too lengthy we will consider them (as [we do] all other stops) only [as they appear] in the organ. Blockpfeife, Blockpipe and Plockpfeife are synonyms, as is Plochflöt. Here there is some disagreement; some give this name to the Gemshorn, but this is incorrect; see Praetorius, *loc. cit.*, p. 135, who says that because of its sound a 4′ Spitzflöt may be called a Blockflöt—it sounds like a Plockpfeife. In this connection one should read what he says about the Spitzflötes or Gemshorns. "A competent master," he writes, "never builds them smaller than 2′. Some build another [type of] Plockflöt, almost a sort of Querflöt, in which the body is twice as long as the proper scale would otherwise call for, yet not stopped; thus it must overblow at the octave."‖ Praetorius has depicted a Spitzflöt with a sketch in Table 37,** thus:

‡ This should read "§.145f."

§ i.e., the instruments themselves; see Praetorius, Vol. II, *Theatrum Instrumentorum*, Table IX.

¶ i.e., between the instruments and their related organ stops.

I have encountered this stop at Lübeck in St. Mary's at 8′, and in St. Petri and in the

‖ In spite of Adlung's quotation marks, this is a free quote.

** Praetorius labels the pipe he depicts "Blockflöte" (no. 12), and does not show a Spitzflöte—though the Blockflöte he gives is clearly conical.

76 Kap. VII. Von den Registern überhaupt und insonderheit.

Dom 4'; in Hamburg zu St. Jacobi, und in Bremen zu St. Stephan 4'. In Buxtehude steht es auch 4' von Holz. Zu St. Marien in Danzig heißt dies Register Spillpfeif oder Blockflöt, und ist 8'. S. Prätor. l. c. S. 163. Zu Bernau in der Markt steht Baurpfeife oder Blockflöte. Im Löbenicht zu Königsberg ists 4'. Ausser diesen Oertern trift man es noch an in Prag zu St. Dominico; in Rudelstadt; zu St. Cosmi in Stade: meistens 2'. Es steht auch zun Predigern in Erfurt.

Die Plochflöt heißt auch Tibia vulgaris, d. i. gemeine Pfeife. In der Disposition von der Orgel zu St. Petri in Lübeck führt Prätorius auch an Blockflötenbaß 16'. l. c. S. 165.

Bock. S. Tremulant.

§. 123.

Bombarda, ist fast wie die Sordunen, und ein Schnarrwerk, doch daß die Auslassung des Resonanzes durch die Löcherchen geändert wird. Auch will es größere Mundstücken und größere Zungen haben, als die Sordunen, daher sichs auch lauterer hören läßt. Geht besser im Pedal als Manual, und ist 16' oder 8', s. Prätorius l. c. S. 147. und 127 in der Tabelle. Man findet auch geschrieben Pombarda, Pombart, Bombart, Bombardo und Bombardone. Der Name ist von bombo, das Summen oder Brummen. Bombyces oder Bombi bedeutet eben das. Eigentlich ist es der Baß zu der Hautbois oder Schalmey. Ausser der Orgel sind sie nicht mehr Mode, s. Mathesons Orchestre I. P. III. c. III. §. 9. p. 269. it. musikal. Trichter Kap. 10; doch in der Orgel brummen sie, wie eine Posaune, und dringen besser durch, als die Bassons. In der Görlitzer Orgel steht es 16' und zu St. Wenzeslai in Naumburg 8'. Pommer oder Bommer ist vielmals eben das. Aber in der kaum angeführten Görlitzer Orgel ist ein Gedaktpommer 4', von welcher Stimme Boxberg in der Beschreibung derselben sagt, sie sey eine starke Quintatön, folglich kann daselbst kein Schnarrwerk verstanden werden. Die Figur suche man beym Prätorio l. c. (**)

(**) In Frankreich wird unter *Bombarde* allezeit die 16füßige Trompete verstanden.

§. 124.

Bordun, ist ein ziemlich gemein Register, und nichts anders als ein großes Gedakt, sonderlich 16': denn die langen Gedakte nennen die Niederländer Bordun, wenn sie zumal enger Mensur sind. s. Prätorius S. 139. l. c. Daher ist im Dom zu Lübeck Bordun oder Gedakt 16'. Von gleicher Größe steht es im Manual zu Haßleben, und in der Stadtkirche zu Jena; it. in Erfurt zun Augustinern ebenfalls 16'. Samber nennt es auch einigemal, z. Ex. S. 154. von gutem Zinn, S. 151; und S. 150. wird es noch einmal angeführt 16' offen. Er schreibt aber jedesmal Portonen. Man findet es auch geschrieben z. Ex. Perduna, wie Biermann S. 1. thut; denn daselbst lieset man Perduna 16', und S. 11. groß Perduna 32. In der Orgel

Ch. VII. Concerning Stops in General and in Particular

Cathedral at 4′; in Hamburg at St. Jacobi and in Bremen at St. Stephan, both at 4′. There is also one at 4′, of wood, at Buxtehude. At St. Mary's in Danzig this stop is called Spillpfeif or Blockflöt, and is an 8′; see Praetorius, *loc. cit.*, p. 163. At Bernau in the Markt* there is a Baurpfeife or Blockflöt. In the Löbenicht[kirche] at Königsberg it is a 4′. Beside these places, it is found in Prague at St. Dominicus, in Rudelstadt, and at St. Cosmi† in Stade, predominantly at 2′. There is also one at the Prediger[kirche] in Erfurt. The Blockflöt is also called *Tibia vulgaris*, i.e., "common pipe" [gemeine Pfeife‡]. In the stoplist of the organ at St. Petri in Lübeck Praetorius also indicates Blockflötenbass (*loc. cit.*, p. 165).

Bock. See Tremulant.

* This should read "Mark" [Brandenburg]."
† i.e., St. Cosmae.
‡ "Tibia" is properly translated "flute."

§. 123.

Bombarda is a reed, and is almost the same as a Sordun, except that the tone is altered as it emerges by little holes. It also requires a larger shallot and tongue than the Sordun, so that it can produce a louder tone. It is either a 16′ or 8′, and is more suited to the pedal than to the manual. See Praetorius, *loc. cit., p.* 147 and 127 in the Table. It is also written Pombarda, Pombart, Bombart, Bombardo and Bombardone. The name comes from *bombo*, a buzzing or growling; *bombyces* or *bombi* mean the same. It is actually the bass of the Oboe or Schalmei. It is no longer fashionable outside the [context of the] organ; see Mattheson's [*Neu-eröffnete*] *Orchestre* I, Part III, Chap. III, §.9, p. 269, as well as [Fuhrmann's] *Musikalischer Trichter*, Chap. 10[, p. 91]. In the organ, though, it rumbles like a Posaune, and is more penetrating than the Basson. It appears at 16′ in the Görlitz organ and at 8′ in St. Wenceslaus in Naumburg. Pommer or Bommer mean the same thing. But in the Görlitz organ just mentioned there is a Gedaktpommer 4′ which according to Boxberg in his *Beschreibung*§ is a strong Quintatön, and thus cannot be understood as a reed stop. A drawing may be found in Praetorius, *loc. cit.*, [Table XI](**)

§ p.[13].

(**) In France "Bombarde" is always understood as the 16′ Trompete. [Agricola]

§. 124.

Bordun is a rather common stop, and is nothing other than a large Gedakt, particularly at 16′. The Dutch call the tall Gedakts "Bordun", especially when they are of a narrow scale; see Praetorius, [*Syntagma musicum II,*] p. 139. Therefore at the Cathedral at Lübeck there is a Bordun or Gedakt 16′. It appears at the same size¶ in the manual at Hassleben,‖ in the Stadtkirche at Jena, and at the Augustiner[kirche] at Erfurt. Samber speaks of it several times, for example, p. 154 (of good tin) and p. 151; on p. 150 it is again mentioned at 16′, open. He always writes Portonen,** though. It may also be found written Perduna, as Biermann does on p. 1; there it appears as Perduna

¶ i.e., 16′.
‖ There is no entry for "Hassleben" among the stoplists Adlung gives in Chap. 10.
** Samber reads "Portunen."

Kap. VII. Von den Registern überhaupt und insonderheit. 77

Orgel zu St. Petri in Lübeck giebt Prätorius S. 165. Borduna 24′ im Manual an: aber das ist wol ein Druckfehler. Denn ein so groß Gedakt schickt sich nicht ins Manual, und es müßte auch nur bis F gehen. Borduna wird es auch eben daselbst in der Kirche zu U. L. Fr. geschrieben. Burdo zu Cambery ist vielleicht gleich viel, weil sonst kein Gedakt daselbst ist. Und ich glaube, daß Burdo mit der lateinischen Endung soviel seyn soll; als bey den Franzosen Bourdon, welches von Burden herzuleiten, [32]) so bey den Niedersachsen bedeutet crepitum emittere einen fahren lassen. f. u. Bourdon heißt daher eine Hummel oder Wespe, die ein groß Geräusch macht, und an einer Orgel bedeutet es die größten hölzernen Pfeifen, die am meisten brummen; s. Frischens Dictionaire, welche generale Beschreibung mit der unsrigen überein kömmt. Hernach wird das Wort Burdo auch von andern tief brummenden Instrumenten genommen. Also heißen z. E. die zwo tiefsten Saiten auf der Bettelmannsleyer, die nicht verändert werden, sondern den Baß in einem sono mit brummen, Burdones. v. de Chales Tom. III. de Musica prop. 34; und die brummenden Hörner oder Pfeifen am Pohlnischen Bocke, heißen daselbst, prop. 37. auch Burdones. Von unserm vorhabenden Register ist nun noch anzuführen, daß es im vollen Werke bessere Dienste thut, als die Quintatön, indem es im Laufen geschwinder anspringt, welches ich besonders vom Manual verstehe. Im Pedal findet sich dies Register z. Ex. in der Görlitzer Orgel, da es heißt Bordun=Subbaß, weil es eben die Größe hat, wie der Subbaß, und also dessen Stelle wol vertreten kann. Es ist von Sordun wohl zu unterscheiden: denn Sordun ist ein Schnarrwerk, daher beyde a part in einem Clavier in einerley Größe gefunden werden, z. Ex. zu Colberg in der Heiligengeistkirche. Oft aber wird es mit Sordun auch verwechselt, und für eine Schnarrstimme gehalten. Z. Ex. Niedt im zweyten Theile seiner Handleitung Kap. 10. S. 114. sagt: „Sordun, aliis Bordun, eine Schnarrstimme, von 16 und 8 Fuß„ton, auf Regalenart." Allein es ist dies bey uns nicht üblich. Man macht dies Register meistens von Holz, mit einer engern Mensur als der Subbaß hat.

Bötze. Es hat Prätorius l. c. S. 168. in der Stralsunder Orgel ein Schnarrwerk angemerkt, mit engen Körpern gleich aus, dabey steht L. B. Bötze. Was daraus zu machen, weis ich nicht: soll die Stimme diesen Namen haben; weis ich abermal nicht, was das für ein Wort sey, und was es bedeute.

§. 125.

Bourdon, s. Bordun.
Brummhorn, s. Krummhorn.
Buccina, s. Posaune.
Burdo, s. Bordun.

[32]) Mit dieser Ableitung ist der Herr von Mattheson nicht zufrieden, wie aus dessen vollkommenen Kapellmeister zu ersehen S. 464. Anmerk. **)

Ch. VII. Concerning Stops in General and in Particular

16′, and on p. 11 as great Perduna 32′. Praetorius* on p. 165 indicates Borduna 24′ in the manual in the organ at St. Petri in Lübeck, but this must be a printing error. For such a large Gedakt is not suited for the manual, and anyway it would only go down to F. It is also written as Borduna in the Kirche zu Unserer Lieben Frau, likewise in Lübeck. *Burdo* at Chambery is perhaps the same thing, since otherwise there is no Gedakt there. And I believe that *Burdo*, with the Latin ending, must be the same as Bourdon in French, which is derived from Burden,[32)] which among the people of lower Saxony means *crepitum emittere*, to break wind; see below. Thus Bourdon means a bumblebee or wasp that makes a great buzzing, and in an organ it means the largest wooden pipes that usually rumble; see Frischen's *Dictionaire*, whose general description agrees with ours. Afterwards the word *Burdo* was given to other deep rumbling instruments as well. Thus for example the two lowest strings on the hurdy-gurdy,† that are not stopped but rumble along in the bass on one pitch, are called Burdones (see De Chales, Vol. III, *de Musica*, prop. 34). The rumbling horns or pipes on a Polish bagpipe (Pohlnischen Bocke) are also called Burdones (ibid., prop. 37). With regard to the stop under consideration, it should only be added that it is of better service in the plenum than the Quintatön, in that it speaks more promptly in running passages; this is particularly true when it is a manual stop. In the pedal this stop is found, for example, in the Görlitz organ, where it is called Bordun-Subbass, since it is of the same size as a Subbas and thus can indeed take its place. It should indeed be distinguished from Sordun, for Sordun is a reed, and thus both may be found together at the same pitch on the same manual, as for example in the Heiligengeistkirche at Colberg. It is, however, often confused with Sordun, and held to be a reed stop. For example, in the second part of his *Handleitung*, Chap. 10, p. 114, Niedt says, "Sordun, alias Bordun, a reed stop of 16 and 8 foot pitch, a sort of Regal." This, however, is not usual with us. [The Bordun] is usually made of wood, with a narrower scale than the Subbass has.

BÖTZE. Praetorius (*l.c.*,‡ p. 168) has made note of a reed in the Stralsund organ, with narrow resonators throughout; he records there "L. B. Bötze." I do not know what to make of this. If the stop actually bears this name, again I do not know what sort of a word it is or what it means.

§. 125.

BOURDON, see Bordun.
BRUMMHORN, see Krummhorn.
BUCCINA, see Posaune.
BURDO, see Bordun.

* *Syntagma musicum*, Vol. II.

† i.e., the drones.

‡ *Syntagma musicum*, Vol. II.

---

32) Mr. Mattheson is not content with this derivation, as can be seen in his *Volkommene Kapellmeister*, p. 464, note **). [Albrecht]

Calcant, ist zwar bisweilen ein besonderes manubrium, aber eigentlich kein Register. Es ist nur, durch einen Zug ein Glöcklein anzuläuten, dadurch der Calcant erweckt und zum Treten angemahnet wird. Es heißt auch Calcantenglöcklein. Es kann durch das manubrium geschehen, zuweilen aber ist unter dem manubrio ein besonderer Drat, oder dergleichen, zu sehen, womit dem Calcanten das Zeichen gegeben wird. Ein anders ist das **Balgregister**, davon oben §. 119. Aber **Balgglocke** §. 293. ist im Dom zu **Erfurt** eben das.

Carillon oder **Campanett Glockenspiel**. s. §. 155.

Chalmovii 8', war ehedessen zu **Merseburg** im Schlosse zu finden, §. 309. Es scheint so viel zu seyn, als chalemie bey den Franzosen, d. i. die Schallmey. Doch gewiß weis ich es nicht. **Chalumeau** ist bey den Franzosen auch so viel, als chalemie. An dessen Stelle steht ißo in **Merseburg Salicet**. (**)

(**) In den meisten Silbermannischen Orgeln heißt ein 8füßiges Rohrwerk **Chalůmeau**.

Choral. s. Anleit. S. 400.

Choralbassset 1' zu **Kindelbrück**. s. unten §. 306.

Choral=Prästant 4' durchs halbe Clavier zu **Lambspring**, wird von Biermann l. c. S. 10. angeführt.

Chormaß ist kein besonder Register, sondern zeigt nur die Größe der Stimme an, welche dabey genennet wird. Z. Er. **Chormaßprincipal** in der (zu Prätorii Zeiten) neuen Orgel zu **Breslau**, d. i. 8'; it. **Gedaktflöt Chormaß**, d. i. 8'; **offen Chormaß**, d. i. Oktave 8'; **Quinta de Tono** (mußte wol a tono heißen, denn ich halte dafür, daß es die Quintatön sey.) **Chormaß**, d. i. die Quint über 8', so viel ich muthmaßen kann. **Mixtur Chormaß**, da wird 8' dabey seyn, u.s.w. **Unterchormaß** hingegen ist 16', z. Er. eben daselbst, wo alle das Zeug vorkömmt, nemlich zu **Breslau**, da ist **Gedaktflöt unter Chormaß**, d. i. 16'; **Dulcian unter Chormaß**, d. i. 16'; **Unterchorbaß**, d. i. Principal oder Oktave 16'; **Posaununterchorbaß**, d. i. 16'; **Posaunenchormaßbaß**, d. i. 8'; **Trompetenbaß Chormaß**, d. i. 8'; **Unterchormaßbaß**, d. i. Baß 16'. Ja es ist daselbst **Grobemixtur Unterchormaß**, da muß 16' dabey seyn, wiewol es fast nicht glaublich; doch sagt Prätorius ausdrücklich daselbst; Unterchormaß ist 16'; Chormaß ist 8'; Oktave aber 4'. Chormaß wird etwan deswegen 8' seyn, weil eines Menschen Stimme die Tiefe hat: oder weil die Orgeln ordentlich, vom Principal an zu rechnen, diese Tiefe haben.

Chormorne, Basse de chormorne, soll so viel seyn als Fagotto. s. unten in F. it. Anleitung S. 401.

Cilinderquint. s. **Cylinder**.
Cimbel. s. **Cymbel**.
Clairon. s. **Anleitung**, S. 401. imgleichen unten in T. bey **Trompete**.
Clarino. s. **Trompete**, it. Anleit. ibid.
Conus, coni, d. i. **Spitzflöten**, s. in S.

§. 126.

Ch. VII. Concerning Stops in General and in Particular

CALCANT is indeed sometimes a separate drawknob, but actually not a [speaking] stop. The drawknob only serves to ring a little bell, by which the bellows-pumper (Calcant) is alerted and admonished to pump. It is also known as Calcantenglöcklein. This may be done by means of a drawknob, but sometimes there is to be seen under the drawknob[s] a special wire or some such, by which the bellows-pumper is given the signal. The Bellows-stop spoken about in §.119 above is something else. Bellows-bell (Ballglocke) in §.293, found in the Cathedral at Erfurt, is however the same thing.

CARILLON or CAMPANETT GLOCKENSPIEL. See §.155.

CHALMOUII 8′ was formerly to be found in the palace at Merseburg (§.309). It appears to be the same as *chalemie* among the French, that is, the Schallmey. But I cannot be certain of this. Chalumeau among the French is also the same as *chalemie*. In Merseburg a Salicet now stands in its place. (**)

(**) In most Silbermann organs an 8′ reed is called CHALÜMEAU [sic]. [Agricola]

CHORAL. See *Anleitung*, p. 400.

CHORALBASSET 1′ at Kindelbruck, see below, §.306.

CHORAL-PRÄSTANT 4′ extending over half the keyboard at Lambspring is mentioned by Biermann, *l.c.*, p. 10.

CHORMASS does not mean a particular stop, but indicates only the size of the stop to which it refers. For example, Chormassprincipal in the new (in Praetorius's day) organ at Breslau means 8′; likewise Gedaktflöt Chormass means 8′; offen Chormass means Oktave 8′; Quinta de Tono (that must surely mean "a tono," since I interpret it as referring to the Quintatön) Chormass means [literally] the "Quint above 8′," as far as I can surmise. Mixtur Chormass means that there is an 8′ in it, etc. On the other hand, Unterchormass means 16′, for example, in that place where all these terms keep recurring, namely at Breslau, there is a Gedaktflöt unter Chormass, meaning 16′; Dulcian unter Chormass, i.e., 16′; Unterchorbass, i.e., Principal or Oktave 16′; Posaunenunterchorbass, i.e., 16′; Posaunenchormassbass, i.e. 8′; Trompetenbass Chormass,* i.e., 8′; Unterchormassbass, i.e. Bass 16′.† Indeed there is even a Grobemixtur Unterchormass there, which must contain a 16′, though this is almost unbelievable; yet Praetorius has expressly said it is there.‡ Unterchormass is 16′; Chormass is 8′; Oktave, however, 4′. Chormass is probably understood to be the same as 8′ because it has the same pitch as the human voice, or because the organ, figuring from the Principal [8′], usually has this pitch.

* i.e., pedal Trumpet 8′.

† presumably pedal Principal 16′.

‡ *Syntagma musicum II*, p. 172.

CHORMORNE [sic], BASSE DE CHORMORNE, amounts to the same thing as *Fagotto*. See below under "F", as well as the *Anleitung*, p. 401.§

§ Here Adlung writes that this stop appears to be the same as "Cromorne."

CILINDERQUINT. See Cylinder.

CIMBEL. See Cymbal.

CLAIRON. See *Anleitung*, p. 401, as well as below under "T" at [the entry] "Trompete."

CLARINO. See "Trompete", as well as *Anleitung*, ibid.

CONUS, CONI, means Spitzflöten; see under "S".

§. 126.

Contrabaß, ist ein Gedakt Pedalregister, und heißt der 32füßige Subbaß ordentlich also; heißt auch Großsubbaß; auch der Untersatz, vor sich klingt er nicht wohl, und sind dessen große Pfeifen fast, als wenn ein Wind gehet. Aber beym Spielen anderer Register spürt man ihn gar eben, und giebt eine besondere Gravität. Je weiter dessen Mensur ist, wie aller Gedakten, desto pompichter und völliger klingt er; braucht aber viel Wind. Ordentlich wird er von Holz gemacht. Wir finden ihn in Jena in der Stadtkirche, und in Mühlhausen in der Kirche St. Blasii, wo er Untersatz 32' heißt. In der Görlitzer Orgel ist der Contrabaß offen 16' von Holz; doch dergleichen nennt man lieber eine Oktave, wenn das Principal 32' ist. Hier aber ist die Oktave 16' auch dabey, muß also der Contrabaß des Holzes wegen einen besondern Klang haben, da die Oktave von Metall ist. Das übrige siehe unten §. 150.

§. 127.

Contraposaune, s. §. 176.

Copendoff 2 und 3 ist im Kneiphof (oder Dom) zu Königsberg. Ich weis eigentlich daraus nichts zu schlüßen; doch muthmaße ich, es sey eben das, was andere das Koppel nennen, wenn dadurch ein Register verstanden wird, das aus doppelten Pfeifen besteht, sonderlich Rauschpfeife. s. §. 128.

Coppeldone (Koppeldone) ist soviel, als Oktave. s. unten in Oktave.

Coppel, oder Koppel. Dieß Wort bedeutet zuweilen den Zug, dadurch die Manualclaviere mit einander verbunden werden, daß durch eines Spielung auch das andere bewegt wird. Es wird dazu das blinde Clavier eigentlich gebraucht. Heut zu Tage koppelt man die Claviere meistens und commoder durch das Verschieben des obern Claviers. Wenn aber das Pedal an das Manual gekoppelt werden soll, so hat man ein absonderliches manubrium und Registratur dazu, welche auch Windkoppel genennet wird. Manche sind so gemacht, daß die Füße können auf dem Pedal stehen bleiben, wenn das Koppel gezogen wird: aber zuweilen ist das Gegentheil. Durch das Koppel wird selten das Manual an das Pedal verbunden: durch besondere Abstrakten, und andere Dinge, wird es dahin gebracht, daß, wenn das Pedal getreten wird, auch die Register des Manuals sich hören lassen. Vom Clavierkoppel s oben §. 22. Zuweilen geht das Manual beständig mit, zuweilen aber nicht. Im ersten Falle braucht es keines Zuges, und werden entweder die Pedalabstrakten an die Manualpalmuln bevestiget, daß sich dieselben mit dem Pedal niederziehen müssen; oder man führt die Pedalabstrakten anders wohin, und hängt sie an die Manualabstrakten. Wo aber das Manual nicht beständig mitgehet im Pedal; so wird solches durch einen Zug zuwege gebracht. Und das geschiehet wieder auf mancherley Weise. Denn man macht entweder die Manuallade mit doppelten Ventilen, oder mit einem. Macht man sie mit einem, so werden zuweilen die Pedalpalmuln durch besondere Abstrakten und Züge mit den Manual-

Ch. VII. Concerning Stops in General and in Particular

§. 126.

CONTRABASS is a stopped pedal register, and thus is normally called the 32′ Subbass; it is also called Grosssubbass, or Untersatz. It does not sound well alone, its large pipes producing hardly more than a gust of wind. But when it is played with other stops one does indeed sense its presence, and it imparts a particular gravity. The wider its scale is (as with all Gedakts), the more pompous and full it sounds; but it requires a lot of wind. It is usually made of wood. It is found at Jena in the Stadtkirche, and at Mühlhausen in the St. Blasius Church, where it is called Untersatz 32′. In the Görlitz organ the Contrabass is an open 16′ of wood; but such a stop ought rather to be called an Oktave when there is a Principal 32′. In this case, however, the Oktave 16′ is also present, and thus the Contrabass must have a special tone due to the wood, since the Oktave is of metal. For more information see §.150 below.*

* under the entry "Gedackt."

§. 127.

CONTRAPOSAUNE, see §.176.

COPPENDOFF 2 and 3 is [found] in the Kneiphof (or Cathedral) at Königsberg. I know nothing really conclusive about it, but I surmise that it is the same thing that others call the Koppel, if by that [term] is understood a stop that consists of two ranks of pipes, in particular the Rauschpfeife. See §.128.

COPPELDONE (KOPPELDONE) is the same as Oktave. See below under "Oktave."

COPPEL, or KOPPEL. At times this word means the mechanism by which the manual keyboards are coupled to each other, so that by playing on one the other moves as well. For this a blind keyboard† is actually used. Nowadays the keyboards are more frequently and conveniently coupled by shoving the upper keyboard. If, however, the manual is to be coupled to the pedal, this is accomplished by means of a special drawknob and mechanism, which is also called Windkoppel. Many are constructed so that the feet may remain on the pedals‡ when the coupler is drawn; but at times the opposite is [the case]. The manual is seldom [directly] connected to the pedal by coupling; rather special trackers and other mechanisms operate to make the manual stops sound when the pedal is played. Concerning the keyboard coupler, see above, §.22. Sometimes the manual always moves with [the pedal], sometimes not. For the former, no drawknob is necessary; the pedal trackers are either fastened to the manual keys, which then of necessity move with the pedal, or the pedal trackers are led off to another spot [in the mechanism] and connected to the manual trackers. Where the manual does not constantly move with the pedal, however, [the coupler] is brought into operation by a drawknob. This is accomplished in a number of ways: the manual chest is constructed either with double pallets, or with one. If it is constructed with one, then sometimes the pedal keys are connected by special trackers and mechanisms to the manual keys,

† Adlung writes more about this in §.22, without, however, ever explaining it thoroughly.

‡ i.e., a pedal key may remain depressed.

nualpalmuln so verbunden, daß sich diese mit niederziehen. Auf solche Art wird in der Orgel zu St. Andreä in Erfurt das untere Clavier an das Pedal verbunden. Oder, welches gemeiner ist, man verbindet durch besondere Züge die Manualabstrakten an das Pedal, daß die Manualpalmuln sich nicht bewegen. Und da können die Füße, wie auch im vorigen Falle, nicht auf dem Pedal stehen bleiben, wenn man das Koppel ziehet. Dieses Koppel ist zu Erfurt in der Kaufmannsorgel, auch an einigen andern Oertern, so, daß man es mit den Füßen schieben kann. Wie solches zugehe, ist besser zu sehen, als zu schreiben. Die andere Hauptart der Koppel ist mit doppelten Ventilen auf der Manuallade. Diese Ventile liegen zuweilen hinten und vornen; da eine Reihe durch die Abstrakten, die an die Manualclaves verbunden sind, aufgezogen wird, die andere Reihe gegenüber durch besondere Abstrakten, so vom Pedal hinauf geführet werden: diese aber gehen nur durch soviel Cancellen, als das Pedal Claves hat. Folglich muß auch ein besonderer Windkasten auf der andern Seite gemacht seyn, und der Wind durch einen besondern Kanal aus dem Manualkanale dahin geführet werden. Aber diese Art hat eine ganz besondere Incommodität bey sich, davon ich anderswo etwas gedenken will. Daher andere die Ventile des Manuals und Pedals auf eine Seite bringen, und neben einander legen, daß z. E. die Cancelle C nur einmal da ist, aber im Windkasten hat sie zwo Oefnungen neben einander, deren jede mit einem besondern Ventile bedeckt wird, und wird das eine durch die Pedalabstrakten, das andere durch das Manual aufgezogen. Ein Orgelmacher, Namens Weise, hat auch Koppel gemacht, da man das Pedal im Manual mitspielt. Zuweilen werden beyde Manualclaviere an das Pedal besonders gekoppelt, wie z. E. zu St. Seueri in Erfurt.

§. 128.

Coppel (Koppel) heißt auch ein gewisses Register mit 2 oder mehr Stimmen. Daher man dabey saget: fach, als Koppel 2 fach, 3fach. Und das geht wohl an: denn man kann auf ein Register viel Pfeifen bringen, wie in den Mixturen geschiehet. Koppel ist also eine gemischte Stimme, aus 2 und zuweilen zerley Stimmen. Samber l. c. hat dieß Register unterschiedliche mal angeführt; aber er schreibt bald Copl, bald copel, und copula. z. E. S. 155. steht Copl von Metall 8'; it. S. 146. schreibt er Copel oder Copula von Holz; S. 146. steht wieder Copula oder Copel von Holz, und da solls ohne Zweifel soviel bedeuten als Oktave 4. Zu Königsberg in der Pfarrorgel steht Koppel 2::3. Dieß sieht aus wie §. 127. das Copendoff 2 und 3. Ich halte es also für ein Register. - Ob aber die 2 und 3 soviel bedeuten sollen, daß auf einmal die Oktave 2' und die Quinte 3' sich hören lassen, weis ich nicht. Es kann wol seyn. Doch wäre es in der Struktur wie die 2fache Rauschpfeife, wenn in derselben die Quinte größer ist als die Oktave. Weil aber ein Unterschied seyn soll zwischen diesen Registern; so glaube ich, es bedeute vielmehr 2 bis 3 fach. In den untern Oktaven ist sie 2fach: aber in den obern Oktaven, da die Pfeifen allzuklein geworden, 3fach. Der Unterschied muß nur in der kleinen Mensur bestehen. Daher zu St. Dominico in

Prag

so that the latter are pulled down at the same time as the former. In the organ at St. Andreas in Erfurt the lower keyboard is connected to the pedal by a special mechanism so that the manual keys do not move [when the pedal is played]. In this case, as in the former, the feet may not be depressing the pedals while the coupler is being drawn. In the Kaufmannskirche organ at Erfurt, as well as in several other places, this coupler is [constructed] so that it can be operated by shoving with the feet; but it is better to see how this works than to write about it. The other main method of coupling is with double pallets in the manual chest. These pallets sometimes lie at the front and back [of the chest], so that one set is drawn open by the trackers that are connected to the manual keys, while the opposite set [is drawn open] by separate trackers that are brought up from the pedal. These, however, are supplied to only as many wind channels as there are pedal keys. Consequently a separate pallet box must be constructed on the other side [of the manual chest], and the wind brought to it through a special duct from the manual duct. This method, however, has a particular disadvantage to it, about which I will speak elsewhere.* Therefore others place the pallets for manual and pedal on the same side and next to each other, so that, for example, there is only one channel for C, but in the pallet box it has two openings next to each other, each of which is covered by a separate pallet, one of which is drawn open by the pedal trackers, the other of which by the manual [trackers]. An organbuilder by the name of Weise has also constructed a coupler that allows the pedal to be played by the manual. Sometimes both manual keyboards are coupled separately to the pedal, as for example at St. Severi in Erfurt.

* See Vol. II, §.390.

§. 128.

COPPEL (KOPPEL) also means a specific stop with two or more ranks. Thus the term "fach" [i.e., "ranks"] appears with it, as Koppel 2 fach, 3 fach. This expression is indeed quite correct, since many pipes can be set on one stop, as happens in mixtures. Thus the Koppel is a compound stop, of two and sometimes 3 ranks. Samber, *l.c.*, has mentioned this stop at various times, but he sometimes writes Copl, sometimes copel or *copula*. For example, [in Vol. II] on p. 155 appears "Copl of Metal" 8'; on p. 146 [& 147] he writes "Copel" or "Copula of wood"; on p. 146† there again appears "Copula or Copel of wood," and there it must certainly mean the same as Oktave 4'.‡ In the Pfarrkirche at Königsberg there is a "Koppel 2-3." This looks to be the same as the "Copendoff 2 and 3" in §.127; thus I consider it to be a single stop. Whether the "2 and 3" mean that the Oktave 2' and Quinte 3' are to be heard together, I do not know; this could well be the case. But then it would be like a 2-rank Rauschpfeife in its composition, one in which the Quinte is larger than the Oktave. Since, however, there ought to be a distinction between these stops [i.e., the Rauschpfeife and the Koppel], I do believe that it more likely means 2-3 ranks. In the lower octaves it is 2 ranks, but in the upper octaves, where the pipes become very small, it is 3 ranks. The distinction must lie in the smaller scale§. Thus at St. Dominicus in Prague the Rauschpfeife, Kop-

† should read "147."

‡ Samber seems to mean "Gedackt 8'." Adlung's presumption, "Oktave 4'," is inconsistent with his statement that the Coppel is a compound stop, but is consistent with his assertion that the stop consists of principal pipes, whatever its composition.

§ presumably of the Koppel; but this is not entirely clear from the text as it stands.

Prag die Rauschpfeife, Koppel und Cymbel scharf auf einem Clavier zu finden, woraus ich schlüßen kann, daß diese Stimmen unterschieden sind. Das Koppel daselbst ist 1½ = 1 Fuß; soll wol die Oktave 1' und Quinte 1½' seyn, da hingegen die Rauschpfeife die Oktave wenigstens 2' bis 4' hat; die Quinte aber 3'. Das Scharf ist mehr fach. Was aber von der Verdoppelung der Stimmen zu merken, das soll bey den Mixturen gesagt werden. Doch kann ich nicht läugnen, es sey eigentlich in dem Koppel dem Orgelmacher keine Gränze zu setzen, als welcher allerhand Stimmen mit einander vermischen kann. Will er sie alsdann Koppel nennen, so kann er es auch thun. Wer also eigentlich wissen will, was die obige 2 = 3 bedeute, der gebe sich die Mühe, es von dem dasigen Organisten zu erfahren. Eben zu Prag l. c. ist im Pedal auch ein Koppel 3fach, nämlich Quinte 3' Superoktave 1', und Terz 2'. NB. Man lache nicht über die Terz 2': denn das kann für sich nie eine Terz e geben, sondern eine Oktave c. Aber der Schreiber der Disposition dasiger Orgel will damit anzeigen, es sey die Terz aus dem 2fußigen Oktavenregister. Mehr davon siehe unten von der Terz. Nach Prätorii Zeugniß hat man vor Alters die Großhohlflöt 8' Ton auch Subbaß, Thunbaß it. Koppel genannt. s. dessen Organogr. Tom. II. p. 132.

§. 129.

Coppelflöt (Koppelfl.) ist von dem vorigen Register wohl zu unterscheiden. Denn dadurch verstehen die Niederländer eben das Register, welches man sonst Gemshorn 8' nennt. s. in Gemshorn. Imgl. Prätor l. c. S. 134. u. Tab. 38. Deswegen ist sie auch 8' bey den Barfüßern in Erfurt, allwo kein besonder Gemshorn zu finden, weil Koppelflöt eben das ist. Koppelflöt 4' ist auch zu Braunschweig in der Orgel St. Blasii, und zu St. Gotthard in Hildesheim zu finden. s. Prätor: S. 178. und 198. (it. Anleitung zur mus. Gel. S. 405. u. f.)

§. 130.

Coppel (Koppel) hat noch eine Bedeutung. Denn wo der Raum enge, oder die Kirche arm ist, da werden zuweilen etliche Register auf solche Weise verfertiget, daß sie durch besondere Züge und manubria im Manual und Pedal jedesmal können allein gebraucht werden. Doch steht an den manubriis ordentlich nicht der Name Koppel, sondern das Register ist selbst genennt. Z. E. in einem Dorfe bey Erfurt, Hohenfelden genannt, sind 2 manubria zu der Quintatön 8'; an beyden steht Quintatön 8', und ist nur ein Register. Wenn das eine gezogen wird, hört man sie im Manual allein: wenn das andere gezogen ist, klingt sie im Pedal. Wenn beyde gezogen sind, geht sie oben und unten. In der Kreuzkirche in Dreßden geht die Mixtur eben so ins Pedal und Manual zugleich. Es ist dies ein compendium für arme Kirchen; aber wenn man in der Arbeit und Windführungen etwas versiehet, entstehet daher viel Ungelegenheit, und klingen solche getheilte Register gar oft falsch, besonders in Schnarrwer-

Ch. VII. Concerning Stops in General and in Particular

pel and Cymbel-scharf are found on the same keyboard*, from which I conclude that these stops are different. The Koppel there is 1 ½- 1′, and must indeed be the Oktave 1′ and Quinte 1 ½′, while on the other hand the Rauschpfeife contains at least the Oktave 2′ or 4′, as well as the Quinte 3′. The Scharf† has multiple ranks. What [is necessary] to note about the doubling of pitches is described under the mixtures.‡ But to tell the truth, there is actually no limit to the variety of stops that an organbuilder can combine with each other in a Koppel. If he wants to call something Koppel, he is free to do so. Anyone who wants to know what the "2-3" mentioned above means should take the trouble to find it out from the incumbent organist. Likewise at St. Dominicus in Prague there is also in the pedal a Koppel 3 ranks, namely Quinte 3′, Superoktave 1′, and Terz 2′. N.B. One ought not to laugh about "Terz 2′"—that would not of course produce a Terz [sounding] "e", but rather an Oktave [sounding] "c". In doing this, however, the writer of the stoplist of the organ there intends to indicate that it is a Terz constructed above a 2-foot Oktave stop. For more on this, see "Terz".§ According to Praetorius's testimony, in times past the Grosshohlflöt 8′ pitch was also called Subbass, Thunbass or Koppel; see his *Organographia,* Vol. II, p. 132.

* If it is correctly translated, then this statement is in error. All three of these stops do indeed appear in this organ, but the first two are in the Ober-Positiv, while the third is in the Brust; see Mattheson's Appendix to Niedt's *Musicalische Handleitung,* p. 194, as well as Chapter 10 below.

† Probably the "Cymbel-scharf" mentioned above.

‡ See §.167 below.

§ See §.197 below.

§. 129.

COPPELFLÖT (KOPPELFL.) is to be distinguished from the stop just described above. By it the Dutch mean the stop that is otherwise called Gemshorn 8′; see under Gemshorn. Note also Praetorius, [Vol. II,] p. 134 and Table 38. Thus it is found at 8′ in the Barfüsserkirche in Erfurt, where there is otherwise found no Gemshorn, since [this] Koppelflöt is indeed [a Gemshorn]. Koppelflöt 4′ is also found at Braunschweig in the organ of St. Blasius Church, and at St. Gotthard in Hildesheim; see Praetorius, [Vol. II,] pp. 178 and 198, as well as the *Anleitung zur musikalischen Gelahrtheit,* pp. 405f.

§. 130.

COPPEL (KOPPEL) has yet another meaning. For where there is limited space, or the church is poor, then sometimes several stops are constructed in such a way that, by means of special mechanisms and drawknobs they may be used separately both in the manual and pedal. Yet the name Koppel does not usually appear on the drawknob, rather the name of the stop itself. For example, in a village near Erfurt called Hohenfelden there are two drawknobs for the Quintatön 8′. Both are called Quintatön 8′, and yet there is only one stop. If one is drawn, the stop is heard only in the manual; if the other is drawn, it sounds in the pedal. If both are drawn, then it speaks both above and below. In the Kreuzkirche at Dresden the Mixtur likewise speaks both in the pedal and the manual. This is an economy measure for poor churches; but if a mistake is made in the construction and the wind conduits, then many problems result. Such divided stops often speak falsely, especially the reeds, if the wind pressure is not completely

82 Kap. VII. Von den Registern überhaupt und insonderheit.

ken, wenn der Zufall des Windes nicht gleich ist: oder wenn der Wind in den Winkeln sich stößt, oder von einem Orte weiter als vom andern zur Pfeife geführet wird, und dahero seine Aequalität verliert. s. **Werkmeisters Orgelprobe**, Kap. 19. S. 42. welcher von diesem compendio nicht viel zu halten scheint, und deswegen den Rath giebt, daß man zuvor alles sehr wohl überlegen solle, ob sichs auch da thun läßt, wo man dergleichen anbringen will.

Coppeloktave. (Koppeloktave.) s. unten in **Oktave**, §. 171.

§. 131.

Cornetto da caccia.
Corne par force.
Corne Sylvestre.
} ist mit **Waldhorn** einerley. S. **Waldhorn**.

Cornu.
Cornettino.
Cornetto.
Corno.
Cornetto torto.
Cornetto muto.
Cornon.
} ist alles einerley mit den Zinken, wenn man dadurch ein gewisses Schnarrwerk verstehet. S. **Zinken**.

§. 132.

Cornet ist etwas besonders: heißt aber zuweilen auch cornu. Man versteht dadurch ein Schnarrwerk, das meistens in Basse gebraucht wird. Es hat Regalmensur, aber etwas enger und länger, 2' oder 4' ton: das corpus aber ist wol 9" hoch bey 4' ton, und bey 2' ton nur 4" bis 5". s. **Prätor.** S. 146. Doch findet man sie auch größer. Dies Register heißt bey uns gemeiniglich **Cornetbaß**. Die Struktur ist konisch, und meistens von Blech: doch können die corpora auch von Metall verfertiget werden. Der **Cornet** wird zuweilen 8' gemacht. s. **Niedt** l. c. Kap. 11. Also ist **Cornet** 8' im Löbenicht zu Königsberg, und zwar im Manual; eben also auch in der Haberbergischen Orgel daselbst. It. zu Sendomir, da steht: **Cornet**, litice 8'; ist also litice eben so viel. Oder es ist der **Cornet** zuweilen mit dem Zinken vermischt worden, z. E. so ist Zink oder Cornet zu U. L. Fr. in **Lübeck**, und zu St. Ulrich in **Magdeburg**. S. **Prätor.** S. 166. u. 175. l. c. Eben derselbe legt dem **Cornet** auch den Namen Spitz bey. s. S. 163. Der Zink ist ordentlich 8', und wird im Manual gebraucht. **Cornetbaß** 8' im Pedal ist zu finden in **Lübeck** in der Orgel zu St. Petri. s. **Prätor.** l. c. In der Barfüsser Orgel in **Erfurt** ist **Singendcornet** im Pedal, da die Intonation etwas angenehmer gemacht seyn soll, als sonst. Eben als wie **Singendregal** soviel ist, als wenn eine Jungfer singt, oder als wenn eine Geige gestrichen wird, weil **Geigenregal** eben

equal, or if the wind gusts about in the corners, or must travel further to the pipe from one location than from another,* and thus is not supplied equally. See Werkmeister's *Orgelprobe*, chap. 19, p. 42, which does not seem to think much of this economy measure, and thus advises that one should carefully consider the whole matter in advance, whether the device will actually work where it is to be installed.

COPPELOKTAVE (KOPPELOKTAVE). See below under Oktave, §.171.

* i.e., the wind comes from two sources to the same pipe, one source being used when the stop sounds in the pedal, and one for the manual; this is not the same as the double-pallet system (Windkoppel) described in §.127.

§. 131.

CORNETTO DA CACCIA.
CORNE PAR FORCE.
CORNE SYLVESTRE.
} is the same as WALDHORN. See WALDHORN.

CORNU.
CORNETTINO.
CORNETTO.
CORNO.
CORNETTO TORTO.
CORNETTO MUTO.
CORNON.
} are all the same as the Zink, if by this [term] is meant a certain reed stop. See ZINK.

§. 132.

CORNET[, however,] is something else, though at times it is also called *cornu*. By this is meant a reed that is used mostly in the pedal. It has the scale of a Regal, but somewhat narrower and longer. It is of 2' or 4' pitch, yet the resonator is a mere 9" tall when it is 4', and only 4"-5" tall when it is 2"; see Praetorius, [Vol. II,] p. 146. It is, however, also found in larger sizes. In this area this stop is usually called Cornetbass. It is conical in structure, and usually of sheet iron, but the resonators may also be constructed of pipe metal. At times the Cornet is made at 8'; see Niedt, *loc. cit.*, chap. II. Thus there is a Cornet 8' in the Löbenichtkirche at Königsberg, and indeed in the manual, as well as in the Haberbergkirche there. Likewise at Sendomir there is a Cornet or *litice* 8', *litice* meaning the same thing [in Czech]. At times the Cornet is confused with the Zink, thus for example there is Zink or Cornet at the Kirche zu Unsrer Lieben Frau in Lübeck, and at St. Ulrich in Magdeburg; see Praetorius, p. 166 and 175, *loc. cit.*. The same [author] assigns the name "Spitz" to the Cornet; see p. 163. The Zink is ordinarily 8' and is used in the manual. Cornetbass 8' in the pedal is to be found in Lübeck in the organ at St. Petri; see Praetorius, *loc. cit.*. There is a Singendcornet in the pedal in the Barfüsserkirche organ in Erfurt, where its voicing is supposed to be somewhat more pleasant than elsewhere. Just as the Singendregal is supposed to imitate a maiden singing, or the Geigenregal a violin being bowed, thus

eben das ist. Also soll auch Singendcornet etwas lieblicher sich hören lassen, als man insgemein vom Cornet gewohnt ist. Denn sonst klingt das Cornet 2′, als wenn die Lämmer schreyen; dahingegen Cornet 4′ dem Tone einer Schalmey ziemlich nahe kömmt. Daher Prätorius im Thum zu Magdeburg, S. 173. anführt; Schallmey oder Cornet 4′, folglich beyde Stimmen für einerley hält. Exempel von Cornetbaß 2′ findet man in vielen Orgeln. Cornet 1′ steht, nach Prätorii Bericht, in der Catharinenkirche zu Magdeburg. Cornettin 2′ ist in Merseburg und in Salzburg zu finden. In der Pfarrkirche zu Danzig ist halber Cornet 8′. Qu. Was bedeutet das? Resp. Ich glaube, es sey so viel, als daß das Register nicht durch das ganze Manual gehe, sondern etwan von oben herab bis ins c̄ oder g. Solche Gedanken hat Mattheson im Anhange zu Niedts 2ten Theile, S. 168. allwo auf gleiche Weise vom halben Zinken steht: und daraus schlüße ich destomehr, das es wol für den Zinken genommen werde. Doch hat die größte Pfeife den 8füßigen Ton nicht, ob er gleich 8′ton genennet wird; sondern der Verstand ist: wenn das Register fortgeführet würde; so würde das C 8′ton haben: oder es ist aus 8′ton gearbeitet, welches eben soviel heißt. Cornet separé heißt ein **abgesondertes Cornet**, und wird davon also genennet, wenn es auf einem besondern Claviere stehet, etwan auf dem dritten. Sonst aber ist **abgesondert** etwas anders, s. unten §. 276. Cornet d'Echo ist auch ein solch Register zum Echo mit einem 4ten Claviere. (S. Anleitung S. 408. Anmerkung t.) (**)

(**) **Cornet.** Wird auch in einem andern Verstande gebraucht, und ist alsdann eine vom vorigen ganz verschiedene Stimme. In dieser zweyten Bedeutung ist **Cornet** eine Art von **Mixturwerk**, gemeiniglich fünf oder auch nur dreyfach. Es ist in Frankreich erfunden worden, und noch so gar lange nicht in Deutschland üblich. Doch findet man es in verschiedenen neuern Orgeln Deutschlands. Es geht gemeiniglich nur durch die zwo obersten Oktaven des Claviers. Bisweilen noch etliche Tone tiefer. Es repetiret nicht, und ist gemeiniglich so zusammengesetzt: aus 8 Fuß, 4 F. 3 F. 2 F. 1⅗ Fuß, wenn es nemlich fünffach ist. Es ist von weiterer Mensur, als die Principalstimmen. In großen Orgeln, zumal in Frankreich, giebt es fast auf jedem Clavier eins: da denn das auf dem Hauptclaviere die weiteste Mensur hat, und le Grand (das große) **Cornet** genennet wird. Ein anderes heißt **Cornet separé**, oder **Cornet de Recit**, und das geht manchmal 3 Oktaven tief, und hat sein eigenes Clavier. Dieses ist von engerer Mensur als das große **Cornet**, das auch gemeiniglich etliche Töne in der Tiefe mehr, als jenes. Noch ein anderes heißt: **Cornet d'Echo**. Dieses hat wieder ein anderes Clavier, und steht am entferntesten oder verstecktesten Orte der Orgel: damit sein Klang gleichsam als von ferne herkommend klingt. Sein Tonumfang und seine Mensur sind dem **Cornet de Recit** gleich. Zuweilen ist es auch von noch engerer Mensur. Diese beyden letzteren Arten der **Cornette** sind in Deutschland noch nicht sehr üblich. Doch findet man das **Cornet d'Echo** in einigen Orgeln, aber so, daß es nicht ein ganz eigenes Claviere und Windlade hat, sondern gemeiniglich zum Oberwerke gehöret. Eins dergleichen ist in der neuen, von Silbermann gebaueten Dresdener Schloßorgel, und noch in einigen andern Werken zu finden. Es kann das **Cornet d'Echo** gar mit einem besondern Kasten von Brettern bedeckt werden. Und in diesem Falle, kann, wenn der Deckel des Kastens beweglich, und so eingerichtet ist, daß er durch einen besondern Zug mehr oder weniger aufgehoben und wieder niedergelassen werden kann, der fortdaurende Ton

Ch. VII. Concerning Stops in General and in Particular 83

a Singendcornet is supposed to be somewhat gentler than a Cornet is usually considered to be. Normally the Cornet 2′ sounds like the bleating of lambs, while the Cornet 4′ approximates the timbre of a Schalmey. Thus Praetorius mentions a Schalmey or Cornet 4′ in the Cathedral at Magdeburg, and consequently considers these stops to be the same. Many organs contain examples of the Cornetbass 2′. Praetorius reports that there is a Cornet 1′ in the Catherinenkirche at Magdeburg. The Cornettin 2′ is to be found at Merseburg and at Salzburg. In the Pfarrkirche at Danzig there is a "halber Cornet 8′." Question: what does that mean? Reply: I believe it means that the stop does not extend through the entire keyboard, rather from the top down to c′ or g. Matheson expresses a similar opinion in the Appendix to Niedt's Part Two, p. 168, where he says the same thing about a "halber Zinken;" thus I conclude all the more confidently that it [i.e., the "halber Cornet 8′"] must be considered as a Zink. The largest pipe, however, is not of 8′ pitch, even though it is labelled that way. Rather one must understand that if the stop were completed, then the C would be of 8′ pitch. In other words, it is constructed at 8′ pitch. *Cornet separe* means a Cornet set apart (abgesondertes), and is so called if it stands on a separate keyboard, usually the third. Otherwise "abgesondert" means something else; see §. 276 below. Cornet d'Echo is also such a stop [built as] an echo from a fourth keyboard (see the *Anleitung, p.* 408, note t.)* (**)

(**) Cornet is also used in another sense, in which it is an entirely different stop from that above. In this second meaning, Cornet is a type of mixture stop, commonly 5 ranks, but also [found as] only 3 ranks. It is found in France, and has not been common all that long in Germany. Nevertheless it is found in various newer organs in Germany. It normally extends only over the two uppermost octaves of the keyboard,† though at times a few notes lower. It does not break back, and is usually composed of 8′, 4′, 3′, 2′, and 1 ⅗′, if indeed it is 5 ranks. It is of wider scale than the principal stops. In large organs, especially in France, there is one on almost every keyboard. The one on the main keyboard has the broadest scale, and is called le Grand (the great) Cornet. Another is called Cornet separé, or Cornet de Recit, and it sometimes extends downward [from c‴] for 3 octaves‡ and has its own keyboard.§ It is of narrower scale than the great Cornet, but also normally goes a few notes lower. Yet another [Cornet] is called Cornet d'Echo. Again it has its own keyboard, and is located in the most distant and concealed spot in the organ [case], so that its sound gives the impression of coming from afar. Its compass and scale are the same as the Cornet de Recit, though sometimes it may be of a yet narrower scale. Both of these last kinds of Cornets are not yet very common in Germany. Yet the Cornet d'Echo is found in several organs, though it does not have its own separate keyboard and windchest, but is commonly part of the Oberwerk. One of these is in the Dresden Palace Church organ, newly built by [Gottfried] Silbermann;¶ a few other organs have it as well. The Cornet d'Echo may be entirely enclosed within a special box of boards. In this case a prolonged tone may to some degree achieve a swelling effect, i.e., become stronger or weaker, if the lid of the box is movable and constructed so that it may be raised and lowered to a greater or lesser ex-

* In the immediately previous sentences Adlung, by considering the *cornet separe* to be related to the German reed Cornet (Kornett), clearly reveals his ignorance of contemporary French organs. If we presume the explanation here dates from 1726 or shortly thereafter, it is interesting to note that by the time Adlung published the *Anleitung* (1758) he knew enough to say that the Cornet could also be a compound flue stop (see the entry Cornet, pp. 407-8)—probably as a result of Gottfried Silbermann's work. It is just such a spot as this that suggests that Albrecht left Adlung's text unaltered; perhaps it was Albrecht who added here the parenthetical reference to the *Anleitung,* or perhaps it was Adlung himself who entered it into his manuscript. Agricola's note immediately following shows, of course, that by the latter half of the 1750's knowledgeable German organists were quite well aware of the characteristics of contemporary French organs.

† i.e., c′ - c‴.

‡ i.e., to tenor c.

§ i.e., the Recit of the French classic organ.

¶ cf. the stoplist of this organ in Chapter 10.

einigermaßen schwellend gemacht, das ist, verstärkt und wieder geschwächet werden. Folglich kann man damit eine cantable Melodie am ähnlichsten ausführen. Was also der seel. Verfasser am Ende des vorigen Absatzes vom Cornet sepaure, und dem Cornet d'Echo sagt: ist von dieser Art der Cornette, und nicht von dem oben von ihm beschriebenen Rohrwerke welches auch Cornet heißt, zu verstehen.

§. 133.

Cors de chasse ist so viel als Waldhorn, daher es unten zu suchen.
Cormorne, und } S. in Krumhorn. §. 164.
Cromorne.

* Cuspida von cuspis, eine Spitze, ist die Spitzflöte, s. unten in S.

* Cylinder, cylindrisch heißt eine Pfeife, welche von oben bis unten einerley Weite hat; als cylinder Quint, zum Unterschiede der spitzigen oder Gemsquinten. Cylinderquint 3′ kömmt vor zu Gera. Ein Cylinder heißt sonst ein Körper der rund ist, aber nicht wie eine Kugel, sondern dabey lang, und der Länge nach ist er allenthalben gleich weit, oder dicke. Z. Ex.  Daraus schlüße ich, daß die Cylinderquint nichts seyn solle, als eine ordentliche Quint, nur daß die Pfeifen cylindrisch sind, nicht, wie bisweilen geschiehet, zugespitzt, wie denn diese Stimme entgegen gesetzt wird der dabey stehenden Gemsquint 6′.

Cymbel bedeutet vielerley. Einmal bedeutet es den sogenannten Stern, oder die Cymbelglöcklein; denn eigentlich nennt man Cymbeln die kleinen hell- und silbermäßig klingenden Glöcklein, deren jede so groß als die runden Schällen, etwan so hoch und breit, als ein Daumen breit ist. Man nimmt sie aber gern von verschiedener Größe. Unten sind sie offen, wie die Glocken, haben unten um den Rand viel Zacken, und werden durch einen kleinen Knöpfel, wie Glocken, klingend gemacht. Dergleichen Cymbeln werden 3, 4, 5, ꝛc. zusammen an eine Welle bevestiget, wie die Glocken an ihren Wellen: diese Welle wird in einen Stuhl, wie in einem Glockenstuhle, horizontal aufgelegt, und an der andern Seite oder Spitze wird ein großes Rad angemacht, wie die Wasserräder in den Mühlen. Je größer es ist, desto besser läuft es herum durch wenig Wind. Wenn dies Rad herum läuft; so drehet es die Welle sammt den Cymbeln herum, wie die Welle vom Wasserrade getrieben wird, und schlägt es an, daß es solchergestalt einen zwar confusen doch artigen Klang von sich giebt. Die Schällen sind nämlich, nach Beschaffenheit ihrer Größe, von verschiedenem Klange. Da nun der Wind das Rad treiben muß; so muß es auch so gemacht werden, daß sich der Wind darinne fängt. Man nimmt eine Welle, etwas dick, deren Diameter nach Proportion der Schällen 1″ oder 1½′ lang seyn kann, schneidet sehr viel Ritze hinein, so enge zusammen, als man kann. Z. Ex  in jeden Ritz leimet man ein gar subtiles Brett, etwan

tent by a special mechanism. Consequently with it a cantabile melody may be performed quite convincingly. Thus what the late author says at the end of the last paragraph about the Cornet separe and the Cornet d'Echo is to be understood [as referring to] this type of Cornet, and not to the reed he describes above, that is also called Cornet. [Agricola]

§. 133.

Cors de chasse is the same as Waldhorn, which may be consulted below.

Cormorne and
Cromorne } see under Krummhorn, §.164.

* Cuspida, from *cuspis*, a point, is the Spitzflöte; see below under S.

* Cylinder or cylindrical refers to a pipe that has the same width from top to bottom; thus cylinder Quint, as distinct from the conical or Gemsquinte. Cylinderquint 3′ appears at Gera. A cylinder moreover means a body that is round, but not like a ball, rather at the same time long, and throughout its length it is always equally wide or thick, for example: 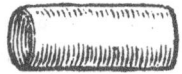 Thus I conclude that a Cylinderquint is nothing more than an ordinary Quint, only that the pipes are cylindrical and not, as sometimes is the case, conical; in this way this stop is distinguished from the Gemsquint 6′ listed next to it [in §.301].

Cymbel means a number of things. For one, it means the so-called star or little tinkling bells; for the small bright and silvery tinkling little bells are properly called Cymbels, each of these being as large as round bells* and about as high and wide as the width of the thumb. But they come in all sorts of sizes. On the bottom they are open like bells, having numerous teeth around the lower [rim], and are made to sound by means of a small clapper, like bells. This sort of Cymbel is fastened to an axle in groups of 3, 4, 5 or more, just like [large] bells on their yokes. This axle is set horizontally into a frame, like a bell mounting, and on the opposite side or end [from the Cymbels] a large wheel is attached, like the water wheels in mills. The larger it is, the less wind it needs to make it revolve. When this wheel turns, it then turns the axle together with the Cymbels (just as an axle is driven by a water wheel), causing them to ring so that they produce a sound indeed confused, but agreeable. The bells are of course of various timbres, according to the nature of their sizes. Since wind must drive the wheel, it must be made in such a way that it catches the [stream of] wind. One takes an axle, rather thick, whose diameter may be 1″ to 1 ½″, depending on the proportions of the bells, and cuts many slots into it, as close together as possible; for example, 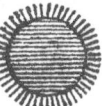 In each slot is

* Adlung's terminology is unclear; he may be referring to the jingles on a tambourine, which is called in German "Schellentrommel."

etwan 2 oder 3 Finger in der größten Breite, und kaum den 10ten Theil eines Zolls dicke. Wenns gut gehen soll; so macht man deren Länge wol 1' lang. Doch hat man auch kürzere Räder. Wenn nun der Wind an deren äusserste Theile anstößt; so läuft das Rad herum. Zuweilen werden auch Papiere, oder dergleichen leichte Materie, auf die ganze Breite des Rads zu beyden Seiten angeklebt, daß also jedes hölzerne Brett eine Kammer präsentirt, die oben offen ist, wo der Wind anstößt; da fängt sich der Wind noch stärker, alsdann wird in den Windkanal, wo man hin will, eine runde oder viereckigte Röhre gesetzt, deren andere Spitze oder Oefnung an das Rad geht. Durch ein besonder Ventil wird der Wind in diese Röhre gelassen; so läuft der Stern herum; oder wieder ausgeschlossen, so steht er wieder stille. Durch einen besondern Registerzug wird das Ventil regieret; daran steht oft Cymbel, zuweilen aber auch wol Stern, oder beydes zugleich, Cymbelstern geschrieben; weil das umtreibende Rad wie ein Stern gestaltet ist; am allermeisten deswegen, weil an die Welle dieses Rads ein Stern von Bildschnitzerarbeit bevestiget wird. In Jena in der Stadtorgel steht Timpani, und ist eben 'as bisher beschriebene Register. Da muß man es von Tympanum unterscheiden, wovon unten §. 203. nachzulesen. Die Welle wird durch das äusserste Gebaude der Orgel geführet, (denn man kann die Cymbel hinbringen, wo man hin will) und an den äussersten Theil der Stern angemacht, vergoldet und sonst wohl geputzt. Dieser läuft also mit herum. Zuweilen sieht man an einer Orgel 2 oder mehr Sterne laufen, welches nicht nur zum Zierrathe dienet, sondern es sind würklich auch so viel Parthien Glocken vorhanden, als sich äusserlich Sterne präsentiren. Z. Er. im Dom zu Naumburg sind drey Sterne, jeder hat 8 Glocken. Dergleichen finden sich auch zun Predigern in Erfurt. Die Struktur des Cymbelstuhls kann auch auf folgende Art verfertiget werden. Man macht an die Welle jede Cymbel für sich beweglich, und die Welle unbeweglich. Jede Cymbel bekömmt ein kleines Zäpfchen; daneben, oder besser, oben darüber geht die bewegliche Welle mit dem Rade, mit eben dergleichen Zapfen. Wenn denn diese Welle durch das Rad umgetrieben wird; so nehmen deren Zapfen die Cymbelzapfen mit herum. Und daß sie nicht zugleich anschlagen, sondern eine nach der andern, so werden sie nicht in gerader, sondern in ungerader Linie an die obere Welle gemacht. Ein Fehler bey dem Sterne ist, wenn die Schällen wie Kuh- oder Schafschällen, und nicht helle klingen; it. wenn das Eingebäude des Sterns nicht fein gefüttert ist, da es denn nothwendig klappert. S. Werkmeisters Orgelprobe, S. 38. Kap. 16. In der Orgel zu St. Gertrud in Hamburg ist ein sonderlicher Stern, in dessen Mitte (von aussen, da er stark vergoldet ist,) ist eine Rose von geschliffenen Stahl auf Diamantenart, welche, wenn die Sonne darauf scheinet, und der Stern läuft, einen Blitz von sich wirft. Auf den Spitzen des Sterns stehen gleichfalls dergleichen kleinere geschlifne Rosen, zwischen welchen gemahlte Flammen herausgehen, welche bey der Wendung einen Regenbogen abbilden. Der Glöcklein sind achte. s. Matthesons Anhang zum Niedt. S. 181. In den Choralgesängen will sie Niedt nicht leiden, und nennt sie absurd. S. dessen 3ten Theil S. 46. Andern wollen sie auch nicht allezeit gefallen, daher

L 3   an

Ch. VII. Concerning Stops in General and in Particular 85

glued a very thin board, at the most about 2–3 fingerwidths wide, and barely 1 $^1/_{10}$ of an inch thick. If it is to work properly, then they ought to be a good 1' long, though there are also shorter wheels.* If the wind now strikes their outer edges, then the wheel turns. Sometimes [a disk of] paper or some other light material is glued over both sides of the wheel, so that each wooden board presents a chamber that is open at the top where the wind strikes. Then the wind catches it even more forcefully. Then at some point in the wind duct a round or square tube is placed, whose other end or opening leads to the wheel. The wind is let into this tube by means of a special valve, and then the wheel revolves. When the valve is shut off, the wheel again stands still. The valve is controlled by means of a special stopknob, which often bears the designation "Cymbel," but sometimes "Stern" or both [words] together: "Cymbelstern." This is because the revolving wheel is shaped like a star, but chiefly it is because a carved wooden star is affixed to the axle of this wheel.† In the Stadtkirche at Jena there is a "Tympani" that is the same as the stop just described. Thus this must be distinguished from Tympanum, about which more may be read in §.203 below. The axle is carried through to the exterior of the organ case (since the Cymbel may be placed wherever desired), and the star, gilded and otherwise ornamented, is affixed to the outer end of it. This [star] thus revolves with [the axle]. Sometimes two or more stars may be seen turning on an organ that serve not only as decoration, but actually bear as many sets of bells as there are exterior stars. For example, at the Cathedral in Naumburg there are three stars, each with 8 bells. The Predigerkirche in Erfurt also has the same. The structure of the Cymbel mounting may also be made in the following way: each Cymbel in itself is made mobile upon an axle, while the axle [itself] is immobile. Each Cymbal receives a small tab. Beside, or better, on top [of the row of Cymbels] moves the axle that revolves with the wheel.‡ [on it are mounted] the same sort of small tabs. When the wheel makes this axle revolve, then the tabs on the axle engage those on the Cymbels. So that they do not all strike simultaneously, but one after another, they§ are affixed to the upper axle not in a straight line, but in an uneven line. The stars are faulty if the bells sound like cow or sheep bells and do not ring brightly; likewise if the star's mounting is not well bushed and has to clatter; see Werkmeister's *Orgelprobe*, Chap. 16, p. 38. In the organ in St. Gertrud at Hamburg there is a remarkable star, in the middle of which (on the side facing forward, where it is heavily gilded) there is a rose of engraved steel, cut like a diamond. When the star turns and the sun shines upon it, it sparkles. On the star's points there are likewise the same engraved roses, but smaller, and between these painted flames shoot outward; these give the impression of a rainbow when the star revolves. There are 8 little bells [on it]; see Mattheson's Appendix to Niedt, p. 181. Niedt cannot stand them during hymn singing, and calls them absurd; see the third part of his [book], p. 46. They do not always please others, either, hence in some places bells have been chosen instead of Cymbels, around

* i.e., these paddles may be made shorter than 1'.

† As the following statement will reveal, the Cymbel may be placed anywhere in the organ. It appears that the Cymbel as Adlung has been describing it is intended to sit somewhere inside the case, but with this sentence he begins to describe another variety of Cymbel that is visible in the organ façade.

‡ this being another axle, not the fixed one upon which the Cymbels swing.

§ i.e., the tabs.

an etlichen Orten anstatt der Cymbeln Glocken genommen werden, etwan viere, welche in lauter Akkordstönen sich hören lassen, und etwas langsam schlagen. Die andere Struktur ist wie bey dem Cymbelstern. Diese Glocken werden nach Gefallen bald groß bald klein genommen. In der Lutherischen Augustinerkirche, it. in der Regler Orgel in Erfurt sind solche Glocken, deren die größte $\bar{g}$, die kleinere $\bar{h}$, die dritte $\bar{\bar{d}}$, die kleinste $\bar{\bar{g}}$ hören läßt. So findet mans auch in Alach, s. §. 284. Wie die Glocken auf einander schlagen sollen, dependirt von der Willkühr des Orgelbauers. Man macht eiserne Hämmerchen daran, und unter ein jedes eine Feder, daß es wieder zurücke prallt, und den Klang nicht verhindert. Sie können auch von Metall seyn wie die Glocken; auch von Meßing. Die Glocken müssen aber recht eingestimmet werden, sonst taugen sie eben so wenig, als die Cymbeln. Mit diesen Glocken darf man ein Register nicht verwechseln, welches aus Pfeifen bestehet, und Glöckleinton genennet wird. s. §. 156.

Communicantenglocke. S. §. 154.

§. 134.

Cymbel ist auch ein Pfeifenregister, welches fast in allen Orgeln zu finden. Es hat den Namen wegen des hellen durchdringenden Klanges, und ist meistens eine gemischte Stimme; denn es hält 2, 3, und mehr Pfeifen, die alle gar klein sind. Zuweilen ist es einfach. Es ist dies Register fast einerley mit den ganz kleinen Mixturen, oder mit dem Scharp oder Scharf; doch will man das Scharf etwas anders disponiren. Denn wenn das Scharf 3fach ist, so sollen die Pfeifchen die Oktav, Quint und Superoktav halten: die 3fache Cymbel aber die Oktav, Terz und Quint. Prätorius l. c. macht unter den Cymbelregistern noch mehr Unterschiede. Er sagt S. 131. **Grober Cymbel** sey von 3 Pfeifen besetzt, oder 3fach. Z. E. in Breßlau führt Prätorius l. c. S. 171. an Zimbel grob. **Klingender Cymbel**, sagt er ferner, sey auch 3fach, repetire aber durch das ganze Clavier, und soll die Kunstreichste seyn. Ist anzutreffen zu St. Jakob in Hamburg 2 mal; it. zu Bernau in der Mark; it. zu St. Nikolai in Leipzig. Was vom repetiren gesagt ist. s. §. 83. Denn die Cymbelpfeifen sind gar klein, und kaum etliche Zoll lang. Die zweysache Cymbel wird etliche mal meist durch alle Oktaven repetirt. **Kleiner Cymbel** ist von einer Pfeife, wird oft repetirt. Man findet ihn zu Breßlau, wie Prätorius l. c. meldet. **Repetirender Cymbel** ist von 2 und 1 Pfeife besetzt, und repetirt sich fort und fort, daher diese Stimme κατ' ἐξοχὴν die repetirende heißt. Z. E. zu St. Lambrecht in Lüneburg. **Klein Repetir-Cymbel** 1fach ist zu Hessen auf dem Schlosse. s. Prätor. S. 189. **Cymbelbässe** werden also gearbeitet, daß sie einmal repetiren, wenn sie $\frac{1}{2}'$ groß sind; die andern, wenn sie geringer sind, werden 2mal repetirt, und doch alle durch 4ten und 5ten disponirt. Man schreibt auch Cimbel für Cymbel: it. Zimbel; und dieser letztern Schreibart bedienet sich Prätorius allenthalben. Cymbel aber ist das beste. s. Matthesons Anmerkung zu Niedts 10ten Kap.

86 Ch. VII. Concerning Stops in General and in Particular

4 bells that form the tones of a chord and strike somewhat [more] slowly [than those in a Cymbelstern]. The rest of their structure is like the Cymbelstern. The bells may be now large, now small, according to preference. In the Lutheran Augustinerkirche as well as in the Reglerkirche organ in Erfurt there are such bells, of which the largest sounds g′, the next smaller b′, the third d″, and the smallest g″. The same thing is found at Alach; see §.284.* In what succession the bells sound depends upon the choice of the organbuilder. Small iron hammers are made [to ring them], under each of which is a spring so that it springs back and does not dampen the sound. They† may also be made of pipe metal like the bells, or of brass. The bells however must be properly tuned, otherwise they are of no better use than the Cymbels. One must be careful not to confuse these bells with a stop that consists of pipes and is called Glöckleinton; see §.156.

COMMUNICANTENGLOCKE. See §.154.

§. 134.

CYMBEL is also a stop composed of pipes, that is to be found in almost all organs. It gets its name from its bright, penetrating sound, and is usually a compound stop containing 2, 3 or more pipes [per key], all of them very small. Sometimes it is 1 rank. This stop is almost identical with a very small‡ mixture, or with the Scharp or Scharf; though the Scharf is usually composed somewhat differently. That is, if the Scharf is 3 ranks, then its pipes ought to stick to the octave, quint and superoctave, while the 3-rank Cymbel [is made up of] the octave, third and fifth. Praetorius, *loc. cit.*, makes yet more distinctions among the Cymbel stops. He says on p. 131 that the Grober Cymbel is made up of 3 pipes [per key], or 3 ranks; for example, on p. 171, *l.c.*, Praetorius mentions a Zimbel grob at Breslau. Klingender Cymbel, he says in addition, is also 3 ranks, but repeats [continually] throughout the entire keyboard, and is considered the most artistic; it is encountered twice at the Jacobikirche in Hamburg, as well as at Bernau in the Mark [Brandenburg] and at the Nicolaikirche in Leipzig. For the meaning of "repeating" see §.83. For the Cymbel pipes are very small, barely a few inches long.§ The 2-rank Cymbel sometimes repeats almost every octave. Kleiner Cymbel is of one rank, and repeats frequently. Praetorius, *loc. cit.*, reports that it is found at Breslau. Repetirender Cymbel consists of 2 or [less commonly] 1 ranks, and repeats constantly, thus this stop is properly called "repeating"; [see,] for example, St. Lambrecht in Lüneburg. Klein Repetir-Cymbel 1 rank is found in the palace at Hesse; see Praetorius, p. 189. Cymbelbass¶ stops are also made that repeat once if they are ½′ high; others, if they are even smaller, repeat twice. All of these, however, are composed of fourths and fifths.‖ The name may also be spelled Cimbel or Zimbel instead of Cymbel; Praetorius always spells it "Zimbel". It is best to spell it "Cymbel," though; see Mattheson's note in Niedt's tenth chapter of the second part, p. 114, that finds fault

---

* See the stoplist for this organ in Chapter 10.

† i.e., presumably the small hammers.

‡ i.e., high-pitched.

§ i.e., this is why this stop must of necessity continually repeat.

¶ i.e., high mixture stops in the pedal.

‖ i.e., of fifth- and octave-sounding ranks (the fifth sounding an interval of a fourth lower than the octave above it), without any thirds.

Kap. VII. Von den Registern überhaupt und insonderheit. 87

Kap. des 2ten Theils, S. 114. als welcher sich über die letztere Schreibart aufhält. Weil die Cymbel mit den Mixturen fast einerley sind; so nennt man sie auch Mixturcymbel. s. Niedt l. c. S. 110. Da steht: „Mixturcymbeln sind Pfeifen-„werke, dreyerley Art; große, mittel, und kleine Mixtur. In der großen waren vor „Alters wol 30. 40. und mehr Pfeifen auf einem claui, nun aber 10 bis 12, deren „größte Pfeife 8' ton hat. Die Mittelmixturen sind von 4, 5 bis 8 Pfeifen, davon die „größte 2 oder 1' ton hält. Die kleine Mixtur heißet sonst Scharf, ist nur von 3 oder „4 Pfeifen, davon die größte 3 Zoll lang." Weil es, wie kaum gedacht, mit Scharf oft eins ist; so findet man auch den Namen: Cymbelscharf, z. Ex. in der Kreuzkirche in Dresden, da das Scharf noch apart dabey ist. Der Klang soll also wie die Cymbel lauten, oder was sonst der Unterschied ist: oder sie stehen nicht in einem Claviere. Scharf Cymbel ist eben das zu St. Petri in Lübeck; desgleichen zu U. L. Fr. ebendaselbst, s. Prätor. l. c. Dies Cymbelscharf ist gar 4fach in der Pfarrorgel zu Königsberg; 3fach zu St. Dominico in Prag, wie sonst die Cymbel meistentheils gefunden wird. In der Pfarrkirche zu Danzig ist Cymbel 1'. Das ist ziemlich groß. Es wird auch dies Register 4fach gefunden unter dem Namen der Cymbel. Z. Ex. zu Mühlhausen in Thüringen, [33]) wie auch zu St. Dominico in Prag: aber in einem andern Clavier, als wo vorhin Cymbelscharf 3fach war.

* Cymbeloktave ist eine helle auf cymbelart klingende Oktave 1', und findet sich diese Oktave 1' unter diesem Namen in der ehemahligen Altdresdener Orgel, wie auch in der Schloßorgel daselbst.

* Cymbelpauke ist zu St. Catharinen in Danzig, ich weis aber nicht was es eigentlich seyn soll: ob durch Ziehung eines Registers sich die Pauke und Cymbal zugleich hören läßt, oder warum es also heißt.

Cymbelregal. In der Grüningischen Orgel, (deren Beschreibung Werkmeister edirt; denn diese verstehe ich allezeit, wenn ich sie allegire,) steht repetirend Cymbelregal. Was das sey, scheinet etwas dunkel. Ich glaube, es sey ein ordentlich Regal; doch wenn dasselbe gezogen wird, läßt sich zugleich eine repetirende Cymbel hören, die also mit dem Regal auf einem Stocke steht. Von der Benennung Regal s. in R. (Man sehe auch hierbey in der Anleitung S. 411. die Anmerkung c nach.) Von dem Cymbelregister ist schlüßlich noch so viel zu sagen, daß es dem vollen Werke das rechte Leben giebt.

§. 135.

Decem, heißt sonst zehen. Decembaß kömmt vor zu St. Petri in Lübeck, s. Prätor. S. 165. welcher dies Register auch Dezehmbaß nennet. Ich vermuthe

es

---

[33]) Hier hat sich der seel. Hr. Verfasser durch die im Niedt stehende falsche Disposition von der Mühlhausischen Obermarktsorgel verführen lassen, ein 4faches Cymbelregister anzugeben, welches doch niemals in dieser Orgel gestanden, wie aus der ächten Disposition dieses kostbaren Werks wird zu ersehen seyn, welche nebst andern, im 10ten Kap. soll beygefüget werden.

Ch. VII. Concerning Stops in General and in Particular 87

with the last-named spelling.* Since Cymbels are almost the same as Mixtures, they are also called "Mixturcymbel"; see Niedt, *loc. cit.*, p. 110, which reads, "Mixturcymbels are stops of three kinds: large, medium and small Mixture[s]. In times past there were indeed actually 30, 40 or more pipes for one key in the large ones, but now [only] 10-12, the largest pipe of which is of 8′ pitch. The small mixture may also be called Scharf, and is [made up] of only 3 or 4 pipes, of which the largest is 3″ long." Because, as has just been mentioned, it is often the same as Scharf,† the name Cymbelscharf is also found, for example in the Kreuzkirche in Dresden, where there is also a separate Scharf as well. Thus it‡ must sound like a Cymbel, or there is some other distinction, or they do not stand on the same manual.§ There is indeed a Scharf Cymbel at St. Petri in Lübeck, as well as at the Kirche zu Unsrer Lieben Frau there; see Praetorius, *loc. cit.*. In the Pfarrkirche organ at Königsberg this Cymbelscharf is actually 4 ranks, but [only] 3 ranks at St. Dominicus in Prague, the usual size at which the Cymbel is found. There is a Cymbel 1′ in the Pfarrkirche at Danzig; that is rather large.¶ This stop is also found with 4 ranks under the name Cymbel; for example, at Mühlhausen in Thuringia,33) as well as at St. Dominicus in Prague, though on a different manual than the 3-rank Cymbelscharf mentioned above.‖

CYMBELOKTAVE is a bright, cymbel-like Oktave 1′. An Octave 1′ under this name was to be found in the former Altdresdenerkirche** organ, as well as in the Palace Church organ there.

CYMBELPAUKE is found at St. Catherine's in Danzig, though I do not know what it is actually supposed to be: whether by pulling a stop the kettle-drum and Cymbel are heard simultaneously, or why it is so called.

CYMBELREGAL. In the Gröningen organ (whose description Werkmeister has published††—this is what I am referring to anytime I mention it) there is a repeating Cymbelregal. What it is seems rather obscure. I believe that it is an ordinary Regal which, when it is drawn, causes a repeating Cymbel, which stands on the same toeboard as the Regal, to be heard at the same time. Concerning the term Regal, see [below] under R (in this connection refer also to note c on p. 411 of the *Anleitung*). All that remains to be said in conclusion about the Cymbel stop is that it imparts a genuine vitality to the full organ.

§. 135.

DECEM, in other words, "ten." Decembass appears at St. Petri in Lübeck; see Praetorius, p. 165, where this stop is also called Detzehmbass. I surmise that it is the

---

* Mattheson prefers "Cymbel" over "Zimbel" or "Zimpel."

† This seems to contradict what Adlung has said earlier in the paragraph, where he makes a distinction between the two.

‡ i.e., the Cymbelscharf.

§ i.e., Adlung is suggesting that Mattheson might have made a mistake listing them on the same manual; see Mattheson's Appendix to Niedt, pp. 169-70, as well as the stoplist of this organ in Chapter 10.

¶ i.e., the pitch is rather low.

‖ The Cimbel [sic] 4 ranks is found on the Werck, while the Cimbel-Scharf 3 ranks is in the Brust; see Mattheson's Appendix to Niedt, p. 194, as well as the stoplist of this organ in Chapter 10.

** apparently the Dreikönigskirche. The area across the Elbe River from Dresden was known as Altendresden until 1685, when it was renamed Dresden-Neustadt. See the stoplist of this organ in Chapter 10.

†† under the title *Organum gruningense redivivum*.

---

33) Here the late author has allowed himself to be led astray by the incorrect stoplist of the Mühlhausen Obermarktskirche [organ] found in [Mattheson's Appendix to] Niedt [second part, pp. 192-3], and cites a 4-rank Cymbel stop that has never existed in this organ, as can be seen in the correct stoplist of this valuable instrument added, together with other [stoplists], to Chapter 10. [Albrecht]

es solle so viel seyn als Decima, die Zehende, oder, welches gleichviel ist, die Tertia composita. Also, wenn das Principal 8′ ist, so wird Decembaß im Pedale die Terz über dem 4füßigen c seyn. Das übrige siehe bey Terz.

Decima, s. bey Terz.

Decima quinta, ist eigentlich eine Oktave, daher es unten bey Oktave zu suchen.

Decima nona, ist eine Quinte, s. Quinte.

* Decupla, eine zehenfache, soll auch die Terz anzeigen.

§. 136.

Dezem, Dezembaß, s. in Terz, auch in Decem §. 135. (s. Anleitung S. 411. Anmerk. e.)

Diapason, ist so viel als Oktave, s. Oktave.

Diapente ist die Quinte, s. Quinte.

Diapente pileata, die gedeckte Quinte, s. Quinte, auch in Gedakten.

Diskantschwiegel, s. in Schwägel.

* Disdiapason, eine erhöhete Oktave.

* Disdiapente, eine erhöhete Quinte.

* Disdisdiapason, eine zweymal erhöhete Oktave.

Dito. Dies Wort steht in der Disposition der Orgel zu St. Ansgarii in Bremen, nemlich: dito 8′. Da wolle niemand so einfältig seyn, und es für einen besonderen Namen eines Registers halten; sondern es ist allezeit das vorhergegangene zu verstehen. Z. Er. daselbst steht erst Trompet 16′ hernach dito 8′, d. i. noch eine Trompet, aber nur von 8′.

§. 137.

Ditonus, ist die Terz, s. in Terz.

Döeff, ist eben soviel, als das Principal, s. Principal.

* Doiflöt, s. Duiflöt.

Dolcan oder Dulcan, wird zwar von Prätorio nicht beschrieben; doch hat er unter den Rissen denselben abgezeichnet, da er 4′ ist, oben weit, unten enge, und ist ein penetrantes Register. Es findet sich zu Gera, s. §. 301. da heißt es Waldflöte oder Dolcan 4′, und zwar mit doppelten labiis. Das letzte ist sonst nicht gewöhnlich, als nur bey der Duiflöt; die aber ganz was anders ist. Die Waldflöte ist auch sonst anders, als deren Körper gleichaus weit sind. Ich habe auch Doscan wo gelesen; aber da hat man wol das l beym Prätorio vor ein s angesehen. Und aus Doscan mag wol Toscan entstanden seyn, weil man nicht allzujust in der Orthographie bey solchen Sachen zu seyn pflegt. Ob auch aus Dulcan das Wort Dusan entstanden, daß das l vor ein s. angesehen worden, und das c gar weggeblieben ist, lasse ich dahin gestellet seyn.

Allein

same as Decima, the tenth, or as the compound third, which amounts to the same thing. Thus, if the Principal is [at] 8′ [pitch] in the pedal, then the Decembass will be the third above the 4′ c.* See further under Terz.

Decima, see under Terz.

Decima quinta ["fifteenth"] is actually an octave, and may be found below under Oktave.

Decima nona ["nineteenth"] is a Quinte; see Quinte.

* *Decupla*, "ten-fold," also indicates a Terz.

§. 136.

Detzem, Detzembass, see under Terz, and also under Decem, §.135 (see *Anleitung, p.* 411, note e).

Diapason is the same as Oktave; see Oktave.

Diapente is the fifth; see Quinte.

Diapente pileata is a stopped Quinte; see Quinte, and also under Gedakt.

Diskantschwiegel, see under Schwägel.

* *Disdiapason*, a Superoctave.†

* *Disdiapente*, an octave above the Quinte [3′].

* *Disdisdiapason*, a Super-superoctave.

Dito. This word appears in the stoplist of the organ at St. Ansgarius in Bremen, namely: Dito 8′. No one would be so naive as to consider it a specific name for a stop; rather it always means "the preceding." For example, in this stoplist there appears first "Trompet 16′," followed by "dito 8′," i.e., again a Trompet, but this time at 8′.

§. 137.

Ditonus is the Terz; see under Terz.

Döeff is the same as Principal; see Principal.

* Doiflöt, see Duiflöt.

Dolcan or Dulcan is not actually described by Praetorius, yet he has represented it among the drawings,‡ where it is a 4′, wide at the top, narrow at the bottom, and is a penetrating stop. There is one at Gera (see §.301§), where it is called Waldflöte or Dolcan 4′, and indeed has double lips. This last, though, is not common except in the Duiflöt, which is however something entirely different. The Waldflöte is also something different, since its body is the same width throughout.¶ Some place I have also read "Doscan", but in this case someone must have read Praetorius's "l" as an "s". And "Toscan" may very well also have come from "Doscan," since the spelling of such things did not used to be very precise. I cannot be sure but that the word Dusan may have come from Dulcan, by reading the "l" for an "s" and dropping the "c"; ex-

* i.e., if one draws the Decembass and plays the lowest C in the pedal.

† See Werkmeister, *Orgelprobe*, p. 55, and Samber, Vol. II, p. 153. At Sendomir (Mattheson's Appendix to Niedt, p. 196) the Superoctava 2′ is called *Disdiapason*, the Superoctava 1′ is called *Disdisdiapason*, and the Quinta 1½′ is called *Disdiapente*; see the stoplist of this organ in Chapter 10.

‡ no. 1, Plate 38 of the "Theatrum Instrumentorum," at the end of *Syntagma musicum*, Vol. II.

§ See the stoplist of this organ in Chapter 10.

¶ i.e., a cylinder, not (as the Dolcan) an inverted cone.

Allein der Duſanbaß, deſſen Prätorius in der Orgel zu St. Petri in Lübeck gedenkt, iſt 16', dergleichen Größe beym Dolcan nicht eben geſehen wird. Dulzain und Dul=
zaen ſind von gleicher Geltung. Beyde Namen findet man beym Prätorio S. 126. und 136. l. c. Unten §. 140. wird auch noch etwas mehr davon zu leſen ſeyn.

Dolciano, ſ. Dulcian und Fagott.

Dolce ſuono, heißt ein lieblicher Klang, und iſt mit Dulcian einerley.

Dolzflöt, ſ. Dulzflöt.

Dolziana, ſ. Dulcian.

Doppelt. Iſt ein Wort, welches keine beſondere Stimme anzeigt, ſondern wird gebraucht, wenn eine Stimme doppelt ſteht. Z. Ex. in Jena iſt Contrabaß 32' doppelt: da 16' offen dabey iſt; ſo könnte man auch ſagen doppelt Baß. Zu Gera iſt Vox humana doppelt, auch Flötedouce 8', ſ. §. 301. Am ſchwerſten kann ich be=
greifen, was es beym Prätorio in der neuen Breßlauer Orgel heißen ſoll, wenn da=
ſelbſt ſtehet Großprincipal, Chormaß=Principal, d. i. Princ. 8', und doppelt Principal mit einem Regiſter. Ob es vielleicht ſo viel iſt, daß Großprincipal 16' und Chormaßprincipal 8, mit einem Zuge regieret werden, welcher Zug, weil er zwey Princi=
pale öfnet, doppelt Principal heiße; oder es iſt ein Regiſter, da jeder clauis 2 Pfei=
fen von einer Größe hat. Hernach kömmt wieder: Gedacktflöt unter Chormaß; Gedacktflöt Chormaß; Doppelflöt: und die auch mit einem Regiſter alle drey. Da iſt eben das zu ſagen von der Doppelflöt. Von dieſer iſt nun nicht unbekannt, daß man auf jeden clauem 2 Pfeifen ſetzt; folglich könnte die Bedeutung wohl zugelaſ=
ſen werden: denn ſo wäre es ſoviel, als Duiflöt, wenn dieſe auch bisweilen ſo genom=
men wird, ſ. §. 137. Und was dieſe Wörter bedeuten, das bedeutet auch das dupli=
cat. Denn ſo folgt alda weiter: Offen Chormaß auf eine beſondere Art, Oktave, duplicat dieſes. Das ſind abermal entweder die vorigen 2 Regiſter, Offen Chormaß und Oktave, hier auf einem Loche; oder ſie werden nur durch einen Zug zugleich re=
girt. Und ſo gehts immerfort. Man ſehe den Prätorius l. c. S. 171. ſelbſt nach.

* Doris, ſ. unten Flauto oder Flute douce.

Drommel, ſo ſchreibt Prätorius l. c. S. 199. anſtatt Trommel, davon un=
ten §. 203.

Duiflöt, Doiflöt, oder Doppelflöt, von duo, zwey, iſt eine Art von gedackten Regiſtern, ordentlich von Holz, mit 2 labiis gerade gegen einander, alſo, daß man über dem Kern durch die 2 labia durchſehen kann, daher ihr Klang anders wird, als der andern Gedackten. Prätorius ſchreibet l. c. S. 140. Daß zu ſeiner Zeit, vor 28 Jahren, einer E. C. (welches Eſaias Compenius bedeuten ſoll) dieſe Art erfun=
den, ungefehr ums Jahr 1590. Man findet ſie etwas ſparſam. Vor dem war ſie in unſerer Regler Orgel in Erfurt; aber da vor einigen Jahren das durchfallende Kirchdach viel verdarb, und man die Orgel mußte repariren laſſen; ſo hielt man die Quinte 6' und

M dieſe

Ch. VII. Concerning Stops in General and in Particular

cept that the Dusanbass, mentioned by Praetorius in the organ at St. Petri in Lübeck, is a 16′, a size that is just not found in the Dolcan. Dulzain and Dulzaen have the same meaning [as Dolcan]. Both names are to be found in Praetorius, pp. 126 and 136, *loc. cit.*. More about this may be read in §.140 below.

Dolciano, see Dulcian and Fagott.

Dolce suono means a "sweet sound," and is the same as Dulcian.

Dolzflöt, see Dulzflöt.

Dolziana, see Dulcian.

Doppelt is a word that does not denote any particular stop, but rather is used if a stop is doubled.* For example at Jena there is a "Contrabass 32′ doppelt"; since an open 16′ is also present.† At Gera there is a "Vox humana doppelt", as well as a Flötedouce 8′; see §.301. I find it most difficult to comprehend what it means in Praetorius's description of the new organ at Breslau‡ when it says "Grossprincipal, Chormass-Principal, i.e., Principal 8′ and 'doppelt Principal with one stop.'" It may perhaps mean that the Grossprincipal 16′ and Chormassprincipal 8′ are controlled by one stop mechanism, which, since it activates two principals, is called "doppelt Principal"; or perhaps it is a stop in which each key has two pipes of the same size. Later on we find: "Gedacktflöt unter Chormass; Gedacktflöt Chormass; Doppelflöt", again all three with one stop. This much may be said about the Doppelflöte: it is not unheard of for two pipes to be placed on each key, and consequently this interpretation is indeed possible. In this case it would be the same as the Duiflöt if the latter is sometimes conceived in the same way; see §.137. "*Duplicat*" likewise means the same thing as these words; for it§ continues: "Offen Chormass of a special type, Oktave, *duplicat* this." Once again, this means either that the previous 2 stops, Offen Chormass and Oktave, are upon the same hole, or that they are both controlled by one stop mechanism. And thus proceeds the rest.¶ One ought to consult Praetorius, *loc. cit.*, for oneself.

* *Doris*, see below under Flauto or Flute douce.

Drommel. Praetorius, *loc. cit.*, *p.* 199, writes this instead of "Trommel;" see below, §.203.

Duiflöt, Doiflöt or Doppelflöt, from "duo", "two", is a sort of stopped register, normally of wood, with two lips exactly opposite each other, so that one may look across the languid through the 2 lips. Thus its tone is different than other Gedakts. Praetorius, *loc. cit.*, discusses it on p. 140. He says that 28 years ago (from his time) a certain E.C. (this must mean Esaias Compenius) discovered this type [of Gedakt], about the year 1590. It is found rather infrequently. Previously it was in the Reglerkirche organ here in Erfurt. Since, however, the church roof collapsed several years ago, causing much damage and requiring the organ to be repaired, the Quinte

---

* i.e. two pipes per key.

† i.e., on the same stopknob, to lend the 32′ the semblance of prompter speech.

‡ *Syntagma musicum*, Vol. II, pp. 171f; see also the stoplist of this organ in Chapter 10.

§ i.e., Praetorius's *Syntagma musicum*, p. 171.

¶ of Praetorius's description.

diese Duiflöt 8′ nicht für so nöthig, als die Sesquialter und Oktave 4′, denen jene also weichen mußten. Zun Kaufmannen und zu St. Severi daselbst, it. zu Udestädt bey Erfurt ist diese Stimme noch zu sehen. Zu Waltershausen steht Flöte dupla 8′, und soll vielleicht eben das bedeuten.

* Dulceon, s. Principal, §. 177.

§. 138.

Dulcian, dolce suono, ist von Dulzain, davon §. 140. wird zu reden seyn, wohl zu unterscheiden; dieses ist ein Flöt= jenes aber ein Schnarrwerk. Dieses Schnarrwerk Dulcian ist mit Fagott nicht einerley, oder doch nur selten; (als z. Er. Prätorius l. c. S. 166. hat es 2 mal dafür gesetzt,) wie man denn ausser der Orgel diese beyden auch unterscheidet. Man müßte denn den deutschen Fagott von dem französischen unterscheiden, wie von etlichen geschiehet, da der deutsche auch Dulcian heißt; der französische aber wäre der eigentliche Fagott. Es ist der Dulcian wie der Fagott ein gefüttert Schnarrwerk, siehe Niedts zweyten Theil, Kap. 10. S. 110. Was das heiße, ist aus dem 104ten §pho klar, da gesagt wurde, daß das Mundstück der Schnarrwerke mit Leder überzogen werde, daß sie nicht allzusehr rasseln. Dies geschiehet nicht bey allen Schnarrwerken, aber wol bey diesem. Prätorius l. c. S. 147. schreibt davon also: „Dulcian ist nur 8′ton; (aber ich will auch Exempel „von 16′ anführen: ja er hat selbst dergleichen 16′, S. 166. und 173.) wird von etlichen „oben zugedeckt, und durch etliche Löcherlein sein Resonanz unten an der einen Seiten ausge= „lassen, welche in denen Regalwerken, so zu Wien in Oesterreich gemacht werden, zu finden. „Etliche aber lassen es oben ganz offen, darum sie auch gleichwol so stille nicht seyn, und sich „dem blasenden Instrument, welches mit diesem Namen genennet wird, gleich arten; „gehöret auch billiger ins Pedal, dann zum Manual." Man findet dies Register an verschiedenen Orten sowol 16′ als auch 8′. Zum Exempel 16′ im Dom zu Bremen 2 mal; zu Elmshorn; zu St. Nikolai, zu St. Petri, zu St. Johannis und zu St. Mariä Magdalenä in Hamburg, fast allenthalben 2 mal. Zu Königsberg in der Altstädter Orgel 2 mal, und noch 8′ darneben; desgleichen im Löbenicht und in der Pfarrorgel daselbst zu St. Michaelis und St. Johannis in Lüneburg; in der neuen Orgel zu Leipzig 2 mal; zu Mühlhausen in Thüringen 2 mal;³⁴) zu Sendomir, da ist auch 8′ dabey, und heißt daselbst auch Dolziana, und zwar ist 16′ zweymal daselbst mit besagtem Namen. 16′ ist auch in Stockholm; zu Cosni in Stade; zu Stralsund in der Klosterorgel; zu Tilse im Brandenburgischen Preußen; im Stift Wurzen. Dulcian unter Chormaß zu Breslau ist beym Prätorio auch 16′; Dulcian von Holz 16′ im Dom zu Magdeburg; Dolcian oder Ranket von Holz 16′ zu Sondershausen; (NB. sonst sind diese Stimmen unterschieden.)

---

34) Man beliebe sich hier dessen zu erinnern, was ich in der vorigen Anmerkung gesagt habe. Diese Stimme ist in keiner Orgel in Mühlhausen zu finden, geschweige daß sie in einer 2 mal sollte anzutreffen seyn.

Ch. VII. Concerning Stops in General and in Particular

6′ and this Duiflöt were not considered as necessary as a Sesqualter and Oktave 4′, and thus they were replaced. This stop may still be seen at the Kaufmannskirche and at St. Severus in Erfurt, as well as at Udestädt near Erfurt. At Waltershausen there is a "Flöte dupla 8′," and that may mean the same thing.

DULCEON, see Principal, §.177.

§. 138.

DULCIAN, DOLCE SUONO, must be carefully distinguished from Dulzain, which will be discussed in §.140; the latter is a flue stop, while the former is a reed. The reed Dulcian is not the same as Fagott, or only seldom the same (as, e.g., in Praetorius, *loc. cit.*, p. 166, who uses it twice in this way), just as both of these are distinct apart from the organ. Were one to distinguish the German Fagott from the French, as some do, by calling the German the Dulcian, then the French would be called the true Fagott. The Dulcian, like the Fagott, is a leathered reed; see Niedt's second part, chap. 10, p. 110. What that means is clear from §.104 [above], where it is stated that the reed shallots are covered with leather to keep them from rattling so much. This is not the case with all reeds, but it is with this one. Praetorius, *loc. cit.*, p. 147, writes about it thus: "The Dulcian is only [at] 8′ pitch (but I* will also cite examples at 16′; indeed, he himself gives it as 16′ on pp. 166 and 173); some [builders] stop it at the top, thus allowing its sound to escape through a number of little holes on one side at the bottom, a characteristic that is found in the regal stops that are made in Vienna, Austria. Some, though, leave it completely unstopped at the top, in which case, however, it is not so quiet, and is similar to the wind instrument that is called by this name. It belongs more properly in the pedal than in the manual." This stop is found at various places, both at 16′ as well as at 8′. At 16′, for example, it is found twice in the Cathedral at Bremen; at Elmshorn; at St. Nikolai, St. Petri, St. Johannis and St. Maria Magdalena in Hamburg, in almost every case twice. At Königsberg it is in the Altstädterkirche organ twice [at 16′], and at 8′ besides; the same in the Löbenichtkirche and Pfarrkirche organs there, and at St. Michaelis and St. Johannis in Lüneburg; twice in the new organ at Leipzig;† twice at Mühlhausen in Thuringia;34) at Sendomir, where it is also at 8′ as well, and indeed appears twice at 16′ under the name "Dolziana." It is also a 16′ at Stockholm, at St. Cosmae in Stade, in the Klosterkirche organ at Stralsund, at Tilse in Prussian Brandenburg, and in the Collegiate Church at Wurzen. Praetorius cites a 16′ Dulcian unter Chormass at Breslau, a 16′ wooden Dulcian in the Cathedral at Magdeburg, a 16′ wooden Dolcian or Rankett at Sondershausen (N.B. in other cases these stops are

* i.e., Adlung.

† The reference is unclear. Mattheson's Appendix to Niedt, p. 189, gives a stoplist for "The new organ in Leipzig," but lists no Dulzian in it (see the stoplist of this organ in Chapter 10).

---

34) It would be well to remember what I have said in the previous note [§.134]. This stop is not to be found in any organ at Mühlhausen, not to mention appearing twice. [Albrecht]

Sordunen Dolcianenart von Holz 16′ zu Riddagshausen im Kloster. Alle diese führt kaum gedachter Prätorius an. 16′ ist auch zu Otterndorf im Lande Hadeln, s. Matthesons Anhang zum Niedt, S. 193. Zu St. Dominico in Prag ist es 2 mal 16′ auch einmal im Manual, und zwar von Holz. Ich sehe also nicht, wie Prätorius mit seinem angegebenen 8′ fortkommt: er müßte denn von der Größe des Körpers reden, da hingegen diese 16′ auf den Ton gehen. Ich habe wenige Exempel dieses Registers von 8′, als im Dom zu Bremen ist 8′, da 16′ auch noch zweymal dabey ist. Auch ist 8′ zu Insterburg in Preussen; it. zu U. L. Fr. in Lübeck 8′ und 16′. Daselbst nennt es Prätorius Dulcian oder Fagott. Sonst weis ich kein Exempel; es müßten denn die Schreiber dieser oder jener Disposition die Größe des Körpers haben exprimiren wollen.

§. 139.

Dulcinus ist bisweilen so viel als **Fagott**, s. Fagott.

Dulzflöt oder **Dolzflöt**, it. **Süßflöt** und **Dulcefloit**, hat seinen Namen vom lateinischen dulcis, **anmuthig**, und Flöt, wegen des angenehmen Klanges den sie hat. Sie heißt sonst **Querpfeife** oder **Querflöt**, nur daß sie wie eine Blockpfeife intonirt wird. Wer also alles begreifen will, der nehme dasjenige dazu, was §. 122. von der Blockflöte gesagt worden ist, und was unten von der Querflöt beygebracht wird. Wie sie ausser der Orgel beschaffen ist, davon ist Prätorius l. c. Kap. VIII. S. 35. nachzulesen. (S. a. Anleitung zur musik. Gelahrtheit S. 515, Anmerk. p.) Tibia angusta ist eben das.

§. 140.

Dulzain oder **Dulzaen**. Den letzten Namen hat Prätorius l. c. S. 126; den ersten aber S. 136. allwo er das Register auch beschreibt. Es ist oben weit, unten aber im labio um ein ziemliches enger. Es stand zu Prätorii Zeiten zu Stralsund im neuen Werke 8′ton; kann auch, wegen der schweren Intonation nicht kleiner seyn. Es klingt darum dem Dulcian etwas ähnlich, weil das corpus oben auch gleichwie der Dulcian erweitert ist, und auch im labio enger gefunden wird. Doch kann es dem Dulcian nicht gar zu ähnlich klingen, weil derselbe eine Rohr- oder Schnarrstimme, der Dulzaen aber ein Flötwerk ist. Man bleibt aber gemeiniglich bey dem Namen, den ihm der Meister Anfangs gegeben hat.

Dunecken 2′ soll in der Danziger Marienorgel stehen, wie Prätorius meldet: ich weis aber nicht, was es eigentlich seyn soll. Soviel sehe ich, es sey eine Oktavstimme, weil sie 2′ angegeben wird: ob es aber eine gedackte Stimme, oder ein Rohrwerk sey, kann ich nicht sagen.

* Duodecima, oder abgekürzt Duodez ist eine erhöhete **Quinte**.

* Dupla sesquialtera ist eine **Terz**.

Duplicat, s. Doppelt. §. 137.

Ch. VII. Concerning Stops in General and in Particular

not the same); a 16′ wooden Dulcian-type Sordun in the Klosterkirche at Riddagshausen. As just mentioned, Praetorius cites all of these.* It is also at 16′ at Otterndorf in Land Hadeln; see Mattheson's Appendix to Niedt, p. 193. At St. Dominicus in Prague it appears twice at 16′, once in the manual (again of wood). Thus I do not see how Praetorius comes up with 8′, as he says; he must have been speaking of the size of the resonator, which nevertheless produces a 16′ tone. I have only a few examples of this stop at 8′, such as in the Cathedral at Bremen where it is 8′, but where it is also twice more at 16′. It is also 8′ at Insterburg in Prussia, and at 8′ and 16′ at the [Kirche zu] Unsrer Lieben Frau in Lübeck (it is there that Praetorius calls it Dulcian or Fagott). I know of no example beyond these; the writers of this or that stoplist must have wanted to express the size of the resonator.

* The sense of this comment seems to be that Praetorius cites all these 16′ examples.

§. 139.

DULCINUS is sometimes the same thing as Fagott; see Fagott.

DULZFLÖT or DOLZFLÖT, likewise SÜSSFLÖT and *DULCEFLOIT*, gets its name from the Latin *dulcis*, pleasant, and Flöt, because of the pleasant sound it has. It is otherwise called QUERPFEIFE or QUERFLÖT, except that it is voiced like a Blockpfeife. Anyone who wants to comprehend everything [about it] should combine what is said in §.122 about the Blockflöte with what is stated below about the Querflöt. For its† characteristics apart from the organ consult Praetorius, *loc. cit.*, chap. VIII, p. 35 (see also *Anleitung zu der musikalischen Gelahrtheit*, p. 515,‡ note p). *Tibia angusta* is the same thing.

† i.e., the traverse flute's
‡ This should read "415."

§. 140.

DULZAIN or DULZAEN. Praetorius uses the latter name, *loc. cit.*, p. 126; but the former on p. 136 where he describes the stop. It is wide on top, but a bit narrower below at the lip. In Praetorius's day it stood in the new organ at Stralsund at 8′ pitch; it cannot really be any smaller because it is so difficult to voice. It sounds somewhat similar to the Dulcian, since the body is broader on top, just like the Dulcian, and is also narrower at the lip.§ Yet it could hardly sound very similar to the Dulcian, since the latter is a reed stop, while the Dulzaen is a flue stop. The name the master¶ gave it at the beginning is, however, the one most commonly adhered to.

DUNECKEN 2′, according to Praetorius, is to be found in the Marienkirche organ at Danzig; I do not know, however, what it actually is. As far as I can see, it must be an Oktave stop, since it is indicated as a 2′. But it might be a stopped register, or a reed—I cannot say.

* *DUODECIMA* ["twelfth"], abbreviated DUODEZ, is a compound fifth.

* *DUPLA SESQUIALTERA* is a Terz.

DUPLICAT, see Doppelt, §.137.

§ up to this point in this entry Adlung has taken his information from Praetorius, Vol. II, p. 136; the rest of the entry is his commentary on Praetorius. Adlung has obviously never encountered the stop himself.

¶ i.e., the organbuilder who invented the stop.

Kap. VII. Von den Registern überhaupt und insonderheit.

Dusanbaß wird von Prätorio S. 165. l. c. in der Disposition der Lübeckischen Orgel zu St. Petri 16′ groß angeführt. Weiter kann ich von der Natur dieses Registers nichts melden, weil ich selber nichts mehr davon weis. s. Dolcan §. 137.

Echo, ist eine Stimme im Manual einen Wiederhall vorzustellen. s. Anleitung S. 415. Cornet d'Echo, s. oben Cornet.

Ellich, ist kein Register, sondern bedeutet 2 Fuß, oder eine Elle groß. Siehe Mixtur.

Engelstimme, s. Angelica. §. 116.

Epistomium, heißt ein Ventil, s. unten in Ventil.

§. 141.

Fagott, italienisch Fagotto, französisch Basson, ist einerley. Man sagt auch dulcinus, dolce suono, und zuweilen vermischt man Dulcian damit. Es ist aber §. 138. gesagt worden, es wären diese Register unterschieden. Siehe davon mehr daselbst. Man nennet es auch den französischen Fagott. Niedt sagt im 10ten Kap. des 2ten Theils, in Orgeln sey es der Dulcian; und es kann wol seyn, daß man in etlichen Exempeln §. 138. den Fagott darunter verstanden, daher ich bey dem Fagott wenig Exempel aufführen kann. Fuhrmann im musikalischen Trichter Kap. 10. nennt den Fagotto auch Dolciano, und unterscheidet ihn vom Bassone, den er den französischen Fagott nennt, dieser sey im Kammer- jener aber im Chorton. Also verstehet er durch den Dolciano den deutschen Fagott. Da nun aber in Orgeln der Kammerton nicht gilt, (**) so kann auch in Orgeln der deutschen Fagott verstanden werden, das

(**) Dies ist nicht allgemein wahr: denn man hat auch in Deutschland schon mehr als eine Kammertönige Orgel. Z. Ex. in Dresden.

ist der Dulcian. Prätorius macht einen Unterschied in dem Klange, daher ich sie auch insbesondere traktire. Vom Fagott sagt er l. c. S. 147. er sey 8′ton, habe gleichaus weite und enge Körper, das größte von 4′ an der Länge, und sey ein Schnarr- oder Rohrwerk, werde im Manual gebraucht. Im Orchestre I. Part. III. cap. III. §. 9. heißt der Basson auch Basse de chormorne. Was dies eigentlich seyn soll, weis ich nicht: sonst aber weis ich von Basse de cromorne, davon unten §. 164. bey dem Krumhorn etwas zu lesen ist. In der Orgel macht man den Fagott theils von Metall, theils auch von Holz. Z. Ex. in Jena in der Collegenkirche ist er im Manual 16′ von Metall:[35] aber in Görlitz ist 16′ von Holz im Pedal. In der Disposition dieser Orgel steht Fagotti. Das ist der italienische pluralis, und ist vermuthlich deswegen

so

[35] Er befindet sich auch hier in Mühlhausen in der Oberstädtischen Hauptkirche B. M. B. 16′, allwo die unterste Oktave von Holz ist, die übrigen aber sind von welschen Blech, und gehet von C bis $\bar{\bar{c}}$. Diese Stimme muß dem superklugen Verfasser der im Niedt befindlichen Disposition so klein gewesen seyn, daß er solche übersehen hat. Vermuthlich hat er auch nicht gewust, daß diese nemliche Stimme auch in der Hauptkirche St. Blasii allhier halbirt von C bis $\bar{c}$ stehet; ob er gleich daselbst Organist gewesen.

Ch. VII. Concerning Stops in General and in Particular

DUSANBASS is cited by Praetorius, *loc. cit.*, p. 165, in the stoplist of the St. Petri organ in Lübeck, at 16′. I can report nothing further about the nature of this stop, since I know nothing more about it. See Dolcan, §.137.

ECHO is a stop in the manual that represents an echo; see *Anleitung*, p. 415. [For] CORNET D'ECHO, see Cornet above.

ELLICH is not a stop, but means "2 feet", or an Ell long.

ENGELSTIMME, see Angelica, §.116.

EPISTOMIUM means a Ventil; see below under Ventil.

§. 141.

FAGOTT, *Fagotto* in Italian, *Basson* in French, are all the same. It is also called *dulcinus, dolce suono*, and sometimes "Dulcian" is confused with it. It has already been said in §.138 (q.v.), however, that these two stops are distinct. It is also called the French Fagott. In the 10th chapter of the second part, Niedt says that in organs it is the Dulcian, and it may well be that some of the examples in §.138 may actually be Fagotts; therefore I can cite only a few examples of the Fagott. In chap. 10 of the *Musikalischer Trichter*[, p. 92,] Fuhrmann also calls the Fagott "*Dolciano*," and distinguishes it from the *Basson*, which he calls the French Fagott, by saying that the latter is in chamber pitch, while the former is in choir pitch.* Thus by *Dolciano* he means the German Fagott. Now since chamber pitch is not used in organs,(**) thus the Fagott in organs

* See §.404. below.

(**) This is not altogether true; there is certainly more than one organ at chamber pitch in Germany, as, for example, in Dresden.† [Agricola]

† See §.287 below.

may be understood as the German one, i.e., the Dulcian. Praetorius makes a distinction in the tone, [however,] and therefore I will also treat them separately. Concerning the Fagott, Praetorius says (*loc. cit.*, p. 147) that it is at 8′ pitch, has either broad or narrow resonators throughout, the largest of which is 4′ long, and is a reed. In the [*Neu-eröffnete*] *Orchestre* I, Part III, chap. III, §.9, [p. 269], the *Basson* is also called the *Basse de chormorne*. I do not know what this actually means; but otherwise I do know about the *Basse de cromorne*, about which there is something to read in §.164 below. In the organ some Fagotts are made of metal, others of wood. For example, at the Collegenkirche in Jena it is in the manual at 16′, of metal;[35] but at Görlitz it is a wooden 16′ in the pedal. The stoplist of this organ‡ reads "Fagotti." That is the Italian plural, and

‡ i.e., Görlitz; see §.301.

[35] It is also found here at Mühlhausen in the Oberstädtischen Hauptkirche B.V.M. at 16′, where the lowest octave is of wood, but the others are of tin-plated sheet iron (von weissen Blech), with a compass of C–c‴. This stop must have seemed so insignificant (klein) to the over-clever author of the stoplist found in Niedt that he overlooked it. Apparently he also did not realize that this very stop also stands in the [organ of the] Hauptkirche St. Blasii here, a half-stop from C–c′, although he has been organist there.§ [Albrecht]

§ The "over-clever author" whom Albrecht is criticizing is apparently Johann Mattheson. Similar criticisms by Albrecht elsewhere in this book cast doubt on the accuracy of Mattheson's stoplists as recorded in his edition of the second part of Niedt. There is no record of Mattheson ever having held a position in Mühlhausen, and thus the final sentence must mean that Mattheson at some time either visited and played the organ at the St. Blasius Church (where J.S. Bach was organist from 1707-8), or that he played a service or a concert there.

so benennet und geschrieben worden, weil jede Pfeife gleichsam einen Fagott vorstellt. Zu St. Nikolai in Stralsund ist auch 16′ von Holz. Auch ist 16′ anzutreffen zu St. Nikolai in Rostock. In Herbstleben ist Fagott 16′ von Holz. Es sind wol 8′ lange Körper, aber sehr enge, eine Hand breit: donnern aber fast wie eine Posaune 16′. Man führt den Fagott oftmals nur durch das halbe Clavier, weil er in der Höhe seine Natur verliehren würde; der andere Theil bleibt ungebohrt, oder man setzt in den obern Oktaven ein Register, welches die Tiefe nicht vertragen kann, und macht einen besondern Zug daraus; wie z. Ex. zu Alach, allwo Fagott 8′ die 2 untern Oktaven von der Menschenstimme giebt. Oder es müßte im Discante die Oboe werden, wozu der Fagott der Baß ist; und die Oboe ist auch würklich in der Orgel, s. unten §. 159.

§. 142.

Feldpfeife, Feldpipe, Feldflöte, (welche zuweilen mit Bauerflöte für einerley gehalten wird, s. §. 121.) ist eine Art der Querflöten, und werden ausser der Orgel auch auf der Seite angeblasen; dies sind aber die kleinen Feldpfeifen, die bey der Trommel und im Felde gebraucht werden, und haben ihre absonderlichen Griffe, die aber mit den Querflöten gar nicht überein kommen. S. Prätor. l. c. S. 35. Kap. 8. Man hat von dieser Art Pfeifen Gelegenheit genommen ein Register in die Orgeln zu machen, und ihm den kaum gedachten Namen beygelegt. Dies Register habe ich bis daher 4′, 2′ und 1′ an verschiedenenen Oertern gefunden. Z. Ex. 4′ zu St. Nikolai in Stralsund; 2′ aber zu St. Marien in Lübeck, wie auch zu Colberg in der Heiligengeistkirche, allwo es Feldflöt heißt; 1′ ists zu St. Lamprecht in Lüneburg. s. Prätorius l. c. Manche halten es mit Schweitzerpfeife für einerley, daher man dasjenige hierbey nachlesen kann, was unten §. 188. davon angeführt wird. (s. Anleitung Seite 416.)

§. 143.

Feldtrommet ist zu St. Petri in Lübeck 16′, wie Prätorius sagt. Sie ist ein Schnarrwerk, und von der Trommet werden wir unten ein mehres bekommen. Ob sie so heiße, weil sie sonderlich etwas wildes an sich hat; oder weil sie der großen Pfeifen wegen craß klingt, weis ich nicht: wir werden aber unten die Trommet selbst auch 16′ finden, s. §. 202.

* Fiffaro, ist die Querpfeife, s. §. 170.

* Fistula, eine Pfeife oder Flöte, kann allerley bedeuten nachdem es einen Beynamen bekömmt, als

* Fistula largior oder minima, s. Schwiegel §. 187.

* Fistula rurestris, s. Feld- oder Bauerflöte §. 121.

§. 144.

Flachflöte oder Flachpfeife, ist ein Flötwerk. (d. i. kein Schnarrwerk: und wo ja in meiner gegenwärtigen Abhandlung nicht ausdrücklich dabey stehet, das dies

Ch. VII. Concerning Stops in General and in Particular

is apparently so called and written because each pipe, as it were, represents one Fagott. At St. Nikolai in Stralsund it is also at 16′ of wood, and is also encountered at 16′ at St. Nikolai in Rostock. In Herbstleben there is a 16′ wooden Fagott. The resonators are indeed 8′ long, but very narrow, the breadth of a hand; yet they thunder almost like a 16′ Posaune. The Fagott is often built only for half the keyboard, since it would lose its characteristic tone in the high [register]. The other part either remains unbored,* or a stop is put in the upper octaves that does not sound well in the bass, thus creating a special stop out of it. At Alach, for example, the two lower octaves of the Vox humana (Menschenstimme) are a Fagott 8′. Alternatively the Oboe is placed in the treble while the Fagott is the bass; the Oboe is indeed found in the organ, too (see §.159 below).

* i.e., no toeholes are bored into the channels of the upper octaves.

§. 142.

FELDPFEIFE, FELDPIPE, FELDFLÖTE (which is sometimes considered the same as the Bauerflöte; see §.121) is a type of traverse flute, and is likewise blown on its side apart from the organ. But this is the small fife, which is used with drums in the field; it has its own special fingering, which is not at all the same as the Querflöte. See Praetorius, *loc. cit.*, chap. 8, p. 35. From this type of pipe someone took the opportunity to build a stop for organs and gave it the above name. Up to now I have found this stop in various places at 4′, 2′ and 1′. For example, it is a 4′ at St. Nikolai in Stralsund, but a 2′ at the Marienkirche in Lübeck, as well as in the Heiligengeistkirche in Colberg, where it is called Feldflöt. It is a 1′ [stop] at St. Lamprecht in Lüneburg; see Praetorius, *loc. cit.*. Many consider it to be the same as the Schweitzerpfeife, and thus one may consult in this regard that which is said about it in §.188 below. (See the *Anleitung*, p. 416.)

§. 143.

FELDTROMMET, according to Praetorius, is a 16′ [stop] at St. Petri in Lübeck. It is a reed stop (we will learn more about the Trommet below). I do not know whether it is so called because it has something especially wild about it, or because it sounds coarse due to its large pipes. Below, however, we will also find the Trommet at 16′; see §.202.

* FIFFARO is the Querpfeife; see §.170.

* FISTULA, a pipe or flute, can mean various things according to the words joined to it, such as

* FISTULA LARGIOR [larger] or MINIMA [very small]; see Schwiegel, §.187.

* FISTULA RURESTRIS, see Feld- or Bauerflöte, §.121.

§. 144.

FLACHFLÖTE or FLACHPFEIFE is a flue stop (i.e., not a reed stop; wherever in the present treatise it is not expressly stated that this or that stop is a reed, then it should

oder jenes ein Schnarrwerk sey; so verstehe ich nie dergleichen.) Von der Flachflöte siehe den Prätor. l. c. S. 136. Sie hat fast die Mensur wie die Spitzflöten; sie ist unten im labio nicht gar weit, mit einem engen niedrigen Aufschnitte, doch gar breit labiirt, daher sie so flach und nicht pompicht klingt, ist auch oben nur ein wenig zugespitzt, deswegen sie auch wol zuweilen Spitzflöte heißt. Z. Er. Spitz- oder Flachflöt 4' zu Riddagshausen im Kloster, wie Prätorius l. c. berichtet. Sonst aber ist zwischen diesen Stimmen ein Unterscheid. It. im Dom zu Magdeburg hat Prätorius Flachflöt 4' an dessen Statt die dasigen Domküster in ihrer Beschreibung Spitzflöte setzen. Ihre Intonation ist etwas schwer, klingen wohl, und flacher als die Gemshörner. Großflachflöt ist 8'; die ordentliche 4'; die kleine 2'. Ich habe sie wenig angetroffen, doch meistens nur 2' z. Er. zun Predigern in Erfurt; im Dom zu Bremen; in der großen Orgel zu St. Nikolai in Hamburg, wie auch zu St. Petri daselbst. Kleinflachflöt 2' zu Bückeburgk führt Prätorius an. Zu Pulsnitz und bey Biermann ist sie 8' angegeben, und heißt daselbst Großflachflöt.

* Flageolet ist mit Schwiegel 1' oder 2' einerley. Flasnet wird wol eben dieses bedeuten sollen. (s. Anleitung zur musik. Gelahrth. S. 417.)

§. 145.

Flauto, im plurali Flauti ist der italienische Name der Flöten.

Flet, schreibt Samber S. 145. da er Flet von Holz, und 146. Flet von Zinn anführt.

Flauto piccolo, kleine Flöte.

Fletna ist die lateinische Endigung beym Janowka. S. 43.

Fleut soll französisch seyn; besser sagt man Fluste, oder nach der neuen Schreibart Flute. Alle drey Arten werden Flüte gelesen.

Flöt oder Flöte ist bey den Deutschen gewöhnlich.

Alle diese Wörter können ihren Ursprung vom lateinischen flare, blasen, haben. Wollte einer sagen, daß die meisten Instrumente geblasen werden, die doch keine Flöten sind, dem dienet zur Antwort, daß vor dem, ehe die Schnarrwerke Mode worden, alles Pfeifwerk Flöten hießen. Da man hernach die Schnarrwerke eingeführt, hat man doch das Wort Flöte für alle Pfeifen genommen, die keine Rohrstimmen waren. Also theilt Prätorius alle Register in Flöten und Schnarwerke; folglich wäre im weitläuftigen Verstande das Principal, Mixtur, Gedakt, 2c. lauter Flöten. Ausser der Orgel haben wir viel Flöten, als: Quartflöte, Altflöte oder Flötedouce, Tenorflötedouce, Baßflötedouce, Flötetraversiere, 2c. In der Orgel haben wir deren noch mehr, da ausser den Schnarrwerken, Principalen, Oktaven und gemischten Stimmen fast alles Flöten kann genennet werden; ja auch die Oktave heißt bey etlichen Flöt; z. Er. Tubalflöt, Jubalflöt. Weil unter diesem Namen so viel begriffen

Ch. VII. Concerning Stops in General and in Particular

always be considered a flue stop). Concerning the Flachflöte, see Praetorius, *loc. cit.*, p. 136. It has almost the same scale as the Spitzflöte, not very wide below at the lip, with a narrow, low cut-up, but the lip itself is quite broad, and thus it sounds quite plain and unpretentious. It is a bit conical, and for that reason is also sometimes called Spitzflöte. For example, Praetorius reports that there is a Spitz- or Flachflöte 4′ in the Klosterkirche at Riddagshausen. But otherwise there is a difference between these two stops. Likewise at the Cathedral at Magdeburg Praetorius gives Flachflöt 4′ in the place where the resident cathedral verger in his description gives Spitzflöte. Its voicing is rather difficult. It sounds well, and smoother than the Gemshorn. A Grossflachflöt is 8′, an ordinary one 4′, a small one 2′. I have not encountered many [examples of this stop], and most of these [are] at 2′, for example, at the Predigerkirche in Erfurt, in the Cathedral at Bremen, in the large organ at St. Nikolai in Hamburg, as well as at St. Petri there. Praetorius cites a 2′ Kleinflachflöt at Bückeburg. At Pulsnitz and in Biermann* it is indicated as 8′, and there it means "Grossflachflöt".

* p. 21, in the pedal at the monastery church at Grauhoff near Goslar.

* FLAGEOLET is the same as Schwiegel 1′ or 2′. "Flasnet" must indeed mean the same thing (see *Anleitung zur musikalischen Gelahrtheit*, p. 417).

§. 145.

FLAUTO, plural *Flauti*, is the Italian name for flute.

FLET† is what Samber writes on p. 145, where he speaks of "Flet of wood", and on p. 146, where he speaks of "Flet of tin."‡

† i.e., flute.
‡ Samber writes "Fleten."

FLAUTO PICCOLO [means] small flute.

FLETNA is the Latin ending§ found in Janowka[, p. 43].

FLEUT is supposed to be French; but it is better to use *Fluste,* or *Flute,* according to the new spelling. All three forms are pronounced "Flüte".

§ i.e., the final "a" is added to the word to make it into a feminine singular noun. In actuality this word has nothing to do with Latin; it is the normal word for "flute" in Czech.

FLÖT or FLÖTE are the usual German spellings.

All these words may have their origin from the Latin *flare*, "to blow". Some may assert that most instruments are blown, including those that are not flutes; a sufficient answer for such people is that in the past, before reeds became fashionable, all wind instruments (Pfeifwerk) were called "flutes". Later on, when reed instruments were introduced, the word "flute" was used for all wind instruments that were not reeds. Thus Praetorius divides all stops into flutes and reeds; consequently principals, mixtures, gedakts, etc., are actually flutes in the general sense.¶ Apart from the organ there are many [types of] flutes, such as: Quartflöte, Altflöte or Flötedouce, Tenorflötedouce, Bassflötedouce, Flötetraversiere, etc. There are still more types within the organ, since with the exception of reeds, principals, octaves and compound stops almost everything can be called a flute. Indeed, some even call the Oktave a flute, e.g., Tubalflöt, Jubalflöt [q.v.]. Since so much is included under this name, it is impossible to indicate any

¶ Adlung also adheres to this method of classification, though he does not make it clear here. This translation of the *Musica mechanica organoedi* distinguishes between the generic and technical senses of the term flute, wherever this distinction is clear from the text, by translating "Flöt" as either "flute" or "flue", and "Flötwerk" as either "flute stop" or "flue stop."

Kap. VII. Von den Registern überhaupt und insonderheit. 95

sen wird; so können wir keinen allgemeinen Begriff davon angeben: denn die Arten haben gar verschiedene Naturen, und kommen in nichts überein, als darinn, daß sie alle Pfeifen sind. Die Engländer heißen die Flöte auch Recordor. s. Prätorius l.c. Kap. 7. S. 33. Wir wollen demnach von der Querflöte insbesondere handeln, auch von der Hohlflöte, Holzflöte, Flötedouce, Sifflöte, Waldflöte, Offenflöte, Spitz= oder Spindelflöte, Rohrflöte, Quintflöte, Pfeiferflöte, Rüzialflöte; ein jedwedes soll an seinem Orte vorkommen, und bey einem jeden kann man die allgemeine Lehre von der Flöte allhier nachlesen. Von etlichen ist schon gehandelt worden. Als von der Bauerflöte §. 121. Blockflöte §. 122. Koppelflöte §. 129. Dulzflöte §. 139. Duiflöte §. 137. Flachflöte §. 144. Doch gehören hierher die Exempel, da das Wort Flöte ohn allen Zusatz gefunden wird. Z. Ex. Flöte 8' steht im Pedal zu St. Petri in Berlin; zu Colberg in der Heiligengeistkirche; in der Marienkirche zu Thoren, und in der Neustadt daselbst; zu St. Bartholomäi in Danzig und zu St. Catharinen daselbst; in der Habergergischen Orgel zu Königsberg, da auch Flöte 4' dabey steht im Manual 2 mal; ebendaselbst, in der Steindammischen Orgel ist Flöte 8' und 4' in einem Claviere, im andern wieder 8'. Was man nun dadurch eigtntlich verstehet, gedeckte oder offene Pfeifen, ist mir nicht bekannt. Es muß was besonders dabey seyn, weil die Gedakte sowol als die Principale und Octaven 8' und 4' ordentlich dabey gefunden werden. Wer die Orgeln durchzuschauen Gelegenheit hat, wird diesen Fehler leicht ersetzen können. Flöte 4' steht in Eisenach. [36] Wenn diese Stimme im Pedal steht; so wird sie meistens mit dem Namen Flötenbaß belegt, wobey ich nur z. Ex. den Flötenbaß 4' in der Stadtkirche zu Jena anführen will. Biermann thut desselbigen S. 19. ebenfalls Erwähnung.

§. 146.

Flute alemande, oder d'alemagne, heißt soviel, als eine Quer= oder Soldatenpfeife. s. unten in Querpf.

Flute traverse oder traversa } s. Querpf.
Flute traversiere

Flute à bec } ist beydes einerley. Bec heißt bey den Franzosen der Mund oder
Flute douce
Schnabel eines Dinges: und haben diese Art Flöten den Namen wegen ihres Schnabels, den sie haben, der wol einen Zoll lang ist. Douce heißt bey ihnen still, angenehm, vom lateinischen dulcis, süß. Demnach wird die in den Orgeln vorkommende Stillflöte wol eben soviel seyn sollen. Man lieset es Flöt a bec und Flöte duse. Die Deutschen sagen oft Flötduse. Man schreibt auch an die Register Fleute douce. Wie man aber dieselben

[36] It. in der D. Blasii Kirche zu Mühlhausen, wo sie im obersten Claviere steht. Im Niedt wird einer offenen Flöte 4' gedacht, welche in der Obermarktsorgel allhier seyn soll: sie hat aber, so, wie viele andere daselbst angegebene Stimmen, niemals in dieser Orgel gestanden.

Ch. VII. Concerning Stops in General and in Particular 95

common conception for it; for the varieties have very different natures, and correspond in nothing except that they are all flue pipes. The English also call the flute the recordor; see Praetorius, *loc. cit.*, chap. 7, p. 33.* The Querflöte will be treated separately later on, as well as the Hohlflöte, Holzflöte, Flötedouce, Sifflöte, Waldflöte, Offenflöte, Spitz- or Spintelflöte, Rohrflöte, Quintflöte, Pfeiferflöte, and Kützialflöte; each of these will appear in its proper place, and the general principles of the flute stated here may be consulted for each one of them. Some of them have already been dealt with, such as Bauerflöte, §.121; Blockflöte, §.122; Koppelflöte, §.129; Dulzflöte, §.139; Duiflöte, §.137; and Flachflöte, §.144. But the examples need to be dealt with here in which simply the word "flute" is found. For example, Flöte 8′ stands in the pedal at St. Petri in Berlin, in the Heiligengeistkirche at Colberg, in the Marienkirche and the Neustadtkirche at Thoren, at St. Bartholomaus and St. Catharinen in Danzig, in the organ of the Haberbergkirche at Königsberg, where the Flöte 4′ appears twice in the manuals; likewise at the Steindammkirche in Königsberg there is a Flöte 8′ and 4′ on one manual and Flöte 8′ on another. What these actually are, stopped or open pipes, I do not know. There must be something special about them, since Gedakts as well as Principals and Oktaves 8′ and 4′ are found there as usual.† Anyone who has the opportunity to examine these organs will easily be able to make up for this lack [of information]. There is a Flöte 4′ at Eisenach.³⁶⁾ If this stop appears in the pedal, it is usually given the name Flötenbass, of which I will only mention for example the Flötenbass 4′ in the Stadtkirche at Jena. Biermann likewise makes mention of this stop on p. 19.‡

*Adlung takes his spelling directly from Praetorius.

† It appears that this statement applies to all the 8′ and 4′ flutes in the organs mentioned directly above it.

‡ Biermann reads "Floit Bass", at 1′.

§. 146.

Flute alemande, or *d'alemagne*, means the same as Quer- or Soldatenpfeife; see below under Querpfeife.

Flute traverse or *traversa*
Flute traversiere } see Querpfeife.

Flute à bec
Flute douce } are both the same. *Bec* in French means something's mouth or beak; so this type of flute gains its name from its mouthpiece, which is a good inch long. In French *douce* means "quiet, pleasant," from Latin *dulcis*, "sweet". Accordingly the Stillflöte that appears in organs is indeed the same thing. It is pronounced "flöt a bec" and "flöte duse". The Germans often say "flötduse". This stop is also spelled "Fleute douce." Just as both large and small ones exist apart from the organ,

---

36) Likewise in the Blasiuskirche at Mühlhausen, where it stands in the uppermost keyboard. In [Mattheson's appendix to] Niedt[, part two,] an Offene Flöte is mentioned that is supposed to be in the Obermarktkirche organ here [in Mühlhausen]; there has never been such a stop in this organ, however, just as many other stops that are indicated there. [Albrecht]

96　Kap. VII.　Von den Registern überhaupt und insonderheit.

ben ausser der Orgel groß und klein hat; so trift man sie auch in derselben von verschiedener Größe an. Doch findet man sie ordentlich 8' und 4'. Z. E. 8' steht zu S. Ansgarii in Bremen, und in der neuen Michaelisorgel in Hamburg (welche aber 1750. durch den Brand mit ruiniret worden;) zu S. Wenceslai in Naumburg; zu Merseburg im Schloße oder Thum, wie auch in Waltershausen. 4' steht in Jena in der Stadtkirche 2 mal; im Löbenicht zu Königsberg; zu Mühlhausen in Thüringen in der Obermarktskirche, ³⁷) und zu S. Nikolai in Stralsund. Doppelt steht sie 4' zu Gera. Zu Alach ist sie 4' von Metall, oben spitzig zu. Um die Natur der Flöten soviel als möglich im Klange nachzuahmen, so machen die Orgelbauer die Pfeifen lieber von Holz, als anderer Materie: sie werden (wie kaum gedacht) so gearbeitet, daß sie oben spitzig zu gehen, und sind schief gedeckt, daß sie nämlich oben nicht ganz offen, aber auch nicht ganz zu sind. Denn das Instrument ausser der Orgel, wovon das in der Orgel den Namen hat, ist unten auch fast zu. Es würden auch die Pfeifen das stille Wesen nicht bekommen, wenn sie nicht so wären. So muß auch die Mensur viel enger seyn, als in Gedackten, und der Aufschnitt nicht so hoch, dadurch sie anmuthiger und nicht so pompicht klingen, als die Gedackten thun. In der Görlitzer Orgel findet sich gedackte Fleut doux 4', denn so hat Boxberg diese Stimme in der Beschreibung genennet: es könnte aber wol Flute douce heißen, weil Flute sonst ein foemininum ist. Er schreibt daselbst, daß es nur ein 4' Gedackt sey; gleiche aber dem Instrumente gänzlich, wovon es benennet worden.

* Flûte dupla, ist halb französisch und halb lateinisch. s. Duiflöt.

§. 147.

Fond d'Orgue wird manchem ein böhmisch Dorf scheinen: ich versichre, daß es mir auch also gehet. Man beliebe nachzuschlagen des de Grigny primier livre d'Orgue, da hat er meistentheils 2 Claviere mit dem Pedale erfordert, hat auch 3 systemata oder Linien; bey jedem Claviere nennt er das Register, so dabey zu ziehen. Unter andern kommen auch in einem Kyrie 3 Linien vor, da über der einen steht Cromorne, über der andern Fond d'Orgue, über der dritten Pedalle. Es scheinet also allerdings ein Orgelregister zu seyn. Orgue heißt die Orgel, und Fond heißt der Grund, also zusammen der Grund der Orgel. Es sind beydes französische Wörter. Was aber die Franzosen für ein Register mit diesem Namen belegen, ist mir nicht bekannt. Weil es im Manual ist; so deucht mir, es könne das Principal dadurch verstanden werden, als das Haupt= und Fundamentalregister. (**)

(**) So ist es auch gewissermaßen. Denn es ist kein eigenes besonderes Register, welches die Franzosen so benennen: sondern sie verstehen durch *Fond*: 1) die **Principal= oder Flötenstimme**, welche zu einem Rohrwerke gezogen werden muß, also sagen sie; Fond de Trompette,

Diese ist von Holz und durch schiefe Stellung eines Brettchens so viel als nöthig gedeckt, der Körper läuft von unten bis hinauf immer enger zu, und der Klang ist viel sanfter wegen der sehr engen Mensur, als eines gemeinen Gedakts 4'. Bey uns ist sie sehr gemein.

they may be met at various sizes within it, though they are normally found at 8' and 4'. For example, there is an 8' at St. Ansgarius in Bremen, and [also] in the new Michaeliskirche organ in Hamburg (which, however, was destroyed in 1750 when the church burned); at St. Wenceslaus in Naumburg; in the palace or Cathedral at Merseburg, and also in Waltershausen. It appears twice in the Stadtkirche at Jena, in the Löbenichtkirche at Königsberg, in the Obermarktkirche at Mühlhausen in Thuringia,37) and at St. Nikolaus in Stralsund. It stands at 4' at Gera, doubled.* At Alach it is a conical metal 4'. Organbuilders prefer to make the pipes of wood rather than some other material, in order to imitate insofar as possible the characteristic flute sound.† Just as mentioned, they are constructed conically, and are stopped [by a flap] at a slant, so they are neither completely open nor completely stopped on top. For the instrument apart from the organ, from which the one in the organ gets its name, is also almost closed at the bottom end. The pipes would not possess their quiet nature if this were not so. Thus the scale must also be much narrower than in Gedakts, and the cut-up not so high, by which they sound more charming and not so pompous as Gedakts. In the Görlitz organ there is a Gedackte Fleut doux 4'—this is the name Boxberg calls it in his *Beschreibung*.‡ It may well mean "Flute douce", since Flute is otherwise feminine.§ There¶ he writes that it is only a 4' Gedackt, but that it exactly resembles the instrument from which it gets its name.

* See §.137.

† i.e., the sound of the recorder.

‡ p.[16].

§ "Doux" is the masculine form of the adjective.

¶ i.e. in the *Beschreibung der Orgel zu Görlitz*, p.[3].

* *FLÛTE DUPLA* is half French and half Latin; see Duiflöt.

§. 147.

FOND D'ORGUE may look to many like [the name of] some Bohemian village;‖ this goes for me, too, let me assure you. One need only consult De Grigny's *Premier Livre d'Orgue*; there he mostly requires 2 keyboards with pedal, and has three *systemata* or staves (Linien). For each keyboard he names the stops that are to be drawn. Among others there is a Kyrie written on three staves, over one of which stands Cromorne, over the second Fond d'Orgue, and over the third Pedalle. Thus it appears certainly to be an organ stop. Orgue means organ, and Fond means foundation, thus combined [they signify] the foundation of the organ. Both are French words. But what sort of stop the French give this name is unknown to me. Because it is in the manual, it seems to me that it could signify the Principal, since this is the main and fundamental stop. (**)

‖ i.e., strange and incomprehensible.

> (**) This is true to a certain extent. For it is not a separate special stop to which the French give this name. Rather they mean by *Fond*: 1) the Principals or flue stop that must be drawn with a reed; thus they say *Fond de Trompette, Fond de Cromorne*, etc. 2) by *Fond d'Orgue,* for which whole pieces are sometimes stipulated, they indicate that the Principal 8' and the Oktave 4' as well as the 16' Bor-

37) This is of wood, and stopped to the degree necessary by a board placed at a slant [over the top of the pipe]. The body is conical, and the sound is much gentler than a normal 4' Gedakt due to the very narrow scale. In this area it is very common. [Albrecht]

pette, Fond de Cromorne, u. f. w. 2) deuten sie durch *Fond d'Orgue*, wofür bisweilen ganze Stücke gesetzt sind, an, wenn das Principal 8 und die Oktave 4 Fuß, auch wol der 16füßige Bordun, und also lauter Oktavenstimmen, ohne Quinten und Terzien, zusammen gezogen werden. In diesem Verstande ist es bey dem vorhin angeführten Werke des de Grigny zu nehmen.

§. 148.

Fornitura, Fourniture, kömmt vor in der Orgel zu Sandomir, da es so viel seyn soll als das Principal, und zwar daselbst 4'. Sonst aber wie aus Frischens französischem Lexico erhellet, ist bey den Franzosen ein solch Register zu verstehen, oder eine solche Reihe Pfeifen, die zur Stärkung dienen, und welches man die Mixtur nennt. Zu Sandomir kann es aber die Mixtur nicht seyn; denn dieselbe ist noch besonders in eben demselben Claviere: wenigstens hat man selten 2 Mixturen in einem Claviere, zumal da dies nicht das Hauptmanual ist. Zu Cambery ist diese Stimme mit der lateinischen Endung Fornitura, s. de Chales Tom. III. propos. 22. Die unten §. 287. anzubringende Disposition der Orgel daselbst zeigt nicht undeutlich, daß es nicht das Principal sey, sondern ein ordo minus praecipuus: denn wäre es das Principal; so hätte es de Chales in der Combination unter diejenigen Stimmen mit gerechnet, die allein können gezogen werden: welches aber von ihm nicht geschehen. E. bedeutet es da etwas anders, und wol die Mixtur. (**)

(**) In Frankreich heißt, ausser allem Streite, die **größere Mixtur**: *Fourniture*.

Französische Posaune 16' stehet im Manual zu Stockholm. Sie wird ohne Zweifel was besonders haben vor der gemeinen Posaune, davon unten zu reden: was es aber sey, ist mir nicht bekannt. Vielleicht hat sie ein stilleres Wesen an sich.

Frontispicium. Dieses Worts bedienet sich Samber S. 153. seiner Continuation, wenn er das Principal anzeigen will, welches im Gesichte stehet.

§. 149.

Fuchsschwanz ist ein Vexierregister, und wird unter den andern manubriis oder Registerknöpfen zuweilen gefunden, um den Vorwitz derjenigen zu bestrafen, welche die Register herausziehen, und doch nichts bey der Orgel zu thun haben. Es findet sich ein solch manubrium in der Orgel zu St. Andreä in Erfurt, wenn das heraus gezogen wird, hat man den Fuchsschwanz in der Hand; und weil er so geschwinde nicht wieder hinein zu bringen ist, so bekommen die Anwesenden Gelegenheit, die Vorwitzigen, die alles durchschnaupern wollen, auszulachen. Man wird es aber freylich nicht daran schreiben. Man kann solcher Arten von Vexierregistern noch mehr erdenken. Vielleicht ist das Noli me tangere zu St. Gertrud in Hamburg auch dergleichen.

Fugara ist mir abermals ein böhmisch Dorf. Janowka in Clave ad Thesaurum magnæ Artis Musicae pag. 91. zählt es unter die gemeinen Register. Es kann auch wol bey uns ein gemein Register seyn: aber wer kann denn eben rathen, was der Böhme für eins mit gedachtem Worte anzeigen will. In Waltershausen findet man

Ch. VII. Concerning Stops in General and in Particular

dun should be drawn, i.e., purely unison-sounding ranks, without fifths and thirds. It is in this sense that both of the De Grigny works cited earlier are to be understood. [Agricola]

§. 148.

FORNITURE, FOURNITURE, appears in the organ at Sandomir [sic] at 4', and must mean the same thing as Principal. As is apparent from Frisch's French dictionary, among the French it means a stop or series of pipes that serves as a strengthener, which is the name given to a mixture. At Sandomir, however, it cannot be the mixture, since one already appears elsewhere in the same keyboard; at any rate there are seldom two mixtures for one keyboard, especially if it is not the main manual. This stop is at Chambery with the Latin ending, "Fournitura"; see De Chales, Vol. III, proposition 22.* The stoplist of the organ there, given below in §.287, shows quite clearly that it is not the Principal, but an *ordo minus praecipuus*;† for if it were the Principal, then DeChales would have included it in his [instructions about] combining [stops] among those stops that may be drawn alone, which however he did not do. Therefore it means something else there, probably the mixture. (**)

(**) In France it means, incontestably, the larger mixture: *Fourniture*. [Agricola]

FRANZÖSISCHE POSAUNE 16' is found on the manual at Stockholm.‡ Doubtless it has something special beyond the common Posaune (which is dealt with below), but I do not know what that is. Perhaps it has a quieter character.

FRONTISPICIUM. Samber makes use of this word on p. 153 of his *Continuation*§ when he wants to indicate the Principal that stands in the façade.¶

§. 149.

FUCHSSCHWANZ is a trick stop, found occasionally among the other *manubriis* or stopknobs, to punish those who are curious enough to pull the stop out; it has nothing to do with the organ. There is such a stopknob in the organ at St. Andreas in Erfurt. The person who draws it out ends up with a foxtail in his hand, and since it cannot be put back in very quickly, those present get a chance to tease the curious one who wants to poke his nose into everything. Of course the name is not written on [the stopknob]. It is possible to invent other such tricks; perhaps the *Noli me tangere*‖ at St. Gertrud in Hamburg is also one of them.

FUGARA again sounds to me like [the name of] some Bohemian village.** On p. 91 of the *Clavis ad Thesaurum magnæ Artis Musicæ* Janowka numbers it among the common stops.†† It may well be a common stop here as well, but who can guess what the Bohemian‡‡ intends to indicate with the word. In Waltershausen there is [a stop] spelled "Vogar 8',"* which I do not know how to make anything of except to believe

---

* This should read "Propositio 15" (p.21).

† a "secondary stop", i.e. not a principal. See §.215 below.

‡ in the "Werck" (Hauptwerk); see Mattheson's Appendix to Niedt, p. 198, as well as the stoplist of this organ in Chapter 10.

§ i.e., Vol. II of the *Manuductio*.

¶ i.e., the Præstant.

‖ Latin "Do not touch me"; a reference to the words of the risen Jesus to Mary Magdelene at the tomb (John 20:17).

** See note to *Fond d'Orgue*, §.147 above.

†† String-toned stops such as this one became common earlier in transalpine Catholic territories than in Protestant areas.

‡‡ i.e., Janowka.

angeschrieben Vogar 8', woraus ich gar nichts zu machen wüßte, wenn ich nicht glaubte, daß diese veränderte Schreibart ihren Ursprung daher habe, weil man diese Stimme nur von Hörensagen nachgeschrieben, ihre rechte Schreibart aber nie gesehen. In Naumburg ist Fugara 4' zu finden. Die Pfeifen sind sehr enge, der Klang folgt etwas langsam, dabey aber ist er schneidend und doch schwach. Es gehört also diese Stimme unter die offenen Flötstimmen, und ist von der Violdigamba 4' wenig unterschieden.

* Fundamentalis, d. i. eine **Grundstimme**. Ist zu **Cambery** das **Principal**.

§. 150.

* **Gar** ist ein Beywort; was dazu gesetzt ist, suche an seinem Orte. Z. Ex. **Gar kleine Flöt**, s. Prätor. S. 172; **gar großer Untersatzgedakt** 32'. S. 178. ꝛc.

Gedackt. Dies Wort ist abermal entweder im weitläuftigen, oder im engern Verstande, anzunehmen. Im weitläuftigen Verstande werden alle Register so genennet, die zugedeckt sind, sie mögen Flöt- oder Rohrwerke, von Metall oder Holz seyn. Z. Ex. der **Subbaß, Contrabaß, Bordun, Barem, Regal, Quintatön**, Flute douce u. s. w. Allein diese Arten haben oft eine besondere Struktur, Intonation und Größe, daher sie auch besondere Namen haben, und am besten an ihrem Orte betrachtet werden. Wir nehmen das Wort etwas enger, und verstehen die gedeckten Register, die keinen besondern Namen führen: sondern also schlechthin benennet werden; oder die doch aus eben einem solchen Fundamente gearbeitet werden. Es können aber alle Arten der Pfeifen gedeckt werden, und weil sie dadurch eine Oktave tiefer klingen; so bekommen sie auch einen Namen, der noch eins so groß ist, als ihre Körper. Also ist das **Gedackt** 4' nur 2' lang; 8' nur 4', 16' nur 8' und s. w. Es werden aber hauptsächlich die Oktavenregister gedeckt, und **Gedackte** genennet. Also haben wir 1) ein 32füßiges Gedackt, doch ist das größte corpus nur 16'. Das hat einen besondern Namen, und heißt: **Contrabaß, Untersatz, Subbaß, Großsubbaß**, s. davon §. 126. 2) ein 16füßiges Gedackt. Wenn das im Pedal ist, heißt es auch **Untersatz** oder **Subbaß**. Zuweilen ist 32' und 16' zugleich im Pedal. Z. Ex. in der Stadtkirche zu Jena. Der wird auch etwas weiter gemacht, daß er pompichter und völliger klingt, weil es ein großer Fehler ist, wenn der Subbaß so schnaubt. Die Körper sind also nur 8' groß. Im Manual heißt es schlechtweg ein **Gedackt** 16'; heißt auch, wenn es zumal etwas enger Mensur ist, **Bordun**, s. § 124. Da muß ohne dies die Weite nicht seyn, die im Pedal gelobet worden, weil es nicht anmuthig lautet. Der Name **Untersatz** ist bey diesen zwo Arten von Gedackten, wenn sie im Pedal stehen, sehr gemein. 16' ist er z. Ex. in **Waltershausen**; zu **Elmshorn**; in **Bützfleth** bey Stade: 32' in der Altstädter Orgel zu **Königsberg**; zu St. Johannis in **Lüneburg** ist 32' und 16', beyde unter dem Namen **Untersatz**, jener ist halb von Holz, und halb von Metall; so ist auch 32' und 16' zugleich unter dem Namen **Subbaß** zu **Mühlhausen** in Thüringen

that this altered spelling is the result of someone writing down this stop after only hearing it spoken, and never seeing its proper spelling. In Naumburg there is found a Fugara 4′. The pipes are very narrow and consequently the speech is rather slow; [this stop] is furthermore cutting and yet delicate. Thus this rank belongs among the open flue stops, and is little different from Violdigamba 4′.

* FUNDAMENTALIS, i.e., foundation stop. At Chambery it is the Principal.†

§. 150.

* GAR ["very"] is an accompanying word; look under the word to which it is prefixed. For example, *Gar kleine Flöt*, see Praetorius, p. 172; *gar grosser Untersatzgedakt* 32′, see p. 178 [*ibid.*], etc.

GEDAKT. This word may be understood either in a broader or narrower sense. In the broad sense, all stops are so called that are stopped, be they flue ranks or reed ranks, metal or wooden; for example, the Subbass, Contrabass, Bordun, Barem, Regal, Quintatön, *Flute douce*, etc. These types [of stops], however, often have their own particular structure, voicing and size; thus they also have their own particular names, and are best considered under their own heading. We will use the word somewhat more narrowly, understanding Gedakt stops as those that bear no special name but are rather simply called thus, or that are constructed according to just such a principle. All types of pipes, however, may be stopped, and since they thereby sound an octave lower, they therefore bear a numeral that is twice as large as their bodies. Thus the Gedakt 4′ is only 2′ long, the 8′ only 4′, the 16′ only 8′, etc. It is primarily the octave-sounding stops‡ that are stopped and called Gedackts. Thus we find: 1) a 32′ Gedackt, whose largest pipe however is only 16′. It has a special name, and is called Contrabass, Untersatz, Subbass, [or] Grosssubbass; concerning these see §.126. 2) a 16′ Gedackt. If it is in the pedal, it is also called Untersatz or Subbass. Sometimes it is in the pedal at both 32′ and 16′, for example in the Stadtkirche in Jena. It is also made [at a] somewhat broader [scale], so that it sounds more pompous and full, since it is a great defect if the Subbass just wheezes. The bodies of these stops are only 8′ tall. In the manual it is simply called a Gedackt 16′, or also (especially if it is of somewhat narrower scale) Bordun; see §.124. Moreover it must not be of the breadth recommended for the pedal, since it would not sound pleasant. The name Untersatz is the most usual one for these two types of Gedackts§ if they stand in the pedal. At 16′ it appears, for example, at Waltershausen, at Elmshorn and in Butzfleth near Stade; at 32′ in the Altstädterkirche organ at Königsberg. At St. Johannis in Lüneburg it is [found at] 32′ and 16′, both bearing the name Untersatz; the former is half wooden and half metal. It is also both at 32′ and 16′ at Mühlhausen in Thuringia, under the name Subbass.[38)] Thus the name is not all that important. In the organ of the royal palace at Königs-

---

* In Adlung's stoplist of the Waltershausen organ, §.314, a stop listed as "Fugar" is found in the Oberwerk. The Oberwerk of this same organ today, however, holds a stop spelled "Vogar". Perhaps either Adlung or Albrecht "corrected" the stoplist.

† See the stoplist of this organ in Chapter 10.

‡ i.e., as opposed to mutations.

§ i.e., 32′ and 16′.

ringen.³⁸) Also ist man an die Namen so sehr nicht gebunden. In der königl. Schloßorgel zu Königsberg ist Unterbaß 26'. Unterbaß ist wol so viel als Subbaß: denn das lateinische sub heißt unter. Aber 26' kann er nicht seyn, und ist gewiß ein Druckfehler in Matthesons Anhange zum Niedt S. 186. Es soll 16' seyn, weil Oktave 8' und 4' dabey stehen. Großunterbaß 32', zu St. Marien in Danzig; imgleichen doppelt Unterbaß zu U. L. Fr. in Lübeck ist beym Prätorio wol eben das; oder ist 16' mit doppelten Pfeifen. Ich glaube das erste, weil Unterbaß besonders dabey ist. Von Bordunsubbaß s. §. 124. In der Pfarrkirche zu Danzig ist im Pedal Untersatz 32', Subbaß 16' und Gedackt 16'. Also muß der Unterschied in der Mensur seyn, wie schon gedacht. In Stockholm ist auch Subbaß 32'; auch in Erfurt zun Barfüßern, soviel ich mich besinne. Der Contrabaß offen 16' ist §. 126. angemerkt. Zu St. Bartholomäi in Danzig ist ein Subbaß 16' offen. Er wird vielleicht anstatt des Principals stehen von Holz, oder was sonst dadurch gemeynt wird; denn ordentlich nennet man das Gedackte einen Subbaß; wiewol es mehr Bedeutungen hat. So heißen z. Ex. die Alten die Großholzflöt 8' ton auch Subbaß oder Thunbaß. (d. i. Tonbaß.) s. Prätor. S. 132. Das Gedackt 16' heißt auch Großgedackt zu St. Dominico in Prag, im Manual. Grobgedackt 16' ist in der Orgel zu St. Michaelis in Erfurt, welches durch besondere Zuge im Manual, und als ein Subbaß im Pedal gebraucht werden kann. (Man vergleiche hiermit §. 130.) 3.) Sonst kann man durch Grobgedackt nicht eben allezeit 16' verstehen, weil auch das 8füßige, wenn die Mensur und der Aufschnitt weit, der Klang aber pompicht ist, so genennet wird. Denn das Gedackt 8' findet sich fast in allen Clavieren; doch wird es in etlichen stiller intonirt, als in andern, daher einige mit dem Namen des Stillen- oder Gelindengedackts beleget werden, welches auch das Musicirgedackt heißt, indem es zur Musik am bequemsten ist. Dies heißt auch Lieblichgedackt; und in der Pfarrorgel zu Königsberg stehet es 8' mit diesem Namen. Wenn sie auf Flötenart gemacht werden, nennet man sie auch Humangedackt. Dies stehet in der Orgel zu St. Gertrud in Hamburg von Holz, sehr lieblich. Die Körper der 8fußigen sind ohngefähr 4' groß. 4) man hat aber auch Kleingedackt von 4' ton und 2fußigen Körpern, auch 2' ton; die aber von andern Flöten genennet werden. Wenn ein Gedackt noch ein größeres oder kleiners neben sich hat; so heißts auch zuweilen Mittelgedackt. Z Ex. zu St. Petri in Magdeburg, s. Prätor. l. c. da es 4' ist. So auch zu St. Catharinen daselbst. id. Großhölzern Gedackt 8' stehet zu Riddagshausen im Kloster, wie Prätor ebenfalls anführet. Gedackt 1' ist die Bauerflöte, davon §. 121. zu lesen. 2' heißt bisweilen auch also, z. Ex. zu Danzig in der Pfarrkirche. Es ist bey den Gedackten weiter zu merken, daß man sie noch mit andern Namen belegt. Z. Ex. Pressior 16' zu Sandomir ist auch ein Gedackt. Pressus heißt gedrückt. Obtusior 8' ist ebendaselbst das Gedackt 8'. Obtusus heißt sonst geschwächt, stumpf, grob; denn so klingen die Gedackte. Pileata 4' ist das Gedackt 4' ebendaselbst. Pileus heißt

---

³⁸) Beyde stehen zwar im Niedt S 193.; aber nur der letztere in der Orgel B. M. V. allhier.

Ch. VII. Concerning Stops in General and in Particular

berg there is an Unterbass 26′. Unterbass is indeed the same as Subbass, since the Latin word "sub" means "under". But it cannot be 26′—this is surely a printing error in Mattheson's Appendix to Niedt, p. 186. It must be 16′, since Oktave 8′ and 4′ are there. The Grossunterbass 32′ at St. Marien in Danzig, as well as the Doppelt Unterbass at the [Kirche zu] Unsrer Lieben Frau in Lübeck (see Praetorius, pp. 163 and 166) are both this sort of stop; or the latter may be a 16′ with doubled pipes.* I believe the first [alternative is correct], since an Unterbass is there as well. Concerning Bordunsubbass, see §.124. In the Pfarrkirche at Danzig there is in the pedal an Untersatz 32′, Subbass 16′ and Gedackt 16′. Thus there must be a difference in the scaling [between the two 16′ stops], as has already been mentioned. In Stockholm there is also a Subbass 32′, as well as at the Barfüsserkirche in Erfurt, to the best of my recollection. The open Contrabass 16′ [at Görlitz] has already been noted in §.126.† At St. Bartholomäus in Danzig there is an open Subbass 16′. It may be a wooden substitute for the Principal [16′], or intended for some other purpose, since normally a Subbass is a Gedackt, although it does have other meanings. For example, in times past the Grossholzflöt was also called Subbass or Thunbass (i.e., Tonbass); see Praetorius, p. 132. The Gedackt 16′ is also called Grossgedackt in the manual at St. Dominicus in Prague. There is a Grobgedackt 16′ in the organ at St. Michaelis in Erfurt, that can be used both in the manual and as a Subbass in the pedal through separate drawknobs (cf. §.130). 3.) The Grobgedackt does not always mean a 16′, though, since an 8′ is so called if its scale and cut-up are wide and its sound pompous. For the Gedackt 8′ is found on almost every manual, though in some it is more quietly voiced than in others. Thus some are given the name Still- or Gelindgedackt, which means the Musicirgedackt,‡ since it is most suitable for figured bass. This is also known as Lieblichgedackt, and stands at 8′ with this name in the Pfarrkirche organ at Königsberg. If it is made to imitate a flute it is also called Humangedackt. Such a stop stands in the organ at St. Gertrud in Hamburg, made of wood and very lovely.§ The bodies of the 8′ are about 4′ tall.¶ 4.) There is also a Kleingedackt of 4′ pitch and 2′ bodies, as well as a 2′ pitch, which is however named for other flutes.‖ If one Gedackt is paired with another one, either larger or smaller, it is sometimes called Mittelgedackt; for example at St. Petri and at St. Catharina in Magdeburg, where it is a 4′; see Praetorius, *loc. cit.* [, pp. 175 and 176]. A Grossholzern Gedackt 8′ stands in the Klosterkirche at Riddagshausen, as Praetorius likewise mentions. The 1′ Gedackt is the Bauerflöte, discussed in §.121; the 2′ sometimes bears this same name, for example at Danzig in the Pfarrkirche. Concerning Gedackts, note furthermore that they are given other names as well: for example, *Pressior* 16′ at Sandomir is a Gedackt (*pressus* means "pressed"). *Obtusior* 8′ there is the Gedackt 8′ (*obtusus* means "weak, dull, thick", and that is the way Gedackts sound). Pileata 4′ there is the Gedackt 4′ (*pileus* means "hat", since Gedackts have caps on top to stop them). All

* See §.137.

† As Adlung has stated earlier in this entry, the Contrabass is normally a stopped rank.

‡ i.e., the one used for realizing figured bass for accompaniments. This stop is also called "Barem"; see §.120.

§ This last comment does not represent Adlung's opinion, but is taken directly from Mattheson's Appendix to Niedt, p. 181.

¶ This statement seems to refer to all 8′ Gedackts, not merely the last instance mentioned.

‖ e.g., Blockflöte, Sifflöte.

38) To be sure, both of these appear in [Mattheson's Appendix to] Niedt, p. 193, yet only the latter is [actually found] in the Marienkirche organ here. [Albrecht]

heißt ein Hut, weil die Gedackte Hüte aufhaben, wodurch sie gedeckt werden. Alle drey Namen schicken sich auf alle Gedackte, groß und klein, und wird darunter Regula verstanden. Will man die Namen behalten, und die Füße nicht dazu setzen, doch aber dieselben unterscheiden; so kann das Gedackt, welches in unserer Orgel das größte ist pileata maxima, obtusior maxima, pressior maxima, heißen; das kleinere pileata, ꝛc. maior, oder media, und das allerkleinste minima, minor. ꝛc. Es sind die bisher erzählten Gedackte 1′, 2′, 4′, 8′, 16′, 32′, lauter Oktavgedackte, die den sonum des Principals angeben, wenn man sie ziehet; aber zuweilen wird ein Gedackt tiefer gestimmt, und behält doch denselben Namen. So ist z. Ex. zu St. Jakobi in Hamburg die Orgel Chormäßig: im Oberwerke aber ist ein Gedackt im Kammerton, damit, wenn man musiciren soll, man des Abschreibens und Transponirens überhoben werde, so oft etwan der Kammerton zu gebrauchen. In ordentlichen Musiken haben sie schon mehr Gedackte. Das ist gar gut. Unter den Flötwerken hat man auch gedeckte Quinten, diapente pileatas. Davon s. unten bey Quinte.

* Gedackte italienische Quinte. s. §. 161.

§. 151.

Gedacktpommer, s. §. 123.

Gedackte Flûte douce, s. in Flûte a bec, §. 146.

Gedackte Quintflöte, s. in Quinte.

* Gedacktflöte ist ein lieblich intonirt Gedackt 16′, 8′ und 4′. In Königsberg im Löbenicht steht es 8′. Biermann führt es S. 25. 4′ an, und Gedacktfl. Oktav, wie auch Gedacktflöt Sedecima ist beym Prätorio l. c. S. 172. angemerkt.

Was sonst für Register vorkommen, die sich von Gedackten anheben, die beliebe man in dem daranhangenden Worte zu suchen. Z. Ex. Gedacktfl. Chormaß und Unterchormaß, ꝛc. s. 125.

§. 152.

Gedämpft Regal, s. unten Regal. §. 183.

Geigenprincipal, s. Principal. §. 177.

Geigenregal, oder Geigendregal ist eine besondere Art des Regals, welches mit der 8füßigen Quintatön im Diskant fast wie eine Geige klingt, daher es auch den Namen bekommen, s. Prätor. l c. Man nennet es auch Jungfernregal, vermuthlich wegen der lieblichen Intonation. Mehr folgt hiervon §. 161. (s. Anleit. S. 423.) Daß es ein Schnarrwerk sey, giebt die Benennung schon zu verstehen. Der Ton ist entweder 8 oder 4füßig. Im Prätorio findet man auch den Namen Geigendregälchen 4′ s. Tom. II. S. 199.

§. 153.

three names apply to all Gedackts, large and small, and [the word] *Regula** is understood as preceding each term.† If one wishes to keep the names without appending the length in feet, yet still to distinguish among them, then the Gedackt, which is the largest in our organs,‡ may be called *pileata maxima*, *obtusior maxima*, or *pressior maxima*; the smaller§ [Gedackt] *pileata*, *major* or *media*, etc.; and the smallest *pileata*, *minima* or *minor*, etc. The Gedackts discussed up to now—1′, 2′, 4′, 8′, 16′, 32′—are only octave-sounding stopped ranks, that produce the pitches of the Principals when they are drawn.¶ Sometimes, however, a Gedackt is tuned lower and still keeps the same name. For example, at St. Jacobi in Hamburg the organ is at choir pitch, yet in the Oberwerk there is a Gedackt at chamber pitch, so that if it is necessary to play figured bass accompaniments the organist is spared the copying and transposing that are so often needed for chamber pitch. Other Gedackts are also there for normal music-making; it all works quite well. Among the flute stops there are also Gedeckte Quinten;‖ see below under Quinte.

* *Gedackte italienische Quinte*. See §.161.

§. 151.

Gedacktpommer, see §.123.
Gedackte *Flöte douce*, see under *Flûte a bec*, §.146.
Gedackte Quintflöte, see under Quinte.
* Gedacktflöte is a sweetly voiced Gedackt 16′, 8′ or 4′. In Königsberg at the Löbenichtkirche it stands at 8′. Biermann mentions it as 4′ on p. 25, and Praetorius, *loc. cit.*, p. 172, notes a Gedacktfl. Oktav as well as a Gedacktflöt Sedecima.

As for other stops that originate from Gedackts, one should seek them under the appended word. For example, Gedacktfl. Chormass and Unterchormass, etc., see [§.]125.

§. 152.

Gedämpft Regal, see below [under] Regal, §.183.
Geigenprincipal, see Principal, §.177.
Geigenregal, or Geigendregal, is a special type of Regal that sounds almost like a violin [when it is combined] with the 8′ Quintatön in the treble; this is how it got its name;** see Praetorius, *loc. cit.*[,p. 146]. It is also called Jungfernregal [maiden regal], apparently because of its lovely voicing. More on this in §.161 (see *Anleitung*, p. 423). Its name makes clear that it is a reed stop. It is either at 8′ or 4′ pitch. Praetorius also uses the name Geigendregälchen ["little Geigendregal"] 4′; see Vol. II, p. 199.

* i.e., "stop, register."
† i.e., *Regula pressa, Regula obtusa, Regula pileata*; see §.184 below.
‡ As this sentence later seems to suggest, Adlung is speaking of the 8′; perhaps he means that the 32′ and 16′ varieties are not normally called simply "Gedackt."
§ i.e., 4′.
¶ i.e., no aliquot stops.
‖ i.e., "Stopped Fifths."
** "Geige" means "fiddle."

§. 153.

Gemshorn ist eine solche Gattung der Flötenwerke, deren Körper oben spitzig oder konisch sind, wie die Spitzflöten: beym labio aber ist sie weiter. Den Namen hat es daher, weil es auf Hornart klingt. Weil sie oben spitzig zu gehen; so können ihre Körper so groß nicht seyn, als anderer offenen Pfeifen, die gleichaus weit sind; denn sie werden durch das Zuspitzen halb gedeckt; die gedeckten Pfeifen aber geben einen tiefern Ton, als die Körper, der Länge nach, sonst austragen würden. Daher das Gemshorn 8' etwann 6' oder 7' lang seyn wird. Doch ist es nicht gar zu; etwan so, daß es oben halb so weit sey, als unten. Das labium wird in fünf Theile getheilet, und ein Theil davon ist des Mundes Breite; alsdann wird die Hälfte aufgeschnitten. f. Prätor l. c. S. 134. I.) Gemshorn 16' ist besser im Pedale zu gebrauchen, wo nicht andere kleine Stimmen dabey sind. Dieß heißt zu Grüningen in der Schloßorgel Großgemshorn, da hingegen im Manual Gemshorn 4' ist; jenes aber, nebst dem kleinen 8' im Pedale und Oberwerke. II.) Das Gemshorn 8' heißt auch äqual Gemshorn. f. Prätor l. c. S. 134. Ist eine sehr liebliche Stimme. Dieß Gemshorn nennen die Niederländer auch Koppelflöt. f. §. 129. Es ist länger als ein Gedackt 8', weil es offen ist, doch kürzer als das Principal 8', weil es wie halb gedeckt ist durch das Zuspitzen. Prätorius sagt: man mögte es dem Klange nach auch wol Violdigamba nennen; allein dieselbe ist itzo bey uns gar ein besonder Register, wie aus deren künftigen Beschreibung §. 206. erhellen wird. So stehen auch z. E. in der Regler Orgel in Erfurt, und in der Orgel B. M. V. in Mühlhausen Gemshorn 8', und Violdigamba 8' in einem Claviere, von gar verschiedener Struktur und Klange. Das Gemshorn klingt weit stiller und stumpfer. Die Violdigamba ist cylindrisch. In der Görlitzer Orgel ist Gemshornbaß 8' im Pedale. Dieß ist eben das, nur daß es im Pedale stehet. III.) Gemshorn 4' heißt auch Oktavengemshorn, auch wol, wie das vorhergehende, Koppelflöte, wie z. E. zu S. Blasii in Braunschweig. Doch heissen alle Arten derselben auch oft, ja ordinär, Gemshorn. Also stehet Gemshorn 4' zu Grüningen im Schlosse, wie zuvor gedacht. It. zu Waltershausen. Dieses heißt zu Hessen auf dem Schlosse Gemshorn oder klein Violn 4': wäre also eine kleine Violdigamba oder Braccio, wie Prätorius will. f. l. c. S. 189. Nach eben desselben Bericht stehet 4' auch im Dom zu Magdeburg, wofür die Domküster Spitzflöte 4' setzen, vermuthlich wegen der Aehnlichkeit ihrer Körper mit der Figur der Spitzflöten. Auch wird Prätorii Großgemshornbaß 8' bey ihnen Spitzflötenbaß genennet. IV.) Gemshorn 2', heißt zuweilen klein Oktavengemshorn. Es stehet in der Kreutzkirche zu Dreßden; zu S. Jakobi in Hamburg; zu S. Stephani in Bremen; in Buxtehude; zu Colberg in der heil. Geistskirche; in der Pfarrkirche zu Danzig; eben daselbst in der mittelsten Orgel; zu Königsberg im Kneiphof; zu Eisenach (§. 288.) nebst 1½' in einem Claviere. Dieß waren lauter Gemshörner, welche die Oktave von sich hören lassen: man kann aber auch V.) Gemshörner machen, welche die Quinte 3' Ton haben. Z. E. Gemshornquinte 3' ist zu Bückeburgk. f.

Ch. VII. Concerning Stops in General and in Particular

§. 153.

Gemshorn is a category of flue stop whose body is tapered or conical on top, like Spitzflötes, but broader at the lip. The name comes from the fact that it sounds rather like a horn. Because it is conical, its body cannot be as tall as other open pipes that are cylindrical, since by being tapered it becomes half-stopped, and stopped pipes produce a deeper pitch than their bodies would otherwise deliver, given their length. Therefore a Gemshorn 8′ will be about 6′ or 7′ long [at low C]. Yet it is not totally stopped, only to the point where it is about half as broad on top as at the bottom. The lip* is divided into five parts, and one of those parts is the width of the mouth; then the cut-up is made one half the width. See Praetorius, *loc. cit.*, p. 134. I.) Gemshorn 16′ is better to use in the pedal if other higher stops are not included.† In the palace organ at Gröningen this stop is called Grossgemshorn [i.e., large Gemshorn], because there is already a Gemshorn 4′ in the manual [i.e., the Rückpositiv]; the 16′, however, is in the Pedal together with a Klein[-Gemshorn, i.e., small Gemshorn] 8′[, as well as a Gemshorn 8′ in the] Oberwerk. II.) The Gemshorn 8′ is also called Aqual Gemshorn; see Praetorius, *loc. cit.*, p. 134. It is a very lovely stop. The Netherlanders also call this Gemshorn "Koppelflöt"; see §. 129. It is longer than a Gedackt 8′, because it is open, yet shorter than the Principal 8′, since it is as it were half-stopped in that it is tapered. Praetorius[, p. 134,] says that in view of its tone it might also well be called Violdigamba; yet that is a completely separate stop today as its description in §.206 below will reveal. For example, in the Reglerkirche organ in Erfurt and in the Marienkirche organ in Mühlhausen, Gemshorn 8′ and Violdigamba 8′ are both found on the same manual, of completely different structure and tone. The Gemshorn sounds far quieter and duller. The Violdigamba is cylindrical. In the Görlitz organ there is a Gemshornbass 8′ in the pedal. That is the same stop, except that it stands in the pedal. III.) Gemshorn 4′ is also called Oktavengemshorn as well as Koppelflöte (like the 8′), as for example at St. Blasius in Braunschweig. Most examples, though, are often, indeed ordinarily, called Gemshorn. Thus a Gemshorn 4′ is found in the palace at Gröningen, as mentioned above, and another at Waltershausen. In the palace at Hesse this stop is called Gemshorn or Klein Violn 4′; this would thus be a little Violdigamba or a Braccio,‡ as Praetorius would have it; see *l.c.*, p. 189. According to this same source § there is also a 4′ in the Cathedral at Magdeburg, which the cathedral vergers give as Spitzflöte 4′,¶ apparently because of the similarity of their bodies with the shape of the Spitzflöte. The stop that Praetorius calls Grossgemshornbass they also call Spitzflötenbass. IV.) Gemshorn 2′ is sometimes called Klein Oktavengemshorn. It stands in the Kreuzkirche at Dresden, at St. Jacobi in Hamburg, at St. Stephani in Bremen, at Buxtehude, at Colberg in the Heilige Geistskirche, in the middle organ in the Pfarrkirche at Danzig, at Königsberg in the Kneiphof, and at Eisenach on the same manual as a 1 ½′ [Gemshorn] (see §.288). All of these are Gemshorns that speak octave-sounding pitches, yet there are also V.) Gemshorns made that speak the pitch of a Quinte 3′. For example, there is a

---

* What Adlung writes here, *labium*, indisputably means "lip"; what he seems to mean, however, is that the circumference of the pipe (perhaps the languid?) is divided into five equal sections, and the mouth of the pipe is made the width of one of those sections.

† It is not clear whether Adlung is discussing registration or the selection of stops for a stoplist.

‡ i.e., Viola.

§ i.e., Praetorius, p. 173.

¶ See §.308 below. Adlung's remark must mean that the vergers have supplied him with the stoplist he publishes here. It is is hardly surprising that the stoplist more than a century later differs in many particulars from the one Praetorius published.

Prätor. Zu Gera (§. 301.) ist sie 6′, und heißt Gemsquint, auch 1½′. Lieblich Gemsquinte 1½′ ist zu Alach. (s. §. 284.) Auch findet man VI.) das Quintgemshorn 6′. Dieß war ehedessen in der Regler Orgel in Erfurt, anstatt dessen nun die Sesquialtera angebracht worden. VII.) Quintgemshorn 1½′ wird von andern Nasat genennet. Wir wollen daran wieder denken bey Nasat. VIII.) Gemshorn 1′ wird von Prätorio mit angeführt in der Disposition der Orgel zu St. Lambrecht in Lüneburg. s. S. 233. Ueberhaupt von allen Gemshörnern noch etwas zu sagen; so bemerken wir, daß sie von andern auch Spillflöte genennet werden, weil sie einer Handspillen gar ähnlich anzusehen. s. Prätor. S. 135. Spillpfeife und Spillpipe ist eben so viel. Daß das Wort Spill soviel heisse als tenuis, subtilis, zeigt Matthesons vollkommener Kapellmeister S. 469. §. 86. an. Andere haben hernach dieß Wort verändert und Spielpfeife oder Spielflöte daraus gemacht. Dieser Name Spielflöte ist zu St. Petri in Berlin 8′; it. zu Insterburg in Preussen; 8′ und 4′ zu Königsberg im Kneiphof; 8′ ist Spielpfeife eben daselbst im Löbenicht; zu Weimar in der Stadtkirche 4′; zu Naumburg in der Kirche St. Wenceslai 8′. Spielpiepe 8′, und klein Spielpiepe 4′ zu S. Petri in Lübeck führt Prätorius an l. c; imgl. Spillpf. 4′ zu S. Lambrecht in Lüneburg Spielflöte 8′ ist zwey mal zu Danzig in der Pfarrkirche. It. zur Dreyfaltigkeit, und zu St. Johannis ebendaselbst. Zu Königsberg in der Schloßorgel; auch in der Habergischen; in der neuen Orgel zu Leipzig In der Disposition der Stralsundischen Orgel zu St. Nikolai wird es auch so erklärt, da ist Spielflöte oder Gemshorn 8′. Ferner merke, daß etliche sie Blockpfeifen nennen. Daher ist zu St. Marien in Danzig Spillpfeife oder Blockflöte 8′. Aber §. 122. ist gezeiget, daß dieses nicht recht sey. Die Spitzflöten haben fast gleiche Struktur; sie sind aber vom Gemshorn unterschieden. s. Spitzflöte. Auch ist in der Disposition der Königsbergischen Pfarrorgel Gemshorn 14′: aber es ist wol ein Druckfehler, weil 14′ kein Register haben kann; es müßte denn die Länge des Körpers, nicht aber der sonus 14′ halten. Doch soll es vielleicht 4′ heißen, als welches man zu Grüningen findet, und zu St. Catharinen in Danzig unter den Namen der Spielflöt 4′; it. zu St. Catharinen in Hamburg; in der mittelsten Orgel der Pfarrkirche zu Danzig. Endlich ist auch nicht zu vergessen, daß Niedt P. II. cap. X. edit. 2dæ sagt: das Gemshorn ist ein schnarrend Register 8′ und 16′ton, gleich einem Regal, doch etwas lieblicher. Das Wort schnarrend soll wol anzeigen, es sey ein Schnarrwerk; weswegen er es auch mit dem Regal vergleicht. Allein ich weis nie dergleichen Gemshorn; wo er dergleichen gesehen haben sollte, ist mir nicht bekannt. Vielleicht ist es bey ihm ein Versehen.

Gingrina, s. §. 184.

§. 154.

Glocken, anstatt des Sterns, s. §. 133. bey Cymbel.

Gemshornquinte 3′ at Bückeburg; see Praetorius[, p. 185]. At Gera (§.301) it is at 6′ as well as 1 ½′, and called Gemsquint. There is a Lieblich Gemsquinte 1 ½′ at Alach (see §.284). One also finds VI.) the Quintgemshorn 6′. There was formerly one in the Reglerkirche organ at Erfurt, which has now been replaced with a Sesqualtera. VII.) Quintgemshorn 1 ½′, which some call Nasat, will be considered further under Nasat. VIII.) Gemshorn 1′ is cited by Praetorius, p. 233, in the stoplist of the organ at St. Lambrecht in Lüneburg. Now to speak a bit about all Gemshorns in general: it should be noted that some call them "Spillflöte", since they look very much like a hand spindle; see Praetorius, p. 135. Spillpfeife and Spillpipe are the same [as Spillflöte]. Mattheson in his *Volkommene Kappellmeister*, §.86, p. 469, indicates that the word "Spill" means the same as *tenuis*, *subtilis*.* This word was later altered and made into Spielpfeife or Spielflöte. The name Spielflöte is [found] at St. Petri in Berlin and at Insterburg in Prussia at 8′, and at 8′ and 4′ in the Kneiphofkirche at Königsberg. There is an 8′ Spielpfeife in the Löbenichtkirche at Königsberg and at Naumburg in the St. Wenceslauskirche; at 4′ in the Stadtkirche in Weimar. Praetorius, *loc. cit.*,† cites a Spielpiepe 8′ and klein Spielpiepe 4′ at St. Petri in Lübeck, as well as Spillpf. 4′ at St. Lambrecht in Lüneburg.‡ Spielflöte appears twice at Danzig in the Pfarrkirche, as well as at the Dreifaltigkeitskirche and at St. Johannis there. It is also in the palace church organ and the Haberbergkirche organ at Königsberg, and in the new organ at Leipzig. In the stoplist of the organ at St. Nikolai in Stralsund it is also stated that there is a Spielflöte or Gemshorn 8′. Note furthermore that some call it Blockpfeife; thus at St. Marien in Danzig there is a Spillpfeife or Blockflöte 8′. It is indicated in §.122, however, that this is not correct.§ The Spitzflötes have almost the same structure, but they are different from the Gemshorn; see "Spitzflöte". In the stoplist of the Pfarrkirche organ at Königsberg there is a Gemshorn 14′; but this is surely a printing error, since no stop can be 14′. 14′ may, though, refer to the length of the body rather than the pitch. Or perhaps it might mean 4′, the same as is found at Gröningen. The same is found at St. Catherine in Danzig under the name "Spielflöt 4′", at St. Catherine in Hamburg, and in the middle organ of the Pfarrkirche at Danzig. Finally, it should not be forgotten that Niedt in Part II, chap. X of the second edition¶ says: the Gemshorn is a rattling (schnarrend) stop of 8′ and 16′ pitch, like a Regal, yet somewhat milder.‖ The word "schnarrend" may well indicate that it is a reed, wherefore it is compared with the Regal. I am not familiar with this type of Gemshorn, however; the place where he is supposed to have seen it is unknown to me. Perhaps it is an error on his part.

GINGRINA, see §.184.

§. 154.

GLOCKEN, instead of the [Cymbel]stern, see §.133 under Cymbel.

---

* Both mean "thin" or "fine" in Latin.

† p. 164; but Praetorius spells the stops "Spilpipe" and "Klein Spilpipe."

‡ p. 233.

§ i.e., that they are not normally considered the same stop.

¶ p. 111.

‖ Niedt actually says: "Gemshorn: ein Schnarrwerk in Orgeln, von 8, und 16 Fuß..." (Gemshorn: an organ reed stop at 8′ and 16′...)

Communicantenglocke ist was anders. Es findet sich dieselbe in einem Dorfe ohnweit Erfurt, Walschleben; und ist so gemacht, daß eine Glocke von beliebiger Größe durch einen Hammer klingend gemacht wird, wie ein Seiger. Es kann dieses nach Belieben gemacht werden, bald so, bald anders. Das Sternrad kann den Anschlag auch verrichten wie bey den 4 Glocken §. 133. doch ist hier nur eine Glocke. Das Rad wird laufend gemacht entweder durch ein Gewicht, wie an der Uhr, oder durch den Wind: Beydes aber kann durch einen Registerzug befördert werden. Hierdurch wird daselbst den Communicanten das Zeichen gegeben, daß sie nach dem Altar gehen sollen. Auch bedeutet der Anschlag dieser Glocke, daß der Prediger auf die Kanzel gehen soll.

§. 155.

Glockenspiel, Glockenregister, Carillon, auch wol Campanetta (von campana die Glocke.) Ausser der Orgel gehört es zum 25. Kapitel: in der Orgel aber hierher. Es ist was kostbares, daher auch was rares. Und habe ich in nicht allzuvielen Orgeln dergleichen angetroffen. In der neuen Orgel zu St. Nikolai in Rostock befindet sich dergleichen, welches im Hinterwerke, nebst andern Registern regieret wird, und aus 48 Glocken bestehet, soviel nämlich auf dem Claviere palmulæ sind. Es hat die Größe 2 Fußton. Nach §. 288. ist in Eisenach dergleichen auch; it. in Gotha. Man kann gleich erachten, daß die Glocken durch die Bälge nicht anzublasen sind, sondern es ist eine jede mit einem Hammer versehen; der durch das Clavier regiert und an die Glocken geschlagen wird. Man muß aber alles auf gebrochen Art spielen, und ein geschickter Organist kann schöne Sachen darauf machen. Solche Claviere aber sind ordinair schwer zu traktiren gegen andere. Durch den Registerzug werden die Hammer unmittelbar mit den palmulis verbunden. Mehr hiervon habe ich in meiner Anleitung §. 159. beygebracht. (**)

(**) In der Schloßkirchen-Orgel in Altenburg ist eines dergleichen.

§. 156.

Glöckleinton ist mit allem diesen nicht zu verwechseln, weil dies ein ordentlich Pfeif- und zwar Flötwerk ist. Es heist auch Tonus faber, (wäre aber wol besser, wenn es Tonus fabri genennet würde) ist weit mensurirt, und klingt, als ob man mit einem Hammer auf einen wohlklingenden Amboß schlüge. Es ist 2′ in der Görlitzer Orgel; und Boxberg sagt dabey, wenn man es zu der Quintatön 16′ ziehe, lasse es sich wohl zu laufenden Sachen gebrauchen, nebst einem douxen (sollte wol doucen heissen) accompagnement eines andern Claviers. Sonst habe ich davon nichts gehöret.

§. 157.

Grobgedackt, s. Gedackt. §. 150.

Grober Cymbel, s. Cymbel. §. 134.

Grob-Regal, s. Regal. §. 183. Und was von Grob sich anhebt, siehe bey dem andern Worte, z. Ex. Grobe Mixtur, Grober Posaunen Untersatz, u. s. w.

Groß

Ch. VII. Concerning Stops in General and in Particular

COMMUNICANTENGLOCKE [Communicants' bell] is something other [than a stop]. There is one of these in Walschleben, a village not far from Erfurt, so constructed that a bell of a certain size is made to ring by a hammer, like a clock [chime]. It may be made in various ways, at will. The [Cymbel]stern wheel may also cause the striking as it does for the 4 bells (§.133), yet here there is just one bell. The wheel may be made to turn either by a weight, as in a clock, or by wind; both [methods], however, may be controlled by a stopknob. By this means the sign is given to the communicants there (at Walschleben) that they may go to the altar. The striking of this bell also means that the preacher is to proceed to the pulpit.

§. 155.

GLOCKENSPIEL, GLOCKENREGISTER, CARILLON, also *CAMPANETTA* (from *campana*, a bell). [Those] apart from the organ are discussed in Chapter 25, but [those] in the organ here. It is an expensive item, and thus a rare one.* I have not encountered them in very many organs. There is one in the new organ at St. Nikolai in Rostock which is played from the Hinterwerk along with other stops, and consists of 48 bells, as many as there are keys on the keyboard. It is at 2′ pitch. According to §.288 † there is also one in Eisenach, as well as in Gotha. It is immediately obvious that the bells are not winded by the bellows. Rather each one is provided with a hammer that strikes it, controlled by the keyboard. It must always be played with a broken touch; a skillful organist can do beautiful things on it. Such keyboards, however, ordinarily have a heavy touch (schwer zu traktieren) compared with others. Pulling the stopknob connects the hammers directly to the keys. I have dealt with this more in my *Anleitung*, §.159[, pp. 425 f.]. (**)

(**)In the Schlosskirche organ in Altenburg there is one of these. [Agricola]

§. 156.

GLÖCKLEINTON is not to be confused with all of the above, since it is a normal stop with pipes, indeed a flue stop. It is also called *Tonus faber* ‡ (it would be better, however, if it were called *Tonus fabri*. § It is widely scaled, and sounds as if someone were striking a sonorous anvil with a hammer. It is a 2′ in the Görlitz organ, and Boxberg¶ says about it that if it is drawn with the 16′ Quintatön it lends itself well to running passages, along with a *douxen*‖ (this should really be *doucen***) accompaniment on another keyboard. I have not heard anything else about it.

§. 157.

GROBGEDACKT, see Gedackt, §.150.
GROBER CYMBEL, see Cymbel, §.134.
GROB-REGAL, see Regal, §.183. As for terms beginning with "Grob", look under the accompanying word; e.g., Grobe Mixtur, Grober Posaunen Untersatz, etc.

---

* Since the Glockenspiel is not uncommon in surviving 18th-century Thuringian organs (even in smaller village organs), one infers from this statement that Adlung wrote it relatively early in the century, and that the Glockenspiel was just beginning to become a popular "accessory stop". Such a conclusion concurs with the growing popularity of color- or effect-stops that is noticeable in the development of Thuringian organs during the 18th century.

† The translation disregards the (superfluous) paragraph numbers in the collection of stoplists; see the stoplist of the organ at Eisenach in Chapter 10.

‡ i.e., "Blacksmith sound."

§ i.e., "Sound of the blacksmith"; Adlung is proving that he knows his Latin.

¶ p.[16].

‖ i.e., "gentle."

** Adlung is proving that he knows his French!

Großhohlflöte, ſ. **Hohlflöte.**

Großquintenbaß, ſ. **Quinte.**

Groß Rankel. ſ. **Rankel.** §. 181.

Großgedackt. ſ. **Gedackt.** §. 150.

Groß Gemshorn. ſ. **Gemshorn.** u. ſ. w. Alle Worte mit **Groß** ſuche man bey dem annexo.

Guckguck iſt auch ein Orgelregiſter, und befindet ſich z. E. zu Sondershauſen, iſt aber nicht viel werth, und noch närriſcher, als der **Vogelgeſang**; beſtehet nur aus 2 Pfeifen, wie der Vogel, davon der Name iſt, auch nur 2 Töne hören läßt, welche eine Terz von einander entfernt ſind. Iſt auch zu St. Catharinen in **Magdeburg.** ſ. **Prätor.** S. 175. Man ſchreibt auch **Ruckuck.** z. E. zu St. Gotthard in **Hildesheim.** ſ. **Prätor.** S. 199. it. 201.

§. 158.

Halbellich. ſ. unten in **Mixtur.**

Halber Cornet. ſ. **Cornet** §. 132.

Halbprincipal, d. i. **Oktave,** daher man es auch daſelbſt zu ſuchen hat.

Harfenprincipal. Dies führt **Prätorius** S. 172 in der Diſpoſition der Breßlauer Orgel an, obwol ohne Größe: was es aber eigentlich ſeyn ſoll, weis ich nicht. Zwar, wenn ich muthmaßen darf, ſo verſtehet man bey ſolchen Stimmen die Davidsharfe, deren Klang man endlich nachmachen kann, auch wol etwas ſchnarrend. Auf dieſe Art iſt zu Gera (ſ. §. 301.) auch ein **Nachthorn** 4′, welches oben den Klang einer Harfe von ſich hören läßt.

Harfenregal, iſt eine beſondere Art des **Regals**: aber aus was für Urſachen es dieſen Namen verdiene, weis ich nicht, weil ich noch keins geſehen: ſie ſind auch rar. Zu St. Petri in **Lübeck** iſt es, wenn die Diſpoſition dieſes Orgelwerks noch gültig iſt, welche **Prätorius** l. c. S. 165. mitgetheilet; doch hat **Prätorius** die Größe deſſelben nicht angegeben. Dagegen führt **Mattheſon** eins an von 8′ton zu **Stockholm,** it. in der Bergiſchen Orgel auf der Inſul **Rügen** von unten bis zum eingeſtrichene e, die beyden obern Oktaven aber haben Trompet 4′. Zu **Mühlhauſen** in Thüringen iſts 16′ton.[39]) Das **Geigenregal** hatte den Klang einer Geige, wenn es mit einem gewiſſen Regiſter gezogen wurde: vielleicht iſt hier auch dergleichen Harfenklang, entweder in dem Regale vor ſich, oder wenn ein gewiß Regiſter dazu gezogen wird.

§. 119.

Hautbois iſt ein franzöſiſch Wort; wird **Hoboä** geleſen, von haut, hoch, und bois, Holz: denn auſſer der Orgel iſt es eine hölzerne Pfeife, die höher gehet, als die

Schall-

---

[39]) So ſtehet zwar in des Herrn von **Mattheſon** Anhange zu **Niedts** zweytem Theile: aber in keiner Orgel zu **Mühlhauſen** iſt dies Regiſter zu finden.

GROSSHOHLFLÖTE, see Hohlflöte.
GROSSQUINTENBASS, see Quinte.
GROSS RANKET, see Ranket, §.181.
GROSSGEDACKT, see Gedackt, §.150.
GROSSGEMSHORN, see Gemshorn, etc. Any word [beginning] with Gross should be sought under the word it precedes.

GUCKGUCK [Cuckoo] is also an organ stop, found for example at Sondershausen. It is practically worthless, however, and is even more foolish than the Vogelgesang.* It consists of 2 pipes, just as the bird for which it is named produces only 2 pitches, a third apart from each other. It is also [found] at St. Catherine in Magdeburg; see Praetorius, p. 175. It is also spelled Kuckuck, e.g., at St. Gotthard in Hildesheim. See Praetorius, pp. 199 and 201.

* i.e., "Birdsong" or "Nightingale", another toy stop; see §.207.

§. 158.

HALBELLICH, see below under Mixtur[, §.167].
HALBER CORNET, see Cornet, §.132.
HALBPRINCIPAL, i.e., Oktave; therefore consult that entry.
HARFENPRINCIPAL. In the stoplist of the organ at Breslau in [*Syntagma musicum* II,] p. 172 Praetorius cites this [stop], but does not give its size. I really do not know what it might be. If I may be permitted to surmise: stops like this refer to [King] David's harp, whose rather twanging tone it has finally been possible to imitate.† There is also a Nachthorn 4′ of this sort at Gera (see §.301) that produces the sound of a harp in its upper register.

† i.e., in the percussive speech of various narrow-scaled string stops, notably the Violdigamba, that were still relatively recent developments in the organ at the time Adlung was writing this treatise.

HARFENREGAL is a separate type of Regal; but for what reason it has earned this name I do not know, since I have never before seen one (they are rare). There is one at St. Petri in Lübeck, if the stoplist of this organ that Praetorius reports, *loc. cit.*, p. 165, is still current; Praetorius, however, does not give its size. Mattheson, on the other hand, cites one at 8′ pitch at Stockholm, as well as in the organ of the church at Bergen on the Island of Rügen, from the bottom [of the compass] up to e′, both upper octaves having, however, a Trompet 4′. At Mühlhausen in Thuringia it is at 16′ pitch.[39] The Geigenregal has the sound of a violin if it is drawn with a given stop; perhaps this stop makes the sound of a harp, either when the Regal is played alone or if a certain stop is drawn with it.

§. 119. [§. 159]

HAUTBOIS is a French word, pronounced "Hoboä", from *haut*, "high", and *bois*, "wood", since apart from the organ it is a woodwind (holzerne Pfeife) that has

---

39) This is indeed what appears in Mr. Mattheson's Appendix to Niedt's second part, but there is no such stop in any organ in Mühlhausen. [Albrecht]

Schallmeyen in Deutschland. Da aber die Hoboä den Klang und Figur faſt wie die Schallmey hat; ſo heißt ſie auch die kleine Schallmey, imgleichen die franzöſiſche Schallmey. Oboe bey den Italienern iſt eben ſo viel. Es hat von der Hautbois der Hotteterre einen kleinen Traktat in Frankreich geſchrieben. ſ. Matthesons Orcheſtre I. P. III. c. III. §. 11. Sie will delikat geblaſen ſeyn ibid. §. 8. und einen Künſtler haben, ſ. muſikal. Trichter Kap. 10. Engliſch heißen ſie Hoboys. Lateiniſch Bombyces oder Bombi. Pommern im Deutſchen, ſoll nach Prätorio auch ſo viel ſeyn. Hautbois d'Amour gehet etwas doucer, weil der Keſſel enger, und ſie alſo wie mehr gedeckt iſt. Man hat in der Orgel dieſe Oboë auch angebracht, da iſt ſie, wie auch auſſer der Orgel ein Rohrwerk. Und da ſie mit Schallmey faſt eins iſt; ſo kann es ſeyn, daß in etlichen Diſpoſitionen auf dieſen Unterſchied nicht geſehen, ſondern Oboe und Schallmey für einerley ſind gehalten und geſchrieben worden. Doch ſoll von der Schallmey unten beſonders gehandelt werden, ſ. §. 186. Hautbois 8' ſtehet zu Görlitz; im Löbenicht zu Königsberg; zu Merſeburg im Schloß; zu Waltershauſen, und zu Hildesheim. 4' ſteht es zu Halle zu U. L. Fr. Der Baß zu Hautbois war §. 123. Bombardo: oder §. 141. der Fagott.

§. 160

Heertrummel ſteht auch in der Orgel, ſ. Tympanum §. 203.

Heerpauke, eben daſelbſt.

Hellpfeife wird beym Prätorio angetroffen zu St. Lamprecht in Lüneburg 8' groß. Ich habe aber davon weiter keinen Begriff; und kann es eine gemeine Oktave oder Principal nicht wohl ſeyn, weil Principal 8' noch beſonders dabey ſtehet.

Hinterſatz war in den alten Orgeln die Mixtur; weil ſie hinter das Hauptregiſter, das Principal, geſetzt wurde, ſ. Mixtur.

Hohlflöt, Holpfeife, iſt ein offen Flötwerk, deſſen Körper gegen das Principal weit, dagegen aber kurz ſind; doch gleichaus weit, faſt wie die Gedackten, aber mit engern labiis: daher ſie ſo hohl klingen, und alſo Hohlflöten heißen. Es ſind deren viererley in Anſehung der Größe. I.) Großhohlflöt 8' iſt zu St. Catharinen in Danzig im Manual und Pedal, unter dem Namen Holflöt; auch zu St. Nikolai in Hamburg; zu St. Wenceslai in Naumburg; in der Pfarrkirche zu Danzig: doch iſt auch in eben dem Claviere Hohlflöt 16', wie auch zu St. Marien daſelbſt. Wenn nun 8' Großhohlflöt beym Prätorio l. c. S. 131. u. f. heißt; wie ſoll denn dieſe heißen? 8' iſt daſelbſt noch einmal im Pedal. Eben daſelbſt iſt in der mittelſten Pfarrorgel 16' und 8' in einem Claviere, und noch 8' im andern. Zu Bartholomäi daſelbſt iſt 8'; it. zu Kreyßen; it. zu St. Marien in Lübeck; zu St. Dominico in Prag; zu Pulsnitz; zu Rudolſtadt; in der Domsorgel zu Hamburg iſt 8', und 4'; in Burtehude; zu Königsberg im Kneiphoſe. Prätorius führt S. 168. in der Orgel zu St. Jakobi in Hamburg an Holpipe 6', welche ſich von F anfängt, (conf. §. 213.) oder es iſt eine Holquinte. Im andern Claviere iſt 8': ſ. ein mehrers in meiner

Ch. VII. Concerning Stops in General and in Particular

a higher range than the Schalmei in Germany. Since however the Hoboä has almost the same timbre and shape as the Schalmei, it is also called the Kleine Schalmei* as well as the French Schalmei. "Oboe" is the same thing in Italian. Hotteterre in France has written a little treatise on the *Hautbois*.† See Mattheson's [*Neu-eröffnete*] *Orchestre*, part III, chap. III, §.11[, p. 271]. It needs to be blown delicately (§.8‡) and played by an artist; see [Fuhrmann's] *Musikalischer Trichter,* chap. 10[, p. 92]. In English it is called *Hoboys*, in Latin *Bombyces* or *Bombi*. According to Praetorius Pommer is the same thing in German. *Hautbois d'Amour* sounds somewhat more gentle, since the bulbous bell is narrower and it is thus a bit more stopped. This oboe has been adopted into the organ, where it is a reed just as apart from the organ. Since it is almost the same as the Schalmei, it may be that some stoplists do not recognize this distinction, but consider Oboe and Schalmei as the same and write it thus.§ Schalmei, though, is treated separately below; see §.186. There is an *Hautbois* 8′ at Görlitz, in the Löbenichtkirche at Königsberg, in the palace at Merseburg, at Waltershausen and at Hildesheim. In the Marienkirche¶ at Halle it stands at 4′. The bass for the *Hautbois* was [stated as] the Bombardo in §.123 or the Fagott in §.141.

* i.e., "Little Schalmei."
† Jacques Martin Hotteterre, *Principes de la flute traversiére,...et du haut-bois*. Paris: Christophe Ballard, 1707.
‡ i.e., §.8 of Mattheson, the source just cited.
§ presumably as "Schalmei."
¶ i.e., the Marktkirche.

§. 160.

HEERTRUMMEL [Military Drum] is also found in the organ; see Tympanum, §.203.

HEERPAUKE [Military Kettledrum], see likewise under Tympanum.

HELLPFEIFE, according to Praetorius,‖ is encountered at St. Lamprecht in Lüneburg at 8′ size. I have no further idea about it. It cannot very well be the common Oktave or Principal, since the Principal 8′ is already there separately.

‖ *Syntagma musicum*, vol. II, p. 233.

HINTERSATZ was the mixture in old organs, because it was placed behind the primary stop, the Principal; see Mixtur.

HOHLFLÖT, HOLPFEIFE, ["hollow flute," "hollow pipe"] is an open flute stop, whose body is wide yet short in comparison with the Principal's, yet not conical, almost like a Gedackt but with narrower lips. Therefore it sounds hollow and is called "Hohlflöt". There are a number of them with respect to size. I.) Grosshohlflöt 8′ is in the manual and pedal at St. Catharine in Danzig, under the name Holflöt. It is also at St. Nikolai in Hamburg and St. Wenceslaus in Naumburg. In the Pfarrkirche and the Marienkirche at Danzig there are a Hohlflöt 16′ and 8′ on the same keyboard. Now if Praetorius, *loc. cit.*, p. 131,** calls the 8′ a Grosshohlflöt, what should this [16′] be called? It appears there once again in the pedal at 8′. It is also at 16′ and 8′ in one keyboard and again at 8′ in another in the middle organ of the Pfarrkirche at Danzig, and at St. Bartholomaus there it is an 8′. It is also an 8′ at Greussen and at the Marienkirche in Lübeck, at St. Dominicus in Prague, at Pulsnitz, and at Rudolstadt. In the Cathedral organ at Hamburg it appears at 8′ and 4′, as well as in Buxtehude and at Königsberg in the Kneiphofkirche. Praetorius, p. 168, cites a Holpipe 6′ in the organ at St. Jacobi in Hamburg, that either begins at [low] F (cf. §.213) or is a Holquinte; on another keyboard [in the same organ] it is an 8′. For further information, see my *Anlei-*

** actually p. 132.

106 Kap. VII. Von den Registern überhaupt und insonderheit.

Anleitung S. 429. in der Anmerk. Im Baſſe tönet die Großhohlflöte ſehr. (conf. Prätor. p. 132.) II.) Hohlflöte 4' iſt zu St. Jakobi in Hamburg; zu Bützfleth bey Stade; zu Colberg in der Heiligengeiſtkirche; in der Heiligendreyfaltigkeit Kirche und zu St. Marien in Danzig; zu St. Gertrud in Hamburg; zu Königsberg im Kneiphofe, it. in der Altſtädter Orgel daſelbſt; in der neuen Orgel zu Leipzig; zu St. Marien in Lübeck; zu Pulsnitz, da ſie auch Süßflöte heißt; zu Bernau in der Mark iſt Hohlflöt 4' oder Oktave von groben Gedackten, ſ. Prätor. S. 177. III.) Hohlflöte 3', iſt eine Quinte nach ſolcher Menſur, daher man ſie Hohlquinte nennt, ſ. Prätor. S. 132. Sie iſt im Schloſſe zu Dresden, und im Schloſſe zu Grüningen, nebſt 4'; Hohlflöt 4' und Hohlquinte 3' befinden ſich in Eiſenach in einem Claviere, ſ. §. 288.; letztere ſtehet auch zu St. Catharinen in Danzig, und in der Orgel zu St. Jakobi in Hamburg iſt, nach Prätorii Nachricht, Quintflöte 3'. IV.) Hohlflöte 2', heißt auch Kleinhohlflöte oder Kleinflöte. Z. Er. zu St. Jakobi und St. Petri in Hamburg, ſ. Prätorius. Etliche nennen dieſe Stimme Nachthorn; aber das iſt was anders, wie unten in Nachthorn wird zu leſen ſeyn. 2' ſtehet auch zu Grüningen im Schloſſe. Es heißt auch dieſe Stimme Kleinflötenbaß, wenn 2' im Pedale ſtehet, wie auch 4' im Pedale Hohlflötenbaß heißt ſie eben zu Grüningen; das iſt aber eben ſo viel als Hohlflöte 4' oder 2', (welche 4' noch nebſt 8' ſtehet zu St. Michaelis in Lüneburg.) V.) 1½' heißt Quintflöte: kann aber auch Hohlflöte heißen, wie die andern alle. Es ſtehet dieſe Quintflöt 1½' zu St. Catharinen in Hamburg; heißt auch Holquintlein, z. E. zu Bückeburgk, ſ. Prätor. S. 185. VI.) Hohlflöte 1' heißt auch Suiflöt, oder Sivflöt, ſo etliche unter die Principalſtimmen rechnen, ſ. in Sifflöt. Sie heißt auch Kleinflötenbaß. Waldflöte wird vom Prätorio auch dazu geſetzt, ſ. davon an ſeinem Orte.

Hohlquinte, ſ. vorher in Hohlflöte.

Holſchelle iſt ſoviel, als Quintatön, daher es allda zu ſuchen.

* Hölzern iſt ein Beyname. Was ſich damit anfängt, das ſuche man bey ſeinem Hauptnamen.

Holzflöte 8', iſt im Dom zu Bremen, zu St. Jakobi und Johannis in Hamburg. Holzpfeife iſt eben ſo viel, und ſteht zu St. Petri daſelbſt. Man ſiehet wol, daß es ein Flötwerk von Holz ſey, und auch einen dunkeln hölzernen Klang habe. Zu Reval iſt Holzflöte oder Gemshorn, §. 313.

Hölzernprincipal, ſ. Principal.

* Horn iſt einerley mit der Sesquialter, ſ. §. 190. Was Samber für dunkle Beſchreibungen davon giebt, ſehe man in der Anleitung S. 429. Anmerk. (t.)

Hornbäßlein 2' iſt zu Bückeburgk, ſ. Prätor. S. 186. Es wird eine ſolche Intonation haben, daß es wie ein Horn klingt, und iſt vielleicht mit Nachthorn eins, wovon §. 168. zu leſen.

Humangedackt, iſt ſo viel, als Stillgedackt, ſ. Gedackt, §. 150.

* Züm-

tung, p.429n.* The Grosshohlflöte is very resonant in the bass; cf. Praetorius, p. 132. II.) The Hohlflöte 4′ is at St. Jakobi in Hamburg, at Butzfleth near Stade, at Colberg in the Heiligengeistkirche, in the Heiligendreyfaltigkeitskirche and at St. Marien in Danzig, at St. Gertrud in Hamburg, at Königsberg in the Kneiphofkirche, at the Marienkirche in Lübeck and at Pulsnitz (where it is also called Süssflöte). At Bernau in the Mark [Brandenburg] there is a Hohlflöt 4′ or Oktave of large Gedackts (von groben Gedackten).† III.) Hohlflöte 3′ is a Quinte with the scale of a Hohlflöte, and thus it gets this name; see Praetorius, p. 132. It is in the palace at Dresden and in the palace at Gröningen, along with the 4′. Hohlflöt 4′ and Hohlquinte 3′ are found on the same manual at Eisenach; see §.288.‡ The Hohlquinte 3′ also stands at St. Catharine in Danzig. In the organ at St. Jacobi in Hamburg there is, according to Praetorius's report, a Quintflöte 3′. IV.) Hohlflöte 2′ is also called Kleinhohlflöte or Kleinflöte, for example, at St. Jakobi and St. Petri in Hamburg; see Praetorius.§ Some call this stop Nachthorn, but that is something else, as may be seen by consulting "Nachthorn" below. There is one at 2′ in the palace at Gröningen. This stop is also called Kleinflötenbass if it stands at 2′ in the pedal, just as it is called Hohlflötenbass when it appears at 4′ in the pedal at Gröningen; this is the same as Hohlflöte 4′ or 2′. A 4′ along with an 8′ is found at St. Michaelis in Lüneburg. V.) The 1½′ [Hohlflöte] is called Quintflöte, but may also be called Hohlflöte like all the rest. Such a Quintflöt 1½′ is found at St. Catharine in Hamburg. This stop is also called Holquintlein, e.g. at Bückeburg; see Praetorius, p. 185. VI.) Hohlflöte 1′ is also called Suiflöte or Sivflöt, though some reckon the latter among the Principal ranks; see under Sifflöte. It is also called Kleinflötenbass. Praetorius also calls it Waldflöte; see under that entry.

 HOHLQUINTE, see above under Hohlflöte.

 HOLSCHELLE is the same as Quintatön; see under that entry.

 * HÖLZERN [wooden] is an accompanying word. For stops that begin with this, consult the entry under the primary name.

 HOLZFLÖTE 8′ is in the Cathedral at Bremen, and at St. Jakobi and St. Johannis in Hamburg. St. Petri there has a Holzpfeife, which is the same thing. It is obvious that it is a wooden flute stop; it also has a dark wooden timbre. At Reval there is a Holzflöte or Gemshorn; see §.313.

 HÖLZERNPRINCIPAL, see Principal.

 * HORN is the same as Sesquialter; see §.190. For the obscure description of it that Samber gives, consult the *Anleitung*, p. 429, note (t).

 HORNBÄSSLEIN 2′ is found at Bückeburg; see Praetorius, p. 186. It must be voiced to sound like a horn; perhaps it is the same thing as Nachthorn, which may be consulted in §.168.

 HUMANGEDACKT is the same as Stillgedackt; see Gedackt, §.150.

* actually pp. 428-9, note s.

† Adlung apparently can make no more sense of this than can we today, but simply reproduces what Praetorius says, for the sake of completeness.

‡ The translation disregards the (superfluous) paragraph numbers in the collection of stoplists; see the stoplist of this organ at Eisenach in Chapter 10.

§ pp. 168 and 169.

Kap. VII.   Von den Registern überhaupt und insonderheit.   107

* Hümmelchen gehört, ausser der Orgel unter die Sackpfeifen, s. Prätorius, S 42.; aber S. 193. schlägt er es vor unter den Nebenzügen, und wird jenes vorstellen sollen.

§. 161.

Italienische Quinte. Was man in Italien für besondere Arten von Quinten hat, weis ich nicht; folglich kann ich auch nicht errathen, was zu Gera §. 301. die Gedackte italienische Quinte 3' bedeuten solle. Von der Quinte, s. §. 171.

Infrabaß, s. §. 126.

Jubal kömmt vor in Kreyßen, und in der Görlitzer Orgel. Boxberg in der Beschreibung der Görlitzer Orgel sagt, daß es eine Oktave 4' sey, s. Oktave §. 171. In besagter Orgel stehet sie im Pedale und ist von Metall. Sie muß von der Oktaven-Mensur abgehen, weil Oktave 4' auf eben derselbigen Lade stehet. Dem ohngeachtet schreibt Boxberg, daß es eine ordentliche Oktave sey. (**)

(**) Es giebt noch mehr dergleichen Vorfälle, daß die Orgelbauer lieber dem Jubal ein Compliment machen, und noch überdies seines Bruders Namen verstümmeln, als gerade heraus: Oktave sagen wollen. S. die Disposition der neuen Königsbergischen Domorgel in Marpurgs Hist. Krit. Beyträgen, im 3 B. S. 514. Eben ein solches Compliment scheint der Verfertiger der Orgel zu Gera, s. oben, mit seiner italienischen Quinte, den Welschen haben machen zu wollen. Dergleichen ungewöhnliche Benennungen ganz gewöhnlicher Register sind, unter andern, auch eine Frucht der Charlatanerie manches Orgelbauers. Einer macht sie dem andern nach. Es ist aber viel schwerer ein altes gewöhnliches Orgelregister gut zu arbeiten, als ihm eine neue Benennung zu geben.

Jula ist die Quinte 6'; und weil diese gespitzt ist, so wird auch dieser Name öfters für Spitzflöte 8' gesetzt. (Mehr siehe in der Anleitung S. 430. Anmerk. w.) s. auch unten in Spitzflöte §. 195.

Jungferregal kommt auch zuweilen vor. Ob es einen so angenehmen Ton von sich hören läßt, wie eine Jungfer, oder warum diese Art der Regale diesen Namen führt, ist mir nicht bekannt. Es steht im Schlosse zu Hessen; 8' in der Altstädtischen Orgel in der Lutherischen Kirche zu Elbingen; in der mittelsten Orgel der Pfarrkirche in Danzig; zu Insterburg in Preussen; im Stift Wurzen: 4' stehet es zu Königsberg in der Pfarrorgel; 8' zu St. Dominico in Prag. 4' stehts zu Görlitz, wobey Boxberg sagt, es wären die Körper und Mundstücke an einander gelöthet, und sey diese Stimme stark und bequem einen Choral im Basse auszuführen; denn dort steht es im Pedale. In der Klosterorgel zu Stralsund ist Geigen= oder Jungferregal 4'; also ist es so viel als das §. 152. genannte Geigenregal. Demnach können alle diese Exempel dort auch gelten: und was daselbst gesagt worden, das gilt auch hier. Prätorius l. c. S. 145. bezeugt es auch, wenn er schreibt: „Jungfrauenregal oder Baß ist „4 Fußton; an ihm selbsten ein klein offen Regal mit einem kleinen geringen corpore, „etwan ein, oder aufs meiste zweene Zoll hoch; wird aber darum also geheißen, weil „es, wenns zu andern Stimmen und Floitwerken im Pedal gebraucht wird, gleich einer

O 2   „Jung=

Ch. VII. Concerning Stops in General and in Particular

* Hümmelchen apart from the organ belongs among the bagpipes; see Praetorius, p. 42. But on p. 193 he names it among the auxiliary stops, as being intended to imitate [the bagpipe].

§. 161.

Italienische Quinte. What special types of Quints there are in Italy, I do not know; consequently I cannot guess what Gedackte Italienische Quinte 3′ at Gera (§.301) is supposed to mean.

Infrabass, see §.126.

Jubal appears in Greussen (Kreysen), and in the Görlitz organ. Boxberg in his description of the Görlitz organ* says that it is an Oktave 4′; see Oktave, §.171. In the organ just mentioned it stands in the pedal and is made of pipe metal. It must deviate from the [normal] Oktave scaling, since an Oktave 4′ stands on the very same chest. In spite of this Boxberg writes that it is an ordinary Oktave (**)

* p.[17].

> (**) There are more cases like this, in which the organbuilder, wanting to honor Jubal, only succeeds in degrading his brother's† name, rather than straightforwardly saying "Oktave". See the stoplist of the new organ in the Cathedral at Königsberg in Marpurg's *Historisch-Kritische Beyträge*, in the third volume, p. 514. The builder of the organ at Gera seems to have wanted to pay the same sort of compliment to the Italians with his Italian Quinte. This sort of unusual terminology for completely common stops is, among other things, also the fruit of many an organbuilder's quackery. It is much more difficult to build the same old stop well than to give it a new name. [Agricola]

† i.e., "fellow musician's" or "fellow organbuilder's."

Jula is the Quinte 6′. Since it is conical, this name is frequently used in place of Spitzflöte 8′ (for further information see the *Anleitung*, p. 430, note "w"); see also below under Spitzflöte, §.195.

Jungfernregal [Maiden Regal] also appears now and then. Whether it produces as pleasant a sound as a maiden, or why this type of Regal bears this name, is unknown to me. It is found in the palace at Hesse; at 8′ in the organ of the Lutheran Church in the old city at Elbingen; in the middle organ of the Pfarrkirche at Danzig; at Insterburg in Prussia; in the Collegiate Church at Wurzen; and at St. Dominicus in Prague. It stands at 4′ in the Pfarrkirche organ in Königsberg, as well as in the pedal at Görlitz, about which Boxberg‡ says that the resonators and shallots have been soldered together, and that this stop is strong and well suited to perform a chorale [*cantus firmus*] in the pedal. In the Klosterkirche organ at Stralsund there is a Geigen- or Jungferregal 4′; thus it is the same as the Geigenregal mentioned in §.152. Accordingly all of these examples also apply there, and what is said there also holds true here. Praetorius, *loc. cit.*, p. 145[-6], also testifies to this when he writes: "Jungfrauenregal or [Jungfrauenregal]bass is at 4′ pitch, a small open Regal with a small, slight body, about one or at

‡ p.[17].

108　　Kap. VII.　Von den Registern überhaupt und insonderheit.

„Jungfrauenstimme, die einen Baß singen wollte, gehöret wird. Es wird auch solch „klein Regal auf 4 Fußton von etlichen Geigen= oder Geigenregal genennet; und „solches darum, daß es, wenn die Quintatön 8 Fußton dazu gezogen, etlicher= „maßen (sonderlich wenns in der rechten Hand zum Diskant allein gebraucht wird) einer „Geigen gar ähnlich klinget." Singendregal §. 193. wird auch wol eben das seyn. Jungfernregalbaß 4' wird vom Prätor. l. c. S. 189. auch besonders angeführet zu Hessen auf dem Schlosse. Jungferstimme (vox virginea) davon §. 208. zu lesen, wird vielleicht eben so viel seyn sollen.

§. 162.

Klein ist ein Beyname, und was sich damit anfängt, ist bey dem Hauptnamen zu suchen. Z. Er.

　Kleiner Cymbel, s. Cymbel, §. 134.
　Kleine Flöte.　　　　　} s. Hohlflöte, §. 160.
　Klein Flötenbaß.　　　}
　Kleingedackt. Man hört schon am Worte, was es sey, und daß es in Ge= dackt zu suchen, §. 150.
　Klein Oktavengemshorn, ist Gemshorn 2', s. §. 153.
　Kleine Hohlflöte, s. Hohlflöte, §. 160.
　Kleinregal, s. Regal, §. 183.
　Kleinschreyer, s. Schryari, §. 186.
　Klingender Cymbel, s. Cymbel, §. 134.
　Knopfregal, s. Apfelregal, §. 116.
　Köpflinregal muß von Knopf= oder Apfelregal §. 116. unterschieden wer= den, s. Prätor. l. c. S. 148. der sagt, es sey 4'ton, habe auch oben ein rundes Knäuflein, als ein Knopf, aber es sey dasselbe in der Mitte von einander gethan, als ein offen Helm, also, daß es den Resonanz gleich wieder ins untere corpus einwendet. Es ist ein kleines Rohrwerk, welches gut und lieblich klingt.
　Koppel, s. in C. §. 127. und 128.
　Koppeldone ist so viel als Oktave, s. Oktave.
　Koppelflöte, s. §. 129.
　Koppeloktave, s. Oktave.

§. 164.

Krumhorn ist etwas merkwürdig. Ausser der Orgel nennt Prätorius S. 40. Kap. 15. Tom. II. den lituum auch das Krumhorn, und italienisch storti oder cor= namuti torti: und an einem andern Orte sagt er, daß Lituus nicht so krumm gewesen, als ein Horn, aber doch auch nicht so gerade als eine Tuba. In der Orgel ists ein Schnarrwerk, s. Prätor. l. c. S. 145. (Werkmeister in Organo grüningensi §. 46. sagt, daß zu Prätorii Zeiten die Bärpfeife oder Krumhorn wäre Vox humana ge= nennet

the most two inches tall. It gets its name from the fact that if it is used with other stops, flute stops in the pedal, it sounds just like a maiden's voice singing in the bass register. Some also call such a small Regal at 4′ pitch a Geigen- or Geigendregal because if the Quintatön 8′ is drawn with it, it sounds to some degree quite similar to a violin (especially if it is used to play the treble in the right hand)." Singendregal in §.193 must also be the same thing. Praetorius, *loc. cit.*, p. 189, also cites in particular a Jungfernregalbass 4′ in the palace at Hesse. Jungferstimme (*vox virginea*), discussed in §.208, is perhaps also the same thing.

§. 162.

KLEIN ["small"] is an accompanying word; whatever begins with it should be consulted under the primary name. For examples:

KLEINER CYMBEL, see Cymbel, §.134.

KLEINE FLÖTE

KLEIN FLÖTENBASS see Hohlflöte, §.160.

KLEINGEDACKT ["small stopped flute"]. What it is may already be perceived from its name; it may be sought under Gedackt, §.150.

KLEIN OKTAVENGEMSHORN is a Gemshorn 2′; see §.153.

KLEINE HOHLFLÖTE, see Hohlflöte, §.160.

KLEINREGAL, see Regal, §.183.

KLEINSCHREYER, see Schryari, §.186.

KLINGENDER CYMBEL, see Cymbel, §.134.

KNOPFREGAL, see Apfelregal, §.116.

KÖPFLINREGAL must be distinguished from the Knopf- or Apfelregal, §.116. Praetorius, *l.c.*, p. 148, says that it is a 4′ pitch and has a little knob on top, like a button; this knob has a cleft in the middle, like an open helmet, so that the sound is immediately reflected back into the lower resonator. It is a reed stop that sounds lovely and well.

KOPPEL, see under C[oppel], §.127 and 128.

KOPPELDONE is the same as Oktave; see Oktave.

KOPPELFLÖTE, see §.129.

KOPPELOKTAVE, see Oktave.

§. 164.*

KRUMHORN ["crooked horn" or "curved horn"] is something remarkable. In [the *Syntagma musicum*,] vol. II, chap. 15, p. 40, Praetorius calls the Krumhorn apart from the organ the lituus,† in Italian *storti* or *cornamuti torti*. In another place he says that the *Lituus* is not as bent as a horn, but also not as straight as a tuba.‡ In the organ it is always a reed; see Praetorius, *l.c.*, p. 145. In his *Organum gruningense*, §.46, Werkmeister says that in Praetorius's time the Bärpfeife or Krumhorn would have been

---

* There is no §.163 in the original publication.

† Latin "curved horn."

‡ Latin "trumpet." This word ought to be in italics in the original publication, but it is not.

Kap. VII. Von den Registern überhaupt und insonderheit. 109

nennet worden.) Auf 16′ ist es nicht wohl zu bringen, klingt auch nicht lieblich im Manuale, weil es so stark und tief ist, sondern ist besser im Pedale zu gebrauchen. Dagegen hat man es 8′, 4′, und 2′. Etliche Orgelmacher wollen solchen Klang, in einem rechten Regalkörper, (der oben mit einem Deckel zugemacht, und 2, 3, ꝛc. Löchlein, entweder oben in selbigem Deckel, oder unten neben dem Mundstücke darein gebohret, hat,) oder sonsten durch andere Arten zuwege bringen. Doch ist die Art, welche 4′ lang, gleichaus weit, und auch offen, die beste. Es kann sie aber nicht ein jeder lieblich machen. Prätorius l. c. Tab. 38. No. 9. theilet uns einen Abriß mit, vom offenen Krumhorn: und eben daselbst No. 16, 17 und 18 siehet man auch, wie die gedeckten Krumhörner gestaltet sind. Man kann beyderley Arten bey ihm selbst besehen. Das Krumhorn 8′ ist den dritten Theil kleiner als die Trompete 8′: die andern Stimmen aber sind nach Proportion. Es soll vom Zinken unterschieden seyn, welches auch ein Rohrwerk von solcher Größe ist. Ob aber in den folgenden Exempeln das Krumhorn nicht damit vermischt worden, wenigstens dann und wann, kann ich nicht wissen. Posito aber, es sey vom Zinken unterschieden, und es solle also den Klang eines krummen Horns nicht vorstellen; so ist die Frage: woher der Name sey, da doch die Pfeife gerade ist? Antwort: aus cromorne ist das Wort gemacht. Chormorne ist was anders s. in Fagott. Aber in des Franzosen de Grigny premier livre d'Orgue kömmt eine Fugue à 5 vor, qui renferme le Chant du Kyrie, mit 2 Clavieren und dem Pedale; mit 3 Linien, da eine das Cornet, die andere dies Cromorne ist. Hernach kommen wieder 3 Linien mit den Registern womit sie zu spielen, als Cromorne en taille, Fond d'Orgue &c. Hernach kömmt Trio en dialogue, da Cromorne und Cornet als Register abwechseln. Auch kömmt darinnen vor Basse de Trompette ou de Cromorne. Als ich nun von Cromorne Frischens französisches Lexicon nachschlug; so fand ich folgende Nachricht: Cromorne ist ein Register, das zum Trompetenregister gehet auf der Orgel, von Cor ein Horn, und morne dunkel, still, traurig; und cromorne wird ebenfalls gefunden unter eben der Bedeutung. Es ist ein Horn, welches einen sehr dunklen Ton hat; die deutschen Orgelbauer, die dieses französische Wort nicht verstanden, haben Krumhorn draus gemacht, und nennen das Register noch so. Denn cor morne kömmt chormorne sehr nahe, so beym Mattheson sich findet in Orchestre I. P. III. c. III. §. 9. allwo Basse de chormorne der Fagott seyn soll: und es kann auch zum Krumhorn der Fagott den Baß agiren. Was also de Grigny Basse de Trompette ou de Cromorne nennet, das wird eben so viel, und der Fagott seyn. (**) In der Orgel zu Sando-

(**) Es bedeutet hier und bey andern französischen Organisten nichts weiter, als ein Stück, dessen Baß mit dem Register Cromorne, und seinem Fond, das ist dem dazu gezogenen Pfeifenwerke, (s. Fond d'Orgue,) ausgeführet wird. So hat man auch Cromorne en taille, wo der Tenor mit diesen Registern, der Baß aber mit dem obligaten Pedale, so wie die übrige Begleitung auf einem von jenem verschiedenen Claviere, mit stillern Registern, ausgeführet wird.

mir heißt das Krumhorn auch Phocinx, und ist im Werk 8′: im Brustpositiv aber heißt es Lituus, und ist 4′. Samber schreibt S. 153. Cromhorne oder Brumhorn von

O 3 Zinn.

Ch. VII. Concerning Stops in General and in Particular

called Vox *humana*. It is not good to carry it down to 16′ in the manual, where because of its intensity and lowness it does not sound beautiful; rather it is better to use it in the pedal [at 16′]. It is found, on the other hand, at 8′, 4′ and 2′. Some organbuilders try to achieve its timbre with an ordinary Regal resonator (covered with a lid on top, and with 2, 3 or more little holes bored either into the lid on top or [into the] lower [section of the resonator] near the shallot), or in some other way. The best type, however, is the one that is 4′ high,* cylindrical and open. Not everybody can make it sound beautiful. Praetorius, *l.c.*, *Tabelle* 38, No. 9, gives us a sketch of an open Krumhorn, and in the same place nos. 16, 17 and 18 show the forms of the stopped Krumhorns. One can examine both types[, open and stopped,] there. The Krumhorn 8′ is a third smaller than the Trompete 8′,† with the other stops being in proportion.‡ It needs to be distinguished from the Zink, which is also a reed of the same size. But I cannot be sure that the Krumhorn is not confused with it in the following examples, at least now and then. In fact, however, it is different from the Zink, and thus is not supposed to represent the sound of a curved horn.§ Thus the question arises, where does the name come from, since the pipe¶ is straight. The answer? The word is derived from *cromorne*. *Chormorne* is something different; see under Fagott. In the Frenchman DeGrigny's *Premier Livre d'Orgue* there appears a *Fugue a 5 qui renferme le Chant du Kyrie*, for 2 keyboards and pedal, on 3 staves, one of which is [designated for] the Cornet, the other for the abovementioned Cromorne. After that these 3 staves recur with the stops to be used in playing them, such as *Cromorne en taille*, *Fond d'Orgue*, etc. Next there appears a *Trio en dialogue*, in which the stops Cromorne and Cornet alternate. In it also appears *Basse de Trompette ou de Cromorne*.‖ When I consulted Frischen's French dictionary, I found the following information: Cromorne is a stop in the organ that is trumpet-like, from *Cor*, "horn", and *morne*, "dark, quiet, sad". Cromorne has this very same meaning; it is a horn that has a very dark tone. German organbuilders who did not understand this French word interpreted it as Krumhorn, and thus gave the stop its name.** *Cor morne* comes very close to *chormorne*, as it is found in Mattheson's [*Neu-eröffnete*] *Orchestre*, part III, chap. III, §.9, where the *Basse de chormorne* is said to be the Fagott. The Fagott may indeed serve as the bass for the Krumhorn; thus what De Grigny calls *Basse de Trompette ou de Cromorne* is nothing more than the Fagott††. (**) In the organ at Sandomir the Krumhorn is called *Phocinx*, and is in the main manual (im Werk) at 8′; but the one in the

(**)Here and [in the works of] other French organists it means nothing more than a piece whose bass is performed on the Cromorne stop and its *Fond*, i.e., the flue stops drawn with it (see *Fond d'Orgue*). There is also the *Cromorne en taille*, in which the tenor is performed with these stops,‡‡ the bass with an obligato pedal, and the rest of the accompaniment on a different keyboard with quiet stops. [Agricola]

Brustpositiv is called *Lituus*, and is at 4′. Samber on p. 153 writes Cromhorne or Brumhorn §§ of tin. At 8′ the Krumhorn stands at St. Petri in Berlin; at Elmshorn; twice in

---

* i.e., half-length resonators.

† This statement still refers to Praetorius's Plate 38, in which the Krummhorn 8′ (No. 9) is pictured next to the Trommet (No. 8); it is obvious that the Krummhorn's resonator is about ²/₃ the height of the Trommet's.

‡ It appears that this is still referring to Praetorius's Plate 38, specifically to the 3 types of stopped Krummhorns (Nos. 16, 17 & 18). The sense of the phrase "in proportion" seems to be that these three have fractional-length resonators, each of which is in some definite proportion to a full-length resonator.

§ which is what the Zink (cornett) is.

¶ i.e., the resonator.

‖ DeGrigny, *Premiere Liver d'Orgue*, 1699, tenth movement, pp. 16-17.

** The origin of the word, whether French or German, is still contested.

†† This is obviously fanciful and incorrect, and shows Adlung's lack of familiarity with the French classic organ.

‡‡ i.e., Cromorne + *Fond*.

§§ i.e., "growling horn."

110 Kap. VII. Von den Registern überhaupt und insonderheit.

Zinn. Das Krumhorn 8′ steht zu St. Petri in Berlin: zu Elmshorn; zu Grünningen im Schlosse 2 mal; zu St. Nikolai in Hamburg; zu St. Jakobi daselbst; in Buxtehude; zu Colberg in der Heiligengeistkirche; in der Pfarrkirche zu Danzig; in der mittelsten Orgel daselbst 2 mal; zur Dreyfaltigkeit daselbst; zu St. Johannis daselbst; zu Königsberg im Kneiphofe ist Krumhorn 4′ 2mal, und 8′ dabey; 8′ in der Altstädter Orgel daselbst; zu St. Marien in Lübeck 2mal; zu St. Johannis in Lüneburg; zu St. Michaelis daselbst; zu St. Lamberti eben daselbst; zu Otterndorf im Lande Hadeln; zu St. Dominico in Prag; zu Rudolstadt 2mal: 4′ aber ist es rarer; z. Ex. zu Sendomir und zu Königsberg im Kneiphofe, wie schon gedacht; 2′ steht im Stift Wurzen: oder ob die Schreiber etwan die Länge des Körpers, nicht aber den Klang dadurch angedeutet haben. 8′ ist also am gemeinsten, welches sich auch noch zu St. Cosmi in Stade findet, und endlich zu St. Marien in Thoren. [40]) Da kann man das Krumhorn oder Cromorne hören; und wenn man den Klang und Struktur des Zinkens auch observirt; so beurtheile man hernach selbst, ob es einerley sey, oder nicht? Deswegen stehen die Exempel häufig da, daß man auf Reisen sie aufsuchen solle. Noch ist zu merken, daß auch zuweilen in den Dispositionen der Orgeln Krumhörner, anstatt Krumhorn, angetroffen wird. Z. Ex. zu St. Ulrich in Magdeburg; it. zu St Blasii in Braunschweig stehet Krumhörner 8′, s. Prätor. Eben derselbe hat auch klein Krumhornbaß 4′, und groß Krumhornbaß 16′. Biermann S. 19. hat dergleichen halbirt, und nennt es in der Anmerkung Hautboe.

§. 165.

Ruckuck ist oben in G da gewesen. §. 157.

Ruzialflöte ist rar, und weis ich eigentlich nicht, worinnen ihr Wesen bestehen soll. Ein Flötregister ist es, wie der Name anzeigt, bald in der Quinte, bald in der Oktave. Zu St. Dominico in Prag ist sie 1′, folglich eine Oktave; in der Kreuzkirche in Dresden ist sie 1½′, und also eine Quinte.

§. 166.

Largior. s. Schwiegel. §. 187.

Lieblichflöt, Lieblichpfeif, Lieblichgedackt, Liebliche Gemsquinte, und alle Wörter, die sich mit dem Beynamen lieblich anfangen, sind bey dem Hauptworte am gehörigen Orte zu suchen. Hier bemerke ich nur noch, daß Lieblichpfeif 4′ zun Predigern in Erfurt, und Liebliche Gemsquinte 1½′ zu Alach, ohnweit Erfurt, anzutreffen sind.

Litice. s. in Cornet §. 132. weil es auch so viel ist.

Lituus,

---

[40]) Krumbhorn 16′ findet man auch. Z. Ex. in der Orgel zu St. Jakobi in Hamburg, allwo es im Pedale stehet, s. Prätor. S. 169. l. c.

the palace at Gröningen; at St. Nikolai and St. Jakobi in Hamburg; in Buxtehude; in the Heiligengeistkirche at Colberg; in the Pfarrkirche organ and in that same church's middle organ (twice), the Dreyfaltigkeitskirche and St. Johannis, all in Danzig; in the Cathedral (Kneiphof) organ (where it also appears twice at 4′) and the Altstädterkirche organ at Königsberg; twice at the Marienkirche in Lübeck; at St. Johannis, St. Michaelis and St. Lamberti in Lüneburg; at Otterndorf in Land Hadeln; at St. Dominicus in Prague; and twice at Rudolstadt. It is rarer, though, at 4′, for example at Sendomir and at Königsberg in the Cathedral (Kneifphofkirche), as already mentioned. It stands at 2′ in the Collegiate Church at Wurzen, though the writer may have indicated the length of the resonators and not the pitch. Thus 8′ [pitch] is the most common, found again at St. Cosmae in Stade and finally at St. Marien in Thoren.[40] If one listens to a Krumhorn or Cromorne and observes that it has the sound and structure of a Zink, then one may judge for himself whether or not they are the same.* There are numerous examples, all waiting to be visited in the course of a journey. It remains to be noted that at times "Krumhörner" is encountered in organ stoplists instead of Krumhorn. For example at St. Ulrich in Magdeburg as well as at St. Blasius in Braunschweig there stands Krumhörner 8′; see Praetorius, who also lists a Klein Krumhornbass 4′ and Gross Krumhornbass 16′.† Biermann [in *Organographia hildesiensis*], p. 19, has the same thing through half the keyboard (halbirt), calling it "Hautboe" in his note.

* This comment refers to the discussion Adlung engages in earlier in this entry.

† These are listed in the "Universal Tabel" including all stops to be found in organs, found as a fold-out insert opposite p. 126 of the *Syntagma musicum*, Vol. II.

§. 165.

Kuckuck has already been [discussed] above under G[uckguck], §.157.

Kützialflöte is rare, and I really know nothing about its character. It is a flute stop, as the name indicates, sometimes at the fifth, other times at the octave. At St. Dominicus in Prague it is 1′, and thus [sounds] an octave; in the Kreuzkirche at Dresden it is 1 ½′, and thus a fifth.

§. 166.

Largior, see Schwiegel, §.187.

Lieblichflöt, Lieblichpfeif, Lieblichgedackt, Liebliche Gemsquinte, and all words that begin with the prefix "lieblich" [i.e., "lovely, gentle"] are to be sought under the entry for the primary word. Here I will only mention that Lieblichpfeif 4′ is to be found at the Predigerkirche in Erfurt, and Liebliche Gemsquinte 1′ at Alach, not far from Erfurt.

Litice, see under Cornet, §.132, since they are the same.

40) Krumbhorn [sic] 16′ is also found; for example, in the organ at St. Jakobi in Hamburg, where it is in the pedal (see Praetorius, *l.c.*, p. 169). [Albrecht]

Kap. VII. Von den Registern überhaupt und insonderheit. 111

Lituus, wenn es das Krumhorn seyn soll; so siehe §. 164. Aber es bedeutet auch den Zinken. s. in Zinken. Liuto ist was anders, und bedeutet eine Laute, so uns aber hier nichts angehet.

Manualkoppel. s. in Coppel. §. 127.

Menschenstimme. s. unten §. 208.: vox humana.

Merula. s. Vogelgesang. §. 207.

Meßing ist ein Beyname; was sich davon anfängt, muß beym Hauptworte gesucht werden. Z. E. Meßingregal singend 4', ist zu Magdeburg im Dom. s. Prätor. Es ist ein Singendregal wie §. 183. vorkömmt; nur daß es von Meßing ist.

Minerici 3' stund ehedessen im Dom zu Merseburg, und soll eine gemeine Quinte gewesen seyn. Itzt steht an deren Stelle Quinte 6'.

§. 167.

Miscella, Mixtur, Mixten, und Mixtum, bedeuten einerley, und haben ihren Ursprung vom lateinischen miscere, mischen. Man deutet demnach eine Mischung der Stimmen dadurch an, da auf ein Register mehr Stimmen, als eine, gesetzt werden. Bey allen solchen gemischten Stimmen kömmt der Terminus vor: fach; als 4 fach, 2 fach, 3 fach, 5 fach, 6 f. Wiewol man nicht gern das f allein dafür gebraucht, weil dieß sonst auch Fuß bedeutet. Man zeigt also dadurch an, wieviel auf jedem clave Pfeifen stehen. Das Wort Chöricht hat gleiche Bedeutung. z. E. Mixtur 3 Chöricht, d. i. 3 fach. So findet man es in der Barfüßerkirche in Halberstadt. Zimbel 2 Chöricht, schreibt Prätorius. Es steht auch wol nur ch. oder chor. geschrieben. Z. E. zu Bückeburg beym Prätorio ist Mixtur 8. 10. 12. 14. chor. Was die vielen Zahlen bedeuten, folgt hernach. Oder man sagt, es ist eine Mixtur von 12. 14. Chören. Z. E. zu St. Gotthardt in Hildesheim; wovon hernach. Es können aber gar mancherley Register mit einander verbunden werden. So ist z. B. in der Bergischen Orgel auf der Insul Rügen eine Trompete 4' und Harfenregal 8' beysammen auf einem Register. So haben wir auch sonst erinnert, daß Vox humana und Fagott ein Register ausmache, da ein jedes das halbe Clavier einnimmt. (s. §. 141.) Wer will es verbieten, daß ein Orgelbauer allerhand Stimmen zusammenbringe, die er sonst nirgends beysammen antrift? wenn nur dieselben sich zusammen gut brauchen lassen. Eine andere Frage ist es: ob man viel solcher Mischungen anbringen solle? Ich sage, es sey nicht rathsam: denn wenn sie besondere Züge haben, können mehr Veränderungen gemacht werden. Dergleichen aber nennt man nicht leicht eine Mixtur: denn dadurch verstehet man ordinär eine Mischung solcher Stimmen, die Principalmensur haben. Nun kann man solcher Stimmen mancherley haben; 16' 8' 12' 6', 4', 3', 2', 1½', 1¼', 1', ꝛc. aber man braucht nicht alle zu der Mixtur. Ordentlich wird 4' die größte seyn in gemischten Stimmen; wiewol zu St. Petri in Lübeck ist Mixturbaß 8'. s. Prätor. it. Mixturbaß un Stuel. ib. zu unser L. Fr. ib. (den Terminum

Stuel

Ch. VII. Concerning Stops in General and in Particular

Lituus, if it is intended to signify the Krumhorn, then see §.164. But it also means the Zink; see under Zink. Liuto is something different; it means a lute, and thus does not concern us here.

Manualkoppel, see under Coppel, §.127.

Menschenstimme, see below, §.208, under *vox humana*.

Merula, see Vogelgesang, §.207.

Messing ["brass"] is an accompanying word. Whatever begins with it is to be sought under the primary word. For example, Messingregal singend 4′ is [found] at Magdeburg Cathedral; see Praetorius.* It is a Singendregal such as is discussed in §.183, except that it is of brass.

* p. 173.

Minerici 3′ formerly stood in the Cathedral at Merseburg, and must have been an ordinary Quinte. A Quinte 6′ now stands in its place.

§. 167.

Miscella, Mixtur, Mixten, and *Mixtum* mean the same thing, and have their origin in the Latin *miscere*, "to mix". Accordingly they indicate a mixture of ranks, since more ranks than one are placed on one stop. The term "fach" [ranks] appears with all such compound stops, i.e., "4 fach", "2 fach", "3 fach", "5 fach", "6 fach". It would be well, however, not to use the letter "f" alone for this [term], since it also means "foot". [Fach] indicates how many pipes stand on each key. The word "Chöricht" has the same meaning, e.g., "Mixtur 3 Chöricht" means "Mixtur 3 fach". This is the way it is found in the Barfüsserkirche in Halberstadt.† Praetorius writes "Zimbel 2 Chöricht", but also just "ch." or "chor."; e.g., at Bückeburg Praetorius gives "Mixtur 8.10.12.14. chor." ‡ What this row of numbers means is explained below. One may also say, "It is a Mixtur of 12.14. Chören ["choirs"]"; e.g., at St. Gotthardt in Hildesheim, mentioned later.§ It is indeed possible to combine many different sorts of stops with each other.¶ Thus there is, for example, a single stop in the Bergkirche on the Island of Rügen in which a Trompete 4′ and Harfenregal 8′ are combined. And we have mentioned elsewhere that a Vox humana and Fagott [combined] may form a stop in which each occupies one half of the keyboard (see §.141). Who would want to forbid an organbuilder to combine diverse stops, stops that are otherwise never encountered together, as long as they are suited to be used together? But as for whether many such combinations ought to be built, that is another question. I do not find it advisable, since more variety [in registration] may be achieved if there are separate drawknobs [for each rank]. One ought not to call such [combinations] a "Mixtur", since this term is ordinarily understood as a combination of ranks of Principal scale. Such [Principal] ranks come of course in many sizes: 16′, 8′, 12′, 6′, 4′, 3′, 2′, 1½′, 1¼′, 1′, etc., but not all are incorporated into a Mixtur. Normally the 4′ is the largest rank in compound stops, although at St. Petri in Lübeck there is a Mixturbass 8′; see Praetorius.‖ Praetorius also mentions a Mixturbass at the [Kirche zu] Unsrer Lieben Frau [at Lübeck] "im Stuel"** (I do not understand the term Stuel ††). In former times there

† See Praetorius, *Syntagma musicum*, Vol. II, p. 183.

‡ *Ibid.*, p. 185.

§ i.e., *Ibid.*, p. 198.

¶ i.e., in the same stop.

‖ p. 165.

** p. 166.

†† The term is indeed obscure; see the note under "Tertia", §.197.

Stuel verstehe ich nicht.) Bey den Alten hatte man gar große Mixturen, da fast die ganze Orgel ein Register, und eine Mixtur ausmachte, s. Prätor. S. 130. l. c. Hernach sonderte man das Principal ab, das übrige blieb alles beysammen, bis man immer mehr davon abgetrennet: sie werden aber in lauter Akkordsintervallen gemischt, und kommen Terzen, Quinten und Oktaven hinein. Wenn sie gar kleine sind, werden sie miscella acuta genennet, und ist ihre größte Pfeife etwann 2' oder 1½' auch wol nur 1' lang; darauf folgt die Quinte, dann die Oktave, auch Terz oder Decima, oder wie man sie mischen will. In etlichen Mixturen bindet man sich, daher bekommen sie andere Namen. Also ist die Sesquialter eine Art gemischter Stimmen, davon in S. zu reden. So auch die Cymbel, von welchen §. 134. verschiedene Arten angeführt worden; da auch der Mixturcymbel gedacht worden. Das Scharp oder Scharf ist auch eine Art der Mixtur, davon in S. zu reden ist. Die Rauschpfeife, Terzian, Coppel ꝛc. sind auch gemischt, von jedem suche an seinem Orte. (s. Prätor. S. 130. l. c.) Wir reden von den eigentlichen und bey uns sogenannten Mixturen. Diese repetiren entweder, oder sie gehen ganz durch. Jenes thun die, welche gar klein anfangen: was aber repetiren sey s. §. 83. Die aus wenig Stimmen zusammen gesetzt sind, heissen auch kleine Mixturen, welche einige mit dem Namen Mixten belegen: die aber viel in sich begreifen heissen große Mixturen. Die alten waren wol 50 Pfeifen stark: aber heutiges Tages macht man sie so ungeschickt nicht mehr. Die kleinesten können 2fach seyn. Ordentlich sind sie 3, 4, 5 oder 6, bisweilen auch 8fach, und das beygeschriebene f. bedeutet nicht Fuß, wie sonst, sondern fach. So ist z. B. Regula mixta (so heißt die Mixtur auch) in Sandomir, in Jena und an viel andern Oertern mehr, 6fach; 6 bis 7fach ist sie auch zu St. Johannis in Lüneburg; 6, 7, 8fach oder chöricht zu Grüningen im Schlosse. Das bedeutet, die untersten claues der Oktaven haben weniger, die obern mehr Pfeifen; weil man 1 oder auch 2 Quinten im Baße wegläßt, und wird sie in etlichen nur 7 oder 6fach. Man müßte denn einerley Pfeifen in solchem Falle doppelt setzen. So war z. E. zu St. Nikolai in Leipzig Mixtur im Baße 4fach, im Tenor 6fach, und im Diskant 8fach. s. Prätor. l. c. It. zu Halberstadt in der Barfüßerkirche Mixtur unten 6fach; im $\overline{c}$ 7fach; im $\overline{\overline{c}}$ 8fach; im $\overline{\overline{\overline{c}}}$ 9fach. s. Prätor. Zu Riddagshausen war in der Klosterorgel Mixtur 4' unten 5fach, mitten 6fach, oben 8fach. s. Prätor. l. c. Mixtur 6 à 8fach ist zu St. Michaelis in Lüneburg, welches eben den Verstand hat. 8fach ist auch in der mittelsten Pfarrorgel zu Danzig; zu St. Dominico in Prag, und zu St. Michaelis in Lüneburg. Ob nun wol da nur 8 stehet; so kann es doch wol seyn, daß in etlichen clauibus 1 oder 2 Pfeifen zu kleine gerathen, und also weggeblieben, und es ist nicht nöthig, es allezeit dazu zu setzen; welches auch bey andern Mixturen zu merken. 9fach ist die Mixtur zu St. Cosmi in Stade; 10fach zu St. Dominico in Prag; zu St. Catharinen in Hamburg; zu St. Wenceslai in Naumburg. Diese und die folgenden sind meistens im Manuale; doch sind auch etliche im Pedale. Also ist 10fach in der mittelsten Pfarrorgel zu Danzig im Werk aber ist sie auch im Kneiphofe zu Königsberg, und eben

daselbst

were very large mixtures, so that almost the entire organ comprised one stop, a Mixtur;* see Praetorius, *l.c.*, p. 130. [In the course of time] more and more [ranks] were separated off. Mixtures, however, are always combinations of chord tones, comprised of thirds, fifths and octaves. If they are very small, they are called *miscella acuta*, and their largest pipe is about 2′ or 1 ½′, or perhaps only 1′ tall; on top of that follows the fifth, then the octave, the third or tenth, or whatever combination is desired. Certain mixtures are comprised of specific ranks, and so get other names. Thus the Sesquialter is a type of compound stop (see below under "S"); likewise the Cymbel, of which various types are cited in §.134 (the Mixturcymbel is also mentioned there). The Scharp or Scharf is also a type of Mixtur; see below under "S". The Rauschpfeife, Terzian and Coppel are also compound, and each may be consulted under its entry (see Praetorius, *l.c.*, p. 130). We are speaking here about the actual Mixtures, as they are called in this area. These either repeat or proceed upward without repeating. If they are very small to begin with, then they repeat; for the meaning of "repeat", see §.83. The ones that are made up of just a few ranks are also called Kleine Mixtur ["small mixture"], though some are labelled [simply] Mixtur. The ones comprised of many [ranks] are called Grosse Mixturen ["large mixtures"]. Old [examples] were as many as 50 ranks strong, but nowadays they are no longer built so clumsy. The smallest may be 2 ranks, but ordinarily they are 3, 4, 5, 6, sometimes even 8 ranks, and the appended "f" means not "foot", as elsewhere, but "fach" [ranks]. Thus for example the mixtures at Sandomir (called *Regula mixta*, another name for Mixtur), Jena and many other places besides are 6 ranks. At St. Johannis in Lüneburg it is 6-7 fach, and in the palace at Gröningen 6,7 and 8 fach or chöricht. This means that the keys in the lowest octaves have fewer pipes, while those above have more, since 1 or 2 quints are omitted in the bass and the mixture is then only 7 or even 6 ranks for some [notes]. In a case like this some of the pipes must double pitches [already present]. Thus at St. Nikolai in Leipzig, for example, the Mixtur was 4 ranks in the bass, 6 ranks in the tenor, and 8 ranks in the treble; see Praetorius, *l.c.*[, p. 179]. At Halberstadt in the Barfüsserkirche the Mixtur was 6 ranks in the lower octaves, 7 ranks at c′, 8 ranks at c″, and 9 ranks at c‴; see Praetorius [p. 182]. At Riddagshausen in the Klosterkirche organ the Mixtur 4′ was 5 ranks at the bottom, 6 ranks in the middle, and 8 ranks on top; see Praetorius[, p. 199]. The Mixtur 6-8 fach at St. Michaelis in Lüneburg is to be understood in the same way. The mixtures in the middle organ in the Pfarrkirche at Danzig, [in the pedal] at St. Dominicus in Prague, and at St. Michaelis in Lüneburg are also 8 ranks. Although all of these are labelled simply "8", it may well be that for certain notes 1 or 2 pipes have gotten too small and have thus been omitted; it is not necessary to indicate this all the time, and this holds true for other mixtures as well. The mixture is 9 ranks at St. Cosmae in Stade, 10 ranks [in the Haupt Werck] at St. Dominicus in Prague, St. Catherine in Hamburg and St. Wenceslaus in Naumburg. Both these and the ones to follow are mostly in the manuals, yet some are also in the pedal. To continue, the middle organ in the Pfarrkirche at Danzig has one of 10 ranks in the Werck, as do the Ca-

* i.e., a Blockwerk.

daselbst in der Altstädter Orgel. 8. 9. 10fach ist sie noch in der großen Orgel zu St. Nikolai in Hamburg; 6. 7. 8. 9. 10fach zu Reval. s. unten §. 313. 11fach ist sie in der Pfarrkirche zu Danzig im Manual, und auch so stark im Pedale. 12fach ist sie zu Königsberg im Kneiphofe im Pedale, da 10fach vorhin 2mal im Manuale war. Zu Stralsund, zu Bernau in der Mark, ist sie ebenfalls 12fach; zu St. Blasii in Braunschweig ist Mixtur 12fach in Diskant, im Basse aber 7fach, s. Prätor. l. c. In Görlitz ist auch eine 12fache Mixtur im Pedal, welche in die Engel und Sonnen vertheilet ist. 15fach im Werke ist zu St. Marien in Lübeck; 12 à 15 fach im Dom zu Magdeburg, s. Prätor. l. c. nach andern wird diese Mixtur 9, 12, 14, bis 16fach angegeben. Zu St. Gotthardt in Hildesheim ist Mixtur im Diskante von 12 Chören; (s. Prätor.) also wird sie unten schwächer seyn. In der Danziger Marienorgel, die Prätorius anführt, soll die Mixtur 24 fach seyn. Nun fragt sichs: wie dies möglich sey? Denn die größte Pfeife ist wol nicht leicht über 4 Fuß lang. Wenn ich nun alle Oktaven nehme, $2'$, $1'$, $\frac{1}{2}'$, $\frac{1}{4}'$, und alle Quinten, $3'$, $1\frac{1}{2}'$, $\frac{3}{4}'$, $\frac{3}{8}'$, auch alle Terzen; so kommt dergleichen Zahl nimmer heraus. Antwort: Wie ich vorhin gedacht, so können viel Stimmen 2, 3, und mehr mal genommen werden, bis die verlangte Zahl herauskömmt. Wollte jemand sagen, daß etliche ganz gleiche Stimmen die Harmonie nicht verstärkten, dem kann ich nicht beypflichten; die Ohren zeigen das Gegentheil. (vergl. §. 233.) Ob aber die Mixturen allezeit in allen Pfeifen klingen, wenn sie gleich nicht so stark sind, ist eine andere Frage. Etliche Orgelmacher, wenn sie in der Stimmung oder Intonation nicht fortkommen können, drücken die labia zu, damit sie kurz davon kommen mögen, und meynen, es werde in der starken Stimme der Mangel einer Pfeife nicht gemerket. Das ist aber nicht gewissenhaft: und einer, der die Orgel probiret, hat sonderlich nachzuforschen, ob die Mixturen richtig sind. Doch wollte ich nicht rathen, allzustarke Mixturen zu machen: besser macht man mehr einzelne oder doppelte Stimmen; denn so giebt es mehr Veränderungen. Was von der Mixtur gesaget worden, gilt auch beym Scharp, davon in S. Fornitura ist gleichviel, s. in F. §. 148. In der Görlitzer Orgel stehet auch Scharfmixtur 1 und $1\frac{1}{2}$ fach; oder ob es etwan Fuß heissen soll; denn daß in den kleinen Mixturen auch durch das F. Fuß angedeutet werde, ist zuweilen aus den Exempeln klar. Es ist ohne dies oft dabey gemeldet, wie groß die größte Pfeife der Mixtur sey. Z. Ex. Mixtur 6fach $4'$, ꝛc. Mixtur ellich, d. i. 2 Fuß oder eine Elle, welches die Länge der größten Pfeife ist. Z. Ex. zu St. Andreä in Erfurt, s. §. 291. Zu Langensalz ist vellicht eben das, §. 307. da halbellich $1'$ ist. Wenn man aber angeschrieben fände Mixtur 1 f. da müßte das f ohnfehlbar Fuß bedeuten: denn eine Stimme ist keine Mixtur, obgleich Prätorius l. c. S. 126. in der Tabelle eine einfache Stimme dafür ausgeben will. Doch zu Görlitz könnte wol die 2fache Mixtur seyn. Denn daß die Quinte $1\frac{1}{2}'$ Fuß größer ist, als das Oktävchen $1'$, ist nicht zu verwundern; man kann eben sowol von der Quinte $1\frac{1}{2}'$ oder $3'$ ꝛc. in Mixturen anheben, als von den Oktavstimmen. Zu Magdeburg, wie Prätorius meldet, ist zu St. Ulrich mixtur graphicalis 10 fach, und mixtur minoralis

Ch. VII. Concerning Stops in General and in Particular

thedral (Kneiphofkirche) and the Altstädterkirche organ at Königsberg. Then in the large organ at St. Nikolai in Hamburg it is 8.9.10 ranks, and at Reval 6.7.8.9.10 ranks; see below, §.313.* It is 11 ranks in the Pfarrkirche at Danzig, both in the manual and pedal, and 12 ranks in the pedal at Königsberg in the Kneiphofkirche, where 2 10-rank manual mixtures were cited above. At Stralsund and at Bernau in the Mark [Brandenburg] the Mixtur is likewise 12 ranks; at Braunschweig it is 12 ranks in the treble, but 7 ranks in the bass; see Praetorius, *l.c.*, [p. 178]. In Görlitz there is also a 12 rank Mixtur in the pedal [the pipes of which] are distributed between the angel and the suns.* [The Mixtur] is 15 ranks in the Werck at St. Marien in Lübeck, and 12-15 ranks in the Cathedral at Magdeburg (see Praetorius, *l.c.* [, p. 173]); [but] according to others† this mixture is indicated as 9.12.14-16 fach. At St. Gotthardt in Hildesheim the Mixtur is of 12 ranks (Chören) in the treble, but weaker‡ below that; see Praetorius[, p. 198]. In the Marienkirche organ at Danzig, as cited by Praetorius[, p. 162,] the Mixtur is reported to be 24 ranks. Now the question arises, "How is this possible?" After all, the largest pipe is not likely to be over 4 feet in length. The sum of all the octaves 2', 1', 1 ½', 1 ¼', the fifths 3', 1 ½', ¾', ⅜', and all the thirds§ in no way equals the number [24]. The answer? As I have mentioned above, many pitches can be doubled 2, 3 or more times, until the required number [of ranks in the Mixtur] is reached. If anyone says that doubling pitches does not strengthen the tone, I cannot agree with him; the ears indicate the contrary (cf. §.233). Whether all the [doubled] pipes in Mixtures are sounding if they are not so strong¶ is another question. Some organbuilders, if they have trouble with tuning or voicing, press the lips closed so that they can quickly be done with it, thinking that the absence of one pipe will not be noticed in a loud stop. This however is not conscientious, and anyone who tests an organ must especially investigate whether the Mixtures are correct. Yet I do not want to suggest making such strong‖ Mixtures; it is better to make more single or double stops,** for these provide more variety. What has been said about the Mixtur also holds true for the Scharp; look under "S". *Fornitura* is the same thing; see under "F", §.148. In the Görlitz organ there stands a Scharfmixtur 1 and 1 ½ fach, but the [word "fach"] may possibly mean "foot", since examples make it clear that small mixtures often bear indications of feet. Moreover, the length of the largest pipe of the mixture is often stated; e.g., Mixtur 6 ranks 4'. "Mixtur ellich" means 2 feet or a yard,†† which is the length of the largest pipe, e.g., at St. Andrea in Erfurt. At Langensalz[a] the "vellicht" (§.307 ‡‡) is the same idea, since "halbellich" is 1'. If one were to find written "Mixtur 1 f", though, that would unmistakably signify "foot", since one rank is hardly a mixture, although Praetorius, *l.c.*, p. 126, tries to pass off a single rank as a mixture in the *Tabel*[*le*]. Yet at Görlitz the 2 ranks§§ could well be a Mixtur. It is not surprising that the Quinte 1 ½' is larger than the little octave 1'; it is just as proper in mixtures to commence with the Quinte 1 ½' or 3' as with the octave ranks. At Magdeburg, as Praetorius reports,¶¶ there

*See Boxberg, p.[18].

† cf. *Sammlung einiger Nachrichten*, p. 61.

‡ i.e., having fewer ranks.

§ i.e., 1 ⅗', ⅘', ⅖'.

¶ i.e., if the Mixtur sounds no louder than a Mixtur composed without doubled pitches.

‖ i.e., with so many ranks.
** i.e., in particular more foundation stops.

†† See §.78.

‡‡ The translation disregards the (superfluous) paragraph numbers in the collection of stoplists; see the stoplist for the organ at Langensalza in Chapter 10

§§ i.e., the example mentioned just above: "Scharfmixtur 1 and 1½ fach."

¶¶ p. 174.

114　Kap. VII.　Von den Registern überhaupt und insonderheit.

lis 8 fach. Das letzte Wort zeigt an, es sey die kleinere Mixtur, weil minor klein heißt. Das erste aber soll von graphicus, künstlich, herkommen: oder von grauis, eine gravitätische oder starke Mixtur. Diese Veränderung des Worts wäre arg genug; doch nutzen sie beyde nicht viel. Mixtur, wobey ein Baß 12′, nämlich vom F an, (conf. §. 213.) ist zu St. Jakobi in Hamburg, s. Prätor. l. c. Grobe Mixtur Unterchormaß, und kleine Mixtur Chormaß sind zu Breßlau. Was das heiße s. in Chormaß. §. 125.

Mittelflöte, s. Flöte.

Mittelgedackt, s. Gedackt.

* Montre; la Montre soll das Principal seyn, s. §. 177. (**)

　　(**) Es ist auch so, nach der französischen Sprache, und in Frankreich.

Musette, s. Schallmey.

§. 168.

Musicirgedackt, ist das Stillegedackt, §. 150.

Musikgedackt ist eben das.

Nachthorn ist ein gedecktes Flötregister, fast wie Quintatön, doch über 2′, 4′ oder 8′ nicht groß; wie denn zu Bernau in der Mark Nachthorn 4′ auch die Oktave von der Quintatön heißt, und sagt Prätorius l. c. S. 138. „Es wird diese „kleine Quintatön von etlichen an der Mensur auf gewisse Maaß erweitert, daher sie einen „Hornklang bekömmt, und die Quinte darinnen wird stiller." Im Pedale heißts zuweilen Nachthornbaß: ist aber eben 4′ und 2′. Es steht z. Ex. 4′ zun Reglern in Erfurt; 2′ aber zu St. Jakobi in Hamburg; und im Dom zu Bremen im Pedale. In Sandomir ist es auch 4′ und wird daselbst Pastorita genennet, von pastor ein Hirt, gleichsam ein Hirtenhorn. Zu Riddagshausen steht in der Klosterorgel Nachthorn oder Baurbäßlein 2′ oder 1′, wie Prätorius meldet; vermuthlich, weil Bauerflöte, wie das Nachthorn, oft eine Art der Quintatön ist. Zu Gera (s. §. 301.) ist Nachthorn 4′ oben aus wie eine Harfe, nämlich wie eine Davidsharfe, etwas schnarrend intonirt. 8′ ist zu Waltershausen. Das Nachthorn klingt gar anmuthig; wenigstens hat es mir wohl gefallen. Die Niederländer (sagt Prätorius zu seiner Zeit) arbeiten das Nachthorn offen (s. die 37. Tabelle seines 2ten Tomis, allwo man es auf zweyerley Art abgebildet findet) wie eine Hohlflöte, doch oben etwas enger, und brechen sie allmählich immer etwas ab; ist auch im labio nicht so hoch aufgeschnitten, als die Hohlflöt, daher es einen sonderlichen Klang bekömmt. Ja etliche, wie er S. 131. sagt, nennen die kleine Hohlflöte 2′ auch Nachthorn, weil sie als ein Hornklang im Resonanz artet: aber dazu schickt sich die Quintatönen Art viel besser. Und weil die Bauerflöte auch aus diesem Fundament zuweilen gearbeitet wird; so heißt sie zuweilen auch Nachthorn. So ist z. Ex. zu Stralsund, laut Prätorii Nachricht, Nachthorn 1′; oder wollte man lieber jedes mit einer eigenen besondern Mensur haben, steht es auch frey. Es ist daselbst im Pedale. Ich habe auch ein Hornbaßlein

is a "Mixtur graphicalis 10 fach" and a "Mixtur minoralis 8 fach" at St. Ulrich. The final word indicates that it is a smaller mixture, since *minor* means "small". In the first instance, however, *graphicalis* must be derived from *graphicus*, meaning "artificial"* (künstlich), or from *gravis*,† a sonorous or strong Mixtur. This variety of terms would indeed be vexing; yet neither of them is much used. A Mixtur with "Bass 12'", i.e., beginning with F (cf. §.213) is at St. Jakobi in Hamburg (see Praetorius, *l.c.*[, p. 169]. There are a Grobe Mixtur Unterchormass and a Kleine Mixtur Chormass at Breslau;‡ for the meaning of this, see "Chormass", §. 125.

* i.e., "skillful, full of artifice."

† i.e., "heavy, grave."

‡ Praetorius, *Syntagma musicum*, Vol. II, p. 172.

MITTELFLÖTE, see Flöte.
MITTELGEDACKT, see Gedackt.
* MONTRE; *la Montre* is said to be the Principal; see §.177.(**)
(**) This is indeed the case, in the French language and in France. [Agricola]
MUSETTE, see Schallmey.

§. 168.

MUSICIRGEDACKT is the Stillgedackt; see §.150.
MUSIKGEDACKT is the same thing.

NACHTHORN is a stopped flute register, almost like a Quintatön, but never larger than 2', 4', or 8'. Thus the Nachthorn 4' at Bernau in the Mark [Brandenburg] is also called the octave of the Quintatön, and Praetorius, *l.c.*, p. 138, says, "Some [builders] broaden the scale of this little Quintatön to a certain degree, so that it takes on a horn-like sound and the fifth in it becomes less prominent." Sometimes it is called Nachthornbass in the pedal, even though it is 4' or 2'. It stands in the pedal at 4', for example at the Reglerkirche in Erfurt, and at 2' at St. Jakobi in Hamburg and the Cathedral at Bremen. It is also a 4' at Sandomir and is called *Pastorita* there, from *pastor*, "a shepherd"—a "shepherd's horn" as it were. In the Klosterkirche organ at Riddagshausen there stands a Nachthorn or Baurbässlein, as Praetorius reports, presumably because the Bauerflöte, like the Nachthorn, is often a type of Quintatön. At Gera (see §.301) there is a Nachthorn 4' [that sounds] like a harp in the upper register, namely like a harp of David,§ voiced with something of a twang. There is an 8' [Nachthorn] at Waltershausen. The Nachthorn sounds quite charming; at least I find it very pleasing. Praetorius¶ says that in his day the Netherlanders constructed the Nachthorn open (see Table 37 of his second volume, where two types are illustrated) like a Hohlflöte, but somewhat conical, and built it with a diminishing scale; the lip also does not have a very high cut-up, and therefore it gets its particular sound. On p. 131‖ he says that some also call the Kleine Hohlflöte 2' a Nachthorn, since it resounds with a horn-like sound; but the Quintatön type is much better suited for this.** Since the Bauerflöte is also at times constructed on this basis, it too is sometimes called Nachthorn. Thus for example there is in the pedal at Stralsund, according to Praetorius, a Nachthorn 1'. But it is also possible for a builder to assign a specific scale to each of these. I have also

§ a reference to the Old Testament King; the common harp of Adlung's day.

¶ p. 138.

‖ actually p. 132.

** Adlung may mean that the stopped pipe can be voiced more stably, or that it can be more readily voiced to sound like a horn.

lein 2′ gefunden zu Bückeburgk beym Prätorio: davon urtheile ich es sey auch ein Nachthorn, nur daß es im Pedale vorkömmt. Nachthorn ist zwar ordentlich gedeckt; doch finde ich zu Sondershausen beym Prätorio auch Nachthorn offen, weiter Mensur, welches lieblich seyn soll. Sie werden am besten von Metall gemacht.

Nachtigal, s. in Vogelgesang, §. 207.

§. 169.

Nasat, Nassat, Nassart, Nazard, Nasarde, Nasatflöte, und was man mehr für gleichgeltende Namen im Druck antrift, ist eine Flötstimme, welche zuweilen offen, meistentheils aber gedeckt angetroffen wird. Prätorius sagt Seite 134.: daß das klein Gemshorn $1\frac{1}{2}$′ gar recht Nasat heiße, weil es wegen seiner Kleine zu andern Stimmen gleichsam nösselt, sonderlich wenn es recht und nicht zu scharf intonirt wird. Aber die Erklärung des Worts scheinet etwas weit her gehohlet zu seyn, wie denn auch die Exempel die Unrichtigkeit solcher Erklärung sattsam an den Tag legen. Es findet sich auch ein größeres Nasat, als $1\frac{1}{2}$′ ist. Etliche Orgelmacher arbeiten das Nasat nach der Mensur des weiten Pfeifenwerks, und labiren es enge. Das Matthesonische Orchestre I. P. III. C. III. §. 15. erklärt Nasat, (wie es auf diese Art am richtigsten geschrieben wird) da es sagt, dies Wort wolle so viel bedeuten, als ein Stimmchen oder Register, so einen Nachsatz und Nachdruck giebt. Zuweilen steht bloß Nasat; da kann man nicht urtheilen, ob es Oktaven- oder Quintenton hören lasse, bis man das Register selbst gehöret: zuweilen aber steht Nasatquinte oder Quintnasat, daraus man sodann deutlich vornehmen kann, es sey eine Quinte auf die Art intonirt. Etliche Exempel dieses Registers, welches vielleicht nicht jedermann kennen möchte, sind diese: In der Domsorgel in Hamburg ist Nasat 3′. Weil es 3′ heißt; so ists eine Quinte: so auch wenn $1\frac{1}{2}$′ vorkömmt. Zu St. Johannis daselbst ist auch 3′; it. zu St. Gertrud daselbst. Nasatquinte ist daselbst zu St. Nikolai: in Bützfleth bey Stade auch 3′. Quintnasat ist $1\frac{1}{2}$′ in Görlitz zu finden, und Nasatquinte 3′ zu Otterndorf im Lande Hadeln. In der Pfarrorgel zu Danzig steht Nasat 5′; aber das ist wol ein Druckfehler: denn 5 Fuß giebt nie eine Quinte. Es soll ohne Zweifel Nasatquinte bedeuten. Diese ist auch 3′ zu Waltershausen 2 mal; it. in der Jenaischen Stadtkirche allwo auch Rohrnasat 6′ ist. Da ist die Mensur, wie das Nasat sonst hat; doch ist auch das kleine Röhrchen drinne, wie die Rohrflöte hat, von welcher aber unten erst zu reden. Assat 2′ soll wol eben so viel bedeuten zu Hildesheim, siehe §. 117. Also zeigen die bisherigen Exempel, daß Nasat nicht allezeit eine Quinte sey, obschon Niedt Part. II. pag. 112. (nach der Matthesonischen Ausgabe) sagt: „Nasat, seil. Nachsatz ist eine gedeckte Quintstimme in der Orgel." In der Lutherischen Augustinerkirche in Erfurt ist Nasat auch zu finden. Mehr hierher gehöriges findet man in meiner Anleitung S. 436. u. 437. in der Anmerkung h.) (**)

(**) In Frankreich heißen alle Quinten, ohne Unterschied: Nazard,

Niederländische Vox humana, s. §. 208.

§. 170.

Ch. VII. Concerning Stops in General and in Particular

found in Praetorius a Hornbässlein 2′ at Bückeburg; from this I judge that it is also a Nachthorn, except that it appears in the pedal. To be sure, the Nachthorn is normally stopped, yet in Praetorius I find an open Nachthorn of wide scale at Sondershausen, said to be lovely. [Nachthorns] are best made of metal.

NACHTIGAL, see under Vogelgesang, §.207.

§. 169.

NASAT, NASSAT, NASSART, NAZARD, NASARDE, NASATFLÖTE and other equivalent names met in print, is a flute stop that is sometimes open, but for the most part found stopped. Praetorius says on p. 134 [of *Syntagma musicum*, vol. II) that the little Gemshorn 1 ½′ is most properly called Nasat, since due to its small size it imparts a nasal quality (nösselt*) to other stops, especially if it is voiced properly and not too penetratingly. But this explanation of the word appears somewhat far-fetched, just as there are sufficient other examples of incorrect derivation current. There is also a Nasat larger than 1 ½′. Some organbuilders construct the Nasat as a wide-scale stop with a narrow lip. Mattheson's [*Neu-eröffnete*] *Orchestre*, Part III, Chap. III,† §.15, explains Nasat (this is the most correct spelling) by saying that this word means the same as a little stop or register that gives a decrease (Nachsatz‡) or emphasis (Nachdruck§). Sometimes just the word Nasat appears; then it is not possible to judge whether it is an octave- or fifth-sounding stop until one has actually heard it.¶ At times, though, Nasatquinte or Quintnasat appears, and from that one may clearly perceive (vornehmen) that it is tuned as a fifth. Some examples of this stop, perhaps not known to everyone, are these: in the Cathedral organ at Hamburg there is a Nasat 3′. Since it is specified as 3′, it is a Quinte, just as when 1 ½′ appears. It is also a 3′ at St. Johannis and at St. Gertrud in Hamburg. The Nasatquinte appears at St. Nikolai in Hamburg and at Butzfleth near Stade at 3′. Quintnasat 1 ½′ may be found at Görlitz, and Nasatquinte 3′ at Otterndorf in Land Hadeln. In the Pfarrkirche organ at Danzig there stands a Nasat 5′, but this is surely a printing error, for 5′ never produces a Quinte. This doubtless means a Nasatquinte, which is also found twice at 3′ at Waltershausen as well as in the Stadtkirche at Jena, where there is also a Rohrnasat 6′. This last has the usual scale of Nasat, but with a little tube in it like a Rohrflöte, discussed below.‖ Assat 2′ at Hildesheim (see §.117) must be the same [as Nasat], and this example shows that the Nasat is not always a Quinte, even though Niedt (in Mattheson's edition) Part II, p. 112, says "Nasat, to wit Nachsatz, is a stopped Quint register in the organ." A Nasat may also be found in the Lutheran Augustinerkirche in Erfurt. Further information on this stop is found in my *Anleitung*, pp. 436-7,** in note "h". (**)

(**) In France all quints are called "Nazard", without distinction. [Agricola]

NIEDERLÄNDISCHE *VOX HUMANA*, see §.208.

---

* Praetorius's use of the verb "nösselt" is unclear. Though the word does not appear in German dictionaries, there are a number of similar ones: nus(s)eln, nüs(s)eln, nuscheln. They all mean "to mumble or mutter, to talk indistinctly through the nose."

† "Part III, Chap. III" is incorrect; the passage cited is in the "Supplementum", §.15, p. 299.

‡ The word "Nachsatz" is no longer in use in modern German. In his *Critica musica*, vol. II, p. 335, Mattheson defines the words "Vorsatz" and "Nachsatz" as "künstlicher Zu- oder Ab-nehmen" (i.e., "artificial arsis and thesis" or "synthetic rise and fall"). It seems that Mattheson was trying to derive "Nasat" from "Nachsatz" by assonance, and that by indicating "Nachsatz" he intended to cast the definition in rhetorical terms; but his meaning is obscure.

§ This would appear to be the opposite of "Nachsatz." again, the meaning is unclear.

¶ This statement is not prepared by what Adlung has already said, but is further elucidated later in this entry.

‖ in §.184.

** This should read "435-6."

§. 170.

Nete ist so viel, als Quinte, s. deswegen unten bey Quinte.

Noli me tangere, ist der Titul eines Registerzuges in der Orgel zu St. Gertrud in Hamburg. Es ist dies gewiß ein Vexierregister, so wie oben §. 149. der Fuchsschwanz war. Die Worte sind lateinisch, und heißen: rühre mich nicht an. Es kann auch propter eurhythmiam hingemacht seyn, um die Zahl der manubriorum voll zu machen.

§. 171.

Oboe, s. Hautbois, §. 159.

Obtusior, ist das Gedackt, s. §. 150. Man schreibt auch oftmals: obtusa.

Oktave ist das gemeinste Orgelregister unter den offenen Flötstimmen. Und wie bekannt, so ist zwar die Oktave zu jedem Register in der That eine Oktave, z. Ex. gegen das Gedackt 8′ ist das Gedackt 4′ die Oktave; oder gegen das Gemshorn 16′ ist das Principal 8′ eine Oktave: denn das kleinere heißt allezeit gegen das große also, wenn es ein oder etliche mal in demselben steckt, daß es in der Division gerade aufgeht. Also: 16 in 8, 2mal. So steckt auch 1 in 8 achtmal, und bleibt nichts übrig. It. 3 in 6 steckt 2mal, also ist 3 zu 6 die Oktave, obschon, gegen die Principale zu rechnen, beydes Quinten sind. Doch diejenigen Stimmen, auf welche das itztgesagte zu appliciren, haben meistens was besonders, und deswegen eigene Namen; und diejenigen Register kommen hier nur in Betrachtung, welche die Principalmensur haben; und unter diesen alle die, welche gegen das Principal 1, 2, 3 oder mehr Oktaven kleiner sind. Daraus siehet ein jeder, daß ein Register bald eine Oktave bald aber ein Principal heißen kann; und nachdem das Principal groß oder klein angenommen wird, darnach sind auch die Oktaven. Unter diesen Registern, die solche Mensur und Intonation haben, wird das größte allezeit das Principal genennet; die andern kleinern hingegen heißen Oktaven. Das Principal kann 16′ 8′ 4′ oder auch 2′ seyn: also sind in der Orgel diese, in der andern andere Oktaven. Beym Principal 16′ sind die Oktaven: 8′, die kleinere 4′, die noch kleinere 2′; beym Principal 8′ sind 4′ und 2′ die Oktaven, auch bisweilen 1′; beym Principal 4′ ist 2′ und etwann 1′ die Oktave; beym Principal 2′ kann nichts als 1′ die Oktave seyn. Kleiner macht man sie nicht; ob sie wol in gemischten Stimmen kleiner vorkommen. Doch man hat im Pedale Principal 32′. Da gehöret 16′ nebst den andern auch zu den Oktaven: es ist aber zwischen Principal 8′ und Oktave 8′, und so auch zwischen den übrigen, kein besonderer Unterschied, als daß die Principale meistens (jedoch nicht allezeit) im Gesichte stehen, und besser Metall halten, als die inwendig stehenden Oktaven: steht aber die Oktave im Gesicht; so heißt sie oft auch Principal, wie z. Ex. in Alach Oktave 4′, nebst Principal 8′ von Zinn im Gesichte stehen. In Waltershausen, findet man den Namen Oktavenprincipal 8′, vermuthlich aus keiner andern Absicht, als dadurch anzuzeigen

§. 170.

NETE is the same as Quinte; therefore see below under Quinte.

NOLI ME TANGERE is the title of a stopknob in the organ at St. Gertrud in Hamburg. Certainly this is a trick stop, just as the foxtail in §.149 above was. The words are Latin, and mean "do not touch me". It may have been constructed for the sake of symmetry, in order to complete the number of stopknobs.*

* i.e., so the layout of stopknobs on both sides of the keyboards is symmetrical.

§. 171.

OBOE, see *Hautbois*, §.159.

OBTUSIOR is the Gedackt; see §.150. It is often written *Obtusa*.

OKTAVE is the most common organ stop among the open flues. As is well-known, the octave of any stop is in fact an Oktave; for example, the Gedackt 4′ is the Oktave in relation to the Gedackt 8′, or the Principal 8′ is an Oktave in relation to the Gemshorn 16′. The smaller [stop] is always called thus in relation to the larger if it is divisible one or more times into it; thus 8 goes into 16 twice. 1 also goes into 8 eight times, with no remainder. 3 likewise goes into 6 twice, and thus 3 is the octave of 6, although both are quints in relation to the principals. Yet those stops to which what has just been said applies usually have some special [characteristic] and therefore [are given] a specific name. Only those stops of principal scale will be considered here, and among those all that are 1, 2, 3 or more octaves higher than the Principal. Anyone may perceive from all this that the same stop may be called Oktave one time, but a Principal† another; as the Principal is established at a higher or lower pitch, so the Oktaves will vary accordingly. Among the stops that have such a scale and voicing, the largest is always called the Principal; the other higher ones, on the other hand, are called Oktaves. The Principal may be 16′, 8′, 4′, or even 2′; when the Principal is 8′, then 4′ and 2′ are the Oktaves, as well as sometimes 1′; when the Principal is 4′, the Oktaves are 2′ and sometimes 1′. When the Principal is 2′, only the 1′ may be the Oktave. No one makes them any smaller [than this], although they do indeed exist smaller in compound stops. Yet there is [such a thing as] a Principal 32′ in the pedal. In that case 16′ also belongs to the Oktaves in addition to the others. There is no particular difference between Principal 8′ and Oktave 8′, nor between the others,‡ except that the Principals usually (though not always) stand in the facade and contain a better [quality of] metal§ than the Oktaves standing inside the case. If the Oktave stands in the façade, it is often called Principal as well, just as for example in Alach the Oktave 4′ as well as the Principal 8′ stand in the facade, both of tin.¶ The name Oktavenprincipal 8′ is found at Waltershausen, presumably for no other reason than to indicate that this stop, just

† i.e., the primary principal rank in a given division.

‡ i.e., Principal 4′ and Oktave 4′, etc.
§ i.e., have a higher tin content.

¶ See the stoplist of the organ at Alach in Chapter 10. Adlung's example does not entirely confirm his statement; the 4′ is not called Principal, though it is of a more expensive metal.

zeigen, daß dasselbe, so, wie das andere Principal, im Gesichte stehe. Eine Oktave, heißt zuweilen Großoktave, wenn es die größte ist nach dem Principal; [41] eine Superoktave, oder suprema octaua, das ist, die obere Oktave: und so heißt allezeit die höchste in eben dem Claviere. (Denn man verstehet allezeit das Principal und Oktaven, die in einem Claviere beysammen stehen.) Der Name aber kann sich an keine Größe binden, sondern er richtet sich nach dem Principale. Wenn z. Er. das Principal 16' ist; so ist 8' die Großoktave; 4' die ordentliche; 2' aber die Superoktave. Im Pedale fehlt beym 16füßigen Principale oftmals die Oktave 2' so heißt in solchem Falle 4' schon die Superoktave, 8' aber schlechtweg die Oktave, oder auch Großoktave. Beym Principale 4' ist 2' nicht die Superoktave, sondern 1'. Man sagt auch zuweilen Kleinoktave, sonderlich bey 2'. Sedetze ist so viel, als Sedecima, die sechszehnte. Wenn ich nun von c durch 16 palmulas fortgehe; so komme ich auf $\bar{\bar{a}}$ nicht aber auf $\bar{\bar{c}}$: kann also die Superoktave nicht seyn; denn diese ist die 15 Klangstufe vom Principal an gerechnet, daher auch einige mit besserm Grunde decima quinta, oder umgekehrt, quinta decima, andere aber der Kürze wegen Quintez schreiben. Doch, diesen Sphum nicht so weitläufig zu machen, will ich in S. von Sedetze mehr sagen, und hier nur noch so viel anmerken, daß man diesen Namen der Oktave beylegt, obgleich derselbe nicht richtig ist. Koppeldone ist auch so viel als Oktave, (einige schreiben Coppeldone,) z. Er. zu St. Johannis in Lüneburg, s. Prätor. l. c. S. 171. Koppeloktave 4' stehet nebst einer Oktave itzo im Schloße zu Dresden. Vielleicht wird darunter ein Gemshorn 4' verstanden, wie Koppelflöte 8' und 4' war §. 129; oder es müßte dieselbe etwan durch zwey besondere Züge im Manual und Pedal können gebraucht werden. In der Disposition, die Prätorius l. c. S. 187. hat, findet man Koppeloktave 4' auch. Bey ebendemselben wird das Wort Oktave insonderheit für 4 Fuß genommen. Z. Er. offen Oktave, Thubalflötoktave, Gedacktflötoktave, u. d. gl. da 8' dort Chormaß, 2' Sedecima, 1' Supercedecima heißen: das Principal aber ist 16 Fuß, s. Prätorii Disposition der Breslauer Orgel, l. c. S. 171 u. folg. Ich habe gefunden Oktave 8' bey Principal 4': aber das ist wol ein Druckfehler, oder sonst ein Versehen gewesen. Es sind zwar wol 8' und 4' gegen einander Oktaven: aber das größte von beyden wird das Principal genennet; und habe ich zuvor schon erinnert, daß nicht eben das Principal auswendig stehen müsse, deswegen bleibt es doch das Principal. In der Disposition der Domorgel in Bremen ist in einem Claviere Oktave 8' und Principal 8'. Das geht noch weniger an. 8' gegen 8' ist ja ein vnisonus und keine Oktave; es soll wol Oktave 4' heißen: denn größer als 8' ist daselbst das Principal nicht, weil es nicht das Hauptmanual ist. Man siehet es auch daher, weil Oktave 4' nicht da ist, die

doch

---

[41] Diese Oktave heißt auch wol Halbprincipal; weil sie an Füßen nur halb so groß ist, als das Principal. Z Ex. zu Bernau in der Mark ist Halbprincipal oder Oktave 4' beym Principal 8', s. Prätor. Tom. 2. S. 176. u. f. Der Hr. Verf. hat unten §. 177. diese Benennung auch mit angeführet.

Ch. VII. Concerning Stops in General and in Particular 117

as the other Principal, stands in the façade. An Oktave may at times be called Grossoktave if it is the next largest after the Principal.[41] A Superoktave or *suprema octava* is an "octave above"; the highest [Oktave] in any given manual is given this name (it is always understood when talking about the Principal and [its] Oktaves that they stand together on the same manual). The name cannot be restricted to any specific size, but is determined by the Principal. If, for example, the Principal is a 16′ pitch, then 8′ is the Grossoktave, 4′ the ordinary [Oktave] and 2′ the Superoktave. If the pedal [is based on] a 16′ Principal, the 2′ Oktave is often lacking; in that case the 4′ is called the Superoktave and the 8′ either simply the Oktave or also the Grossoktave. When the Principal is 4′, 1′ is the Superoktave, not 2′. Sometimes the term Kleinoktave is used, especially when referring to the 2′. Sedetze is the same as Sedecima, the 16th; however, if I proceed upward 16 keys from c, then I arrive at d″ rather than c″. This cannot be the Superoktave, since [the Superoktave] is 15 tones higher than the Principal; thus some [authors] write more appropriately *decima quinta,* or the reverse, *quinta decima,* or just Quintez for the sake of brevity. But in order not to make this paragraph too lengthy, I will say more about Sedetze under "S", and only note here that this name is given to the Oktave even though it is not correct. Koppeldone (some write Coppeldone) is also the same as Oktave, for example at St. Johannis is Lüneburg; see Praetorius, *l.c.,* p. 171. A Koppeloktave 4′ stands at present in the palace at Dresden in addition to an Oktave.* Perhaps this means a Gemshorn 4′, just as Koppelflöte 8′ and 4′ were [both Gemshorns] in §.129; this stop must be able to be used in some way in both manual and pedal by means of 2 separate stopknobs. Koppeloktave is also found in the stoplist [of the palace organ at Dresden] that Praetorius gives, *l.c.,* p. 187. By the word "Oktave" this author often means the 4′ in particular, e.g., Offen Oktave, Thubalflötoktave, Gedacktflötoktave and the like, while calling 8′ "Chormass", 2′ Sedecima and 1′ Supercedecima [sic]. The 16′, however, is called the Principal; see Praetorius's stoplist of the Breslau organ, *l.c.,* p. 171f. I have found Oktave 8′ where there is a Principal 4′,† but that is surely a printing error or some other oversight.‡ 8′ and 4′ are octaves in relation to each other to be sure, but the larger of the two is called Principal, and as I have already mentioned, the Principal need not stand outside [the case§] in order to be designated as the Principal. In the stoplist of the Cathedral organ at Bremen Oktave 8′ and Principal 8′ appear on the same keyboard; that is even less felicitous. 8′ versus 8′ produces a unison, not an octave. It must mean Oktave 4′, for there is no Principal there larger than 8′ since it it not the primary manual. One reaches this conclusion because an Oktave 4′, which always appears with a Principal 8′, is not pres-

* See Mattheson's Appendix to Niedt, p. 171, as well as the stoplist of the organ in the Palace [church] in Dresden in Chapter 10.

† i.e., in the Rückpositiv at Sendomir; see Mattheson's Appendix to Niedt, Part Two, p. 196.

‡ In §.177 (under Prästant) Adlung does indeed suggest a reason for having an Oktave 8′ with a Principal 4′.

§ i.e., in the façade. Adlung is presuming that the 4′ at Sendomir may have been called "Principal" because it stood in the facade.

41) This Oktave may well also be called Halbprincipal, because it is only half as large as the Principal. For example, at Bernau in the Mark [Brandenburg] there is a Halbprincipal or Oktave 4′ in conjunction with the Principal 8′; see Praetorius, vol. 11, p. 176f. The author has also cited this term in §.177 below. [Albrecht]

doch allezeit bey Principal 8′ ist. In der Dresdener Orgel ist im Pedale Superoktave 1′, 2′, 4,′ 8′ und 16′. NB. obwol kein Principal 32′ da ist; so heißt doch die Oktave 16′ nur Oktave, und nicht Principal; sie wird also inwendig stehen und von Holz seyn, und in Ansehung des Subbasses also heißen; wiewol ich mich nicht besinne, ob ich ihn daselbst 32′ angetroffen. Wo aber Principal 32′ ist, da heißt 16′ freylich Oktave, wie z. Ex. zu Hamburg in der großen Nikolaiorgel, auch zu St. Jakobi daselbst. Großoktave 8′ ist zu Görlitz, und heißt auch Tubal: denn Tubal oder Thubal ist so viel als Okave, wie Boxberg in deren Beschreibung meldet. So ist, teste Prætorio, Thubalflötchormaß, d. i. 8′ Thubalflötoktave, d. i. 4′, zu Breslau eine Oktave auf Flötenart; oder auch nur eine schlechte Oktave. Denn so heißt auch die Oktave 4′ Tubalflöte in Görlitz, wobey Boxberg erinnert, sie heiße bloß zum Unterschiede also. Ebendaselbst ist auch Oktave 4′ unter dem Namen Jubal. Bey den Griechen heißt die Oktave διὰ πασῶν. Daher auch diese Namen von der Oktave in Orgeln gebraucht werden. So ist zu Sendomir Regula Diapason 4′; Superoctaua, oder Disdiapason 2′; Superoctaua; oder Disdisdiapason 1′. Nachdem nun das Principal ist, so heißt auch entweder 8′ oder 16′ oder 4′ Diapason, und die Kleinern nach Proportion. S. Superoctaua aber soll ein Oktave anzeigen, welche noch kleiner ist, als Superoctaua, welche einige Supersuperoctauam nennen. Eben daselbst ist Principal im Rückpositive 4′, Diapason 8′ Disdiapason 2′. Dies scheint verdruckt zu seyn. Das Principal wird wol 8′ seyn sollen. Decima quinta, (welcher Name vorher erwähnt worden) ist eigentlich so viel, als Octaua composita, oder Superoctaua. So findet man es z. B. in Cambery. Eben daselbst ist auch Vigesima secunda fortis. Dies wäre noch um eine Oktave höher. Fortis bedeutet, daß es eine scharfe Intonation habe. Vigesima secunda suauis, und Octaua suauis, welche beyde daselbst ebenfalls angetroffen werden, haben eine liebliche und sanftklingende Intonation. Oktavenbaß ist auch bekannt genug. Er stehet 16′ zu Görlitz. Zuweilen aber führt 32′ und 16′ zugleich den Namen Principal. Oktave 1′, heißt auch Sifflöt, davon unten. Cymbeloktave 1′ ist §. 134. erklärt worden. Im Löbenicht zu Königsberg stehet im Pedale Principal 16′, Oktave 8′, Superoktave 4′, und S. Superoktave 4′; das letzte muß wol 2′ heißen. Oktave 6′ ist zu St. Petri in Hamburg, d. i. vom F an gezählet, (conf. §. 213.) s. Prätor. l. c. Doch genug zu einer Einleitung von der Oktave.

§. 172.

Oktavengemshorn. s. Gemshorn §. 153.

Oktavagiol kömmt beym Prätorio vor in der Orgel zu St. Ulrici in Magdeburg S. 174. Mehr weis ich nicht davon. Vielleicht ist es allda eine Oktave 4′, weil Principal 8′ und Superoktave dabey stehen. Wiewol die letztere in einem Clavicre zwey mal stehet, und Sedetz noch dazu, diese aber stehet etwann für 1′, da sie doch nach der Rechnung 2′ halten sollte. Oder sie sind vielleicht nach zweyerley Mensur gearbeitet.

Offen

ent. In the pedal of the organ at Dresden there are Superoktave 1′, 2′, 4′, 8′ and 16′.[*] N.B. Although no 32′ Principal is present, the Oktave 16′ is still called just Oktave and not Principal; it must stand inside [the case] and be made of wood, and be given this name in view of the Subbass [32′?], though I do not recall encountering one of those at 32′ there.[†] Where there is a 32′ Principal, then the 16′ is of course called Oktave, as e.g. at Hamburg in the large organ at St. Nikolai and also in St. Jakobi. There is a Grossoktave 8′ at Görlitz, also called Tubal; Tubal or Thubal is the same as Oktave, as Boxberg reports in its description.[‡] Thus at Breslau Thubalflötchormass (i.e., at 8′) and Thubalflötoktave (i.e., 4′) are according to Praetorius a flute-like Oktave, or just an ordinary Oktave.[§] The Oktave 4′ at Görlitz is likewise called Tubalflöte, concerning which Boxberg mentions that this name is only for the sake of distinction.[¶] The Oktave 4′ also stands there under the name Jubal. Among the Greeks the Oktave is called διὰ πασῶν [dia pason]; thus this name is also used in organs for the Oktave. Therefore at Sendomir there is *Regula diapason* 4′, Superoctava or *Disdiapason* 2′, and [S.[∥]] Superoctava or *Disdisdiapason* 1′. The 8′, the 16′ or the 4′ may be called Diapason, according to the [length of the] Principal. *S. Superoctava*, however, should indicate an Oktave that is even smaller than Superoctava; some refer to this as "Supersuperoctava". Also at Sendomir are Principal 4′, *Diapason* 8′ and *Disdiapason* 2′ in the Rückpositiv. This appears to be a misprint. It is the Principal that ought to be as 8′. *Decima quinta* (a name mentioned above) is actually the same as *Octava composita* or Superoctava. It is found thus at Chambery, where there is also a *Vigesima secunda fortis*; this [latter] would be yet another octave higher. *Fortis* means that it is voiced strongly. *Vigesima secunda suavis* and *Octava suavis*, both of which are also encountered at Chambery, are voiced to be lovely and gentle-sounding. [The term] Oktavenbass is also familiar enough; it stands at 16′ at Görlitz. At times both 32′ and 16′ alike bear the name Principal. The 1′ Oktave is also called Sifflöt; see below [under Sifflöte, §.192]. Cymbeloktave 1′ is explained in §.134. In the Löbenichtkirche at Königsberg there stand in the pedal Principal 16′, Oktave 8′, Superoktave 4′ and S. Superoktave 4′; the last must mean "2′". At St. Petri in Hamburg there is an Oktave 6′, i.e., counting from F upwards (cf. §.213); see Praetorius, *l.c.*[, p. 169]. But this is enough to introduce the Oktave.

§. 172.

OKTAVENGEMSHORN, see Gemshorn, §. 153.

OKTAVAGIOL appears in Praetorius in the organ at St. Ulrich in Magdeburg, [*Syntagma musicum*, Vol. II,] p. 174. I know nothing more about it. Perhaps it is an Oktave 4′ there, since a Principal 8′ and a Superoktave are present. The latter, though, appears twice in the same keyboard, with a Sedetz there as well. Perhaps [the Sedetz] stands for a 1′, though it is normally considered a 2′. Or perhaps they[**] are constructed according to two different scales.

---

[*] There are Principals at these pitches in the Altdresdener organ (i.e., the organ of the Dreikönigskirche); see Mattheson's Appendix to Niedt, Part Two, p. 170, as well as the stoplist of the Alt-Dresdener organ in Chapter 10.

[†] The reference is obscure. There is no Oktave 16′ in the Dresden Dreikönigskirche organ, only a Principal 16′; there is likewise a 16′ Subbass, but not one at 32′.

[‡] See Boxberg, *Beschreibung der Görlitzer Orgel*, p.[17].

[§] Yet another obscure reference; Praetorius, p. 171, lists these stops, but says nothing about either of them.

[¶] Boxberg, p.[17].

[∥] "S." (i.e., "Super") appears in the Sendomir stoplist in Mattheson's Appendix to Niedt's Second Part, p. 196; its omission here is an oversight, since Adlung discusses "S. Superoctava" immediately below.

[**] i.e., the two Superoktaves? (this passage is equally confused in the original German).

Offen ist ein solches Wort, welches zu etlichen Stimmen einer Orgel gesetzt wird, und nur bedeutet, daß die Pfeifen nicht gedeckt seyn, ohne in der Mensur etwas besonders zu haben. Zuweilen aber hat es etwas besonders. So ist in der Breslauischen Orgel bey Prätorio: **Offen Chormaß besondere Art.** Was Chormaß sey, s. oben in C. §. 125. In eben der Disposition findet man auch **Offen Oktave**, d. i. 4', welches wol nichts besonders ist. It. Sedecima offen, 2 mal, auch Supersedecima offen; mag auch wol nur eine gemeine Oktave seyn. Daselbst steht auch ausdrücklich: Sedecima offen, principalart; it. ist Sedecima und Supersedecima offen daselbst auf andere Art. Wo sonst das Wort offen vorkömmt, da schlage man allezeit das dabey befindliche Hauptwort auf. Z. E. **Offener Subbaß.** s. Subbaß. ꝛc. ꝛc.

Offenflöt, heißt aperta, oder tibia aperta bey den Lateinern, und findet man den lateinischen Namen zu Sandomir, da sie 4' ist. Der Name zeigt schon an, daß es kein gedackt Register sey. Zu Danzig in der Marienkirche ist die Offenflöte auch, da heißt sie zugleich Viol, und ist 3'; also wäre es eine offene Quintflöte. s. Prätor. S. 162. l. c. 4' ist sie auch in der Pfarrkirche zu Danzig 2 mal; it. zu St. Marien, und zu St. Johannis daselbst; zu Insterburg in Preussen; zu Königsberg im Kneiphofe; it. in der Altstädter Orgel daselbst, wie auch in der Pfarrorgel eben daselbst; zu St. Dominico in Prag; zu Rudolstadt, und zu Görlitz, wobey Boxberg sagt, diese offene Fleut mit dem groß Principal 16' Oktava oder Violdigamba 8' gezogen, lasse sich bey einer starken Musik wohl hören, und überschreye sie nicht, weil sie stumpfer ist als Oktave und Salicet. Quintviol ist die Quinte der Viol. Vergleiche §. 204. Offenflöt 8' und 4' ist zu Uns. L. Fr. in Lübeck; 4' von Elfenbein zu Bückeburg. von beyden s. Prätor. l. c.

Offenquerflöte. s. Querflöte.

§. 173.

Onda maris, oder besser **Vnda maris**, dieß Register soll in manchen Orgeln die strudlenden Wasserwellen vorstellen. Auf deutsch heissen vorhin angeführte Wörter, das Meerwasser. Es steht dieß Register in Görlitz 8'. Boxberg giebt uns davon diese Beschreibung: Onda maris 8', welche (Stimme) ein hölzern Principal ist, klingt noch annehmlicher, (als das, wovon er vorhin geredet) und ist zur schwachen Musik bequemer, als das Principal. Sie wird zu keinem Register mehr als zum Principale gebraucht, über welches sie ein wenig höher gestimmt ist, und daher eine artige Schwebung erhält, gleichsam als wie ein Wasser, von einem gelinden Winde bewegt, kleine fluctus macht. Daher sie auch den Namen empfangen. Daß sie aber etwas höher gestimmt, ist gegen das gelinde gezogene Pedal beym Generalbasse wenig zu merken, weil der schwebende Effekt mehr in Accorden zu hören, wenn sie mit dem Principal gezogen. Diese Stimme klingt, als ob sie von Zinn wäre, wozu die Invetriatur das meiste hilft. In Waltershausen ist Vnda maris 8 Fuß eine Pfeife mit doppelten labiis, welche 2 Klänge

Ch. VII. Concerning Stops in General and in Particular

OFFEN [open] is a word placed with certain organ stops, merely indicating that the pipes are not stopped, and having nothing in particular to do with the scaling. At times, though, it does indicate something particular. Thus in the Breslau organ Praetorius gives: "Offen Chormass besondere Art."* For the meaning of "Chormass", see above under "C", §.125. In the same stoplist there is also "Offen Oktave", i.e., 4'; that is surely nothing out of the ordinary. "Sedecima offen" likewise [appears] twice, as well as "Supersedecima Offen"; [the latter] may well be an ordinary Oktave [1']. There [in the Breslau stoplist] is expressly stated: "Sedecima offen, principal-like, and also Sedecima and Supersedecima offen, of another sort." Wherever the word "offen" appears, consult the primary word found with it; e.g., Offener Subbass, see Subbass, etc.

OFFENFLÖT means *aperta* [open] or *tibia aperta* [open flute] in Latin; the Latin names are found at Sandomir, where this flute is at 4'. The name already indicates that it is not a stopped register. There is also an Offenflöte in the Marienkirche at Danzig, where it is called Viol at the same time and is a 3'; thus it would be an open Quintflöte; see Praetorius, *l.c.*, p. 162. It appears twice as a 4' in the Pfarrkirche at Danzig, as well as at St. Marien and St. Johannis in the same city; at Insterburg in Prussia; in the Kneiphofkirche, the Altstädterkirche organ and the Pfarrkirche organ at Königsberg; at St. Dominicus in Prague; at Rudolstadt; and in Görlitz, concerning which Boxberg says that this open flute, drawn with the Gross Principal 16' and the Oktave or Violdigamba 8', sounds particularly well in loud ensemble music, and does not stick out, since it is duller than the Oktave and Salicet.† Quintviol is the Quinte of the Viol; see §.204.‡ There is an Offenflöte at 8' and one at 4' at the Marienkirche in Lübeck, and also one at 4', made of ivory, at Bückeburg; for both of these, see Praetorius.§

OFFENQUERFLÖTE, see Querflöte.

§. 173.

ONDA MARIS, or better *Unda maris*, is a stop that represents swirling waves of water in some organs. The words cited above mean "ocean water" in German.¶ At Görlitz this stop stands at 8'. Concerning it Boxberg gives us this description: "*Onda maris* 8', a stop that is a wooden Principal, sounds even more pleasant,‖ and is more suitable for soft ensemble music than the Principal.** It is used with no other stop than the Principal, and is tuned a bit sharp to it, and thus produces a continuous, agreeable undulation, just as water, when agitated by a gentle wind, produces small waves. Thence it gets its name. When it is played in figured bass above a gentle pedal registration, it is hardly noticeable that it is tuned somewhat sharp, since the undulating effect is perceived more in chords if it is drawn with the Principal. This stop sounds as if it were of tin, an effect produced mostly by the Invetriatur."†† At Waltershausen the *Unda*

---

* Vol. II, p. 171.

† See Boxberg, p.[14].

‡ §.204 makes it clear that Quintviol is considered by some a synonym for Offenflöt; cf. the remark earlier in this entry about the "Offenflöte or Viol 3'" at the Marienkirche in Danzig.

§ *Syntagma musicum*, Vol. II, pp. 166 & 185.

¶ This translation is incorrect; the Latin *Unda maris* means "wave of the sea."

‖ Adlung writes "annehmlicher," but Boxberg writes "*delikater,*" making it clear that the *Onda maris* is softer than the Principal 8' on the Oberwerk, with which it is paired.

** In his previous paragraph, p. [14], Boxberg has recommended the use of the Oberwerk Principal 8' "for figured bass in a moderately loud ensemble (*Concert*, das nicht allzu starck gebraucht werden). He now proposes the *Onda maris* for the figured bass registration in soft ensemble music, and continues by saying that its being tuned slightly sharp is not noticeable in ensemble music. It is clear that Boxberg is not proposing that the Principal and *Onda maris* be drawn together for figured bass realizations.

†† See §.38 above. The entire passage in quotation marks is a (selective) quote from Boxberg, p.[15].

120   Kap. VII. Von den Registern überhaupt und insonderheit.

Klänge hören läßt, davon der eine etwas höher ist, als der andere. Zu St. Wenceslai in Naumburg ist diese Stimme auch, und geht von a bis oben durch. Sonst habe ich diese Art nicht gesehen, auch von derselben nichts gehöret.

§. 174.

Passunen. s. §. 176.
Pastorita ist das Nachthorn. s. §. 168.
Pauke. s. unten Tympanum. §. 203.
Päurlin. s. Bäuerlein §. 121.
Pedalkoppel. s. in Coppel §. 127.
Perduna. s. Bordun §. 124.

Petite soll der Name einer Orgelstimme zu Anspach seyn. Dieß Wort zeigt was kleines an, und man könnte etwan das Flageolet, Schwiegel 1′ u. d. gl. darunter verstehen.

Pfeiferflöte ist die gedeckte Quinte 3′ Ton, wie sie von etlichen genennet wird. s. Prätor. l. c. S. 139. Nasat, welches §. 169 beschrieben worden, ist nach einiger Meynung eben das. s. Anleitung S. 436. Anmerk. (m.) allwo ich angeführt, daß Gregorius Vogel die gedeckte Quinte 3′ Pfeiferflöte genennet. Weil Nasat weder allemal gedeckt, noch jedesmal eine Quinte ist; so thut man besser, beyde für verschiedene Stimmen zu halten.

§. 175.

Phocinx. s. Krumhorn. §. 164.
Piffaro. s. Schallmey. §. 186.
Pileata.
Pileata minor.
Pileata maior. } von allen diesen s. §. 150. Gedackt.
Pileata maxima.
Pileata diapente.

Platterspiel wird von Werkmeistern in der Orgel zu Grüningen mit angeführet §. 46; er setzt aber nicht dazu, was es damit zu sagen habe.

Plockflöte }
Plockpfeife } s. in Blockflöte §. 122.

Pommer.
Pombart.
Pomart. } s. theils §. 159. bey der Hautbois; theils §. 123. bey Bombarda.
Pömmert.
Pombarda.

Portunen. s. Bordun. §. 124.

§. 176.

maris 8′ is a rank with double lips that produces two sounds, one of which is somewhat sharper than the other. This stop is also found at St. Wenceslaus in Naumburg, commencing with tenor a. I have not seen or heard anything else about this sort [of stop].

§. 174.

PASSUNEN, see §.176.

PASTORITA is the Nachthorn; see §.168.

PAUKE, see below under Tympanum, §.203.

PÄURLIN, see Bäuerlein, §.121.

PEDALKOPPEL, see under Coppel, §. 127.

PERDUNA, see Bordun, §.124.

PETITE is reported to be the name of an organ stop at Ansbach. This [French] word indicates something that is small, and perhaps [this stop] may be understood as a Flageolet, Schwiegel 1′ or something of that sort.

PFEIFERFLÖTE, as some call it, is a stopped Quinte of 3′ pitch; see Praetorius, *l.c.*, p. 139.* The Nasat, described in §.169, is in the opinion of some the same thing; see the *Anleitung, p.* 436, note (m),† where I have mentioned that Gregorius Vogel calls the stopped Quinte 3′ a Pfeiferflöte. Since the Nasat is neither always stopped nor always a Quinte, if would be better to consider each of these as a separate stop.

* actually p. 140.

† This should read "note (h)."

§. 175.

PHOCINX, see Krumhorn, §.164.

PIFFARO, see Schallmey, §.164.

PILEATA.
PILEATA MINOR.
PILEATA MAJOR. } for all of these see Gedackt, §.150.
PILEATA MAXIMA.
PILEATA DIAPENTE.

PLATTERSPIEL is cited by Werkmeister in [his publication about] the organ at Gröningen, §.46; he does not have anything to say anything about it, though.

PLOCKFLÖTE
PLOCKPFEIFE } see under Blockflöte, §. 122.

POMMER.
POMBART.
POMART. } see variously §.159 under Hautbois and
PAMMERT.   §.123 under Bombarda.
POMBARDA.

PORTUNEN, see Bordun, §.124.

§. 176.

Posaune, Posaunenbaß, ist ein gar bekannt Register, und zwar ist es ein offenes Pedalschnarrwerk, und wol unter allen das stärkeste und nachdrücklichste. Man hat dessen Größe 32′, 16′ und 8′; doch nur am Tone: denn die Körper findet man selten, oder niemals, so lang, und ist auch dieses nicht nöthig. Prätorius sagt, der Posaunenbaß 16′ werde am besten gemacht von 12füßigen Körpern; und so bekommt er schon die gehörige Gravität: denn in Schnarrwerken kann die Tiefe auch bey kleinen Körpern seyn. (confer. §. 105.) Daher nach Proportion die 32füßigen etwann 24′, die 8füßigen 6 Fuß groß seyn könnten. Wollte man sagen: wenn die Tiefe bey kleinern Körpern auch zu erhalten, warum nimmt man dieselben so groß? dem dient zur Antwort, daß dem zwar so sey; allein bey einer solchen Tiefe der kleinen Körper ist die gehörige force und Gravität nicht, so wenig, als ein kleiner Junge den Baß singen kann: und wenn mancher noch so tief singt; so kann doch wol demselben die Stärke und die Gravität mangeln. Etliche machen sie auch kleiner, und nehmen 5′ oder 6′ zu der 16 füßigen Posaune: und um die Intonation auch in der Tiefe leichter zu erhalten, decken sie dieselbe etwas, doch so, daß oben ein Loch bleibt. Da aber die Körper so kleine sind; so ist auch der Klang gar flach und platt weg. s. Prätor. l. c. S. 142. Die Materie, von welcher die Körper der Posaunen verfertiget werden, ist zuweilen Zinn, auch Meßing, welches aber sehr kostbar ist; zuweilen Blech, und alsdann muß man sie recht stark machen, sonst rasselt der Körper mit, da doch nur das Mundstück allein klingen sollte. Am gemeinsten und besten macht man die Posaune von Holz, und da jene rund werden, so bekommen dagegen die hölzernen eine viereckigte Figur. Sie klingen gut und stehen vest; die Körper bewegen sich nicht so leicht, daher nicht sowol die Materie klingt, als das Mundstück. Ueberall aber sind die Körper unten enge und oben weit. Die Köpfe sind viereckigt, wie auch die Stiefel; die Mundstücke und Blätter müssen stark seyn, damit sie nicht fladdern. Man versieht diese Blätter meistens mit Krücken, wie andere Rohrwerke; aber wenn man Schrauben bekommen kann, so ists desto besser, und lassen sie sich geschwinder und auch accurater stimmen: oder noch besser sind Krücken und Schrauben zugleich, wie z. E. in Jena. Die Krücken werden besser geschmiedet, als von Drat gemacht. Die eisernen werden verstaniolt, daß sie nicht rosten: die stählernen aber nicht, daß sie nicht weich werden. Wo man dazu kommen kann im Stimmen, ists besser, sie haben keinen Haken, um sie heraus nehmen zu können. s. was §. 105. steht. Prätorius l. c. erinnert, daß die Körper, ob sie schon ihre Größe nicht haben, die der Sonus anzeigt, doch müßten proportionirt seyn. Also würde 24′, 16′, 12′, 8′, 6′, ꝛc. den Klang leicht von sich hören lassen, den man verlangt: da hingegen eine Zahl, die ungeschickt aussieht, auch im Klange nicht wohl zu hören. Also würde eine Pfeife 10½′ lang schwerlich den 16füßigen Ton von sich geben, da es doch 8′ thut, so kleiner, und 12′, so größer ist. Was das für raison habe, ist hier zu untersuchen zu weitläuftig; genug, daß die Proportion der großen Körper gegen die kleinern richtig seyn muß, sonst klingen sie nicht nach Proportion schwach oder gravitätisch. Wenn man unten mit

§. 176.

POSAUNE or POSAUNENBASS is a very familiar stop, an open pedal reed, and is the strongest and most emphatic of all [reeds]. It comes in 32′, 16′ and 8′ sizes, but these are only with regard to pitch, for the resonators are seldom if ever found this long, nor is this necessary. Praetorius says the Posaunenbass 16′ is best constructed with 12′ resonators,* and in this way it acquires the requisite gravity. Note that a low pitch may be [achieved] with shorter resonators (cf. §.105). Thus according to proportion the 32′ could be about 24′ and the 8′ about 6′ [tall]. Should someone ask "Why make the resonators so large if the low pitch can be achieved with smaller ones," let this answer suffice: this is indeed the case, except that the proper force and gravity cannot be achieved at such low pitches with the small resonators any more than a little boy can sing bass. Even if many [boys] sing that low, [their voices] most certainly lack strength and gravity. Some [builders] make [the resonators] smaller, [giving] a 16′ Posaune a 5′ or 6′ resonator. Then, in order more easily to preserve the voicing in the low register, they stop them to some degree, leaving a hole in the top. But since the resonators are so small, the sound goes accordingly quite flat and dull; see Praetorius, *l.c.*, p. 142. The material from which the resonators of Posaunes are constructed is sometimes tin, but [sometimes] also brass (which is however very expensive), sometimes sheet iron, in which case they have to be made very strong or otherwise the resonator rattles along, when only the shallot should sound. While these metal ones are made round, the Posaune is best and most commonly made of wood, and wooden ones are on the other hand made in a quadrangular shape. [The wooden ones] sound well and are stable; their resonators are not so easily set into vibration, and thus the material† does not sound along with the shallot. The resonators are uniformly made narrow at the bottom and wide at the top. The blocks are quadrangular, as are the boots. The shallots and reed tongues must be strong so that they do not flutter. The reeds are usually provided with tuning wires, like other reeds, but if screws are available, all the better; these allow more rapid and accurate tuning. Crooks and screws together are even better, as e.g. [in the Stadtkirche] at Jena.‡ It is better to forge the crooks than to make them of wire. The iron ones are plated with tin so that they do not rust, but the steel ones are not, so that they do not become soft.§ If [the Posaune pipes] are accessible for tuning, it is better that they have no latches,¶ so that they may be taken out; see what is said in §.105. Praetorius, *l.c.*[, p. 142], mentions that the resonators, although they are not of the full length indicated by the pitch, must nevertheless be in proportion. Thus 24′, 16′, 12′, 8′, 6′, etc., can easily produce the required pitch, while on the other hand a number that looks awkward will not produce the pitch well. Thus a pipe 10 ½′ long would produce a 16′ pitch only with difficulty, whereas an 8′, which is shorter, would do it, as would a 12′ which is longer. The reason for this is too detailed to examine here; suffice it to say that the proportion of the large resonators in relation to the small ones must be correct, otherwise they will sound proportionately weaker or fuller. If the lowest pipe begins with an awkward number, then the cal-

* *Syntagma musicum*, Vol. II, p. 142.

† i.e., the wood.

‡ See the stoplist of the organ at Jena in Chapter 10.

§ In the process of reheating the steel tuning wires to plate them with tin, they lose their temper and again become soft.

¶ i.e., to attach the block and resonator to the boot. In §.105 Adlung uses the term "Haken" to refer to the devices that anchor the resonator to the block, and the term "Vorschlage" (latches) to describe the devices that secure the block and resonator to the boot. Here the context suggests that he means the latter, even though he writes "Haken".

keiner geschickten Zahl anhebt, so wird auch die Rechnung schwerer. Wenn ferner die Mundstücke länglicht und schmal sind, so geben sie vielmehr einen lieblichern Klang, als wenn sie breit und kurz sind, (sagt Prätorius l. c. S. 143.;) doch sind alle enge Mensuren nicht so leicht zu intoniren. ⁴²) Eine Tugend der Posaune ist, daß sie nicht so sehr rassele, oder knastere, welches geschiehet, wenn die starken messingenen Blätter ohne Unterlaß auf die harten Mundstücke schlagen. Dieses zu vermeiden, füttert man billig die Mundstücke mit Leder aus. Buccina ist der lateinische Name der Posaune, unter welchem sie Samber 153. unter die Manualstimmen zählet, und zwar von Zinn gearbeitet. Wollte etwan jemanden wunderlich scheinen, die Posaune 8' zu haben, da es doch ein grober Baß seyn solle, der erwäge, daß man ausser der Orgel auch kleine und große, Alt- Tenor- und Baßposaunen hat, die alle von der Trompete unterschieden sind, und haben weitere Körper, auch stärkere Blätter, als die Trompeten von gleichem Tone. Doch wer darauf nicht genau Acht hat, der verwechselt auch leichtlich die Namen mit einander, wie denn die Posaune 8' bey Prätorio im Dom zu Magdeburg bey den dasigen Domküstern Trompet heißt. Posaune 32' ist rar; doch ist sie im Dom zu Bremen, unter dem Namen der Contraposaune, und ist eine andere Posaune 16' noch dabey. Posaune 32' und 16' ist auch zu St. Johannis in Lüneburg, deren jene halb von Holz seyn soll. 32' und 16' ist zu Hamburg in der großen Orgel zu St. Nikolai; it. zu Königsberg im Löbenicht; it. zu St. Jakobi in Hamburg; it. zu St. Catharinen daselbst; zu St. Michaelis in Lüneburg; it. zu Mühlhausen in Thüringen in der Hauptkirche B. M. V; 16' steht eben daselbst in der Hauptkirche D. Blasii; beyde aber trift man noch an zu St. Dominico in Prag; zu Magdeburg in der Johanniskirche; (s. §. 308.) it. zu Reval, (s. §. 313.) und im Dom zu Upsal; sonst ist 32' allein in Stockholm, und in Waltershausen. In der Orgel zu St. Marien in Lübeck ist Großposaune 24' und Posaune 16'. Was 24' bedeuten sollen, weis ich nicht. Vielleicht ist das größte Korpus 24 Fuß lang; der

42) Um die Posaune prächtig, und nicht etwann wie ein Jungferregal zu intoniren, macht man die Zungen und Kellen besser lang, schmahl und stark, als kurz, breit und schwach, wie als hier in der Obermarktskirche B. M. V. an der Posaune 32' und 16' zu sehen, welche beyde stark gefüttert, dahero auch sehr donnern und schüttern: nicht aber (wie man vielmals anderwärts hört) auf eine elende Weise rasseln. Doch ist die Größe des Körpers, wie oben ganz recht erinnert worden, die Hauptursache dieses donnernden Klanges: denn der hölzerne Körper von der Posaune 16' ist 12', und wol noch etwas drüber, und der hölzerne Körper von der Posaune 32' ist gut 24' groß; obgleich, wegen Mangel der Höhe, von den größten Pfeifenkörpern etliche haben müssen gekröpfet werden. Die Körper von beyden sind überdieß noch sehr weit. Das Gegentheil von dem hier angeführten findet sich an der Posaune 16' in hiesiger Untermarktskirche Div. Blasii. Denn da sind Zungen und Kellen kurz, breit und schwach, und der Körper in C. kaum 8' lang, und noch dazu sehr enge, daher man beym Gebrauch dieser Posaune wol ein Fladdern und Rasseln, aber keinen Posaunenton, vernimmt. Starker Wind gehört auch zu solchen pompösen Schnarrwerken: und wo der ist, da kann man Posaune 32' und 16' glücklich zusammen ziehen, wie z. E. in hiesiger Obermarktskirche B. M. V. da die drey Pedalbälge 40 volle Grad, und die Manualbälge 36 Grad Wind geben.

culation will also be more difficult. Furthermore, if the shallots are oblong and narrow they will produce a much more gentle tone than if they are wide and short (so says Praetorius, *l.c.*, p. 143); all narrow scales, on the other hand, are not as easy to voice.[42)] It is a virtue if a Posaune does not rattle or crackle so much, which happens if the strong brass tongues beat continuously upon the hard shallots. To prevent this, the shallots are best faced with leather. *Buccina* is the Latin name for the Posaune; under this name Samber, p. 153, counts it among the manual stops, constructed of tin. If someone should perhaps think it strange to find an 8′ Posaune,[*] since it should be a heavy bass [stop], he should consider that there are also small and large, alto, tenor and bass Posaunes apart from the organ, all of which are different from the Trumpet, having broader bodies and stronger tongues than trumpets at the same pitch. Yet someone who does not pay precise attention to this can easily confuse the names with each other, just as the Posaune 8′ listed by Praetorius in the Cathedral at Magdeburg[†] is called Trompet by the Cathedral Sacristan there.[‡] The Posaune 32′ is rare; it is found in the Cathedral at Bremen, though, under the name Contraposaune, and a Posaune 16′ is also present. Posaune 32′ and 16′ are also at St. Johannis in Lüneburg, of which the former is half of wood. [Posaune] 32′ and 16′ are at Hamburg in the large organ at St. Nikolai, at St. Jakobi and at St. Catharine; likewise at Königsberg in the Löbenichtkirche, St. Michaelis in Lüneburg; also at Mühlhausen in Thuringia in the Hauptkirche B.M.V. (there is a 16′ [example] in the Hauptkirche Divi Blasii there). Both are encountered at St. Dominicus in Prague, at Magdeburg in the Johanniskirche (see §.308 [§]), at Reval (see §.313 [¶]) and at the Cathedral in Upsala. Moreover, it appears only at 32′ in Stockholm and in Waltershausen. In the organ at St. Marien in Lübeck there are Grossposaune 24′ and Posaune 16′. I do not know what 24′ is supposed to mean. Perhaps the longest resonator is 24′ long, but the sound 32′; or [perhaps] it be-

[*] i.e., rather than an 8′ Trompete.

[†] *Syntagma musicum*, Vol. II, p. 173.

[‡] See §.308; but it is obvious when comparing this stoplist with that given by Praetorius that the organ had undergone many changes between 1619 and the 1720's.

[§] The translation disregards the (superfluous) paragraph numbers in the collection of stoplists; see the stoplist of the organ at the Johanniskirche in Magdeburg in Chapter 10.

[¶] See the stoplist of the organ at Reval in Chapter 10.

[||] i.e., too weak and thin; with too little fundamental.

42) In order to voice the Posaune magnificently, and not like some kind of Jungferregal,[||] the tongues and shallots (Kellen) are better constructed long, narrow and strong than short, wide and weak, as may be seen here [at Mühlhausen] in the Obermarktskirche of the Blessed Virgin Mary in the Posaune 32′ and 16′, both of whose [shallots] are heavily faced [with leather]; thus they truly thunder and vibrate without that miserable rattling that one often hears elsewhere. However the size of the resonators is, as has been quite correctly noted above, the primary cause of this thundering tone, for the wooden resonator of the Posaune 16′ is 12′ and indeed a bit beyond that, and the wooden resonator of the Posaune 32′ is a full 24′ tall, although due to lack of height some of the largest resonators have had to be mitered. Moreover, the resonators of both [stops] are very wide. The opposite of what has just been described is to be found in the Posaune 16′ of the Untermarktskirche of St. Blasius here.[**] There the reed tongues and shallots are short, broad and weak, and the resonators barely 8′ long at low C; furthermore they are also very narrow, so that in using this Posaune one indeed perceives a fluttering and rattling, but no Posaune tone. Heavier wind [pressure] also suits such pompous reeds; where it is found, the Posaune 32′ and 16′ may happily be drawn togther, as e.g. in the Obermarktskirche B.M.V. here, in which the three pedal bellows produce a full 40 degrees of wind and the manual bellows 36 degrees.[††] [Albrecht]

[**] i.e., the organ whose rebuilding and expansion J.S. Bach oversaw in 1708f. Albrecht's remark seems to establish that Bach was not successful in achieving all the changes he listed as desirable for this organ in his Memorandum to the Church Council in 1708; cf. David, Hans T., and Arthur Mendel, rev. & enlarged by Christoph Wolff, *The New Bach Reader* (N.Y: W.W. Norton, c. 1998), p. 55 (Bach-Dokumente I, p. 152).

[††] See §.441.

Kap. VII. Von den Registern überhaupt und insonderheit. 123

der Klang aber 32′: oder sie fängt im F an, (conf. §. 213.) 16′ heißt zu Breslau Posaunenbaß Unterchormaß; 8′ aber Posaunenbaß Chormaß. Man sagt auch Posaunenuntersatz. Daher ist zu Halle in der Marienkirche Groberposaunenuntersatz 16′ s. Prätor. It. Subbaßposaunen 16′ zu Dresden im Schlosse, siehe Prätor. Im Schlosse zu Schöningen ist, nach Prätorii Erzählung, ganz vergoldete Posaune, dem äusserlichen Ansehen nach; sonsten soll es Kromhörnerart seyn; und so heißt daselbst das erste und vörderste Principal 8′. Da sind auch Posaunen auf Dolcianen Art. It. kleine Trompeten oder Posaunen zum vördersten Principal zum Augenschein, und daß es dem obersten Werke respondire; sind aber blind, und an deren Statt stehet eine Bärpfeife 8′. Posaunenuntersatz 32′ und 16′ zu Gera, s. §. 301. Zu Königsberg im Kneiphofe steht 16′ und 8′, und Trompete 8′ auch dabey im Pedale; daher man siehet, daß Posaune 8′ und Trompete 8′ nicht einerley seyn, indem die Trompete mehr sladdert, auch nicht gefüttert ist. Wie Anfangs gesagt worden, so gehört die Posaune ins Pedal: aber man findet dieselbe auch im Manual; doch selten. In Stockholm ist sie 16′, unter dem Namen der französischen Posaune: Ob vielleicht die Intonation angenehmer als sonst? weis ich nicht. Prätorius l. c. sagt: „In Hessen in einem Kloster ist eine sonderliche Art von Posaunen „gefunden worden, da auf das Mundstück ein meßingener Boden aufgelöthet, und in „der Mitte ein ziemlich länglicht Löchlein drinnen, darüber denn allererst das rechte „Züngelein oder Blättlein geleget, und mit geglüeten Sayten darauf gebunden wird, „daß es nicht allzusehr schnarren und plerren kann, und geht wie eine ordentliche Posau„ne, wenn man die Intonation trift, weil sie gedämpft ist, und doch so nicht schnarrt; „doch müssen sie gleichwol mit Auf= und Niederziehung des obersten Körpers gestimmt „werden." Zu Bückeburgt ist Posaune oder Bombardbaß 16′. s. Prätor. Soll also einerley seyn, da sie doch sonst unterschieden sind. (conf. §. 123.)

§. 177.

Pressior, s. Gedackt, §. 150.

Prästant, Primaria, Principal, ist alles einerley. Es ist dieses das vornehmste Register in der Orgel; deswegen ihm alle diese Namen beygeleget werden. Regula primaria heißt das vornehmste Register, und diese Benennung wird zu Sandomir gebraucht, s. Matthesons Anhang zum Niedt. Principal heißt eben so viel, und ist die gemeineste Benennung. [43]) Prästant, von præstans, kann so viel
bedeu=

Q 2

---

[43]) Das Wort Principal beziehet sich nicht nur auf die Größe, sondern auch bisweilen auf die Güte der Materie. Wenn z. B. ein zinnern Register von 4′ im Gesichte stehet, und inwendig ist ein metallenes 8′; so heißt man lieber das erstere Principal, weil es, theils wegen der Härte der Materie, besser klingt, theils auch, weil es in der Stimmung beständiger und reiner bleibt, so, daß man die übrigen Stimmen darnach stimmen kann. Man hat ohne Zweifel hierinne auf den Ursprung des Worts gesehen; weil princeps und primus oft eins ist: dies aber bedeutet was bey einer Orgel voran in Gesichte stehet. Diese besondere Bedeutung des Worts

Ch. VII. Concerning Stops in General and in Particular

gins at F (cf. §.213). The 16′ at Breslau is called Posaunenbass Unterchormass, while the 8′ is Posaunenbass Chormass. The term Posaunenuntersatz is also used; thus in the Marienkirche at Halle there is a Groberposaunenuntersatz 16′; see Praetorius.* In the palace at Schöningen, as Praetorius relates, there is a Posaune completely gilded, for the sake of appearance; moreover, it is said to be Krumhorn-like and is called the first and furthest forward Principal 8′† there. There are also Dolcian-like Posaunes; thus [Praetorius lists at Schöningen] a little Trompete or Posaune as the furthest forward Principal in the façade, belonging to the uppermost division; but it is mute, and in its place there is a Barpfeife 8′. At Gera are Posaunenuntersatz 32′ and 16′; see §.301.‡ In the Kneiphofkirche at Königsberg stand 16′ and 8′ [examples], along with Trompete 8′, in the pedal; thus one may see that Posaune 8′ and Trompete 8′ are not the same, since the Trompete vibrates more, and [its shallot] is not faced [with leather]. As stated at the beginning, the Posaune belongs in the pedal; yet they are also found in the manual, though rarely. There is one at 16′ in Stockholm, under the name French Posaune; whether this means that the intonation is perhaps more pleasant than usual, I do not know. Praetorius, *l.c.*[, p. 143], says, "In a monastery at Hesse is found a special type of Posaune in which a brass plate is soldered onto the shallot, with a somewhat oblong little hole in the middle of it. Only then is the actual tongue or reed laid on top of it and bound with red-hot wires. Thus it cannot rattle and howl too much, and behaves like an ordinary Posaune when it comes to voicing, since it is dampened and does not rattle. It must be tuned, however, by making the resonator above it it shorter or longer."§ At Bückeburg there is a Posaune or Bombardbass 16′; see Praetorius.¶ Here they must be the same, though as a rule they are different (see §.123).

* *Syntagma musicum*, Vol. II, p. 187.

† This is Adlung's interpretation of Praetorius's term "Principalia"; by this term Praetorius means the pipes seen in the façade.

‡ See the stoplist of the organ at Gera in Chapter 10.

§ i.e., it has no tuning wire.

¶ *Syntagma musicum*, Vol. II, p. 186.

§. 177.

Pressior, see Gedackt, §.150.

Prästant, Primaria, Principal, are all the same. This is the primary stop in an organ, and it is for this reason it is given these various names. *Regula primaria* means the primary stop, and this is the term used at Sandomir; see Mattheson's Appendix to Niedt[, pp. 196-7]. Principal means the same thing, and is the most common term.[43] Prästant, from *praestans*, may mean the same as "useful, excellent", yet it may also

---

43) The word "Principal" refers not only to the size, but also at times to the quality of the material. If, e.g., there is a 4′ stop in the façade of tin, and an 8′ within the case of [pipe] metal, then the former is preferably called Principal, since it sounds better, partly due to the hardness of the material, partly also because it stays more constant and pure in its tuning, and the other stops may be tuned from it. The reader has doubtless grasped the origin of the word, since *princeps* [Latin "prince"] and *primus* [Latin "first"] often mean the same thing; in an organ this signifies [the rank] that stands in the façade. I have noticed this special meaning of the word in Praetorius, specifically in

bedeuten, als: nützlich, vortreflich; doch kann es auch so viel heißen, als: was vornen stehet: denn die Principale stehen gemeiniglich vorn im Gesichte um den Staat zu vergrößern. Deswegen auch z. Ex. die Oktave 4′ in Alach Principal heißt, weil sie von Zinn gemacht ist, und im Gesichte stehet. Etliche heißen es Döeff, s. Prät. l. c. S. 127. Zu Sandomir heißt es auch Fourniture; wodurch sonst die Mixturen angedeutet werden: doch siehe davon oben §. 148. Ob Fond d'Orgue auch das Principal bedeute, ist oben §. 147. zu sehen. Zu Cambery heißt es Fundamentalis oder Grundstimme, s. de Chales Tom. III. p. 20. da er sagt: la Monstre sey französisch eben so viel; welche Bedeutung mir nicht bekannt, weil dies Wort sonst eine Mißgeburt anzeigt: man müßte es denn vom lateinischen monstrare, vorzeigen, ableiten wollen, aus der Ursach, weil das Principalregister im Gesichte stehet; aber auf solche Weise müßte es vielmehr montre (von montrer) heißen. Jedoch in uerbis simus faciles &c. Es sind die Principale Oktavenregister, daher ihre Proportion allezeit in folgenden Zahlen auszudrücken: 32′, 16′, 8′, 4′, 2′, und ihre Mensur ist die ordentliche, so, daß die Länge durch besagte Zahlen angedeutet wird, nach welcher die Breite einzurichten. Doch kann in der Mensur wol ein Unterschied seyn, und eins weiter als das andere gemacht werden; es muß nur nicht viel austragen, sonst verliehren sie den Namen. Das findet man auch zuweilen, daß in einer Orgel jedes Clavier eine besondere Mensur im Principale hat. So sind sie in Görlitz gemacht, da eins weitere, das andere engere Mensur hat; daher das Hauptwerk prächtig, das Oberwerk sehr spitzig und scharf, und das Brustpositiv scharf und angenehm klingt. Denn nach der Principalmensur sind auch alle Oktavenregister, oder andere, die die Principalmensur zu haben pflegen, zu machen; daher im ganzen Werke die Aenderung gespüret wird. Es ist, wie aus dem bisherigen, und aus dem §. 171. erhellet, unter den Principalen und Oktaven kein großer Unterschied; nur daß die Principale das beste Metall bekommen, damit die Stimmung reiner bleibe, weil darnach die ganze Orgel zu stimmen ist. Doch ist auch das Principal in jedem Claviere das größte unter den Oktavenregistern, und nachdem jenes ist, werden auch diese genennet. Zuweilen giebt man den Namen Prästant oder Principal der Oktave auch. Z. Ex. zu St. Ulrich in Magdeburg, bey Prätorio, ist Prästant 16′, und Principal 8′ in einem Claviere. Jedes Clavier in einer Orgel pflegt ein Principal zu haben. §. 171. ist angeführet, daß irgendwo Principal 4′ und Oktave 8′ sey; it. beydes 8′ ꝛc.; welches aber, wie dort erinnert, nicht recht ist. Die Oktaven sind kleiner als das Principal. Doch hat eine Gemeinde zuweilen zu großen Principalen keine Mittel; daher man sie von Holz macht, und setzt sie inwendig ein; da verliehren sie vielmals den Namen Principal, und heißen Oktaven:

Principal habe ich im Prätorio, und zwar in der Disposition der Dreßdener Schloßorgel, angemerkt: denn da steht unter dem Namen Principal eine Trommet 8′ ganz übergoldet; it. eine schöne zinnerne Oktave; it. schön zinnern Principal. Dabey steht: 3 Principale. Hernach steht wieder Regal ganz vergoldet 8′; it. Superoktave 2′; und Principal 4′. Dabey steht abermals: 3 Principale.

Ch. VII. Concerning Stops in General and in Particular

mean "that which stands in front", since Principals usually stand in the façade to increase the impression of splendor. It is for this reason that the Oktave 4′ at Alach is called Principal, because it is made of tin and stands in the façade.* Some call [the Principal] "Döeff"; see Praetorius, *l.c.*, p. 127. At Sandomir it is also called Fourniture, a term that normally indicates a mixture; concerning this, see §. 148 above. Whether *Fond d'Orgue* also means the Principal has already been discussed in §.147 above. At Chambery it is called *Fundamentalis* or foundation stop (Grundstimme); see DeChales, Vol. III, p. 20, where he says that the *Monstre* is the same thing in French. This meaning is unknown to me, since this word otherwise indicates a monster. [*Monstre* †] must be derived from the Latin *monstrare,* "to show, display", for the reason that the Principal rank stands in the facade; but in this case it ought rather to be called *montre* (from [the French] *montrer*). Yet *in verbis simus faciles, etc.* [let us not quibble over words]. Principals are octave [-speaking] stops, and thus their proportions are always to be expressed in the following numbers: 32′, 16′, 8′, 4′, 2′.‡ Their scale is the ordinary one, so that the widths are to be determined by the lengths indicated by the abovementioned numbers. But scales may indeed vary, and one be made wider than another; this must not be overdone, however, or otherwise they would lose the name [Principal].§ At times one may discover that each manual in an organ has its own particular scale for the Principal. This is the way they are made in Görlitz, where one has a wider scale, the other a narrower one. Thus the Hauptwerk is splendid, the Oberwerk very keen and sharp, and the Brustpositiv keen but gentle.¶ [The scales of] all the octave stops, or other [stops] that normally have principal scale, are determined by the scale of the Principal. Thus the variation is to be perceived throughout the entire organ. As is apparent from §.171 and from what has already been said, there is no great distinction between Principals and Oktaves, only that Principals get the best metal, so that their tuning remains purer, since the entire organ must be tuned from them. Yet the Principal is also the largest of the octave[-sounding principal] stops in each manual, and the names of the octaves are determined by it. Sometimes the name Prastant or Principal is also given to the Oktave; e.g., at St. Ulrich in Magdeburg there are Prastant 16′ and Principal 8′, according to Praetorius, on the same manual. Each manual in an organ normally has a Principal. §.171 mentions that at a certain place there is a Principal 4′ and an Oktave 8′,‖ and elsewhere both are at 8′,** but as was stated there, this is not correct.†† The octaves are smaller than the Principal. Yet at times a congregation does not have the means to afford large Principals; in that case they are made of wood and set inside the case, and then they often lose the name Principal, and are called Oktaves. The smaller [octave rank], however, the one [made] of

the stoplist of the Dresden palace organ[, p. 187]; a Trommet, completely gilded, stands there under the name Principal[ia], along with a beautiful tin Oktave and a beautiful tin Principal. Next to them ‡‡ stands [the indication] "3 Principale." §§ Later there appears "Regal, completely gilded, 8′," along with Superoktave 2′ and Principal 4′. Next to them again stands "3 Principale". [Albrecht]

---

* In the stoplist of this organ this stop is called Octave, not Principal; see the stoplist of the organ at Alach in Chapter 10.

† This is the old spelling of *Montre* that became obsolete during the 17th century.

‡ By this statement Adlung is not suggesting that mutation ranks cannot be of principal scale (see, e.g., §.179, "Quinta"), rather that only octave-sounding stops may bear the name "Principal".

§ i.e., they would become either strings or flutes.

¶ See Boxberg, p.[11].

‖ i.e., at Sendomir; see Mattheson's Appendix to Niedt, p. 196, as well as the stoplist of the organ at Sendomir in Chapter 10.

** i.e., in the Cathedral organ at Bremen; see Mattheson's Appendix to Niedt, p. 158, as well as the stoplist of the organ in the Cathedral at Bremen in Chapter 10.

†† i.e., it is a printing error.

‡‡ in the stoplist given by Praetorius.

§§ sic; should read "3 Principalia."

ven: das kleinere aber, so von gutem Metall ist, und im Gesicht stehet, wird Principal genennet. Auf solche Art wird wol Oktave 8' bey Principal 4' gefunden. Im Pedale hat man zuweilen Principale, als 32', 16', selten 8', als welches meistens Oktave genennet wird. Im Manuale sind sie nicht größer, als 16', 8', 4', und nicht kleiner als 2'. Das Principal 32' ist rar, und sehr kostbar, zumal da es im Gesichte von gutem Metall zu machen ist, wenn es, wie alle Principale, was taugen soll. Daher es auch bisweilen von Holz gemacht wird, oder doch nur was die größten Pfeifen betrift. Es schickt sich ins Manual gar nicht; denn es spricht so geschwinde nicht an, und ist mehr ein Sausen des Windes, als ein vernehmlicher Klang zu hören. Doch wenn andere Register dabey sind; so giebt es dem Werke eine Gravität. Wenn dies Principal im Pedale stehet; so heißt es zuweilen Großprincipalbaß, auch nur Principalbaß, oder Principal. Man findet auch den Namen Großbaß, z. Er. in Breslau, da Unterchorbaß, Chorbaß und Oktave dabey sind, d. i. 4', 8', 16', und 32'. Dieses letztere, nämlich Principal 32', ist zu St. Nikolai in Hamburg in der großen Orgel; it. zu St. Jakobi daselbst; it. zu Görlitz von englischem Zinn; es stehet aber nur bis ins F 24' ton im Gesichte (wie Borberg sagt) die tiefern Claves sind von Holz, und stehen inwendig; it. zu St. Catharinen in Hamburg; zu Cassel in der Freiheiterkirche; it. zu Buckeburgk ist Subprincipalbaß 32', ist aber eben das; zu St. Marien in Lübeck und zu St. Petri daselbst; zu St. Dominico in Prag, und im Dom zu Upsal. Zu U. L. Fr. in Halle ist Großprincipalunterbaß wol eben so wiel. Großprincipal 24' aus dem F (conf. §. 213.) ist zu St. Jakobi und zu St. Petri in Hamburg. Principalgroßerunterbaß bis F 24' ist im Dom zu Magdeburg, s. von allen diesen den Prätorium l. c. Principal 16' im Pedale ist schon gemeiner, als 32', und man trift sie beyde zuweilen in einer Orgel an. Eigentlich sollte das erstere gegen das letzte eine Oktave 16' heißen, wie auch vielmal geschiehet: aber man setzt es zuweilen ins Gesicht, sammt dem großen 32füßigen, und daher führt es auch nicht unbillig den Namen Principal. Im Manual ist Principal 16' rarer; doch giebt es eine feine Gravität, wenn man nur nicht so in der Tiefe zusammen greift. Es schlägt nothwendig 16' deutlicher und geschwinder an, als 32', wird auch von Werkmeistern demselben vorgezogen, der das 32füßige Principal Prahlsachte nennet, s. Orgelprobe S. 42. 16' wird auch eher zur reinen Intonation gebracht, als 32'. Im Manuale wird es ordentlich zum Hauptwerke gesetzt. Und so findet es sich z. Er. im Dom zu Bremen; daher heißt dasselbe Clavier, oder auch die ganze Orgel 16füßig. Wo nur Principal 8' oder 4' oder 2' ist, heißt es eine 8füßige, 4füßige und 2füßige Orgel. Z. U. L. Fr. in Bremen ist Principal 17': es ist aber wol verdruckt, und soll 16' heißen. Ich will hier einige Exempel beybringen, wo das 16füßige Principal angetroffen wird. Nämlich man findet es zu St. Johannis in Lüneburg; zu St. Lambrecht daselbst; zu St. Nikolai in Hamburg; zu St. Jacobi und St. Catharinen daselbst; zu Danzig in der Pfarrorgel; zur Dreyfaltigkeit und zu St. Johannis, wie auch zu St. Bartholomäi daselbst, wiewol an letzterm Orte 6' anstatt 16' ge-

Ch. VII. Concerning Stops in General and in Particular

good metal and standing in the case, is called Principal. In this manner it might indeed be possible to find an Oktave 8' with a Principal 4'.* In the pedal the Principals are sometimes 32', sometimes 16', but seldom 8', since this is usually called Oktave. In the manual they are never larger than 16', 8' or 4', and never smaller than 2'. The 32' Principal is rare and very expensive, especially since it needs to be made of good metal for the façade, if it (like all Principals) is to be worth its salt. Thus† it is sometimes also made of wood, at least as concerns the largest pipes. It is not at all suited for the manual, since it does not speak very quickly and is heard more as a gust of wind than as a perceptible pitch. Yet if it is used in combination with other stops it imparts a gravity to the ensemble. If this Principal stands in the pedal it is sometimes called Grossprincipalbass, but also only Principalbass or Principal. The name Grossbass is also found, e.g. in Breslau, along with Unterchorbass, Chorbass and Oktave, i.e., 32', 16', 8' and 4'. The Principal 32' is found in the large organ at St. Nikolai and at St. Jakobi in Hamburg; at Görlitz, [made] of English tin (it stands in the façade, though, only down to F 24' pitch, as Boxberg says; the pipes lower [than this] are wooden and stand inside the case;‡ at St. Catharine in Hamburg; in the Freiheiterkirche at Cassel; at Bückeburg the Subprincipalbass 32' is the same thing; at St. Marien and St. Petri in Lübeck; at St. Dominicus in Prague; and in the Cathedral in Upsala. At the Marienkirche in Halle the Grossprincipalunterbass is no doubt the same thing.§ The Grossprincipals at St. Jakobi and St. Petri in Hamburg begin at 24' (cf. §.213¶). There is a Principalgrossunterbass from F 24' in the Cathedral at Magdeburg; for all of these‖ see Praetorius, *l.c.* [, pp. 169, 170 and 172]. Principal 16' in the pedal is indeed more common than the 32'; at times they are both encountered in the same organ. The former should properly be called an Oktave 16' over against the latter, as often happens; yet sometimes it also not unjustly bears the name Principal. The Principal 16' is rarer in the manual, yet it lends an excellent gravity if only the player refrains from playing big chords in the bass. Naturally the 16' attacks more clearly and quickly than the 32'; Werkmeister prefers it to the latter, and calls the 32' ostentatious; see the *Orgelprobe*, p. 42.** The 16' is more likely to speak cleanly than the 32'. In the manual it is ordinarily placed in the Hauptwerk. That is the way it is, e.g., in the Cathedral at Bremen, and therefore that manual, or indeed the entire organ, is called "16-foot". Where there is only a Principal 8', 4' or 2', then the organ is called "8-foot", "4-foot", or "2-foot". At the Marienkirche in Bremen there is a Principal 17',†† but this is no doubt a misprint, and should read "16'". At this point I want to cite a number of examples where the 16' Principal is to be encountered. It is found at St. Johannis and St. Lambrecht in Lüneburg, at St. Nikolai, St. Jakobi, St. Catharine and St. Petri in Hamburg (it was also [found] there in the former Michaeliskirche organ], in the organs of the Pfarrkirche, the Dreifaltigkeitskirche, St. Johannis and St. Bartholomai at Danzig—although at the last-named place 6' is printed instead of 16'—, at Görlitz, where it is of English tin, at St. Petri in

---

* Cf. §.171 ("Oktave"), where Adlung censures calling an 8' (principal-scale) stop an "Oktave" when there is a Principal 4'.

† i.e., because it is so expensive.

‡ Boxberg, p.[17], says that these pipes are C, D, D# and E.

§ Neither Praetorius's nor Adlung's stoplist show such a stop in this organ. Praetorius lists one at the Marienkirche in Lübeck; see *Syntagma musicum*, Vol. II., p. 166.

¶ The translation disregards the (superfluous) paragraph numbers in the collection of stoplists; see the stoplists of these organs in Chapter 10.

‖ i.e., the two organs in Hamburg and the one in Magdeburg.

** This should read "p. 52."

†† See Mattheson's Appendix to Niedt, p. 161, as well as the stoplist of the organ in the Marienkirche at Bremen in Chapter 10.

druckt worden; zu Görlitz ist 16′ von englischen Zinn; zu St. Petri in Hamburg; (in der ehmahligen Michaelisorgel daselbst war es auch.) zu St. Petri in Lübeck; it. zu St. Marien daselbst im Werke. Die Disposition giebt hier auch 16′ in der Brust vor, so aber wol schwerlich recht ist. Zwey 16füßige Claviere in einer Orgel weiß ich nie. Vielleicht soll es 8′ heißen, zumal da die Oktave 8′ nicht da ist. It. zu St. Michaelis in Lüneburg; zu St. Lamberti daselbst; zu St. Dominico in Prag; zu St. Nikolai in Rostock; zu St. Cosmi in Stade; zu Stockholm; zu St. Nikolai in Stralsund; im Dom zu Upsal. Zu Rostock heißt es auch Weitprincipal, s. Prätor. S. 164. Großprincipal zu Breslau ist eben nichts anders, als Principal. 16′; zu St. Gotthard in Hildesheim findet man es unter dem Namen Großprästant 16′. Wenn es in einigen Orgeln 12′ angegeben wird, wie z. Ex. zu St. Jakobi und zu St. Petri in Hamburg; so fängt es im F. an, (conf. §. 213.) wie schon mehrmals erinnert worden. Zu Reval ist Principal 16′ von englischem Zinn, s. unten §. 313. Principal 8′ ist in den meisten Orgeln, und wenigstens in einem Claviere; zuweilen auch in 2 oder mehrern Clavieren. Es heißt auch Aequalprincipal, weil es an der Tiefe und Höhe der Menschenstimme gleich kömmt. It. Chormaßprincipal, (s. von Chormaß §. 125.) Es ist die beste Stimme in einer Orgel, und am schönsten zu gebrauchen. Principal 4′ ist in der Höhe so anmuthig nicht, als das vorige, daher ordentlich das Gedackt oder Quintatön 8′ dabey gezogen wird. Stillprincipal 4′ findet sich zu Waltershausen. It. Geigenprincipal 4′ ebendaselbst im Gesichte, sehr enge. Ist wol mit Viola eins; klingt auch so, wie eine continuirte Violdigamba. Principal 2′ ist noch geringer. Kleiner aber wird, wie schon gesagt, kein Principal genennet. Es kömmt in der Disposition der Orgel in der Kreutzkirche zu Dresden Principal 4′ im Pedale vor: allein man nennet es nie also, und ist folglich ein Fehler, und soll wol 16′ heißen, weil Oktave 8′ und 4′ dabey stehen. Zu St. Bartholomäi in Danzig ist in der Brust Principal 4′, und Oktave 8′. Vielleicht soll es umgekehrt seyn. In der Dresdener Schloßorgel ist Principal 8′ und noch lieblich Principal 8′ von Holz in einem Claviere. In der altstädtischen Orgel in der lutherischen Kirche zu Elbingen ist Principal 8′ von Metall, und Principal 8′ von Holz; ferner Principal 4′ von Holz, und noch Oktave 4′ alles in einem Claviere. Hölzern Principal 8′ ist zu Dresden im Schlosse: it. zu Hessen auf dem Schlosse 8′ von Holz, und noch Kleinprincipal 4′ von Elfenbein und Ebenholz; zu Sondershausen ist Hölzernprincipal 8′ enge, nebst Schönprincipal 8′; dies letztere wird von Zinn seyn. Von Doppelprincipal, s. oben §. 137. Halbprincipal ist die Oktave: [44]) Was aber Harfenprincipal zu Breslau bey Prätorio seyn soll, weiß ich nicht eigentlich. Was ich davon muthmaße, s. oben §. 158. Dulceon und Frontispicium sind auch ein paar Namen, die dem Principale beygeleget werden. Zu St. Petri in Hamburg ist 24′ im Pedale; nicht daß das C 24′ groß wäre, denn das gienge nicht an, sondern, daß es nur bis ins F reichet: die größere Pfeifen sind gar nicht da;

[44]) Hievon die 41ste Anmerkung bey §. 171.

Ch. VII. Concerning Stops in General and in Particular

Lübeck, and also at St. Marien there, where it is in the Werck. Here* the stoplist also gives a 16′ in the Brust[werk], but that can hardly be correct. I have never known an organ to have two 16-foot manuals. Perhaps it should read 8′, especially since the Oktave 8′ is not listed. There is also a 16′ Principal at St. Michaelis in Lüneburg, at St. Lamberti there,† at St. Dominicus in Prague, St. Nikolai in Stralsund, and in the Cathedral at Uppsala. At Rostock it is called Weitprincipal; see Praetorius, p. 164. The Grossprincipal at Breslau is surely nothing other than a Principal 16′. At St. Gotthard in Hildesheim it is found under the name Grossprastant 16′. If it is cited as 12′ in some organs, such as e.g. at St. Jakobi and St. Petri in Hamburg, then it begins at [low] F (cf. §.213‡), as has already been mentioned several times. At Reval there is a Principal 16′ of English tin; see §.313§ below. There is a Principal 8′ in most organs, at least in one manual; sometimes also in 2 or more manuals. It is also called Aequalprincipal because it matches the range of the human voice. It is likewise called Chormassprincipal (see Chormass, §.125). It is the finest stop in an organ, and the most beautiful to use. The Principal 4′ is not so pleasant in the upper register (in der Höhe) as the [Principal 8′], and thus a Gedackt or Quintatön 8′ is ordinarily drawn with it. There is a Stillprincipal 4′ at Waltershausen, as well as a Geigenprincipal 4′ at the same place, in the façade and of very narrow [scale]. It is no doubt the same as a Viola, and sounds like an extension of the Violdigamba. The Principal 2′ is even smaller. As has already been mentioned, however, nothing smaller [than 2′] is ever called Principal. A Principal 4′ appears in the pedal in the stoplist of the organ in the Kreutzkirche at Dresden; but a [4′ in the pedal] is never called by this name, and consequently this is a mistake.¶ It should read 16′, since Oktave 8′ and 4′ are present. In the Brust[werk] at St. Bartholomai in Danzig there are a Principal 4′ and Oktave 8′; perhaps it should be the reverse. In the Dresden palace organ there is a Principal 8′ together with a Lieblich Principal 8′ of wood, both on the same keyboard. In the Altstädtische organ in the Lutheran Church at Elbingen there is a Principal 8′ of metal and a Principal 8′ of wood, as well as a Principal 4′ of wood and an Oktave 4′, all on the same manual. There is a wooden Principal 8′ in the palace organ at Dresden,‖ and in the palace at Hesse there is also a wooden one at 8′, together with a Kleinprincipal 4′ of ivory and ebony. At Sondershausen there is a narrow-scale wooden Principal 8′, together with a Schönprincipal 8′, the latter being made of tin. Concerning the Doppelprincipal, see §.137 above. Halbprincipal is the Oktave.⁴⁴⁾ I do not really know, however, what Praetorius** means by Harfenprincipal at Breslau; for what I surmise, see §.158 above. Dulceon and Frontispicium are several names that have also been conferred upon the Principal. At St. Petri in Hamburg there is a [Principal] 24′ in the pedal; not that the [low] C would be 24′ long, however (that would not suffice), but rather that it extends down only to F—the larger pipes are simply not there. If they were there, however,

---

* i.e., at the Marienkirche in Lübeck; see Mattheson's Appendix to Niedt, p. 189.

† Adlung has already mentioned this above; the duplication probably arose because Adlung consulted consecutively both Praetorius and Mattheson/Niedt, who spell the name differently ("Lambrecht" vs. "Lamberti").

‡ See the stoplist of the organ in St. Petri, Hamburg, in Chapter 10.

§ See the stoplist of the organ at Reval in Chapter 10.

¶ i.e., a printing error.

‖ Adlung has just mentioned this two sentences above.

** *Syntagma musicum*, Vol. II, p. 172.

---

44) In this regard see also note 41 in §.171. [Albrecht]

da; wären sie aber da, so würde das C 32′ seyn. Zu Königsberg in der Pfarrorgel ist im Pedale Principal 16′ enger Mensur. Zu St. Dominico in Prag ist im Rückpositive Principal 12′ und 8′. 12′ kann nicht richtig seyn. Zu Sandomir ist im Rückpositive Principal 4′; die Oktave aber 8′ und die andere 2′. Vielleicht ist 8′ und 4′ versetzt. Wie vorhin gemeldet, so bekommen die Orgeln von dem Manual= (nicht aber vom Pedal=) Principal die Namen, daß sie 16=, 8=, 4= und 2füßige Werke genennet werden. Man nennet es von dem größten unter allen, so man in einer jeden Orgel hat. Es ist aber noch eine Benennung der Orgeln bekannt, da einige ganze, andere halbe, andere 4tels oder 8tels Orgeln heißen. Dies erklären einige durch die Zahl der Register, daß das eine ganze Orgel seyn soll, wo alle Register zu finden. Allein solchergestalt ist in der ganzen Welt keine ganze Orgel; denn man kann ja immer noch mehr Register machen. Vielmehr ist das eine ganze Orgel, wo im Manual Principal 16′ ist; eine halbe, wo 8′ ist; eine Viertelsorgel, wo 4′ ist, und eine Achtelsorgel wo 2′ anzutreffen. Das wird hier nur angeführt, daß man die Reden verstehe, welche darnach eingerichtet sind, s. Werkmeisters Orgelprobe Kap 22. S. 54. und Samber S. 156. it. Fuhrmann in der Vorrede zum musikal. Trichter S. 4. als welcher 32′ eine ganze Orgel nennt, (ex opinione vulgi) und es vielleicht vom Pedale will verstanden wissen, da denn im Manuale auch würde 16′ seyn müssen. Wo Principal 16′ im Manuale ist, da heißt die Orgel auch ein Großprincipalwerk; wo 8′ ist, heißt sie Aequal= oder Chorprincipalwerk; wo 4′ ist, heißt sie Kleinprincipalwerk, s. Prätor. Tom II. Kap. 1. des 4ten Theils, S. 121. und folg. So viel mag von den Principalen genug seyn. Doch noch eins; aus dem äusserlichen Ansehen kann man das Principal und die Orgel nicht allezeit beurtheilen; weil das Principal zuweilen inwendig steht, und die Oktave im Gesichte, wegen Mangel des Raums. Z. Ex. in Jena ist im Brustpositive 2′ im Gesichte, das Principal 4′ aber steht inwendig, wegen Mangel der Höhe. Inwendig kann man kleine Füßchen machen, auch im Nothfalle die Pfeifen kröpfen. (**)

(**) In Frankreich heißt die Oktave: *Prestant*, so wie das Principal: *Montre*.

§. 178.

Quarta 3′ kömmt vor in der Disposition der mittelsten Orgel in der Pfarrkirche zu Danzig. Aber es scheint ein Fehler vorgegangen zu seyn: denn es schicken sich keine andere als Accordsklänge in die Orgel. Es soll vielleicht Quinta 3′ heissen; zumal da die Quinta ordentlich 3′ gesetzt wird.

Quarta decima (die 14te) verstehe ich nicht. Und obgleich in Ulm dieselbige 3fach durch das halbe Clavier angegeben wird; so kann doch wol ein Fehler mit untergelaufen, und quarta decima anstatt quinta decima geschrieben worden seyn. Demnach wäre es eine Oktava, und gehöret zum 17:sten Spho.

Querflöte, Querpfeife, welche die Italiener Traversa und Fiffaro nennen, (**) wie Prätorius T. II. P. II. C. VIII. S. 35. sagt, ist ausser der Orgel ein bekanntes

Ch. VII. Concerning Stops in General and in Particular

then the C would be 32′. In the Pfarrkirche organ at Königsberg there is a Principal 16′ in the pedal of narrow scale. At St. Dominicus in Prague there is a Principal 12′ and 8′ in the Rückpositiv; 12′ cannot be correct. At Sandomir there is a Principal 4′ in the Rückpositiv, but with an Oktave 8′ and another [Oktave] 2′. Perhaps 8′ and 4′ have been reversed. As stated earlier, organs get their names from the manual Principal (and not from the one in the pedal), being termed 16′, 8′, 4′ or 2′ instruments (Werke). The designation comes from the largest of all [the principals] that are found in a given organ. There is, however, yet another way of designating organs, in which some are whole-, others half-, others quarter- or eighth-organs. Some explain these [terms] by the number of stops, calling an organ "whole" in which every stop is to be found. But such being the case, there is no whole-organ in the entire world, since people are always making new stops. Rather a whole-organ is one in which there is a manual Principal 16′; a half-organ, one with an 8′; a quarter-organ one with a 4′, and an eighth-organ one where a 2′ is found.* This is only mentioned here to clarify the ways of speaking that have been established in this matter; see Werkmeister's *Orgelprobe*, Chap. 22, p. 54, and Samber, [Vol. II,] p. 156, as well as Fuhrmann in the foreword to his *Musikalischer Trichter*, p. 4, who calls a 32′ a whole-organ (*ex opinione vulgi* †), perhaps trying to derive this from the pedal [32′], in which organ there would also have to be a 16′ [Principal] in the manual. Where there is a Principal 16′ in the manual, there the organ is also called a Grossprincipalwerk; where an 8′, it is called an Aequal- or Chorprincipalwerk; where a 4′ is, it is called a Kleinprincipalwerk; see Praetorius, Vol. II, chap. 1 of the fourth part, pp. 121f.‡ This much [information] about principals should suffice. Yet there is one other thing: one cannot always judge the [size of the] Principal and the organ by outward appearance, since the Principal sometimes stands within the case, and the Oktave in the façade, due to lack of space. For example, at Jena in the Brustpositiv § there is a 2′ [Superoktave] in the façade, but the Principal 4′ stands within the case, due to the lack of height. Inside the case very small feet can be made [for the larger pipes], or if necessary the pipes can be mitered. (**)

(**) In France the Oktave is called *Prestant*, and the Principal is called *Montre*. [Agricola]

§. 178.

Quarta 3′ appears in the stoplist of the middle organ in the Pfarrkirche at Danzig. It appears, however, that an error has been made, for nothing other than chord tones ¶ are suited to the organ.‖ Perhaps it should read Quinta 3′, especially since the Quinta is ordinarily designated as 3′.

Quarta decima (the 14.th) I do not understand. And although a 3-rank example of this is cited at Ulm, encompassing half the manual, it may well be that an error has crept in and that *quarta decima* has been written instead of *quinta decima*. In that case it would be an Oktave, treated in §.171.

Querflöte, Querpfeife [Traverse flute], called Traversa and Fiffaro by the Italians, (**) as Praetorius says, Vol. II, Part II, chap. VIII, p. 35, is a familiar instru-

* Cf. §.20, where this scheme is also mentioned.

† Latin "according to common/vulgar opinion."

‡ actually pp. 112-3

§ i.e, the Unterwerk; see the stoplist of the organ at Jena in Chapter 10.

¶ i.e., octaves, fifths and thirds.
‖ Adlung is referring here not to the pitch indication, "3", but to the name "Quarta", which means "fourth".

128 Kap. VII. Von den Registern überhaupt und insonderheit.

Instrument, welches seinen Namen daher erhalten, weil man auf der Seite hineinblasen und das Instrument in der Quere halten muß. Man hat davon ein gewisses Orgelregister benennet, welches Prätorius l. c. S. 138. also beschreibt: " Es ist aus der Invention der Quintatön, gedeckt; der Querflötenklang kömmt aber nicht aus der natürlichen Intonation, sondern aus dem Uebersetzen oder Uebergallen; dieses kömmt daher, weil das corpus, wegen seiner Enge fast noch eins, und fast noch anderthalb mal so lang ist. Z. E. wenn der Ton ist 4', so ist der Körper so, daß er der Länge wegen 12' Ton geben sollte: aber es intonirt nur die Quinte, weil es so lang ist. Sie sind gut; aber man hat noch eine offene Art, so noch besser gefallen, und die noch eins so lang sind. Diese werden von Holz und auch von Metall gemacht: denn es ist natürlicher, daß es sich in die Oktave übersetzen, als daß es noch weiter und ferner übersetzen sollte. Sie sind am Klange den andern Querpfeifen ähnlicher, als die gedeckten, und lauten etliche davon, als ob man auf einer Braccio und gesponnenen Seyten anschlüge." Querpipe heißt eben so viel. Die Franzosen sagen Traversiere, Flute allemande, oder Flute d'Allemagne, d. i. deutsche Flöte. s. Matthesons Orchestre I. P. III. C. III. §. 11. Kircher nennt die Querflöte fistulam militarem. Doch ist dieß eigentlich die kleine Feldpfeife, davon oben §. 142. Bis dato habe ich die Querflöte 16', 8', 4' und 2' angetroffen. So ist z. E. in Kreyßen und in Sondershausen, in der neuen Schloßorgel, Traversenbaß 16' im Pedale; zu Waltershausen Flöte traversa 8'; zu Grüningen ist Großquerfl. 8', und Kleinquerflöte 4'; im Pedale ist wieder Großquerflöte 4', ist aber wol versehen, und soll 8' heissen: denn so hat es Werkmeister in der Beschreibung; jenes steht in Matthesons Anhange beym Niedt. 8' ist auch zu St. Catharinen in Hamburg; it. im Löbenicht zu Königsberg. Querflötenbaß 4' ist zu Hessen im Schlosse; it. 4' zu Riddagshausen in der Klosterorgel. s. Prätor. 4' zu St. Gotthard in Hildesheim; 4' zu Sondershausen. Querpipe 6' Ton, 12' lang führt Prätorius an zu St. Jakobi in Hamburg; ist aber vom F. angezählt; (conf. §. 213.) eben daselbst ist auch Offenquerflöt 4' Ton, 8' lang. Querpf. 8' ist zu St. Lambrecht in Lüneburg. s. Prätor. und ebendas. ist dieselbe noch 1 mal halbirt 8'. Zu Breßlau ist sie auch 2 mal. 4' steht sie zu St. Petri in Magdeburg; 8' zu St. Marien in Halle; auch 8' zu St. Blasii in Braunschweig; 4' 2 mal bey den Barfüßern in Halberstadt; it. zu Cassel in der Freyheit und in der Brüderkirche; zu Bückeburg 4', und Querflötenbaß von Holz 8'. 4' aber steht sie auch noch zu St. Jakobi in Hamburg; zu Collberg in der heil. Geisteskirche; zur heil. Dreyfaltigkeit in Danzig; zu St. Johannis ebendaselbst; zu Königsberg im Kneiphofe 2 mal; in der Altstädter Orgel daselbst; it. in der Königl. Schloßorgel daselbst ist sie 4', und noch einmal, dabey steht aber halb; Vielleicht geht sie nur durch das halbe Clavier, wie sie denn nach Prätorii Zeugniß zu Stralsund auch nur im Discante ist; d. i. nur in den 2 obern Oktaven, oder nur bis ins a, weil sie unten ihre Natur nicht wohl behält. 4' und 2' ist sie in der Haberbergischen Orgel in Königsberg; it. 4' in der Steindammischen Orgel daselbst. 4' zu St. Dominico in Prag, und zu Sendomir, allwo sie Tibia trans-

ment apart from the organ. It gets its name from the fact that it is blown on its side and must be held crosswise. A specific organ stop has been named after it, which Praetorius, *l.c.*, p. 138, describes as follows: "It is based on the invention of the Quintatön, and is stopped. The Querflöte does not sound its fundamental pitch, but rather overblows to an upper partial. This happens because the body [of the pipe] is almost three times* as long as its scale would require. For example, if the pitch is [to be] 4′, then the body is long enough that it ought to produce a 12′ pitch; but it is voiced to speak only the Quinte† because it is so long. This type is good, yet there is also a kind that is open and is even more pleasing, but only twice as long.‡ These are made of wood and also of metal. It is more natural to overblow at the octave than at more distant and higher [pitches]. They are more similar in sound to the other Querpfeifen§ than the stopped [variety]; some of them sound as if someone were bowing a viola (*Braccio*) with spun strings."¶ The French say *Traversiere*, *Flute allemande*, or *Flute d'Allemagne*, i.e., "German flute"; see Mattheson's [*Neu-eröffnete*] *Orchestre* I, Part III, chap. III, §.11[, p. 270]. Kircher calls the Querflöte *fistula militaris*.‖ This, however, is properly the little fife (Feldpfeife), discussed in §.142 above. Up to this time I have encountered the Querflöte at 16′, 8′, 4′ and 2′. Thus at Greussen and in the new palace organ at Sondershausen** there is a Traversenbass 16′ in the pedal. At Waltershausen there is a Flöte traversa 8′. At Gröningen there is a Grossquerfl. 8′ and Kleinquerflöte 4′, and again in the pedal a Grossquerflöte 4′, according to Mattheson's Appendix [to Niedt, pp. 172-3]; this however must be a mistake, and ought to read 8′, since Werkmeister notes it as such in his *Beschreibung*.†† There is also an 8′ [example] at St. Catharine in Hamburg, as well as in the Löbenichtkirche at Königsberg. In the palace at Hesse, as well as in the Klosterkirche organ at Riddagshausen, there is a Querflötenbass 4′; see Praetorius.‡‡ It is at 4′ at St. Gotthard in Hildesheim, and at Sondershausen.§§ Praetorius cites a Querpipe 6′ pitch, 12′ long, at St. Jakobi in Hamburg, counting however from [low] F (cf. §.213); at the same place there is also an Offenquerflöt 4′ pitch, 8′ long. There is a Querpf. 8′ at St. Lambrecht in Lüneburg (see Praetorius[, p. 233]), as well as yet another one at 8′, encompassing half the keyboard. It also appears twice at Breslau. It stands at 4′ at St. Petri in Magdeburg, at 8′ at St. Marien in Halle and St. Blasius in Braunschweig, twice at 4′ in the Barfüsserkirche in Halberstadt, as well as at Cassel in the Freiheiterkirche and the Bruderkirche, and at 4′ in Bückeburg, together with a Querflötenbass 8′ of wood. To continue, it also stands at 4′ at St. Jakobi in Hamburg, in the Heiliggeisteskirche at Colberg, at the Heiligdreifaltigkeitskirche and at St. Johannis in Danzig, twice in the Kneiphofkirche and in the Altstädterkirche at Königsberg. In the organ at the royal palace in Königsberg there is a 4′ [Querflöte], and also a second one that is, however, labeled "half"; perhaps it extends through only half the keyboard, just as the one at Stralsund also does, according to Praetorius's testimony, only in the treble, i.e., only in the 2 upper octaves or down to [tenor] a, since it does not retain its character well in the bass. It is at both 4′ and 2′ in the Haberbergkirche organ in Königsberg, also at 4′ in the Steindammkirche organ there, 4′ at St.

* literally, "almost once, and almost yet half again as long."

† i.e., the second overtone, an octave and a fifth above the fundamental.

‡ i.e., as the length called for by the pitch it produces; thus it overblows to its octave.

§ i.e., the actual instruments.

¶ i.e., made of gut wound with wire. It may seems strange that Adlung likens the sound of this stop both to a flute and a stringed instrument; he seems to be thinking of the stop's incisive speech (similar to the organ stop Violdigamba).

‖ See *Musurgia universalis*, p. 500.

** Praetorius neither lists a Traversenbass 16′ in the palace organ at Sondershausen (*Syntagma musicum*, Vol. II, p. 197), nor does he label the organ "new". There is no such stop, in fact, at any pitch anywhere in this organ. One might be tempted to think that Adlung intended to write "Altenburg" (the stoplist of which is found on p. 286 of the *Musica mechanica organoedi*, and which is the only 'palace organ' with a "Flötetraversiere 16′" in the pedal) instead of "Sondershausen", except that Agricola added the Altenburg stoplist as an appendix before publication in 1768, six years after Adlung's death.

†† i.e., *Organum gruningense redivivum*, §.3.

‡‡ pp. 189 and 200. Praetorius lists no such stop in the pedal at Riddagshausen; he does list one, however, in the pedal at Hildesheim (p. 199), the immediately preceding stoplist.

§§ Praetorius, pp. 197 & 199.

transuersa heißt. 4′ Im Dom und zu U. L. Fr. in Lübeck. 2′ steht sie in der großen Orgel zu St. Nikolai in Hamburg; it. zu St. Petri daselbst; zu Thoren in der Marienkirche steht auch Querpfeife, aber nicht, wie groß? —— Man hat sie auch wie die Spitzpfeife gemacht. So ist z. E. Spitzpfeife oder Querflöte 4′ von Holz zu Dresden auf dem Schlosse. s. Prätor. Im Generalbasse kömmt zuweilen eine Traversa vor, welche mit diesem Register zu spielen. Doch davon s. das 8. Kap. §. 238.

(**) Traversa heißt im italienischen ein Querbalken, eine Schürze, u. s. w.; nicht eine Flöte. Fiffaro ist gar nicht mehr gebräuchlich. Der rechte italienische Name der Querflöte ist: *Flauto traverso.*

§. 179.

Quinta ist ein bekannt Register in den Orgeln; doch werden einige Dinge dabey zu erinnern seyn. Ordentlich ist es eine offene Pfeife, Principalmensur; zuweilen ist sie aber auch gedeckt, da es meistens dabey steht. Man hat Quinten 6′, 3′ und 1½′. In den Mixturen und andern gemischten Stimmen sind sie auch kleiner, etwann ¾′, ⅜′ 2c. Es entstehet aber durch gar zu große Quinten ein harter Klang, deswegen man über 6′ nicht geht; denn sonst könnte 12′ und 24′ auch eine Quinte abgeben. Ja, die Quinte 6′ ist schon sehr craß, zumal in der Tiefe; daher sie meistens etwas zugespitzt wird, daß sie, als halb zugedeckt, nicht zu scharf klinge. Nachdem das Principal ist, nach dem müssen die Quinten seyn; das Principal muß allezeit die Quinte übertreffen an der Größe. 3′ ist die gemeinste; in kleinen Orgeln aber 1½′. Wenn also der clauis c angeschlagen wird; so geben die Quinten g, als die Quinte von c. Und so gehts durch alle claves. Die Quinte heißt auch Diapente. Also ist Regula diapente 3′ zu Sandomir; und Disdiapente 1½′. Wäre aber die Quinte 6′ da; so könnte 3′ schon Disdiapente heißen. Ebendaselbst heißt die Quinte 3′ auch Nete. Wer dieß Wort weiter verstehen will, der muß die antiquitates musicas zu Hülfe nehmen. [45] Die Quinte 1½′ wird von etlichen Quintez genennet: allein Quintez ist von quindecima entstanden; dieß aber ist keine Quinte, sondern eine Superoktave. (conf. Praetor. l. c. pag. 130.) Etliche Quinten sind gedeckt. So ist z. Ex. zu Grüningen im Schlosse gedackte Quinte 3′ und 1½′: Sonst aber haben diese gedeckten Quinten einen besondern Namen, daß sie Nasat heißen; wiewol bey dem Worte mehr zu erinnern, welches man §. 169. lesen kann. Gedackte italienische Quinte kam oben §. 161. vor. Zu Görlitz steht decima nona 3′; welcher Name sich beym Samber S. 153. auch findet. Es ist auch eine Quinte: eigentlich aber heißt es das neunzehnte Intervall, nämlich von dem Principal an zu rechnen, das in eben demselben Clavier ist. Wenn ich

[45] Man kann hievon nachlesen Wallisii Vergleichung der alten Musik mit der zu seiner Zeit. Sie befindet sich in Mizlers musikal. Bibliothek, im 1sten Bande, und dessen zweyten Theile. S. 1 s 27. Imgleichen Marpurgs kritische Einleitung in die Geschichte und Lehrsätze der alten und neuen Musik, besonders in dem daselbst eingeschalteten Kapitel von der Beschaffenheit der alten Musik.

Ch. VII. Concerning Stops in General and in Particular

Dominicus in Prague and at Sendomir, where it is called *Tibia transversa*, 4' in the Cathedral and the Marienkirche at Lübeck. It stands at 2' in the large organ at St. Nikolai and at St. Petri in Hamburg. In the Marienkirche at Thoren a Querpfeife is listed, but without any size. [Querflötes] have also been constructed like Spitzflötes; thus, e.g., in the palace at Dresden there is a Spitzpfeife or Querflöte 4' of wood; see Praetorius[, p. 187]. In figured basses there sometimes appears [the word] *Traversa*, which is to be played with this stop; yet in this regard see Chap. 8, §.238 [below].*

* See §. 259, as well.

(**) In Italian *Traversa* means "crossbeam" or an "apron", etc., not a flute. *Fiffaro* is not in use any more at all. The proper Italian name for the Querflöte is *Flauto traverso*. [Agricola]

§. 179.

QUINTA† is a familiar organ stop, yet there are several things to be kept in mind concerning it. Ordinarily it is an open pipe of principal scale, but at times it is also stopped, in which case it is usually so labeled. There are Quints at 6', 3' and 1 ½". In mixtures and other compound stops they are also smaller, say, ¾' or ⅜" etc. Quints that are too large, though, create a crude sound, and for this reason 6' is not exceeded, for otherwise 12' and 24' could also produce a Quint. Indeed, the Quinte 6' is already very crude, especially in the lower register, and thus it is usually somewhat tapered so that, being half-stopped, it does not sound too harsh. The Quinte must always accord with the scale of the Principal, the latter always exceeding the former in size. The most common [size] is 3'; in small organs, though, 1 ½'. If the key c is played, then the Quints will sound g as the fifth of c, and so forth through all the keys. Quints are also called *Diapente*; thus there is a *Regula diapente* 3' and a *Disdiapente* 1 ½' at Sandomir. If, however, the Quinte 6' were there, then the 3' could be called *Disdiapente*. At Sandomir the Quinte 3' is called *Nete*. Whoever would like to understand more about this word [*Nete*] must make use of the *antiquitates musicas*.[45] ‡ Some call the Quinte 1 ½' "Quintez", but Quintez grew out of Quindecima which is no Quinte, but rather a Superoktave (cf. Praetorius, *l.c.*, p. 130). Some Quints are stopped; thus, e.g., in the palace at Gröningen there is a Gedackte Quinte 3' and [also one at] 1 ½'. As a rule, however, these stopped Quints have a special name, being called "Nasat"; yet there is more to keep in mind about this [latter] word, as may be read in §.169. Gedackte italienische Quinte has been discussed in §.161 above. At Görlitz there stands a *decima nona* 3', a name also found in Samber, p. 153. It is also a Quinte; but properly speaking it means the interval of a nineteenth, that is, figuring from the Principal that is in the same manual. If the Principal at Görlitz is a 16', then the Quinte is properly 12'; one octave

† Adlung writes this form of the word, with a Latin ending, interchangeably with "Quinte," the form with a German ending.

‡ the "antiquities of music", i.e., volumes describing the music of antiquity, specifically of Greece.

---

45) In this regard one may consult Wallisius' comparison of early music with that of his time, found in Mizler's *Musikalische Bibliothek*, Vol. I, Part 2, pp. 1-27; likewise Marpurg's *Kritische Einleitung in die Geschichte und Lehrsatze der alten und neuen Musik*, particularly in the chapter he has inserted into it, "von der Beschaffenheit der alten Musik." § [Albrecht]

§ "Concerning the Character of Old Music."

ich nun daselbst das Principal 16′ habe, so ist die Quinte eigentlich 12′; eine Oktave höher 6′, ist eigentlich duodecima; noch eine Oktave höher ist 3′, das ist das 19te, oder wie vorher steht: decima nona. Wenn also das c angeschlagen wird; so giebt das Register $\frac{g}{c}$ dazu. Eben daselbst ist vigesima nona, 1½′, das 29ste: aber das kann nicht recht seyn, weil von Principal 16′ an die 29ste palmula wirklich $\frac{e}{c}$ angiebt. Die Quinte 1½′ aber ist vielmehr vigesima sexta, d. i. 26. Wenn aber das Principal anders zum Grunde geleget wird; so kömmt auch eine andere Rechnung heraus. Denn bey 8′. wird 3′ die duodecima, 1½′ die decima nona; ¾′ die vigesima sexta. Quintnasat ist §. 169. bey Nasat zu suchen. Rohrflötquinte, ist wie eine Rohrflöte, aber sie giebt die Quinte an, s. Rohrflöte. Zu Görlitz steht Großquintenbaß, weil er im Pedale ist. Zu Königsberg im Kneiphofe oder Dom ist keine Quinte 3′ im ganzen Werke da doch drey Claviere und 59 Stimmen sind. Gedackte Quintflöte 3′ ist in der Altstädter Orgel daselbst. Prätorius giebt zu St. Johannis in Magdeburg eine Quintflöte 4′ an: aber das kann nicht seyn, wenn nicht der 213. §. dieser Abhandlung zu Hülfe kömmt. Spitzquinte ist eine Art der Spitzpfeife oder Spitzflöte, wovon in S zu reden. Sie steht 3′ zu Königsberg im Kneiphofe. Dagegen heißt die gleichaus weite Quinte zuweilen Cylinderquint, s. oben in C. Gemshornquinte 3′ und 1½′ auch 6′, ist eine Art von Gemshörnern, welche die Quinte von sich hören läßt, s. §. 153. In der Altstädter Orgel zu Königsberg ist eine Quinte von 2 Pfeifen 4′ und 1½′. Dies ist eine besondere Mischung einer Quinte und Oktave, dergleichen fast die Rauschquinte ist, doch würde bey der Rauschquinte oder Rauschpfeife die Oktave nicht so groß seyn. Von der Rauschquinte, s §. 182. Zu Bernau in der Mark soll, nach Pratorio, die Quinte vom groben Principale 8′ (so also 6′ wäre) Jula heißen. Sonst ist Jula die Spitzflöte. Endlich fragt es sich: ob die Quinte könne eigentlich 6′, 3′, 1½′, 2c. seyn? Antwort: nach der Rechnung kommen diese Zahlen für die Quarte; denn wenn ich eine Sayte, 4 Fuß lang, um einen Fuß verkürze, durch Fortrückung des Steges; so bleiben 3 Füße übrig, und das giebt die Quarte f zu dem 4füßigen sono. Also wäre die Oktave 1½′ auch f, 6′ auch. Die Quinte aber $\frac{g}{c}$. Er. g gegen c ist 2⅔′: denn wenn ich die Sayte in 4 theile, und 2′ nehme, und von dem 3ten noch ⅔′; so giebt es das g. Folglich ist die tiefere Oktave 5⅓′, und die höhere Oktave 1⅓′. Weil man sich aber nicht gerne mit Brüchen behängt; so hat man für 2⅔′, 3′ voll genennet, und die andern auch darnach gerechnet. Von Sedezemquint, s. §. 189. Quinta ex octaua ist zu Breslau, d. i. Quinte 3′; denn daselbst ist Oktave 4′ gemeynet. Quintbaß 12′ ist zu Kindelbrück, s. §. 306.

§. 180.

Quinta ex sedecima ist in Breßlau, s. Prätor. in Dispositionibus. Es soll, so viel ich begreife, die Quinte über der sedecima seyn. Sedecima aber soll allda beym Principal 16′ die Superoktave 2′ seyn, und eine Quinte höher, ist die quinta ex sedecima, i. e. 1½′; aber sedecima ist nicht eigentlich eine Oktave; wovon unten. Daher auch dieses nicht accurat geredt ist. Sedezemquint ist gleich viel. §. 189

Quinta

higher, 6′, is the *duodecima*, strictly speaking. Yet another octave higher is 3′, which is the nineteenth or, as has already been stated, the *decima nona*. If then c* is played, this stop sounds g′. Likewise at Görlitz there is a *vigesima nona* 1 ½′, the 29th; but that cannot be correct, since the 29th note above the Principal 16′ actually sounds c‴.† The Quinte 1 ½′ is rather the *vigesima sexta*, i.e., the 26th. If the Principal sounds some other fundamental pitch, then another set of numbers will result. For an 8′ [fundamental], 3′ will be the *duodecima*, 1 ½′ the *decima nona* and ¾′ the *vigesima sexta*. Quintnasat may be found in §.169 under Nasat. Rohrflötquinte is like a Rohrflöte, except that it sounds the fifth; see "Rohrflöte‡." At Görlitz there stands a Grossquintenbass [6′], since it is in the pedal.§ At Königsberg in the Cathedral or Kneiphofkirche there is not a single Quinte 3′ in the entire organ, even though there are three manuals and 59 stops. There is a stopped Quintflöte 3′ in the Altstädterkirche organ at Königsberg. Praetorius cites a Quintflöte 4′ at St. Johannis in Magdeburg,¶ but that cannot be [correct], unless §.213 of this treatise be taken into consideration.‖ Spitzquinte is a variety of Spitzpfeife or Spitzflöte, discussed under "S";** it stands at 3′ in the Kneiphofkirche at Königsberg. On the other hand, the non-tapered Quinte is sometimes called Cylinderquint; see above under "C".†† Gemshornquinte 3′ and 1 ½′ (as well as 6′) is a type of Gemshorn that sounds a fifth; see §.153. In the Altstädterkirche organ at Königsberg there is a Quinte of 2 ranks, 4′ and 1 ½′. This is an exceptional combination of a Quinte and an Oktave that is almost [the same as] a Rauschquinte, except that the Oktave would not be so large in a Rauschquinte or Rauschpfeife; concerning the Rauschquinte, see §.182. Praetorius‡‡ says that at Bernau in the Mark [Brandenburg] the Quinte of the Grober Principal 8′ (thus it would be a 6′) is called "Jula"; as a rule Jula is a Spitzflöte. Finally, the question arises, can a Quinte actually be 6′, 3′, 1 ½′, etc.? The answer: figuring precisely, these numbers come out to a fourth, §§ for if I shorten a 4-foot long string by one foot, by advancing the bridge, then 3 feet are left, which [when plucked] produce the fourth, f, above the 4′ pitch. Thus the octaves [of 3′], 1 ½′ as well as 6′, would also be f. The Quinte on the other hand, e.g., g against c, is 2¾′,¶¶ for if I divide the string into four 1-foot sections, taking 2′ plus ⅔′ of the third [foot], this produces a g. Consequently the lower Oktave is 5⅓′ and the higher Oktave 1 ⅓′. Because no one wants to be overrun with fractions, though, 2⅔′ gets labelled a full 3′ and the other [Quints] are figured from it. Concerning Sedetzemquint see §.189. There is a *Quinta ex octava* at Breslau, i.e., a Quinte 3′, since there it is the Oktave 4′ that is meant [by *ex octava*]. There is a Quintbass 12′ at Kindelbrück; see §.306.

§. 180.

QUINTA EX SEDECIMA is at Breslau; see Praetorius's stoplists.‖‖ As far as I can comprehend, it must be the Quinte above the *sedecima*. There, however, with the Principal 16′ the *sedecima* should be the Oktave 2′;*** thus a fifth higher is the *quinta ex sedecima*, i.e., 1 ½′. But *sedecima* is not properly speaking an Oktave, as [I have explained] below [in §.189]. Therefore this [term *Quinte ex sedecima*] is also not properly phrased. Sedetzemquint is the same thing; [see] §.189.

* This perhaps should read "C".

† i.e., figuring from great C of the Principal 16′.

‡ §.184 below.

§ i.e., this is the reason it has the word "bass" appended to it.

¶ *Syntagma musicum*, Vol. II, p. 174.

‖ i.e., the stop may begin at F instead of C.

** §.195 below.

†† §.133.

‡‡ *Syntagma musicum*, Vol. II, p. 177.

§§ i.e., 6′ produces a pitch a fourth above an 8′.

¶¶ This appears to be a misprint; Adlung writes "2 ⅔′" just below.

‖‖ *Syntagma musicum*, Vol. II, p. 171.

*** Praetorius lists the Gross Principal in that manual as an 8′, not a 16′; figuring from the 8′, the *sedecima* would indeed be an Oktave 2′.

Kap. VII. Von den Registern überhaupt und insonderheit. 131

Quinta dulcis ist 6′ zu Dresden im Schlosse. Es heißt zu deutsch: die anmuthigen Quinte: was sie aber besonders und anmuthiges an sich hat, kann ich nicht sagen.

Quinta decima, quindecima, heißt der 15te clauis vom Grundton an. Das ist just 2 Oktaven: also wäre es eine Superoktave; und das ist besser geredt als Sedecima. Es steht quinta decima 2′ zu St. Bartholomäi in Danzig; quindecima aber zu St. Catharina daselbst. Quintadetz ist eben das zu Sondershausen, s. Prätorius. Man sagt auch Quintetz; wie bald folget.

Quintflöte $1\frac{1}{2}′$ ist zu St. Catharinen in **Hamburg**, s. §. 160.

Quintetz, ist wol von quinta decima entstanden, und also mit demselben einerley, s. §. 171. Eigentlich ist es eine Superoktave. Es wird dies Wort aber auch gebraucht für eine gemischte Stimme, und alsdann ists so viel als Scharpquintetz, davon §. 186. zu lesen. So ist z. Ex. im Dom zu Naumburg das Quintetz 3 fach im Rückpositive; zu St. Ulrich in Magdeburg ist Quintetz im Brustpositive; doch ist nicht angezeiget wie groß oder vielfach es sey, s. Prätor., welcher es S. 191. noch einmal gesetzt hat, und zwar mit der Bemerkung: Anderthalb.

Quintviole 8′ steht in der Altdresdener Orgel. Daß es ein Quintregister seyn soll, siehet man wol aus der Benennung: aber was für Art, weis ich nicht. Wiewol auch das erste nicht gar zu gewiß scheint, weil 8′ dabey steht, welches keine Quinte, wol aber ein Oktavenregister ausmachen kann. Was sonst Viole sey, s. §. 172. und 204.

Quintadön, Quintathön, Quintadena, Quintiden, Quintadeens, Quintitenens, Quinta ad una, Quintadehn, für welche Worte man besser schreibt Quintatön, weil das Tönen der Quinte dadurch bemerkt wird, als wenn es hieße Quintgetön. Es ist der Name daher entstanden, weil nebst dem ordentlichen Oktavenklange auch die Quinte über sich einigermaßen dabey gehöret wird; doch ists nicht die quinta prima, wie 3 : 2, sondern die secunda, wie 3 : 1., d. i. eine Superquinte, wie der Herr Hofrath Henfling sagt in Epistola de nouo Syst. music. §. 14. Die unterschiedene Schreibart ist aus der Unwissenheit entstanden. Daß aber eine offene Pfeife also könne abgerichtet werden, daß man allemal eine Oktave mit höret; eine gedeckte aber so, daß man die Quinte mit höret, bezeugt Werkmeisters musikalisches Sieb, Kap. 3. S. 5. Wie es denn auch alle Orgelmacher wissen. Prätorius T. II. P. IV. c. II. p. 137. sagt: „sie sey vor 50 Jahren (von seiner Zeit an gerechnet) aufge-
„kommen, und werde von etlichen Holschelle genannt; habe 2 Laute, ut, sol, (das ist
„aus der Solmisation, ist aber eben so viel als c und g; im d aber d und a u. s. w.)
„Daher sie Anfangs genennet worden ist: quinta ad una. Sie ist etwas weiter als die
„Principale an der Mensur, doch eine Oktave tiefer, weil sie gedeckt ist." Es scheint, daß quint de tono zu Breßlau auch so viel sey, und zwar 8′, weil das Wort Chormaß dabey steht 2 mal, (s. Prätor.) und Quintenor auch. Zu Magdeburg in

Ch. VII. Concerning Stops in General and in Particular

Quinta dulcis is at 6′ in the palace at Dresden.* In German it means "pleasant Quinte", though what about it is special and pleasant, I cannot say.

Quinta decima, quindecima, means the 15th note above the fundamental. This is exactly 2 octaves; thus it would be a Superoktave, and it is better to speak of it thus than as a *Sedecima*.† A *Quinta decima* 2′ stands in St. Bartholomai at Danzig, while *quindecima* is at St. Catharine there. Quintadetz at Sondershausen is the same thing; see Praetorius.‡ The term "Quintetz" is also used, that follows just below.

Quintflöte 1 ½′ is at St. Catharine in Hamburg; see §.160.

Quintetz no doubt arises from *quinta decima*, and thus is identical to it; see §.171. It is actually a Superoktave. This word, however, is also used for a compound stop, and then it is the same as Scharpquintetz, discussed in §.186. Thus in the Cathedral at Naumburg, e.g., there is a Quintetz 3 ranks in the Rückpositiv. At St. Ulrich in Magdeburg there is a Quintetz in the Brustpositiv, but without any indication of how large or how many ranks it is; see Praetorius,§ who records it once again on p. 191.¶ this time with the indication "1 ½′."

Quintviole 8′ stands in the organ of the Altdresdenerkirche.‖ One may perceive from its name that it is a Quint stop, but of what kind, I do not know. Yet even the former [assertion**] does not seem to be all that certain, since 8′ stands beside it, which would produce no fifth, but rather an octave[-speaking] stop. For what Viole as a rule is, see §.172 and 204.

Quintadön, Quintathön, Quintadena, Quintiden, Quintadeens, Quintitenens, *Quinta ad una*, Quintadehn, are all better written as "Quintatön", since one notes in [the spelling of the word] the sounding of the fifth, as though it were called "Quint-sound". The name has arisen from the fact that, in addition to the normal octave sound†† the fifth above it is also heard to some degree. Yet this is not the primary fifth, as 3:2, but rather the secondary one, as 3:1, i.e., the "Superquinte", as Privy Councillor Henfling says in *Epistola de novo syst. music.*, §.14. The various spellings are the result of ignorance. Werkmeister's *Cribrum musicum*, Chap. 3, p. 5, attests that an open pipe may be voiced so that one always hears an octave with [the fundamental], while a stopped pipe may be voiced so that one hears a fifth with [the fundamental]. Every organbuilder already knows this. Praetorius, Vol. II, Part IV, Chap. II, p. 137, says "they came into use 50 years ago (figuring from his time), and that some [people] call them "Holschelle"; they have 2 sounds, ut and sol (that is, from solmization; this is the same as c and g or, [based] on d, d and a, etc). Thus in the beginning it was called *quinta ad una*. It is somewhat wider in scale than the Principal, yet an octave lower, because it is stopped." It appears that *quint de tono* at Breslau is the same thing, and indeed at 8′, since the word "Chormass" stands next to it in two instances; see Praetorius[, p. 172]. The same holds true for Quintenor. In the Ulrichskirche at Magdeburg

---

* According to Mattheson's Appendix to Niedt, p. 171; see the stoplist of this organ in Chapter 10.

† See §.189.

‡ *Syntagma musicum*, Vol. II, p. 197; but it is unlikely that Adlung's assertion is true. There are already two 2′ stops in the same manual, one an Octav; see "Quintetz" below.

§ *Syntagma musicum*, Vol. II, p. 174; but Praetorius spells the name "Quindetz".

¶ in one of his sample stoplists.

‖ See Mattheson's Appendix to Niedt, p. 170, as well as the stoplist of the Alt-Dresdener organ, under "Dresden" in Chapter 10.

** i.e., that this is a Quint stop.

†† i.e., the unison or fundamental pitch.

der Ulrichskirche, heißt sie Holschelle 4' allwo aber Quintatön 4' noch besonders zu finden, und scheint demnach, daß man sie bisweilen zu unterscheiden habe, s. Prät. l. c. S. 174. Man hat sie 16', 8' und 4', auch 2', obschon Prätorius sagt, sie lasse sich kleiner, als 4' nicht arbeiten. Zu St. Bartholomäi in Danzig steht sie 2'. So viel ist war, daß solch Register überall schwer zu intoniren, wegen des engen Aufschnitts; es überschreyet sich leicht in die Quinte; und deswegen macht man ihnen Bärte an. Niedt im 2ten Theile, S. 113. nach der Matthesonischen Ausgabe, gedenkt auch der Quintathön 32': die ist aber gewiß rar; und sagt Mattheson dabey, daß er sie auch noch nie gesehen. 16' und 8' sind die gemeinsten. 4' steht sie in der Altstädtischen Orgel in der lutherischen Kirche zu Elbingen. Daß die Quintatön 4' auch oft Nachthorn heiße, s. in N. H. 168. Zu Görlitz ist Quintatönbaß 8' im Pedale von Holz: sonst macht man sie ordentlich von Metall, da man sie leichter zurechte bringt; wie denn der Orgelmacher Casparini daran, wie auch an der dasigen Quintatön 16' ein besonder Meisterstück sehen lassen. Es schlagen die Quintatönen etwas langsam an, sonderlich die großen von 16'; deswegen sie zum Laufen nicht so wohl dienen im vollen Werke, als der Bordun. Eben zu Görlitz ist ein gedackter Pommer 4' vom welchem Boxberg sagt, es sey eine starke Quintatön. Zu Sondershausen ist bey Prätorio Quintatönsubbaß 16', d. i. sie steht im Pedale.

§. 181.

Racket führt Werkmeister in Organo grüningensi §. 46. unter den fast in Vergessenheit gerathenen Schnarrwerken an. Es ist vom Ranket unterschieden. Außer der Orgel werden die Rackete vom Prätorio S. 39. und folg. beschrieben.

Ranket ist ein Schnarrwerk 16' und 8'ton, deren jenes groß Ranket, dies aber klein Ranket heißt, s. Prätor. S. 147. l. c. der sagt: es sind schöne liebliche Arten von Schnarrwerken, ganz stille zu intoniren. Sie haben gleich kleine corpora; ihr größtes ist einer guten Spannen lang oder 9", und haben in sich noch ein verborgen corpus wie die Sordunen. Den Abriß davon hat Prätorius ebenfalls mitgetheilet. Werkmeister in Organo grüningensi sagt, daß das Ranket 8' zu Grüningen sey, da es sehr wohl klinge: aber es sey in wenig Werken heut zu Tage, weil die Körper einen accuraten Meister erfordern; sie hätten auch innerliche Röhren. Es steht daselbst in der kleinen Brust, auch noch einmal im Pedale. Auch ists 16' von Holz zu Bückeburgk, und zu Hessen auf dem Schlosse findet man es auch 16', s. Prätor. S. 186. und 89. Zu Sondershausen ist Ranket oder Baerpfeife 8'; zu Riddagshausen in Kloster Ranket oder Krumhorn; it. zu Sondershausen Dolcian oder Ranket 16' von Holz: da doch sonst alle diese Stimmen unterschieden sind. Zu Reval ist Ranket 8', s. §. 313. Sonst erinnere ich mich nicht, dergleichen irgendwo gefunden zu haben.

§. 182.

it is called Holschelle 4′, but a Quintatön is also found there separately, and accordingly it appears that it is sometimes necessary to distinguish [between] them; see Praetorius, *l.c.*, p. 174. They are found at 16′, 8′, 4′ and also 2′, although Praetorius* says they ought not to be built smaller than 4′. There is an example at 2′ at St. Bartholomai in Danzig. This much is certain, that this stop is always difficult to voice, because of its low cut-up; it overblows easily to the fifth, and for that reason is constructed with beards. Mattheson's edition of Niedt's Second Part, p. 113, also mentions a Quintatön 32′, but that is certainly rare, and moreover Mattheson says that he has never seen one. 16′ and 8′ are the most common. It stands at 4′ in the Altstädtische organ in the Lutheran Church at Elbingen. The Quintatön 4′ is also often called Nachthorn; see under "N", §.168. At Görlitz there is a Quintatönbass 8′ of wood in the pedal; otherwise they are usually made of metal, in order to make their regulation easier. Thus the organbuilder Casparini† has shown in it‡ a singular masterpiece, as also in the Quintatön 16′ that is there as well.§ Quintatöns speak somewhat slowly, especially the larger ones at 16′; therefore they do not serve as well in running passages on the plenum (im vollen Werke) as the Bordun. At Görlitz there is likewise a Gedackt Pommer 4′, about which Boxberg¶ says that it is a strong Quintatön. At Sondershausen there is, according to Praetorius, a Quintatönsubbass 16′, i.e., it stands in the pedal.‖

* *Syntagma musicum*, Vol. II, p. 137.

† builder of the Görlitz organ.
‡ i.e., the wooden Quintatönbass 8′.
§ Adlung is extrapolating from Boxberg, p.[15], who praises only the wooden Quintadena 16′ in the Oberwerk.
¶ p.[13].
‖ See *Syntagma musicum*, Vol. II, p. 197.

§. 181.

RACKET. In the *Organum gruningense*[, §.46], Werkmeister mentions this stop among those reeds that have almost fallen into oblivion. It is not the same as Ranket. Rackets apart from the organ are described by Praetorius, pp. 39f.

RANKET is a reed stop of 16′ and 8′ tone, the former being called "Gross Ranket", the latter "Klein Ranket"; see Praetorius, *l.c.*, p. 147, who says that they are a beautiful, lovely variety of reed, to be voiced very quietly. They all have small resonators, their largest being a good [hand]span or 9″ long, and they contain within themselves a concealed body like the Sorduns.** Praetorius has provided a sketch of one.†† Werkmeister in his *Organum gruningense*[, §.46,] says that there is a Ranket 8′ at Gröningen and that it sounds very well, but it‡‡ is found in few organs nowadays, since [the construction of] the bodies require[s] an exacting master. He also says that they have interior tubes.§§ At Gröningen¶¶ it stands in the small Brust, and once again in the pedal. There is also a 16′ [example] at Bückeburg, as well as at the palace in Hesse; see Praetorius, pp. 186 and [1]89. At Sondershausen there is a Ranket or Baerpfeife 8′, and at Riddagshausen in the Klosterkirche a Ranket or Krumhorn. Likewise at Sondershausen there is a Dolcian or Ranket 16′ of wood, though otherwise all of these stops are distinct.‖‖ At Reval there is a Ranket 8′; see §.313.*** Otherwise I cannot remember ever having found one anywhere else.

** i.e., the bore coils around a number of times within the resonator, and this coil is not visible from the exterior of the pipe.
†† *Syntagma musicum*, Vol. II, "Theatrum instrumentorum", Table 38.
‡‡ i.e., the Ranket stop
§§ i.e., the invisible bore coiled within the resonator.
¶¶ See Mattheson's Appendix to Niedt, p. 173.
‖‖ i.e., each of the two names given for the three stops just mentioned (with double names) is ordinarily a different stop.
*** The translation disregards the (superfluous) paragraph numbers in the collection of stoplists; see the stoplist for the organ at Reval in Chapter 10.

§. 182.

Rauschpfeife, Rauschflöte, Rauschwerk, Rauschquinte, Ruschquint, Rußpipe, ist alles einerley. Es wird dadurch eine gemischte Stimme angedeutet, wo die Oktave und Quinte mit einander auf einem Stocke stehen. Doch nimmt man die Oktave 2′, und die Quinte 3′, oder 1½′, daß also bald die Oktave, bald die Quinte größer ist. Ueber 3′ nimmt man wol nicht, weil es ein schärfendes Register seyn soll. Hat sie jemand nicht gehöret, der kann nur in seiner Orgel Quinte 3′ und Oktave 2′ zu ammen ziehen, so hat er gleichen Klang. Man macht sie nach Principalmensur, siehe Prätor. l. c. S. 130. welcher sagt, daß der Name dieser Stimme schon alt sey. Etliche wollen Rauschquinte nennen, wenn die Quinte die Oktave an Größe übertrift: Rauschpfeife aber, wenn die Oktave größer ist. Andere brauchen diese Wörter ohne Unterschied. Prätorius gedenkt nur der 2fachen Rauschpfeifen; aber die 3fachen sind auch gemein; ja man hat sie auch mehrfach; da werden die Quinten und Oktaven stets kleiner repetirt, und sie sind hernach von den Mixturen in nichts unterschieden, als daß sie keine Terzen haben. 2fach steht sie in der Orgel zu Elmshorn; zu St. Jakobi in Hamburg in 2 Clavieren, und zu St. Catharinen in Magdeburg; (an beyden Orten wird sie Rauschflöt genennet) zu U. L. Fr. in Bremen; in Buxtehude; in Görlitz, da dabey steht: aus 2 Fußton, d. i. die größte Pfeife ist 2′; zu St. Stephani in Bremen; zu Otterndorf im Lande Hadeln. Rauschquinte 4′ führt Prätorius zu St. Petri in Lübeck an. Ob etwan Oktave 4′ dabey ist, oder ob es soll bedeuten über 4′; oder ob es verdruckt? Weis ich nicht. 3fach ist sie in der großen Orgel zu St. Nikolai in Hamburg 2 mal; zu St. Johannis daselbst 2mal; zu U. L. Fr. in Bremen; in der mittelsten Orgel der Danziger Pfarrkirche; zu St. Dominico in Prag; in der Kirche zu St. Johannes in Danzig; zu Königsberg im Kneiphofe oder Dom 2 mal; in der Altstädter Orgel daselbst; it. in der königlichen Schloßorgel allda. Manchmal heißt sie Rauschpfeif, zuweilen aber Rauschquint. Prätorius l. c. sagt, daß man auch einen Rauschpfeifenbaß habe, der noch in usu sey: aber dergleichen habe unter diesem Namen nirgends gefunden. Er würde wol ins Pedal gehören müssen, wie denn davon hier unten noch einige Exempel sollen beygebracht werden, wo dies Register im Pedale gefunden wird; deswegen aber könnten doch die Pfeifen von eben der Größe seyn im Manuale. Zuweilen ist es nicht an die Registerzüge geschrieben, wie vielfach sie sind. Also ist es in Jena in der Stadtorgel; zu Danzig: aber in andern Dispositionen ist es determinirt, wie aus vorhin angeführten Exempel zu ersehen, welchen noch beyzusetzen: zu St. Petri in Berlin 3fach; im Dom zu Bremen, im Manuale und Pedale 3fach; zu St. Ansgarii daselbst ist im Pedale 3 f, und noch dabey im Werke Rauchpfeife 2 f; aber das ist ein offenbarer Druckfehler, und muß Rauschpfeife heißen. Von Copendorf, welches auch hierher zu ziehen, s. §. 127. Es kömmt bey Prätorio auch vor Ruschquint, z. Er. zu U. L. Fr. in Lübeck. Das ist aber wol durch einen besondern Baurendialekt anstatt Rauschquint gesagt. Und hieraus mag wol durch eine fernere Corruption die Rußpipe, Rußpfeif,

§. 182.

Rauschpfeife, Rauschflöte, Rauschwerk, Rauschquinte, Ruschquint, Russ- pipe are all the same. They all indicate a compound stop in which an octave and a fifth stand together on the same toeboard. The octave is 2′, and the fifth either 3′ or 1 ½′, so that at times the octave is the lower [pitch] and at times the fifth. Pitches lower than 3′ are never used, since this is supposed to be a penetrating stop. If there is someone who has never heard it, he need only draw the Quinte 3′ and Oktave 2′ together on his organ and he will get the same sound. It is constructed according to principal scale; see Praetorius, *l.c.*, p. 130, who says that the name of this stop is already old. Some prefer to call it a Rauschquinte if the Quinte exceeds the Oktave in size, but Rauschpfeife if the Oktave is larger. Others use these words without distinguishing between them. Praetorius mentions only 2-rank Rauschpfeifen, but those of 3 ranks are also common; indeed, they also come with multiple ranks, composed of smaller and smaller fifths and octaves, and thus differ from mixtures in no other way than that they have no thirds. [This stop] stands with 2 ranks in the organ at Elmshorn, at St. Jakobi in Hamburg on 2 manuals, and at St. Catharine in Magdeburg (at both of [these last-mentioned] places it is called Rauschflöt), at the Marienkirche in Bremen, at Buxtehude, at Görlitz (where "from 2-foot pitch" appears with it, i.e., the largest pipe is 2′), at St. Stephani in Bremen, and at Otterndorf in Land Hadeln. Praetorius cites a Rauschquinte 4′ at St. Petri in Lübeck.* Whether there is a 4′ Oktave in it, or whether it is supposed to mean "above 4′", or whether it is a misprint, I do not know. It appears twice at 3 ranks in the large organ at St. Nikolai in Hamburg, and twice at St. Johannis there, at the Marienkirche in Bremen, in the middle organ of the Pfarrkirche in Danzig, at St. Dominicus in Prague, in the St. Johanneskirche in Danzig, and in the Kneiphofkirche or Cathedral twice, in the Altstädterkirche organ and in the organ in the royal palace, all at Königsberg. Sometimes it is called Rauschpfeif, other times however Rauschquint. Praetorius, *l.c.*, [p. 130,] says that there is also a Rauschpfeifenbass that is still in use, but [I] have never found such a thing under this name. It no doubt must belong to the pedal; there are several examples to be cited below in which this stop is found in the pedal. For that reason,† though, the pipes could be of just the same size [as] in the manual. At times it is not written on the drawknob how many ranks it is. This is the case in the Stadtkirche at Jena, and at Danzig. Yet in other stoplists it is stated, as may be seen in the examples cited above, to which may be added: 3 ranks at St. Petri in Berlin, 3 ranks in the manual and pedal in the Cathedral at Bremen, and 3 ranks in the pedal at St. Ansgarius there, in addition to a "Rauchpfeife" 2 ranks in the [Haupt]werk, but that is an obvious printing error, and should be called Rauschpfeife. Concerning Copendorf, which also needs to be mentioned here, see §.127.‡ "Ruschquint" also appears in Praetorius, e.g., at the Marienkirche in Lübeck. That is however no doubt cast in a specific peasant dialect in place of Rauschquint. Through further corruption of this [word] may well have arisen the [terms] Russpipe, Russpfeif and Russ-

* *Syntagma musicum*, Vol. II, p. 164-5.

† i.e., because the "bass" in the title indicates location in the pedal division and not size.

‡ There the word is spelled "Copendoff."

134 Kap. VII. Von den Registern überhaupt und insonderheit.

Rußflöt, entstanden seyn, welche Namen alle bey besagtem Prätorio vorkommen. Samber hat von diesem Register auch nicht stille geschwiegen: um aber dessen dunkle Ausdrücke hier nicht nochmals wiederholen zu dürfen; so verweise ich meine Leser auf meine Anleitung zur musikal. Gelahrtheit, woselbst man S. 454. das hierher gehörige finden wird.

§. 183.

Rechte Heerpaucken nennt Prätorius l. c. S. 197. hier gehören sie zum 223. Spho.

Recordor, ist englisch, und soll so viel bedeuten als Flauto, eine Flöte, s. davon §. 145. auch 122.

Regal, s. Prätor. Tom. II. Part. II. c. XLV. p. 72. u. folg. der viel davon geschrieben. Es werden dadurch Schnarrwerke, entweder in oder ausser der Orgel, angezeiget. Diese gehören ins 21ste Kapitel; jene aber gehören hierher. In der Orgel, sagt er, mögte man es zum Unterschiede Regalpfeife nennen. Regal kömmt von Rex, und heißt königlich, weil der erste Erfinder es einem Könige zum Präsent offerirt, und es daher regale, dignum rege, regium uel regale opus, geheißen. Die Pfeifen sind gar klein, haben 3, 4, 5, und mehr Löcherchen; sonst sind sie unten ganz zu. Man macht sie 16′, meistens aber 8′, auch 4′. Das Quärsen will nicht allen gefallen. Mattheson sagt in einer Anmerkung zum Niedt: „Wenn ich nur vom Re„gal lese oder schreibe, so wird mir übel. Es dringt ein solches infames Schnarrwerk „zwar weit durch, aber ohne die geringste Lieblichkeit." Siehe Niedts 2ten Theil, S. 114. Anmerk. i.) Sie verstimmen sich auch sehr. Und ob schon einer (secundum *Prætorium*) sie hat machen wollen, daß sie ein Jahr dauerten; so hat man es doch noch nie dahin gebracht. Ordentlich sind die Pfeifen von Meßing. Auch hat man sie von Blech; welches aber das Trichterregal ist, weil die Pfeifen wie ein Trichter, oder wie eine blecherne Trompete gemacht werden; doch kaum 1′ groß. Davon siehe in T. §. 201. Von Harfenregal, s. §. 158. Von Singendregal, s. §. 193. Von Jungferregal, s. §. 161. Vom Cymbelregal, s. §. 134. Scharfregal, s. §. 186. Von Geigendregal, §. 161. Von Knopfregal, s. §. 115.; eben daselbst ist auch Apfelregal. Köpflinregal findet man §. 163. Grobsordunenregal, Grobgedacktregal, und Gedämpftregal, sind bey Prätorio, und Suptilregal bey Sambern, S. 153. zu suchen. Sonst gehört hierher noch, daß man auch findet Großregal, Kleinregal; jenes ist zu Grüningen 8′; dieses auch, aber nur 2′, wo es nicht etwan verdruckt, welches doch nicht glaublich, weil es Werkmeister auch sagt, der es nennt: Kleinregalbaß; weil dies zum Pedale, 8′ aber zum Manuale gehört. Kleinregal ist auch zu St. Petri in Magdeburg. So steht auch 16′ zu St. Dominico in Prag; dies könnte noch eher Großregal heißen. Weil dies Regal durch den Wind angeblasen wird; so heißt es Regale a vent, von uentus, der Wind; wovon

flöt, all of which names appear in the abovementioned Praetorius. Samber also does not refrain from mentioning this stop, but to avoid having to repeat again his obscure statements, I refer the reader to my *Anleitung zur musikalischen Gelahrtheit,* where what is pertinent here may be found on p. 454.

§. 183.

RECHTE HEERPAUCKEN [Military drums] are mentioned by Praetorius, *l.c.*, p. 197; here they belong in §.223.*

* This should read "§.203."

RECORDOR is English, and is said to mean the same thing as *Flauto*, a flute; see in this regard §.145 as well as §.122.

REGAL, see Praetorius, Vol. II, Part II, Chap. XLV, pp. 72f., who has written a great deal about it. The term indicates a reed, either within or apart from the organ. The latter† belongs to Chap. 21, while the former belongs here. In the organ, he says, it may be called Regalpfeife to distinguish [it from the instrument]. "Regal" comes from *Rex* [Latin "King"], and means royal, since its first inventor offered it as a present to a king, and thus it came to be called *regale, dignum rege, regium,* or *regale opus.* The pipes are very small and have 3, 4, 5 or more little holes; otherwise they are completely closed underneath. They are built at 16′, but mostly at 8′, and also at 4′. Their squawking is not pleasing to everyone. Mattheson in a note to Niedt says, "It irritates me just to read or write about the Regal. Granted that such an infamous reed penetrates right through, yet [it does so] without the slightest charm;" see Niedt's Second Part, p. 114, note i). They are also very prone to be out of tune. And although a certain person (according to Praetorius‡) claimed he could make them stay [in tune] a year, his method of doing this has not been preserved. Ordinarily the pipes are of brass, but they may also be of sheet iron, as is the Trichterregal, since the pipes are made like a funnel or like a Trompete [resonator] of sheet iron, yet barely 1′ tall; concerning it, look under "T", §.201. Concerning the Harfenregal, see §.158. Concerning the Singendregal, see §.193; concerning the Jungferregal, see §.161; concerning the Cymbalregal, see §.134; for Scharfregal, see §.186; for Geigenregal, see §.161; concerning Knopfregal as well as Apfelregal, see §.115. Köpflinregal is found in §.163. Grobsordunenregal, Grobgedacktregal and Gedampftregal are to be found in Praetorius,§ and Suptilregal in Samber, p.153. Otherwise it remains to be said here that there is also a Grossregal and a Kleinregal; the former is an 8′ at Gröningen, as is the latter, but only at 2′. One might suspect [its being a 2′] to be a misprint, but this hardly seems likely; Werkmeister makes this clear by calling it Kleinregalbass because it belongs in the pedal, while the 8′ [Grossregal] belongs in the manual.¶ There is also a Kleinregal at St. Petri in Magdeburg, as well as at 16′ at St. Dominicus in Prag; the latter should rather be called Grossregal. Because this Regal‖ is blown by wind, it is called *Regale a vent*, from *ventus*, "the wind", and is to be distinguished from *Regale de percussion*, which is

† "the instrument apart from the organ"; i.e., the independent keyboard instrument, as opposed to the organ stop of the same name.

‡ *Syntagma musicum*, Vol. II, p. 74.

§ *Syntagma musicum*, pp. 179 & 181, and "Theatrum instrumentorum," Plate 38, no. 15.

¶ See: Werkmeister, *Organum gruningense redivivum*, §.3.

‖ i.e., the type of Regal that has been discussed up to this point under this entry.

Kap. VII. Von den Registern überhaupt und insonderheit.   135

wovon Regale de percussion zu unterscheiden, welches mit Schlägeln, wie eine Stroh=
fiedel geschlagen wird, s. Matthesons Orchestre III. P. I. c. IV. §. 16. in not.
S. 434.

§. 184.

*Regula bedeutet einen jeden Registerzug, daher ist

Regula mixta (d. i. die Mixtur) oben §. 167. zu suchen, und

Regula primaria (d. i. das Principal) ist oben §. 168. anzutreffen. Und so ist
es auch mit den übrigen: denn Regula heißt ein Register überhaupt; und kann man
nur die dazu gefügten Wörter nachschlagen, so wird man alles finden.

Repetirende Cymbel. s. Cymbel §. 134.

Rohrflöte, Rhorquinte, Rohrschelle, und Rohrnasat, dieses sind lauter
solche Register, deren Pfeifen gedeckt sind, doch so, daß in des Deckels Mitte eine
runde Oefnung bleibt, wodurch ein kleines Röhrchen gesteckt wird, daß es also zwo Pfei=
fen sind, etwann auf folgende Art:

das kleine Pfeifchen (a) kann heraus ragen, auch ganz hineingerückt werden; und muß
damit eben sowol die Proportion beobachtet werden, als in der Pfeife selbst. s. Prätor.
S. 141. Wenn diese Röhrchen ganz hineingerückt werden, daß man auswendig nichts
davon siehet als das Loch; so sind sie beständiger: denn sonst wird daran leicht etwas
zerstoßen. Dergleichen Register klingen heller als andere Gedackte, und haben gleich=
sam 2 Töne. (conf. §. 109.) Man hat sie 16', 8', 12', 6', 4', 3', 2', 1½', 1'.
Großrohrflöte 16' Ton ist besser zu gebrauchen im Manuale, als das große Gedackt
16'; denn es klingt lauter und reiner, und läßt dabey doch eine wohlklingende Quinte
mit hören. Sie steht in der großen Orgel zu St. Nikolai in Hamburg; in der Stadt=
orgel zu Rudolstadt, 46) Großrohrflötenbaß 16' ist zu Bückeburg; Rohrflöten=
baß 16' zu Sondershausen; Großrohrflöte 16' im Manuale und Pedale abge=
sondert zu Riddageshausen in der Klosterorgel; s. von allen den Prätorium l. c. Rohr=
flöte 8' ist zu Jena in der Stadtkirche; zu Grüningen; in der Altstädter Orgel zu
Königsberg; in der Predigerkirche zu Erfurt; 47) zu St. Stephani in Bremen ist
8' und 4' in einem Claviere; so auch zu St. Johannis in Lüneburg; zu Grüningen
ist auch noch 4', und heißt es daselbst Rohrflöt oder Gedackt; 4' ist im Dom, und
zu St. Ansgarii in Bremen; zu St. Jakobi in Hamburg; im Löbenicht zu Königs=
berg,

46) Und in der Hauptkirche B. M. V. zu Mühlhausen im Hauptmanual, von weiter Mensur
und starker Intonation. Sie hat ein herausragendes Rohr.

47) Auch in der Oberstädtischen Hauptkirche B. M. V. alhier im Oberwerke, von eben der Struk=
tur, wie die vorher gedachte 16füßige.

Ch. VII. Concerning Stops in General and in Particular

struck with mallets like a xylophone (Strohfiedel); see Mattheson's [*Forschende*] *Orchestre* III, Part I, Chap. IV, §.16, in note [9] on p. 434.

§. 184.

REGULA[, Latin "rule" or "guide",] means each single stopknob. Thus
REGULA MIXTA (i.e., a mixture) is to be sought above in §.167, and
REGULA PRIMARIA (i.e., a Principal) is met with in §.168 above. And so it is with the other [stops having names beginning with the word *Regula*], since *Regula* means in general a stop. One need only consult the words added to it, and one will find everything.

REPETIRENDE CYMBEL, see Cymbel, §.134.

ROHRFLÖTE, RHORQUINTE, ROHRSCHELLE, and ROHRNASAT are simply stops whose pipes are stopped, yet leaving in the middle of the cap a round opening, through which a little tube (Röhrchen) is inserted, so that [each pipe] is thus two pipes,* rather in the manner as follows:

* i.e., the normal pipe plus the chimney in its cap.

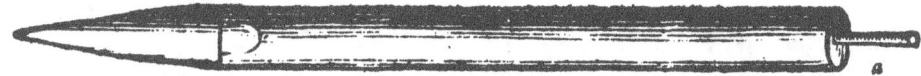

The little chimney at *a*) may project [upward] out [of the cap], or it may extend entirely down into [the pipe]. [The chimney] must observe the same proportion as the pipe itself; see Praetorius, [Vol. II,] p. 141. If the chimneys extend entirely down into the pipe, so that nothing is seen on the exterior except the hole, they are more durable, for otherwise something can easily damage them. Such stops† sound brighter than other Gedackts, and likewise speak two pitches simultaneously (cf. §.109‡). They are found at 16', 8', 12', 6', 4', 3', 2', 1½' and 1'. Grossrohrflöte 16' is better to use in the manual than the low Gedackt 16', since it sounds louder and clearer and produces in addition a euphonious quint. It stands in the large organ at St. Nikolai in Hamburg and in the Stadtkirche organ at Rudolstadt.46) There is a Grossrohrflötenbass 16' at Bückeburg, a Rohrflötenbass 16' at Sondershausen, and a Grossrohrflöte 16' [available] separately in the manual and pedal in the Klosterkirche organ at Riddagshausen; for all of these, see Praetorius, *l.c.*§ There is a Rohrflöte 8' in the Stadtkirche at Jena, at Gröningen, in the Altstädterkirche organ at Königsberg, and in the Predigerkirche at Erfurt.47) At St. Stephani in Bremen and at St. Johannis in Lüneburg it is at 8' and 4' in the same manual. It also appears at 4' in the Cathedral and at St. Ansgarii in Bremen, at St. Jakobi in Hamburg, in the Löbenichtkirche at Königsberg, in the

† i.e. Rohrflötes in general.

‡ Adlung writes nothing in §.109 about two pitches; presumably he is referring here to the quint that (along with the fundamental) is prominent in Rohrflöte timbre; cf. §. 180, "Quintadon".

§ *Syntagma musicum*, Vol. II, pp. 186, 197 & 199.

---

46) and in the main manual of the Hauptkirche of the BVM at Mühlhausen, of wide scale and strong voicing. It has chimneys that project outward. [Albrecht]

47) Also here [at Mühlhausen] in the Oberstädtische Hauptkirche BVM, in the Oberwerk, of the same structure as the 16' mentioned above [in note 46]. [Albrecht]

136 Kap. VII. Von den Registern überhaupt und insonderheit.

berg; in der neuen Orgel zu Leipzig; im Dom und zu St. Catharinen in Magdeburg, wie auch zu Waltershausen 2 mal. 2′ habe ich nicht gesehen, als im Dom zu Magdeburg: Aber 1′ ist im Pedale zuweilen zu finden, und giebt es gute Bauerflöten, oder Bauerflötbaß. (conf. §. 121.) So ist sie z. E. zun Reglern und Augustinern (evangelischer Seite) in Erfurt. Diese Rohrflöte 1′ wird von etlichen Rohrschelle genennet, weil es eine helle Quinte in sich hat: es errinnert aber Prätorius S. 141. daß diese Benennung nicht accurat sey. Einige nennen sie Bauerflöt, z. E. wenn Prätorius im Dom zu Magdeburg anführt Bauerflötbaß 1′ (weil es im Pedale ist;) so schreiben die dasigen Domküster Rohrflöt 1′ dafür. 6′, 12′, 3′, 1½′ sind Quinten; und wenn sie nach Rohrflötenart gemacht sind, können sie Rohrflöten heissen: aber besser ists, man druckt es mit aus, daß es Quinten sind, und nennt sie Rohrflötquint, und so kömmt 6′ vor in Görlitz: oder Rohrquint, und so kam dieß Wort vor in der neuen Michaelisorgel (so aber 1750 mit verbrannt) in Hamburg, da sie gar 12′ war. 6′ ist zu Jena, und heißt daselbst Rohrnasat. Rohrquint 3′ weis ich nirgends. Rohrflöte 2′ heißt auch Superrohrflöte. Endlich muß man diese Rohrflöt nicht mit den Rohrwerken verwechseln. Denn Rohrwerke sind Schnarrwerke.

Rurestris (scil. tibia) von rus, das Feld, s. bey Bauerflöt §. 121. it. §. 188. bey Schweizerpfeife.

Rußpipe ist ein unbekannt Register, wenigstens hier zu Lande. Ich habe eine Anzeige dieses Worts gesehen beym Prätorio, der in seinen Dispositionen sagt, sie stehe in Hamburg zu St. Jakobi, und an andern Orten mehr. Ich glaube es sey eine Corruption des Worts Rauschpfeife, oder Rauschpipe, wovon oben §. 182. nachzulesen.

§. 185.

Salcional. s. Matthesons Anhang zu Niedts zweytem Theile, S. 168. da er sagt: „Bey diesem Worte, daferne es italienischer Abkunft ist (wie wol zu vermuthen) „könnte observirt werden, daß es von Salcio oder Salce, so ein Weidenbaum heißet, „herkommen, und so viel bedeuten könne, als eine aus Weidenästen geschnittene „Pfeife, oder eine Schäferflöte. Es klinget dieses Stimmwerk sonst einer Viola „di Gamba nicht ungleich." Wer es siehet, der weis am besten, wie es aussiehet. Es müßte nach dem italienischen Saltschonal gelesen werden. Salycional, welches weiter unten sagt, ist vielleicht eben das. Salicional steht, nach §. 313., zu Reval. Die Leute hören zuweilen ein Register nennen, aber nicht recht; und auf solche Weise werden hernach aus Unwissenheit dergleichen verschiedene Namen einer Sache eingeführt. Ich habe es 16′, 8′, und 4′ angetroffen. Es ist von Metall, offen, und die Mensur desselben ist noch enger, als die Violdigambe, und klinget doch stumpfer und platter, als dieselbe; wegen der schweren Intonation bekommt es Bärte an den labiis. Am klange ist es sehr schwach; wie ich denn diejenigen, die ich gehört habe,

new organ at Leipzig,* in the Cathedral and at St. Catharine in Magdeburg, and also twice at Waltershausen. I have never seen a 2′ [Rohrflöte] other than in the Cathedral at Magdeburg; but it is sometimes found at 1′ in the pedal, where it makes a good Bauerflöte or Bauerflötbass (cf. §.121). This is the case, e.g., at the Reglerkirche and the Augustinerkirche (the Protestant part of it) in Erfurt. Some call this 1′ Rohrflöte "Rohrschelle"† because it includes a bright quint within its [sound]; but Praetorius mentions on p. 141 that this term is inaccurate. Some call it Bauerflöt; e.g., whereas Praetorius cites a Bauerflötbass 1′ (since it is in the pedal) in the Cathedral at Magdeburg, the Cathedral vergers there write "Rohrflöt 1‴" for this [stop].‡ 6′, 12′, 3′ and 1 ½″ are Quints, and if they are built as Rohrflötes, then they may be called "Rohrflöte". But it is preferable to state expressly that they are Quints and call them Rohrflötquint, as in the 6′ that appears in Görlitz; or Rohrquint, a word that appeared in the new Michaeliskirche organ in Hamburg (which burned with the church in 1750), where it was indeed a 12′. There is a 6′ at Jena that is called Rohrnasat. I know of no [example of a] Rohrquint 3′. The Rohrflöte 2′ is also called Superrohrflöte. Finally, the Rohrflöt must not be confused with the reeds (Rohrwerken), for "Rohrwerke" are reeds (Schnarrwerke).

Rurestris (namely *tibia* ["flute"]), from *rus*, "field": see under Bauerflöt, §.121, likewise under Schweizerpfeife, §.188.

Russpipe is an unfamiliar stop, at least in these parts. I have seen this word mentioned in Praetorius, who says in his stoplists that it stands at St. Jakobi in Hamburg and other places as well. I believe it is a corruption of the word Rauschpfeife or Rauschpipe, discussed in §.182 above.

§. 185.

Salcional. See Mattheson's Appendix to Niedt's Second Part, p. 168, where he says: "In connection with this word, provided it is of Italian origin (as may well be surmised), it may be observed that it derives from *Salcio* or *Salce*, as a willow tree is called, and may mean the same as a whistle cut from a willow branch, or a shepherd's pipe. This stop sounds similar to a Viola di Gamba." It is best actually to see it in order to know what it looks like. It must be pronounced "Saltschonal" after the Italian fashion. Salycional, spoken of further below, is perhaps the same thing. According to §.313 there is a Salicional at Reval.§ At times people hear the pronunciation of a stop incorrectly, and in this way such variant names for things subsequently get established out of ignorance.¶ I have encountered it at 16′, 8′ and 4′. It is of metal, open, and its scale is even narrower than the Violdigambe, yet it sounds duller and flatter than the latter. Because it is difficult to voice it is provided with beards on its lips. It is very weak in sound. I have found those that I have heard to be little different in sound than a

* See Mattheson's Appendix to Niedt, p. 189, as well as "The New Organ in Leipzig," under "Leipzig" in Chapter 10.

† "Schelle" is a little bell.

‡ Presumably it is they who have supplied Adlung with the stoplist he prints in §.308 of the original publication, in which there is a Rohrflöte 1′ in the pedal.

§ but spelled "Salcional;" see the stoplist of the organ at Reval in Chapter 10.

¶ Adlung is probably referring to the variant spelling "Salicional" mentioned in his previous sentence, which has since become the standard spelling for this stop.

Kap. VII. Von den Registern überhaupt und insonderheit. 137

habe, am Klange einer Violdigambe nicht weit unterschieden befunden. 16′ steht es in der Pfarrkirche zu Danzig; zu St. Dominico in Prag 2 mal. 8′ findet man schon mehr; als in der großen Orgel zu St. Nikolai in Hamburg; in der vorhin gedachten Pfarrkirche zu Danzig; zu St. Johannis daselbst; zur Dreyfaltigkeit daselbst; zu St. Bartholomäi daselbst; zu St. Catharinen daselbst 2 mal; in der Haberbergischen Orgel zu Königsberg; zu St. Michaelis in Lüneburg; zu Stockholm; in der Marienkirche zu Thoren; im Dom zu Upsal. 4′ habe ich nur angetroffen zu Königsberg in der Altstädter Orgel; zu St. Bartholomäi in Danzig, und zu Waltershausen. 48) Solacinal, welches ich zu Naumburg in der Otternskirche angeschrieben gefunden und besehen, ist eben das.

Salicet hat mit Salcional einerley Ursprung, nämlich von Salix ein Weidenbaum, oder von salce, da jenes lateinisch und dieses italienisch ist. Ich habe es nirgends gefunden, als zu Görlitz, wobey Borberg sagt, es gleiche seiner engen Mensur wegen einer Weidenpfeife, und habe auch davon den Namen; sey eins der artigsten Register, und lasse sich zu einem laufenden Basse mit dem großen Principal 16′, Oktave oder Violdigamba 8′ gar wohl brauchen; dahingegen es mit der Offenflöt 4′ bey einer starken Musik sich hören läßt, und von solcher, weil sie stumpfer als Oktav und Salicet intonirt, nicht überschrieen wird. 49)

Salycinale. Ob dies mit Salcional einerley seyn soll, weis ich nicht, und habe ich es bis dato nirgends gefunden. Doch denkt Janowka in claue daran, da er es S. 91. unter die gemeinen Register zählt.

Sanftgedackt, s. Gedackt, §. 150.

§. 186.

Scarpa. Dies Register führt Samber S. 155. in der Salzburger Domorgel 4′ an, und zwar als ein Zungenwerk; (d.i. ein Schnarrwerk: sonst aber ist es mir niemals zu Gesicht gekommen, und weis auch deswegen keine weitere Nachricht zu geben. Man findet das Wort nicht einmal in einem Lexiko. Sollte eine kleine Harfe dadurch angedeutet werden; so wundert michs, das er nicht den rechten Namen Harpa behalten und gebraucht, da er doch denselben eben daselbst im 2ten Claviere gesetzt hat, da er geschrieben: Harpa von meßingen Rohren in 16 Fuß.   Schall-

---

48) Es findet sich auch in Mühlhausen in der Kirche D. Blasii 4′ im Rückpositiv.

49) Bey uns befindet es sich allhier in mehrgedachter Hauptkirche B. M. V. in Oberwerk 4′, und ist der Mensur nach enger, als eine Violdigambe, doch fehlet ihm die Stärke einer solchen, indem es bey seinem schneidenden Wesen dennoch etwas stumpf, schwach und langsam anspricht. Die veränderten Schreibarten dieses Worts, als: Salcional, Salycional, Salicinal, Salicet, Solacinal, Salcionale, rc. rc. veranlaßten den Verfasser des musikalischen Wörterbuchs zween besondere Artikel im Lexiko unter Salicet und Salcional (doch NB. beyde unter einer Disinition, welche auch der compendiöse Lexikonschreiber getrost nachgeschrieben) zu machen. Salcional, Salicional und Salicet, ist die beste Schreibart, und was sich nicht so schreibet, ist obstante deriuatione grundfalsch.

S

Violdigambe. It stands at 16' in the Pfarrkirche at Danzig, and twice at St. Dominicus in Prague. It is found more often at 8', such as in the large organ at St. Nikolai in Hamburg, in the abovementioned Pfarrkirche, St. Johannis, the Dreifaltigkeitskirche, St. Bartholomai and St. Catharinen (twice) in Danzig, in the Haberbergkirche organ at Königsberg, at St. Michaelis in Lüneburg, at Stockholm, in the Marienkirche at Thoren and in the Cathedral at Uppsala. At 4' I have encountered it only at Königsberg in the Altstädterkirche organ, at St. Bartholomai in Danzig, and at Waltershausen.[48] Solacinal, which I have found written and examined in the Ottmarskirche at Naumburg, is the same thing.

SALICET is of the same derivation as Salcional, namely from *Salix*, "a willow tree", or from *salce*, the former being Latin, the latter Italian. I have never found it anywhere except at Görlitz [at 4'], about which Boxberg says that due to its narrow scale it resembles a willow pipe, that it is one of the most pleasing stops, and that it is well suited to use for running bass passages with the great Principal 16' and the Oktave or Violdigamba 8'; on the other hand, it* may be used with the Offenflöt 4' [to realize the figured bass] in loud ensemble music, and will not stick out in it, since [the Offenflöt] is voiced more dully than the Oktav [4'] and the Salicet.† [49]

SALYCINALE. I do not know if this is supposed to be the equivalent of "Salicional"; to date I have never encountered one. Yet Janowka mentions it in his *Clavis*, p. 91, counting it among the common stops.

SANFTGEDACKT, see Gedackt, §.150.

§. 186.

SCARPA. Samber, p. 155, cites this stop at 4' in the Salzburg Cathedral organ, specifically as a "Zungenwerk" (i.e., a reed (Schnarrwerk)). I have never seen it anywhere else, though, and therefore I have no further information about it. The word is not to be found anywhere in a dictionary. If by this [Samber] means a small harp, I find it strange that he did not hold to and use the proper name *Harpa*, which he has in fact recorded there in the second manual, writing: "*Harpa* with brass tubes (Rohren) at 16 foot."

---

48) It is also found in Mühlhausen in the St. Blasiuskirche at 4' in the Rückpositiv. [Albrecht]

49) Here [in Mühlhausen] it is found in the aforementioned Hauptkirche BMV at 4' in the Oberwerk, narrower in scale than a Violdigambe, yet lacking the strength of that stop, in that in spite of its penetrating character it nevertheless speaks somewhat dully, weakly and slowly. The various spellings of this word, such as: Salcional, Salycional, Salicinal, Salicet, Solacinal, Salcionale, etc., have occasioned the author of the musical dictionary‡ to make two separate articles in the dictionary under "Salicet" and "Salcional"§, giving definition[s] for both of them, definitions which the author of the compendious lexicon has cheerfully copied.¶ Salcional, Salicional and Salicet are the best spellings, and anything not spelled thus is fundamentally incorrect, in spite of its source. [Albrecht]

---

* This might appear to refer to the Salicet 4', but Boxberg, p.[14] makes it clear that the Offenflöt is to be combined with the stops just listed (i.e., Principal 16', Oktave or Violdigamba 8') for (moderately) loud ensemble music; cf. §.172, "Offenflöt." Therefore "it" must be understood as referring to the combination of stops previously enumerated.

† See Boxberg, p.[14].

‡ i.e., Johann Gottfried Walther, *Musicalisches Lexicon*. Leipzig: Wolffgang Deer, 1732.

§ p. 538; the two entries are actually under "Salicet" and "Salicianal, oder Salcional."

¶ i.e., [Barnickel?], *Kurzgefaßtes Musicalisches Lexicon*. Chemnitz: J.C. and J.D. Stößel, 1737, p. 327.

Schallmey, französisch chalumeau, oder chalemie, ist ausser der Orgel fast der Hautbois gleich, daher auch die Hautbois eine französische Schalmey heißt, s. davon §. 159. Genug für uns, daß es in der Orgel ein Schnarrwerk ist im Oktavenklange: und habe ich die Schalmey 16' 8' und 4' angetroffen, da sie denn wol können dem Instrumente gleich intonirt werden, weil es auch ein Rohrwerk ist. Den Riß davon kann man beym Prätorio sehen. Dieser will daß die Schallmeyenkörper allezeit halb so groß seyn sollen, als der Trompete, und dieser Körper halb so groß als der Posaune; doch achte ich dieses nicht eben für gar nöthig, s. unten das 10te Kapitel. Bey der Disposition der Orgel zu St. Ansgarii in Bremen §. 270. steht Trompet oder Schalmey 4', als wenn es einerley wäre: allein, man kann sie in der Figur, Größe und Intonation schon unterscheiden. Sonst steht Schallmey 4' zun Predigern in Erfurt 2 mal; im Dom zu Magdeburg, allwo Prätor. aber setzt: Schallmey oder Cornet; zu Naumburg in der großen Stadtorgel 2 mal; zu Königsberg im Dom und im Löbenicht. 8' ist in der Michaelskirche zu Erfurt. 16' zu Insterburg in Preußen. Wenn aber dies Register mit der Hautbois in der Orgel sollte eins seyn; so könnten §. 159. mehr Exempel gesehen werden. Schallmeybaß, der wie Geigen klinget, Chormaß, i. e. 8', ist zu Breßlau, s. Prätorius. Schallmey 2' weis ich nirgends; doch gedenkt Prätorius daran, auch an die 3' da er sagt: „wenn Trompete 6' ist, muß die Schallmey 3' seyn." Es ist aber anzunehmen nicht vom Ton, sondern von den Körpern. Der sonus ist bey beyden allezeit in der Oktave, und also in proportione geminata 2', 4', 8', 16'. Chalmonii ist vielleicht auch so viel, als die Schallmey, s. §. 125. Piffaro, italienisch, und Gingrina, lateinisch sollen so viel seyn, als Schallmey, da das Lateinische vom Gänseförmigen Gacken her seyn soll, wie Prätorius l. c. S. 37. meynet. Lituus soll auch nach Prätorio S. 3. l. c. eine Schallmey seyn. Andere brauchen noch die Namen Musette und Pomart, anstatt daß sie Schallmey sagen sollten, s. Samber S. 55. allwo man unter andern bereits erwähnten Namen auch den ordentlichen Namen Schallmey findet, mit dem Zusatze: von Meßing, Zungenwerk, 4fach. Wo nicht für fach etwan Fuß stehen soll; so weis ich nicht, was damit soll gemeynt seyn. In eben demselbigen Claviere hat er auch Piffaro 4', wovon er aber nicht sagt, daß es ein Zungenwerk sey.

Scharf oder **Scharp** ist eine Art gemischter Stimmen, und werden die kleinen Mixturen also genennet. Prätorius sagt, S. 131. „es sey eine rechte scharfe Stim„me, habe nur 3 Pfeifen, Oktave, Quinte, und noch eine Oktave. Etliche neh„men gar kleine Pfeifen 3 Zoll lang, oder 3 oder 4 Pfeifen in unisono und ein Oktäv„lein, aber keine Quinte; repetiren alle Oktaven (davon s. §. 83.) deswegen sotha„nes Register nicht allein zu gebrauchen. Hæc ille." Dreyfach ist das gemeinste Scharp, und wird vielfältig in Orgeln angetroffen: aber 4fach findet sich U. L. Fr. in Bremen, und eben daselbst ists im Dom 4, 5, 6fach 2mal; 4, 5fach zu St. Marien in Lübeck. Dies und das vorige, sammt allen dergleichen, ist zu verstehen, wie §. 167. dergleichen Mixturen erkläret worden: 4fach ist auch zu St. Ansgarii in Bremen;

SCHALLMEY, in French *chalumeau* or *chalemie*, is, apart from the organ, almost identical to the oboe, and thus the oboe is also called a French Schallmey; concerning this, see §.159. [It is] sufficient for us [to know] that in the organ it is an octave-sounding* reed. I have encountered the Schalmey at 16′, 8′ and 4′; they can indeed be voiced [to sound] just like the instrument, since it is also a reed instrument. Praetorius provides a sketch of it,† and suggests that Schalmey resonators should always be half as large as the Trompete, and Trompete resonators half as large as the Posaune.‡ Yet I do not consider this absolutely necessary; see Chap. 10[, §.270,] below. In the stoplist of the organ at St. Ansgarius in Bremen, §.270,§ there stands Trompet or Schalmey 4′, as if these were the same; however, they may indeed be different in shape, size and voicing. In addition the Schalmey 4′ is found twice at the Predigerkirche in Erfurt, in the Cathedral at Magdeburg, where Praetorius however writes "Schallmey or Cornet", twice in the organ of the great Stadtkirche¶ in Naumburg, and in the Cathedral and the Löbenichtkirche at Königsberg. It is at 8′ in the Michaelskirche at Erfurt, and at 16′ at Insterburg in Prussia. But if this stop is considered the same as the organ Oboe, then more examples may be seen in §.159. At Breslau there is a Schallmeybass that sounds like a violin, Chormass, i.e., at 8′; see Praetorius.‖ I have never known a 2′ Schallmey; yet Praetorius mentions it, as well as a 3′, when he says, "if the Trompete is 6′, then the Schallmey must be 3′."** This presumably refers not to pitch, but to the [length of the] resonators.†† The pitch of both is always at the octave, and in double proportion: 2′, 4′, 8′, 16′. *Chalmonii* is perhaps the same as Schallmey; see §.125. *Piffaro* in Italian and *Gingrina* in Latin are said to be the same as Schallmey, since the Latin is said to come from its gooselike honking, as Praetorius believes, *l.c.*, p. 37. According to Praetorius, *l.c.*, p. 3, *Lituus* is also supposed to be a Schallmey. Yet others use the names Musette and Pomart instead of saying Schallmey; see Samber, p. 55‡‡ where, among other names already mentioned, the usual name "Schallmey" is also found, with the addendum: "of brass, a reed, 4 ranks." If "foot" (Fuss) does not belong there instead of "ranks" (fach), then I do not know what this means. In the same manual he also has Piffaro 4′, but does not say that it is a reed.

SCHARF or SCHARP is a variety of compound stop; small mixtures§§ are called by this name. Praetorius says on p. 131 that it is a very penetrating stop, having only 3 ranks (Pfeifen), an octave, a fifth and another octave; that some [builders] use very small pipes 3″ long, or 3 or 4 pipes in unison and an octave higher, without a fifth; and that it repeats every octave (concerning this, see §.83 above), for which reason such a stop is not to be used alone. (Haec ille¶¶). The most common Scharp is 3 ranks, and is frequently met with in organs, but there is a 4 rank [specimen] at the Marienkirche in Bremen and a 4-5-6-rank at St. Marien in Lübeck. What was explained in §.167 about mixtures also applies to the stops just mentioned here, together with all like them. There is also a 4-rank at St. Ansgarius in Bremen. Biermann, p. 17, mentions a 5-rank

---

* i.e., it is never a mutation stop.

† *Syntagma musicum*, Vol II, "Theatrum instrumentorum," Plate 38.

‡ *Ibid.*, p. 142.

§ Adlung discusses this matter in §.270, but the organ at St. Ansgarius in Bremen is listed in §.285, and the actual stoplist is found in Mattheson's Appendix to Niedt, p. 159.

¶ i.e., St. Wenceslaus—the organ built by Zacharias Thayssner.

‖ *Syntagma musicum* II, p. 172.

** *Ibid.*, p. 142.

†† See §.176, "Posaune."

‡‡ This page number should be "155."

§§ i.e., presumably ones that are high-pitches, with small pipes.

¶¶ This cryptic Latin statement seems to mean, "This is where the quote from Praetorius ends."

Bremen: 5fach führt Biermann an S. 17; 4 à 5fach zu Elmshorn; auch ist 3 à 4fach zu St. Stephani daselbst; in der großen Nikolaiorgel in Hamburg ist es in einem Claviere 3fach, im andern 6fach, im dritten 4, 5, 6fach; zu St. Jakobi daselbst ist 5fach und 4, 5, 6fach; 4, 5, 6fach zu St. Martini in Bremen; 5fach zu St. Cosmi in Stade; 5, 6 à 7fach ist zu St. Joh. in Lüneburg, 7 fach zu St. Catharinen in Hamburg, und zu St. Johannis in Magdeburg, s. H. 308. 7, 8, u. 9fach in der großen Nikolaiorgel zu Hamburg, im Rückpositiv; hat also diese Orgel das Scharf 4mal. 8fach zu St. Catharinen in Hamburg. So starke Scharf sind auch wol mit den Mixturen in einem Claviere, und müssen folglich gewaltig schärfen. Man sieht wol, daß die meisten Pfeifen in unisono gehen müssen.

Scharf ist vielmals auch ein Beyname; daher man sich da, wo es in diesem Falle vorkömmt, an den Hauptnamen zu halten hat. Z. Er.

Scharfcymbel, s. oben H. 134. allwo Cymbel scharf vorkam, welches mit diesem einerley ist.

Scharflöte 2' ist zu Merseburg, H. 309. d. i. sie hat eine scharfe Intonation, s. a. Flöte.

Scharfoktave, s. Oktave.

Scharfregal, s. Regal. Es soll gedachtes Scharfregal zu St. Petri in Lübeck stehen, wie Prätorius zu seiner Zeit meldete. Vielleicht soll es soviel heißen als daß es eine besondere Schärfe oder Stärke habe, und könnte man es auch Starckregal nennen, welcher Name auch würklich vorkömmt zu Bernau in der Mark, s. Prätor. l. c.

Scharpquintez ist 3fach zun Predigern in Erfurt, und ist wol eben so viel als ein ander Scharp; und Quintez ist vor Quinta decima gesetzt, welches, wie H. 180. erinnert worden, eine Superoktave. Quintez ist oft eben so viel, siehe suo loco. Es ist aber das dasige Principal 4'; also ist die Superoktave 1', und das Scharp auch etwan 1' groß im Größten.

Schlangenrohr. Was dasselbe ausser der Orgel sey, davon ist Kirchers Musurgie nachzuschlagen, als welcher im sechsten Buche S. 505. den krummen Riß mitgetheilet hat. Dabey sagt er, daß es in Frankreich sehr gebräuchlich sey, und stärker klinge, als ein Fagott, aber nicht so lieblich. In der Orgel scheint es Marpurg in der Anweisung zur Fuge 16' groß gefunden zu haben, wenn er nemlich daselbst im 7ten Kapitel des 1sten Theils, H. 3. vom vesten Gesange in der Mittelstimme schreibet, „daß derselbe durch ein im Tone sechszehnfüßiges Instrument, z. Er. einen Baßbrum„mer (bombardo) ein Schlangenrohr, (fr. serpent) oder dergleichen Register auf „der Orgel hervorgebracht werde."

* Schön ist als ein Beywort anzusehen, und was dabey steht sucht man am gehörigen Orte: als

Schönprincipal, s. H. 177.

Ch. VII. Concerning Stops in General and in Particular

[at Goslar]. There is a 4-5-rank at Elmshorn, and also a 3-4-rank at St. Stephanus in Bremen. In the large organ of the Nikolaikirche in Hamburg it is 3 ranks in one manual, 6 ranks in a second, and 4-5-6 ranks in a third; at St. Jakobi there it is 5 ranks and 4-5-6 ranks. [There is a] 4-5-6-rank at St. Martini in Bremen, a 5-rank at St. Cosmae in Stade, a 5-6-7-rank at St. Johannis in Lüneburg, a 7-rank at St. Catharinen in Hamburg and at St. Johannis in Magdeburg; see §.308.* There is a 7-8-9-rank in the Rückpositiv of the large organ in the Nikolaikirche in Hamburg; thus this organ has the Scharf four times.† There is an 8-rank at St. Catharinen in Hamburg. Such strong Scharfs are in addition to the mixtures in a manual, and consequently they must be powerfully penetrating. It is easy to see that most of the pipes must speak in unison.‡

SCHARF is also frequently a prefix; where this is the case, one need only consult the primary name. For example,

SCHARFCYMBEL, see §.134 above, where Cymbelscharf appears, which is the same thing.

SCHARFLÖTE 2′ is at Merseburg, §.309;§ i.e., it is keenly voiced; see also Flöte.

SCHARFOKTAVE, see Oktave.

SCHARFREGAL, see Regal. The said Scharfregal is supposed to stand at St. Petri in Lübeck, as Praetorius¶ reported in his day. Perhaps it means that it has a special keenness or power, and thus it could also be called Starckregal, a name than actually appears at Bernau in the Mark [Brandenburg]; see Praetorius, *l.c.*‖

SCHARPQUINTEZ appears at 3 ranks in the Predigerkirche at Erfurt, and is without doubt the same as any other Scharp. Quintez is written for Quinta decima, which is, as was mentioned in §.180, a Superoktave; Quintez is often just exactly that; see under that entry. Since the Principal there is a 4′, thus the Superoktave is a 1′, and the largest [pipe] of the Scharp is therefore about 1′ high.

SCHLANGENROHR [Serpent]. For what this is apart from the organ, consult Kircher's *Musurgia*, the sixth book of which, p. 505, provides a sketch [of its] crooked [shape]. Regarding it, he says that it is very common in France, and sounds stronger than the Fagott, but not as pleasing. Within the organ, it seems that Marpurg in the *Anweisung zur Fuge*** has found large [examples], since in the seventh chapter of the first part of this publication, §.3, he writes concerning the cantus firmus in the middle voice, that it should be made prominent by an instrument of 16′ pitch, e.g., a Bassbrummer (bombardo),†† a Schlangenrohr (French *serpent*), or some such stop on the organ.‡‡

* SCHÖN [beautiful] is to be considered a modifying word, the word that stands with it being the one to consult at its proper entry; thus

SCHÖNPRINCIPAL, see §.177.

---

* See the stoplists of these organs in Chapter 10.

† the other three having been mentioned just above.

‡ i.e., many pipes duplicate the same pitch, since in such large mixtures so many of the pipes are so high-pitched and tiny.

§ See the stoplist of the organ at Merseburg in Chapter 10.

¶ *Syntagma musicum*, Vol. II, p. 165.

‖ p. 177.

** actually the *Abhandlung von der Fuge*, p. 154.

†† i.e., a bass schalmei or pommer.

‡‡ Marpurg is not referring to organ stops, but to the instruments, bombardo or serpent, then still in use in French church music as an accompaniment to chant.

140 Kap. VII. Von den Registern überhaupt und insonderheit.

Schreyer, Schreyerpfeife, Schryari, ist ausser der Orgel eine offene Pfeife, stark am Laut, hat hinten und vorn Löcher, fast wie die Corna-Musen, aber stärker am Klange weil sie unten offen und einfach ist. Und wiewol der des Diskant unten zugedeckt ist; so hat er doch viel Nebenlöcher, da der Wind heraus kommen kann. Prätorius beschreibt sie S. 42. l. c. Den Namen haben sie vom Schreyen; denn sie gehen stark, sagt Fuhrmann im musikalischen Trichter Kap. 10. Prätorius in seinen Orgeldispositionen S. 174. meldet, daß in Magdeburg zu St. Ulrich Kleinschreyer in der Orgel sey, und zwar in 2 Registern, d. i. wenn ein Zug für die untern, der andere aber für die obern Oktaven angebracht wird. Sonst habe ich dergleichen in Orgeln nicht gefunden. Es ist ohne Zweifel ein offen Flötregister. Werkmeister in Organo grüningensi §. 46. zählt es unter die unbekannten Register einer Orgel.

§. 187.

Schwägel, Schwiegel, oder auch Stamentienpfeife, in so ferne solche ausser der Orgel gewöhnlich, s. Prätor. S. 34. Diese Pfeifen haben nur 2 Löcher unten, und hinten eins; sind an der Länge der Querpfeife gleich, wird aber wie eine Plockflöte intonirt, ꝛc. Man hat sie auch in der Orgel, s. Prätor. l. c. S. 133. Da sind sie gleichaus weit, doch nicht so weit, als die Hohlflöte. Sie sind von den Niederländern so genennet, weil sie, gegen ander engmensurirtes Pfeifwerk zu rechnen, auch hohl und doch sanft auf Querflötenart klingen. Man findet sie bisweilen auf Gemshornart gearbeitet; doch unten und oben etwas weiter, und gleichwol oben wieder zugeschmiegt. Das labium ist schmahl; und der Klang ist stiller als die Spillflöten. Woher der sanfte Laut komme, ist nicht ausgemacht. Große Schwiegel sind 8'; Kleine Schwiegel 4'; man hat sie aber auch kleiner, und die ich gefunden, sind alle 1'. Z. Er. Schwiegel 1' in der Pfarrkirche zu Danzig; it. zu St. Catharinen daselbst, wobey Mattheson auch von der Erklärung des Worts was hat, daß es nämlich von Schweigen herzuleiten, weil sie so sanft klingen. Zu Königsberg in der Pfarrorgel ist Schwiegel auch 1', it. in der Pfarrorgel zu Stolpe in Pommern.. Zun Barfüssern in Erfurt ist Schwiegeldiskant, weil er nur die beyden obern Oktaven einnimmt. Also könnte man die 2' nennen Schwiegelalt, die 4' Schwiegeltenor, und die 8' Schwiegelbaß, oder wie man wil: Denn ausser der Orgel sind sie auch verschiedentlich. Die ganz kleinen werden Fistula minima genennet, und werden mit Flageolet oft für einerley gehalten. Largior ist auch ein Beynamen der Schwiegelpf., welche Samber in der Beschreibung der Orgel zu Salzburg S. 155. Swegl nennt.

§. 188.

Schweizerpfeife ist die Feldpfeife, s. §. 142. und Prätor. S. 35. sonderlich aber S. 128., da er sie beschreibt; in der Orgel soll sie enger Mensur seyn. Den Namen hat sie von den Nieder- und Holländern bekommen, weil sie so lang ist, und gegen

die

SCHREYER, SCHREYERPFEIFE, *SCHRYARI*, is (apart from the organ) an open pipe, strong in tone, having holes back and front, almost like a cornamuse, but stronger in sound because it is open and plain at the end.* And although the treble variety is stopped at the end, yet it has auxiliary holes so that the wind can escape.† Praetorius describes it on p. 42, *l.c.*. Fuhrmann in his *Musikalischer Trichter*, Chap. 10, [p. 92,] says that they get their name from *Schreyen*, "to cry," for they produce a lot of sound. On p. 174 in his organ stoplists Praetorius reports that there is a Kleinschreyer in the organ at St. Ulrich in Magdeburg, and that it is in fact two stops, i.e., there is one drawknob for the bass and another for the treble. Otherwise I have never found such a thing in an organ. It is without doubt an open flue stop.‡ Werkmeister in his *Organum gruningense*, §.46, counts it among the unfamiliar organ stops.§

* Adlung takes this assertion directly from Praetorius, p. 42 (on p. 41 Praetorius describes the "Corna Muse" as stopped at the end).

† As is often the case when Adlung discusses obsolete instruments, this description is taken entirely from Praetorius; this explains why it is so imprecise (it is doubtful that Adlung himself ever saw such an instrument).

‡ Presumably Adlung is referring to the Kleinschreyer at Magdeburg, mentioned by Praetorius; at any rate, it is unclear why he is so sure it is an open flue.

§ In fact, Werkmeister in this source seems to include it among the reeds with short resonators.

§. 187.

SCHWÄGEL, SCHWIEGEL, or also STAMENTIENPFEIFE; this is [reported to be] common apart from the organ, see Praetorius, p. 34. These pipes¶ have only two holes at the end and one at the back; they are similar in length to a Querpfeife, but blown (intonirt) like a Blockflöte, etc.‖ It also appears in the organ; see Praetorius, *l.c.*, p. 133. There they are cylindrical, yet not so wide as the Hohlflöte. The Netherlanders call them by the name [Hohlflöte] because, compared with other pipes of narrow scale, they also sound hollow and yet gentle like a Querflöte. They are sometimes found built like a Gemshorn, yet somewhat wider below and on top,** though still conical. The lip is narrow, and the sound is quieter than a Spillflöte. It is not certain what causes the gentle tone. The great Schwiegel is 8′, the small Schwiegel 4′; but they also come smaller, and the ones I have found are all 1′. For example, there is a Schwiegel 1′ in the Pfarrkirche and the St. Catharinenkirche in Danzig; in listing these Mattheson also includes some explanation of the word, namely that it is derived from *Schweigen* (to be still or silent), since it sounds so soft.†† At Königsberg in the Pfarrkirche organ there is a Schwiegel 1′, as in the Pfarrkirche organ at Stolpe in Pomerania. At the Barfüsserkirche in Erfurt there is a Schwiegeldiskant that extends only over the two upper octaves. Thus the 2′ could be called an alto Schwiegel, the 4′ a tenor Schwiegel, and the 8′ a bass Schwiegel, or whatever one likes—apart from the organ they also come in various sizes. The very small ones are called *Fistula minima*, and are often considered the same at a Flageolet. *Largior* is also a surname for the Schwiegelpfeife. Samber calls it "Swegl" in his *Beschreibung der Orgel zu Salzburg*, p. 155.

¶ Adlung is speaking of the instrument, not the organ stop.

‖ Again Adlung has simply reported what Praetorius writes about the instrument in the *Syntagma musicum*, Vol. II, p. 34.

** i.e., of wider scale than a typical Gemshorn.

†† See Mattheson's Appendix to Niedt, p. 169.

§. 188.

SCHWEITZERPFEIFE is the fife; see §.142 [above] and Praetorius, p. 35, but especially p. 128 where he describes it. In the organ it is of narrow scale. It gets its name from the Netherlanders and Hollanders, because it is so long and due to its propor-

Kap. VII. Von den Registern überhaupt und insonderheit. 141

die Enge des Körpers in Ansehen der Proportion einer Schweitzerpfeife gleichet. Der Klang ist lieblich und scharf, bald wie eine Viole, wegen der Engigkeit. Man macht sie mit Seitenbärten und Unterleisten, sonst wären sie schwer zu intoniren wegen der engen Mensur; deswegen sie auch im Diskant und kleinen Pfeifen etwas weiter zu machen sind. Die große Schweitzerpfeife ist 8' ton; die kleine 4'. Aus dieser kleinen wird von etlichen Orgelmachern nur der Diskant gearbeitet, welcher alsdann Schweizerdiskant genennet wird. Desgleichen auch im Pedale findet man 1' ton und bekömmt den Namen Schweizerbaß, oder Schweizerpfeifenbaß, oder auch Schweizerflöte. Schweizerbaß 2' findet sich zu St. Catharinen in Magdeburg, s. Prät. Und zu Eisenach (s. §. 288.) ist Schweizerflöte 2'. Die große Schweitzerpfeife giebt im Pedale einen Klang wie eine Baßgeige von sich. Diese Stimme muß mit langsamen Takt und reinen Griffen, ohne Coloraturen, gebraucht werden, sonst spricht sie nicht an. Diese Beschreibung sollte uns fast glaubend machen, daß es unsere heutige Violdigamba oder vielmehr das Salicet in der Orgel sey, als von welchem wir alles das sagen können. Die Orgelmacher treffen sie selten recht. Es giebt eine andere Art von Schweizerpfeifen, die oben gedeckt sind, (jene aber sind offen) und Principalmensur haben; und ungeacht sie daher sich nothwendig überblasen müssen; so fallen sie doch in ihren rechten Ton, gleich als wären sie nicht gedeckt. In Erfurt zun Barfüssern ist die Schweizerflöte; it. zu Stralsund, da sie 1' ist, s. Prätor. 8' aber steht sie zu St Catharinen in Magdeburg im Manuale. Die kleine befindet sich in Gotha sowohl im Schloß, als auch zu St. Margarethen. Sonst wüßte ich sie nirgends. Wo aber die erste Art die Violdigamba seyn sollte; so wäre sie fast in den meisten Orgeln.

§. 189.

Sedetz, Sedex, Sedecima, ist wol alles einerley, und von Sedecim, sechzehn, hergeleitet. Dem zu folge sollte man 16 palmulas diatonas fortschreiten, da man aber nicht auf c, sondern auf d, oder auf eine Sekunde käme, die aber in der Orgel nicht klingt. Also ist es klar, es müsse in der Rechnung ein Fehler, und Sedecima anstatt decima quinta gesetzt seyn: denn es soll ein Oktavenregister seyn, weil man es 2' und 1' hat. Es ist davon §. 171. etwas gemeldet worden. Nachdem das Principal groß ist, ist die Sedecima auch groß. Bey 4' ist die Sedecima 1'; bey 8' aber 2'. Bey Principal 16' aber ist sie der Rechnung nach 4'. So ist bey Prätorio zu St. Ulrich in Magdeburg Sedetz 4', S. 174. 175. Sedecima wird diese Superoktave 2' oder 1' genennet z. Ex. in Danzig. (vid. *Prætorius* in Dispositionibus.) Zu Colberg in der Heiligengeistkirche ist sie 2'; it. zu Danzig in der Pfarrkirche; in der mittelsten Orgel selbiger Pfarrkirche; zu St. Johannis daselbst; in Görlitz. 1' ist sie zu St. Petri in Berlin; zur Dreyfaltigkeit in Danzig; zu Görlitz; zu Königsberg im Dom; in der Steindammischen Orgel daselbst; zu Cosmi in Stade; in der Neustadt in Thoren. Wer aber in diesen Exempeln die Principale dagegen hält, der wird

S 3   finden,

Ch. VII. Concerning Stops in General and in Particular 141

tionately narrow body resembles a Schweitzerpfeife.* The tone is gentle and keen, almost like a Viole, due to its narrowness. It is made with boxbeards, otherwise it would be difficult to voice due to its narrow scale. For the same reason it is also made [with a] somewhat wider [scale] in the small treble pipes. The great Schweitzerpfeife is 8′ pitch; the small one, 4′. Some organbuilders only build the treble of the smaller variety,† which is then called Schweitzerdiskant. It is also found in the pedal at 1′ pitch and gets the name Schweizerbass or Schweizerpfeifenbass, or also Schweizerflöte. There is a Schweizerbass 2′ at St. Catharinen in Magdeburg (see Praetorius[, p. 176]), and a Schweizerflöte 2′ at Eisenach (see §.288).‡ The great Schweizerpfeife in the pedal produces a sound like a bass viol. This stop must be used for slow tempi and with simple chords, without runs, otherwise it does not speak. This description§ is almost enough to make us believe that [the Schweizerpfeife] is [the same as] the Violdigamba or rather the Salicet in our present-day organs, since we can say all the same things about these stops. Organbuilders often do not make them successfully. There is another type of Schweizerpfeife that is stopped on top (the former ones are open) and has a principal scale; thus it cannot help but overblow, and thus drops down to its proper pitch, just as if it were not stopped. At the Barfüsserkirche in Erfurt there is a Schweizerflöte; likewise at Stralsund, where it is a 1′ (see Praetorius, p. 168). At St. Catharinen in Magdeburg, however, it is an 8′ in the manual. The small [Schweizerpfeife] is found both in the palace [organ] as well as at St. Margarethen in Gotha. I know of it nowhere else. If the first type should be the Violdigamba, however, then it would be in almost every organ.

§. 189.

SEDETZE, SEDEX, SEDECIMA, are indeed all the same, and are derived from *Sedecim*, "sixteen". Accordingly, if one were to proceed upward [from C] for 16 diatonic notes, one would end up not on c[′], but on d[′], or a second above c[′], which does not sound [well] on the organ.¶ Thus it is clear that this must be a mistake in the figuring, and that *Sedecima* is written instead of *decima quinta* [i.e., fifteenth]; for it is supposed to be an octave stop, because it is at 2′ and 1′. Something more is said about this in §.171 [above]. The size of the *Sedecima* is in proportion to that of the Principal; with a 4′ the *Sedecima* is 1′, with an 8′ it is 2′, and with a 16′ Principal it is calculated at 4′. Thus in Praetorius, p. 174-75, there is a Sedetz 4′ at St. Ulrich in Magdeburg. The Superoktave 2′ or 1′ is called *Sedecima*, e.g., in Danzig (see Praetorius's stoplists[, pp. 162-3]). At Colberg in the Heiligengeistkirche it is a 2′, as well as in the Pfarrkirche organ at Danzig and in the middle organ in the same church, at St. Johannis in Danzig, and at Görlitz. At 1′ it is at St. Petri in Berlin, at the Dreyfaltigkeitskirche in Danzig, at Görlitz, in the Cathedral and Steindammkirche organs at Königsberg, at St. Cosmae in Stade and in the Neustadtkirche in Thoren. Anyone, however, who compares the [pitch of the] Principal in these examples [with the pitch of the *Sedecima*]

* i.e., a fife: a narrow-scale traverse flute, though not necessarily of very high pitch.

† i.e., the 4′.

‡ There is no such stop listed for the organ at Eisenach; see the stoplist of the organ at Eisenach in Chapter 10.

§ Adlung has taken all of the above description from Praetorius, p. 128.

¶ i.e., the dissonance that results when C and d′ are sounded simultaneously.

finden, daß die Rechnung gar oft nicht zutrift. Denn da findet man z. Er. bey Principal 16′ sedecima 1′, welches nimmer accurat ist; denn 4′ sollte schon so heißen: bey 8′ aber 2′. So finde ich auch bey Principal 2′ Sedecimam 1′; da es doch nur eine simple Oktave ist. Sedecima offen kommt vor §. 172. da es bald Principalart hat, bald nicht. Gedacktflöt Sedecima d. i. 2′ s. in G §. 151. Sedex ist dem Ursprunge nach auch so viel, und obschon Niedt in zweyten Theile der Handleitung, in der ersten Ausgabe Kap. XII. es für die Sesquialter ausgegeben; so hat ihn doch darinnen Mattheson in der 2ten Edition corrigiret, der ausdrücklich sagt, es sey ein Superoktävchen 1′ : 2′ Ton. Der Name Sedeze kömmt bey Prätorio vor, da er von den Oktaven handelt. Doch bleibt allezeit richtig, daß es der Rechnung nach sollte quinta decima, oder kurz weg Quintez heißen. Man kann aber auch stets Oktave sagen.

Sedezenquint ist herzuleiten von Sedecima, davon zuvor gesagt worden. Die Sedecima qua talis, man mag sie 2′ oder 1′ setzen, kann keine Quinte abgeben: also muß man durch Sedezemquint verstehen die Quinte über der Sedecima. So steht zu St. Lambrecht in Lüneburg bey Prätorio Sedezemquint 1½′, d. i. die Quinte über 2′. Quinta ex sedecima würde eben so viel seyn, wovon §. 172. nachzusehen.

§. 190.

Serpent, s. Schlangenrohr, §. 186.

Sesquialter, sesquialtera, (proportio) ist ein bekannt Orgelregister. Sesqui heißt so viel als ganz, und altera halb; ganz und ein halb: denn die 3, welche die sesquialter ist, steckt in der Oktave 2′ einmal, und noch ein halbmal. Also ist 10 sesquinona, weil die 10 die 9 einmal ganz in sich hält, und noch $\frac{1}{9}$ dazu, s. Orchestre I. P. I. c. I. §. 8. Also wäre es die ordentliche Quinte, und zwar meistens 3′, wie sie denn auch schon bey den alten ist, s. Werkmeisters Orgelprobe S. 73. Kap. 30. ganz. Daß Sedex bey Niedten so viel seyn sollte, als Sesquialtera, und daß es falsch sey, ist schon §. 189. erinnert worden. Man nennt aber heut zu Tage Sesquialter, wenn zu der Quinte noch die Terz gesetzt wird. Also ist es eine gemischte Stimme. Es kann aber die Terz größer seyn als die Quinte, und alsdann heißt es mit einem besondern Namen Tertian, davon unten §. 198. zu lesen. Doch wissen viel Orgelmacher den Unterschied nicht, und nennen es auch Sesquialter, da es doch nur alsdann so heißt, wenn die Terz kleiner ist, als die Quinte, und da ist die Benennung a potiori. Man sieht also, wenn die Sesquialter aus 2 Stimmen bestehet, so kann sie nicht gebraucht werden, ohne ein Oktavenregister dabey zu ziehen; und da wird ordentlich Oktave 4′ gebraucht. Um aber es noch besser zu machen, setzt man oft diese Oktave 4′ noch besonders auf den Stock der Sesquialter, daß also die Sesquialter 3fach wird: alsdann muß aber Oktave 4′ noch einmal im Claviere seyn. Zuweilen will man mehr Veränderungen machen, und macht aus der Quinte ein besonder Register, und aus der Terz auch, da wird, wiewol gar nicht accurat diese Terz von manchen auch Sesquialter

will find that the figuring very often does not come out right. For example, a *sedecima* 1′ is found with a Principal 16′, which is not at all accurate, since it should be thus with a 4′ [Principal], and 2′ with an 8′ [Principal]. I also find a *Sedecima* 1′ with a Principal 2′, yet it is just a plain Oktave. It appears in §.172 that the *Sedecima* sometimes has the characteristics of a Principal, and sometimes not. For a Gedacktflöt *Sedecima*, i.e., 2′, look under "G[edacktflöte]", §. 151. *Sedex* is the same thing by origin; although Niedt in the second part of his *Handleitung*, first edition, chap. XII, presents it as a Sesquialter, Mattheson in the second edition* nevertheless corrects him by saying expressly that it is a little Superoktave at 1′ or 2′ pitch. The name "Sedetze" appears in Praetorius when he deals with Oktaves.† Yet according to correct calculation it ought always to be called *quinta decima*, or Quintez for short. It is always possible to say Oktave, too.

SEDETZENQUINT [sic] is derived from *Sedecima*, which has already been discussed. The *Sedecima* as such, be it a 2′ or a 1′, cannot produce any Quinte; thus by Sedetzemquint must be understood the Quint above the *Sedecima*. Thus in Praetorius[, p. 233,] a Sedetzemquint 1 ½′, i.e., the Quinte above 2′, stands at St. Lambrecht in Lüneburg. *Quinta ex sedecima*, discussed in §.172, would be the same thing.

§. 190.

SERPENT, see Schlangenrohr, §.186.

SESQUIALTER, *SESQUIALTERA* (*PROPORTIO*), is a familiar organ stop. "Sesqui-" means the same as "whole" (ganz), and "altera", "half": [thus] "whole and a half". For the 3, which the Sesqualter is,‡ is divisible by the Oktave 2′, once and then half again.§ Thus 10 is *sesquinona*,¶ since it contains 9 once plus 1/9th; see [Mattheson's *Neu-eröffnete*] Orchestre I, Part I, Chap. 1, §.8. Thus [the Sesquialter] would be an ordinary Quinte, i.e., mostly at 3′, as was indeed the case in the past; see Werkmeister's *Orgelprobe*, p. 73, Chap. 30 in its entirety. Niedt states that the Sedex is the same as Sesquialtera, but it has already been mentioned in §.189 that this is false. Nowadays, though, the Quint combined with the Terz is called the Sesquialter; thus it is a compound stop. The Terz may be larger than the Quinte, in which case it is called a specific name, Tertian; consult §.189 below. Many organbuilders do not know the difference, though, and thus also call it Sesquialter, which it should be called only if the Terz is smaller than the Quinte, since it gains its name from the more important rank.‖ It is obvious that, since the Sesquialter consists of 2 ranks, [each speaking a different pitch,] it cannot be used without drawing an Oktave[-sounding] rank with it, and for this purpose the Oktave 4′ is ordinarily used. To make things even better, however, this Oktave 4′ is often specifically placed on the Sesquialter toe-board, thus making the Sesquialter 3 ranks. Then the Oktave 4′, however, must appear once again [separately] in that manual. Sometimes there are even further variants: the Quint is made a separate stop as well as the Terz. And, although it is completely inaccurate, many call this Terz

* Chapter 10, pp. 114, note (k). Chapter 10 of Mattheson's edition of the second part of Niedt's *Musikalischer Handleitung* is a re-working of the material contained in Chapter 12 of Niedt's original publication.

† *Syntagma musicum*, Vol. II, p. 129.

‡ Here Adlung is referring to the (by now ancient) *proportio sesquialtera*, that signified triple meter in mensural music notation.

§ Roughly speaking, as Adlung knows, since he has already discussed the accurate figure, 2 2/3′, in §.179.

¶ this term signifies the relation 10:9.

‖ i.e., the larger rank; in the case of the Sesquialter, the Quint.

Kap. VII. Von den Registern überhaupt und insonderheit. 143

quialter $1\tfrac{1}{3}'$ oder $1\tfrac{3}{5}'$ genennet. Weil dies Register allerwegen zu sehen; so führe ich kein Exempel an. Es kan aber in kleinen Werken, wo Principal nur 4' ist, die Sesquialter auch nur Quint $1\tfrac{1}{3}'$ haben; und die Terz über der Oktave 1'. Die Alt: dreßdener Orgel hat große Sesquialter im Alt und Diskant; das ist, sie geht nicht durch das ganze Clavier, weil sie in den untern clauibus etwas craß klingt, wegen der großen Quinte und Terz. Doch meistens führt man sie durch, weil ja im vollen Werk auch sonst die Quinte 3' auch wol 6' durchgeführet wird, so auch die Terz. In Görlitz wird die Sesquialter Zynk genennet. Aber Zink ist ganz was anders, wenn es mit dem i geschrieben wird. Daß aber das vorhin angeführte Tertian von der Sesquialtera zu unterscheiden, sieht man daher, weil sie beyde zugleich in einem Claviere stehen können, z. Er. in Bremen zu U. L. Frauen und zu St. Martini. Samber führt diese Stimme auch an S. 155. und nennet sie Horn oder Sesquialtra.

§. 191.

* Sesquiquarta und
* Sesquioctaua, suche §. 197. bey Terz.

Sexta, ist auch ein Orgelregister, und steht 2' groß zu St. Petri in Berlin; zu St. Catharinen in Danzig; in der altstädtischen Orgel in der lutherischen Kirche zu Elbingen; in Cößlin; in der Pfarrkirche zu Danzig; zur Dreyfaltigkeit daselbst 2mal; zu St. Johannis daselbst 2mal; zu Königsberg im Kneiphofe; im Löbenicht daselbst; in der königlichen Schloßorgel daselbst; zu St. Dominico in Prag. Es scheint alles gar paradox zu seyn, theils, daß eine Sexte klingen soll, da doch bekannt, daß alle Register in Akkordstönen seyn müssen; denn was würde das werden, wenn ich C hätte, und dazu die Quinte zöge, welche g angiebt; auch die Sexte, so a wäre? Theils daß 2' soll eine Sexte geben, das doch sonst eine Oktave ausmacht. Allein es dient folgendes zur Nachricht. Man hat, wie oben gemeldet, die Sesquialter mit der Terz verbunden, daß also meistens die Quinte 3' und die Terz über dem c 2' die Sesquialter ausmachen. Diese Terz über der 2füßigen Oktave ist von andern so genennet worden 2'; nicht als wäre deren größte Pfeife 2', sondern weil sie aus 2' Oktave gearbeitet worden ist, und wenn sie solte tiefer, bis ins c gebracht werden, würde es die Oktave 2' seyn. Und das wollen gewiß die anzeigen, welche nicht schreiben Sexta 2', sondern Sexta aus 2'. So kömmt es auch vor in der Disposition der Altstädter Orgel in Königsberg; in der Orgel im Löbenicht daselbst. Und eben das wird auch bedeuten sollen Sexta von 2' in der dasigen königlichen Schloßorgel. Man hat hernach diese Terz besonders in die Orgeln gesetzt, und sie bisweilen Terz genennet, bisweilen aber auch Sexte, nicht, als wär es eine Sexte, vom großen C, oder von einem andern c an zu rechnen, sondern von der Quinte an zu zählen, mit welcher sie in der Sesquialter vereinigt ist. Denn in der Sesquialter ist g und e, so eine Sexte von einander entfernet sind. Daher im Kreyßen würklich stehet Sexte aus 3', oder von der Quinte an. Ja, es wird durch Sexte zuweilen die Sesquialter doppelt verstanden,

Ch. VII. Concerning Stops in General and in Particular 143

also Sesquialter 1 1/5' [sic] or 1 3/5'. Since this stop may be seen everywhere and always, I will not cite any examples. In small organs, however, where there is only a Principal 4', the Sesquialter may have only a Quint 1 ½' and the Terz above the Oktave 1'.* The Altdresdener organ† has a Grosse Sesquialter im Alt und Diskant [great Sesquialter in the alto and treble]; i.e., it does not go throughout the entire manual, since it sounds somewhat coarse in the lower register, due to the low Quinte and Terz. Yet usually they are carried all the way down, since in the plenum the Quinte 3' and even 6' are carried to the bottom, as well as the Terz. At Görlitz the Sesquialter is called Zynk. Zink, however, is something entirely different, if it is spelled with an "i". That the abovementioned Tertian is to be distinguished from the Sesquialtera may be seen from the fact that both of them may stand together on the same manual, e.g., at the Marienkirche and at St. Martini in Bremen. Samber also cites this stop on p. 155, calling it "Horn or Sesquialtra."

* i.e., the 4/5'.
† See the stoplist of the Alt-Dresdener organ, under "Dresden" in Chapter 10.

§. 191.

* SESQUIQUARTA   and
* SESQUIOCTAVA,   see §.197 under Terz.

SEXTA is also an organ stop, and stands at 2' pitch at St. Petri in Berlin, at St. Catharinen in Danzig, in the altstädtische organ in the Lutheran Church at Elbingen, at Cösslin, in the Pfarrkirche, the Dreyfaltigkeitskirche (twice) and St. Johannis (twice) at Danzig, in the Kneiphofkirche, the Löbenichtkirche and the royal palace organ at Königsberg, and at St. Dominicus in Prague. It appears to be completely paradoxical, partly that a sixth should be sounding [at all], since it is well-known that all stops must be in chord tones (what would it sound like if I began with C, drew with it the Quinte that sounds g, and then also the Sexte, which would be a?), and partly that a 2' should produce a sixth, that would otherwise create an Oktave. But the following should settle the matter. As reported above, the Sesquialter was combined with the Terz, so that the Quinte 3' and the Terz above the 2' c thus usually comprise the Sesquialter. Some have called this Terz above the 2-foot Oktave a 2'; not that its largest pipe would be a 2', but because it is above the 2' Oktave, and if it were to be carried lower, down to c, then it would be a 2' Oktave. And this is certainly what people intend to indicate when they write not Sexta 2', but Sexta aus 2'.‡ This is how it appears in the stoplist of the Altstädterkirche organ in Königsberg and in the Löbenichtkirche organ there. The "Sexta von 2'" in the royal palace organ there no doubt also means the same thing. Later on this Terz was put into organs separately, and sometimes called Terz, but sometimes also Sexte; not that it would be a Sexte figuring from great C or from some other c, but rather counting upward from the Quinte with which it is united in the Sesquialter. For in the Sesquialter are found g and e', these being a sixth apart from each other. Thus in Greussen there actually stands a Sexte aus 3', or above the Quinte.§ Indeed, at times Sexte is meant to indicate both ranks of the Sesquialter, since

‡ "sixth from [i.e., above] 2'."

§ This would presumably be a 1 3/5'; but there is no such stop listed in the stoplist Adlung gives in §.306; see the stoplist of the organ at Kreyssen in Chapter 10.

Kap. VII. Von den Registern überhaupt und insonderheit.

standen, eben deswegen, weil sie eine Stimme darinnen ist, wie von der Quinte die Sesquialter Sesquialter heißt, weil die Sesquialter oder Quinte dabey ist, s. Niedts 2ten Theil Kap 11. der Matthesonischen Ausgabe. In der Schloßorgel zu Dresden ist Sexta $2\frac{4}{5}$; aber das ist nimmer richtig. Warum hieße es nicht $3\frac{1}{5}'$? Das giebt aber keine Terz. Ich weis daraus nichts zu machen; in der Disposition steht es so.

§. 192.

Sifflöt, Siefflöt, Siefflit, Suiflöt, Sufflöt, Subflöt, Zifflöt, und dergleichen wunderliche Schreibarten mehr, gehören zu den Hohlflöten, §. 160. Wollte einer fragen: was die Sifflöt bey den Hohlflöten mache, da ich sie §. 171. unter die Oktavenregister gezählet, und ihr also Principalmensur beygeleget? Dem dienet zur Antwort, daß Oktave 1', weil sie so klein wird, etwas weiter gemacht werde, doch hingegen etwas kürzer: weil nun die Hohlflöten darinn von den Oktaven abgehen, daß sie weiter, aber kürzer sind; so ist Hohlflöt 1' und Octave oder Sifflöte 1' einerley. Es steht diese Sifflöt an verschiedenen Oertern nicht nur 1' sondern auch $1\frac{1}{2}'$, da es sodann eine kleine Quinte ist; ja man trift sie auch 2' an. 1' ist in der Stadtkirche zu Jena; zu Grüningen im Schlosse; zu St. Catharinen in Hamburg, und zu St. Petri daselbst. $1\frac{1}{2}'$ ist im Dom zu Bremen; in der großen Nikolaiorgel in Hamburg, eben dasselbe in der kleinen Orgel; zu St. Jakobi allda; zu St. Johannis und St. Gertrud daselbst; zu St. Ansgarii in Bremen; zu St. Marien in Lübeck, und zu St. Michaelis in Lüneburg; it. zu St. Cosmi in Stade. Zu Schöningen im Schlosse findet man Sieflöt oder Schwiegelpfeif 1'. 2' ist in der mittelsten Orgel der Pfarrkirche zu Danzig, und in der Marienkirche zu Thoren. Ich glaube aber, daß Sifflöt $1\frac{1}{2}'$ und 2' nichts anders sind, als ordentliche Quinten und Oktaven von solcher Größe in Principalmensur.

§. 193.

Singendcornet, s. Cornet, §. 132.

Singendregal, kömmt in Prätorii Orgeldispositionen vor. Es wird von Metall, Blech, Meßing, ꝛc. gearbeitet. Daher steht im Dom zu Magdeburg Meßingregal singend 4' und eben daselbst ist zu St. Ulrich Singendregal 4', it. zu St. Marien in Halle; auch soll es zu St. Marien in Danzig stehen: Doch ist diese Orgel wol nicht mehr. Was besonders an dem Regal sey, daß es den Namen eines singenden verdiene, weis ich nicht eigentlich. Was sonst ein Regal sey, ist §. 183. zu sehen.

§. 194.

Solacinal, ist §. 185. zu suchen.

* Sonne, s. Anleitung zur musikal. Gelartheit, S. 464.

Sordun,

it is one rank within it, just as the Sesquialter* gets its name from the Quinte† because the Sesquialter or Quinte is present [within it]; see Niedt's Second Part, Chap. 11,‡ in Mattheson's edition. In the palace organ at Dresden there is a Sexta 2 ⁵/₄'; but that is certainly incorrect. Why would it not be called 3 ¼'? But that does not produce a Terz [either]. I do not know what to make of it; it reads that way in the stoplist.§

* i.e., the compound stop.

† See §.190 above.

‡ This should read "Chap. 10", p. 114.

§ i.e., in Mattheson's Appendix to Niedt, p. 171.

§. 192.

Sifflöt, Siefflöt, Siefflit, Suiflöt, Sufflöt, Subflöt, Zifflöt, and other such fanciful spellings, belong to the Hohlflöte family, §.160. If anyone should ask what the Sifflöt is doing among the Hohlflöten, since in §.171 I included it among the Oktave stops and thus assigned it a Principal scaling, this will serve as an answer: the Oktave 1', since it is so little, is built somewhat wider, yet on the other hand somewhat shorter. Now since the Hohlflötes deviate from the Oktaves in that they are wider but shorter, thus the Hohlflöt 1' and the Octave or Sifflöte 1' are the same. The Sifflöt is found at various places, not only at 1', but also at 1 ½', in which case it is a little Quinte; indeed, it is also encountered at 2'. It is 1' in the Stadtkirche at Jena, in the palace [organ] at Gröningen, and at St. Catharine and St. Petri in Hamburg. At 1 ½' it is in the Cathedral and St. Ansgarius in Bremen, in the large and small organs of the Nikolaikirche, at St. Jakobi, St. Johannis and St. Gertrud in Hamburg, at St. Marien in Lübeck, St. Michaelis in Lüneburg and St. Cosmae in Stade. In the palace at Schöningen there is a Sieflöt or Schwiegelpfeif 1'. It is at 2' in the middle organ of the Pfarrkirche at Danzig, and in the Marienkirche at Thoren. I believe, though, that the Sifflötes 1 ½' and 2' are nothing other than ordinary Quints and Oktaves at those sizes and at Principal scale.

§. 193.

Singendcornet, see Cornet, §.132.

Singendregal appears in Praetorius's organ stoplists. It is constructed of pipe metal, sheet iron, brass, etc. Thus there stands in the Cathedral at Magdeburg a Messingregal singend [i.e., singing brass regal] 4' and at St. Ulrich in the same city a Singendregal 4'. There is also one at St. Marien in Halle, and one is said to have stood at St. Marien in Danzig, yet that organ no longer exists. What there is special about this Regal that earns it the name "Singend", I really do not know. For what a Regal is otherwise, see §.183.

§. 194.

Solacinal may be found in §.185.

* Sonne; see *Anleitung zur musikalischen Gelahrtheit*, p. 464.

Kap. VII.   Von den Registern überhaupt und insonderheit.   145

Sordun, italienisch Sordoni, (etliche nennen es Dolzianen) ist sonst ausser der Orgel fast den Corna-Musen am Resonanz gleich, oder den stillen Krumhörnern, ꝛc. s. Prätor. S. 28. l. c. In der Orgel ist es ein Schnarrwerk, und Prätorius hat auf der 38. Tabelle den Riß davon mitgetheilet, wobey er sagt, es könnten die Orgelsordunen nicht wohl höher als 16′ Ton von sich geben, weil sie gedeckt wären, und in sich noch ein verborgen corpus mit ziemlichen langen Röhren hätten. Ihr auswendiger Körper ist zwar ohngefähr 2′ hoch, und seine Weite als ein Nachthornkörper von 4′ Ton: ist aber sehr lieblich und stille, wenn es der Meister recht trift. Es wird im Manuale und im Pedale gebraucht. Aus Niedts zweyten Theile habe ich gesehen, daß es auch auf 8′ gemacht werde, und zwar auf Regalenart, und der Name soll herkommen von surdus, taub, stille, weil es still und lieblich anzuhören ist. Er nennet es ad mentem quorumdam auch Bordun; doch haben wir von Bordun als von einem Gedackte oben gehandelt, und kann wol seyn, daß es etliche vor eins nehmen, aus einer Confusion: von andern aber wird es auch ausdrücklich unterschieden, wie denn beyde 16′ in einem Claviere stehen zu Colberg in der Heiligengeistkirche; also muß es zweyerley seyn. Sonst ist Sordun 16′ auch zu Grüningen 2 mal, allwo es einmal im Pedale stehet, und Sordunbaß heißt. In Merseburg zu St Maximi findet man Sordin 8′, welches diese Stimme vielleicht seyn wird. Zu St. Dominico in Prag ist Sordun 16′, welches dem lateinischen noch näher kömmt. Samber schreibt Sordun von Zungenwerk 2fach 8′ im Pedale: welches aber ein seltsamer Ausdruck ist.

Sordunenregal mag wol von Sordun die Benennung haben. Und weil Sordun nach der vorigen Beschreibung still und tief ist; so mag dies Regal auch groß und stille seyn. So findet sich Grobsordunenregal auf 16′, nebst Regal 8′ und 4′ beysammen zu St. Nikolai in Leipzig, s. Prätor. l. c.

§. 195.

Sperrventile werden auch unter den manubriis gefunden; was man dadurch verstehe, s. §. 74

Spielflöt, Spillflöt, Spielpfeife, Spillpipe, ist alles einerley, und ist meistentheils mit dem Gemshorn eins, daher davon §. 153. nachzuschlagen.

Spitz, s. Cornet.

Spitzflöte, Spindelflöte, Spitzquinte, ist abermal einerley, und hat den Namen bekommen von der Figur der Pfeifen, welche auch so zugespitzt sind, wie die Gemshörner, oder wie eine Spindel, s. Prätor. S. 153. Allein, sie sind im labio weiter, und oben noch mehr zugespitzt, als das Gemshorn. Auch giebts deren welche, die oben gar wenig offen, und unten gar enge labirt sind, daher sie zwar lieblich klingen, aber schwer rein zu intoniren sind. Wenn es Spitzquinte heißt, so ist es eine Quinte auf dieser Manier gemacht. In Hamburg (wie aus Prätorii Dispositionen zu ersehen war sonst eine Spitzquinte; es ist aber dieselbe auch in der Altstädter Orgel zu

T   Königs=

Ch. VII. Concerning Stops in General and in Particular

Sordun, *Sordoni* in Italian (some call it Dolzianen) is, apart from the organ, almost identical to the Cornamuse in sound, or to a quiet Krumhorn; see Praetorius, *l.c.*, p. 28.* Within the organ, it is a reed, and Praetorius has provided a sketch of it in [his *Syntagma musicum*, Vol. II, "Theatrum instrumentorum",] Plate 38, about which he says that organ Sorduns ought not to produce anything higher than a 16′ pitch,† since they are stopped, and contain within themselves a hidden body with rather long tubes.‡ Their outer bodies are about 2 feet tall, and their width that of a Nachthorn pipe (Nachthornkörper) of 4′ pitch. It is very lovely and gentle if properly built by a master. It is used in the manual and in the pedal. In Niedt's second part§ I have noted that it is also made at 8′ [pitch], indeed like a Regal, and that the name is said to derive from *surdus,* [Latin] "deaf", "quiet", because it is quiet and gentle in tone. He also calls it, according to the usage of some, "Bordun", but we have treated the Bordun above as a Gedackt. It may well be that some out of confusion consider them the same; but others expressly distinguish between them. Since they both stand at 16′ on the same manual in the Heiligengeistkirche at Colberg, they must be different. In addition, the Sordun 16′ also appears twice at Gröningen (once in the pedal, called Sordunbass). At St. Maximi in Merseburg there is a Sordin 8′ that is perhaps this [same] stop. At St. Dominicus in Prague there is a Sordun 16′; this approximates more closely the Latin [form of the word¶]. Samber‖ writes "Sordun von Zungenwerk 2 fach im Pedale" [Sordun, a reed of two ranks in the pedal]; that is certainly an odd expression.

Sordunenregal may well get its name from Sordun. And because the Sordun according to the above description is quiet and low [in pitch], thus this Regal may also be large** and quiet. There is a Grobsordunenregal 16′, together with Regals 8′ and 4′, at St. Nikolai in Leipzig; see Praetorius, *l.c.* [, p. 179].

§. 195.

Sperrventile [cut-out ventils] are also found among the stopknobs; for what these are, see §.74 [and §.204 below].

Spielflöt, Spillflöt, Spielpfeife, Spillpipe, are all the same, and are usually the same thing as a Gemshorn; therefore consult §.153.

Spitz, see Cornet[, §.132].

Spitzflöte, Spindelflöte, Spitzquinte, are once again all the same. The names come from the shape of the pipes, which are conical like the Gemshorns, or like a spindle; see Praetorius, p. 153.†† They are wider at the lip, however, and come to more of a point on top than the Gemshorn. There is also a variety that is barely open on top, with a very narrow lip below; it indeed sounds gentle, but is difficult to voice purely. If the name Spitzquinte is used, then it is a Quinte constructed in this way. In Hamburg there was formerly a Spitzquinte (as may be noted in Praetorius's stoplists‡‡);

---

* This should read "p. 39."

† p. 146.

‡ For a further explanation of this, see "Ranket," §.181.

§ as edited by Mattheson, p. 114.

¶ perhaps because it ends with "un" rather than with "in".

‖ Vol. II, p. 155.

** i.e., of low pitch.

†† This should read "p. 135."

‡‡ at the Jakobikirche; *Syntagma musicum*, Vol. II, p. 169.

146   Kap. VII.   Von den Registern überhaupt und insonderheit.

Königsberg 3′, und zu Stockholm; item 1½′ zu Danzig in der Pfarrkirche. Man kann aber diese Quinte auch schlechtweg Spitzflöte heißen; wie denn auf solche Art Spitzfleut 3′ zu Görlitz gefunden wird. Spitz- oder Flachflöt 4′ steht im Kloster Riddagshausen, nach Prätorio: sonst aber sind sie unterschieden. Spitzflöte 8′ ist zu St. Marien in Lübeck; zu St. Lambert in Lüneburg; it. im Dom zu Upsal. 4′ steht sie zu St. Jakobi in Hamburg. 2′ wird sie zum Reglern in Erfurt, und zu Halle gefunden, an welchem letztern Orte Prätorius den Namen Spitzflöte gesetzt hat. Dies Werk ist aber nicht mehr vorhanden. Das Wort Spindelflöte ist zu sehen in Niedtens zweytem Theile der musikal. Handleitung. Jula ist auch soviel, als Spitzflöte: denn in Prätorii Orgeldispositionen steht sie in der Orgel zu St. Lambrecht in Lüneburg 8′, da steht: Jula oder Spitzflöt. Auch kömmt daselbst Jula vor im Pedale zu Riddagshausen in der Klosterorgel. Jule soll zu Bernau in der Mark die Quinte seyn vom groben Principal, und also 6′, weil das Principal 8′ ist, s. Prätor. Lateinisch heißt sie Flauta cuspida, von cuspis, eine Spitze; dieser Name kömmt vor zu Sandomir, da sie 4′ ist: daselbst steht auch Flauta cuspida 8′; man sieht aber leicht, daß es ein Druckfehler sey. Coni oder Kegel sind bey Sambern S. 153. eben das.

§. 196.

* Stahlspiel ist zu Merseburg im Thum, das ist, wenn anstatt der Glocken Stahlstangen angeschlagen werden. Es liegt unmittelbar über den Manualtastaturen.

Stamentienpfeif, ist Schwiegel, s. §. 187.

Stark ist ein Beywort; daher sind Starkgedackt, Starkposaun, Starkregal, Starksubbaß u. s. w. bey dem Hauptworte zu suchen.

Stern, s. §. 133. bey Cymbel.

Still. Wenn dies Beywort mit andern Wörtern zusammengesetzt wird; so hat man sich jedesmal an das dabey stehende Hauptwort zu halten.

Stillflöte ist vielleicht das deutsche Wort von Flute douce, s. davon §. 146.

Suauis, ist ebenfalls ein Beywort.

Subbaß 32′, und 16′, s. oben von Gedackten §. 150. Wenn aber dies Wort als ein Beyname gebracht wird, als z. Ex. Subbaßposaune; so suche man das Hauptwort auf.

Subprincipalbaß, s. Principal.

* Sub ist aber auch ein Beywort, so die Tiefe anzeigt, wobey man sich nur um das Hauptwort zu bemühen hat.

Suptil ist ein Beyname; suche also

Subtiles Regal, bey Regal.

Sufflöt und Suiflöt, it. Suffloit, s. Sifflöt.

Super

there is still one in the Altstädterkirche organ at Königsberg and at Stockholm, at 3′, as well as at 1 ½′ in the Pfarrkirche at Danzig. This Quinte, however, may simply be called Spitzflöte; this is why there is a Spitzfleut 3′ to be found at Görlitz. According to Praetorius there is a Spitz- or Flachflöt 4′ in the Klosterkirche at Riddagshausen, but otherwise these are different. There is a Spitzflöte 8′ at St. Marien in Lübeck, at St. Lambert in Lüneburg, and in the Cathedral at Uppsala. It stands at 4′ at St. Jakobi in Hamburg. At 2′ it is found in the Reglerkirche in Erfurt and at Halle; at the last-named place Praetorius records the name Spitzflöte,* but this organ is no longer extant. The word Spindelflöte may be seen in the second part of Niedt's *Musikalische Handleitung*.† Jula often means the same thing as Spitzflöte; in the organ at St. Lambrecht in Lüneburg, found in Praetorius's stoplists[, p. 233-4], there stands "Jula or Spitzflöt". This same Jula appears in the pedal in the Klosterkirche organ at Riddagshausen. At Bernau in the Mark [Brandenburg] Jule is reported to be the Quinte of the Groben Principal [16′], and thus a 6′, since the [ordinary] Principal is at 8′; see Praetorius[, p. 177]. The Latin name is *Flauta cuspida*, from *cuspis*, "a point"; this name appears at Sandomir, where it is a 4′. There is also a *Flauta cuspida* 8′ recorded there, but it is easy to see that this is a printing error.‡ Samber on p. 153 calls the same thing *Coni* or Kegel.

* *Syntagma musicum*, Vol. II, p. 178.

† p. 111, under "Flöten."

‡ This last statement makes no sense; the entry appears to be quite correct, since there is no other 8′ flute on the Hauptwerk. See Mattheson's Appendix to Niedt, p. 196.

§. 196.

* STAHLSPIEL appears in the Cathedral [organ] at Merseburg, where steel rods are struck instead of bells. It is located directly above the manual keyboards.

STAMENTIENPFEIF is the Schwiegel; see §.187.

STARK ["strong, loud"] is a prefix; therefore Starkgedackt, Starkposaun, Starkregal, Starksubbass, etc., are to be consulted under the primary word.

STERN, see §.133, under Cymbel.

STILL ["soft, gentle"]. If this accompanying word is prefixed to other words, then in each case the primary word that stands with it must be consulted.

STILLFLÖTE is perhaps the German word for *Flute douce*, q.v., §.146.

SUAVIS [Latin "gentle, soft"] is likewise an accompanying word.

SUBBASS 32′ and 16′, see above under Gedackt, §.150. If however this word is used as an accompanying word, as e.g. Subbassposaune, then the primary word must be consulted.

SUBPRINCIPALBASS, see Principal.

SUB is also an accompanying word, indicating deep [pitch]; in connection with it one only need trouble oneself with the primary word.

SUPTIL is an accompanying word; thus consult

SUBTILES REGAL under Regal.

SUFFLÖTE and SUIFLÖT, likewise SUFFLOIT, see Sifflöte.

Supergedackt, s. Gedackt, §. 150.

Supergedacktflöte, s. Flöte.

Superfedez ist eine Oktave höher als Sedecima, davon §. 189. zu sehen. Wie denn alle die, so das Super vor sich haben, in dem andern dabeystehenden Worte zu suchen. Also auch

Superoktave, s. in Oktave, §. 171.

Süßflöte oder Hohlflöte, s. Dulzflöte.

Swegl, s. Schwiegel.

Sylvestris, s. Waldflöt.

§. 197.

Tambour, s. Tympanum.

Tarantantara, s. Trompet, §. 202.

Tertia ist ein bekannt Register in der Orgel. Es heißt auch Ditonus. So steht zu Sandomir. Die erhöhete Tertia heißt auch Decima. Daher man auch Decem findet. So hat Prätorius das Wort in der Lübecker Orgel zu St. Petri, da steht Decembaß, so sonst Detzehm heißt, z. Er. eben daselbst im Dom, und zu U. L. Fr. daselbst ist Detzembaß im Stuel. Was der Stuel bey der Orgel sey, weis ich nicht. Decima ist in der Altstädter Orgel, in Königsberg. Zu Stockholm ist Decima $2\frac{2}{3}'$. Im Dom zu Upsal ist Decima $4'$. Zu Prag ist im Pedale die Tertia $2'$. Besiehe oben §. 128. In der neuen Orgel zu St. Nikolai in Rostock ist Diatonus $1\frac{3}{5}'$ 3mal, und zu Sandomir ist $2'$ 2mal. Zu St. Nikolai in Stralsund ist Tertia $1\frac{3}{5}'$. Zu Sandomir heißt die Tertia $2'$ auch Sesquioctava. Die vorigen Benennungen sind leicht zu verstehen: aber was Sesquioctava hier thun soll, weiß ich nicht. Nach der Erklärung des Worts sesqui §. 190. müßte es heißen einmal ganz, und noch den achten Theil: aber diese Proportion bringe ich nicht heraus. Denn nehme ich die Oktave ganz, und noch den 8ten Theil; so giebt das keine Terz. Es mußte die Proportion wie 9 zu 8 seyn, da die 8 einmal in der 9 steckt, rc. Doch wem hilft das was? — Sonst wird die Proportion der Terz gar verschieden angegeben. Die größte ist $4'$: aber es kann ein Fehler seyn; denn so groß macht man sie deswegen nicht gern, weil sie allzucraß klinget. Wenn es aber so wäre; so fragt sichs: wie die Terz $4'$ oder $2'$ seyn könne, da ja dieses Oktaven geben? Antwort: es ist eben so anzunehmen, als bey der Sexte §. 191. erinnert worden, daß es von der Oktave in besagter Größe die Terz sey. Also wird sie kleiner werden, welches in die Brüche kömmt; und hätte man auch sagen können Tertia aus $4'$, oder aus $2'$, wie Sexte aus $2'$ oder von $2'$, rc. Was aber die wahre Proportion betrift; so zeigen die vorigen Exempel meistens $1\frac{3}{5}'$: andere setzen was anders, in welche Rechnung wir uns nicht einlassen. In der Jenaischen Collegenorgel steht auch Tertia $1\frac{3}{5}'$. Sonst ist noch wohl zu merken, daß durch die Terz zuweilen die Sesquialter verstanden wird, weil sie aus der Quinte und Terz besteht. Auch ist in Erfurt zu St. Andrea würklich die

Ch. VII. Concerning Stops in General and in Particular

Supergedackt, see Gedackt, §.150.

Supergedacktflöte, see Flöte[, §.145].

Supersedez is an octave higher than a Sedecima; thus see §.189. In the same way, everything that is prefixed by "Super" should be sought under the word that it accompanies. Thus

Superoktave, see under Oktave, §.171.

Swegl, see Schwiegel.

Sylvestris, see Waldflöte.

§. 197.

Tambour, see Tympanum.

Tarantantara, see Trompet, §.202.

Tertia is a familiar stop in the organ. It is also called *Ditonus*, as at Sandomir. The octave *Tertia* is also called *Decima*, which is also written as *Decem*. This word occurs in Praetorius in the organ of the St. Petrikirche at Lübeck, where there is a Decembass, elsewhere spelled Detzehm; e.g., in the Cathedral and the Marienkirche one finds "Detzembass im Stuel."* I do not know the meaning of "Stuel" as it applies to the organ.† There is a *Decima* in the Altstädterkirche at Königsberg. At Stockholm there is a *Decima* 2 3/5'.‡ In the Cathedral at Uppsala there is a *Decima* 4'. At Prague there is a *Tertia* 2' in the pedal; see above, §.128[, also §.191]. In the new organ at St. Nikolai in Rostock there are three examples of a *Diatonus* 1 3/5',§ and at Sandomir two examples of this stop at 2'. At St. Nikolai in Stralsund there is a *Tertia* 1 3/5'. At Sandomir the *Tertia* 2' is also called *Sesquioctava*. The earlier terms are easy to understand, but I cannot understand what *Sesquioctava* is doing here [at Sandomir]. According to the explanation of the word "sesqui" in §.190, [*Sesquioctava*] should mean a whole plus one eighth,¶ but I cannot figure this proportion out. Moreover, the proportion of the Terz is indicated in many and various ways. The largest is 4', but this must be a mistake; no one likes to make it this large, since it would sound far too coarse. Yet if it were of this size, the question arises, how could the Terz be 4' or 2', since these produce octaves? The answer: it is to be taken in the same sense as has been mentioned with regard to the Sexte in §.191, that the Terz comes from the Oktave in the size stated. Thus it would be smaller, which gets into fractions. It could also be expressed as "*Tertia* out of the 4'", or "out of the 2'", just like the Sexte out of 2' or from 2'. As concerns the true proportion, most of the previous examples indicate 1 3/5'. Others put down different figures, but we will not get involved in them. A *Tertia* 1 3/5' also stands in the Collegenkirche organ at Jena. Moreover, it would be well to note that by the Terz is meant at times the Sesquialter, since [the Sesquialter] consists of the Quinte and the Terz. Furthermore, at St. Andrea in Erfurt, as at Naumburg, the Terz is actually labeled with

---

* Praetorius, *Syntagma musicum*, Vol. II, p. 166. Though there is a Detzembass in the pedal of both of these organs, it is only to the one in the Marienkirche that Praetorius adds "im Stuel."

† The meaning of this word is no more certain today than in Adlung's time. The most frequent interpretation of the word is "Rückpositiv" (i.e., "Stuhl" ("chair"), in the same sense that the corresponding division in England was sometimes called the "Chair organ". But in his *Orgelwörterbuch* (3. Auflage. Mainz: Rheingold-Verlag [1949], p. 60) Carl Elis defines the word "Orgelstuhl" as follows: "The old term for the lower case (das untere Stockwerk) of the organ in which is located the mechanism, and where pipes, especially pedal pipes, may occasionally be placed." This description suggests that "im Stuhl" (or "Stuel") may also mean "in Brustwerk position" (cf.: J.F. van Os, "A 15th-century Organ reconstructed in Switzerland...," trans. James L. Wallmann. *The American Organist*, Vol. 24, No. 3 (March 1990), p. 62, note 13). See also the note under "Mixtur", §.167.

‡ sic; see Mattheson's Appendix to Niedt, p. 199.

§ Mattheson's Appendix to Niedt, p. 195; the term, however, is spelled "Ditonus."

¶ "Sesquioctava" is the proportion 9:8.

Terz mit dem Namen Sesquialter belegt; it. zu Naumburg, wovon oben bey der Sesquialter. Will man also da die Sesquialter voll haben; so muß man die Quinte 3′ dazu ziehen, sammt der Oktave 4′ s. Sesquialter, §. 190. Sesquialter aus 2′ ist eben das. Wer sonst fremde Namen brauchen will, (sagt Werkmeister in der Orgelprobe S. 74.) der kann die Tertia nach ihrer Proportion 4 zu 5, oder 2 : 5 sessesquiquartam, oder duplam sesquiquartam, oder vom Principal 8′ an zu rechnen quintuplam 1 : 5, und von 16 an, decuplam, 1 : 10, nennen. Es ist übrigens hierbey noch zu merken, daß diese hier beschriebene Terz eine offene Flötstimme nach Principalmensur sey; imgleichen daß man allezeit unter dem Namen Terz die große Terz zu verstehen habe, die aber nicht über sich schweben darf, wie sie sonst bey der Temperatur aufwärts schweben muß.

§. 198.

Tertian ist eine gemischte Flötstimme, fast wie die Sesquialter, daher sie auch zuweilen Sesquialter heißt, s. §. 90. Doch ist in diesen die Terz größer als die Quinte, also giebt das große C an e g, da in der Sesquialter g c̄ war. Man macht es meistens 2fach. Z. E. im Dom zu Bremen; it. zu Ansgarii u. St. Stephani daselbst; zu St. Joh. in Hamburg; in der neuen Orgel in Leipzig; zu St. Cosmi in Stade. Doch steht es auch 3fach in der großen Orgel zu St. Nikolai in Hamburg, und da wird vielleicht die Oktave dabey seyn, wie bey der Sesquialter bisweilen Oktave 4′ ist. Was damit gemeynet sey, wenn man sagt: Tertian 2 fuß, weis ich nicht: es müßte etwan die Terz und Quinte über Oktave 2′, oder aus 2′ gearbeitet seyn, s. dergl. bey Sexta, §. 191. So ist Tertian 2′ in der Altdresdener Orgel; zu Rudelstadt; im Stift Wurzen. Wo nicht etwan hier einige Irrungen vorgegangen, daß Fuß anstatt Fach gesetzt worden, als welches was gar gemeines ist: oder es bedeutet, daß es sich über der Oktave 2′ anhebe. Tertian 2 fach steht noch zu St. Martini in Bremen; zu Colberg in der Heiligengeistkirche; in der Sackheimischen Orgel. It. in der Pfarrorgel zu Königsberg; zu Kleinbrembach, einem Dorfe bey Erfurt, ist es 2fach unter dem Namen der Sesquialter. Zu St. Petri in Berlin ist Tertian 1⅘′. Was das ist, weis ich nicht. Vielleicht soll der Name von der größten Pfeife, als von der Terz, genommen seyn. Doch 1⅘′ ist kein Ton.

§. 199.

Thubal, s. §. 171. bey der Oktave.

Thubalflöt, s. eben dasselbe. Man findet auch Tubal.

Thunbaß. Eine Orgelstimme. Es führte die große Hohlflöte 8′ ton, teste Praetorio, sonst diesen Namen, von thönen, weil sie weit und thönend gewesen. Sie heißt auch wol Subbaß oder Koppel, s. Prätor. S. 132.

Tibia

the name Sesquialter; see above under Sesquialter[, §.190,] for an explanation of this. Thus if one wants to have the complete Sesquialter, one must draw the Quinte 3′ with it, together with the Oktave 4′; see Sesquialter, §.190. The same thing goes for "Sesquialter out of 2′" [as has been said above concerning "Sesquialter out of 4′"]. Anyone who wants to use other strange names (as Werkmeister says in his *Orgelprobe*, p. 74) may name the *Tertia* a *sesquiquartam* (from the proportion 4:5) or *duplam sesquiquartam* (from 2:5), or figuring from the Principal 8′, *quintuplam* (from 1:5) or from the [Principal] 16′, *decuplam* (from 1:10). Furthermore, it should be noted here that the Terz described here is an open flue stop of principal scale, and also that the name Terz always signifies the major third, which however must be tuned pure; otherwise it must beat sharp when it is tempered.

§. 198.

TERTIAN is a compound flue stop, almost like the Sesquialter, and is therefore sometimes called Sesquialter; see §.[1]90. Yet in it the Terz is lower than the Quinte, so that low C produces [the pitches] e[′] and g[′], while in the Sesquialter [low C] produces g and e above it. It is at least 2 ranks in size, e.g., in the Cathedral, St. Ansgarii and St. Stephani at Bremen, at St. Johannis in Hamburg, in the new organ at Leipzig,* and at St. Cosmae in Stade. Yet it stands at 3 ranks in the large organ at St. Nikolai in Hamburg; perhaps the Oktave [2′?] is included with it there, just as the Oktave 4′ is sometimes included in the Sesquialter. What is meant by the expression "Tertian 2 foot", I do not know; perhaps it signifies the "Terz and Quinte above the Oktave 2′", or that they are made out of the 2′, as is the case with the Sexta in §.191. Thus there is a Tertian 2′ in the Altdresdener organ, at Rudelstadt, and in the Stiftskirche at Wurzen. Perhaps several errors have been committed here, and "foot" has been written instead of "ranks", as very often happens; or it may mean that it rises above the Oktave 2′. Furthermore, Tertian 2 ranks stands at St. Martini in Bremen, at the Heiligengeistkirche at Colberg, and in the organs of the Sackheimkirche and the Pfarrkirche at Königsberg. At Kleinbrembach, a village near Erfurt, it is at 2 ranks under the name Sesqualter. At St. Petri in Berlin there is a Tertian 1 4/5′; what this is, I do not know. Perhaps the name has been taken from the largest pipe, that is, from the Terz; yet 1 4/5′ is not a [proper] pitch.

* See "The New Organ in Leipzig," under "Leipzig" in Chapter 10.

§. 199.

THUBAL, see §.171 under Oktave.

THUBALFLÖT, see the same entry. [The spelling] "Tubal" is also found.

THUNBASS. An organ stop. According to Praetorius the large Hohlflöte at 8′ pitch was also given this name, from "thönen" ["to ring, to resound"], because it was broad and ringing. It is also called Subbass or Koppel; see Praetorius, p. 132.

Tibia heißt überhaupt eine Pfeife, und bedeutet also eigentlich kein besonder Register; aber wenn sie durch ein ander Wort determinirt wird: so ist es was besonders. Jedes kann man suchen in dem Buchstaben des dabey stehenden Worts, oder in einem, so gleich viel gilt. Z. Ex.

Tibia angusta, ist die **Dulzflöt**, s. §. 139.
Tibia syluestris, ist die **Waldflöt**, oder **Waldhorn**, s. §. 209. u. 210.
Tibia transuersa, s. **Querflöt**, §. 170.
Tibia uulgaris, s. **Blockflöt**, §. 122. u. s. w.
Timbales, s. Tympanum, §. 203.
Timpani, ist der Stern, s. §. 133.
Tonus faber, s. **Glöckleinton**, §. 156.
Transuersa.
Trauersa.   } s. **Querflöte**, §. 170.
Trauersiere.
Toscan, s. Dolcan.

§. 200.

Tremulant, ist kein Klingregister, sondern etwas, dadurch der Klang der Pfeifen zitternd oder bebend gemacht wird, von Tremulo. Die Struktur ist ohngefehr diese: man macht eine Oefnung oben auf dem Hauptkanale, über diese Oefnung legt man ein länglicht 4eckigtes Bret, etwan 1 Fuß lang, und von beliebiger Breite. An den Kanal bevestiget man es mit Leder, doch fornen etwas weiter als hinten; hinten muß es ganz genau durch das Leder aufliegen, fornen aber muß es sich aufheben lassen durch das Blasen des Windes, wie sich ein Balg aufthut. In dieses Bret macht man wieder eine kleinere Oefnung, und bevestiget darüber abermal ein Bretchen, wie vorhin, daß nirgends der Wind herauskommen kann. Ich habe gesehen, daß auf diesem Bretchen noch ein kleiners gelegen: glaube aber, daß dies so nöthig nicht sey. Wenn der Wind diese Maschine wie einen Balg in die Höhe treibt; so ist sie viel zu leicht, als daß sie den Wind sollte zurückschlagen können. Da nun das Beben eben daher entstehet, wenn der Wind die Maschine bald aufhebt, bald aber dieselbe sich wieder zuthut; so kann dieses ohne Gewicht nicht erhalten werden. Demnach bevestiget man forne an das Bretchen, wo es sich aufthut, eine Drat- oder Zinnstange, etwan eine Spanne lang, zuweilen auch länger, und hänget daran ein Stück Bley, oder dergleichen, welches schwer genug ist, dem Winde zu widerstehen. Weil nun durch das erste Anblasen der Maschine dieses Gewicht gleich zu schwanken und zu beben anhebt und damit fortfähret, bis durch eine andere Gewalt alles gehindert wird; so wird der Wind auch zittern, und endlich auch der Klang der Pfeifen. Durch das manubrium aber kan der Organist den Tremulanten aufhalten, indem dadurch die Bretter fein aufgedruckt werden auf den Ca-

Ch. VII. Concerning Stops in General and in Particular

Tibia means in general "a pipe", and thus does not actually signify any particular stop. But when it is modified by another word, then it becomes something specific. Each [of these specific meanings] may be sought under the [first] letter of the accompanying word, or under a [word] that means the same thing. For example:

Tibia angusta is the Dulzflöte; see §.139.

Tibia sylvestria is the Waldflöte or Waldhorn; see §.209 and 210.

Tibia transversa, see Querflöte, §.170.

Tibia vulgaris, see Blockflöt, § .122, etc.*

Timbales, see Tympanum, §.203.

Tympani is the [Cymbel]stern; see §.133.

Tonus faber, see Glockleinton, §.156.

Transversa.
Traversa. } see Querflöte, §.170.
Traversiere.

Toscan, see Dolcan[, §.137].

* i.e., this marks the end of Adlung's remarks on the Tibia.

§. 200.

Tremulant, from Tremulo, is not a sounding stop, but rather something by which the sound of the pipes is made to flutter or shake. The structure is approximately as follows: an opening is made on the top of the main wind duct. On top of this opening is placed an oblong rectangular board, about 1 foot long and of whatever width desired. It is fastened to the duct with leather, somewhat broader in front than at the back. At the back the leather must bind it right against [the duct], but at the front the force of the wind must be able to lift it, just like a bellows. A smaller opening is then made in this board, and a little board must once again be fastened over it, as before,† so that none of the wind can escape. I have seen an even smaller board affixed to this little board, but do not believe that it is so necessary. If the wind forces this device upward like a bellows, then it is much too light to be able to drive back the wind. Now since the shaking arises from the device alternately being lifted by the wind and then closing again, this [action] cannot be sustained without a weight. Accordingly a wire or tin rod is fastened to the front of the little board, the side on which it expands. This rod is about a "Spanne"‡ long, sometimes longer, and is tipped with a piece of lead or something similar that is able to offer resistance to the wind. Then, because this weight immediately begins to bob and shake from the first time the device expands, and continues to do this until prevented by an opposing force, the wind flutters, and consequently the sound of the pipes [flutters with it]. The organist, however, can stop the Tremulant by means of a stopknob that causes the boards to be tightly pressed against the

† i.e., in the same manner as the larger board has been fastened above the wind duct.

‡ An old unit for measuring length (a hand-span), slightly over 20 centimeters.

150 Kap. VII. Von den Registern überhaupt und insonderheit.

nal, daß der Wind sie nicht aufblasen kann. Nachdem einer das Schlagen geschwind oder langsam haben will, nachdem rückt er das Gewicht weiter nach dem Tremulanten hin, oder von demselben ab: deswegen das Gewicht beweglich seyn muß an der Stange. Man kann sie auch ohne Gewicht machen, da aber die Stange alsdann dessen Stelle vertreten muß. Es muß der Tremulant fein sanfte beben, die Mensur halten, und darf ein Werk nicht dämpfen, daß es faul und falsch gehe, welches geschiehet, wenn die Tremulanten in Canale liegen. Besser liegen sie aussen. Er soll nicht klappern; deswegen alles mit Tuch und Leder zu futtern ist. Er soll auch verbauet seyn, daß er kein Gelächter verursache. Auch kann man zuweilen zwey Tremulanten haben, einen langsamen und einen geschwinden. Im Dom zu Naumburg ist deswegen einer mit der Schwankfeder, der andere ohne dieselbe. Ja man kann auch zu jedem Claviere einen besondern haben, da sie aber nicht auf den Hauptkanal, sondern auf die Arme, welche nach jeder Lade gehen, zu legen sind. Vom Tremulanten handelt Werkmeister im 16. Kap. der Orgelprobe. Samber, S. 153. schreibt Tremulus. Es wird auch der Tremulant Bock genennet, welches man bey Prätorio etlichemal antrift, doch sonderlich beym Rückpositiv. Denn so sagt er Tom. II. S. 201. „Tremulant zum „Rückpositiv absonderlich wird sonsten der Bock genennet." Er hat dieses Bocks auch gedacht zu Schöningen im Schlosse, da Bock zum Rückpositiv absonderlich ist. Auch hat er zu Riddagshausen in der Klosterorgel den Bocktremulant zum Rückpositive. Die Ursach solcher Benennung kann ich nicht errathen. Vielleicht ist sie daher gekommen, weil im Rückpositive ordinär kleine, scharfe und quäksende Stimmen sind, welche, wenn der Tremulant gehet, wie Böcke meckern.

§. 201.

Trichterregal. Vom Regal, s §. 183. Dies ist eine besondere Art, da die Pfeifen wie ein Trichter aussehen; Dieses Schnarrwerk habe ich nur 8′ gefunden. Z. Ex. zu St Ansgarii in Bremen, dabey gemeldet wird, es solle dieses von einer neuen Invention sey, fast auf die Art, wie eine Vox humana. In der bremischen Orgel sind deren 4 von solcher neuen Art, und müssen also von den alten Trichterregalen, davon Orchestre I. p. 299. gehandelt worden, wohl unterschieden werden. So redet Mattheson im Anhange zu Niedts 2ten Theile. Sonst geht das ordentliche Trichterregal nicht besser, als andere Regale. Zu St. Stephani in Bremen ist auch die neue Art; it. zu U. L. Fr. daselbst. Sonst steht es auch (doch, wie ich glaube, meist nach der alten Art) zu Elmshorn 8′; in der großen Orgel zu St. Nikolai in Hamburg; zu St. Jakobi daselbst; zu St. Petri daselbst; it. in der Domsorgel, und zu St. Marie Magdelenen allda, da die Pfeifen ganz kurz, und oben sehr weit sind; zu St. Marien in Lübeck; zu St. Michaelis in Lüneburg; zu Otterndorf im Lande Hadeln; zu St. Cosmi in Stade, ꝛc. Alle sind sie 8′ Ton.

§. 202.

duct so that the wind cannot inflate them. The weight is moved further back toward the Tremulant or away from it, according to whether a faster or slower beat is desired, and for this reason the weight must be moveable on the rod. [The Tremulant] may also be made without a weight, in which case the rod [alone] must serve in its place. A Tremulant must beat delicately and gently, keep an even beat, and must not suffocate an organ by working poorly or falsely, which happens if Tremulants are placed in wind ducts. Better that they should be located on the exterior [of a duct]. [The Tremulant] ought not to clatter, and therefore everything should be faced with cloth and leather. It ought also to be enclosed, so that it does not cause people to laugh.* It is possible at times to have two Tremulants, a slow one and a fast one. In the Cathedral at Naumburg, therefore, there is one with the bobbing spring† and one without. Indeed, every keyboard may have its own separate one, in which case they must be placed not upon the main wind duct, but rather on the ones that branch off to each [individual] chest. Werkmeister covers Tremulants in the 16th chapter of the *Orgelprobe*. Samber on p. 153 writes "Tremulus". The Tremulant is also called the "Bock", [a term] that one sometimes encounters in Praetorius, especially in the Rückpositiv. He says as much in Vol. II, p. 201[-202]: "The Tremulant specifically for the Rückpositiv is otherwise called the 'Bock'." He has also mentioned this "Bock" in the palace at Schöningen, where there is a separate Bock for the Rückpositiv alone. He also lists a Bocktremulant for the Rückpositiv in the Klosterkirche organ at Riddagshausen. I cannot fathom the origin of such a name. Perhaps it arose because there are ordinarily small, shrill and squawking stops in the Rückpositiv that bleat like billy goats (Böcke) when the tremulant is going.

* i.e., by hearing the thumping noise of the mechanism, or by watching it bob up and down.

† i.e., the rod described above.

§. 201.

Trichterregal. From Regal; see §.183. This is a special variety in which the pipes look like funnels (Trichter). I have found this reed only at 8′, e.g., at St. Ansgarii in Bremen, about which it is reported that this [Trichterregal] is a newly invented variety, almost like a *Vox humana*. There are 4 of this new type in the organ in Bremen, and these must be distinguished from the ordinary Trichterregals, such as are discussed in the [*Neu-eröffnete*] *Orchestre* 1, p. 299; this is what Mattheson says in the Appendix to Niedt's Second Part[, p. 160]. Otherwise there is nothing better about the ordinary Trichterregal than other Regals. The new type is also [found] at St. Stephani and the Marienkirche in Bremen. Moreover, it is found (though, I believe, mostly of the old variety) at Elmshorn at 8′, in the large organ at St. Nikolai, at St. Jakobi, St. Petri, and in the organ at the Cathedral in Hamburg, at St. Marie Magdelena there (in which the pipes are very short and very wide at the top), at St. Marien in Lübeck, St. Michaelis in Lüneburg, Otterndorf in Land Hadeln, and at St. Cosmae in Stade, etc. All are at 8′ pitch.

Kap. VII.   Von den Registern überhaupt und insonderheit.   151

§. 202.

Tromba, Trommet, Trompet, Trummet, Taratantara, Clarin, Clairon, davon die Trombonen zu unterscheiden, welches die Posaunen sind. Ausser der Orgel ist die Trompet bekannt genug. In der Orgel ist sie eine Schnarrstimme 16' oder 8', 4' oder 2' Ton. Die Körper werden von Blech gemacht, unten enge und oben weit; doch sind sie lang, und Trompet 8' wird wol einen Körper 6' lang haben. So weit sind sie aber nicht, als die Posaunenbässe, deswegen sie auch das donnernde Wesen nicht so an sich haben. Man macht sie auch von Metall in cylindrischer Form. Die Mundstücke sind nicht gefüttert; die Blätter sind auch nicht so dicke als bey den Posaunen, daher sie in der Tiefe mehr sladdern. 8' und 4' ist gar gemein; daher ich nur die Exempel von 16' anführe, oder wo etwan mancherley Trompeten zugleich in einer Orgel sind. 16' wollen einige nicht leiden, weil es eine Posaune werde; allein es bleibt wol ein Unterscheid, und steht zu St. Ansgarit in Bremen, nebst 8'; in der großen Orgel zu St. Nikolai in Hamburg; zu St. Jakobi daselbst; 16' und 8' in einem Claviere stand ehemals in der Orgel zu St. Michaelis daselbst; zu St. Catharinen ist Trommel 16' und 8' 2mal und noch 4' dabey. Zu U. L. Fr. in Bremen ist 16', 8' und 4' in einem Claviere; zu St. Petri in Hamburg ist 16'; in der Domsorgel daselbst ist 16' und 8'. Zu Königsberg im Löbenicht steht 16'; zu St. Marien in Lübeck 16' und 8' in einem Claviere; zu St. Cosmi in Stade 16' und 8; in Stockholm auch. 16' zu St. Johannis in Lüneburg; it. zu St. Michaelis und zu St. Lamberti allda; zu Sandomir, da sie Tuba heißt, allda ist sie 16' 8' 4' und 2'. 16' noch zu St. Nikolai in Stralsund; da auch noch eine ist von $\bar{c}$ bis $\bar{\bar{c}}$, und dergleichen ist auch in der neuen Orgel zu St. Nikolai in Rostock. Im Dom zu Upsal ist 16' und 8'. Trompet 4' wird mit der Schallmey fast eins seyn, deswegen zu Ansgarii in Bremen steht: *Trombet* oder *Schallmey* 4': doch können sie unterschieden werden. Zu U. L. Fr. in Bremen ist im Pedale noch 8' und 4', obschon vorhin im Manuale 16', 8' und 4' waren. So ist auch mehrmal (z. Ex. in Hildesheim) 8' und 4' beysammen. Feldtrommet 16' in Lübeck ist oben §. 143. berührt worden. Zur Dreyfaltigkeit in Danzig ist Trompet 9': es soll aber vielleicht 8' heißen. Zu Görlitz ist sie 8' von englischem Zinn, und heißt Tromba. Daß es aber nicht eben nöthig, daß die Trompete noch halb so klein als die Posaune, und präcise noch eins so groß, als die Schallmey, seyn müsse, wie Prätorius und Niedt wollen, ist §. 184. erinnert worden: und findet man auch Posaune 16' und Trompete 16' beysammen; ihr Klang ist auch gar wohl zu unterscheiden. In Jena sind beyde Trompeten mit Krücken, die aber doch geschraubt werden können. Ordentlicher Weise sind sie mit gemeinen Krücken. Die Köpfe sind meistens rund. Trompetenbaß Chormaß, d. i. 8' in Breslau führt Prätorius an. Trommetbaß 8' ist nach §. 301. zu Gera, da die Körper von Blech, die Mundstücke aber von Elsebeern Holz, das in Leinöl gesotten ist, gemacht sind. Die Zungen sind mit Papier belegt, um das Knastern zu verhindern. Zu Großen Gottern sind die Körper halb von Blech, halb aber von Holz.

Zu

Ch. VII. Concerning Stops in General and in Particular   151

§. 202.

TROMBA, TROMMET, TROMPET, TARATANTARA, CLARIN, CLARION, are [all] to be distinguished from the Trombones or Posaunes. The trumpet is familiar enough apart from the organ. In the organ it is a reed stop at 16′, 8′, 4, or 2′ pitch. The resonators are made of sheet iron, narrow beneath and wide on top; yet they are long—a Trompet 8′ will have a resonator 6′ long. They are not as wide[scale] as the pedal Posaunes, and for that reason they do not have that thundering quality about them. They are made of [pipe] metal in a round shape.* The shallots are not faced [with leather, like the Posaune], nor are the tongues as thick as [those] in Posaunes, and thus they vibrate more in the bass.† It is very common at 8′ and 4′; therefore I will cite only examples at 16′, or perhaps where several trumpets stand together in [the same] organ. Some would like to forbid it at 16′, because [then] it would be a Posaune. But there is indeed a difference. [At 16′] it stands at St. Ansgarii in Bremen, together with an 8′ [Trompet], and in the large organ at St. Nikolai and at St. Jakobi in Hamburg. It used to stand at 16′ and 8′ in one manual of the organ at St. Michaelis there.‡ At St. Catharine [in Hamburg] there is a Trommel§ 16′, 2 at 8′ and one at 4′ besides. At the Marienkirche in Bremen it is at 16′, 8′ and 4′ in one manual. There is a 16′ at St. Petri in Hamburg, and a 16′ and an 8′ in the Cathedral organ there. At Königsberg there is a 16′ in the Löbenichtkirche, and at St. Marien in Lübeck a 16′ and 8′ in the same keyboard. At St. Cosmae in Stade it is at 16′ and 8′, as well as at Stockholm. It is at 16′ at St. Johannis, St. Michaelis and St. Lamberti in Lüneburg, and at Sandomir, where it is called *Tuba*—there it is at 16′, 8′, 4′ and 2′. Furthermore there is a 16′ at St. Nikolai in Stralsund, where there is also another one from c′ to c′′′; the same holds true for the new organ at St. Nikolai in Rostock. There is a 16′ and 8′ in the Cathedral at Uppsala. The Trompet 4′ is almost the same as a Schallmey; thus at [St.] Ansgarii in Bremen there stands a "Trombet or Schallmey 4′". These [two] can be different, though. At the Marienkirche in Bremen [the Trompet] is in the pedal at 8′ and 4′, even though 16′, 8′ and 4′ were [mentioned] above in the manual. Often 8′ and 4′ are together [in the same division], e.g., in Hildesheim.¶ Feldtrommet 16′ in Lübeck has been alluded to above in §.143. At the Dreyfaltigkeitskirche in Danzig there is a Trompet 9′; this should probably read "8′", however. At Görlitz it is at 8′, [made] of English tin, and is called "Tromba". It has already been mentioned in §.184‖ that it is not really necessary for the Trompete [resonators] to be half as small as the Posaune and precisely twice as large as the Schallmey, as Praetorius** and Niedt†† maintain.‡‡ The Posaune 16′ and the Trompete 16′ are indeed found side by side [in the same organ]; their sound is most assuredly different. Both of the Trompetes in Jena are [supplied] with tuning wires, but may also [be adjusted with] screws as well. Ordinarily [Trompetes] are [provided] only with tuning wires. The blocks are mostly round.§§ Praetorius cites a Trompetenbass Chormass, i.e., 8′, in Breslau. According to §.301 there is a Trommetbass 8′ at Gera in which the resonators are of tin-plate, but the shallots are made of wild service-tree wood that has been boiled in linseed oil. The tongues are coated with paper to prevent the crackling sound. At Grossgottern the resonators are half of tin-plate and half of wood. At Kindelbruck [the Trompete] is doubled from e′. Biermann

---

* in contrast to the Posaune, which may be made of wood in a square or rectangular shape.
† Cf. §.176.

‡ i.e., the organ by Arp Schnitger that burned with the church in 1750.
§ a misprint. Mattheson spells the word "Trommete"; see Mattheson's Appendix to Niedt, p. 177, as well as the stoplist of the organ at St. Catherine, under "Hamburg" in Chapter 10.

¶ See Biermann, p. 7, as well as the stoplist of the organ at Hildesheim in Chapter 10.

‖ This should read "§.186."
** *Syntagma musicum*, Vol. II, p. 142.
†† *Musicalische Handleitung*, Anderer Theil, p. 114.
‡‡ See also §.270 below.

§§ They might also be square if they were made with wood.

Zu Kindelbrück ist sie von e eingestrichen an doppelt. Trompet halbirt steht bey Biermann S. 26. und soll anzeigen, daß solche nur 2 Oktaven einnehme. Ganz übergüldete Trommet 8' ist zu Dresden im Schlosse unter dem Namen eines Principals, weil sie im Gesichte stand, s. Principal.

* Trompeterzug zu Giebichenstein zu Halle ist unter den Nebenzügen, von dessen Einrichtung ist mir nichts mehr bekannt.

§. 203.

Trommel, Trummel, s. Tympanum.
Tuba, s. Trompete.
Tubal } s. bey Oktave. §. 171.
Tubalflöt

Tympanum, siehe davon ausser der Orgel Janowka in Claue, und Prätorium S. 427. imgl. S. 77. da er de Tympano Hieronymi handelt. Es ist die Pauke. Die Ital. nennen sie Timpani, und die Franz. Timbales, conf. Orch. I. P. III. c. III. §. 12. Man nennt sie auch Tamburo und Tambour, s. Niedts 2ten Theil. In der Orgel hat man es vorstellen wollen durch 2 Pfeifen in der Tiefe des Subbasses. Ich halte aber nichts davon. Diese 2 Pfeifen lassen die Töne c g von sich hören. Sonst ist die Trummel oder Trommel von Tympano unterschieden: in der Orgel aber dürfte es wol einerley seyn. Niedt zählt es auch unter die absurden Register. Daß die Trommel auch so sey, wie die Pauke, sehe ich aus Prätorii Disposition der Braunschweigischen Orgel, da die Trommel 2 Pfeifen stark ist. Sonst könnte man eine rechte Trommel machen, die mit Klöpfeln geschlagen, und durch ein Gewicht gezogen würde: aber das gehört nicht in die Kirche. Zu Colberg in der Heiligengeistkirche ist die Pauke auch. Zu Görlitz ist Tambur 16', das ist: es sind 2 Pfeifen aus dem 16füßigen Subbasse. Cymbelpauke ist zu St. Catharinen in Danzig, s. davon §. 134. bey der Cymbel. Timpani sind auch in der Stadtkirche in Jena; bedeuten aber daselbst den Stern. Trommel ist zun Predigern in Erfurt. Heertrummel ist eben das zun Barfüßern in Erfurt. Sonst findet man diesen Namen Heertrummel auch bey Prätorio S. 187. in der Dresdener Schloßorgel angeführt, welche Heertrummel aus den 2 Tönen E und F bestehen soll. Drommel steht zu St. Gotthard in Hildesheim, s. Prätor. Rechte Heerpaucken sollen in Sondershausen seyn, s. Prätor. l. c. S. 197.

§. 204.

Ventile sind auch unter den Register-Manubriis, und wird dadurch der Wind aus den Canalen in die Lade gelassen, und so lange die nicht gezogen sind, geht keine Pfeife. Siehe davon mehr §. 74. Sie heißen auch epistomia, und Sperrventile. Bey vielen Orgelwerken sind keine; bey einigen ist ein allgemeines für alle Claviere; bey einigen hat jedes Clavier sein eigenes: und diese letztere Einrichtung ist die beste, weil durch Einstoßen des Ventils das Heulen geschwinder gehindert wird, als auf eine andere Art.

Vige-

Ch. VII. Concerning Stops in General and in Particular

records a "Trompet halbirt" on p. 26, and that is meant to indicate that it encompasses only 2 octaves. "Ganz übergüldete Trommet 8'" [completely gilded Trumpet 8'] is in the palace at Dresden under the name "Principal[ia]", since it stood in the façade; see Principal[, §. 177].

* TROMPETERZUG at Giebichenstein near Halle is [listed] among the auxiliary stops; I know nothing about its construction.

§. 203.

TROMMEL, TRUMMEL, see Tympanum.

TUBA, see Trompete.

TUBAL } see under Oktave, §.171.
TUBALFLÖT

TYMPANUM. Concerning this [instrument] apart from the organ, see Janowka in his *Clavis*[, p. 319] and Praetorius, p. 427* and also p. 77 where he deals with the *Tympanum Hieronymi*. This is the kettledrum [Pauke]. The Italians call it *Tympani* and the French *Timbales*; cf. [Mattheson's *Neu-eröffnete*] *Orchestre* I, Part III, Chap. III, §.12[, p. 272]. It is also called *Tamburo* or *Tambour*; see Niedt's Second Part.† [Builders] have tried to imitate it in the organ by means of 2 low Subbass pipes. I do not think much of this, though. These two pipes produce the pitches c and g. Elsewhere the "Trummel" or "Trommel" [drum] is different from the *Tympanum*; in the organ, however, they may well be the same. Niedt counts it among the absurd stops.‡ That the Trommel may be the same as the kettledrum, I note from Praetorius's stoplist of the Braunschweig organ, in which the Trommel consists of 2 pipes. One could construct a proper drum, struck with drumsticks and driven by a weight, but that has no business being in a church. There is also a kettledrum in the Heiligengeistkirche at Colberg. At Görlitz there is a Tambur§ 16', that is, it consists of 2 pipes from the 16' Subbass. At St. Catharinen in Danzig there is a Cymbelpaucke; concerning this see §.134 under Cymbel. There are also Tympani in the Stadtkirche in Jena, but there [the name] signifies the [Cymbel]stern. There is a Trommel at the Predigerkirche in Erfurt. Heertrummel at the Barfüsserkirche in Erfurt is the same thing. Moreover, this name Heertrummel is cited in Praetorius, p. 187, in the palace organ at Dresden, reported as consisting of two pitches, E and F. There is a "Drommel" at St. Gotthard in Hildesheim; see Praetorius[, p. 199]. "Rechte Heerpaucken" is also reported in Sondershausen; see Praetorius, *l.c.*, p. 197.

[UNDA MARIS:¶ see below, §. 207.]
[UNTERBASS: see below, §.207.]
[UNTERSATZ: see below, §.207.]

§. 204.

VENTILS are also [found] among the stopknobs; by means of them the wind is released from the ducts into the chest, and so long as they are not drawn, no pipe will sound (for more about them see §.74). They are also called *epistomia* or Sperrventile.‖ Many organs do not have them; some have a universal one for all the keyboards,** and some have one for each manual.†† This last arrangement is the best one, since shoving the ventil closed stops the ciphering more quickly than any other method.

---

* sic; the Tympanum is mentioned on pp. 4 and 77 of the Syntagma musicum, Vol. II, and is pictured in Plate 23 of the accompanying *Theatrum instrumentorum*; the volume has only 236 pages.

† There is an entry under "Timpano" in Niedt, part two, p. 114, but it does not mention the names Tamburo or Tambour.

‡ *Musicalischer Handleitung*, Part III, §.5, p. 46.

§ sic; Boxberg, p.[5], spells the stop "Tamburo."

¶ Following the practice of his day, Adlung considers "U" and "V" as the same letter, and thus places this and the following two entries after "Violdigamba".

‖ "Cut-out ventils;" see §.195 above.

** i.e., one for the entire organ.

†† i.e., each division.

Kap. VII. Von den Registern überhaupt und insonderheit. 153

Vigesima nona soll die Quinte seyn: aber siehe davon bey Quinte §. 171.

Vigesima secunda, s. Oktave.

Viola, oder Viole, ist eine offene Flötstimme, wodurch man den Klang eines Bogenstrichs auf einer Alt= oder Tenorgeige vorstellen will. Man trift dies Register meistentheils 8′ und 4′ an, und giebt der kleinern auch zuweilen den Namen Violet, wie z. Er. zu Kindelbrück und zu Kreyßen geschehen. Viole 4′ könnte auch der so genannten Viole oder Braccio gleich kommen, und wäre also der Alt zur Violdigambe 8′; wiewol sie auch Violdigamba heißen könnte, weil man diese auch 4′ hat. Einige nennen die Offenflöte so, von welcher §. 172. gehandelt worden, welches man hierbey nachschlagen kann. Man kann sich auch desjenigen hier wieder erinnern, was bey Gelegenheit des Geigenprincipals, oder der Schweizerpfeife §. 177. und §. 188. vorgetragen worden. Wenn die Viole 3′ groß ist; so nennt man sie Quintviole. Man lese hiervon Sambers Continuation, S. 148. nach.

§. 205.

Violone, der Violon, oder Violonbaß, ist ein offenes Pedalregister 16′ und 8′ von Metall oder Holz, womit man den Bogenstrich eines Contraviolons ausser der Orgel nachahmen will. Es hat mit der Violdigamba gleiche Art, indem es engere Mensur hat, als die Principale, daher die Körper länger, der Aufschnitt aber niedriger ist. Es thut im Pedale gute Dienste, und schnurrt gleich einem Violon oder Baßgeige, wenn es recht getroffen wird. Aber es ist schwer zu intoniren, daher die Orgelmacher selten die Mensur recht enge nehmen, folglich thut es nicht gleichen Effekt. Von Metall setzt man es zuweilen ins Gesichte, und da darf man keine Bärte daran machen; und wiewol sie inwendig nicht so gesehen werden, so sind sie doch ein Zeichen der Schwachheit. Sie überblasen sich oft in die Oktave, auch wol in die Quinte, welches letztere größern Schaden thut, als das erste, und die Harmonie verdirbt. Werden sie aber recht getroffen; so thun sie fast bessere Dienste als der Principalbaß 16′. Zuweilen hat man sie beyde beysammen. Da sie nun von Metall so schwer sind, wie vielmehr im Holze; doch hat man auch hölzerne Violonbässe. Ob aber die Mensur enge genug genommen worden, ist eine andere Frage. In der Reglerkirche zu Erfurt steht er von Zinn im Gesichte, und wird eben daran erkannt, das er nicht so weite Pfeifen hat, als Principal 16′. Zu Königsberg in Löbenicht findet man den Namen Violenbaß angeschrieben. Und zu Gera §. 301. ist Violdigambenbaß eben das; doch werden daselbst bey jedem Clave 3 Töne gehört, s. den folgenden 206. §.

§. 206.

Violadigamba, Violdigamba, ist ein schönes Orgelregister, offen, und viel engerer Mensur, als die Principale von gleicher Größe. Es stellt die Violdigamba wohl vor, wenn es recht getroffen ist, und schnarrt sehr durchdringend, und ist gleichsam

U   der

Ch. VII. Concerning Stops in General and in Particular 153

Vigesima nona is intended to be a Quinte; see §.171* about this, however.

Vigesima secunda, see Oktave.

Viola, or Viole, is an open flue stop that is intended to imitate the sound of a bow stroking a VIOLA OR A TENOR VIOLIN. This stop is encountered mostly at 8' and 4', and at times the smaller one† is given the name Violet, as for example at Kindelbruck and Greussen. The Viole 4' may also approach [in timbre] to the so-called *Viole* or *Braccio*, and would be the alto for the Violdigambe 8', although it might also be called Violdigamba, since these appear at 4' as well. Some call the Offenflöte by this name, [a stop] that has been dealt with in §.172, which may be consulted in this regard. It would also be well to remember what has been explained in connection with the Geigenprincipal in §.177 and the Schweizerpfeife in §.188. If the Viole is 3' in size, then it is called Quintviole. Concerning this [stop], consult Samber's *Continuation*, p. 148.

* This should read "§.179."

† i.e., the one at 4'.

§. 205.

VIOLONE, the VIOLON or VIOLONBASS, is an open pedal stop at 16' and 8' of metal or wood, that is intended to imitate a bow stroking a Contraviolon‡ apart from the organ. It has the same characteristics as the Violdigamba, in that it has a narrower scale than the Principals, and therefore the body is longer, while the cut-up is lower. It serves well in the pedal, purring just like a Violon or Bassgeige when it is properly built. It is difficult to voice, however; therefore organbuilders seldom make the scale really narrow, and as a result it does not produce the same effect. Metal ones are sometimes placed in the façade, and then one dare not put any beards on them; and even though [the beards] are not visible when [the stop] is inside the case, they nevertheless indicate a lack of skill. They often overblow at the octave or at the fifth; the latter is more harmful than the former, spoiling the harmony. If however they are built properly, then they are almost more useful than the Principalbass 16'. At times both of these are present together [in the same pedal division]. As heavy as they are [when made] of metal, they are all the heavier in wood; yet there are also wooden Violonbasses. Whether the scale is made narrow enough, though, is another question. In the Reglerkirche at Erfurt [this stop] is of tin and stands in the façade; it may be recognized because it does not have such wide pipes as the Principal 16'. At the Löbenichtkirche at Königsberg the name is found written "Violenbass". And at Gera, §.301, the Violdigambenbass is the same thing; yet there one hears 3 pitches from every pipe; see §.206 following.

‡ i.e., a double bass.

§. 206.

VIOLADIGAMBA, VIOLDIGAMBA, is a beautiful organ stop, open and of much narrower scale than the Principal of the same size. It does indeed imitate a Violdigamba if it is properly made, and sizzles very penetratingly; it is as it were the tenor where the

der Tenor, da der Violon der Baß war. Es ist dies Register eins mit von den schweren, und die Intonation macht den Orgelmachern um so viel mehr Mühe, je enger die Mensur genommen wird; deswegen man es oft weiter machet, als es sich gehöret: welches aber ein Fehler ist, indem es seine Art verliehret, und den Oktavenregistern im Klange ähnlicher wird. Man macht den Pfeifen oft Bärte an, um die Intonation zu erleichtern: aber ohne Bärte sind sie ein Zeichen eines accuraten Meisters. Man macht sie von Metall, und was für Fehler beym Violon getadelt worden, die sind auch hier zu merken. Man macht sie 8′ und 4′, welche letztere den Alt kann vorstellen. Wer diese Beschreibung gegen die Beschreibung der Schweitzerflöte §. 188. hält, dürfte sie fast mit jener für einerley halten. In Niedts zweytem Theile der Handleitung Kap. 11. der 2ten Auflage lautet es so: „daß die Violdigamba 8′ seyn müsse, ver=„steht sich von selbsten." Allein, obschon 8′ gemeiner ist, und ich deswegen auch kein Exempel anführe; so ist doch 4′ auch gar bekannt. Prätorius l. c. S. 134. sagt, daß das Aequalgemshorn 8′ auch wol dem Klange nach Violdigamba heißen könnte: aber es ist ein großer Unterschied zwischen dem Gemshorn und der Violdigamba; jenes klingt viel stiller, ist oben enge und unten weit, dahingegen diese stärker schnurret, und unten und oben gleich weit ist; wenigstens so viel ich deren gesehen. Wenn Viole so viel ist, als Violdigamba 4′, wie es denn seyn sollte; so kömmt ein Exempel vor in sensu Prætorii zu Hessen auf dem Schlosse, da steht Gemshorn oder Klein Violn 4′. Violdigambenbaß, 8′ könnte eben diese Stimme seyn, nur daß sie im Pedale wäre; doch findet man, daß man auch denselben 16′ gemacht. Und da glaube ich ihn mit Violon 16′, eins zu seyn. So ist er §. 301. zu Gera 16′, wobey gemeldet wird, daß man zu jedem Clave 3 Töne höre. Dies ist nicht unmöglich. Hört man doch bey der Quintatön auch nebst der Oktave die Quinte, und bey engen Intonationen ist nichts leichters, als daß die Pfeifen sich überblasen, zum Exempel bey der Querpfeife. Qu. Was wären das für Töne? Resp. Es können keine andere seyn, als die Oktave darüber, d. i. 8′ und die Quinte; doch wird man solche 2 Töne nicht so stark hören, als den Ton 16′, sondern so, wie es bey der Quintatön ist. Ob aber die Arbeit hierbey allezeit so gerathen, daß nicht zuweilen die Pfeife sich sollte überblasen, und der tiefe Ton gar aussen bleibe, werden die wissen, so es gehöret haben.

§. 207.

Vnda maris, s. Onda maris, §. 173.

Unterbaß, ist wol so viel, als Subbaß, s. davon §. 150.

Untersatz, ist auch soviel, siehe eben daselbst §. 150. Er steht noch 16′ in der Kirche St. Andreä in Erfurt unter diesem Namen. Sonst ist das Wort general, daher man findet Grober Posaunen=Untersatz zu St. Marien in Halle, s. Posaune.

Vogar, ist vermuthlich mit Fugara §. 149. einerley.

Vogelgesang heißt auch wol Nachtigal. Jener Name ist gar gemein. Zu Magdeburg zu St. Ulrich ist Vogelgesang oder Nachtigall, s. Prätorii Dispositionen. Man sagt auch Vogelgeschrey, z. Er. zu St. Cathartnen in Magdeburg, s. Prätor.

Ch. VII. Concerning Stops in General and in Particular

Violon is the bass. It is equivalent to [the Violon] being difficult [to voice], the voicing being more and more troublesome for the organbuilder the narrower the scale is. For this reason it is often made wider than is proper, which is a fault in that it loses its character and becomes more similar in sound to the Oktave* stops. Beards are often attached to them to make voicing easier, but [when built] without beards they are the mark of an exacting master [craftsman]. They are made of metal. What has been censured as a fault with the Violon also applies here.† They are made at 8′ and 4′—the latter may represent the alto. Anyone who compares this description with the description of the Schweitzerflöte in §.188 may well consider [these stops] to be the same. The second part of Niedt's *Handleitung*, second edition, Chap. II, [p. 115,] reads as follows: "It goes without saying that the Violdigamba must be an 8′." However, although 8′ is more common (and thus I cite no examples of it), yet the 4′ is also quite familiar. Praetorius, *l.c.*, p.134, says that with respect to timbre the Aequalgemshorn 8′ might well also be called Violdigamba, but there is a major difference between the Gemshorn and the Violdigamba: the former sounds much quieter and is conical, while the latter purrs more strongly and is cylindrical—at least the ones that I have seen. If the Viole is the same as the Violdigamba 4′, as it should be, then an example in Praetorius's sense appears in the palace at Hesse, where there stands a Gemshorn or Klein Violn 4′. Violdigambenbass could be this same stop, except that it would be in the pedal; yet one also finds [Violdigambas] built at 16′. And in that case I believe it is the same as the Violon 16′. Thus in §.301 there is a 16′ at Gera, about which it is reported that each pipe produces 3 pitches. This is not impossible. Indeed, the Quintatön also produces a quint together with an octave, and with a narrow scale there is nothing easier than for pipes to overblow, [as happens] for example with the Querpfeife. Question: What would those [3] pitches be? Answer: They could be none other than the octave above, i.e. 8′, and the fifth[, i.e., 5 ⅓′]. Yet one would not hear these two pitches as distinctly as the 16′ pitch, but rather in the way the Quintatön speaks them. Whether the workmanship in them has been so completely successful that a pipe does not occasionally overblow and omit the fundamental entirely, those who have heard it will know.

* i.e., principal-scale.

† presumably the tendency to overblow.

§. 207.

UNDA MARIS,‡ see Onda maris, §.173.

UNTERBASS is indeed the same as Subbass; in this regard see §.150.

UNTERSATZ is also the same [as the Subbass]; again, see §.150. It stands at 16′ in the St. Andrea Kirche in Erfurt under this name. Otherwise this is a generic word, and thus Grober Posaunen-Untersatz is found at St. Marien in Halle; see Posaune[, §.176].

VOGAR is apparently the same as Fugara; see §.149.

VOGELGESANG [birdsong] is also called Nachtigal [nightingale]. The former name is very common. At St. Ulrich in Magdeburg there is a "Vogelgesang or Nachtigall;" see Praetorius's stoplists.§ "Vogelgeschrey" [birdcall] is another name for it,

‡ Following the practice of his day, Adlung considers "U" and "V" as the same letter, and thus places "Unda maris" (written "Vnda maris" in the book) after "Violdigamba".

§ *Syntagma musicum* II, p. 174.

Kap. VII. Von den Registern überhaupt und insonderheit. 155

s. Prätor. Es ist ein von Metall gemachtes Kästgen, von beliebiger Größe, etwan 4" breit, hoch und lang; unten ist ein kurz Röhrchen, dadurch der Wind in das Kästchen bläset, wenn es auf den Windcanal gesetzt wird. Oben drauf setzt man 3, 4, oder mehrere kleine Pfeifchen, etliche Zolle lang, nach Proportion, deckt sie oben zu u. s. w. und die werden zugleich angeblasen. Wenn man das Register ziehen will, füllet man das Kästchen mit Wasser als wozu oben ein Trichter darauf ist: und kann man es schon bereiten, daß nichts von Wasser in die Canäle kommt. Da giebt es einen zitternden Klang, wie die Eulen, oder wie man sie nennt, welche die Jungen auf den Jahrmärkten dem Töpfer für etliche Pfennige abkaufen, und sich darnach lustig machen. In neuen Orgeln wird es als ein absurd Register weggelassen, wofür es Niedt schon ausgiebt im 3ten Theile seiner Handleitung. Einige machen einen Unterschied unter der Nachtigall und dem Vogelgesang; deswegen in der Görlitzer Orgel beyde besonders zu stehen gekommen: worinne derselbe bestehe; ist mir unbekannt. Bey Prätorio findet man S. 175. auch allerley Vogelgesang geschrieben, welches wol mit Vogelgesang, wenn es ohne Zusatz geschrieben wird, eins ist: Was aber gedachter Prätorius S. 201. mit Vogelgesang durch das ganze Pedal zu verstehen geben wollen, weis ich nicht. Weil er es nicht unter die Nebenzüge, sondern unter die ordentlichen Baßstimmen im Pedale setzt; so schlüße ich, daß es eine ordentliche Stimme sey, etwan nach Art eines Flageolets, oder sonst was anders, das diesem ähnlicht.

§. 208.

Vox humana, die Menschenstimme ist ein Schnarrwerk 8' weil ein Mensch ordentlich so tief singen kann. Ich habe sie angetroffen im Dom zu Bremen; zu St. Ansgarii daselbst; zu St. Stephani daselbst; in der großen Orgel zu St. Nikolai in Hamburg; im Löbenicht zu Königsberg; in der neuen Orgel in Leipzig; zu St. Marien in Lübeck; zu St. Johannis in Lüneburg; zu St. Michaelis daselbst; zu St. Lamberti daselbst; in der neuen Orgel zu St. Nikolai in Rostock ist sie von $\bar{c}$ bis $\bar{\bar{c}}$; in der Altdresdener Orgel von a bis $\bar{\bar{c}}$. Vielleicht gehen auch einige unter den übrigen nicht gar durchs ganze Clavier, ob es schon dabey nicht gemeldet wird. Im 10ten Kapitel werden noch mehr Exempel vorkommen, wo Vox humana anzutreffen. Sie heißt auch Anthropoglossa, von ἄνθρωπος ein Mensch, und γλῶσσα die Zunge, conf. Kircheri Musurg. L. VI. Part. III. C. III. Probl. IX. allwo er die Proportion der Pfeifen vorgestellt, die die vocem humanam von sich sollen hören lassen. Es steht auch dieselbe zun Augustinern in Erfurt; it. in Görlitz, woselbst sie ein Flötwerk ist. Wie aber die Körper eigentlich zu machen, sammt den Mundstücken, daß es einen Klang von sich gebe, welcher der Menschenstimme gleicht, ist eine hohe Frage. Nichts ist schöner, als die Stimme des Menschen: nichts ist aber auch schwerer nachzumachen, als eben dieselbe. Deswegen hat man zwar vielerley Inventionen; aber keine hat vollkommen geleistet, was sie leisten sollen, und es wird doch allemal ein großer Unterschied bleiben unter dem Klange einer solchen Pfeife, und der natürlichen Stimme eines Menschen.

e.g., at St. Catharinen in Magdeburg; see Praetorius.* It is a little box made of metal, of indeterminate size, about 4" square. At the bottom there is a short little tube, through which the wind blows into the box when it is attached to the wind duct. On top [of the tube] are set 3, 4 or more little pipes, several inches long, at the proper proportion.† Then the box is covered on top, etc., and [the pipes] are all blown at the same time. If one wishes to use the stop, then one fills the little box with water, for which purpose there is a funnel on top. [The system] can indeed be fashioned so that none of the water gets into the duct. It produces a twittering sound, like the owls or whatever you call them that boys buy from the potter for a few pennies at fairs and then have fun with. In new organs it is omitted as an absurd stop; indeed Niedt already considers it so in the third part of his *Handleitung*.‡ Some make a distinction between the Nachtigall (nightingale) and the Vogelgesang; thus both of them have come to appear separately in the Görlitz organ. Wherein this distinction lies is unknown to me. In Praetorius, p. 175, one finds "allerley Vogelgesang" (all sorts of birdcalls) written, which is doubtless the same as Vogelgesang written without a modifier. What the abovementioned Praetorius, however, means to indicate on p. 201 by "Vogelgesang durch das ganze Pedal" [birdsong throughout the entire pedal], I do not know. Since he does not list it among the auxiliary stops, but rather among the pedal stops proper, I conclude that it is a regular stop, perhaps something along the line of a Flageolet, or some other sort of thing that resembles it.

Ibid., p. 175.

† i.e., to make the proper twittering sound.

‡ §.5, p. 46. Niedt died in 1708; the volume was published in 1717.

§. 208.

Vox humana, the human voice, is a reed stop at 8′, since a man can normally sing at that pitch. I have encountered it in the Cathedral, St. Ansgarii and St. Stephani at Bremen, in the large organ at St. Nikolai in Hamburg, in the Löbenichtkirche at Königsberg, in the new organ in Leipzig,§ at St. Marien in Lübeck, at St. Johannis, St. Michaelis and St. Lamberti in Lüneburg. In the new organ at St. Nikolai in Rostock it extends from c′ to c‴, and in the Altdresden organ¶ from a to c‴. Perhaps some of the others also do not go through the whole keyboard, although this is not reported about them. More examples of where the Vox *humana* may be found will be given in Chapter 10. It is also called *Anthropoglossa*, from ανδρωποσ‖ "a human being", and γλωσσα, "tongue"; cf. Kircher's *Musurgia*, Book VI., Part III, Chap. III, Probl. IX[, pp. 514-5], where he explains the proportion of pipes that are intended to reproduce the sound of the human voice. This [stop] is also found at the Augustinerkirche in Erfurt, as well as in Görlitz, where it is a flue stop.** How actually to make the resonators, together with the shallots, so that [the stop] produces a sound that resembles a human voice, is a good question. Nothing is more beautiful than the human voice, yet nothing is more difficult to imitate. Therefore all sorts of things have indeed been invented, but no one has ever fully achieved what needs to be, and there always remains a great difference between the sound of such a pipe and the natural human voice. Part of the reason for

§ See "The New Organ in Leipzig," under "Leipzig" in Chapter 10.

¶ See the stoplist of the Alt-Dresdener organ, under "Dresden" in Chapter 10.

‖ sic; this should read "ανθρωποσ."

** Not a reed stop, rather an Italian "Voce umana."

156 **Kap. VII. Von den Registern überhaupt und insonderheit.**

Es thut auch etwas, daß die Orgelmacher in der Anatomie nicht bewandert sind, und daher nicht wissen, wie der Klang in unsere Kehle formiret wird. Und welche Stimme will man denn nachmachen? Die Diskantstimme? oder Tenor= Alt= oder Baßstimme? Man sieht also, daß dabey noch verschiedenes zu erinnern. Es giebt derselben viel Arten in der Welt, dabey ich mich aber nicht aufhalte. Ich kenne auch nicht eine jede besonders, sondern bin zufrieden, wenn ein Organist weis, es sey (wie schon gesagt) ein Schnarrwerk 8′. Etwas mehres davon habe ich in meiner Anleitung zu der musikalischen Gelahrtheit, §. 200. S. 476. u. folg. besonders in der Anmerkung (w) beygebracht, wohin ich den geehrtesten Leser verweise, um es hier nicht noch einmal abschreiben zu dürfen.

Vox virginea, die Jungferstimme, ist vielleicht einerley mit dem oben §. 161. angeführten Jungfernregal. Ihre Intonation muß lieblicher seyn, als der vorhergedachten vocis humanae. Vermuthlich ist sie engerer Mensur, eine Oktave höher, und auch nur in den obern Oktaven gebräuchlich.

Vulgaris tibia, s. Blockflöte.

§. 209.

Waldflöte, Waldpfeife (Tibia syluestris) ist eine offene Flötstimme, weiter aber desto kürzerer Mensur. Sie klingt hölzern, grob und hohl, daher sie auch den Namen bekommen. Ich habe sie 8′, 6′, 4′, 3′, 2′, 1½′, und 1′ gesehen. 6′ ist eigentlich eine Quinte, und wird Waldquinte genennet, und soll zu U. L. Fr. in Bremen stehen. 4′ ist in der Pfarrkirche zu Danzig. Zu Gera (§. 301.) ist Waldflöte, oder Dolcan 4′ mit doppelten labiis, s. oben Dolcan. §. 137. 3′ ist auch eine Quinte, und ist in der Altstadter Orgel zu Königsberg. 2 ist sehr gemein, z. Ex. zu Jena in der Stadtkirche; zun Augustinern in Erfurt, im Stift Severi daselbst; in Naumburg im Dom und zu St. Ottmar. 1½′ ist abermal eine Quinte dem Laute nach, und nennet Prätorius S. 131. l. c. die Hohlquinte 1½′ Waldflöt; und wird auch wol überhaupt zwischen der Hohl= und Waldflöte wenig oder gar kein Unterschied seyn. 1′ ist die Waldflöte im Dom zu Upsal; it. zu Halle in U. L. Frauenkirche; auch zu St. Lambert in Lüneburg, s. Prätor. l. c.

§. 210.

Waldhörner, Corni da Caccia, Parforce=(Jagd=) Horn, Cornu sylvestre, Cors de chasse. s. Orchestre I. P. III. C. III. §. 7. Ausser der Orgel sind sie bekannt. In der Orgel ist es ein Schnarrwerk 8′, 4′ oder 2′ Ton, so dieß Instrument imitiren soll. Wie aber das Waldhorn überall noch nicht gar zu alt ist; so ist es auch in der Orgel noch nicht gemein. Zu Colberg in der Heil. Geisteskirche ists 8′ im Pedale, und zu Königsberg im Kneiphofe ist es 2′. Von dessen Natur weis ich nichts zu sagen, weil ich es niemals gesehen.

Weite

this is that organbuilders have never delved into anatomy, and thus do not know how sound is formed in our throats. And then, which voice should be imitated? The treble? or the tenor, alto or bass? One can well see that there is a variety of things to consider. There are many types of [Vox humana stops] in the world, but I will not dwell on this topic. I am not familiar with each and every one of them individually, but will be content if an organist knows (as has already been said) that it is an 8′ reed. I have gone into more detail about it in my *Anleitung zu der musikalischen Gelahrtheit*, §.200, p. 476f., especially in note (w)[, pp. 477-8], about which I inform my honored reader to save having to copy it here again.

Vox virginea, the "maiden's voice," is perhaps the same as the Jungfernregal mentioned above in §.161. Its voicing must be gentler than that of the abovementioned *Vox humana*. It is likely of narrower scale, an octave higher, and also usable only in the upper octaves.*

Vulgaris tibia ["common flute"], see Blockflöte[, §.122 above].

§. 209.

Waldflöte, Waldpfeife (*Tibia sylvestris*) ["forest flute"] is an open flute stop, broader in scale and thus shorter in height. It sounds wooden, rough and hollow, whence it gets its name. I have seen it at 8′, 6′, 4′, 3′, 2′, 1½′ and 1′. The 6′ is actually a Quinte, called Waldquinte, and is listed at the Marienkirche at Bremen. There is a 4′ in the Pfarrkirche at Danzig. At Gera (§.301†) there is a Waldflöte or Dolcan 4′ with doubled lips; see Dolcan, §.137 above.‡ The 3′ is also a Quinte, and is found in the Altstädterkirche organ at Königsberg. The 2′ is very common, e.g., in the Stadtkirche at Jena, the Augustinerkirche and the Collegiate Church St. Severi in Erfurt, and in the Cathedral and St. Ottmar in Naumburg. The 1½′ is once again a Quinte, according to its pitch. On p. 131, *l.c.*, Praetorius calls the Hohlquinte 1½′ a Waldflöte, and there is indeed little or no difference between the Hohlflöte and Waldflöte. There is a Waldflöte 1′ in the Cathedral at Uppsala, in the Marienkirche at Halle, and also at St. Lambert in Lüneburg; see Praetorius, *l.c.*[, p. 233].

§. 210.

Waldhörner, Corni da Caccia, Parforce-(Jagd-)horn, Cornu sylvestre, Cors de chasse, see [Mattheson's *Neueröffnete*] *Orchestre* I, Part III, Chap. III, §.7 [, pp. 267-8]. They are familiar apart from the organ. In the organ it is a reed at 8′, 4′ or 2′ pitch intended to imitate this instrument. Since however the Waldhorn has not come into universal use until recently, it is also not yet common in the organ. It is an 8′ in the pedal in the Heiliggeisteskirche at Colberg, and a 2′ at Königsberg in the Kneiphofkirche. I cannot say anything about its character, since I have never seen it.

---

* all of this, presumably, to represent a very high female voice. It is likely, however, that Adlung has never heard the stop, and that he is making these assumptions based on the stop's name.

† The translation disregards the (superfluous) paragraph numbers in the collection of stoplists; see the stoplist of the organ at Gera in Chapter 10.

‡ in §.137 Adlung states that the Waldflöte has cylindrical pipes.

Kap. VII.   Von den Registern überhaupt und insonderheit.   157

Weite Pfeife 8′ ist in der großen Orgel zu St. Nikolai in Hamburg. Es deucht mir dieses das Principal weiter Mensur zu seyn; doch demonstrativisch kann ich es nicht sagen, weil ich es nicht gesehen, auch nie gehört. Weit Principal 16′ führt Prätorius S. 163. l. c. zu Rostock an.

Windkoppel in Waltershausen, vermöge dessen man eine Manualstimme soll ins Pedal bringen können, ohne dazu einen doppelten Zug nöthig zu haben. s. oben Coppel. §. 127.

§. 211.

Zifflöt. s. Sifflöt. §. 192.

Zimbel. s. in Cymbel §. 133. u. 134.

Zimbelbaß. s. Cymbelbaß. §. 134.

Zink, heißt auch Cornetto ausser der Orgel, im plurali Cornetti. conf. Prätorius l. c. S. 35. it. Cornettino: auf französisch aber Cornet a bouquin. s. Orchest. I. l. c. Man findet auch Lirice, Cornetto torto, Cornetto muto, Corno und Cornon in eben dem Verstande gebraucht. Es ist ein bekanntes krummes Instrument, welches sehr schwer zu blasen ist. In der Orgel hat man es schon längst gesucht nachzumachen. s. Prätor. von Schnarrwerken. Tom. II. P. IV. C. 2: denn es ist ein Schnarrwerk. Er sagt, sie wären 8′ Ton, und würden nur durchs halbe Clavier im Diskant gebraucht, hätten gleichaus weite Körper, unten etwas zugespitzt, oben offen, darum sie etwas hohl klingen, und nicht so schnarren, als welches durch die starken Blätter und starken Wind, (so diese Stimme erfordert) verhindert wird. Es ist bis dato dieß Register noch etwas rar, und habe ich es gefunden 8′ zu St. Petri in Berlin; zu St. Marien in Lübeck; zu St. Marien in Danzig 2 mal; zu Otterndorf im Lande Hadeln; zu St. Catharinen in Hamburg; zur Dreyfaltigkeit in Danzig ist halber Zink 8′, und zu St. Bartholomäi daselbst, wobey Mattheson im Anhange zum Niedt erinnert, es wolle vermuthlich nur so viel sagen, daß solch Stimmwerk nicht weiter reiche, als etwann auf die Hälfte des Claviers, oder auf den sogenannten Diskant. Und so ist §. 132. auch der halbe Cornet erkläret worden. Oder es ist Cornet und Zink zuweilen eins. s. §. 132. Cornetti sind auf eine besondere Art in Görlitz, da sie aus 3 Pfeifen bestehen, als Quinte 6′, Oktave 4′ und aus der Terz über 4′ Ton, und klingt, als ob es ein 8füßiges Schnarrwerk wäre, da doch keine 8füßige Pfeife drinnen ist: geht aber nicht tiefer als Vox humana, d. i. von a bis $\bar{\bar{c}}$; weil es sonst unangenehm werden würde. Es läßt sich wohl mit der rechten Hand zu dem Bombart 16′, und andern bequemen Stimmen brauchen, und giebt eine artige Harmonie, so ich (sagt Borberg) noch nie in einer andern Orgel gehöret. Das wäre also kein Schnarrwerk. (**) Eben daselbst ist auch Zynck für die Sesquialter genommen, so also auch kein Schnarrwerk, sondern eine gemischte Stimme ist, 2fach, aus 3′ it. 2′ Ton, das ist, wie es Borberg erklärt, aus Quinta 3′ und Terz über 2′ Ton, wie die Sesquialter ordentlich ist, davon §. 196. gehandelt worden. Ich glaube, daß es eins, ob man Zynck oder Zinck schreibe,

U 3

Ch. VII. Concerning Stops in General and in Particular

WEITE PFEIFE 8′ is found in the large organ at St. Nikolai in Hamburg. It would seem to me to be a Principal of broad scale, but I cannot say conclusively because I have never seen nor heard it. Praetorius, *l.c.*, p. 163, cites a Weit Principal 16′ at Rostock.

WINDKOPPEL at Waltershausen; by virtue of this stop it is said to be possible to bring a manual stop to the pedal without a second stop mechanism being necessary; see Coppel, §.127 above.

§. 211.

ZIFFLÖT, see Sifflöte, §.192.
ZIMBEL, see under Cymbel, §.133 and 134.
ZIMBELBASS, see Cymbelbass, §.134.

ZINK is also called *Cornetto* or *Cornettino* apart from the organ, plural *Cornetti*; cf. Praetorius, *l.c.*, p. 35. In French, however, it is *Cornet a bouquin*; see [Mattheson's *Neu-eröffnete*] *Orchestre* I, *l.c.*[,p. 269]. One also finds *Litice, Cornetto torto, Cornetto muto, Corno* and *Cornon* used in the same sense. This is a familiar curved instrument that is very hard to blow. [Builders] have long sought to imitate it in the organ; see Praetorius concerning reeds, Vol. II, Part IV, Chap. 2[, p. 146], [who says] it is a reed stop. He says that it is at 8′ pitch, and is used only in the treble through half the manual, that it has somewhat cylindrical resonators, tapered at the bottom and open on top, and thus it sounds rather hollow and does not rattle so much, this being prevented by the heavy tongues and high wind pressure that this stop requires. Up to the present this stop has been somewhat rare; I have found it at 8′ at St. Petri in Berlin, at St. Marien in Lübeck, twice at St. Marien in Danzig, at Otterndorf in Land Hadeln, and at St. Catharinen in Hamburg. At the Dreyfaltigkeitskirche and at St. Bartholomai in Danzig there is a "halber Zink 8′", about which Mattheson mentions in his Appendix to Niedt* that this is apparently as much as to say that such a reed does not extend further than over about half the keyboard, or over the so-called treble. The Halbe Cornet has been explained in the same way in §.132. That the Cornet and Zink are sometimes identical, see also §.132. There is also a special sort of *Cornetti* in [the Oberwerk at] Görlitz consisting of 3 pipes, Quinte 6′, Oktave 4′ and the Terz above 4′ pitch,† that sounds as if it were an 8′ reed yet has no 8′ pipe in it; it does not go, however, any lower than a Vox *humana,* i.e., from a to c′′′, since it would otherwise become unpleasant. It lends itself well for use in the right hand WITH the Bombart 16′ and other suitable stops, and produces an agreeable TIMBRE, such as I (says Boxberg‡) have never heard in another organ. This would then not be a reed stop.(**) [The name] Zynk is also used there for the Sesquialter, and thus it is also not a reed, but a compound stop of 2 ranks, i.e., as Boxberg explains,§ from Quinta 3′ and the Terz over 2′ pitch,¶ just like an ordinary Sesquialter dealt with in §.190. I believe it is immaterial whether it is spelled "Zynck" or "Zinck"; at least I have read the word "Zinck" used for such a compound

* p. 168.

† i.e., 3 1/5′.

‡ p.[16].

§ p.[13].
¶ i.e. 1 3/5′.

Kap. VII. Von den Registern überhaupt und insonderheit.

be, wenigstens habe ich das Wort Zinck auch gebraucht gelesen für eine solche gemischte Stimme, und soll vermuthlich auch die Sesquialter seyn. So ist Zink 2fach in der Altdresdener Orgel. Prätorius hat auf der 38sten Tabelle den Riß, wobey er geschrieben: Zink; Cornetdiskant; und in der Tabelle zu S. 126. setzt er Zinkdiskant 8'. S. 168. hat er den Zink 8' von f $\bar{a}$, und setzt dazu: wie gebräuchlich; vielleicht weil die Orgeln damals selten höher giengen. — Wer über eine Orgel kömmt, der bekümmere sich wohl darum, was durch den Zink zu verstehen; ob es ein Schnarrwerk oder Sesquialter seyn soll. (**) Siehe oben unter Cornet.

Zyfflöt. s. Sifflöt §. 192.

Zymbel. s. Cymbel. §. 133. u. 134.

Zynk ist kaum mit dem i geschrieben und erkläret worden: soll es aber mit der Sesquialter einerley seyn; so s. §. 190.

§. 212.

Und soviel habe ich endlich, Gott sey Dank! von den Orgelstimmen beybringen können. Es sind deren sehr viel, und deswegen ist das Kapitel so weitläuftig gerathen: aber ich wollte doch nicht gerne, daß ein Organist etwas vergebens suchen sollte. Aus diesem Grunde habe ich auch die alphabetische Ordnung beybehalten, um alles desto geschwinder finden zu können. Ich glaube, ein Organist habe daran genug, daß er sich nicht sonderlich vergehen sollte, wenn er auf eine Orgel kommt, und läßt sich die Register vorsagen.

§. 213.

In den Namen sind manchmal große Verwirrungen gewesen, welche theils von mir sind gehoben worden, theils nicht. Viel Wörter hätten aus allerhand Sprachen können erläutert werden; und bisweilen habe ich mir die Mühe gegeben, und etwas beygefügt; bisweilen aber habe ich es unterlassen. Aber wer daraus die Register nach dem folgenden Kapitel will brauchen lernen, der hat die Derivation nicht eben nöthig. Ich konnte auch zuweilen die Wörter nicht finden, weil ich im niederdeutschen, holländischen rc. nicht bewandert war.

Alle Orgelregister können auf diese folgenden drey Classen reducirt werden; (wie schon anderswo erinnert worden) Nämlich 1.) auf Oktavenregister, d. i. solche, deren großes C auch wirklich C angiebt, es sey ein hohes oder niedriges. Das sind diejenigen, welche in proportione dupla steigen oder fallen, als $\frac{1}{2}'$, 1', 2', 4', 8', 16', 32'. 2.) auf Quintenregister, deren großes C eine Quinte höher angiebt, nämlich G. Diese sind $1\frac{1}{2}'$, 3', 6', 12', 24'. 3.) Auf Terzenregister, die selten anders sind, als $1\frac{1}{3}'$ oder nach anderer Rechnung $1\frac{3}{5}'$. Nun merke man wohl dabey, wenn ein Register seiner Natur nach eine Oktavstimme, oder eine andere, ist; so ist es ein Fehler des Buchdruckers, oder des Auktoris, wenn solche durch falsche Zahlen bisweilen zu fol-

stop, apparently intended to be the Sesquialter. Thus there is a Zink of 2 ranks in the Altdresden organ.* Praetorius has a sketch [of it] in Table 38, next to which he has written: "Zink; Cornetdiskant", and in the Table at p. 126 he lists "Zinkdiskant 8′." On p. 168 he has a Zink 8′ from f to a′,† adding to it "as usual", perhaps because organs at that time seldom went any higher. Anyone who encounters an organ [that has one] might well take the trouble [to find out] what is meant by "Zink", whether it is a reed or a Sesqualter. (**) See above under Cornet. [Agricola]

ZYFFLÖT, see Sifflöte, §.192.

ZYMBEL, see Cymbel, §.133 and 134.

ZYNK has been spelled with an "i" and explained just above; if it should be the same as the Sesquialter, then see §.190.

* See the stoplist of the Alt-Dresdener organ, under "Dresden" in Chapter 10.

† Praetorius, *Syntagma musicum* II, p. 168, writes "a″;" "a′" may simply be a printing error in Adlung's book.

§. 212.

I have finally been able to [finish] imparting all of this [information] about organ stops—thanks be to God! There are a great many of them, and it is for that reason that this chapter has become so extensive. It would never suit me, however, to have an organist look up something in vain. For this reason I have adhered to an alphabetical arrangement, so everything could be found that much quicker. I believe there are enough of them to keep an organist from going wrong when he gets to an organ and comes face to face with the stops.

§. 213.

Now and again a great deal of confusion has crept into the names, which I have in part cleared up, but in part not. [The derivation of] many words from all sorts of languages could have been explained; sometimes I have taken the trouble to add something about this, but sometimes I have let it pass. But anyone who wants to use this chapter to learn how to use the stops according to the following chapter does not really need the derivations. Sometimes I also could not find the [meaning of] words, since I am not conversant with low German, Dutch, etc.

All organ stops may be reduced to the following three classes (as has already been mentioned elsewhere), namely: 1) octave stops, i.e., those whose lowest C actually sounds C, be it a high or low one. Those are the ones that ascend or descend in double proportion, such as ½′, 1′, 2′, 4′, 8′, 16′, 32′. 2) quint stops, whose lowest C sounds a fifth higher, namely G. These are 1 ½′, 3′, 6′, 12′, 24′. 3) Terz stops, that are seldom other than 1 1/5′‡ or, according to an alternate computation, 1 3/5′. One should take note whether a stop is by nature an octave stop or one of the others, for it is either a printer's error or an author's mistake if such a stop is sometimes, by incorrect numbers,

‡ sic; cf. §.190, "Sesquialter."

Kap. VII. Von den Registern überhaupt und insonderheit. 159

solchen Stimmen gemacht worden, die es entweder nicht sind, oder vielmals auch nicht seyn können. Also, wenn oben zuweilen vorgekommen Principal 6′, Oktave 5′ u. d. gl.; so habe ich es oft corrigirt, weil das Principal und die Oktaven nicht in der 6 stecken, die 5′ aber, nebst andern vorher nicht genannten Zahlen, sich zu keiner Stimme reimt. Ich will aber nicht sagen, daß ich im corrigiren es allezeit getroffen habe: denn es haben mich die Umstände zuweilen können betrügen, auf welche ich meine Aenderung gegründet. Auch gehen bey den Alten nicht alle Orgeln bis ins C, sondern nur zuweilen bis ins F. Und da hat denn Prätorius oft die Stimmen von solchem F an gezählet, daher nothwendig die Zahl sich geändert. Z. E. eine Orgel geht ins F, und das Principal vom C an zu rechnen wäre 16′, da sagt er 12′; vor 8′ sagt er 6′. Sonst aber kann man doch solche Stimmen vom C an rechnen, um die Confusion zu vermeiden. Dieß kann zuweilen oben nicht seyn regardirt worden. Oder zuweilen sind die Orgeln bis ins C; allein es sind etliche Stimmen nicht bis dahin geführet worden, daher auch ihre Größe nicht so angegeben wird. Z. E. in Hamburg zu St. Jakob hat Prätorius im Manuale Principal 12′. Wer das wollte corrigiren, der würde fehlen, weil zwar C nicht 12′ ist, aber diese Stimme geht daselbst nur bis ins F. So steht auch die Quintatön 12′ dabey, anstatt 16′; Hohlpipe 6′, anstatt 8′; 3′ anstatt 4′; Querpipe 6′ Ton, 12′ lang, offen, anstatt 12′ Ton 16′ lang. Andere Stimmen aber daselbst sind richtig angegeben. Im Pedale aber ist Basaune (wie er schreibt) 16′, auch Krumhorn 16′ ꝛc. Da hingegen das große Principal 24′ ist, nämlich es geht nur bis ins F, sonst wäre es 32′. It. die Mixtur, wobey ein Baß von 12′, anstatt 16′, ist. Daher steht zuweilen C und F dabey, zu zeigen, wovon man rechnen müsse. Z. E. zu St. Petri in Hamburg ist Gedackt 8′. C; Hohlflöt 3′. F. Das merke man, daß man nicht zur Unzeit die Dispositionen corrigire. Wo aber 5. 7. 9. u. d. gl. vorkommen, die kann man schon sicherer für falsch halten. Wo man auch auf Reisen etwas anmerkt, das mit diesem und jenem allegato nicht übereinstimmet, so kann man es corrigiren. Ob eine Stelle aus Prätorio, oder sonst woher sey, ist nicht allezeit angemerkt. Genug, daß, wo sie nicht in meinen hernachfolgenden Orgeldispositionen steht, oder in Matthesons Anhang zum Niedt, sie gewiß aus Prätorio ist, wobey man also zu zweifeln hat, ob die Orgel noch so stehe. Wundert sich jemand endlich, daß ich zuweilen so viele Oerter angeführt, wo die Stimme zu finden, der wisse, daß es für Reisende gut ist, und kann man sie am besten kennen lernen, wenn man sie siehet und höret: weis man aber nicht, wo sie stehen; so kann man sie destoweniger aufsuchen. Auch hätte ein Orgelmacher zweifeln mögen, daß bisweilen eine Stimme so groß oder klein zu machen: durch die Exempel aber wird er überführet. Doch genug von dieser Materie.

Ch. VII. Concerning Stops in General and in Particular

labeled as a stop that it either is not or cannot be. Thus when Principal 6′, Oktave 5′ and the like have at times appeared above,* I have often corrected them, since the Principal and Oktave can never fit into 6′, and 5′, in addition to other numbers not mentioned above, does not tally with any stop. I will not say, though, that I have always made the correction right, for at times the circumstances on which I have based my correction may have deceived me. In former times not all organs extended down to C, rather sometimes only to F. Praetorius has often figured the stops from this F upward, and so the number must necessarily be different. For example: if an organ goes down to F, and the Principal (figuring from C) would be 16′, then he says 12′; for 8′ he says 6′. Otherwise these stops may be figured from C, however, to avoid confusion. This† may at times not have been taken into account [in the text] above. Then sometimes organs will go down to C, but some stops may not have been carried that low, and thus their size is indicated differently. For example, at St. Jakobi in Hamburg Praetorius lists a Principal 12′ in the manual.‡ It would be a mistake to correct this; C is indeed not 12′, but this stop only goes down to F there. There is also a Quintatön 12′ there instead of 16′, Hohlpipe 6′ instead of 8′ and 3′ instead of 4′, Querpipe 6′ pitch, 12′ tall, open, instead of 12′§ pitch, 16′ tall. Other stops there, though, are indicated correctly.¶ In the pedal there is a "Bassaune" (as he spells it) 16′ and also a Krummhorn 16′, etc., while on the other hand the Great Principal is 24′, namely it only goes down to F; otherwise it would be 32′. It is the same with the Mixtur, next to which stands "Bass of 12′" instead of 16′. Therefore at times C or F stands next to [the stop name] to show from which pitch one must figure. For example, at St. Petri in Hamburg there is a Gedackt 8′ C and a Hohlflöt 3′ F. One needs to be careful not to correct a stoplist prematurely. Where 5, 7, 9 and the like appear, however, one can be more confident that these are wrong. If in the course of travel someone should note something that does not agree with this or that piece of information [in this book], he may correct it. Whether a citation comes from Praetorius or somewhere else is not always noted. Suffice to say that if it is not found in the organ stoplists that follow in this book, or in Mattheson's Appendix to Niedt, it is for sure out of Praetorius, in which case one must entertain the suspicion that the organ [in question] has been altered. Finally, if anyone should wonder why I have at times cited so many places where a stop may be found, let him keep in mind that it is helpful for travelers; one can get to know [the various stops] best by seeing and hearing them, but if one does not know where they are, then one has all the more trouble seeking them out. An organ builder might also sometimes doubt whether a [particular] stop is [customarily built] that large or small; the examples will then convince him [one way or the other]. But enough about these matters.

* from the stoplists that Adlung gathered while preparing to write the *Musica mechanica organœdi*.

† i.e., an organ's compass extending only to low F.

‡ *Syntagma musicum*, Vol. II, p. 168.

§ sic; the length should read "8′."

¶ i.e., beginning from low C.

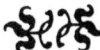

Das VIII. Kapitel.
Vom Gebrauch der Register.

Inhalt.

§. 214. Warum davon zu handeln. §. 215. Oktavenregister müssen die Quinten und Terzen überwiegen. §. 216. Sonderlich in der Tiefe. §. 217. Jedes Clavier ist für sich zu betrachten. §. 218. Die Register müssen nicht weit von einander seyn. §. 219. Von dem Tertian §. 220 Man muß die Bedeutung jedes Namens wissen. §. 221. Von Mixturen, Scharpen, Cimbeln, und andern gemischten Stimmen. §. 222. Wenn man mit viel Clavieren spielt. §. 223. Wie kleine Stimmen groß und große Stimmen klein gemacht werden. §. 224. Wie man gemischte Stimmen zuwege bringt §. 225. Von Schnarrwerken. §. 226. Man ziehe die Stimmen den Einfällen gemäß. §. 227. Man sehe auf des Orts Umstände, wie auch §. 228 der Zeit. §. 229. Onda maris; Violdigamba; Vox humana. §. 230. Von der prädominirenden Stimme. §. 231. Vom vollen Werke. §. 232. Ob Aequalstimmen zusammen zu ziehen. §. 233. Ob sie schärfen §. 234. Von Pedalstimmen. §. 235. Musicirstimmen. §. 236. Fantasirregister. §. 237. Choralstimmen. §. 238. Vom Echo.

§. 214.

Dieses Kapitel ist blos für die Organisten; als worinne gezeiget werden soll, wie jedes Register, seiner Natur nach, zu brauchen sey. Zwar gehört dies nicht eigentlich zur Mechanik, sondern theils zu den Choralen, theils zum Generalbasse und theils zur Fantasie. Allein es kann allhier füglicher eingerückt werden: sintemal es sich auf die Natur eines jeden Registers gründet. Da nun im vorigen Kapitel dieses Fundament, so viel mir möglich, erklärt worden; so wird hier die Application und der rechte Gebrauch der Register desto leichter verstanden werden.

§. 215.

Hier muß man nun einen großen Unterscheid machen unter den Stimmen welche man brauchen will. Dieser Unterschied ist schon im vorhergehenden 7ten Kapitel §. 213. angemerkt worden. Hier können wir diejenige Eintheilung am besten brauchen, welche de Chales macht, da er die Stimmen in ordines *præcipuos*, und in *minus præcipuos* unterscheidet. Præcipuos nenne ich die einfachen Oktav= oder Hauptstimmen; die gemischten aber, wie auch die Quinten und Terzen sind minus præcipui. Wenn ein modus oder Ton angegeben wird; so ist allezeit die Absicht auf solche Hauptregister (ordines præcipuos) die einfach und ihrer Natur nach 32', 16', 8', 4', 2', und 1', sind, zu machen. Folglich müssen diese Register allezeit der Grund und der vornehmste oder prädominirende Theil der Harmonie seyn. Wenn also der modus z. Ex. D soll gebraucht werden; so darf ich nicht die Quinte allein gebrauchen, weil diese den verlangten Ton nicht angiebt, sondern eine Quinte höher. So verhält sichs auch mit andern,

zum

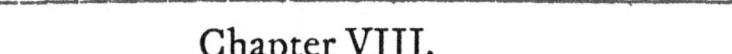

Chapter VIII.
Concerning the Use of the Stops.

Contents:

§.214. Why discuss this? §.215. Octave-sounding stops must predominate over fifths and thirds. §.216. Especially in the bass. §.217. Each keyboard must be considered independently. §.218. There must not be big gaps between stops. §.219. Concerning the Tertian. §.220. One must know the meaning of each name. §.221. Concerning Mixtures, Scharffs, Cymbels and other compound stops. §.222. Playing on several keyboards at once. §.223. How to make high stops low and low stops high. §.224. How to simulate compound stops. §.225. Concerning the reeds. §.226. Stops must be chosen with a purpose in mind. §.227. One must consider the customs of a place, §.228. as well as the occasion. §.229. *Onda maris*, Violdigamba and *Vox humana*. §.230. Soloing out a particular voice. §.231. Concerning the plenum. §.232. Whether 8′ stops should be drawn together. §.233. Whether they intensify each other. §.234. Concerning pedal stops. §.235. Figured bass stops. §.236. Registrations for improvisation. §.237. Stops for [accompanying] chorales. §.238. Concerning echo [effects].

§. 214.

This chapter is solely for organists. Its intention is to indicate how each stop is to be used, according to its character. To be sure, this is not really a matter of mechanics, but rather partly of [accompanying] chorales, partly of figured bass, and partly of improvisation. But it may more reasonably be inserted here, since it is based upon the character of each individual stop. Now since this basic information has been explained to the best of my ability in the previous chapter, its application, the proper use of the stops, will be all the more easily understood here.

§. 215.

Here a basic distinction must be made among the stops that one might wish to use. This distinction has already been noted in Chapter 7 above, §.213. Here it will best serve our purposes to use the classification made by De Chales,* dividing the stops into "primary stops" and "secondary stops." By "primary" I mean simply the octave-sounding or principal stops; the compound stops, on the other hand, as well as the quints and thirds, are the "secondary" ones. When a mode or key† is indicated, it is always intended that the primary stops should be used, the ones that naturally sound at 32′, 16′, 8′, 4′, 2′ and 1′. Consequently these stops must always be the foundation and the chief or predominating element in the harmony. If, for example, I decide to play in the key of D, then I dare not use the Quints alone, since they do not produce the requisite pitch, but a fifth higher. The same holds true for the other [stops], such as Terzes or compound

* *Cursus seu mundus mathematicus*, Vol. III, p. 21.

† For Adlung these words are synonymous.

Kap. VIII Vom Gebrauch der Register.

zum Ex. mit Terzen oder gemischten Stimmen, wo die Quinte oder Terz prädominiren. Die Oktavenregister, sie mögen offen oder gedeckt; Flöt= oder Rohrwerke seyn, können aber gar wohl allein gebraucht werden, weil sie stets den verlangten Ton von sich hören lassen. Will man ja die Quinten brauchen; so müssen von solchen Oktavenregistern soviel dabey seyn, daß sie die Quinte überschreyen, und ihr wildes Wesen nicht allzusehr gemerkt werde. Deswegen ist die erste Regel bey de Chales l. c. diese: ne in combinationibus ordines minus principales soli educantur. Eins aber von solchen Oktavenregistern muß größer seyn, als die Quinte und Terz. Dies will die zwote Regel des de Chales, welche so heißt: ne Quintae et Tertiae inferiorem locum obtineant. Z. Ex. die 6füßige Quinte ist ohne Principal 8' nicht zu gebrauchen: oder man nehme andere 8füßige Register, so gleichen Effekt haben. Wollte man die Quinte 3' und Oktave 2' zusammen ziehen, und weiter kein Register in einem Manual; so wäre es gleichfalls ein Fehler, weil die Quinte größer ist, als die Oktave. Wenigstens muß bey Quinte 3' Oktave 4' seyn, oder andere von gleicher Würkung. Doch dürfen uns die Zahlen nicht betrügen, wie uns der §. 213. gelehret.

§. 216.

Ja, wenn auch eine größere Oktave bey den Quinten ist, und keine andere Register in gehöriger Anzahl dabey sind; so wollen sie doch in der Tiefe gar verzweifelt klingen, da man in der Höhe die Harmonie viel erleidlicher findet. Z. Ex. ich habe bey der Quinte 6' das Principal 8', nebst dem Bordun 16' und Rohrflöt 8', gehört, welches in der Höhe wohl lautete, aber in der Tiefe war die Quinte viel zu widrig anzuhören: wäre aber nur die Oktave 4' noch dabey gewesen; so hätte man den Klang um ein merkliches verbessert. Daß aber die Quinte kleiner seyn müsse, als das Oktavenregister, erhellet daraus, weil ausser dem die Harmonie aus bloßen und beständig fortschreitenden Quarten bestehen würde. In Quarten aber fortzugehen, ist auch einem Tironi nicht vergönnet. Es sey z. Ex. die Quinte 3' und die Oktave 2': wenn ich nun die Claves c d e f g u. s. w. anschlage, so wird die Oktave 2' geben c̄ d̄ ē f̄ ḡ a. ꝛc.; die Quinte 3' aber, weil sie tiefer ist g a h c d ē, ꝛc. Sind das nicht lauter Schafquarten? Wäre aber die Oktave 4; so hätte sie c d e f g a angegeben, und also wären es Quinten worden. Wolte jemand einwenden, daß ja die Quinten auch verboten wären; dem dient zur Antwort, daß die Generalbaßisten es zwar im Spielen, nicht aber im Registerziehen schlechterdings verbieten. Es wird aber, um dieses Kapitul nicht allzuweitläuftig zu machen, im 28sten Kapitel mehr davon beygebracht werden. Diesen §phum erläutert de Chales mit folgender dritten Regel: Tertia et Quintae ita *praecipuis ordinibus* iunguntur, vt *praecipui praeualeant*; unde, si *Quinta* educatur, ad minimum *duo ordines praecipui* cum ea iungantur,

§. 217.

Man verstehe mich wohl. Denn ich betrachte jedes Clavier für sich, ohne Rücksicht auf das andere. Wolte einer dieser Anweisung nach, indem er mit 2 Clavieren zugleich

X

Chap. VIII.   The Use of the Stops

stops, in which fifths or thirds predominate. The octave-sounding stops, be they open or stopped, flues or reeds, may very readily be used alone, since they always produce the requisite pitch. If one wishes to use the Quints, then there must be a sufficient number of such octave-sounding stops with them to overpower the fifth, so that its rough character is not too noticeable. For this reason, the first rule in De Chales, *l.c.** is: "combinations of secondary stops may never be drawn alone." One of the octave-sounding stops must be lower than the Quinte and Terz. This is the intention of De Chales's second rule, which reads as follows: "Quints and Terzes may not occupy the lowest pitch level." For example, the 6′ Quinte is not to be used without the Principal 8′ or other 8′ stops that have the same effect. If the Quinte 3′ and Oktave 2′ were to be drawn together on the same manual without any other stop, that would likewise be an error, since the Quinte is lower than the Oktave. At the least there must be an Oktave 4′, or some other [stop] that has the same effect, with the Quinte 3′. But we must not allow ourselves to be tricked by numbers,† as we have learned in §.213.

* This rule and all that follow it are found in Vol. III, p. 21.

† i.e., a stop may be labeled incorrectly, or may begin at F instead of C; the organist should try it out.

§. 216.

Indeed, even if there is a lower Oktave with the Quints, and other stops are not drawn in sufficient number, then [the Quints] will sound simply dreadful in the bass, while in the treble the harmony‡ will seem much more bearable. For example, I have heard the Principal 8′, Bordun 16′ and Rohrflöt 8′ together with the Quinte 6′, [a combination] that sounded well in the treble; but in the bass the Quinte was much too unpleasant to listen to. If only the Oktave 4′ had been added to it, the sound would have been noticeably improved. It is apparent, however, that a Quinte must be smaller than an octave-sounding stop, because otherwise the harmony would consist entirely of a constant progression of fourths. A string of successive fourths is not even permitted an amateur. Take, for example, the Quinte 3′ and the Oktave 2′; if I play the keys c d e f g a,§ etc., the Oktave 2′ would sound c′ d′ e′ f′ g′ a′, etc., but the Quinte [3′ would sound] g a b c′ d′ e′, etc., because it is lower. Aren't those just plain old parallel fourths? If however the Oktave had been a 4′, then it would have sounded c d e f g a, and then there would have been [parallel] fifths. If anyone should object that fifths are indeed also forbidden, let this answer suffice: it is absolutely forbidden to figured bass players in performance, but not in registration. To avoid making this chapter too extensive, however, Chapter 28 will say more about this. De Chales explains this paragraph¶ with the following third rule: thirds and fifths should be combined with the primary stops in such a way that the primary ones predominate; thus, if the Quinte be drawn, at least two primary stops should be combined with it.

‡ i.e., the notes played by the right hand in the treble. Adlung has in mind the typical texture of figured bass: a single bass note in the left hand, realized by chords played in the treble by the right hand.

§ By setting these notes an octave lower (C D E F G A), all of the following pitches are correct as printed; otherwise they are all an octave too low.

¶ i.e., the matter that Adlung has been writing about in this paragraph, §.216.

§. 217.

Do not misunderstand me. I am considering each keyboard separately, without regard to the other[s]. If anyone should, in following these principles, while playing

gleich spielte, in einem die Quinte 3′ ziehen, ohne 4′ oder 8′; im andern aber wollte er es durch 4′ gut machen, der hätte die Sache nicht wohl getroffen. Jedes Clavier muß für sich richtig seyn. Wer nun aus dem vorigen Kapitel gelernet hat, was für Register die Quinten in sich halten, der wird auf alle dieselben das vorgemeldete zu appliciren wissen. Also ist Nasat auch eine Quinte, folglich auch auf gleiche Art zu gebrauchen. Item, weil die Rauschpfeife die Quint in sich hält, auch die Sesquialtera; so sind sie ebenfalls nicht zu gebrauchen, wo nicht etwan größere Oktavenstimmen zum Grunde geleget werden. Doch bey der Sesquialtera ist oft die Oktave 4′ mit auf einem Stocke, und da hat man nicht nöthig, sie noch besonders dazu zu ziehen. Man erkundige sich demnach wie vielfach sie sey, wenn man sie brauchen will.

§. 218.

Es muß aber das Oktavenregister von diesen Registern nicht allzuweit entfernet seyn; z. Ex. die Sesquialtera (wenn die Oktave 4′ nicht auf dem Stocke steht) lautet weit übeler, wenn man anstatt 4′ das 8′ zieht. Denn 8′ giebt C an; die Sesquialtera hat die Quinte 3′, die giebt g an, das eine Duodez von 8′ entfernet ist; die Terz ist noch höher, und ist 17 Claves von C entfernet. Der große hiatus zwischen 2 Stimmen ist etwas verdrießlich, und die Quinte wird dadurch nicht so gut bedeckt. So ist auch das Tertian, welches wenig von der Sesquialter unterschieden ist. Wollen doch nicht einmal die Oktavenstimmen wohl lauten, wenn sie allzuweit von einander entfernet sind. Z. Ex. 16′ zu 2′ oder 1′.

§. 219.

Die Tertiane sind noch härter, weil zumal in allen Mollaccorden *mi* contra *fa* gehöret wird, welches Diabolus in Musica heißt. Z. Ex. wenn ich den Akkord c moll angebe; so giebt das Tertian die große Terz zu c, nämlich e, an; (denn es hat allezeit die große Terz) ich aber greife es als die kleine Terz: das ist *mi* contra *fa*, die kleine und große Terz zugleich. Mein angeschlagenes es giebt wegen der Terz g, und die Quinte des Accords ist auch g, schickt sich also dieses besser als das vorige, nur daß mein g niedriger steht, weil es in der Temperatur etwas entbehren müssen: die Stimmung aber der Quinten- und Terzenregister gegen die Oktaven richten sich nach keiner Temperatur. Ferner die Quinte g giebt wegen der Terz h mit an. Nun betrachte man den Klang, wenn c̄, ē, ē, ḡ, h̄, c̄, zusammen klingen soll: daraus auch ein Kind begreift, daß die Terzen und das Tertian nicht anders zu brauchen, als wenn sie mit andern Stimmen stark genug bedeckt werden. Sonderlich können sie in modis minoribus die Harmonie verderben; denn in modis maioribus ist es so arg nicht. Es kömmt zwar auch *mi* contra *fa* bey der Quinte vor; aber etwas höher, und nicht so craß, und es wird der Klang auf folgende Weise sich hören lassen: c̄, ē, ḡ, gis, h̄, c̄. Hier wird von mir der Accord c̄, ē, ḡ, c̄, gegriffen: die Terz aber läßt e auch hören, als die

Ter-

on two keyboards at the same time,* draw a Quinte 3′ on one (without a 4′ or an 8′) and hope to set it right by using a 4′ on the other, that person will not have understood the matter very well. Each keyboard must be right in itself. Whoever has learned from the previous chapter what stops are included in the Quints will understand that what has just been said applies to all of them. Thus the Nasat is also a Quinte, and consequently must be used in the same way. Likewise, because the Rauschpfeife contains a Quint, as does the Sesquialtera, these are not to be used unless some other lower octave-sounding stops are present as a foundation. Yet the Oktave 4′ is often on the same toeboard† as the Sesquialtera, and then it is not necessary to draw it again‡ separately. One should accordingly ascertain how many ranks [the Sesquialtera] is, if one wishes to use it.

§. 218.

The octave-sounding stops must not be too far distant [in pitch] from these stops; e.g., the Sesquialtera (unless the Oktave 4′ stands [with it]) on the toeboard) sounds far worse if an 8′ is drawn instead of a 4′. For the 8′ sounds C, the Sesquialtera with the Quinte 3′ sounds g (a twelfth removed from the 8′), and the Terz is even higher, seventeen keys removed from C. The great gap between these two stops is rather disagreeable, and with this [combination] the Quinte is less well absorbed. The same also hold true for the Tertian, which is little different from the Sesquialter. Even the octave-sounding stops will not sound well if they are too far removed from each other, e.g., 16′ and 2′, or [16′ and] 1′.

§. 219.

The Tertians are even harsher [than the Sesqualtera], especially since *mi contra fa* is heard in all minor chords; this is called the *Diabolus in Musica*.§ For example, if I play the chord of c minor, the Tertian sounds the major third of c, namely e (since [this stop] always has the major third); I am playing e-flat, however, the minor third. This is *mi contra fa*, the minor and major third [sounding] simultaneously.¶ Because of the Terz, the e-flat I am playing sounds g, and the fifth of the chord is also g. These two fit together better than the preceding, except that my g‖ is tuned lower, since it must be adjusted to fit the temperament, while the tuning of the Quint and Terz stops is pure and untempered in relation to the octave[-speaking] stops. Furthermore the fifth [of the chord], g, sounds b-natural due to the Terz. Just think what it would sound like, now, if c′, e-flat′, e′, g′, b-natural′ and c″ were to sound together. Even a child would understand from this that the Terzes and the Tertian are never to be used except when they are adequately absorbed by other stops. Especially in minor keys they can spoil the harmony; in the major keys, though, [this problem] is not so vexing. To be sure, *mi contra fa* also arises [in major keys] with the fifth, but somewhat higher and not so coarse. Here the sound is composed of the following: c′, e′, g′, g#′, b-natural′, c″. In this case I play the chord c′, e′, g′, c″, but the Terz also sounds e, the third above c, as

* presumably, in this instance, uncoupled: one hand on the upper keyboard, the other hand on the lower.

† i.e., on the same channel with the Sesqualtera; see §.190 under "Sesqualter."

‡ i.e., to pull another, independent 4′ Oktave.

§ the "Devil in Music"; Adlung's understanding of this expression differs from its traditional connotation, the augmented fourth or tritone. The Tertian may indeed produce a more biting sound than the Sesqualter, since it sounds higher pitches, but the phenomenon of *mi contra fa* (as Adlung explains it) is created by the third in the Sesqualtera as well as the third in the Tertian.

¶ *Mi contra fa*, "mi against fa", refers to the simultaneous sounding of the third and fourth degrees of the major scale, or of a half step. Its application to the simultaneous sounding of the major and minor third is obvious.

‖ i.e., the one from the octave-sounding rank.

Kap. VIII. Vom Gebrauch der Register. 163

Terz zu c. Imgleichen gis als die große Terz zu e. Das klingt mit g freylich nicht, und ist *mi* contra *fa*; allein es ist schon höher, als in modis minoribus, und folglich so merklich nicht.   h wird als die Terz zu g auch wie vorhin gegen c dissoniren. Dies ist unter andern die Ursach, warum die **Sesquialter** lieblicher klingt, als das **Tertian**, weil das letztere die Terz, die erstere aber die Quinte größer hat.   In viel Stimmen ist also die Terz zu brauchen; sonst aber nicht. Man macht sie auch ordentlich gar klein, wie §. 197. zu sehen, damit sie nicht allzuhart klingen möge.   In der Sesquialter ist die Terz schon klein; sonst wäre es eben so zu halten.   Davon sagt **de Chales** in Regula quarta; Vix 2. Quintae educantur, nisi illis addantur 4 ordines fundamentales. Denn die minus praecipui mischen so viel Sekunden und Septimen mit ein, die dem Gehör unangenehm sind, wo sie von andern Okavstimmen nicht überschrieen werden.

§. 220.

Wer auf eine Orgel kömmt, der examinire die Namen wohl, und frage: was darunter zu verstehen? Z. Ex. wenn **Zink** daran steht, muß er sich erkundigen, ob es ein Schnarrwerk sey, oder eine Sesquialter u. s. w.   Deswegen ist im vorigen Kapitel die vielfältige Bedeutung eines Worts angeführet worden. Also wenn **Cimbel** daran geschrieben stehet; so muß man forschen, ob es ein Pfeifenregister oder der Stern sey; wiewol das letztere ordentlich an dem Zuge erkannt wird, da die Schiebestange sich in eine Kerbe einhängt: **das Cimbelregister aber wird gleich heraus gezogen, wie andere Stimmen.**

§. 221.

Bey **Mixturen, Scharpen, Cimbelregistern**, und überhaupt bey allen gemischten Stimmen, hat man sich gleichfalls nach der obigen Anweisung zu richten. Alleine sind sie nicht zu gebrauchen; denn die meisten haben zur größten Pfeife keine Octave, sondern die Quinte; und wenn sie gleich solche hätten, so sind doch der Quinten und Terzen so viel, wenigstens sind sie zu stark, als daß solche Oktave sie genugsam überschreyen könnte.   Im vollen Werke kann man sie brauchen.   Es kömmt auch darzu, daß sie oft repetiren.   Wenn ich nun setze, daß bey einer Mixtur Oktave 4' die größte Pfeife wäre, darauf die Quinte 3' folgte, ic.; so wird die Octave 4' in der 2 gestrichenen Oktave 1' groß; die Quinte 1½ oder ¾" werden oben repetirt, und also größer, als sie ordentlich seyn sollten; die **Oktave 4'** aber, oder 2' werden nicht repetirt: also werden sie gar klein gegen die Quinten.

§. 222.

Wer mit viel Clavieren spielt, der muß in dem, welches am tiefsten geht, oder welches er mit der linken Hand traktirt, gröbere Register ziehen, als in dem andern; wenigstens sollten die Hauptregister in der Tiefe gleich seyn.   Denn wenn die Hände nahe beysammen sind, oder wenn die rechte Hand tiefer zu stehen kömmt, als die Linke, so

Chap. VIII. The Use of the Stops

well as g#, the major third above e. That is of course not consonant with g, and is *mi contra fa*, though it is indeed higher than in the minor keys and consequently not so noticeable. B-natural, the third above g, is also dissonant against c, as before. This is one reason, among others, why the Sesquialter sounds milder than the Tertian, because in the latter the Terz is lower, while in the former the Quinte is lower. Thus the Terz is to be used exclusively in [combinations of] many stops. It is ordinarily built [at a] very high [pitch], as may be seen in §.197, to prevent it from sounding too harsh. In the Sesqualtera the Terz is already high by the very nature of this stop. De Chales speaks about this in his fourth rule: two Quints should not be drawn unless 4 primary stops be added to them. For the secondary stops introduce any number of seconds and sevenths* that are unpleasant to listen to if they are not absorbed by the other octave-sounding stops.

* i.e., dissonant intervals.

§. 220.

Anyone who visits an organ should carefully examine the [stop] names and ask [himself], "What do they mean?" For example, if [the stop] is labeled "Zink," he must ascertain whether it is a reed or a Sesquialter,† and so forth. It is for this reason that multiple meanings of a word have been cited in the previous chapter. Thus if [the stop] is labeled "Cimbel," one must investigate whether it is a stop with pipes or the Cymbelstern, although the latter may normally be recognized by its drawknob, since the draw-rod hooks into a notch. The Cimbel stop,‡ however, may be drawn right out, just like other stops.

† See §.211 above.

‡ i.e., the mixture.

§. 221.

With Mixtures, Scharffs, Cimbels, and with all compound stops in general, one must likewise be guided by the above instructions. They must not be used alone, for most of them have as their lowest pipe not an octave but a fifth, and even if they had [an octave as their lowest pipe], there are still so many fifths and thirds, or at least they are so loud, that the octave cannot sufficiently absorb them. They may be used in the plenum. There is also this to consider: they repeat often. If I establish that an Oktave 4′ is to be the lowest pipe in a Mixtur, followed by the Quinte 3′, etc., then in the two-stroke octave the Oktave 4′ would be 1′ tall. The Quinte 1½′ and ¾′ break back in the treble, and thus [become] lower than they ordinarily would be;§ yet the Oktave 4′ and 2′ do not break back, and thus they become very high in relation to the Quints.

§ i.e., if they were independent stops and did not break back.

§. 222.

[An organist] who plays on more than one keyboard [simultaneously] must draw deeper stops in the one that goes the lowest (the one that he plays with the left hand) than in the other; the primary stops¶ must at least be at the same pitch level [in both manuals]. For if the hands‖ are near together, or if the right hand passes below the left,

¶ See §.223. What Adlung seems to mean here is "the lowest (octave-) sounding pitch."

‖ i.e., the pitches played on each manual.

werden Fehler verursachet. Z. Er. wenn der Gang durch Sexten sammt der dazwischen liegenden Terz gebraucht wird, man wollte aber in der rechten tiefere Stimmen haben, als in der linken; so würden die Stimmen nicht mehr in Quarten einhergehen, welches wohl angehet, wenn die Terz noch darunter ist, sondern in puren Quinten. Es sey denn, daß einer mit der Rechten beständig in der Höhe, und mit der Linken in der Tiefe bleiben wollte, woran man sich aber nicht zu binden pflegt. Wiewol wer stets also spielt, daß per contrapunctum solche Stimmen können verwechselt werden, braucht solcher Erinnerung nicht. Wo sind sie aber? — — —

§. 223.

Wer in einer Orgel wenig große Stimmen hat, der spiele eine Oktave tiefer, so ist es eben so gut. Also, wer mit Principal 4′ spielt, kann den 8fußigen Klang bekommen, wenn er eine Oktave tiefer spielt. Es kann auch wol sich zutragen, daß in einer Orgel irgendswo das Gedackt 8′ nicht zu brauchen, wegen allerhand Ursachen. Da nun in der Musik dasselbe nöthig ist, (oder auch an dessen Statt die Quintatön 8′) und aber keins zu ziehen taugt, oder wol gar nicht da ist; so ziehe man die Quintatön 16′, und spiele stets in der 2gestrichnen Oktave, denn damit kömmt man dem 8fußigen gleich. Und so kann (und muß) man sich öfters behelfen, daß man aus kleinen große, und aus großen kleine Register macht.

Hier wollen wir zeigen, wie man durch die artem combinatoriam mit wenig Stimmen viele Veränderungen machen könne, wenn man sie nur so braucht, daß solche Veränderung und Ziehung der Register den obigen Regeln nicht zuwider ist, und hernach ex regulis prudentiae beurtheilet, was zu der oder jeder Zeit, an dem und jenem Orte, bey der und jener Melodie, für eine Combination sich füglich schicke; wovon im folgenden etwas vorkommen wird. In der Arithmetik wird gezeigt, daß die ars combinatoria lehre, alle Veränderungen zu finden, die man in Versetzung gewisser Zahlen oder Sachen vornehmen könne. Z. Er. wenn 12 Personen einmal so, das andermal anders rangiret würden, und man wissen wollte, wie vielmal sie anders geordnet werden könnten, daß sie nie einmal wie das anderemal zusammen geordnet wären. Dies lehrt die ars combinatoria. Wie es zu rechnen, mag einer aus der Arithmetik erlernen. [50]) Wir wollen nur durch ein Exempel zeigen, wie sich solches appliciren lasse. Wir wollen ein Clavier setzen von 8 Stimmen, nämlich:

1) Principal 8′.	5) Quintatön 8′.
2) Oktave 4′.	6) Mixtur.
3) Oktave 2′.	7) Cimbel.
4) Gedackt 16′.	8) Quinte 3′.

Da muß man die ordines præcipuos von den minus præcipuis unterscheiden. Præcipui sind die ersten 5 von diesem Werke, deren jedes allein gezogen werden kann: also sind

---

[50]) Siehe des seel. Hrn. Verfassers Anleitung zu der musikal. Gelahrtheit. §. 209. S. 497.

then the result will be blemishes.* For example, if a progression of 6/3 chords is played in which the right hand plays on stops [an octave] lower than the left hand,† then the voices would no longer proceed in [parallel] fourths, which are permissible when a third lies beneath them, but rather in pure [parallel] fifths. [To avoid this] would mean that a player would have to remain constantly high up [in the treble] with the right hand and down low [in the bass] with the left, but players are not accustomed to restrict themselves to this. Anyone who plays consistently, though, in invertible counterpoint does not need such reminders. But where are such players to be found? — — —

* i.e., false relations.

† Adlung is envisioning a hypothetical situation here in which the right hand is playing the root of the chord in the upper voice with, e.g., 16′ as the lowest pitch, while the left hand is playing the third and fifth of the chord (below the root) on another manual at 8′ pitch.

§. 223.

Anyone who has [too] few low stops in an organ should play an octave lower; this works just as well. Thus anyone can get an 8′ sound by playing an octave lower on the Principal 4′. It may well also happen that in some organ or another the Gedackt 8′ is unusable, for whatever reason. Since this stop is necessary for ensemble music‡ (or the Quintatön 8′ in its place), if there is not one fit to be used, or if there simply is not one at all, one should draw the Quintatön 16′ and play constantly in the 2-stroke octave;§ this is just like playing on an 8′. Thus frequently one can (and must) make do by making low stops out of high ones and high ones out of low ones.

‡ i.e., for the realization of figured bass.

§ i.e., an octave higher; this is an incidental clue as to the range within which figured bass should ordinarily be realized: the one-stroke octave.

Here I want to show how it is possible to achieve a great deal of variety with a few stops by means of the art of combining, as long as one uses it so that, in varying and choosing the stops, the above rules are observed, and [as long as] hereafter good common sense dictates what combination is appropriate for this or that occasion, at this or that place, with this or that melody (more about this below). [The study of] arithmetic shows that the *ars combinatoria* teaches [us] how to find all [possible] variations; this is done by determining the permutations of given numbers or objects. For example, if 12 persons may be arranged one way at one time and another way at another, and one wishes to know how many different ways they may be arranged without repeating any previous order--this is what the *ars combinatoria* teaches. Anyone may learn how to calculate it by arithmetic. We will merely show by means of an example how to apply it. We will first posit a manual with 8 stops, namely:

1) Principal 8′   5) Quintatön 8′
2) Oktave 4′   6) Mixtur
3) Oktave 2′   7) Cimbel
4) Gedakt 16′   8) Quinte 3′

Then we must distinguish the primary stops from the secondary. The primary are the first 5 of this manual, any one of which may be drawn alone; thus this already

50) See the late author's *Anleitung zu der musikalischen Gelahrtheit*, §.209, p. 497. [Albrecht]

sind dies schon 5 Veränderungen. Hernach kann man 2 und 2 zusammen nehmen, und da werden folgende combinationes entstehen, dabey ich, der Kürze wegen, die Stimmen durch die Zahlen andeuten will. Es kann beysammen stehen:

1. 2. imgleichen 2. 3.
1. 3.   2. 4.
1. 4.   2. 5.
1. 5.   3. 4.
                3. 5.
                4. 5.

Ferner kann man drey Stimmen zugleich zusammen nehmen, und folgendermaßen verändern:

1.2.3. | 1.2.4. | 1.2.5. | 1.3.4. | 1.3.5. | 1.4.5. | 2.3.4. | 2.3.5. | 3.4.5. |

Will man es vierstimmig haben; so finden sich folgende Veränderungen:

1.2.3.4. | 1.2.4.5. | 1.3.4.5. | 2.3.4.5. | 1.2.3.5. |

Man kann auch alle 5 Hauptregister zusammenziehen. Dies zusammen giebt schon 30 Veränderungen, die mit den Regeln übereinkommen. Nun kann man die drey ordines minus principales anziehen; so werden noch gar viel Veränderungen entstehen, ob sie schon nicht alle gut sind. Doch kann man wol die folgenden gebrauchen:

1.2.8. | 1.6.5.8. | 2.3.8. | 1.4.2.8. |

Oder die Mixtur dabey, z. Ex.

1. 2. 3. 6. | 1. 2. 4. 6. | 1. 2. 3. 5. 6. | ꝛc.

So auch mit der Cymbel, die ich nicht mag hersetzen, weil aus dem besagten schon begreiflich ist, was man durch die artem combinatoriam bey dem Registerziehen verstehe. Es hat diese artem combinatoriam bey dem Registerziehen der De Chales gar artig abgehandelt, l. c. Prop. XV. pag 20. 21. 22. Da er auch exempli loco eine Orgel mit 10 klingenden Stimmen annimmt, nämlich die zu Cambery, welche hernach inserirt werden soll. Er merkt an, daß solche 10 Stimmen über 300 gute combinationes haben könnten: sonst aber wol 1023, wenn man die unbrauchbaren, die wider die obigen Regeln sind, mitzählen wollte. Wenn man diese Combination auf mehr Stimmen, z. E. auf 40, 50, u. s. w. it. auf mehr als ein Clavier zusammen erstreckt; so kommen so viel Veränderungen heraus, daß ein Organist wol in etlichen 100 Jahren nicht durchkäme, wenn er jede brauchen wollte. Dennach sehe ich nicht warum etliche Organisten immer bey einerley bleiben. Die Veränderung ist und bleibt doch die Seele der Musik.

§. 224.

Will einer mit gemischten Stimmen eine Veränderung machen: aber er hat dergleichen nicht; so kann er durch Zusammenziehung anderer Register solche zuweilen zuwege

Chap. VIII.   The Use of the Stops

produces 5 variations. Next we may combine by twos, and in this way the following combinations are formed, for which I will indicate the stops by their numbers, for the sake of brevity. The following may be combined:

1. 2.	as well as	2. 3.
1. 3.		2. 4.
1. 4.		2. 5.
1. 5.		3. 4.
		3. 5.
		4. 5.

Furthermore, we may combine three voices at once, and come up with the following variations:

1.2.3. / 1.2.4. / 1.2.5. / 1.3.4. / 1.3.5. / 1.4.5. / 2.3.4. / 2.3.5. / 3.4.5./

By combining four stops the following variations result:

1. 2. 3. 4. / 1. 2. 4. 5. / 1. 3. 4. 5. / 2. 3. 4. 5. / 1. 2. 3. 5. /

We may also draw all 5 primary stops together. These already produce altogether 30 variations that conform to the rules. Now we may introduce the three secondary stops; in this way a great many additional variations will be formed, although they are not all good ones. Yet we may well use the following:

1. 2. 8. / 1. 6. 5. 8. / 2. 3. 8. / 1. 4. 2. 8. /

With the Mixtur added, e.g.,

1. 2. 3. 6. / 1. 2. 4. 6. / 1. 2 .3. 5. 6. / etc.

The same holds true for the Cymbel, but I will refrain from writing it out, since what has already been said is sufficient to grasp what is meant by [applying] the *ars combinatoria* to the selection of stops. De Chales has treated this *ars combinatoria* [applied] to choosing registration very skillfully [in Vol. III], Prop. XV, pp. 20, 21 and 22. There he takes as an example an organ with 10 sounding stops, namely the one at Chambery, [the stoplist of] which will be given below.* He notes that 10 stops such as these can afford over 300 good combinations; the number swells to 1023 if the unusable [combinations], the ones against the above rules, are included. If this combining is extended to more stops, e.g., to 40, 50, etc., on more than one keyboard, so many variations result that an organist could not get through them all in some 100 years if he wanted to use them all. Thus I do not see why some organists keep on using the same few. Variety is and remains the soul of music.

* See the stoplist of this organ in Chapter 10.

§. 224.

If anyone wants to devise a registration with compound stops, but has none of them, he can sometimes create them by combining other stops. For example, if he wants

wege bringen. Z. E. wer die **Rauschpfeife** hören will, der ziehe die **Oktave** 2' und **Quinte** 3' zusammen; so hat er sie: will er die **Sesquialter** hören 2fach; so ziehe er die **Quinte** 3' und die **Terz** über **Oktave** 2': soll sie 3fach seyn; so muß **Oktave** oder **Principal** 4' dazu. Hat man keine **Terz**; so kann man sie im Spielen auch nicht gebrauchen: aber man kann sie doch hören, wenn in einem Clavier die **Quinte** 3', und im andern die **Oktave** 2' gezogen wird, daß eine Hand im c anhebe, die andere eine große **Terz** höher oder tiefer, nachdem die Hand die **Quinte** oder **Terz** greift. Wer hören will, wie das **Tertian** klingt, der ziehe die **Terz** über 2' und die **Quinte** $1\frac{1}{2}$: denn die **Terz** über 4' hat man nicht leicht, sonst könnte man die **Quinte** 3' dazu nehmen. Oder man nehme mit einer Hand in einem Claviere die **Quinte** in solcher Größe, und mit der andern ziehe man die **Oktave** 4' und spiele sie im andern Claviere, doch eine **Sexte** tiefer als solche **Quinte**. Hier mögte ein Kritikus einwenden, daß man nicht eigentlich also hören könnte, wie solche Register klingen, weil ein Register gegen das andere nicht temperirt wird, wohl aber ein Clavis gegen den andern; also wird die dazu gegriffene **große Terz** nicht so hoch seyn, als wenn sie in einem besondern Register dazu gezogen wird, weil jene durch die Temperatur etwas hat leiden müssen. Hierauf dienet zur Antwort, daß solches wol wahr sey: aber ich will nur einigermaaßen den Lehrlingen weisen, wie sie solche Register in etwas können kennen lernen, ob es schon nicht allzuvollkommen geschehen kann. Zu **Prag** ist ein **Koppel** (confer. §. 128.) Da **Quinte** 3', **Superoktave** 2' und **Terz** 2' (i. e. die Terz drüber) auf einem Stocke stehen. Dieß kann man durch drey besondere Register auch nachmachen.

§. 225.

Wo **Schnarrwerke** sind, vergreife man sich nur nicht dran, es sey denn, daß man versichert sey, daß sie gestimmt worden. Könnte jemand davon, item von dem, was von der mannigfaltigen Bedeutung eines Worts gesagt worden, nicht Nachricht bekommen, der nehme auf dem Clavier solche Register, derer Natur er kennt, und spiele; unter dem Spielen ziehe er bald das, bald jenes heraus, um zu hören, was es in der Harmonie für eine Aenderung mache, darnach sich alsdann beurtheilen läßt, in was für einem Verstande es gebraucht worden. Daraus wird er bald merken, ob z. E. der **Zink** ein **Schnarrwerk** oder eine **Sesquialter** sey, u. s. w. Auf dem andern Claviere kann er auch die Stimmen probiren, wenn er unter dem Spielen eine nach der andern anzieht, und darnach hurtig auf die Palmuln dipt. (wie wir bey uns reden.) Dieß Mittel kann auch gebraucht werden, wenn wir gar keine Namen an den Registerzügen angeschrieben finden. Item, wenn wir nicht wissen, in welches Clavier jedes Register gehöre.

§. 226.

Etliche Stimmen schicken sich besser zum laufen, als zum langsamen spielen; andere kehren es um. Die **Quintatön** schlägt nicht gerne an, wenn man laufen will; also lasse man sie weg im vollen Werke, oder wenn man sonst geschwinde spielt. Besser ist

ein

a Rauschpfeife, he should draw the Oktave 2′ and the Quinte 3′ together, and he has it. If he wants a Sesquialter 2 ranks, he should pull the Quinte 3′ and the Terz above the Oktave 2′;* if he wants a 3 rank [Sesquialtera], then the Oktave or Principal 4′ must be added to these. If no Terz is available, then it cannot be used in playing; yet it is possible to hear it [for purposes of demonstration] by drawing a Quinte 3′ in one manual and an Oktave 2′ in another. Then one hand commences at c while the other begins [either] a major third higher or lower, depending on which hand is playing the Quinte or the Terz. Anyone who wants to hear how a Tertian sounds may draw the Terz above 2′ and the Quinte 1⅓′—the Terz above 4′† is not often available, otherwise [the sound of a Tertian could be reproduced by] adding the Quinte 3′ to it. Or one could draw for one hand on one manual the Quinte of this size, draw the Oktave 4′‡ for the other [hand] on a second manual, and play it a sixth below the Quinte. Here a critic might object that [in doing this] one can not actually hear how [Terz stops] sound, since one stop is not tempered against the other, but rather one note against the other. Thus the major third played in this way§ will not be as wide as if it is played on a separate stop drawn for that purpose,¶ since it will lose a bit due to its being tempered. Let this serve as an answer: this [objection] is indeed valid, but I am only trying to instruct novices to some degree how to become a bit familiar with such stops, even if imperfectly. At Prague‖ there is a Koppel (cf. §.128) in which the Quinte 3′, Superoktave 2′ and Terz 2′ (i.e., the Terz above [2′]**) stand together on one toeboard.†† This stop can also be imitated by [drawing] 3 separate stops.

* i.e., the 1 3/5′.

† i.e., 3 1/5′.

‡ sic; the pitch should read "2′".

§ i.e., by means of 2 keys on tempered keyboards.

¶ This statement seems to be exactly reversed; the major third would be wider when played on the tempered stops than in the Tertian.

‖ See the stoplist of the organ at St. Dominicus in Prague., in Chapter 10.

** i.e., the 1 3/5′.

†† i.e., on the same channel.

§. 225.

Where there are reeds, one should be sure they are in tune before playing on them. If one cannot find out anything about [their tuning], or about that which has been said concerning multiple meanings of [the same] word,‡‡ he should draw on the manual the stops whose character he is familiar with, and play. While playing he should add first this [stop], then that one, in order to hear what kind of difference it makes in the ensemble. From that he can decide in what sense it is used [in the particular instance]. In doing this he will soon note, e.g., whether the Zink is a reed or a Sesquialter, etc. He can also try out the stops by drawing first one and then another on a second manual while playing, and then by tapping quickly on the keys (as we say around here).§§ This method may also be used if no names are found written on the stopknobs, or if it is not known to which manual each stop belongs.

‡‡ See §.112 above.

§§ The extraordinary caution Adlung recommends in determining the character and condition of stops presupposes his imagining an organist doing it while others are listening (as for example in worship).

§. 226.

Some stops are better suited for runs than for slow playing, while others are the opposite. The Quintaton speaks slowly if runs [are played on it]; thus it ought to be omitted from the plenum or whenever one is playing quickly. A Grob Gedackt or

Kap. VIII. Vom Gebrauch der Register.

ein Grob Gedackt, oder Bordun, wenn man dergleichen hat. Klare Register gehen besser, wenn man geschwinde spielt. Also spiele man entweder den Registern gemäß; oder man ziehe die Register dem Spielen gemäß.

§. 227.

Wenn man an einen Ort kömmt, da die Leute an ein starkes Spielen gewöhnt sind, und an starke Register; so wird man sich schlecht recommandiren, wenn man oft schwachklingende allein braucht: denn sie denken, man könne nichts, man sey nicht munter, u. s. w. Andere aber hören schwache Register lieber, als Gedackte, Quintatönen, Gemshörner ꝛc. Also muß man sich darnach zu richten wissen, wenn deren Gunst soll erhalten werden. Siehe *Janowka* in Clau. pag. 92.

§. 228.

In der Musik ist die Veränderung die Seele. Deswegen läßt man viel Stimmen machen, Flöt-und Schnarrwerke, damit man destomehr abwechseln könne. Man soll also bald dies, bald jenes, gebrauchen; bald diese, bald jene zusammen ziehen. Dies aber kömmt aufs Gehör an, und nachdem die Einfälle sind, nachdem muß man ziehen. Man gehe demnach zuweilen alleine in die Kirche, und probire es so und so. s. Werkmeisters Orgelprobe S. 72. Ich habe an Orten gelebt wol etliche Jahre, und kann wol sagen, daß in so vielen Jahren nicht alle Register gezogen worden, auch nicht ein einziges mal. Allein, warum werden sie in die Orgeln gesetzt? Könnte man das Geld nicht besser anwenden? —— Man muß aber zugleich auf die Zeit sehen. Denn so spielt man allerdings auf Ostern schärfer, als bey einer Leiche, oder am Charfreytage, da man sich weit stiller aufzuführen pflegt. Man hat auch auf den Ort zu sehen. Denn in kleinen Kirchen kann z. E. in einem Chorale zuweilen das Gedackt allein gebraucht werden, welches in einer großen Hauptkirche lächerlich wäre, da man kaum das volle Werk vor der Gemeinde vernimmt.

§. 229.

Sollte ich das vorige Kapitel durchgehen, und bey jedem Register dessen Gebrauch zeigen; so wurde es allzuweitläuftig fallen. Es hat ein Anfänger aus dem obigen Vortrage schon soviel gehört, daß er auf jedes Register leicht die Anwendung machen kann, wenn er nur dessen Natur zu untersuchen sich die Mühe nicht verdrießen läßt. Daß insbesondere bey der Onda maris das Principal von gleicher Größe zu ziehen sey, und weiter nichts, ist aus dem §. 173. zu ersehen. Wie das Salicet insbesondere zu brauchen, siehe §. 185. Die Violdigamba wird am besten in laufenden Bässen gebraucht: denn wenn sie nicht recht gemacht ist, überschreyet sie sich gern, wenn man lange auf einem Ton halten will. Zur Voce humana wird das Principal 8′ gezogen. (**)

(**) Noch lieber aber die Hohlflöte 8′, wenn sie anders vorhanden ist.

§. 230.

Wenn man mit 2 Clavieren so spielt, daß die Hauptmelodie vor andern gehört werden soll; so verstehet es sich von freyen Stücken, daß man auch stärkere Register nehmen

Chap. VIII.   The Use of the Stops

Bordun is better if one is available. Clear stops are better for playing quickly. Thus one should [either adjust one's] playing to conform to the stops, or else choose stops to conform to one's [style of] playing.

§. 227.

If one finds oneself at a place where people are accustomed to loud playing and to a loud registration, then one would make a bad impression by frequently using soft stops alone. For [listeners] would think that you are incompetent or a gloomy sort, etc. Others prefer to hear soft stops such as Gedackts, Quintatöns, Gemshorns, etc. Thus one must know how to accomodate oneself in order to maintain favor; see Janowka's *Clavis*, p. 92.

§. 228.

Variety is the soul of music. This is why so many stops are built, [both] flues and reeds, the better to achieve variety. One ought to use first this, then that [stop], first this combination, then that. This all depends, though, on one's [sense of] hearing—one must register according to one's fancy. Accordingly one should at times go into the church alone and try out this and that; see Werkmeister's *Orgelprobe*, p. 72. I have lived at [various] places over a period of years, and can indeed assert that in all those years I never exhausted all the registrational possibilities, not even once. After all, why are they put in the organ? Couldn't the money be put to better use?* — At the same time, however, one must take into account the occasion. One of course plays more brilliantly at Easter than at a funeral or on Good Friday, when it is customary to play far more quietly. One must also take the place into consideration. For example, in small churches the Gedackt alone may sometimes be used for a chorale; this would be ridiculous in a large principal church where one can barely perceive the plenum over [the singing of] the congregation.

* than buying stops that the organist does not use.

§. 229.

If I had gone through the previous chapter indicating for each stop its use, [the chapter] would have become far too extensive. A novice [should] already have gathered enough from the above discourse to easily make out the use of each stop, as long as he does not shrink from the task of investigating its character. It has already been observed in particular in §.173 that only the Principal of the same pitch is to be drawn with the *Onda maris*, and nothing else. For the particular use of the Salicet, see §.185. The Violdigamba is best used for running basses, for if it is not properly made it readily overblows if one dwells too long on one pitch. The Principal 8′ is drawn with the *Vox humana*.(**)

(**) A Hohlflöte 8′ would be preferable, if it is otherwise available.† [Agricola]

† In his article in F.W. Marpurg's *Historisch-Kritische Beyträge*, Vol. 3, p. 504, Agricola elaborates on these suggestions:

A reed is seldom used alone. One always draws with it a flue stop of the same pitch, to cover the reed's rattling. Thus, for example, the Principal 8′ belongs with the Trompete 8′. The Vox humana, in order to achieve any resemblance of the human voice, must always be joined, if not by the Principal (as Mr. [Gottfried] Silbermann calls for), at least by the Gedackt 8′ or Rohrflöte 8′. Best suited of all for this purpose, however, is the Hohlflöte 8′, if it is available. Yet it is also possible to use an 8′ reed with a 4′ flue, and vice versa. Several higher-pitched stops may also conveniently serve as the foundation for such a reed.

§. 230.

If one is playing on 2 manuals in such a way that the main melody is to be heard as a solo, it is self-evident that the manual on which the melody is played must have

nehmen müsse in demselbigen Claviere, wo die Melodie gespielt wird. Z. E. wenn in einem Clavier das Gedackt wäre; so könnte im andern das Gedackt und Rohrflöte oder sonst etwas, für die dominirende Stimme schon genug seyn. Will ich aber zu der dominirenden Stimme etwann das Principal 8', Rauschpfeife, Rohrflöte u. d. gl. brauchen; so kann das andere Clavier mit dem Principal oder Gemshorn verstärkt werden, damit man es auch höre.

§. 231.

Wollte jemand wissen, was im Manuale zum vollen Werke zu ziehen, der merke nur so viel: Man muß Register haben, die schärfen. Dazu dient das Principal, sammt allen Oktaven; item die Quinten, Terzen; und am meisten schärfen die gemischten Stimmen, als das Terzian, Sesquialter, Mixturen, Scharp, Cimbelregister, ꝛc. Will man es nicht allzustark haben; so lasse man etwas weg, was man will. Soll es aber noch schärfer werden; so ziehe man die Register des andern Clavieres eben so, und koppele sie zusammen. Man muß aber auch Register haben, die die Gravität geben. Dazu dienen die Gedackte, als die Quintatön 16', oder besser das Gedackt 16', oder Rohrflöte 16', oder der gleich große Bordun; (wie man sie hat) Gedackt 8', Quintatön 8', Rohrflöte 8', Gemshorn 8', ꝛc. Denn der Meynung bin ich nicht, daß man mit der Quintatön 16' könne alleine zufrieden seyn. Man kann ja wol: (wenn man muß,) aber wenn man mehr dergleichen hat, warum sollte man sie nicht ziehen? Ja sagst du: sie werden wenig gehöret, und rauben doch so viel Wind, verderben also die Orgel. Antwort: Was das letzte anlanget; so präsupponire ich gute Bälge, und genugsamen Wind: denn wo der Wind fehlt, da urgire ich diese vielen Register nicht. Aber wo derselbe vorhanden ist, wird dadurch die Orgel nicht verderbt. Daß sie aber wenig gehört werden sollen, deucht uns nur so. Wer z. Ex. den Subbaß oder Contrabaß alleine höret, dem scheint es, als ob ein Wind gehe, und ist wenig Klang dabey. Aber wenn andere Register dabey sind; so spürt man ihn gar eben. Und so ist es auch mit allen Gedackten.

§. 232.

Es fragt sich hier: ob zwey oder mehr Aequalstimmen dürfen zusammen gezogen werden? Es hat dieses Niedt im 2ten Theile der Handleitung in Zweifel gezogen; und noch itzo sind etliche, die seine Meynung unterschreiben. [51] Im 12ten Kapitel der ersten Auflage (in der andern ists das 11te) giebt er die Ursach an, weil sie allezeit würden stark schweben. Daher sieht man oft, daß das Gedackt 8', und Principal 8' nicht beysammen gelitten werden; oder das Principal 8' und Trompet 8'. Ich habe einen Organisten in Erfurt gekannt, der nichts weniger leiden konnte, als daß

[51] **Werkmeister** will auch nicht gerne daran, wie man aus dessen Orgelprobe S. 72. ersiehet, allwo er die Ursach davon anführet. Man sehe auch im Hodego das 20. Kapitel, besonders S. 52. hiervon nach.

stronger stops. For example, if there were a Gedackt in one manual, then in the other a Gedackt and Rohrflöte* or something of the sort would be sufficient for the dominant voice. However, if I wanted to use, say, the Principal 8′, Rauschpfeife, Rohrflöte and such for the dominant voice, then the other manual may be reinforced with the Principal or Gemshorn so that it may also be heard.

* Gedackt 8′ and Rohrflöte (8′? 4′?).

§. 231.

Anyone who would like to know what to draw for a manual plenum need note only this: the required registers are those that intensify (schärfen†). The Principal, together with all the Oktaves, as well as the Quints and Terzes all serve this purpose, but the compound stops intensify the most: the Terzian, Sesquialter, Mixtures, Scharp, Cimbel, etc. If a less powerful combination is desired, then something should be omitted, whatever one wishes. If one wants an even louder [plenum], then one should draw the appropriate stops on the second manual and couple the manuals together. Yet it is also necessary to have stops that produce gravity. The stopped flutes serve to do this, [such] as the Quintatön 16′, or better yet, the Gedackt 16′, Rohrflöte 16′ or Bordun of the same size; also the Gedackt 8′, Quintatön 8′, Rohrflöte 8′, Gemshorn 8′, etc. (according to what is available). I am not of the opinion that one should be satisfied with the Quintatön 16′ alone.‡ One indeed can be (if one must), but if several of this sort of stop§ are available, why shouldn't they be used? You may say, they are hardly audible and yet steal so much wind that they spoil the organ.¶ With regard to the latter [assertion], I am presupposing good bellows and an ample [supply of] wind; where [ample] wind is lacking, I do not urge [drawing] so many stops. But where [ample wind] is available, the organ will not be spoiled by [adding a number of stopped flutes to the plenum]. [The assertion] that they are hardly audible, however, is deceiving. For example, anyone who hears a Subbass or Contrabass alone would suppose that it was a gust of wind with little sound. Yet when other stops are [sounding] with it, one indeed senses it presence. The same thing goes for all the stopped flutes.

† Adlung continues to use this word in the following paragraphs (and indeed in the following chapters as well), but it conveys a meaning that can only be expressed in English by two words: to strengthen (i.e., to make louder; e.g., §.233) and to make brilliant (e.g., §.234). I have accordingly translated it in various ways, depending on its context.

‡ i.e., as the only stop drawn to add gravity to the plenum.

§ i.e., stopped flutes at 16′ or 8′.

¶ i.e., by exposing its lack of ample winding.

§. 232.

This paragraph is concerned with whether two or more stops at eight-foot pitch may be drawn at the same time. Niedt has called this into question in the second part of his *Handleitung*,‖ and even now there are some that subscribe to his opinion.(51) In the twelfth chapter of the first edition (the eleventh chapter of the second) he gives as a reason that they would always beat [out of tune] so badly. Thus one often sees** that the Gedackt 8′ and Principal 8′ should not be tolerated together, or the Principal 8′ with the Trompet 8′. I knew an organist in Erfurt who simply could not tolerate having

‖ p. 116.

** in discussions about organ registration.

---

51) Werkmeister also does not approve of this, as can be seen from his *Orgelprobe*, p. 72, where he gives the reason for it. In this regard consult also [Werkmeister's] *Hodegus*, Chapter 20, in particular p. 52. [Albrecht]

Kap. VIII. Vom Gebrauch der Register. 169

daß man den Subbaß 16' mit dem Posaunbasse 16' zog; jenen stieß er allezeit weg. — — Fragt man: woher das Schweben komme? so dienet zur Antwort, daß eine Pfeife der andern den Wind raube, wenn sie auf einer Lade stehen. (denn davon ist die Rede.) Dieser Meynung pflichte ich auch gerne bey, wenn man Orgeln hat, darin der Zufall des Windes nicht stark genug ist, und darinne man wegläßt, was nur zu entrathen ist. Aber wenn der Zufall des Windes stark genug ist, und die Bälge groß und wohl gemacht sind; so halte ich von dieser Regel nichts, sondern ich ziehe ohne Bedenken solche äquale Register zusammen. Mattheson erinnert gleichfalls in einer Anmerkung zum 11ten Kapitel des 2ten Theils des Niedts, S. 116. der 2ten Ausgabe, daß dabey eine Ausnahme zu machen. Borberg, in der Beschreibung der Görlitzer Orgel, hält diese Regel daselbst deswegen, für unnütze, weil jede Pfeife ihren besondern Kanal hat, und keine der andern den Wind rauben kann. Wenn aber gleich die Kanäle so nicht sind; so kann man doch satt Wind haben, und folglich in einem Claviere das Principal 8', Gedackt 8', Gemshorn 8', Rohrflöte 8', zusammen ziehen. Eben so kann es auch mit 16= und 4füßigen Registern gehalten werden, sowol im Manuale als Pedale. Und wie kommt es denn, daß 8', dem andern 8füßigen den Wind raubt: aber 16' thut dergleichen dem 8' nicht; so auch in andern? Geschieht es aber etwan auch, (wenn die Orgel zu wenig Wind hat) warum verbietet man sie nicht neben 8'? Doch ich merke gleich was man antworten will. Nämlich: es gebe 16' eine Gravität, und schaffe also einen Nutzen; demnach könne man es ehe gebrauchen, als ein anders, das eben die Tiefe und Höhe hätte, folglich die Harmonie nicht verstärke: denn Aequalestimmen verstärken nicht. Diese Entschuldigung aber ist nicht weit her, und wollen wir sie im folgenden §pho kürzlich beleuchten. Ich hätte vielmehr gesagt: in Oktaven höre man die Schwebung und Unreinigkeit so nicht, als im Unisono, 8' gegen 8' aber ist der Unisonus; 16' gegen 8' die Oktave. Je weiter nun die Soni von einander sind, desto weniger wird eine solche Kleinigkeit gemerkt. Das wäre eine bessere Entschuldigung.

§. 233.

Daß man aber sagt: zwo Aequalestimmen schärften nicht, ist wol nicht so ausgemacht. Man probire es, und lasse von ferne einen urtheilen, der unpartheyisch ist. Warum macht man denn die Sesquialter mit der Oktave 4' auf einen Stock, da man sie leicht dazu ziehen, und also das Geld sparen könnte? Gewiß nicht nur der Commodität wegen, daß man nicht so viel ziehen müße, sondern damit es im vollen Werke schärfe. Oder verwirft man das; so müßte man auch verwerfen, daß man die Claviere koppelt, da in jedem etwan Principal 8', Oktave 4' und 2', Quinte 3' nebst der Sesquialter, und dergl. zu finden, die, wenn sie vollkommen reine gestimmt, den Registern des andern Claviers äqual sind. Ja, sagest du, sie stehen nicht auf einer Lade; Antwort: von fern hört man es nicht, daß sie auf 2 Laden stehen; genung, daß man die Schärfe wohl hört. Was nun von allen überhaupt gesagt wird, daß sie die Harmonie

Y

Chap. VIII.   The Use of the Stops

the Subbass drawn with the Posaunbass; he always pushed off the former [when the Posaunbass was drawn]. —— If anyone should ask whence the beating arises, let this serve as an answer: one pipe robs another of wind if they are standing on the same chest (this is the heart of the matter). I hasten to concur with this opinion, if the organ in question is not winded amply enough; in that case what is dispensable should be omitted. But if there is an ample supply of wind and the bellows are large and well made, I see no reason to abide by this rule, and draw such stops of the same pitch together without a second thought. Mattheson likewise mentions in note [(m)] to the eleventh chapter of [his] second edition of the second part of Niedt, p. 116, that an exception to this [rule] may be made. In his description of the Görlitz organ Boxberg* considers this rule inapplicable there, since each pipe has its own channel and cannot steal the wind from other pipes. Even though the channels are not like [the ones at Görlitz], though, it is possible to have ample wind, and consequently to draw the Principal 8′, Gedackt 8′, Gemshorn 8′ and Rohrflöte 8′ together on the same manual. The same holds true for 16′ and 4′ stops, both in the manual and in the pedal. How does it happen that one 8′ can rob wind from from another 8′, but a 16′ or some other [stop] will not? Given the fact that this sometimes happens (if the organ has insufficient wind), why not forbid [16′ and other stops] with the 8′? Now, I know right away what the answer to this will be: namely, that the 16′ provides gravity and thus serves a purpose. Accordingly its use is to be preferred over another [stop] at the same [8′] pitch level that does not strengthen the ensemble, for stops of the same pitch do not strengthen. This excuse, however, will not hold water, and we will make short work of it in the following paragraph. A better reason† would be that the beats and out-of-tuneness are not as noticeable at the octaves as at the unison, and 8′ versus 8′ is unison, while 16′ versus 8′ is an octave. The further apart the pitches are, the less noticeable such trifles are—that would be a better excuse.

* pp.[8] & [13].

† for drawing a 16′ with an 8′, but not two 8′s together.

§. 233.

The assertion that 2 stops of the same pitch do not strengthen, however, is indeed a moot question. It should be tested and judged by someone who is impartial and is standing at some distance [from the organ]. After all, why build a Sesquialter together with an Oktave 4′ on the same toeboard, when [the 4′] can easily be drawn in addition and thus money be saved? Certainly not for the sake of convenience, to save so much stop-pulling, but rather because it strengthens the plenum. Rejecting this [statement] inevitably means rejecting coupling manuals together, since in each of them there are to be found more or less a Principal 8′, Oktave 4′ and 2′, and Quinte 3′, together with a Sesquialter and [other] such [compound stops] that (providing they are in tune) are at the same pitches as the stops on the other manuals. Yes, you may say, but they do not stand on the same chest. I answer: no one [standing] at a distance can hear that they are on 2 [separate] chests, but they do indeed perceive the [added] strength. Now what may be said about all of them in general,‡ that they redouble and strengthen the

‡ i.e., about the combination of one entire manual with another.

monie verdoppeln und verstärken, dasselbe ist auch von jeden insbesondere anzunehmen. Oder man muß im vollen Werke nichts ziehen, als das Gedackte 16′, Principal 8′, und die 4füßige Mixtur, wenn sie etwan 6, 8 = 10fach ist. Die Sesquialter, Rauschpfeife, Quinte, Scharp, Oktave 4′, Oktave 2′, müssen wegbleiben. Wie so? Antw. Eine Mixtur, welche so vielfach ist, hat ohngefehr folgende Stimmen: Oktave 4′, 2′, 1′, $\frac{1}{2}$′, Quinte 3′, $\frac{1}{2}$′, $\frac{3}{4}$′, $\frac{3}{8}$′, Terz, ꝛc. Was brauch ich denn der Oktave 4′ und 2′ besonders; die stecken ja darinnen? So auch die Quinte 3′ und 1$\frac{1}{2}$′. Die Sesquialter und das Terzian bestehen aus der Quinte und Terz, die stecken auch darinnen, ꝛc. ꝛc. Wer wird wol glauben, daß, wenn Quintatön 16′, Principal 8′ und die große Mixtur gezogen wird, das eine so völlige und starke Harmonie werde, als wenn über dies die Sesquialter, Quinte, Terz, Tertian, Rauschpfeife, Scharp, Oktave 4′ und 2′ gezogen werden? Dies sind aber gegen die 4füßige Mixtur, Aequal=stimmen, also müssen sie ja verstärken; und dies habe ich eben damit beweisen wollen. Was hülfe es denn, daß z. Ex. zu Kindelbrück §. 306. die Trompet von c̄ hinaus doppelt gemacht ist? und in andern Orgeln findet man das Principal 8′ also. [52])

§. 234.

[52]) Die Jünger des von mir vorhin allegirten Werkmeisters werden vielleicht hierbey noch etwas excipiren, nemlich, daß Werkmeister diese Regel nicht deswegen gegeben, weil er gemeynet, es raube eine Stimme der andern den Wind; sondern er rede von solchen Stimmen, die nicht aus einem Fundamento oder Mensur gemacht wären, z. Ex. Weitprincipal und Engeviol=digamba von einerley Ton und dergleichen, die können wegen ihrer ungleichen Proportion nicht harmoniren: also mögte man immer zwo Oktaven 4′, oder andere dergleichen, zusammen ziehen, die NB. aus einerley Fundamento gearbeitet wären, und folglich einerley Weite hätten. Und dies ist auch würklich Werkmeisters Meynung im 29sten Kapitel der Orgelprobe, besonders S. 72.; und im 20sten Kapitel des Hodegi S. 52. und folg. Am ersten Orte schreibt er ausdrücklich: „Zwo Aequalstimmen zieht man nicht gerne zusammen, so nicht aus „einem Fundament gearbeitet; denn obschon dieselben so accurat zusammen gestimmt sind, „wollen sich doch die proportiones der Pfeifen, was die Weite der Pfeifen betrift, nicht wohl „vertragen, u. s. w." Im Hodego sagt er: „Die weite Pfeife bekömmt einen weitern Auf= „schnitt und stärkern Wind; und ist ihr Klang pompichter, bey den engern aber gelinder. Das „ist auch die Ursach, warum wir in den Orgeln nicht zwo Aequalstimmen zusammenziehen dür= „fen; denn obschon die Gleichheit in der Länge der Pfeifen bey nahe zutrift; so ist es doch die Un= „gleichheit in der Weite, so die Unreinigkeit verursachet." Allein, obgleich von niemanden wird geläugnet werden, daß der Klang in zwo Aequalstimmen von ungleicher Weite verschieden ist; so folgt doch daraus keinesweges, das sie nicht zusammen dürften gezogen werden, weil bey rein=gestimmten Pfeifen die Vibrationes nie gegen einander laufen. Man bemerkt zwar eine Ver= schiedenheit des Klanges: aber es befindet sich dazwischen keine Anarmonie. Muß es doch klin= gen, wenn man zwey Knaben mit einander singen läßt, da einer mit der weitern Kehle völliger singt, als der andere mit der engern. Wollte man solches nicht leiden, so mögte ich wol fra= gen: wo man wollte solche Sänger herbekommen, die einander hierinnen vollkommen gleich wä= ren? Ich sage, daß die Varietät der Stimmen so groß sey, daß man fast so wenig gleiche Stim= men, als gleiche Gesichter antreffen wird. Nun glaube ich nicht, daß Werkmeister verboten, daß zween Vokalisten zugleich eine Stimme singen sollten. Ingleichen: man leidet ja auch zwo Violinen, da eine ein weiteres, oder höheres corpus hat, als die andere, oder mit stärkeren Sayten bezogen ist als die andere, beysammen; warum sollten denn die Organisten allein so ekel seyn, daß sie solche Stimmen nicht leiden wollten?

ensemble, may also be admitted for each [stop] in particular. Otherwise the plenum should consist of nothing but the Gedackt 16′, Principal 8′ and the 4′ Mixture, if it is, say, 6 or 8 to 10 ranks. The Sesquialter, Rauschpfeife, Quinte, Scharp, Oktave 4′, and Oktave 2′ all must be omitted. Why? My answer: a Mixtur of that many ranks contains approximately the following pitches: Oktave 4′, 2′, 1′, ½′, Quinte 3′, [1]½′, ¾′, ⅜′, Terz, etc. Why would I need the Oktave 4′ and 2′ separately, when they are already contained in it? The same goes for the Quinte 3′ and 1½′. The Sesquialter and the Terzian consist of the Quinte and Terz, that are also contained in [the Mixtur], etc. Is there anyone who would believe that as full and strong an ensemble would result from just the Quintatön 16′, Principal 8′ and the large Mixtur as [would result from] the Sesquialter, Quinte, Terz, Tertian, Rauschpfeife, Scharp, Oktave 4′ and 2′ being drawn in addition? These are, however, stops of the same pitch in relation to the 4′ Mixtur; yet they do indeed strengthen, and with this I believe I have proved my point. Otherwise what sense does it make that, e.g., at Kindelbrück* the Trompet is doubled from c′ upwards, or that the Principal 8′ is made like this in other organs?(52)

* See the stoplist of this organ in Chapter 10.

52) The disciples of the abovementioned† Werkmeister would perhaps at this point take exception, in that Werkmeister did not intend this rule to mean that one stop would rob the wind from another. Rather he was speaking about those stops that are not constructed according to the same principle or scale, e.g., a broad-scale Principal and a narrow-scale Violdigamba of the same pitch, and other such [stops] that cannot blend well because of their dissimilar proportions. Thus one would always be free to draw 2 Oktaves 4′ or the like, that are constructed according to the same principle and are thus of the same breadth. This is actually Werkmeister's opinion in the 29th chapter of the *Orgelprobe*, in particular on p. 72, and also in the 20th chapter of the *Hodegus*, p. 52f. In the first source he expressly writes, "It is not good to draw two stops of the same pitch together, ones that are not constructed according to the same principle, for no matter how accurately they are tuned to each other, the proportions of the pipes, as concerns their width, will simply not be compatible, etc." In the *Hodegus* he says, "The broad[-scale] pipes get a higher cut-up and heavier wind; their sound is more pompous, while that of the narrow[-scale stops] is gentler. That is the reason, then, why two stops of the same pitch ought not to be drawn together in organs, for although the pipes are almost equal in length, it is their unequal width that causes the incompatibility." Although no one would deny that the sound of two stops of the same pitch but dissimilar widths is different, in no way does it follow that they may not be drawn together, because the overtones never clash with each other if the pipes are carefully tuned. The difference in tone is indeed noticeable, but they do not clash. It sounds just the same as if two boys are made to sing next to each other, one of whom sings with a wider throat and a fuller sound than the other with a more constricted throat. If there is anyone who wants to forbid this, I should like to ask him where he is going to find singers who are perfectly identical in vocal quality. I maintain that the variety in voices is so great that one is no more likely to encounter two identical voices than two identical faces. Now I do not believe that Werkmeister has forbidden two vocalists to sing the same voice part together. In the same way, it is permissible for two violins to play together, one of which has a wider or longer body, or louder strings, than the other. Why should it be just the organists who are so disagreeable as not to allow stops [of the same pitch to sound together]? [Albrecht]

† §.232, note 51.

Tabelle 3.

Fig. 1.

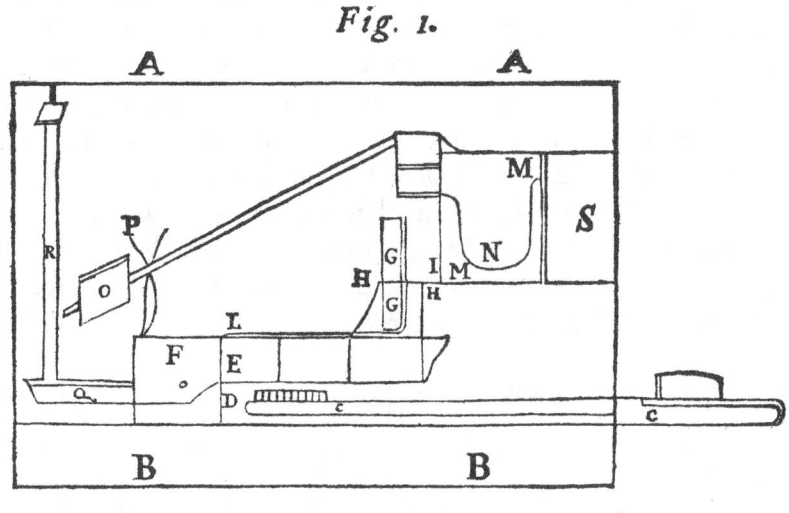

ad Pag. 118. — 119.

Fig. 2.   Fig. 3.   Fig. 4.

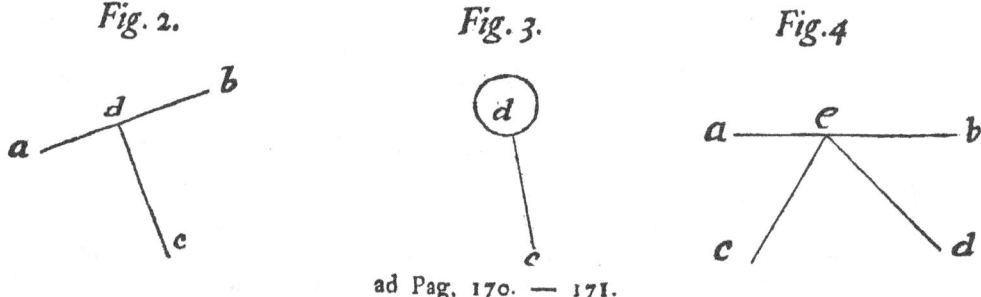

ad Pag. 170. — 171.

Tabelle 3.

Fig. 1.

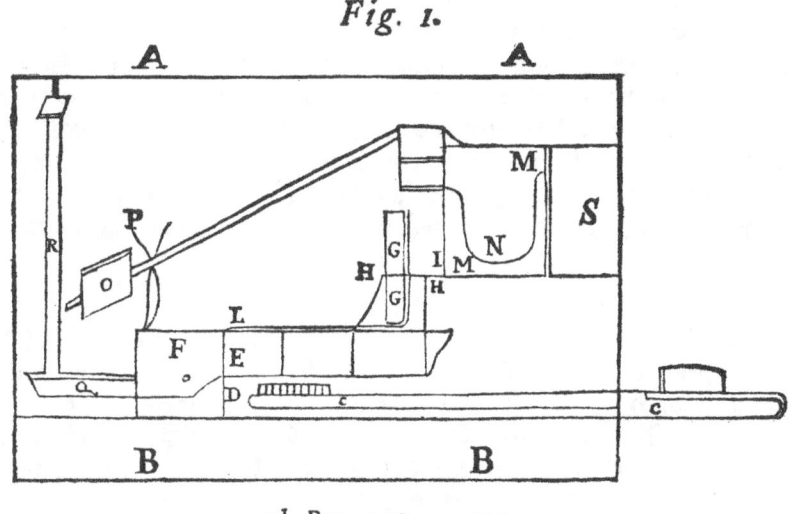

ad Pag. 118. — 119.

Fig. 2.   Fig. 3.   Fig. 4.

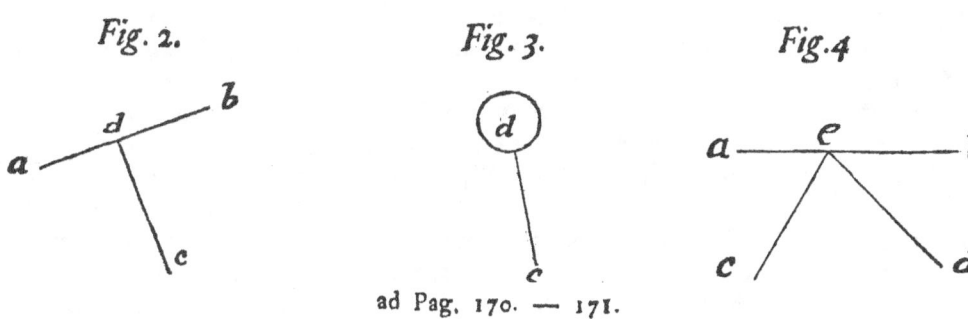

ad Pag. 170. — 171.

§. 234.

Was von den Manualstimmen gesagt ist, das gilt auch im Pedale. Denn das muß im vollen Werke auch stark seyn, daß man es gegen das Manual höre. Doch sieht man da mehr auf die Gravität; zuweilen schärft man es auch. Die Gravität befördern der Contrabaß 32′, Subbaß 16′, Gedackt 8′, Principal 32′ und 16′, Violon 16′, Oktave 8′. Diese können alle zugleich gezogen werden, wenn eine Orgel satt Wind hat, und sonderlich etliche Bälge besonders zum Pedale gehören. Zuweilen macht man schärfende Stimmen ins Pedal, z. Ex. Oktave 4′ und 2′, auch wol Mixturen. Die können auch gebraucht werden. Hat man aber solche schärfende Stimmen nicht; so kann man die Manualstimmen durch das Koppel ins Pedal bringen: sind aber ohne Koppel die Manualstimmen dem Pedale gemein; so braucht man es nicht. Die Posaune 32′ und 16′ sammt der Trompete können, wie auch die andern Schnarrwerke, auch dabey seyn. Sonst aber kann die Posaune 16′ genug seyn. Zumal man im geschwinden Spielen die 16füßigen Register bequemer gebraucht, als die 32füßigen.

§. 235.

Es könnte dieses schon genug seyn, wenn jemand überhaupt von dieser Materie was wissen wollte; denn was insbesondere beym Fantasiren, Generalbasse, Choral u. s. w. für Register zu brauchen, könnte an jeztgedachten Orten in einem besondern Kapitel beygebracht werden. Nur einige Stücke davon zu berühren; so muß im Generalbasse ein Unterschied gemacht werden, nachdem entweder der volle Chor, oder doch viel Stimmen sich hören lassen, oder wenige. Bey einzelnen oder wenig Stimmen kann das Gedackt 8′ oder Quintatön 8′ genug seyn. Wo zweyerley Gedackte sind, als z. Ex. Grobgedackt, und Still- oder Musicirgedackt; so nimmt man das Stillgedackt. Wer aber nur ein Clavier hat, der muß den Subbaß im Pedale mit dazu nehmen, welcher auch den Violon, oder die Oktave 8′ bey sich haben kann, oder wenigstens noch ein Gedackt, es sey denn, daß das Manual-Gedackt auch ins Pedal gehöre, als welche in kleinen Kirchen schon das Fundament der Kirchenmusik abgeben können: und alsdann spielen beyde Hände das Gedackt im Manuale. Wenn aber mehr Stimmen oder gar der ganze Chor musiciren; so kann man das Principal dazu ziehen. Werden Choralverse gesungen; so kann man das Principal behalten, auch wol eine Quinte oder Oktave dazu nehmen, weil die Gemeinde oft mitsinget. Wo ein Clavier ist, da muß der Organist die Register gar oft im Ziehen verändern. Wo aber zwey Claviere vorhanden, da kann man in dem einen das Gedackt haben, in dem andern aber das Principal 8′ oder 16′ und noch (wenn man will) den Bordun, oder Quintatön, oder dergleichen dabey, damit man gleich hinauf fahren und stärker spielen könne, wenn es nöthig ist, ohne vieles Ziehen. Es kann aber auch die linke Hand auf solchem Claviere mit den großen Registern die Baßnoten spielen, anstatt des Pedals, und in laufenden Bässen kann zuweilen die Violdigamba 8′ dabey gebraucht werden, mit oder ohne

Chap. VIII. The Use of the Stops

§. 234.

What has been said about manual stops also holds true for the pedal; its plenum must also be loud in order to balance the manual. One pays more attention to its gravity, though at times also to its brilliance. The Contrabass 32′, Subbass 16′, Gedackt 8′, Principal 32′ and 16′, Violon 16′ and Oktave 8′ all promote gravity. All of these may be drawn together if the organ has sufficient wind, and especially if there are several bellows provided specifically for the pedal. Sometimes brighter stops are included in the pedal, e.g., Oktave 4′ and 2′, or even Mixtures. These may also be used. If these brighter stops are not available, then stops from the manual may be brought into the pedal by means of a coupler; but if the manual stops are also available in the pedal,* then coupling is not necessary. The Posaune 32′ and 16′ together with the Trompete [8′] may also be included [in the plenum], as well as the other reeds. But the Posaune 16′ can be sufficient. In particular, the 16′ stops are more suitable for use in playing rapid [passages] than the 32′.

* Adlung is referring to the Windkoppel; see §.127 above and §.269 below.

§. 235.

This should suffice for anyone who would like to know something in general about this matter. What stops to use in particular for improvisation, figured bass, hymn accompaniment, etc., could be the subjects of separate chapters for each of them. To mention a few important points about these: in figured bass there must be a difference [in registration] according to whether the full choir (or at least many voices) is singing or only a few [voices]. For one or several voices, the Gedackt 8′ or Quintatön 8′ may be sufficient. Where there are two kinds of Gedackts, e.g., Grobgedackt and Still- or Musicirgedackt, the Stillgedackt should be used.† If there is only one manual, then the Subbass in the pedal must be used with it, to which may be added the Violon [8′] or the Oktave 8′, or at least another Gedackt, unless the manual Gedackt is already sounding in the the pedal.‡ This may indeed [be sufficient to] provide support for church music [ensembles] in small churches. Then both hands [would] play on the Gedackt in the manual. If however a number of voices or an entire choir are singing, then the Principal [8′?] may be added to it. When chorale verses are being sung,§ the Principal may be retained and even a Quinte or Oktave drawn with it, since the congregation often sings along. Where there is only one manual the organist must do a lot of stop-pulling to vary the registration. Where two keyboards are available, however, a Gedackt [8′] may be drawn in one, while in the other Principal 8′ or 16′ plus (if desired) the Bordun or Quintatön are available, so that the player may quickly switch manuals and play more loudly if necessary, without a lot of stop-pulling. The left hand, however, may also play the bass line on the manual with the more prominent stops, instead of the pedal. In running basses the Violdigamba 8′ may at times be used, with or without the Principal

† cf. §.150.

‡ As the following sentences confirm, the sense of this sentence is that the bass line needs to be reinforced by playing it on a louder registration; see also §.259 and §.266. If there is only one manual, this can only be accomplished by playing the bass line in the pedal.

§ in the context of concerted music.

ohne Principal: denn laufende Noten können im Pedale nicht so bequem herausgebracht werden als im Manuale. Kommen langsame Noten; so kann das Pedal wieder genommen, das Manual aber verlassen werden. Z. Er. in Recitativen. Oder man nimmt beyde Claviere, und das Pedal auch dabey. In schweren Recitativen, wenn die Sänger für sich nicht just sind, und das Gedackt von ihnen nicht gehört wird, kann man das Principal oder Gemshorn brauchen, mit oder anstatt des Gedackts; das hören die Sänger besser, und lassen sich dadurch wieder in den rechten Weg leiten. Zum Beschluß des Stückes geht es am vollstimmigsten; also spielt man auch am schärfsten, auch wol mit vollem Werke, sonderlich auf unsern Dorfkirmsen. Aber oft wird alle Harmonie dadurch bedeckt, oder ich will sagen, man hört gar keinen Sänger oder Instrumentisten, welche zusammen doch die Musik ausmachen. Man braucht ordentlich das Gedackt; im geringern Claviere, damit die großen Register im Hauptwerke den Baß mit hören lassen können.

§. 236.

Im Fantasiren ist man noch weniger gebunden: denn es kann mit schwachen und starken Registern geschehen, nachdem die Einfälle sind, oder nachdem man auf ein trauriges oder lustiges Stück oder Choral zu präludiren hat. Beym Anfange und Beschluß des Gottesdienstes läßt es besser mit dem vollen Werke zu spielen. Präambuliret man aber auf etwas; so kann es entweder durch eine gemeine Fantasie geschehen, und da kann man das volle Werk nehmen; aber auch zur Abwechselung zuweilen stille klingende Register ziehen; oder man spielt mit 2 Clavieren, die beyde besondere Register haben, nicht allzustark, eines aber pflegt zu prädominiren, und diese prädominirende Stimme läßt den Choral hören, oder doch etwas davon, wenn man auf den Choral präambuliret.

§. 237.

In den Choralen pflegt man mit den Registern fleißig abzuwechseln; dabey aber wenig zu erinnern ist. Es beobachte einer nur die obigen Lehrsätze, daß er die Register nicht wieder die Natur derselben brauche; übrigens, ob er schwach oder stark ziehen solle, dependirt von seinem Willen, und von andern Umständen der Zeit, des Affekts und des Orts. Wer auch gar zu kleine Register zieht, ob es wol Oktavenregister sind, der thut nicht wohl, weil man auch etwas auf die Gravität und Anmuth zu sehen hat. Wer etwan ein Register insbesondere wollte hören lassen, muß in demselben Claviere nicht so viel andere dazu ziehen. Z. Er. die Vox humana würde nicht gehöret werden, wenn Principal 8', Oktave 4', und 2'. it. Quinte 3,' nebst Quintatön 16', rc. dabey wären.

§. 238.

Wenn ein Echo vorzustellen ist, kann ein Clavier schwächer gezogen werden, als das andere: zuweilen kann auch das Gedackte mit dem vollen Werke abwechseln. Ist eine

[8'?], since running passages cannot be performed as conveniently in the pedal as in the manual. With the return to slow notes the pedal may again be used and the manual relinquished,* e.g. in recitatives. Or both keyboards may be used as well as the pedal.† In difficult recitatives, if the singers do not hear the Gedackt and stray from pitch, the Principal or Gemshorn may be used with or instead of the Gedackt. The singers hear these better, and are again guided into the proper path. The close of a piece‡ is always the fullest; here one plays the most brilliantly, even with the plenum, especially at our village church festivals. But this often drowns out the ensemble; what I mean to say is that the singers and instruments cannot be heard, even though they are the essence of the concerted music. Normally the Gedackt is used on the subsidiary manual, so that the more prominent stops may play the bass on the Hauptwerk.

* i.e., there is no need to double the bass with both left hand and pedal.
† i.e., the pedal may double the left hand if the organist wishes.
‡ Presumably Adlung is thinking of an extended concerted choral piece.

§. 236.

One is less restricted in improvisation; it may be done on soft or loud stops, according to one's fancy, or according to whether one must prelude on a sad or cheerful piece or chorale. At the beginning and close of the service it is best to play on the plenum. If one is preluding on something,§ however, this may be accomplished either by a normal improvisation, in which case the plenum may be used, or by drawing soft-sounding stops for variety. Or one may play on two keyboards, each having a different registration, not too loudly; one of these normally predominates, and the predominating voice plays the chorale or some [motives or phrases] from it, if one is preluding on a chorale.

§ e.g., a chorale or a choral work.

§. 237.

In [playing] chorales it is usual to vary the stops regularly; there is little [more] to mention about this; One need only observe the above precepts, so as not to use the stops [in a way] contrary to their nature. Moreover, whether a player uses a soft or loud registration depends upon his fancy and upon other circumstances [such as] occasion, *Affekt* and place. Anyone who uses stops that are simply too high, even though they are octave-sounding stops, provides no satisfaction, since it is necessary to give some consideration to gravity and charm. Anyone who wishes to feature one stop in particular must not draw too many other [stops] with it on the same keyboard. For example, the *Vox humana* would not be heard if the Principal 8', Oktave 4' and 2', as well as the Quinte 3' and the Quintatön 16' were sounding with it.

§. 238.

If an echo effect is desired, one manual may be registered more softly than the other; at times the Gedackt [8'] may even alternate with the plenum. If there is a Quintatön

eine Quintatön oder so etwas dabey, so geht es nicht gar zu stille. Wenn eine Piece im Generalbasse mit der Flötetraverse zu machen wäre, und dieselbe nicht bey der Hand ist, kann die Violdigamba dazu gebraucht werden, als die ihr etwas ähnlich ist; oder man nehme das Principal 8′: will man es aber mit schärfen Registern thun, kann die Sesquialter sammt der Oktave 4′ oder das Tertian, oder die Rauschpfeife dazu gebraucht werden. Das andere Clavier aber spielt mit der linken Hand die Accorde mit dem Gedackte; das Pedal kann die Noten mit brummen. Es können bey solchen Traversen im Generalbasse noch andere Register gebraucht werden, sonderlich Flöten. Hat man die Rauschpfeife, Sesquialter, oder dergleichen gemischte Stimmen nicht, so ziehe man andere zusammen, die einerley Klang mit ihnen haben, wie §. 224. gelehret worden ist.

So viel habe ich für diesesmal vom Gebrauch der Register melden wollen. Es ist für gar unwissende und nicht für schon erfahrne Organisten, die es besser wissen. Es hätten mehr Specialia können beygefügt werden: allein ich besorgte, es mögte zu weitläuftig werden; auch wird ein jeder, der nicht gar ein Gänsegehirn hat, aus dem bisher gesagten, und aus der Natur eines jeden Registers mehr Veränderungen machen können. In die Pauke, Vogelgesang, Trummel u. d. gl. wird sich auch keiner so leicht verlieben, wenn er aus dem vorigen Kapitel ihre Eigenschaften hat kennen lernen.

Das IX. Kapitel.
Von Verdüng= und Bauung einer Orgel.

Inhalt.

§. 239. Die Nothwendigkeit dieses Kapitels. §. 240 Man soll einen Baudirektor über das Werk setzen. §. 241. Man soll sich in Erwählung eines Orgelmachers behutsam aufführen. §. 242. Man soll einen schriftlichen Contrakt machen. §. 243. Man soll nicht allzugenau handeln; doch der Kirche nichts verschenken §. 244. Man schreibt dem Orgelmacher vor, wie vielfach die gemischten Stimmen werden sollen §. 245. Die Materie der Pfeifen. §. 246. 247. Noch andere Kleinigkeiten. §. 248. Vom Rückpositive, Stimswerk und Clavieren. § 249. Spring= und Schleiflade. §. 250. Man bemerkt die Anzahl der Bälge. §. 251. Behutsamkeit bey Orgelcontrakten. §. 252. Kost der Orgelmacher. §. 253. Ob man ihnen die Materialien dazu geben soll? §. 254. Ein Exempel kömmt nicht dazu. §. 255. Wenn man keinen Direktorem des Baues hat, muß man dem Orgelmacher trauen. §. 256. Man mache die Lade breiter, daß nachher mehr Stimmen können darauf gebracht werden.

§. 239.

Mir ist keiner bekannt, der diese Materie ex professo abgehandelt. Es hat zwar Michael Prätorius Tom. II. Syntagmatis Mus. etlichemal eines Traktats gedacht, den er von Verdüngung, Bauen und Lieferung einer Orgel hat ediren wollen, z. Ex. S. 203. l. c. sonderlich Tom. III. P. III. S. 224. aber meines Wissens

[8′] or some such [stop] available [to add to the Gedackt], it would not be so very quiet. If there is a piece to perform with figured bass and a Flötetraverse,* and this [stop] is not available, the Violdigamba may be used in its place, since it is somewhat similar. Or the Principal 8′ might be used. If a performance with more brilliant stops is desired, the Sesqualter plus Oktave 4′, or the Tertian, or the Rauschpfeife may be used. The left hand, however, plays the chords on the second manual with the Gedackt [8′], and the pedal may growl along on the [bass] notes. Other stops may be used for such traverse-flute [pieces] with figured bass, especially flutes. If the Rauschpfeife, Sesqualter or some such compound stop is not available, then other stops may be combined to produce the same sound, as has been discussed in §.224.

 This is all I want to say for the present about the use of the stops. It is [intended] for the completely inexperienced and not for already seasoned organists who are more familiar with [such principles]. More details could have been added, but I was concerned that it would become too lengthy. Anybody who is not a complete featherbrain will be able to create more variations from what has already been said and from the character of each individual stop. Perhaps [a player] will not be so quick to become enamored of the Kettledrum, Birdsong, Drum and such [toy stops] if he has become familiar with their characteristics from the previous chapter.

* Adlung seems to have in mind a traverse-flute solo accompanied by a figured bass, the solo line of which is played by the organ stop of that name. See also the end of §.178, as well as §.259.

Chapter IX.
Contracting for and Building an Organ.
Contents:

§.239. The need for this chapter. §.240. A director should be in charge of the work [of building the organ]. §. 241. Care must be exercized in choosing an organbuilder. §.242. A written contract should be drawn up. §.243. Dealings [with the organbuilder] ought not be too stingy, yet the church should not be cheated. §.244. The number of ranks in the compound stops should be prescribed to the organbuilder. §.245. The material for the pipes. §.246-247. Other details. §.248. The Rückpositiv, the moldings, and the keyboards. §.249. Spring- and slider-chests. §.250. The number of bellows should be noted. §.251. Caution in [drawing up] organ contracts. §.252. Board for the organbuilder. §.253. Should the church provide the builder with the materials for [the organ]? §.254. An example [of a contract] is not provided. §.255. If there is no director for the building, the organbuilder must be trusted. §.256. The chest should be made wider [than needed], so that later more stops can be set upon it.

§. 239.

I know of no one who has treated this matter expressly.* To be sure, Michael Praetorius in Vol. II of his Syntagma musicum made mention several times of a treatise he intended to publish on contracting for, building and delivering an organ; e.g., p. 203 in particular, or Vol. III, Part III, p. 224. To [the best of] my knowledge,

* i.e., no one has written an entire treatise on it.

sens ist er nie zum Vorschein gekommen. Ich habe ihn im Manuscripte.⁵³) Andere haben in denen von mir im ersten Kapitel angeführten Büchern zwar etwas von dieser Sache berührt: aber nur im Vorbeygehen. Gleichwol wird von einem Organisten erfordert, daß er sich in diesen Dingen eine Erkänntniß zuwege bringe, weil sie meistentheils den Orgelbau anzugeben und zu dirigiren haben. Inspektores und Vorsteher der Kirchen wissen oft wenig von solchen Dingen; daher man bey dem Organisten sich pflegt Raths zu erhohlen. Wollte der nun sagen: er verstehe es nicht; so würde er zwar wol besser thun, als wenn er es über sich nähme, und durch Unwissenheit die Kirchen in Schaden brächte: doch ist es auch für ihn keine Ehre, wenn man aus andern Orten Künstler holen muß. — Wir wollen demnach etliche Dinge anmerken, woraus hernach in andern leicht abzusehen, wie behutsam man sich in Bauung der Orgeln aufzuführen habe. Man bauet sie nicht alle Jahre von neuem auf, und müssen deswegen alle solche Sachen gar wohl bedacht werden, daß man den Schaden nicht hernach zu bereuen habe.

§. 240.

Das erste Momentum ist, daß man einen verständigen Organisten das ganze Werk dirigiren lasse. Ein solcher Direktor muß hernach nach seinem Sinne einen Entwurf des ganzen Werks machen, wie er denkt, daß es am besten sey; (NB. wenn er erst vorher ohngefehr weis, was die Kirche dazu anwenden wolle.) Alle Register muß er vorschreiben, und wie die Materie zu jedem Theile der Orgel seyn solle, muß er aufs genaueste anzugeben wissen. Diesen Entwurf kann er hernach den Vorstehern übergeben, welche ihn andern Kunstverständigen an fremden Oertern communiciren, und von denselben vernehmen, ob er in allen Stücken so sey, wie es seyn muß. Dieses ist für den Direktor gut, weil ihm hernach nicht alles kann beygemessen werden, und man desto eher mit ihm zufrieden seyn muß. Nach angehörten Censuren macht man mit dem Orgelmacher den Contrakt, und zwar so, daß er in allem seine Arbeit nach des Direktors oder Baumeisters Willen einrichten müsse. Auf solche Art ist ehedessen die Jenaische Stadtorgel gebauet worden, da man den dasigen Organisten, Herrn Johann Nikol. Bachen, den ganzen Bau dirigiren lassen. Doch ist noch zu merken, daß man bey Aussendung des Entwurfs den Namen des Baudirektors nicht melde, damit nicht der eine aus Haß, der andere aus Freundschaft den Entwurf tadeln oder gutheißen möge. Und obschon diese Censuren ohne Entgeld nicht leicht zu erhalten; so lasse man sich doch dieses nicht dauern, weil der daraus erwachsende Nutzen sehr groß ist. Man muß den Baudirektor aber auch anhalten, daß er beständig dabey sey, wenn etwas gemacht wird, damit nichts versehen werde: und weil dadurch bey dem Orgelmacher wenig Dank pfleget verdienet zu werden, auch viel Zeit verdorben wird; so muß ein raisonabler Recompens

---

⁵³(Daß ich dieses Manuscript jetzo im Besitz habe, und solches künftig ans Licht zu stellen willens sey, ist bereits in eine Anmerkung zum 9ten §pho angezeiget worden.

however, this never appeared. I have a manuscript of it.⁽⁵³⁾ Indeed, other [authors] have touched on some [aspects] of this matter in the books I have cited in Chapter I, but only in passing. Nevertheless it is incumbent on organists that they gain some acquaintance with these things, since it is usually they who have to specify and direct the building of an organ. The inspectors and administrators of the church often know little about such things; therefore they are accustomed to seek the organist's counsel. Now were he to say that he did not understand [the matter], that would indeed be better than his assuming [the direction of the project] and through his ignorance causing the church [to incur] a loss. Yet on the other hand it is no honor to him if an expert has to be brought in from somewhere else.— Accordingly we will mention a number of things from which it will be easy to see how carefully one must proceed in building an organ. [Organs] are not built new again every year, and thus all these matters must be very well thought out, so that later on there are no misfortunes to regret.

§. 240.

The first thing to keep in mind is that a competent organist should be put in charge of the entire project. Such a director must then draw up a plan of the entire project according to the best of his understanding (N.B. He must first know in advance approximately how much the church wants to spend on it). He must specify all the stops, and he must know how to indicate very precisely what materials are to be used for each part of the organ. He may then hand this plan over to the church authorities to pass on to various outside experts, in order to learn from them whether all particulars are as they should be. This is in the best interests of the director, since it keeps him from being saddled with all the responsibility for it later, and there is all the more reason to be satisfied with him. After considering all criticisms [of the plan], a contract is drawn up with the organbuilder, specifying that he must carry out all his work in accordance with the director's wishes. This is how the organ in the Jena Stadtkirche was built a while ago, in which the resident organist Mr. Johann Nikolaus Bach was assigned to direct the entire project. Yet it is also to be noted that the name of the director should not be revealed when sending out the plan,* so that no one may fault or praise the plan either out of enmity or friendship. And although one need not expect to get these criticisms without remunerating [the experts for them], one should not hesitate to do this, since the benefit that derives from them is very great. The director must also be admonished to be in constant attendance while anything is being built so that nothing is overlooked. Since it is unlikely that the organbuilder will thank him much [for this pains] and he will spend a lot of time [fulfilling his charge], some reasonable recompense must not be

* Adlung has reverted to speaking about his suggestion, made several sentences earlier, to send the plan out to various experts at other places.

53) I have already indicated in a note to §.9 that I have this manuscript in my possession and intend to publish it at a future date.† [Albrecht]

† The treatise has been published in a modern edition as: Michael Praetorius and Esaias Compenius, *Orgeln Verdingnis*. (Kieler Beiträge zur Musikwissenschaft, hrsg. Friedrich Blume, Heft 4. Wolfenbüttel & Berlin: Georg Kallmeyer, 1936). A second modern edition with an English translation and a helpful preface has been published: Vincent Panetta, "An Early Handbook for Organ Inspection: the 'Kurtzer Bericht' of Michael Praetorius and Esaias Compenius." (in: *The Organ Yearbook*, Vol. XXI (1990), pp. 5-33). Mr. Panetta has also published a detailed account of this treatise's influence on subsequent manuals regarding the testing of organs: "Praetorius, Compenius, Werckmeister: A Tale of Two Treatises" (in: *Church, Stage, and Studio: music and its contexts in seventeenth-century Germany*, ed. Paul Walker. Ann Arbor, MI: UMI Research Press, c. 1990, pp. 67-85). See also §.9.

Kap. IX. Von Verdůng- und Bauung einer Orgel. 175

pens dem Direktor nicht abgeschlagen werden; (⁵⁴) zumal da in solcher Verfassung bey der Probe alles von dem Direktor gefordert wird, und der Orgelmacher sich um weiter nichts bekümmert, als daß er macht, was ihm jener angiebt.

§. 241.

Hernach siehet man sich nach einem Orgelmacher um, der so viel Geschicklichkeit besitzt, daß er alles vorgeschriebene verfertigen kann, sonderlich einem, der bey einem braven Meister gelernet hat, und brav gereiset ist, und die Struktur der Register selbst in Augenschein genommen, welche was besonders haben; der auch in andern Werken allbereit seine Probe sehen lassen. Denn obschon eine Orgel des Orgelmachers erste seyn muß; so läßt man doch gern anderwärts solche Proben erst machen, oder übergiebt Anfängern nur kleine Werke. Billig soll auch ein Orgelmacher angesessen seyn, und in eben dem Lande unter eine Obrigkeit gehören, damit man sich allenfalls Raths erhohlen könne, wenn er nicht treu wäre. Ist er nicht angesessen, oder nicht unter gleicher Obrigkeit; muß man sehen, daß er Caution stelle. Man hat auch zu regadiren, ob einer ein guter Tischler sey, oder dergleichen Gesellen führe; weil dadurch die Orgelwerke am ansehnlichsten werden.

§. 242.

Ist dergleichen Künstler vorhanden; so schließe man einen förmlichen Contrakt; in demselben schreibe man ihm alles vor, was, wie, und auch von was für Materie es zu machen sey; man vernehme ihn darüber wegen der Kosten und seines Verdienstes, und vergleiche sich desfalls. Man kann sich auch nach der Zeit erkundigen, wann er mit der Arbeit fertig seyn will; it. was er für Leute zu Gehülfen habe. ꝛc. Man schließe aber solchen Contrakt in Beyseyn der Vornehmsten, und sonderlich der Inspektoren, daß hernach keine Verdrießlichkeiten entstehen. Wenn alles schriftlich abgefaßt worden; so schreibet man es ab und giebt es dem Orgelmacher, dem Direktor und der Gemeinde, und läßt alle Abschriften von allen Theilen unterschreiben. Denn daß man die Größe der Orgel und der Stimmen einem überhaupt vorschreiben, weiter aber nichts determiniren wolle, solches ist wegen vieler Untreu manches Orgelmachers und vieler anderer Umstände nicht zu rathen.

§. 243.

Es ist heut zu Tage so weit gekommen, daß man den Orgelmachern fast wenig für die Arbeit zahlt, daß man sich auch billig wundern muß, wie manche dabey auskommen können: Allein ich wollte nicht rathen, daß man sie sehr drücke; es ist gar eine mühsame Arbeit, und erfordert einen klugen Kopf, und auch fleißiges Nachsinnen, daher man ja mehr davor zahlen sollte, als wenn sonst einem Zimmermanne das Tagelohn vor

---

⁵⁴) Der Baudirektor muß aber nicht eines Recompenses wegen mit dem Orgelmacher, zum Schaden der Kirche, unter einer Decke liegen; doch auch nicht ohne dringende Noth sich mit demselben in Streit und Zank verwickeln, sonst entsteht nichts gutes daraus.

Chap. IX. Contracting for and Building an Organ

denied to the director,(54) in particular since with such an arrangement the director will be responsible for everything at the final examination, and the organbuilder only need worry about doing whatever someone else tells him to do.

§. 241.

Next one must search out an organbuilder who has enough skill to construct everything that has been prescribed, especially one who has apprenticed with a worthy master and is well-traveled, so that he has seen for himself how stops are constructed and what their special characteristics are, also one whose past projects have passed their examinations. For although some one organ must be an organbuilder's first, it would be better to let such test-cases be done elsewhere, or to entrust only small projects to beginners. It is also proper that an organbuilder be resident and subject to the governing authority in the same territory [where the organ is being built], so that there is at least some recourse if he turns out to be undependable. If he is not resident, or not under the same authority, one must see to it that he furnishes a performance bond. It is also necessary to take note if he is a good woodworker, or if he employs competent journeymen, since [the woodwork] is what makes an organ the most imposing.

§. 242.

If such an artist is available, then a formal contract should be executed with him. In it everything should be prescribed for him: what, how and also with what sort of materials [the organ] is to be built. He should be questioned about his board and wages, and an agreement on this should be reached. One may also inquire about the time it will take him to be finished with the work, as well as what sort of helpers he has, etc. Such a contract should be executed in the presence of the [church] authorities, especially the Inspectors, so that no unpleasantness later arises. When everything has been drawn up in writing, copies should be made and given to the organbuilder, the director and the congregation, and all copies should be signed by all parties. Prescribing to a [builder only] the size of the organ and its stops in general without determining anything more specific is inadvisable, due to the undependability of many an organbuilder and many other circumstances.

§. 243.

Nowadays it has gotten to the point that organbuilders are paid almost [too] little for their work, giving just cause to wonder how many of them can make ends meet. So I would not advise that they be pressed too hard. It is a very difficult occupation, and demands a clever head and thorough consideration; thus it indeed deserves higher pay than a carpenter's daily wage for building a pigsty. [Organbuilders] must also continue

---

54) The director must not however enter into collusion with the organbuilder for the sake of a recompense, to the detriment of the church; neither, on the other hand, should he get himself entangled in squabbling and wrangling with the builder without a pressing reason, for otherwise no good will come of it. [Albrecht]

vor die Aufrichtung eines Säustalles gezahlt wird. Auch müssen solche Leute beständig davon leben, indem nicht allezeit Orgeln gebauet werden. Wollten sie nun nicht mehr daran verdienen, als daß sie von Zeit zu Zeit davon leben könnten; was hätten sie denn zu der Zeit, da keine Orgeln zu bauen sind? Eine Orgel kann ja, wenn sie wohl gemacht, gar lange stehen. Es entstehet aus solchen genau eingerichteten Contrakten das Incommodum, das solche Gemüther über der Arbeit verdrüßlich werden; nicht alles so accurat, dauerhaft und so sauber machen, als sie sonst wol könnten. Ist der Schade hernach nicht der Kirche? Damit aber die Kirchen nicht allzusehr übertheuert werden; so muß man die Kosten ohngefehr überschlagen; alle Materialien, alle Zeit, die darauf geht, Essen und Erhaltung des Künstlers sammt dessen Gesellen, die Arbeit, alles dieses muß in Ueberlegung genommen, und über dasselbe auch noch ein ehrlicher und NB. erlaubter Profit in Rechnung und Anschlag gebracht werden; alsdann richte man sich darnach einigermaßen: denn vollkommen kann man nicht alles determiniren. Also kömmt es in großen Werken auf 100 Rthlr. nicht an. Sonderlich kann man das Pretium der Register rechnen; doch sowohl nach ihrem Metalle oder anderer Materie, (weil Holz freylich dem Metalle nicht gleich hoch kömmt,) als auch nach ihrer Schwere zu machen; it. nach ihrer Größe, da man denn die Proportionen wohl verstehen muß, daß man nicht etwa denke, 16′ sey noch einmal so groß, als 8′, deswegen koste es auch noch einmal soviel als 8′. Das wäre falsch. Denn 16′ ist noch einmal so lang, als 8′: wenn es also auch gleich weit wäre; so wäre es schon noch einmal so theuer: nun aber ist es zugleich um etliche mal weiter; folglich kostet es auch mehr, als noch einmal so viel.

§. 244.

Im Contrakte muß man das specificiren, was im Bauen zu beobachten. Als da setzt man hin, wieviel Register werden sollen; was es für Stimmen seyn sollen; wie vielfach die gemischten Stimmen werden sollen, und wie groß die größte Pfeife in denselben werden soll. Denn darinne gehen viele Betrügereyen vor, wenn z. Ex. die **Mixtur** oder **Scharp** ꝛc. überhaupt gesetzt werden, da man doch bestimmen sollte, ob sie 4, 5, oder 6 fach u. s. w. werden müsse. Imgleichen, ob die **Mixtur** 4 oder 2, oder mehr füßig seyn solle. Man schreibt auch wol die Töne vor, die sie haben soll, z. Ex. c, e, g; oder 6 fach: c, g, c, e, g, c, auch bestimmet man genau, wo sie anheben soll zu repetiren. Die Exempel im folgenden 10ten Kapitel werden dieses deutlich machen. Es ist auch anzuzeigen, ob die Sesquialter 3 oder 2 fach seyn solle; it. ob sie die Quinte 3′ und die Terz über 4′ bekommen solle; und so in andern gemischten Stimmen. Was aber hierinne die Klugheit rathe, wird im Kapitel von der Disposition vorgetragen. Denn dem Orgelmacher läßt man solche Sachen nicht frey, sonst setzt er etwan anstatt der Sesquialter eine Terz hin, **wie Tayßner zu Naumburg und Jena** gethan: oder er sucht sonst seinen Profit.

§. 245.

to live on [the money they receive for an organ], since they are not continuously building organs. Now if they could earn no more than what is necessary to live on while they are employed, what would they have for the time[s] when there are no organs to build? If an organ is well made, it can indeed last a very long time. Such precisely specified contracts* give rise to the disadvantage that the poor souls get fed up with the work and do not make everything so accurately, durably and neatly as otherwise they could. Is not the church then the loser? So that churches are not too much overcharged, however, the expenses need to be roughly calculated: all materials and the time that goes with them, board and keep for the master together with his workers, the work-- all this must be taken into consideration, and beyond them also an honest and, indeed, justifiable profit must be included in the figuring and calculation. These may then be used as rough guidelines, since it is not possible to determine everything absolutely. In large instruments the total will not exceed 100 Reichsthaler.† It is possible to figure the cost of each stop separately, taking into acount both the metal or other material (since wood is of course not as expensive as metal) as well as weight and size. In this case one must have a thorough understanding of proportions, in order not to think, say, that 16′, since it is twice as large as 8′, will then cost twice as much as 8′. This would be incorrect. 16′ is twice the length of 8′, and if it were also of equal width, then it would indeed be twice as expensive. In truth, however, it is a good bit wider, and consequently it costs more than twice as much.

* i.e., those that hold the builder too closely to expenses.

† beyond the price originally contracted.

§. 244.

The contract must specify what is to be observed in constructing [the organ]. In it are established such things as: how many stops there are to be; what specific stops are to be [included]; how many ranks the compound stops are to be, and how large the largest pipe should be in each of them. A good deal of deceit goes on in this last point, if for example merely "Mixtur" or "Scharp" is stated instead of specifying whether it is to be 4, 5, 6, etc., ranks; as well as whether the Mixtur is to begin at 4′ or 2′ or some other length. It is also wise to prescribe the pitches [each Mixtur] is to have, e.g., c,e,g, or (6 ranks) c,g,c,e,g,c′.‡ Where they are to begin repeating should also be precisely specified. The examples in Chapter 10 below will make all this clear. It should also be indicated whether the Sesquialter should be 3 or 2 ranks, as well as whether it is to contain the Quinte 3′ and the Terz above 4′.§ The same goes for the other compound stops. The most prudent alternatives will be reported in the chapter on stoplists.¶ Such matters ought not to be left to the organbuilder's fancy; otherwise he may substitute a Terz for the Sesquialter, as Tayssner did at Naumburg and Jena, or seek his own profit in some other way.

‡ It is interesting to note that Adlung presumes Mixtures will be composed with thirds as well as with fifths and octaves.

§ This statement is somewhat obscure. When Adlung writes "... ob sie die Quinte 3′ und die Terz über 4′ bekommen solle", it is also possible that he has made a mistake, intending to write "...Terz über 2′". In any event, it seems clear that he is referring to the Quinte $2\frac{2}{3}'$ and the Terz $1\frac{3}{5}'$. See §.191, "Sesquialter".

¶ Chapter 10.

§. 245.

Man schreibt ihm auch die Materie jedes Registers vor: denn darauf werden die Kosten auch gerechnet. So wird freylich die **Oktave** 8′ von Metall höher kommen, als von Holz. Wollte man nichts bestimmen; so könnte man auch dem Orgelmacher nichts anhaben, wenn er sie zu seinem Vortheile von Holz machte. Manche Pfeifen klingen besser von Holz, andere von Metall: und folglich muß ein Direktor des Baues solches verstehen, und den Entwurf darnach machen. Z. Er. die Flute douce wird besser von Holz gemacht; die **Quintatön** aber besser von Metall. Hat man metallene Stimmen; so muß man determiniren, ob sie von **Blech** (wie der **Cornetbaß, Trompet, Posaune, Regal,** ꝛc. oft gemacht werden) oder **Meßing,** oder **Zinn, Gold, Silber** oder **Bley** seyn sollen: Ob das Zinn englisches oder gemeines Bergzinn seyn, oder ob man Zinn und Bley vermischen solle, welche Masse alsdann insonderheit Metall genennet wird. Pur Bley ist nie zu rathen; weil der Salpeter die von purem Bley gemachte Pfeifen bald durchfrißt; pur Zinn zur ganzen Orgel zu nehmen, ist zu kostbar, deswegen man heut zu Tage nur zu den im Gesichte stehenden Stimmen (welches ordentlich die **Principale** sind) Zinn nimmt: zu den innern Pfeifen aber nimmt man Metall. Wie viel aber Bley zu dem Zinn gethan werden solle, muß dem Orgelmacher abermal vorgeschrieben werden, sonst nimmt er dessen zu viel, weil es sich besser arbeiten läßt. Man kann die **Legirung** (so nennt man die Proportion des Zinnes und Bleyes) machen, wie man will, oder so gut, als man es bezahlen kann. Halb Zinn und halb Bley geht noch mit: nimmt man aber zu viel Bley; so dauren die Pfeifen destoweniger. Denn unten, wo der Wind einbläset, setzt sich der Salpeter desto häufiger an, und zerfrißt die Pfeifen: weil er nun auch süße ist; so gerathen die Mäuse auch leicht darüber, und fressen die Pfeifen. [55] Im Gesichte nimmt man es ordentlich besser, und entweder pur Zinn, oder wenig Bley mit unter, um es besser arbeiten zu können; etwan unter 10 Pfund Zinn, 1 Pfd. Bley u. s. w. Auch sieht das Zinn besser aus; wie es denn auch der **Principale** wegen nöthig, weil diese am besten müssen reine bleiben, als darnach die andern Register müssen gestimmt werden. Man drückt diese Legirung aus durch **Lothe**; und sagt z. Er. es solle das Metall 10löthig, 12löthig ꝛc. seyn; 16löthig ist das beste, und je weniger es hält, je mehr Zusatz von Bley ist dabey. Weil aber nicht alle diese terminos verstehen; so rede man lieber deutlich, und sage: zu so und so viel Pfund Zinn sollen so und so viel Pfund Bley kommen; so versteht es ein jeder. **Halbrecht** ist, wenn so viel Bley als Zinn genommen wird. Um denen zu dienen, die auch diese Zinngießersprache verstehen wollen; so dient zur Nachricht, daß die Zinngießer

---

[55] Je härter die Materie des Pfeifwerks ist, desto besser und reiner wird auch der Klang seyn. und wenn einige der itzigen gebaueten Orgeln nicht so klingen wollen, als die alten; so rührt solches daher, weil man die Pfeifen von solcher Materie arbeitet, die zu weich ist. Man kann auch solchem schlechten Pfeifwerke solchen guten starken Wind nicht geben, als dem harten und guten Pfeifwerke.

§. 245.

The material for each stop should also be prescribed to [the organbuilder], since the expenses are calculated from them. Thus an Oktave 8′ of metal will of course be more expensive than [one] of wood. If nothing is specified, then the organbuilder cannot be held at fault if he makes them of wood, to his advantage. Many pipes sound better [if they are made] of wood, [while] others [sound better made of] metal; consequently the director of the project must understand such things, and draw up the plans accordingly. E.g., a Flute douce is better made of wood, while the Quintatön is better made of metal. If the stops are to be made of metal, it must be determined whether they are to be of tin-plate (as the Cornetbass, Trompet, Posaune, Regal, etc., are often made) or of brass, tin, gold, silver or lead; also whether the tin is to be English or common native tin, or whether tin and lead are to be mixed, in which case the [resulting] substance is specifically referred to as "pipe metal." Pure lead is never to be recommended, since saltpeter quickly corrodes pipes made of pure lead. Using pure tin for the whole organ is too expensive, and thus it is used nowadays only for the stops that stand in the façade (which are ordinarily the principals), while the interior pipes are of pipe metal. The ratio of lead to tin must also be prescribed to the organbuilder, or otherwise he will use too much of the former, since it is easier to work with. The alloy (this is the term for the proportion of tin to lead) may be chosen as desired, or as fine as can be afforded. Half tin and half lead is still acceptable, but if too much lead is used, the pipes are all the less durable. For at the bottom, where the wind enters, saltpeter sets in all the more frequently, and corrodes the pipes; and since it is sweet, the mice are quick to get to it and eat the pipes.(55) The façade pipes ordinarily get a better [quality metal], either pure tin or [tin] mixed with a little lead to make it more workable, something around 10 pounds of tin to 1 pound of lead.* Tin also makes a better appearance, and it is also necessary for the principals; these must remain the best in tune, since the other stops must then be tuned from them. This alloy is expressed in terms of 'weights'; e.g., it is said that the metal should be 10-weight, 12-weight, etc. 16-weight is the best, and the lower the number, the more admixture of lead there is. Since not everyone understands these terms, however, it is better to speak plainly and to say, "so many pounds of tin are to be added to so many pounds of lead." Then everyone understands it. "Halbrecht" means that equal parts of lead and tin are used. For the sake of those who would also like to understand the tinfounders' language, it is useful to know that tinfounders say

* See also §.87.

---

55) The harder the material the pipes are made of, the better and purer the sound will be. If some of the organs built today do not sound as well as the old ones, this fact may be traced to making pipes of material that is too soft. It is also not possible to provide such poor pipework with good strong wind as [it is] good, hard pipes. [Albrecht]

14löthig nennen, wenn zu 14 Loth Zinn noch 1 Loth Bley gethan wird; 11löthig, wenn zu 11 Lothen Zinn noch 1 Loth Bley kömmt. ꝛc. Manche irren sich, und meynen, 14löthig wäre, wenn unter 14 Lothe Zinn 1 Loth Bley sey, also 13 Lothe Zinn und 1 Loth Bley: aber das ist unrichtig, und müssen 14 Lothe Zinn und 1 Loth Bley seyn, zusammen 15 Lothe, wenn es 14löthig heißen soll. Das dependirt von dem Gebrauche. Auch muß man vorschreiben, wo etwan die Pfeifen sollen verdoppelt werden; denn ein grobes Register geht in der Tiefe allzuschwach, deswegen zuweilen 2 Pfeifen auf jeden Clavem in der Tiefe gesetzt werden, um eine Stärke zu geben. Z. Ex. zu **Sondershausen**, teste *Prætorio*, sind C, D, E, im *Principalsubbasse* von reinem Zinn 16' doppelt klingend gesetzt, also, daß die großen Pfeifen auf beyden Seiten an der Größe und Länge einander respondiren. In der Höhe geschiehet dergleichen auch, wie desfalls die Mixturen im Diskante oft verstärket werden. conf. §. 167. und in **Cassel** ist in der Schloßkirche das *Principal* 8' halb hinaus doppelt, s. **Prätor.** Ordentlich aber thut man es nicht.

§. 246.

Man schreibt dem Orgelmacher ferner vor die Materie zur ganzen Orgel, wo er nämlich Cedern, Eichen oder Tannenholz u. s. w. nehmen soll; wo Eisen oder Meßing zu brauchen; wo Schrauben oder gemeine Nägel anzubringen; wo Thüren hin sollen, u. d. gl. Was aber bey jedem Theile am besten zu brauchen, und wie das ganze Gebäude vollkommen werden müsse, wird im 12ten und 13ten Kapitel vorgetragen; deswegen ich hier nichts besonders anzuführen habe.

§. 247.

Man schreibt ihm auch vor, daß er die Pfeifen alle anhänge und an Pfeifenbrettern verwahre. Zu allen Theilen der Orgel, sonderlich darinne der Wind muß aufbehalten werden, ꝛc. muß das Holz recht dürre genommen werden; sonderlich zu den hölzernen Pfeifen, Parallelen, Dämmen, Windladen, Windröhren oder Kanälen und Bälgen. Denn wenn sie um etwas weniges eindorren, so ist es nichts nutz. Das Holz muß viel Jahre gelegen haben; und darauf muß man auch dringen im Contrakte. Hat der Orgelmacher dergleichen nicht; so ist es besser den Bau so lange aufzuschieben, bis das Holz dazu recht dürre und brauchbar wird. Man schreibt ihm auch vor, wie groß die Orgel in der Breite seyn solle. Denn je mehr er sie ausbreitet, desto besser ist es. Einige Orgelmacher haben die Gewohnheit, das ganze Gebäude so in einander zu stecken, daß man nirgends dazu kommen kann; welches ihnen zwar zum Nutzen gereicht, weil sie nicht so viel Materialien zum Gebäude gebrauchen: allein es steht übel, und ist auch unbequem, weil man nirgends dazu kommen kann. Man sollte billig um alle Laden herum gehen können.

"14-weight" when one part lead is added to 14 parts tin, or "11-weight" when one part lead is added to 11 parts tin. Many err in thinking that 14-weight means one part lead is added to 13 parts tin for a total of 14 parts. But that is incorrect; for 14-weight there must be 14 parts tin and 1 part lead for a total of 15 parts.* This depends on custom. If pipes are to be doubled, where this needs to be done must also be prescribed. Since a deep stop gets too weak in the bass, two pipes are sometimes provided for each bass note, to give strength. For example, at Sondershausen, according to Praetorius, [Vol. II, p. 197,] C, D and E of the pure-tin Principalsubbass 16′ each have two sounding pipes, so that the large pipes on both sides [of the case in the façade] correspond with each other in size and length. The same thing happens in the treble [of some stops†], and on that account mixtures are often reinforced in the treble; cf. §.167. In the palace church at Cassel the upper half of the Principal 8′ is doubled; see Praetorius[, p. 184]. Ordinarily, however, this is not done.

* See §.87; in a note there, Agricola states that Adlung's interpretation of the term "— -weight" as explained here is incorrect.

† i.e., the treble becomes too weak.

§. 246.

Furthermore, the materials for the entire organ should be prescribed to the organbuilder: where he should use cedar, oak, firwood, etc.; where to use iron or brass; where to use screws or ordinary nails; where doors need to be placed, and the like. The best [material] to use for each part and how to make the entire structure perfect is presented in Chapters 12 and 13, however, and therefore I have nothing in particular to mention here.

§. 247.

The organbuilder also needs to be told to secure all the pipes on pipe racks. He must use very dry wood for all parts of the organ, in particular for those that must contain the wind, such as the wooden pipes, sliders, spacers, windchests, wind conduits or ducts and bellows, for if these shrink even the least bit they are good for nothing. The wood must have aged for many years—the contract must insist upon this. If the organbuilder does not have this sort [of wood], then it is better to postpone the building long enough for the wood to get very dry and usable for it. He also needs to be told how wide the organ should be; the more he spreads it out, the better. Several organbuilders have the habit of crowding everything in the structure so close together that it is completely inaccessible. This is of course to their advantage, since they do not need to use so much material to build it. But it is a defect, and also inconvenient, since everything is inaccessible. One ought to be able to get around all the chests with ease.‡

‡ The insistence on leaving ample space between ranks represents a change from the older ideal of keeping the case small and compact, thus making the organ's sound focused and present. Adlung's instructions are a first step in the direction of the 19th-century organ with its large, deep and spacious chests, often without any case, fronted by façade pipes. J.S. Bach concurred with Adlung in this matter; see: *New Bach Reader*, no. 59, p. 75 (*Bach-Dokumente I*, Nr. 85, S. 158).

Kap. IX. Von Verdűng- und Bauung einer Orgel. 179

§. 248.

Man verstatte ihm nicht, ein Rückpositiv hinter den Rücken des Organisten zu bauen, (**) es sey denn gar kein Raum da. Es sieht nicht wohl aus, und kann der Organist nichts sehen; auch wenn er solches spielt, hört er vor dem Geschrey desselben keine Musik. Es können 2 Claviere und nur eine Lade seyn. Große Simse werden ihm zu machen billig auferlegt, als welche das beste Ansehen geben. Man schreibt ihm auch vor, ob er die Manualclaves von Elfenbein, die Chromatischen aber von Ebenholz machen soll, (nämlich von solchem Holze fournirt) oder was er sonst für Holz nehmen solle. Man bemerkt auch, wie viel Claves im Manuale so wol als im Pedale zu machen, und ob Cis, Dis, und im Pedale das $\overline{cis}$ und $\overline{d}$ wegbleiben sollen. Ob dies rathsam gehört ins 13te Kapitel.

(**) Daß nicht alle Leute hierinn von der Meynung des seel. Verfassers sind, ist schon oben angemerkt worden.

§. 249.

Wie viel Claviere zu machen, wird ohne dies gleich ausgedungen. Auch muß ein Orgelmacher die Registerknöpfe fein ordentlich disponiren. Man merkt auch an, daß er das Pfeifwerk nicht so dünne ausarbeite; daß er Koppel und Ventile machen solle; it. Tremulanten, Stern, und dergleichen. Man schreibt ihm auch vor, ob er eine Schleif- oder Springlade machen solle, und daß jene, wo sie zu machen verlanget worden, kein Durchstechen hören lasse, sondern daß alles accurat gearbeitet sey. Die Vorschläge an den Spünder werden auch angemerkt. Imgleichen, das er die Pfeifen nicht kröpfe, Stücke oben anflicke oder eindrücke u. dergl.

§. 250.

Die Zahl der Bälge, ihre Länge und Breite, werden auch berührt; auch daß sie nur eine Falte haben sollen; it. daß sie mit Schrauben und Roßadern wohl versehen werden; imgleichen daß sie doppelte Fangventile bekommen ꝛc. auch ob etliche ins Pedal allein, andere aber ins Manual allein gehen sollen. Die Grade des Windes giebt man auch einigermaßen an. Man bedingt sich auch aus, daß er zuletzt das Werk wohl temperire und recht reine stimme. Man behält sich auch vor, daß er ein Jahr nach der Probe vor das Werk sorgen solle, wo es mangelbar würde. Will man bey einem Register, oder sonst, etwas beydingen; so ist am gehörigen Orte, nämlich Kap. 13. it. Kap. 7. da die Register betrachtet worden, genugsame Nachricht zu finden, daraus das benöthigte zu erlernen und in den Contrakt zu setzen ist. Man lasse sich auch von dem Direktor, oder Orgelmacher einen Riß machen von der Orgel, wie er solche im Kopfe hat, um zu sehen, wie es alles lasse.

§. 251.

Was für Register in einer Orgel am nöthigsten, wird im folgenden 10ten Kapitel bey der Disposition vorgetragen. Itzt erinnere ich weiter, daß man das Geld für die

Z 2

Chap. IX. Contracting for and Building an Organ

§. 248.

The organbuilder should not be permitted to build a Rückpositiv behind the organist's back,(**) unless there is absolutely no room elsewhere. It does not look well, and the organist cannot see anything.* Furthermore, if he plays on it he cannot hear any music for all the noise. Two keyboards may be accommodated on only one chest.† He should rightly be required to make heavy moldings, since these make the best appearance. The organbuilder also should be told whether to make the manual naturals of ivory and the chromatics of ebony (i.e., veneered with this wood), or what other type of wood he should use. It should also be noted how many keys are to be made for the manual as well as the pedal, and whether C# and D# are to be omitted, as well as the [upper] c#' and d' in the pedal. Chapter 13‡ discusses whether this is advisable.

(**) It has already been remarked [in Vol. II, §.324 and 344] above§ that not everyone is of the same opinion in this matter as the late author. [Agricola].

* i.e., his view of the nave (and also the choir at the Predigerkirche in Erfurt, where Adlung was organist) is blocked by the Rückpositiv case.

† thereby obviating the need for a Rückpositiv.

‡ In §.351, Adlung calls the short octave a major defect in organs.

§ Agricola has not previously countered Adlung's objection to the Rückpositiv.

§. 249.

Moreover the contract should specify how many keyboards are to be made. The organbuilder must also arrange the stopknobs in a neat, orderly fashion. It should also be stated that he is not to construct the pipes too thin, [and whether] he is to make couplers and ventils, etc., as well as tremulants, a cymbelstern and the like. It should also be prescribed whether he is to make a slider or a spring chest, and that the former, if it is required, be very accurately constructed so it is free of runs. The latches on the bungboards are also to be mentioned; also that he is not to miter the pipes, pinch them in or patch pieces on the top, and the like.

§. 250.

[The contract] should also touch upon the number of bellows and their length and breadth, that they should have only a single fold, and that they are to be well provided with screws and horse-veins; likewise that they are to receive double intake valves, and whether some are to serve the pedal alone and others only the manual[s]. The approximate degree of wind [pressure] should also be indicated. The contract should specify that the builder give the organ a good temperament¶ at the close [of his work] and tune it precisely. The contract should also provide that [for a period of] one year after the [final] examination he should repair anything that is wrong with the instrument. If anyone wishes to specify something in greater detail about a stop or anything else, there is ample information to be found in the pertinent place, namely Chapter 13 and Chapter 7 (in which stops are discussed), from which to learn what is necessary and put it into the contract. The director or organbuilder should also be required to prepare a sketch of the organ as he envisions it, in order to see how it all will look.

¶ Chapter 14 makes it clear that the organ should at least be tuned in a well temperament, if not in equal temperament.

§. 251.

The organ stops that are the most necessary will be explained in Chapter 10 below, in connection with the stoplist[s]. I will mention further that the money for the work

Arbeit nicht voraus verspreche, sondern zum wenigsten einen ziemlichen Theil desselben, bis nach der Probe zurück behalte, damit, wenn etwas versehen, man sich Raths erhohlen, und ihn solches zu ändern zwingen könne. Etliche machen den Contrakt so, daß jedes Stück der Orgel, und jede Stimme an ein gewiß Geld geschlagen wird, und so bald es fertig, wird dafür das Geld gezahlt: aber das gefällt mir nicht; und was für Schaden daraus entstehen könne, ist leicht zu erachten Denn wenn die Kirche nicht allezeit das Geld parat hat (wie es denn gemeiniglich zu gehen pflegt;) so thut der Orgelmacher auch nichts, es sey denn das vorige erst bezahlt, und folglich werden die wenigen Stimmen, welche zuerst gesetzt worden, erst wieder verdorben, ehe die andern nachkommen. Wenn doch die Menschen zuvor bedächten, ob sie die Mittel dazu könnten möglich machen, ehe sie sich einer Sache unterfiengen!

§. 252.

Es versteht sich von selbst, daß die Schnarrwerke frey stehen müssen, daß man im Stimmen ungehindert dazu kommen könne. Es wird auch gemeiniglich für die Arbeiter und den Orgelmacher die Kost bey der Gemeine auf eine gewisse Zeit bedungen; da man denn genau zu bestimmen hat, wie lange die Kost währen soll; it. wie viel Personen beköstiget werden sollen. Ordentlich gilt dieß nur die Zeit über, da die Orgel gesetzt wird. Zuweilen aber wird alles zugleich an ein Geld geschlagen, daß sie sich selbst verköstigen müssen, welches fast noch besser: und dürfen sie weniger faullenzen.

§. 253.

Man macht entweder den Contrakt so, daß der Orgelmacher für alle Materialien stehen muß, auch für die Schmiede- und andere Arbeit: oder die Gemeine besorgt solches, jener thut nur die Orgelmacherarbeit. Beydes hat seine Commoda und Incommoda. Schafft der Orgelmacher die Materialien; so sind sie oft nicht tauglich: sonderlich ist das Holz nicht allezeit recht dürre. Auch setzt er sie oft zu hoch an, und schonet sie doch hernach auf alle Weise. Stehet aber die Gemeine für die Materialien; so können die Vorsteher derselben solche bey Zeit und guter Gelegenheit anschaffen, auf daß sonderlich das Holz erst recht ausdorre: und alsdann wissen sie, ob es tauglich sey, oder nicht. Allein, wenn zumal die Orgelmacher das Werk in ihren Häusern machen, tauschen sie es zuweilen aus, behalten es zum Theil, oder schwänzen, wie man hier redet. Oder sie hausiren darein und verwüsten es vergeblich, weil ihnen dadurch kein Schade geschiehet. Was übrig bleibet, ist der Gemeine nichts nütze, da sie es doch vorher anschaffen müssen: der Orgelmacher aber kann es anderswo nutzen. Wo aber der Orgelmacher das ganze Werk bey der Gemeine verfertiget, und nicht zu Hause; so ist doch das sicherste, wenn man die Materialien selbst bey Gelegenheit anschaft. Was gilts, das Pfeifwerk wird so dünne nicht geschunden werden, als wo der Orgelmacher das Metall schaffen muß! Und so verhält sichs auch mit andern Stücken. Wenn ein Direktor da ist; so muß auch derselbe beständig dabey seyn. Also ist das Werk nicht in des Orgelmachers

Hause

should not be promised in advance, but rather at least a fair percentage of it withheld until after the examination, so that if anything is wrong there is some recourse to force [the builder] to rectify it. Some people make the contract so that each part of the organ and each stop is set at a specific sum, and as soon as [that component] is finished the money is paid for it. But this does not seem wise to me, and it is easy to judge what sort of harm may arise from it. For if the church does not always have the money at hand (as is usually the case), then the organbuilder is idle until what is due him is paid, and consequently the few stops that were first put into place would be spoiled before the others could join them.* If only people would think ahead whether they can produce the requisite means before undertaking something!

§. 252.

It goes without saying that the reeds must not be hemmed in so that they may be accessible for tuning without hindrance. It is also normal for the congregation to contract to furnish board for the organbuilder and his workers for a set [period of] time, but it is necessary to stipulate precisely how long this board will last, as well as how many persons will be fed. It normally lasts only as long as it takes to erect the organ. Sometimes, however, the entire cost is agreed upon in a lump sum, so that [the builder and his workers] are responsible for providing their own food. This is almost better, since they have less temptation to be idle.

§. 253.

The contract is either drawn up so that the organbuilder is to be responsible for all materials, including the wrought-iron work and all other labor, or the parish takes care of such things and he does only the [actual] work of organbuilding. Either one has its advantages and disadvantages. If the organbuilder procures the materials, they are often substandard; in particular, the wood is not always completely cured. He also often puts too high a price on them, and then afterward cuts all kinds of corners. If however the parish is responsible for the materials, then the parish authorities can procure them at the most opportune time, especially so that the wood may first have the opportunity to cure thoroughly. Then they know whether or not it is of suitable quality. Especially if the organbuilder constructs the instrument in his own shop, however, he sometimes switches materials, keeping part of them for himself, or as we say here, he plays loose with them. Or [organbuilders] misuse it and idly waste it, since they have nothing to lose. What is left over is of no use to the parish, since they have had to buy it in advance, and thus the organbuilder gets to use it somewhere else. But if the organbuilder constructs the entire instrument on site and not in his own shop, the safest procedure is for the parish itself to procure the materials when the opportunity presents itself. I'll wager that pipework is never made so thin as when the organbuilder must procure the metal on his own! The same holds true for other parts. If there is a director, then he must constantly be in attendance. Thus it is best that the instrument be built on site and

---

* The German text is quite clear. It unclear, however, why some stops would be spoiled for lack of others; perhaps Adlung means that the few stops would not sound well without their mates, or that pipes might be prone to collapse without a full complement of pipe racks; or he may simply be engaging here in rhetorical exaggeration.

Hause, sondern in der Gemeine zu bauen. Halten aber der Direktor und Orgelmacher zusammen, und haben beyde Lust zu betrügen; so sieht es übel aus. Doch wird von verständigen Leuten bey der Orgelprobe bald entdecket werden, ob alles mit dem Contrakte eintreffe, oder nicht.

§. 254.

Ich könnte wol ein Exempel eines Contrakts hersetzen, um zu zeigen, wie dergleichen werden müsse: allein es würde zu weitläuftig und noch dazu von wenig Nutzen seyn, weil die allerwenigsten recht eingerichtet sind. Wer das Kapitel von den **Vollkommenheiten und Fehlern einer Orgel** aufmerksam durchlieset, der wird wol wissen, was vorzuschreiben sey, oder nicht.

§. 255.

Wenn man aber keinen Inspektor oder Direktor des ganzen Werks hat; so muß man auf Treu und Glauben des Orgelmachers handeln, und wenigstens beym Contrakte einen Verständigen consuliren. NB. Es kömmt aber hierinne nicht darauf an, ob einer eine große Auctorität habe; ob er alt oder jung, oder ob er ein excellenter Organist sey: sondern es wird erfordert, daß er wenigstens theoretice ein guter Mechanikus sey, und dabey die principia physica und mathematica wohl inne habe, welches oft bey den größten Organisten nicht ist. Es muß einer gereiset seyn, viel Orgeln, Register u. s. w. gesehen haben, und dabey von gutem Verstande seyn, sonst hilft sein Rathgeben nichts, wo es nicht gar schädlich ist. Welches alles auch von dem Baudirektor zu merken ist, davon oben Meldung geschehen; denn daß man dazu keinen Dummkopf, sondern einen klugen, verständigen und erfahrnen Mann wählen müsse, ist wol von selbst zu ermessen. Was sonst die Musik der Mathematik zu danken hat, das ist sonderlich in der Mechanik; also muß einer solche Principia gründlich verstehen.

§. 256.

Man kan auch ausdingen, daß die Laden etwas breiter gemacht werden sollen, als die Register erfordern; und daß man etliche blinde Parallelen darauf lege, damit, wenn mit der Zeit einmal mehr Geld vorhanden, noch einige Register können darein gebracht werden. Die zu vermeidenden vornehmsten Fehler, davon im 13ten Kapitel zu reden, sollen auch vorgeschrieben werden, z. Er. daß er keine schwedischen Stiche (man nennt sie auch spanische Reuter; it. Laufgraben,) machen solle, auch keine Fliegenschnäpper, u. d. gl. welches aus dem kaum angeführten 13ten Kapitel zu ersehen seyn wird.

Chap. IX. Contracting for and Building an Organ

not in the organbuilder's shop. It is a sorry state of affairs, however, if the director and organbuilder conspire together in an attempt to swindle [the parish]. Yet in the final examination the experts will soon discover whether everything is in accord with the contract or not.

§. 254.

I could easily have provided an example of a contract to show how it must be [drawn up]; but it would have been too lengthy and furthermore of little use, since very few are well drawn up [that might be used as an example]. Anyone who reads attentively the chapter on the virtues and faults of an organ* will surely know what to specify and what not to.

* Chapter 13 below.

§. 255.

If there is no inspector or director for the entire project, then it is necessary to put faith and trust in [the integrity of] the organbuilder, while at least consulting an expert about the contract. N.B. In this matter it is not important whether a [director] is in a position of great authority, whether he is young or old, or whether he is an excellent organist. Rather what is required is that he has a good grasp of mechanics, at least in theory, and in addition is thoroughly acquainted with the principles of physics and mathematics, which is often not the case with the most renowned organists. He must be well-traveled, must have seen many organs and [various kinds of] stops, and have good common sense as well, otherwise his counsel will be useless, if not downright harmful. A report has been given above of everything that the director of the project needs to keep in mind; one may judge for oneself that the person chosen for this [responsibility] must not be a blockhead, but rather a clever, intelligent and experienced man. That for which music is indebted to mathematics is especially [to be seen] in mechanics, and such a man must therefore have a thorough understanding of such principles.

§. 256.

It is also possible to specify that the chests should be made somewhat wider than the stops require and that a number of blank sliders† be placed upon them, so that a few more stops may be added when in time more money becomes available. The chief faults to be avoided, which are described in Chapter 13, should also be specified, e.g., that [the builder] not make any scoring or bleed grooves (schwedische Stiche‡) (these are also called "spanische Reuter" or "Laufgraben"), nor any "flycatchers" (Fliegenschnäpper§), etc.; these may be noted in Chapter 13 just mentioned.

† i.e., sliders without holes.

‡ See §.362, and §.444.

§ Adlung mentions these again in §.444, together with "Sternlöcher". He describes the latter in his Anleitung, p. 538: star-shaped holes (instead of perfectly round ones) in which the pipe feet rest, creating tiny channels to let the wind escape. He does not describe "Fliegenschnäpper", but the context suggests they are some variety of scoring/bleed groves.

Das X. Kapitel.
Von der Disposition.

Inhalt.

§. 257. Was dadurch zu verstehen? §. 258. Der Orgelmacher soll sie nicht machen. §. 259. Man mache 2 Claviere. §. 260. Die Stimmen sind schärfend und douce. §. 261. Von den groben Stimmen. §. 262. Schärfende. §. 263. Douce. §. 264. Andere. §. 265. Was in 8füßigen Werken zu thun. §. 266. Wo ein Clavier ist; it. 3 Claviere. §. 267. Schnarrwerke sind verdrüßlich. §. 268. Mehr Stimmen. § 269. Das Pedal soll abgesondert seyn. §. 270. Die Proportion der Trompet, Posaune und Schallmey. §. 271. Eine Stimme steht etlichemal. §. 272. Auch wol von einerley Größe. §. 273. Von gemischten Stimmen. §. 274. Von Quinten. §. 275. Principal 8′ ist was schönes. §. 276. Man soll zu einem Register 2 Züge machen, ins Pedal und Manual. §. 277. Von Kammerregistern. §. 278. Von Kammerkoppel. §. 279. Von Manualkoppeln. § 280. Guckguck, Vogelgesang, ꝛc. sind nichts nutz. §. 281. Vom Tremulanten. §. 282. Von den Ventilen. §. 283. Von den folgenden Dispositionen. §. 284 ⁚ 315. Stehen die Dispositionen nach dem Alphabet.

§. 257.

Durch die **Disposition** verstehet man die **Ordnung und Rangirung der Orgelregister**. Wenn also die Disposition eines Werks verlangt wird; so will man wissen, wie viel Register es habe; wie sie heißen; zu welchem Claviere sie gehören, ꝛc. Nun ist vor allen Dingen nöthig, daß der Baumeister, oder ein anderer, eine Disposition seiner zu bauenden Orgel dem Orgelmacher vorschreibe; also ist auch nöthig, hiervon mit wenigem zu reden; weil öfters wider die Klugheit hierinne gehandelt wird.

§. 258.

Man lasse aber nicht den Orgelmacher die Disposition nach seinem Willen machen, ohne sie von andern censiren zu lassen; denn sonst setzt er viel kleine und wohlfeile Stimmen hinein, die doch oft hoch angerechnet werden, wegen der Vielheit: oder er setzt solche hin, die ihm am leichtesten zu machen sind. Man überlasse es vielmehr einem verständigen Organisten, welcher jedoch allezeit wohl bedenken muß, ob die Kirche viel oder wenig anwenden könne und wolle, auch was für Raum da sey.

§. 259.

Ist es möglich, so mache man die Disposition auf 2 Claviere: denn so hat man mehr Abwechselungen, und darf nicht immer die Register an- und abziehen. Ja in der Musik sind 2 Claviere sonderlich nöthig, weil man sonst den Baß nicht sattsam verstärken kann, wenn er obligat ist. Denn die Accorde dürfen selten mit starken Stimmen gespielet werden, als welches alle Anmuth verdirbt; es wäre denn bey einem vollen

Chapter X.
Concerning the Stoplist.

Contents:

§.257. What is meant by ["the stoplist"]? §.258. The organbuilder ought not to draw it up. §.259. There should be two manuals. §.260. There are both penetrating and gentle stops. §.261. The low stops. §.262. Intensifying [stops]. §.263. Gentle [stops]. §.264. Other [stops]. §.265. What to do with 8′ divisions. §.266. If there is one manual; if there are 3 manuals. §.267. Reeds are annoying. §.268. Additional stops. §.269. Stops should be available separately in the [manual and] pedal. §.270. The proportions of the Trompet, Posaune and Schallmey. §.271. One stop appears several times. §.272. Even at the same size. §.273. Compound stops. §.274. Quints. §.275. Principal 8′ is a beautiful stop. §.276. Two drawknobs should be made for a stop, one for the pedal and one for the manual. §.277. Stops at chamber pitch. §.278. Chamber-pitch couplers. §.279. Manual couplers. §.280. Cuckoo, birdsong, etc., are worthless. §.281. Tremulants. §.282. Ventils. §.283. About the following stoplists. §.284-315. Alphabetical arrangement of stoplists.

§. 257.

By "stoplist" is meant the order and arrangement of the stops in an organ. Thus if the stoplist of an instrument is asked for, the information sought is: how many stops does it have, what are they called, what keyboard do they belong to, etc. What is necessary above all is that the director or someone else dictate to the organbuilder the stoplist of the organ he is to build. Thus it is also necessary to speak a bit about it [here], since foolish things are often done in dealing with it.

§. 258.

The organbuilder should not be allowed to draw up the stoplist according to his own wishes without it being critiqued by others; for otherwise he will put a lot of small and cheap stops into it that people often consider valuable because there are so many of them. Or he will include those [stops] that he finds the easiest to build. Rather this [matter] is best turned over to a knowledgeable organist, who must however always keep in mind how much or little the church is willing and able to spend and how much space is available.

§. 259.

If possible, the stoplist should be drawn up with 2 manuals, for thus more variety may be had, and stops do not constantly have to be put on or off. Indeed, 2 manuals are especially necessary when playing figured bass for an ensemble, because otherwise it is not possible sufficiently to reinforce the bass if it is an obligato part.* For chords may seldom be played with loud stops, since this destroys all the charm. They might be used

* cf. §. 235 and 266.

Kap. X. Von der Disposition.

len Chöre: doch ist auch dabey Behutsamkeit nöthig, und ein Organist hat sich billig zu bescheiden, daß er sich im Registerziehen also mäßige, um die andern mitmusicirenden Personen durch allzustarkes Spielen nicht zu übertäuben. In langsamen Noten kann das Pedal die Harmonie verstärken: nicht aber so wohl in geschwinden Läufen. Und wenn man im andern Claviere nichts hätte, als ein **Gedackt**; so wollte ich doch rathen, 2 Claviere zu machen. Auf solche Art kann im Fantasiren ein **Echo** gemacht, und im Generalbasse eine **Traversiere** gespielet werden, wenn die Griffe im andern Claviere, wo das **Musicirgedackt** ist, die Traversiere im Hauptmanual, und die Baßnoten im Pedale genommen werden. Kurz, keiner weis, was ein einzelnes Clavier für Incommoda bey sich hat, als der es erfahren. Zumal geht es mit 2 Clavieren desto eher an bey armen Kirchen, wenn man nach §. 256. auf der Windlade hat Raum gelassen, damit nach der Zeit, wenn mehr Mittel vorhanden, noch etwas könne darauf gesetzt werden. Zwar findet man auch **getheilte Claviere**, die dieses in etwas können prästiren: allein, mir gefallen sie nicht. Sie sind von dieser Beschaffenheit: die Lade wird in zwey Stücke getheilt, von allen Registern werden die Pfeifen von C bis c̄ auf die eine Hälfte gesetzt, und die von c̄ bis c̿ auf die andere Hälfte. Folglich bekömmt jedes Register 2 Parallelen, in jedem Theile eine. Wenn ich nun die manubria zur rechten Hand ziehe; so geht nur das eine Theil des Claviers, von 2 Oktaven; Ziehe ich auf der andern Seite; so gehen die andern 2 Oktaven auch. Zu jeder Stimme müssen also auch 2 Züge oder manubria seyn, eins zur rechten, und eins zur linken Hand. Folglich wird eine solche Orgel noch einmal soviel Register zu haben scheinen, als sie wirklich hat. Will man also den Diskant mit andern Registern haben, als den Baß; so kann man darnach ziehen. Z. E. im Generalbasse könnte man im Basse nebst dem **Gedackt** auch das **Principal** oder dergleichen ziehen, um den Baß zu verstärken, da im Diskante die Accorde nur mit dem Gedackt allein könnten gespielet werden, weil man nicht beyde manubria des **Principals** gezogen. u. s. w. Noch heut zu Tage findet man solche getheilte Claviere, und **Prätorius** recommendirt dergleichen zuweilen. Allein 1.) hat man doppelte Arbeit mit ziehen. 2.) muß man die Hände sehr binden, daß keine weder auf- noch unterwärts das c̄ überschreite. Es ist also, wo es je möglich zu machen, besser, auch nur das einzige **Musicirgedackt** auf eine besondere Lade und Clavier zu setzen, und (wie gesagt) Raum zu laßen, daß man noch mehrere Stimmen nach und nach hinzu thun könne.

§. 260.

Ueberhaupt hat man die Stimmen einzutheilen in **nöthige** und in **unnöthige**. Denn wer alle Stimmen, die im 7ten Kapitel erwähnt worden, in eine Orgel wollte bringen laßen, der unternähme sich was, welches doch nicht möglich zu machen. Wo wollte ein solch Werk stehen? Was würde es kosten? — Tonnen Goldes würden nicht hinreichen, die Unkosten eines solchen Werks zu bestreiten. Daher muß man die nöthigen von den andern separiren. Wollen wir wissen, was für nöthig zu halten; so dürfen wir

for the full choir, yet even there it is necessary to exercise caution. An organist simply must acquiesce in being moderate with registration so as not to drown out his fellow musicians by playing too loudly. In [playing] slow notes the pedal may reinforce the harmony, but not so readily in fast passages. Even if there were nothing but a Gedackt in the second manual, I would still advise making 2 manuals.* It is possible in that way to play an echo when improvising, and to play a traverse flute solo with continuo, by playing the chords on the second manual where the continuo-Gedackt is, the traverse flute [melody] on the main manual, and the bass part with the pedals.† In short, no one knows what inconveniences a single manual causes until he has experienced it. It is easier to arrange for 2 manuals, especially in poor churches, if in accord with §.256 space is left on the windchest so that in time, when more [financial] means are available, more stops may be added to it. To be sure, there are also divided keyboards that can serve to some degree as a substitute, but I am not in favor of them. This is how they are constituted: the chest is divided into two parts,‡ and the pipes of all stops from C to c' are placed on one half while those from c' to c''' are put on the other half. Consequently each stop gets two sliders, one for each half. If the stopknobs for the right hand are drawn, then only one section of the keyboard, 2 octaves, sounds; if the [stops on the] other side are drawn, then the other 2 octaves sound as well. Thus there must be 2 stopknobs for each stop, one on the right side and one on the left. Consequently such an organ will appear to have twice as many stops as it actually has. If the organist wishes to have a different registration in the treble than in the bass, the stops may be drawn accordingly. E.g., in playing figured bass the Principal [8'] or some such may be drawn in the bass along with the Gedackt [8'] in order to reinforce the bass [line], while the chords in the treble may be played on the Gedackt alone,§ since only one of the Principal stopknobs is drawn. Such divided keyboards may still be found nowadays, and at times Praetorius recommends them.¶ However: 1.) there is twice as much work changing registration, and 2.) the hands must be very much restrained so that they do not pass above or below c'. Thus it is better if at all possible to put even a single continuo-Gedackt on a separate chest and keyboard and (as already stated) leave room [on the chest] for several more stops to be added gradually.

§. 260.

In general the stops may be divided into those that are necessary and those that are not. For anyone who would try to put all the stops mentioned in Chapter 7 into one organ would be undertaking something that is impossible. Where would there be room for such an instrument? What would it cost? Tons of gold would not suffice to cover the expenses of such an instrument. Thus the necessary [stops] must be distinguished from the others. If we want to know what to consider necessary, we need only take the

---

* Adlung considers it best to play the bass line on a louder manual with 16' and 8' stops, while playing the realization above it with the right hand on a gentle 8' Gedackt; see §.235 and §.266.

† See also §.178 and §.238.

‡ See §.43.

§ See also §.235.

¶ *Syntagma musicum*, Vol. II, p. 193.

wir nur den Endzweck des Spielens zur Richtschnur nehmen. Daraus erhellet, daß man **grobe** oder **tiefe** Stimmen brauche, damit im Basse die nöthige Gravität erhalten werde. Ferner müssen auch **scharfe** Stimmen da seyn, damit in Choralen, und auch sonst das Werk vor der Gemeinde gehöret werde. Es müssen auch **stillklingende** Register, der Musik wegen, mit eingerückt werden. Wenn wir mit diesen Sätzen die Natur der Register, aus dem 7ten Kapitel, vergleichen, so wird sich bald zeigen was für **nöthig** oder **unnöthig** zu halten. Unter den **tiefen** Stimmen waren **gedeckte** und **offene**, **Flöt-** und **Schnarrwerke**.

§. 261.

Die **Schnarr-** oder **Zungenwerke** können in der Musik nicht so bequem gebraucht werden, als die andern, daher man bey den andern bleibt, und jene wegläßt. Unter den gedeckten Stimmen hat man den **Contrabaß** 32', aber weil er, zumal in der Tiefe so wohl nicht klingt, und doch theuer ist; so läßt man ihn in der Classe der unnöthigen Register, und bleibt bey 16', welches im Manuale ein **Gedackt** und im Pedale **Subbaß** heißt. Ist das corpus etwas enge, so heißt es auch **Bordun**. Und wer 16' Gedackt in die Hauptmanuale haben will, wie es denn zum 8füßigen Manuale nöthig scheint, der wähle lieber dergleichen, als die **Quintatön** 16'; denn diese schlägt im Laufen so geschwinde nicht an, da hingegen jenes allezeit eine vortrefliche Gravität giebt.

§. 262.

Nun folgen auch **schärfende Stimmen**: denn die gedeckten schärfen nicht. Je kleiner die Stimmen sind, desto mehr schärfen sie: doch wenn im Hauptmanuale Bordun oder Quintatön 16' ist; so ist unter den offenen Stimmen eine 8füßige nöthig, daß keine Lücke zwischen den Stimmen sey. Wenn aber das 8füßige noch sehr groß ist, und wenig schärft; so nimmt man 4', auch wol 2' dazu. Unter diesen Oktavenregistern heißt das größte das **Principal**, die andern werden **Oktaven** und **Superoktaven** genennet. Will man es noch schärfer haben, so kommen die Quinten dazu; it **Sesquialter, Terz, Tertian, Rauschpfeife, Mixtur, Scharp, Cymbelregister** ꝛc. Doch nicht alle auf einmal; sondern nachdem man es will scharf haben, und nachdem man viel bezahlen kann.

§. 263.

Man muß aber auch **douce Register** haben, sonderlich der Musik wegen: daher ein Gedackt 8' hinein zu setzen ist; doch von stillerer Intonation, als sie sonst zu seyn pflegen. Dies nennt man das **Musicir-** oder **Stillgedackt**. An dessen Stelle kann auch die Quintatön 8' hinein gesetzt werden. Das wären die Hauptstimmen zu einem mittelmäßigen 8füßigen Werke. Wenn man die Manualstimmen durch besondere Züge, oder durch ein Koppel ins Pedal führt; so braucht man keine mehr nothwendig: wollte man aber ja noch was ins Pedal bringen, so könnte es die **Oktave** 8' seyn.

§. 264.

ultimate purpose of [organ]playing as a guiding principle. From this it is evident that heavy or low stops are needed in order that the bass may receive its proper gravity.* Furthermore, intensifying stops must also be included, so that in chorales and such the instrument may be heard above the congregation. Quiet-sounding stops must also be included for the sake of playing figured bass. If we compare the character of the stops from Chapter 7 with these principles, it will soon become clear what to consider necessary or unnecessary. Among the low stops there would be stopped and open registers, both flues and reeds.

* cf. §.231

§. 261.

Reeds cannot be used as satisfactorily for playing figured bass as can the [flue stops], and therefore one should stick to the latter and omit the former. Among the stopped registers is the Contrabass 32',† but because it does not sound well, especially in the bass, and is expensive to boot, one should assign it to the category of unnecessary stops, and begin with 16', which is called a Gedackt in the manual and a Subbass in the pedal. If the body is somewhat narrow[-scaled], it is also called Bordun. If anyone wishes to have a 16' stopped flute in the primary manual, as would seem necessary for an 8' manual, he should choose [a 16' Gedackt or Bordun] over a Quintatön 16', since the latter does not speak so promptly in running passages, while on the other hand the former always provides an excellent gravity.

† i.e., a 32' Subbass; see §.126.

§. 262.

Next come the intensifying‡ stops, since stopped flutes do not provide intensity. The higher-pitched the stops are, the more they intensify. However if there is a Bordun or Quintatön 16' in the primary manual, then an 8' must be included among the open stops, so that there is no gap between the stops.§ But if the 8' is very large[-scaled] and adds little intensity, then a 4' or even a 4' and 2' is used with it. Among these octave-speaking stops the largest is called the Principal, while the others are called octaves and superoctaves. If more brilliance is desired, then the Quints are added [to the stoplist], as well as the Sesquialter, Terz, Tertian, Rauschpfeife, Mixtur, Scharp, Cymbel, etc.— yet not all at once, rather according to how much brilliance is desired and how much can be afforded.

‡ "schärfende;" see §.231.

§ The sense of this statement seems to be that without an 8' Principal there is too great a gap between the depth provided by a stopped 16' and the higher center of gravity that results when a 4' Principal is the primary stop.

§. 263.

Gentle stops are also required, especially for the sake of playing figured bass. Therefore a Gedackt 8' is to be included, but more quietly voiced than is otherwise customary. This is called the Musicir- or Stillgedackt.¶ A Quintatön 8' may also be substituted for it. These would be the most important stops for a medium-sized 8' division. If the manual stops are made available in the pedal on separate stopknobs, or by means of a coupler, then nothing else is necessary.‖ Yet if something more is desired in the pedal, it might be the Oktave 8'.

¶ cf. §.150.

‖ The sentence following this one makes it unclear whether this statement refers only to gentle stops or to all manual stops.

Kap. X. Von der Disposition.

§. 264.

Wenn die Unkosten reichen wollen, so kann man nun andere dazu thun. Also kann ins Pedal eine offene 16fußige Stimme gebracht werden, z. E. der Violon oder Principalbaß 16′; oder beyde; auch wol eine Oktave 4′, und andere Stimmen. So kann der Posaunbaß 8′, oder besser 16′, eine besondere Stärke bringen. Im Hauptmanuale könnte die Trompete stehen, etwann 8′. ꝛc. Im andern Manuale eine scharfe Stimme, etwann Principal 4′, daß man es auch in Choralen brauchen könne, auch wol Oktave 2′, Mixtur oder Scharp, oder sonst was schärfendes.

§. 265.

Wenn aber zu 8füßigen Werken entweder kein Raum oder kein Geld vorhanden ist; so muß man freylich das Principal 4′ anstatt 8′ nehmen, und anstatt des Gedackts oder Quintatön 16′ nur 8′. Hernach können die Oktave 2′ Quinte 1½′, Mixtur, Sesquialter, Cymbel ꝛc. folgen. Das andere Manual wird alsdann ordentlich das Principal 2′ bekommen, und noch wenige Stimmen dazu. Doch ists auch wohl möglich auf einem kleinen Reviere ein groß Werk zu bauen, wenn man die Pfeifen enge ineinander und hintereinander setzt, oder ein Rückpositiv anbringt, wenn der Raum in der Höhe oder Breite, oder hinterwärts, mangelt. Fehlt der Raum aber nur in der Breite; so können im Nothfall auch die Laden hinter einander gesetzt werden; auch setzt man Röhren auf die Stöcke, und auf dieselben die Pfeifen, daß sie oben aus einandergehen, wie es in der Erfurthischen Augustinerorgel ist im Mittelwerke. Fehlt es an der Höhe, so gebe man dem Werke die rechte Breite, so gut man kann; allein man setze die großen Pfeifen inwendig, da man des Staats wegen so große Füße nicht vonnöthen hat, als auswendig. Man kann auch inwendig die Pfeifen kröpfen. Es ist zwar sonst dieses ein Fehler; allein man muß ja zuweilen aus der Noth eine Tugend machen. Auch kann man sich zuweilen helfen, wenn man die Pfeifen abwärts hängt, welches alsdann am bequemsten angehet, wenn die große Stimme die äußerste ist auf der Windlade, forn oder hinten, da kann man es also anbringen:

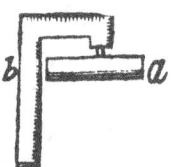

Die Windlade ist hier *a*, darauf hängt die Pfeife *b* hinten herunter. Das wird nun freylich keinen Staat machen: aber wer kann sich helfen, wenn der Raum fehlt? Trost meldet in der Beschreibung der Weißenfelsischen Orgel S. 13. daß die 3 größten Pfeifen vom Subbasse daselbst umgekehrt und hinunter gehänget worden.

Chap. X. Concerning the Stoplist

§. 264.

Then other stops may be added if finances are adequate. An open 16′ stop may be placed in the pedal, e.g., a Violon or Principalbass 16′, or both, as well as an Oktave 4′ and other stops. A Posaunbass 8′, or better 16′, can add a special power. A Trompete could stand in the primary manual, perhaps an 8′. An intensifying stop, perhaps a Principal 4′, [could be placed] in the second manual, as well as an Oktave 2′, Mixture or Scharp, or something else penetrating, so that it could also be used for [accompanying congregational] chorales.

§. 265.

If there is either insufficient space or money available for an 8′ division, then of course a Principal 4′ must be used instead of an 8′, with only an 8′ Gedackt or Quintatön instead of a 16′. After these could come an Oktave 2′, Quinte 1½′, Mixtur, Sesquialter, Cymbel, etc. The second manual will then normally have a Principal 2′ plus a few other stops. Yet it is also quite possible to build a large instrument in a small space, if the pipes are set very close to each other or a Rückpositiv is built, in the event that space (either height, width or depth) is lacking. If only width is lacking, then the chests may be placed one behind the other, if need be. Tubes may also be set upon the toeboards and the pipes set on these tubes, so they may expand into the space above [the other pipes sitting directly on the chest], as is the case in the Mittelwerk of the organ in the Augustinerkirche at Erfurt. If height is lacking, the instrument should be given its proper width insofar as possible, but the large pipes should be placed inside the case, since there the tall feet that are needed for purposes of display are not necessary, as they are in the façade. When they are inside the case the pipes can also be mitered. This is a shortcoming, to be sure, but one must sometimes make a virtue of necessity. Another solution to this problem is to hang the pipes downward, which can most conveniently be accomplished if the largest stop is on the edge of the windchest, either in back or in front; then [the largest stop] may be constructed thus;

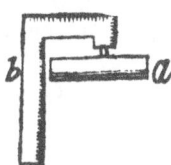

Here the windchest is *a*, and the pipe *b* hangs down behind it. This does not look very elegant, of course, but what else is there to do if space is lacking? In his *Beschreibung der Weißenfelsischen Orgel*, p. 13, Trost reports that the 3 largest pipes of the Subbass there are turned upside down* and hung downward.

---

* i.e., twice mitered, as in the diagram above.

§. 266.

Wo nur ein Clavier ist, wird die Disposition eben so gemacht; nur daß das Musicirgedackt nicht vergessen wird, und die Quintatön 8'. Kann man nun dabey nicht Principal 8' im Manuale haben; so suche man doch die Oktave 8', nebst dem Subbasse 16' im Pedale anzubringen. Wo drey Claviere gemacht werden, da wird eins das Hauptwerk, in welchem man die Stimmen nach §. 261 und 262. ordnen kann. Das andere wird entweder 8= oder 4füßig. Wenn jenes ist, so ist es gut in der Musik zu gebrauchen, indem man auf dem Werke präambulirt, auf dem andern Claviere aber die Baßnoten spielt, auf dem dritten, dahin das Musicirgedackt zu stehen kommt, die Accorde. In das mittlere Werk können auch die vorigen schärfenden Stimmen gesetzt werden, wenn man will: man kann aber auch andere hineinbringen, die wir sonst unter die unnöthigen zählen. Zuweilen sind beyde Arten da; zuweilen nur eine. Doch pflegt man es so scharf nicht zu machen, als das Hauptwerk, weil es wenig Nutzen hätte. Was aber noch für Register dahin können gesetzt werden, die kann man aus dem 7ten Kapitel suchen. Wenn diese 2 größten Claviere scharf werden; so kommt eins oben, das andere in die Mitte, daß man sie koppeln kann: wird aber das andere nicht scharf; so wird etwan das dritte scharf, und alsdann wird dieses zum Hauptmanual gesetzt, daß man sie koppeln kann. Das Principal des letztern wird eine Oktave höher, als die vorigen beyde, weil es eben nicht nöthig, 3 Principale, einer Größe zu haben. Ist etwan das erste und andere Clavier 8'; so wird dies 4'. Wird das erste 8', das andere 4', so wird das dritte 2'. Wird aber das erste 16'; so wird das andere 8', und das dritte 8' oder 4'. Drey Claviere sind ziemlich oft anzutreffen, und wird man im folgenden unterschiedliche Dispositiones von dergleichen Orgeln antreffen. Z. Ex. zu Naumburg in der Wenceslaikirche, §. 310. Zun Augustinern in Erfurt, §. 289. Zu Gera, §. 301. Zu Görlitz, §. 301. Zu Jena, §. 302. Zu Langensalza, §. 307. Zu Magdeburg, §. 308. Zu Reval, § 313. Ohne die vielen Orgeln mit 3 Clavieren, welche Mattheson und Prätorius recensiret. Die kann man zum Muster sich vorstellen, und alles richtig überlegen, so wird man finden, was gut sey, oder nicht. Soll man die Disposition auf 4 Claviere richten; so ist eben das zu observiren, und kann man die Stimmen ordnen, wie man will, wenn nur die 2 schärfsten Claviere des Koppelns wegen oben an einander stehen. Vier Claviere sind schon rar. Ich habe dergleichen zu Eisenach angeführet §. 288.; und zu Merseburg §. 309. Sonst hat Mattheson dergleichen Werke mit 4 Clavieren zu Hamburg angeführet zu St. Nikolai; it. zu St. Jakobi; zu St. Catharinen, welche eins 16' hat, die andern alle 8'; zu St. Petri daselbst. Zu St. Dominico in Prag ist dergleichen auch. Man siehet leicht, daß alsdann viel Stimmen erfordert werden. Daher kömmt, daß solche Orgelwerke 40, 50, 60, 70. und wol noch mehrere Stimmen haben.

§. 267.

Ob es nun zwar eins ist, aus den unnöthigen Stimmen zu wählen, welche man will, indem einer diese, der andere jene liebt: denn einer hat gerne Schnarrwerke;

ein

§. 266.

Where there is only one manual, the stoplist should be drawn up in just the same way, except that the figured-bass Gedackt should not be forgotten, and* the Quintatön 8′. If it proves impossible to have a Principal 8′ in the manual, then one should at least try to include an Oktave 8′ along with the Subbass 16′ in the pedal. Where three manuals are built, one will be the Hauptwerk, in which the stops may be arranged according to §.261 and 262. The second [manual] will be [based] either on an 8′ or 4′ [Principal]. When it has a [Principal] 8′, then this is of good use in ensemble music, since the organist plays a prelude on the Werk [plenum]; then [he plays] the bass line on the second keyboard, while playing the chords on the third, where the figured-bass Gedackt is located.† The intensifying stops mentioned above may also be placed in the middle division‡ if desired; but other stops may also be included, ones that we have otherwise assigned to the [category of] unnecessary [stops]. Sometimes both of these types [of stops§] are present, sometimes only one. Yet it is customary to make it less intense than the Hauptwerk, since it would be less useful. As to which stops to put on it, they may be chosen from Chapter 7. If these two largest manuals are [both] made loud, then one is placed on top and the other in the middle so that they may be coupled.¶ If however the second [manual] is not made loud, then perhaps the third will be; then the latter is placed next to the primary manual so that they may be coupled.‖ The Principal of the last manual will be an octave higher than the previous two, since it is unnecessary to have 3 Principals of the same size. If the first and second manuals have, say, 8′, then the third will be a 4′. If the first is an 8′ and the second a 4′, then the third will be a 2′. If however the first is a 16′, then the second will be an 8′ and the third 8′ or 4′. Three manuals are encountered rather frequently, and in the following [pages] one will find various stoplists of such organs: e.g., in the Wenzelskirche in Naumburg, §.310; at the Augustinerkirche in Erfurt, §.289; at Gera, §.301; at Görlitz, §.301; at Jena, §.302; at Langensalza, §.307; at Magdeburg, §.308; and at Reval, §.313; not to mention the many organs with 3 manuals that [both] Mattheson and Praetorius have published.** These may be taken as models and pondered thoroughly; they will reveal what is good and what is not. If the stoplist is drawn up with 4 manuals, the same [principles] are to be observed. The stops may be arranged at will, as long as the two loudest manuals lie one atop the other for the purpose of coupling. Four keyboards are indeed rare. I have cited one at Eisenach,†† §.288, and at Merseburg, §.309. Mattheson has also cited similar instruments with 4 keyboards in Hamburg at St. Nikolai, St. Jakobi and St. Catharinen, [all of] which have one 16′ [division] and all the others 8′; likewise at St. Petri there.‡‡ There is also one at St. Dominicus in Prague. It is easy to see that many stops are then required; this is why such organs have 40, 50, 60, 70 or even more stops.

§. 267.

Although one may choose whatever unnecessary stops one wishes, since some prefer this and others that (one prefers reeds, another Hohlflötes, a third Spitzflötes,

---

* Perhaps this "and" should be understood as "or"; see §.263.

† cf. §.235 and §.259.

‡ i.e., the second manual.

§ i.e., intensifying and unnecessary.

¶ Adlung is speaking not of the position of the chests, but of the arrangement of the keyboards.

‖ Adlung is presuming the likelihood that only two manuals can be coupled. In his time, coupling three manuals was still unusual enough for him to make particular mention of this feature in the stoplist.

** See the alphabetical collection of stoplists beginning in Chapter 10, §. 284.

†† See Chap. 2, §.21 and note 22.

‡‡ This organ is listed as having two 16′ divisions and two 8′.

Kap. X.   Von der Disposition.   187

ein anderer Hohlflöten; ein anderer Spitzflöten, ꝛc.; so wollte ich doch nicht rathen, allzuviel Schnarrwerke in eine Orgel zu setzen, wegen der gräulichen Arbeit, die deren Stimmung verursacht: und wo nicht rechte fleißige Organisten sind, da sind sie fast nichts nütze, und kosten doch viel Geld. Siehe *Prätorii* Synt. T. II. p. 194. In der Grüningischen Orgel sind 14 Schnarrwerke, die können einem Organisten den Kopf zu Zeiten warm machen.

(**) In der St. Catharinenkirchenorgel in Hamburg sind gar 16 Rohrwerke. Der seel. Capelmeister, Hr. J. S. Bach in Leipzig, welcher sich einsmals 2 Stunden lang auf diesem, wie er sagte, in allen Stücken vortrefflichen Werke hat hören lassen, konnte die Schönheit und Verschiedenheit des Klanges dieser Rohrwerke nicht genug rühmen. Man weis auch, daß der ehmalige berühmte Organist an dieser Kirche, Hr. Johann Adam Reinken, sie beständig selbst in der besten Stimmung erhalten hat. In den großen Orgeln in Frankreich sind auch sehr viele Rohrwerke.

§. 268.

Dieses könnte genug seyn. Doch will ich zur Curiösität noch etliches berühren. Ich habe oben folgende Stimmen ins Pedal gesetzt: Subbaß 32' oder 16', oder beyde; Principal 32' oder 16', oder beyde; Oktave 8' und 4'; Violon 16'; zu diesen können aus dem vorhergehenden 7ten Kapitel noch viel Stimmen ins Pedal ausgesetzt werden, als: Bauerflöte, Schnarrwerke, sonderlich Posaune 16' oder 32', oder beyde; Trompete 16', oder 8'; Cornet; Regal; Waldflöte, ꝛc. Bey dem Subbasse 32' vergesse man ja Subbaß 16' nicht. Jener kann in geschwinden Noten nicht so gut gebraucht werden, als dieser; hat auch bey andern wenigen Stimmen weniger Kraft als 16', welcher in der Musik was vortrefliches ist. Principal 32' ist allzukostbar, und thut nicht eben gar zu große Dienste, und deswegen rathe ich nicht dazu. Zwar mögte jemand einwerfen: wenn gleichwol im Manuale 16' die Grundstimme wäre, wie denn oft Principal 16' vorkommt; so müßte ja wohl das Pedal eine Oktave tiefer gehen. Und dieses *dubium* schrieb ehemals ein gewisser Organist an Hr. Bachen in Jena, da er 2 Punkte von ihm wissen wollte, nemlich: 1) Ob die Eisenachische Orgel im Manuale 53 *clavos* und im Pedale 29 *clavos* habe? (Wenn er hätte *definiren* gelernet, hätte er *claves* gesagt; denn sonst wären es Nägel.) Und ob die Jenaische Orgel auch dergleichen habe? Das ist, daß das Manual bis ins $\bar{\bar{e}}$ und das Pedal bis ins $\bar{e}$ gienge. 2) Ob man im Pedale nothwendig 32' haben müsse, wenn im Manual 16' die Grundstimme wäre? Dies letztere suchte er zu behaupten: doch war die Raison nicht dabey. Ich glaube er habe gemeynet, das Pedal sey der Baß zu dem Manuale, und müsse also tiefer gehen. Ich will, um dem Argumente noch mehr Kraft zu geben, noch dazu thun, daß man zuweilen im Manuale tiefer spielt, als im Pedale: wo nun die Stimmen im Pedale nicht größer; so ists eben so viel, als habe man die *Palmulas* versetzt, daß der Baß der Tenor worden, der Tenor aber in der linken Hand ist zum Basse worden. Wir wissen aber, daß durch Versetzung der Stimmen, die vorher gut gewesene Sätze falsch werden können; also kann es auch hier geschehen. Was nun dies Argument betrifft; so ist es wahr, daß dadurch *vitiöse Progreßiones* entstehen können. Doch 1) kann durch ein ge-

Chap. X. Concerning the Stoplist

etc.), I would nevertheless advise against putting too many reeds into an organ because of the dreadful task of tuning them. If the organist is not very conscientious [in tuning them], then they are practically useless and cost a lot of money to boot; see Praetorius, *Syntagma* [*musicum*], Vol. II, p. 194. In the organ at Gröningen there are 14 reeds, enough to cause an organist at times to work up a sweat.(**)

(**) In the organ at the Catharinenkirche in Hamburg there are all of 16 reeds. The late Kapellmeister Mr. J. S. Bach in Leipzig, who once performed for two hours on this instrument which he proclaimed splendid in every way, could hardly praise highly enough the beauty and variety of sound made by those reeds. It is also known that the renowned organist of this church, Mr. Johann Adam Reinken (now deceased), always kept them in excellent tune. There are also many reeds in the large organs in France. [Agricola]

§. 268.

[What has been said up to this point] could suffice. Yet I will touch on several other points as curiosities. I have placed the following stops above in the pedal: Subbass 32′* or 16′ or both, Principal 32′ or 16′ or both, Oktave 8′ or 4′; Violon 16′. In addition to these, many other stops from Chapter 7 above could be placed in the pedal, such as: a Bauerflöte; reeds, especially a Posaune 16′ or 32′, or both; a Trompete 16′ or 8′; a Cornet; a Regal; a Waldflöte, etc. Do not forget to include a Subbass 16′ with the Subbass 32′; the latter cannot so readily be used in rapid passages as the former, and also has less power than the 16′ when playing with a few stops. The 16′ is a great benefit for ensemble music. A Principal 32′ is terribly expensive and is not of all that much use, and therefore I advise against it. Someone might object: if the foundation stop in the manual were a 16′ (for a 16′ Principal is often found), then the pedal must indeed play an octave lower. A certain organist once expressed this doubt in writing to Mr [Johann Nikolaus] Bach† in Jena, by questioning him about two particulars: 1) whether the organ at Eisenach had 53 keys (*clavos*) in the manual and 29 keys (*clavos*) in the pedal (if he had learned his [Latin] declensions he would have said *claves*; what he wrote means "nails"), and whether the organ at Jena has the same, i.e., the manuals extending up to e‴ and the pedal to e′; 2) whether it is necessary to have a 32′ in the pedal if the foundation tone in the manual is 16′. This latter [was the opinion] he was trying to assert, but he gave no reason for it. I think he meant that since the pedal provides the bass for the manual, it ought to play lower. To give this argument more force, I will add to it that at times one plays lower in the manual than in the pedal; were then the pedal stops not lower, it would be the same as inverting the notes so that the bass becomes the tenor while the tenor in the left hand becomes the bass.‡ We know that many previously acceptable passages can become unacceptable by inverting the voices, and thus it could happen in this instance. With regard to this argument, it is true that faulty progressions may arise in this way. Yet: 1) through clever playing the organist may indeed prepare himself to

* In §.261 above Adlung suggests omitting the 32′ Contrabass (i.e., Subbass), but there he may be thinking of a smaller organ.

† Johann Nikolaus Bach [1669-1753], a cousin of J. S. Bach, whom Adlung came to know during his student years in Jena; see Adlung's biography in the foreword to Vol. II, p. VI.

‡ This situation would create false relations between tenor and bass.

scheutes Spielen der Organist sich schon darnach richten, daß er in solchem Falle dergleichen Sätze erwähle, welche die Verkehrung der Stimmen leiden können. 2) Muß es ja nicht eben der Principalbaß 32' seyn, sondern der Subbaß 32' thut gleiche Dienste. 3) Werden ja die 32füßigen Stimmen wenig gehöret, wenn viele andere dabey sind. 4) Was soll denn endlich die Grundstimme 16' im Pedale seyn? Denn es kömmt nicht allein auf Principal 16' an; andere 16füßige Stimmen thun eben das, daß sie die Harmonie vertiefen, sonst müßte folgen, daß, so oft die Quintatön 16', oder Bordun 16', oder dergleichen Stimmen in einem Claviere sich fände, allezeit im Pedale 32' seyn müsse: jenes aber ist ordinär in 8füßigen Werken; also müßte auch dies allezeit geschehen. Das letzte aber will bis dato keiner sagen. Uebrigens mache ich aus Principal 16' im Manuale keinen Staat; genug, wenn es von solcher Größe einmal im Gesichte steht, so ist es Zierde genug. Nun fragt es sich: ob die schärfenden Stimmen im Pedale stehen sollen? Z. Er. die Cymbel, welche im Pedale auch wol Cymbelbaß heißt; die Mixtur; Rauschpfeife, welche alsdann auch Rauschpfeifenbaß genennet wied. So ist z. Er. Mixtur 4fach zu St. Wenceslai in Naumburg im Pedale; zu Görlitz ist sie 5fach, da auch im Pedale Scharp 2fach anzutreffen, ja es steht noch eine Mixtur 12fach im Pedale daselbst. Prätorius l. c. S. 234. daß in Lüneburg zu St. Lamprecht unter andern Pedalstimmen auch die Spitzquinte 3', Rauschpfeife, Zimbel und Mixtur sey. Ratio dubitandi, ob sie ins Pedal gehören, ist, weil es wider die Gravität des Basses, und schicke sich nicht, daß kleine Jungens den Baß mitsängen, s. Janowka in claue pag. 91. Und, ich halte es in dem Punkte mit ihm, zumal da ich nicht sehe, wozu es soll. Die vorigen Register haben force genug, daß man sie im vollen Werke hören kann, und das Gequickse geht so schön eben nicht im Pedale, zumal da die Quinten in der Tiefe gräulicher klingen, als in der Höhe. Will man aber ja scharfe Stimmen im Pedale haben; so kann ein Koppel die Manualstimmen herunter ins Pedal leiten, oder man kann die Stimmen absondern. Was brauchts der Kosten? Dafür kann man andere Stimmen setzen lassen.

§. 269.

Weil ich eben an das Pedalkoppel gedenke; so erinnere ich hieben, daß man sehr wohl thue, wenn man die Stimmen im Manuale nicht alsbald im Pedale mit gehen läßt; sondern man bringe sie lieber durch das Koppel ins Pedal, so kann man nach Belieben das Pedal verstärken wie man will, und kömmt nicht gleich jede quicksende Stimme ins Pedal. Man hat aber auch noch andere Koppel, da besondere Abstrakten nach den clauibus des untern Manuals gehen, und an dieselben angeschraubt sind, daß die palmulae durch das Pedal mit niedergezogen werden. Dadurch kann man auch den Baß verstärken. Doch wie gesagt, es ist selten nöthig, es sey denn, daß im Pedale entweder wegen Mangel des Raums, oder wegen Armuth der Kirchen, allzuwenig Stimmen haben können gesetzt werden. Das vorige Koppel aber gehet nach der Manuallade, und werden durch das Pedal die palmulae nicht mit niedergezogen. In alten kleinen

Werken

seek out in such cases those passages that can allow the inversion of voices;* 2) [the stop sounding an octave lower in the pedal] need not necessarily be a Principal 32′—a Subbass 32′ will serve just as well; 3) 32′ stops are little perceived when many other [stops] are sounding with them; 4) in the final analysis, what should the 16′ foundation stop in the pedal be? The Principal 16′ is not the only one [possible]; other 16′ stops do exactly the same thing by deepening the harmony. Thus it must follow that as long as there is a Quintatön or Bordun or some similar 16′ stop in the manual there must always be a 32′ in the pedal. [A 16′ Quintatön or Bordun] is common in 8′ divisions, and thus [a 32′] would always have to be drawn with it. Up to now, however, there is no one who has gone so far as to insist on this. Furthermore, a Principal 16′ in the manual is no great virtue; one [stop] of that size† standing in the façade is sufficient. Now the question arises, should there be brilliant stops in the pedal, e.g., a Cymbel (which in the pedal would actually be called "Cymbelbass"), a Mixtur or a Rauschpfeife (which would then be called Rauschpfeifenbass)? Thus for example there is a 4-rank Mixtur in the pedal at St. Wenceslaus in Naumburg; at Görlitz there is one of 5 ranks, together with a pedal Scharp 2 ranks, and yet another Mixtur of 12 ranks. Praetorius, *l.c.*, p. 234, [records] that among other pedal stops at St. Lamprecht in Lüneburg are a Spitzquinte 3′, Rauschpfeife, Zimbel and Mixtur. The reason for doubting whether they belong in the pedal is because they detract from the gravity of the bass; it is not becoming that little boys should sing along with the bass; see Janowka's *Clavis*, p. 91.‡ I concur with him in this matter, especially since I do not see what purpose they serve. The other stops have sufficient force to be heard in the plenum, and the squeaking does not sound at all well in the pedal, especially since the Quints sound more strident in the bass than in the higher range. If brilliant stops are desired in the pedal, then the manual stops may be coupled down to the pedal, or the stops may be borrowed. Why spend the money when it can be used to build other stops.

* Adlung presumes that the organist will be improvising.

† i.e., the pedal Principal 16′.

‡ Janowka says, "Since the cymbel and mixture, however, do not provide a grave sound suitable for a foundation or basis, not everyone approves of them in the pedal."

§. 269.

While I am speaking about the pedal coupler, let me mention that it would be a very good idea not to have the manual stops play automatically in the pedal,§ but rather to bring them to the pedal by means of a coupler, so that one can choose when to reinforce the pedal, and every squeaking stop does not automatically sound in the pedal. There are other types of couplers besides those in which separate trackers are run [from the pedals] to the keys of the lower manual and are screwed to them, so that the keys move up and down with the pedals. This is indeed a way to reinforce the bass. But as I have already said, it is seldom necessary unless it has been impossible to put enough stops in the pedal, either because of lack of space or the church's financial restraints. The previous coupler¶ proceeds to the manual windchest, and the [manual] keys are not drawn down by the pedal.‖ In old, small instruments there is often no pedal

§ i.e., by coupling the manual to the pedal permanently.

¶ i.e., the one Adlung writes about above, saying that "one can choose when to reinforce the pedal."

‖ Adlung is referring to the "Windkoppel"; each pipe or note of the stops that do double duty is provided with two pallet boxes (for manual and pedal), and has two stopknobs (manual and pedal).

Kap. X. Von der Disposition. 189

Werken ist oft kein Pedal; da kann man, um das Spielen zu erleichtern ein solch Pedal anhängen, dadurch das Clavier niedergezogen wird, obschon kein besonderer Baß da ist.

§. 270.

Es sagt ferner Niedt im zweyten Theile der Variation des Generalbasses, im 12ten Kapitel, wenn der Posaunenbaß 32' sey müsse die Trompete 16' und die Schallmey 8' seyn: wäre hingegen der erste 16', so müsse jene 8' und diese 4' seyn. Es fragt sich: was hiervon zu halten? Antwort: Wenn man supponirt, daß in der Trompete 16' und Posaune 16' die Körper gleich groß sind, und die Blätter der Mundstücke auch gleich; so wird auch der Klang wenig von einander unterschieden seyn: folglich wäre eins von beyden unnöthig. Allein da in der Trompete 16' die Körper kleiner, und zumal etwas enger, gemacht werden, als in der Posaune 16'; so können sie wol einerley Tiefe haben, und doch zweyerley Art oder Klanges seyn, weil die Posaune mehr donnern und völliger klingen wird, als die Trompete; auch werden die Blätter in dieser so stark nicht gemacht, als in jener. Auf solche Weise ist es nicht absurd, Posaune 16' und Trompete 16' in ein Pedal zu bringen. Und eben so könnte auch wol die Trompete 8' und Schallmey 8' beysammen stehen, mit verschiedenen Körpern und Blättern; denn wie sich die Trompete zur Posaune gleiches Tons verhält, so verhält sich die Schallmey zur Trompete gleiches Tons. Und so trägt es Prätorius vor Tom. II. Part. IV. pag. 142.: aber er redet von der Mensur, daß Trompet 16' und Posaune 16', imgleichen Trompete 8', Schallmey 8' und Posaune 8'', wie auch Trompete 4' und Schallmey 4' nicht sollen einerley Mensur oder Größe der Körper haben. Das muß man also nicht unrecht verstehen. Niedt hat Prätorium nicht recht verstanden: denn die Tiefe dependirt nicht von der Größe der Körper allein. Man findet also diese Stimmen in einem Claviere oder Pedale oft beysammen von einerley Größe, was den Ton anlangt. Z. Ex. zu Königsberg im Kneiphofe ist im Pedale Posaune 16' und 8'. Item Trompete 8'.

§. 271.

Ferner bey Gelegenheit der Posaune 16' und 8' beysammen, merke ich an, daß in vielen Dispositionen eine Stimme vielmal stehe von verschiedener Größe, entweder in einem Claviere, oder in verschiedenen. Wo es die Kosten leiden, kann man es auch theils der Stärke, theils der Veränderung wegen, wohl thun. Z. Ex. im Dom zu Bremen ist Posaune 32' und 16', wie auch zu St. Johannis in Lüneburg. Mehrere Exempel wird man in den bald folgenden Dispositionen anmerken.

§. 272.

Ja man hat oft ein Register zweymal in einem Claviere von einerley Größe und Ton, doch von verschiedener Intonation. Weite und Materie. So ist z. Ex. in der Schloßkirche in Dresden Principal 8' von Metall, und noch lieblich Principal 8' von Holz in einem Claviere; in der Altstädtischen Orgel in der Lutherischen Kirche in Elbingen ist

[division]; in that case to make playing easier a pedal[board] may be appended that draws down the keys,* even though no separate pedal stops are there.

§. 270.

Furthermore, in the second part of his [*Musicalische Handleitung*†], Chap. 12,‡ Niedt says that if the Posaunenbass is 32', the Trompete must be 16' and the Schallmey 8'; if on the other hand the [Posaunenbass] is 16', then the Trompete must be 8' and the Schallmey 4'. The question arises, is this to be believed? The answer: if it is presupposed that the resonators of the Trompete 16' and Posaune 16' are of the same size, and that the tongues on the shallots are also identical, then their tone would differ very little, and consequently one of each would be unnecessary. But since the resonators of the Trompete 16' are made smaller and in particular somewhat narrower than those of the Posaune 16', it is quite possible that they could be of the same size and still have distinct tonal characteristics, since the Posaune has a fuller and more thundering sound than the Trompete and the tongues of the latter are not made as heavy as those of the former. For this reason it is not ridiculous to have a Posaune 16' and Trompete 16' in the same pedal [division]. And in the same way the Trompete 8' and Schallmey 8' could well appear together [in the same pedal division] with different resonators and tongues, for as the Trompete is related to the Posaune of the same pitch, so is the Schallmey related to the Trompete of the same pitch.§ Praetorius says the same thing in Vol. II, Part IV, p. 142, but he expresses it in terms of scaling, saying that the Trompete 16' and Posaune 16', the Trompete 8', Schallmey 8' and Posaune 8', and the Trompete 4' and Schallmey 4' should not have the same scale or resonator size. One must not understand this incorrectly. Niedt did not understand Praetorius correctly.¶ Low pitch does not depend on resonator size alone. Thus these stops are often found at the same pitch in the same manual or pedal [division]; e.g., in the Kneiphofkirche at Königsberg in the pedal there is a Posaune 16' and 8' as well as a Trompete 8'.

§. 271.

Since I have just mentioned a Posaune 16' and 8' together, let me note further that in many stoplists the same stop appears multiple times at various pitches, either in the same manual or in different ones. If money allows, this may well be done, both for the sake of volume and for variety. E.g., in the Cathedral at Bremen as well as at St. Johannis in Lüneburg there is a Posaune at 32' and 16'. Several examples [of this] may be noted in the stoplists soon to follow.

§. 272.

Indeed, the same stop often appears twice in the same manual at the same pitch, but with different voicing, scale and material. Thus in the Dresden palace church, e.g., there is a Principal 8' of metal and also a Lieblich Principal 8' of wood, both on the same manual, and in the Altstädtische organ of the Lutheran Church in Elbingen there

* This is the permanent coupler Adlung has censured at the beginning of this paragraph.

† Adlung writes "Variation des Generalbasses"; this is the title of the second part of Niedt's *Musicalische Handleitung*.

‡ The passage Adlung is referring to is on p. 114 of the 1721 edition of this publication (edited by Johann Mattheson); p. 114 is in Chapter 10, not Chapter 12. In the first edition (1706), however, Chapter 12 is essentially the same as Chapter 10 of the second edition. Other citations from this source seem to indicate that Adlung was working from the 1721 edition (e.g., the 1706 edition had no organ stoplists); but it is possible that at this point in writing his treatise he had access to the first edition.

§ i.e., a Schallmey has a smaller, narrower resonator and a thinner tongue than a Trompete, just as a Trompete has a smaller, narrower resonator and a thinner tongue than a Posaune.

¶ Praetorius writes that if these stops appear at the same pitch, they must have different scales and resonator sizes. Niedt misunderstood Praetorius and thought he was asserting that these stops must not appear at the same pitch.

190   Kap. X. Von der Disposition.

Principal 8′ von Metall und 8′ von Holz, it. Oktave 4′ von Metall und 4′ von Holz, alles in einem Claviere. Hat man aber in zweyerley Clavieren einerley Register einer Größe; so ists kein Wunder, und ist fast allerwegen also zu finden. Zuweilen ist in den Clavieren einerley Mensur oder Weite behalten; zuweilen aber hat man in einem Claviere die weite Mensur, im andern die enge, daher, ob man schon einerley Stimmen in beyden ziehet, der Klang doch verschiedentlich ist. Ex hoc capite wird die Görlitzer Orgel gelobet, als darinne das Hauptwerk prächtig klingt, weil das Principal, und alle Stimmen, so Principalmensur lieben, weite Mensur hat; das Oberwerk klingt sehr spitzig und scharf, wegen der engen Mensur. Dies kann man merken, und bey Gelegenheit dergleichen auch angeben. **) Die weite Mensur klinget allezeit völliger, daher man sie zum Hauptwerke behält; widrigen Falls hat das Werk seine Gravität und force nicht, wie man in der Lutherischen Augustinerorgel zu Erfurt wahr nimmt.

(**) Die Orgeln von Silbermann, Friderici und Hildebrand ꝛc. sind alle so eingerichtet.

§. 273.

Die gemischten Stimmen nehme man immer fein vielfach, wenn es die Gelder verstatten; auch nicht so gar klein. Z. Er. die Sesquialter ordne man 3fach, daß die Oktave 4′ dabey ist bey der Quinte 3′ und Terz über 2′. Wollte einer sagen, daß man die Oktave könne dazu ziehen, und man deren nicht brauche, weil Aequalstimmen nicht schärften: dem dient zur Antwort, daß man sodann des vielen Registerziehens entübriget seyn könne, wenn die Sesquialter allein zu gebrauchen. Daß aber Aequalstimmen die Harmonie verstärken, ist §. 233. zur Gnüge bewiesen. Die Cymbel 3fach ist am besten zu brauchen. Die Mixtur kann nach Beschaffenheit der Kirche und deren Größe, auch nach Beschaffenheit der andern Stimmen 4: 5: oder 6fach seyn. Stärker achte ich sie nicht für nöthig, zumal wo man die Claviere koppeln kann. Auch haben die gar zu starken Mixturen selten Wind genug, und schärfen daher oft kaum so viel als eine andere. So habe ich z. Er. an der 10fachen Mixtur zu Naumburg in der Kirche zu St. Wenceslai, in der vorigen Orgel, nichts besonders schärfendes gefunden. Der Organist gab die Schuld dem, daß sie nur 2füßig sey: aber das macht es wol nicht aus; denn so wäre die Oktave 4′ und etwan Quinte 3′ noch dazu kommen. Gesetzt nun, man zöge sie dazu, etwan durch Koppelung zweyer Claviere; so würde sie doch kaum den Effekt haben, den ich bey kleinern Mixturen observirt. Ja wenn man allen Pfeifen satt Wind schaffte: aber so setzt man sie alle zusammen, und macht durch die Parallele ein einziges Loch, dadurch alle Pfeifen zugleich angeblasen werden: Wenn ich nun das Loch ausrechne gegen andere; so ist es ordentlich viel zu klein. So ließe ich es gelten: wenn zu jeder Pfeife im Stocke ein Loch durchgebohrt würde, und auch so viel Löcher in der Cancelle und Parallele neben einander in der Breite. Man müßte aber diese Mixturparallelen breiter machen, als die andern, so bekäme jede Pfeife den gehörigen Wind, der sonst oft mangelt, zumal wenn die Grade des Windes wenig sind. Ja, sagt man, wäre der Wind nicht zulänglich; so gienge die Mixtur nicht reine, sondern faul und zu tief:

is a Principal 8' of metal and also one at 8' of wood, as well as an Oktave 4' of metal and another at 4' of wood, all on the same manual. It is no surprise to find the same stop at the same pitch in two different manuals; this may be found almost everywhere. Sometimes the same scale is maintained throughout all keyboards; but at other times one keyboard is of wide scale while the other is of narrow scale, and therefore even though the identical stops are drawn in both, their sound is different. For this reason the Görlitz organ is praised: its Hauptwerk sounds broad and grand because its Principal and all the [other] stops of principal scale are wide-scaled, while the Oberwerk sounds very acute and penetrating due to its narrow scale.* One may take note of this and specify this† when the opportunity arises.(**) A wide scale always sounds fuller and thus should be preserved for the Hauptwerk; otherwise the instrument will have no gravity and power, as may be observed in the organ of the Lutheran Augustinerkirche at Erfurt.

* Boxberg, *Beschreibung der Görlitzer Orgel*, p.[11].
† in an organ contract.

(**) The organs of Silbermann, Friderici and Hildebrandt, etc., are all constructed like this. [Agricola]

§. 273.

The compound stops should always be built with a generous number of ranks if money permits, and not be so very small. E.g., the Sesquialter should be specified as 3 ranks, so that the Oktave 4' is in it along with the Quinte 3' and the Terz above 2' [i.e., $1\,3/5'$]. If anyone should say that an Oktave [4'] may be drawn with [the Sesquialter] and that [the Oktave 4' within the Sesquialter] is unnecessary since multiple stops at the same pitch do not provide added intensity, let the following answer suffice: the organist may be spared so much stop-pulling if the Sesquialter may be used alone. It has been sufficiently proved in §.233, however, that stops of the same pitch do strengthen the ensemble. Three ranks is the best choice for a Cymbel. A Mixtur may be 4, 5 or 6 ranks, according to the characteristics of the church and its size, and also according to the character of the other stops. I consider it unnecessary to make it any stronger,‡ especially if the manuals can be coupled. In addition, over-large mixtures seldom have ample wind, and therefore provide no more brilliance than another [of smaller size]. Thus I have found, for example, that the 10-rank Mixtur in the previous organ§ in St. Wenceslaus Church at Naumburg does not add any particular brilliance. The organist [there] blamed this on its beginning only at 2', but that is not the reason for it, for then the Oktave 4' and perhaps the Quinte 3' might be added to it. Supposing now that these had been added to it, perhaps by coupling two keyboards together—they [all] would not have anywhere near the effect that I have observed in smaller mixtures. Everything is fine if the pipes are provided with ample wind; but [builders] put all [the pipes belonging to a given note] together and bore a single hole through the slider through which all the pipes are blown at the same time. When I compare this hole against others,¶ [I find that] it is ordinarily much too small. Thus it would be best in my opinion to bore a [separate] hole in the toeboard for each pipe, and also [to bore] the same number of holes across the breadth of the wind channels and sliders. Such mixture-sliders, however, must be made broader than other [sliders]; then each pipe would get ample wind, wind that is otherwise often lacking, especially if the wind pressure is low. Yes, one might say, but if the wind were not adequate the Mixtur would

‡ i.e., to provide it with any more ranks.

§ i.e., the instrument build by Thayssner in 1700. In §.310 below Adlung notes that this organ was in all respects substandard and had to be rebuilt by Hildebrandt in 1743-46; only the case could be retained.

¶ presumably those that serve a single pipe.

Kap. X. Von der Disposition. 191

tief: das findet sich aber nicht. Antwort: das kann sich nicht finden, weil nach diesem schwachen Winde das Pfeifwerk auch eingestimmet wird. Wenn Oktave 4′ und die Sesquialter auch mit Oktave 4′ da ist; so achte ich es vor desto unnöthiger die Mixtur 4füßig zu machen. Hat man eine starke Mixtur; so kann man auch wol die Quinten daraus in der Tiefe weglassen, daß sie im Pedale nicht gehöret werden, weil sie in der Tiefe ohne dies sehr widrig klingen, und über dieses die Quinte noch besonders ist, auch in der Sesquialter, Rauschpfeife, u. d. gl. die Quinte mit begriffen ist. Daher hatten wir oben §. 167. oft die Mixtur 6: 7: auch 8fach. Das ist, unten ist sie 6fach, hernach in der Mitte 7fach, oben 8fach, und so im übrigen. So führt Prätorius an, daß im Kloster zu Riddagshausen die Mixtur unten 4fach, mitten 6fach, oben 8fach sey, da er also diese Sache ohngefehr erkläret.

§. 274.

Weil wir eben von Quinten reden; so merke ich an, daß etliche sie unverständig hinsetzen: andere aber sie allzusehr meiden. Das Pricipal muß freylich um ein merkliches größer seyn, als die Quinte, damit diese besser bedeckt werde: und wenn das Principal viel größer ist; so sind auch mehr Oktavstimmen da, die sie decken helfen. Also wäre es zu hart, bey Principal 8′ die große Quinte 6′, gleich weit und offen, zu setzen: denn sie ist zu widrig, und in der Tiefe ist stefast nicht zu erleiden. Daher macht man sie bey uns ordentlich oben spitzig zu, daß sie als halb gedeckt etwas stiller gehe. Die Quinte 3′ ist zu Principal 8′ recht; denn so hat man folgende Oktavstimmen, die sie decken: 1) Principal 8′; 2) Oktave 4′; 3) Oktave 2′; 4) Bordun oder Gedackt; 5) drey oder mehr Oktaven in der Mixtur. ꝛc. Zum Principal 4′ ist die Quinte 3′ etwas zu groß, zumal wenn sie offen, und oben nicht spitzig zulaufend, gemacht ist; obschon Werkmeister in Organo grüningensi es für eine Faute achtet, daß daselbst im Rückpositiv, wo das Principal 4′ ist, keine Quinte 3′ gewesen, deswegen man sie noch anstatt der anderthalbfüßigen hineingesetzt. Ich habe solcher Dispositionen etliche gesehen, da bey Principal 4′ Quinte 3′ war, und in der Sesquialter noch einmal 3′, und noch Quinte 1½′, item die Quinte 2 mal in der Mixtur, auch in der Zimbel. Die Quintatön hält auch die Quinte mit in sich; was ist das für ein Klang? Und bey allen den Quinten waren kaum etliche Oktavstimmen, als Principal 4′, Oktave 2′, und Gedackt oder Quintatön 8′, und noch 2 Oktaven in der Mixtur. Andere werfen die Quinten mehr weg, als es nöthig. So wollen manche die Spitzquinte 6′ nicht leiden bey Principal 8′: da kann sie aber wol bleiben. So ist auch im Kneiphofe zu Königsberg ein Werk mit 59 Stimmen, (**) und ist Principal 8′, da; doch ist im ganzen Werke keine Quinte 3′, vielweniger 6′. Wollte einer hier die Frage aufwerfen: warum man hier Quinten sollte einrücken, welche doch sonst in der Harmonie verboten? dem dient zur Antwort, daß davon etwas im 28sten Kapitel dieses Werks zu reden seyn wird.

(**) Der Hr. Verfasser redet von dem vorigen.

§. 275.

not sound in tune, but off-pitch and too low; but this is not the case. The answer? This cannot be the case, because the pipes [of the Mixtur] are tuned according to this weak wind. If the Oktave 4' and the Sesquialter with its own Oktave 4' are present, I consider it all the more unnecessary to make the Mixtur begin at 4'. If the Mixtur is strong, the fifths [in it] may readily be omitted in the lower register so that they will not be heard in the pedal,* because they sound more unpleasant in the lower register anyway, and furthermore there is a separate Quinte [stop] as well as a quint included in the Sesquialter, the Rauschpfeife and such. Therefore in §.167 above mixtures were often seen with 6-7-8 ranks: that is, in the lower register it is 6 ranks, in the middle 7 ranks, and on top 8 ranks, and thus it goes with other [similar examples]. Praetorius states that the Mixtur in the Klosterkirche at Riddagshausen is 4 ranks down low, 6 ranks in the middle and 8 ranks on top, thus explaining this matter in an indirect way.

* i.e., if the manual is coupled to the pedal, or if the Mixtur appears on separate stopknobs in both manual and pedal.

§. 274.

While we are speaking about Quints, let me mention that some call for them unwisely, while others avoid them too frequently. The Principal must of course be at a considerably lower pitch than the Quinte so that the latter may be better absorbed; and if the Principal is much lower, then there are also several octave ranks present to help absorb it. Thus it would be too harsh to put a low Quinte 6', cylindrical and open, with the Principal 8', since it is too grating and almost unbearable in the low register. Therefore it is normal in these parts to make [6' Quinte stops] conical, so that they are half-stopped and thus somewhat quieter. A Quinte 3' is proper for a Principal 8'; then there are the following Oktave stops to absorb it: 1) Principal 8'; 2) Oktave 4'; Oktave 2'; Bordun or Gedackt [16'?]; three or more Oktaves in the Mixtur. For a Principal 4', a Quinte 3' is somewhat too low, especially if it is made open and cylindrical, although Werkmeister in his *Organum gruningense*,† considers it a fault that in the Rückpositiv [at Gröningen], which is based on a Principal 4', there is no Quinte 3'; therefore [he says that the Quinte 3'] should have been put into [the organ] instead of the 1½'. I have seen a number of stoplists like this, in which a Quinte 3' was put with a Principal 4'; in the Sesquialter there was another 3', and then a Quinte 1½' on top of these. There were likewise two Quints in the Mixtur, and also in the Zimbel. The Quintatön also produces a Quint as part of its timbre. Now what kind of a sound would that make? And with all of these Quints there were hardly any octave-sounding stops such as Principal 4', Oktave 2', Gedackt or Quintatön 8' or 2 Oktaves in the Mixtur. Others [on the other hand] reject Quinte stops more than is necessary. Many would not allow a Spitzquinte 6' with a Principal 8', but this is quite acceptable. Thus there is an instrument in the Kneiphofkirche at Königsberg with 59 stops,(**) based on an 8' Principal, yet there is not a single Quinte 3' in the entire organ, much less a 6'. If anyone should raise the question why Quints should be put into [an organ] that are otherwise forbidden by the rules of harmony,‡ let him be advised that there will be something to read about this subject in Chapter 28 of this treatise.§

† §.28.

‡ i.e., they produce parallel fifths against the octave-speaking stops.

§ See Vol. II, pp. 177-79. Adlung has already written something about this matter in §.216.

¶ See the collection of stoplists at the end of Chapter 10, under "Königsberg."

(**) The author is speaking about the previous [organ there¶]. [Agricola]

§. 275.

Weil es gar zu was schönes ist um ein 8füßiges Principal, und die Kosten doch zuweilen es nicht gestatten, dergleichen zu machen; so lasse man doch wenigstens ein hölzernes 8′ verfertigen, und setze es inwendig, welches am Klange dem metallenen zwar nicht gleich kömmt; doch thut es gute Dienste und kostet nicht viel, zumal wenn man es durch einen besondern Zug ins Pedal bringt; denn auf solche Weise hat man nicht nöthig im Pedale eine besondere Oktave zu machen. Also halte ich es für eine Faute, wenn in der Orgel zu Büseleben (ist ein Dorf ohnweit Erfurt) im Manuale nur Principal 4′ steht, im Pedale aber Principal 8′ von Zinn im Gesichte, s. davon §. 286. Der die Disposition gemacht, hätte ja 8′ sollen ins Manual setzen: im Pedale wäre eine hölzerne Oktave gut genug gewesen. Oder man hätte es durch 2 Züge im Manuale und Pedale besonders brauchbar gemacht, und zwar mit eben den Kosten. Im Nothfalle hätte ja auch die Oktave 4′, die bey der Sesquialter 3fach ist, dafür wegbleiben können, weil Principal 4′ schon da war. Ja sagst du: wo Principal 8′ ist, da muß Quintaton oder Bordun 16′ seyn? Antwort: Wo stehet das geschrieben? Wenn man es nicht haben kann, muß es ja eben nicht so seyn. Mit dem 8füßigen Register hätte man im Choralen und Generalbasse die Stärke und Tiefe bekommen.

§. 276.

Für arme Kirchen wird ohnedies als ein großer Vortheil recommendirt, daß in der Disposition etliche Stimmen durch zweyerley Züge ins Pedal und Manual gebracht werden. Denn ob man zwar alle Stimmen der Manuallade mit dem Pedale durch das Koppel verknüpfen kann, oder sie sind auch ohne Koppel an das Pedal verbunden, daß sie nicht können abgesondert werden: so hat doch dies viel incommoda bey sich, und man kann nicht die nöthigen Veränderungen haben, sondern alles gequickse ist gleich mit im Pedale. Aber wenn zu denen Stimmen, die man aus dem Manuale gern im Pedal hätte, doppelte Züge gemacht werden, kan man alle Veränderungen machen, die man wünscht. Z. Ex. in der Orgel zu St. Michaelis in Erfurt ist Principal 8′, aber kein Gedackt oder Quintatön 16′. Um nun diesem Mangel abzuhelfen, hat man den Subbaß 16′ durch einen besondern Zug ins Manual gebracht. Eben die Pfeifen, welche im Pedale den Subbaß 16′ ausmachen, die machen im Manuale das Gedackt 16′ aus. Ziehe ich den einen Zug, wo Subbaß daran steht; so geht es nur im Pedale allein: ziehe ich den andern Zug, wo Gedackt 16′ daran steht; so geht es nur im Manuale; zieht man beyde; so geht es im Manuale und Pedale zugleich. Solchergestalt hat man mit einem Gelde 2 Register. Doch muß der Subbaß etwas enge werden, daß im Manuale der Klang etwas lieblich heraus komme. Auch müssen solche abgesonderte Stimmen durchs ganze Manual geführet werden, obschon sonst im Pedale nur zwo Oktaven nöthig wären; doch die obern Oktaven kosten nicht viel. Zun Predigern in Erfurt ist Quintatön 16′ im Manual doppelt, und auch nur eine Stimme. Auch im Rückpositive stehen die Trompete 8′ und Schallmey 4′, so durch besondere Züge

§. 275.

Since there is something especially beautiful about an 8′ Principal and yet cost at times prohibits its being built, at least a wooden 8′ [Principal] should be built and placed inside the case. This does not measure up to the sound of a metal one, to be sure, yet it will provide good service and does not cost much. This is especially [true] if it is made available in the the pedal with a separate stopknob,* since in this way it is not necessary to make an independent Oktave [8′] in the pedal. I also consider it a fault that the organ at Büseleben (a village near Erfurt) has only a Principal 4′ in the manual, and yet a pedal Principal 8′ of tin in the façade; see §.286. The person who drew up the stoplist should have put the 8′ in the manual; a wooden Oktave would have sufficed for the pedal. Or it should have been made available separately in the manual and pedal on two drawknobs; the cost would have been the same. If necessary the Oktave 4′ that is part of the Sesquialter 3 ranks could have been omitted, since there was already a Principal 4′ present. Do I hear you saying, "Where there is a Principal 8′ there must also be a Quintatön or Bordun 16′?" I answer in return, "Where do you find that written?" If it is not possible to have [a 16′ in the manual], then that is how it has to be. An 8′ stop could provide the intensity and depth in chorales and figured bass.

* i.e., a Windkoppel; see §.269 above.

§. 276.

Moreover, it is recommended as a great advantage for poor churches that several stops in the stoplist be made available in the pedal and manual by means of two stopknobs.† For even though it is indeed possible to link all the stops on the manual chest with the pedal by means of a coupler, or to connect them permanently to the pedal without a coupler, yet these are attended by much inconvenience, and it is not possible to achieve the necessary variety, but rather all the little squeaking stops have to play along with the pedal. But if double stopknobs are made for those manual stops that are desirable for the pedal,‡ then it is possible to achieve all the variety one might desire. For example, in the organ at St. Michaelis in Erfurt there is a Principal 8′ [in the manual], but no Gedackt or Quintatön 16′. In order to remedy this deficiency the Subbass 16′ has been made available on a separate stopknob in the manual. The very same pipes that constitute the Pedal 16′ Subbass form the manual Gedackt 16′. If I draw the stopknob that bears the name "Subbass", it sounds only in the pedal; if I draw the other stopknob that says "Gedackt 16′", then it sounds only in the manual. If both stops are drawn, then it plays both in the manual and pedal. In this way 2 stops may be had for the price of one. The Subbass must be somewhat narrow-scaled, however, so that the sound is gentle enough for the manual. Such divided stops must be extended throughout the entire manual, even though only two octaves would otherwise be necessary for the pedal, but the upper octaves do not cost much. In the Predigerkirche at Erfurt there is a manual Quintatön 16′ that is doubled (doppelt§), but is only a single stop. In the Rückpositiv [of this organ] there stand a Trompete 8′ and Schallmey 4′ that may also be used in

† Ibid.

‡ In Adlung's view, the "desirable" stops are those that have weight and gravity; see §.268, as well as §.269 with accompanying notes.

§ Adlung's use of the word "doppelt" (doubled) is odd (cf. §.137), but both its context here as well as the stoplist (see the collection of stoplists later in Chapter 10, under "Erfurt") make it clear that the stop is "abgesondert", i.e., it also appears on a separate stopknob for the pedal.

Kap. X. Von der Disposition. 193

Züge auch ins Pedal gebracht werden können. Und dergleichen sind hin und wieder noch mehr. Zu St. Ulrich in Magdeburg sind etliche Stimmen halbirt, d. i. mit 2 Zügen versehen, z. Er. Posaune, Regal, Kleinschreyer. Sonst ist halbirt was anders. Werkmeister zwar in seiner Orgelprobe, Kap. 19. S. 42. hält es nicht für rathsam, weil es oft falsch klinge, sonderlich in Schnarrwerken, wenn der Zufall des Windes nicht gleich sey, oder wenn der Wind in den Winkeln sich stößt, oder von einem Orte weiter als vom andern zu der Pfeife geführt wird, und daher seine Aequalität verliert; ob es wol sonst für ein fein compendium hält in armen Kirchen: Allein es kann von dem Orgelmacher die nöthige Klugheit dabey schon gebraucht und alles accurat gemacht werden, so hat man keins zu besorgen, s. oben §. 130.

§. 277.

Wo es die Umstände leiden, kann man auch Kammerregister in die Orgel bringen, d. i. solche Register, welche 1 oder 1½ Ton tiefer gestimmt sind, als das Werk selbst, als welches, wie gebräuchlich, im Chortone stehen muß. Quaer. Warum dieses? Resp. Nicht des Fantasirens wegen: denn da mag ein Organist spielen woraus er will; auch nicht des Chorals wegen, weil es auch leicht ist, sie aus allerhand Tönen zu spielen: sondern der Musik wegen. Es geschiehet nämlich zuweilen daß ein Stück, welches z. Er. mit Waldhörnern aus dem d gesetzt ist, mit Trompeten soll gemacht werden; da müßte man entweder den Generalbaß anders abschreiben, und aus dem d ins c transponiren: oder der Organist müßte transponiren. Zu dem ersten hat man nicht allezeit Musse, und das andere kann nicht ein jeder Organist; In solchem Falle ist es gut, daß man Kammerregister habe, die 1 oder 1½ Ton tiefer sind; denn so spielt der Organist mit diesen Registern wie die Noten stehen. Wäre z. Er. das Stück aus dem d, und er sollte aus dem c spielen; so präambulirte er mit dem vollen Werke aus dem c, weil das c in Chorton dem d im Kammerton gleich ist. Hernach zieht er das Kammergedackt, den Kammersubbaß, Kammertonoktave im Pedale, und was dergleichen mehr ist, und spielt aus dem d, wie die Noten stehen. Den andern Subbaß, Gedackt, Oktav, ꝛc. thut er weg, so ist die Musik richtig, wenn nur die besayteten Instrumente einem Ton tiefer stimmen. Dies kann man auch prakticiren, wenn im feuchten Wetter die Sayten nicht halten. Es müssen aber so viel besondere Register im Kammertone seyn, daß der Baß in gehöriger force mit gehen kann. Unten §. 309. ist zu sehen, daß zu Merseburg im Schlosse etliche Kammerstimmen seyn sollen. Zu St. Jakobi in Hamburg ist das Gedackt allein im Kammertone. Das ist aber in der Musik allein nicht genug. Doch eben diese Stimmen müssen auch im Chortone da seyn. [56]) Wollte man sagen: der Organist müsse das Transponiren lernen: so dient

zur

---

[56]) In der Frauenkirche zu Dresden ist eine ganze Orgel im Kammertone von dem berühmten Silbermann verfertiget worden, s. Reinholds poetische Gedanken bey Gelegenheit der schönen neuen Orgel, ꝛc. S. 28. (1736. in 4to.)

(**) Und dergleichen giebt es ißo, nicht nur in Dresden sondern, auch an andern Orten, mehr.

the pedal by means of separate stopknobs.* Here and there are to be found yet other examples of this practice. Some of the stops at St. Ulrich in Magdeburg are "halved" (halbirt), i.e., provided with two stopknobs, e.g., the Posaune, Regal, Kleinschreyer.† Otherwise "halbirt" means something else.‡ To be sure, Werkmeister in his *Orgelprobe*, Chap. 19, p. 42, considers [the practice of borrowing stops] inadvisable, because [the stops] often sound out-of-tune, especially reeds, if the supply of wind is not identical, or if the wind gusts about in the corners, or must travel further to the pipe from one [wind source] than from another, and thus is not equally supplied.§ For poor churches, though, he still considers it a good means of economizing. As long as the organbuilder exercises the necessary intelligence and builds everything correctly, there is no need to worry; see §.130 above.

§. 277.

Where circumstances permit, stops at chamber pitch may be included in an organ, i.e., stops that are tuned 1 or 1½′ [whole] steps lower than the rest of the instrument, which must, as is customary, be at choir pitch. Question: why do this? Reply: not for the sake of improvising, for then an organist may play in any key he will, and also not for the sake of accompanying hymn-singing, because it is simple to play [hymns] in a variety of keys, but for the sake of ensemble music.¶ For it sometimes happens that a piece that is set, e.g., with horns in *d* needs to be played with trumpets [in *c*]. Then either the figured bass has to be copied over to transpose it from *d* to *c*, or the organist must transpose [at sight]. One does not always have the spare time for the former, and not every organist can do the latter. For such cases it is well to have stops at chamber pitch, ones that are 1 or 1½′ tones lower. On these stops the organist may play the notes as they stand. If for example the piece were in *d*, and he needed to play in *c*, then he improvises the prelude on the plenum in *c*, since *c* in choir pitch is the same as *d* in chamber pitch. Then he draws the Kammergedackt [in the manual] and the Kammersubbass [16′] and Kammeroktave [8′] in the pedal, plus whatever similar stops are available, and plays in *d*, as the notes are written. The other Subbass, Gedackt, Oktave, etc., he retires; in this way the ensemble is all at the same pitch, so long as the stringed instruments tune a whole step lower. This may also be done if the strings [of the stringed instruments] do not hold [their pitch] in damp weather. There must, however, be enough separate stops at chamber pitch so that the [figured] bass may accompany [the ensemble] with appropriate strength. It may be noted in §.309 below that in the [organ of the] palace at Merseburg‖ there are reported to be several stops at chamber pitch. At St. Jakobi in Hamburg there is a single Gedackt at chamber pitch. That alone does not suffice, however, for ensemble music. The very same stops, though, [that are present at chamber pitch] must also be there at choir pitch.(56)(**) If anyone should say, the organist must learn to transpose, let this answer suffice: this is easier to do with slow

* In the stoplist these two stops are listed both in the manual and the pedal.
† In the stoplist of this organ (Praetorius, *Syntagma musicum*, Vol. II, pp. 174-5) there seems to be no independent pedal division; all the pedal stops are borrowed from various manual stops.
‡ Praetorius may not be using the term "halbirt" to refer to the pedal stops; rather he may be using "halbirt" in the same sense that Adlung uses it in §.164, 178 and 202: a stop that speaks only through half the compass of the manual.
§ cf. §.130 above.

¶ i.e., realization of the figured bass.

‖ i.e., in the Cathedral.

56) The renowned [Gottfried] Silbermann has built an entire organ at chamber pitch in the Frauenkirche at Dresden; see Reinhold's *Poetische Gedanken bei Gelegenheit der schönen neuen Orgel* ..., p. 28 ([published in] 1736 in quarto). [Albrecht].
(**) The same [situation] prevails today, not only in Dresden, but at other places as well. [Agricola]

zur Antwort, daß es leichter in langsamen Bässen gehe, als in andern, die geschwinder Capriolen voll sind. Freylich sollten sie es lernen: aber es heißt auch hier: Das Wort fasset nicht jedermann. An manchen Oertern differirt Chor- und Kammerton nur um einen Ton, an andern um anderthalb Töne. Daher eins von beyden kann gewählet werden.

§. 278.

Noch besser ists, wenn die ganze Orgel in Kammerton kann transponirt werden. Bey Clavicymbeln ist es leicht, weil blos die Claviere auf und nieder gerückt werden, dadurch man einen halben Ton, auch wol einen ganzen Ton, oder wol gar anderthalbe Töne, mit größter Kommodität transponiren kann; weil allezeit andere palmulae unter die Docken und Saiten zu stehen kommen. Man hat es aber nicht nur jetzo, sondern auch schon in ältern Zeiten auf der Orgel applicirt, da man durch ein Koppel, welches das Kammerkoppel heißt, die ganze Orgel, oder wenigstens ein Clavier, ganz in Kammerton bringt. Ich habe zwar selbst keins gesehen; doch kann man sich endlich modos possibiles davon vorstellen. Daß zu Naumburg im Dom dergleichen sey, obschon diese Orgel die neueste nicht ist, hat man mich ganz gewiß versichert. Der Hr. Wender aus Mühlhausen, der zu Merseburg in der Stadt ein schön Werk gemacht, soll auch daselbst ein Kammerkoppel angebracht haben. Man sieht leicht, daß solche Orgeln eine gute Temperatur haben müssen, wenn es angehen soll.

§. 179.

Die Manualkoppel anlangend, so wollte ich lieber rathen; man schriebe eins vor, da die palmulae des obern Claviers unten, und die palmulae des untern Claviers oben mit Klötzgen versehen wären, welche, wenn das obere Clavier hinter geschoben wird, auf einander treten, daß solchergestalt ein Clavier das andere drückt. Es bleiben solche Koppel beständiger, und so ja eins aus Versehen abgedrückt wird, kann man das Clavier leicht losschrauben, und es wieder anleimen. Doch um dieses zu verhüten, werden sie von einigen eingebohrt. Machte man eine Parthey mit Schrauben; so könnte man auch die Höhe nach Belieben ändern. Wenn das Hauptwerk im obern Claviere seyn kann; so wollte ich rathen, es dahin zu bringen, weil unten meistens Druckwerke sind, welche sich so gut nicht spielen. Das andere bringe man in die Mitte, daß man die stärksten Manuale koppeln könne; das geringste unten, wenn man deren 3 hat. Die Ursach ist, daß man, wenn das Koppel gezogen ist, doch kann ein Echo spielen, wenn das Nebenwerk unten angebracht worden, wo zwey Claviere sind, welches nicht angehet, wo das Hauptwerk unten stehet.

§. 280.

Der Guckguck, Trommel, Pauke und Vogelgesang werden als abgeschmackt in den neuesten Orgeln weggelassen; sie haben keinen Nutzen, als daß sie die Zuhörer lachend machen. Der Stern wird noch zuweilen gebraucht; doch will er vielen nicht anstehen: daher sie Glocken nehmen, und sie in Accordstönen ordnen, wie §. 133. mit mehrerm geredet worden.

§. 281.

basses than with others that are full of rapid flourishes. Of course they should learn to do it, but as the saying goes, "Not everyone understands this." In many places choir- and chamber-pitch are only a [whole] step apart, in others a step and a half. Thus either of the two may be chosen [when building an organ].

§. 278.

It is even better if the entire organ can be transposed into chamber pitch. This is easy with harpsichords, since the keyboards are merely moved up or down. With this [arrangement] it is possible to transpose a half step, a whole step, or even a step and a half with the greatest of ease, since different keys come to lie under the jacks and strings each time. This is not only applied to the organ of today; already in former times an entire organ, or at least one manual, was shifted into chamber pitch by means of a coupler called the "Kammerkoppel". To be sure, I have not seen one myself, but it is possible to imagine innumerable ways in which this could be done. I have been given absolute assurance that such a coupler is to be found in the Cathedral at Naumburg, even though this organ is not all that new. [The organbuilder] Mr. Wender of Mühlhausen has built a lovely instrument at Merseburg and is said also to have built a chamber coupler there. It is easy to see that such organs must be well-tempered if such a device is to work.

§. 179 [sic; should be "§.279].

With regard to manual couplers, I would advise it as preferable to specify that small blocks be affixed under the keys of the upper manual and atop the keys of the lower manual. When the upper manual is shoved back, these blocks come into contact with each other in such a way that one manual depresses the other.* Such couplers are more durable, and if one [of the little blocks] accidentally gets broken off, the manual can easily be unscrewed and the block re-glued. But to guard against this, some [builders] bore holes in [the blocks].† If a series [of blocks] is made with [regulating] screws, then the height can also be altered at will [in order to regulate the coupler]. If it is possible for the Hauptwerk to be the upper manual, I would suggest that this be done, since the lowest manuals are mostly backfall actions‡ that are not so easy to play.§ The second [manual] should be set in the middle, so that the two loudest manuals may be coupled. The least important manual should then be the lowest, if there are 3 manuals. The reason for this [arrangement of the keyboards] is that on a 2-manual instrument an echo can be played while the coupler is drawn if the secondary manual is placed beneath [the Hauptwerk]. This cannot be done when the Hauptwerk stands beneath [the secondary manual].¶

§. 280.

The Cuckoo, Drum, Tympani and Birdsong are omitted as tasteless in the most recent organs. They have no use except to make listeners laugh. The [Cymbel]stern is still sometimes built, but many find it inappropriate. Therefore they use bells, arranging them into chord tones, as has been mentioned among other things in §.133.

---

* cf. §.22 and §.472.

† i.e., and screw or peg them to the key levers.

‡ "Druckwerke;" see §.52 above.

§ i.e., since the Hauptwerk usually has the stiffest action, better that it should be built with the more sensitive and lighter suspended action than as a backfall action (§.52).

¶ i.e., given the coupling system Adlung recommends, one could play the two manuals coupled together only on the upper manual, which in this case would contain the softer stops; thus the Hauptwerk would sound on both of the two manuals, making it impossible to achieve an echo effect.

§. 281.

Die Tremulanten aber sind noch beybehalten. Sie sind nicht theuer, daher man deren mehr in eine Orgel bringen kann, so, daß etwan der Manualladen jede einen besondern bekömmt. Im Pedale ist er so viel nicht nütze. Etliche ordnen einen Tremulanten mit der Schwangfeder, einen aber ohne Schwangfeder. So ist im Dom zu Naumburg einer mit, der andere ohne die Schwangfeder, daß einer langsam, der andere geschwinde schlägt.

§. 282.

Wer die Disposition eines Orgelwerks angiebt, der vergesse ja die Ventile nicht, dadurch der Wind von der Lade abgehalten wird, bis man spielen will. Dadurch wird mancher Fehler verhütet, weil man sie nicht eher öfnet, bis man anhebt zu spielen: da im Gegentheil ein Werk oft heulet, und allerhand Unlust macht. Soll man dann erst alle Register hinein stoßen, so währt es zu lange; mit dem einzigen Ventile wird gleich alles gestillt. Zu dem Endzwecke könnte ein Hauptventil genug seyn, wenn es in den Generalkanal gelegt würde, da der Wind aller Bälge noch beysammen ist. Wären zu dem Pedale besondere Bälge; so müßte in deren Hauptkanal auch ein besonder Ventil gemacht werden. Aber es ist auch hübsch, wenn zu jeder Lade und Clavier ein besonder Sperrventil ist, damit nicht ein jeder leyren kann wie er will, wenn er über die Orgel geht, s. Prätor. l. c. S. 202. Sonderlich aber deswegen, damit, wenn ein Clavier anhebt zu heulen, man nicht die ganze Orgel, sondern nur dasselbe Clavier müsse lassen stille schweigen. Andere haben noch mehr Ventile als Claviere. So sind z. Er. in Görlitz 8 Ventile, §. 301. Und die Orgel im Löbenicht zu Königsberg hat 4 Sperrventile und ein Hauptventil; damit alles auf einmal kann abgeschlossen werden.

§. 283.

Das wird das meiste seyn, was von der Disposition eines Werks zu merken. Man sieht hieraus, daß man in solchen Dingen Verstand brauchen müsse. Verlangt einer auf allerhand Fälle Exempel der Dispositionen; so hat Prätorius l. c. Tom. II. P. V. pag. 161. bis 203. eine ziemliche Anzahl derselben eingerückt; die mag ich nicht hierher setzen, obschon das Buch etwas rar worden, zumal da wol die wenigsten Orgeln noch so stehen, wie er sie gesetzt. Denn sein Buch, wenigstens dieser andere Tomus ist Ao. 1619. schon gedruckt, und die meisten Orgeln, die er beschreibt, sind lange vorher gebauet, können also wenig derselben mehr stehen. Wer sie auch mit Matthesons Dispositionen conserirt, der wird vollends davon überzeuget werden. Doch habe ich das merkwürdigste daraus im 7ten Kapitel angezeigt. Weil aber die Orgeln allezeit sammt dem Orte und Stadt genennet sind; so will ich seine Dispositionen dem Alphabet nach hier nur anführen zwischen den andern, sie selbst aber nicht hersetzen, nur damit einer, welcher in der und der Stadt eine Stimme Kap. 7 angeführt findet, hier sehen könne, ob die Disposition aus dem Prätorio sey, und ob sie probabiliter noch stehe, oder nicht.

Chap. X. Concerning the Stoplist

§. 281.

Tremulants, however, have been retained. They are not expensive, and thus several of them may be constructed in the same organ, so that perhaps each of the manual chests gets a separate one. It is not of much use in the pedal. Some regulate a tremulant with a bobbing spring, others without it.* Thus in the Cathedral at Naumburg there is one with a bobbing spring and one without, so that one beats slowly and the other quickly.

* See §.200 above.

§. 282.

Anyone who draws up a stoplist for an organ should not omit the ventils that block the wind from the chests until [the organist] is ready to play. They prevent many a fault, since they are not opened until right before playing. If they are not there, a division often ciphers and makes all sorts of disagreeable [noises]. If one were [to have] to shove off all the stops, it would take too long; with a single ventil everything is silenced at once. One primary ventil would be enough for this purpose, if it were placed in the primary wind duct that holds all the wind from the bellows. If the pedal has a separate bellows, then a separate ventil must also be built in its main wind duct. But it is also nice to have a separate cut-out ventil for each chest and manual, so that not everyone can play around at will if he gets to the organ (see Praetorius, *l.c.*, p. 202); more importantly, though, so that when one manual begins to cipher, it is not necessary to silence the entire organ, but only that particular manual. Other [organs] have more ventils than manuals; thus, for example, there are 8 ventils at Görlitz; see §.301. And the organ in the Löbenichtkirche at Königsberg has 4 cut-out ventils and a universal ventil, [the latter] so that everything can be shut off at once.

§. 283.

This is most of what needs to be noted about the stoplist of an organ. From this it may readily be seen that it is necessary to use one's wits in such things. If anyone should require examples of stoplists for whatever reason, Praetorius has included a considerable number of them in [the *Syntagma musicum*], Vol. II, Part V, pp. 161-203 [and 233-4]. I will not bother to reproduce them here, although the book has become rather rare, in particular since only a very few of the organs still exist as he describes them. For his book, at least the second volume of it, was printed way back in the year 1619, and most of the organs he describes were built long before that; thus few of them could still exist. Anyone who compares them with Mattheson's stoplists will be completely convinced of this.† Even so, I have cited the most noteworthy of [Praetorius's stoplists] in Chapter 7. Since organs are always labeled by their city and location, I will cite [the titles of] his stoplists alphabetically among the others, but omit the stoplists themselves. In this way anyone who finds a stop cited in this or that city in Chap. 7 may take note here whether the stoplist is in Praetorius and whether or not it is probably still standing. Anyone

† In the Appendix to the second edition of Niedt's *Musicalische Handleitung*, Mattheson printed more recent stoplists of many of the same organs described by Praetorius, showing that most had been rebuilt or altered.

Matthesons Dispositionen kann auch ein jeder in Niedtens zweytem Theile der Handleitung zur Variation des G. B. im Anhange leicht selber lesen, und mag ich sie nicht abschreiben; denn das Buch ist leicht zu haben. Doch sollen die Oerter, daraus er sie hat, auch dem Alphabet nach hier genennet werden, daß, wer von der oder jener Stadt nach der Disposition fragen wollte, hier kann nachsehen, ob ich sie habe, oder ob er sie bey Mattheson oder Prätorio, oder sonst wo, finden könne. Ist etwan in einem Traktate nur eine Disposition, die will ich hier einschalten, daß man nicht einen ganzen Traktat kaufen oder borgen müsse um einer einzigen Disposition willen. Kommt etwas zu loben oder zu tadeln vor, will ich es dann und wann bescheiden anmerken. Kommt aber eine Sache allzuoft vor; so verweise ich auf das vorige. Sollte nicht allezeit die Orgel so stehen, wie die Disposition zeigt; so beliebe man zu erwägen, daß man durch Correspondenzen kann betrogen werden. Die alphabetische Ordnung geht auf die teutschen Namen der Städte und Oerter, und ist deswegen erwählet worden, daß man alles gleich finden könne. (**)

(**) Wie schon in der Vorrede erinnert worden, sind noch viel mehrere Dispositionen hierbey theils ganz eingeschaltet worden; theils hat man nur angezeiget wo sie zu lesen sind. Im übrigen hat man der Absicht des Hrn. Autors nachzufolgen gesuchet. Das neueingeschaltete ist durch kleinere Schrift, und durch das Zeichen der (**) von des Hrn. **Adlung** Arbeit unterschieden worden.

may also easily read Mattheson's stoplists in the second part of Niedt's *Musicalische Handleitung* for himself, and these I will not bother to reproduce, since the book is easily obtainable. The locations at which he reports [the organs], however, will also be listed here alphabetically, so that whoever would like to consult a stoplist from this or that city can check here if I have it, or if he can find it in Mattheson, Praetorius or somewhere else. If there is just a single stoplist in some treatise I will insert it here, to spare someone buying or borrowing an entire treatise for the sake of a single stoplist. It there appears to be anything to praise or to censure, I will make a modest note of it from time to time. If the same thing occurs too frequently, however, then I will refer to the former [instance of it]. If the organs do not always stand as the stoplists indicate, then I ask the reader graciously to take into account that one may be led astray by correspondence.* The arrangement proceeds alphabetically by the German names of the cities and locations; this method has been chosen in order that everything may be found immediately.(**)

* i.e., Adlung did not personally gather all of these stoplists, but got some of them by writing the officials of a particular church and asking them to send him the stoplist.

(**) As has already been mentioned in the Foreword, many more stoplists have been inserted here, in part in their entirety, in part with just an indication where they may be consulted. In other respects I have attempted to carry out the intentions of the author. That which has been newly inserted is distinguished from Mr. Adlung's work by smaller print and by the sign (**). [Agricola]

The End of Part I†

† In the 1768 edition, Volume I continued with a 95-page collection of stoplists. In the present publication, this collection of stoplists is augmented and appears following the end of Volume II.

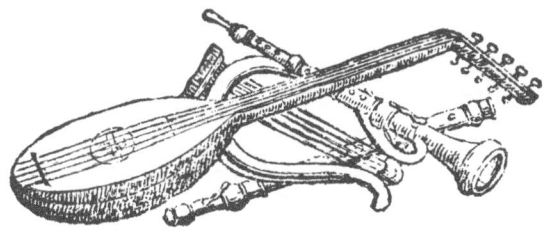